Keystone

JOHN MASEFIELD

P O E M S

BY JOHN MASEFIELD

COMPLETE EDITION
WITH RECENT POEMS

NEW YORK
THE MACMILLAN COMPANY
1 9 5 3

PRINTED IN THE UNITED STATES OF AMERICA

PREFACE

I have been asked to write a preface to this new collected edition of my poems. The work of many years has been gathered together here. Some has been weeded out; some that has been omitted from past collections has been included; some few misprints and other errors, of placing, have been corrected; most of the work here printed now appears in the order in which it was composed.

I have been asked to say something about the making of these verses. I began to write them in boyhood. Delight in poetry, like other delights, is strongest in youth. Although I wrote some verses in childhood with pleasure to myself, I first felt the real delight of poetry in a room in Yonkers, New York. It was there that I decided that I had rather write verse than do anything else in the world.

My earliest verses reflected clearly my enthusiasm for certain English poets, for Chaucer first, then Keats, then Milton, then Shelley. The fruits of these enthusiasms are now, I trust, scattered ashes. Afterwards, while I was still playing with words and measures, I met with the work of A. C. Swinburne. Like most young writers of that time I at once succumbed to his talent. He could do easily and supremely all those tricks with words and measures which the young craftsman longed to be able to perform. In my enthusiasm for him I paid pilgrimages to Putney and watched outside "The Pines" until the little figure of the Master appeared and went trotting up the hill. I never spoke with him. A few years later, when he had ceased to seem the miraculous Master of the art, it was my fortune for many days together to sit at the same table with him in the reading-room of the British Museum. He was then very old, frail, and deaf. The magnificent head was all that remained of the prophet and seer; the rest was a little shrunken stalk. The late Mr. Watts-Dunton used to bring him there, see him to his chair, and order his books for him; he would then bellow in his ear that he would return at one o'clock and take him out to lunch. This message had to be repeated several times before the old man could grasp it, and by that time the reading-room was aroused. Grave heads from every table turned to watch. Presently, after Mr. Watts-Dunton had gone, Swinburne would turn to his books. I know not what they were, but imagine that they were of a merry impropriety, for the old man used to roar with laughter over them and, being deaf, never knew what disturbance he was causing. An Anglican Bishop and an Abbot of the Roman Church haunted the same table, and from time to time in that room a little, smiling, erect, cynical man, with a face which none could forget, would pass. This was Lenin, then studying, I believe, the psychology of revolution.

While the work of Swinburne influenced me, I came to know the work of the writers of a later time: James Thomson, John Davidson, Ernest Dowson, and some of the contributors to the *Yellow Book* and the *Savoy*. I read all these writers with enthusiasm; a young mind needs the thought of the time.

In those early years when I made verses, I tried to make what I called "pictures in verse," or clear statements of things seen. The contemporary writers who seemed to me to do this with the greatest success were William Morris and Robert Louis Stevenson; many clear-cut passages from their verse and prose were ever in my thoughts.

In 1899, the best literary paper in England was the *Daily Chronicle,* then edited by Mr. H. W. Massingham. Late in that year I read in that paper a review by Mr. H. W. Nevinson of poems by Mr. W. B. Yeats. The fragments quoted in the review so excited me that I bought the book that morning, and read it that night, feeling that a new world of romance and beauty had been opened to me. In a few weeks, I knew all the published writings of Mr. Yeats. About a year later I had the very great privilege of meeting him.

He lived then, when in London, in one of the older lanes of Bloomsbury, a little street or gully containing small, well-built, and pretty houses of about the year 1820, all rather come down in the world, but shaded with a few plane-trees and always strange and romantic-looking. They have tidied up the ends of the lane now, so that on the whole it looks rather brighter and trimmer, but the house (No. 18, Woburn Buildings), when I last saw it, looked very much as it looked in those days. Mr. Yeats described his house as being "next door to a lapidary's shop." The lapidary has now gone, and the brass plate that once bore the name of Yeats has gone, but the holes of the screws may still be seen. The lane is now more brightly lit at night than it was thirty-five years ago.

Woburn Buildings lies between Woburn Place and St. Pancras Church. In Woburn Place at that time, just at the turn into Woburn Buildings, there were two small houses built with those bulges, or gazebos, so popular in 1820 and 1830. There were plane-trees in front of these houses, so that at night, when lamps were lit, the shadows of the trees moved continually on the pale yellow houses, which were always closely shuttered. Just outside those houses a blind beggar had his stand. Usually he waved a couple of boxes of matches with some boot-laces, and mumbled his request for alms. Beggar, plane-trees, and houses are now all gone, and a smart hotel stands where they once stood; I cannot pass that place to-day, nor see the caryatids in the Church of St. Pancras, without a quickening of the pulse.

Mr. Yeats has ever been the great encourager of his time. It was his custom then to receive his friends on Monday evenings from eight o'clock till midnight, or after midnight. Perhaps no happier gatherings have ever been at any time in London: I have known none so fruitful: all who went there came away resolved to achieve and seeing something of the way.

In the excitement of this stimulus I began to try to write verses and stories.

I was then living wholly in London, and thinking it a dark, dismal, and oppressive city. I longed for the open spaces and freedom of life that I had known in the past. My early verses were written in that mood of longing for escape which marked a good deal of the writing of that time. In those days it was more difficult to get out of London than it is to-day. My first book of verses, written mainly in six exciting weeks, consisted chiefly of ballads expressing a longing for fresh air.

After this first book (which met with no welcome at the time), I wrote little verse for some years. I made experiments in other ways of writing. In the course of these experiments, I became interested in dramatic writing, as a form of art demanding powers of directness and simplicity for which all writers ought to strive. It is not a way of writing for which I much care, but as discipline it is invaluable to all young talents. Perhaps time pleasantly spent should never be considered wasted.

In 1911, I first found what I could do. In this year, I began a way of writing in which I continued for several years. Towards the end of May in that most beautiful sunny year, it chanced that I went for a lonely evening walk in lonely country. I had walked for some miles; I cannot now recollect where; but was certainly returning home on a northerly course through a beech-wood. As I thrust through the hedge which parted the beech-wood from a stretch of common land I said to myself, "Now I will write a poem about a blackguard who becomes converted." Immediately as I broke into the common land, the beginning of the poem floated up into my mind and I began to compose it. When I reached home I wrote down what I had composed, and wrote on with great eagerness until nearly midnight. I should, no doubt, have stopped up all night, writing, had I not received a sudden shock. I was alone in the house, which was a little old farm in remote country. I was writing hard, when suddenly, without any warning, the door of the room in which I sat opened violently, exactly as though someone had thrust it open. I was scared out of my wits and thought it better to break off for that night and go to bed. Next morning I continued to write the poem, and wrote hard for the next three weeks, by which time the tale of *The Everlasting Mercy* was finished. I then went into Wales with two friends who were bent on trout-fishing. On our arrival in Wales, it began to rain. On the first day I went fishing with the two friends, one of whom caught a small fish two inches long, which he returned to the water; the others did not get a bite. The next day it poured again with rain. I went out with them and saw them begin their pastime, but myself returned to the inn, and, after watching the rain pouring in a grey sheet, decided that I would write a poem as a complement to the other, and that, as I had shown in the one a bad man made happy through no virtue, so, in the other, I would show a good woman made wretched through no fault. I started to compose the poem and continued writing until the fishing party broke up. They caught in all their stay no fish save the little one which they put back; but in fishing, as in religion, Hope is a third part of the matter. On my return home I finished the poem. Like the other it took me exactly three weeks and three days to complete.

Until that summer of 1911, most of the little verse I had written had been the outcome of a longing for freedom. After that walk in 1911 most of my work, for some years, sprang from the effort to fill a certain countryside, perhaps twelve miles square, with the imagined figures of men and women, whose doings might perhaps please the dwellers in that land by making the familiar scenes significant.

The mention of a place in a book, even in a bad book, written many years ago, will give that place a curious meaning to those who pass it and remember the allusion. Few who care for the work of Thomas Hardy can move anywhere in the Southern counties without thinking, "Ah, it was here in this valley, or there, or yonder, in that house among the trees, that one or other of the characters in the Wessex novels lived." I longed to give to my little plot some measure of the interest which Burns gave to the fields, the bridge, and the river of his village, and Hardy to the counties of his birth and adoption.

Less than a mile from me, at this moment, there is an old farm, once an inn. It is mentioned in a bad satire, now almost wholly forgotten, written in the late eighteenth century by an imitator of Henry Fielding. I pass the old house almost every day, but never without an increased interest from the fact that that almost forgotten author must once have come there, seeking lodging when it was crowded with hundreds of sportsmen and scoundrels who had come there for the races.

The moods which govern a writer's production change with the years; few moods can last for more than seven years: the mood which drove me to make tales in verse presently changed.

After the war, many people, looking out upon England, felt that her social structure needed to be remade nearer to the heart's desire. Reformers do best when they keep their efforts to themselves, their families, and their parishes. Throughout England, this feeling led to the establishment of countless theatrical and musical societies designed to brighten and gladden the national leisure.

As we saw that in our part of England there was not enough amusement for the young men and women, my wife and I decided to try to start an amateur theatrical company. With the help of a few friends and well-wishers we gathered together a company sufficiently big to attempt a Shakespearian play. Most of the company had never acted anywhere, very few had ever read a line of verse, but we decided to start with Shakespeare's *King Lear*, thinking that the play, at least, should be good whatever the acting might be, and having also thought that if we set the actors a big task they might be prompted to make a great effort. A good Shakespearian actor promised to play the part of King Lear. Encouraged by his promise we rehearsed the rest of the play and borrowed some admirable costumes. Two days before the advertised performance the actor withdrew his promise. I had to play King Lear myself, reading most of the part from manuscript stitched inside my sleeves and elsewhere. We will draw a veil over the performance, but at the end of it the chief feeling of the company was that it had been great fun and that we must do more plays together, which we did. After some years of play-production, we built a small theatre in which the plays might be done with rather greater ease to ourselves: for the next few years this theatre was the main interest in our lives. I wrote for the company several plays and translated others.

About twelve years ago, while judging the verse-speaking at the Edinburgh Musical Festival, I became for the first time absorbingly and burningly interested in the speaking of verse. Certain Scotch speakers spoke at that festival with such beauty that I could not sleep for three nights. These speakers had been trained by Miss Marjorie Gullan, a teacher of genius, who had put into effective practice the principles and theories of Mr. W. B. Yeats, who began the reform of verse-speaking at the beginning of this century. My wife, who was as deeply delighted as myself with these speakers, suggested that we should organize a similar contest in verse-speaking at Oxford, during the next Summer. This contest was attended by the very best of the speakers of Great Britain. The beauty of the speech was beyond all telling. Lovely as the Scotch speakers were, they met their matches among the English. We had never heard anything more lovely than the speaking of the last day, when none but the winners of the different classes were competing. We were so pleased with the results that we determined to hold a similar festival the next year. For several years in succession this festival was the great delight of ourselves and of the poets who helped us. From the first we had been helped by poets. We felt that the only kinds of verse-speaking worth having were such as poets could approve.

After some years we knew that there were no less than fifty excellent speakers of verse in these islands. We felt that there had been enough competition among them, and that now it was for the poets to invent poems and plays for these excellent speakers to speak and act. We modified the form of the recitations, dispensing with the contest and asking the poets, our helpers, to write work for their favourite speakers to perform. This they did with great effect. For some years our chief delight was to organize performances by these exquisite speakers of work specially written for them by their admirers, the poets. Very nearly all my work for the last ten years was written for performance by them.

But that way now has come to an end; the mood has changed; what is to come is still unsure. The preparation of a poetical mood is slow and unseen in the caverns of the mind. What gathers there secretly may break forth suddenly. All writers live longing for the day when the rocks burst and the living waters rush forth singing.

JOHN MASEFIELD.

CONTENTS

PART ONE

Salt-Water Ballads

CONTENTS

PART TWO

confession

CONTENTS

PART ONE

SALT-WATER BALLADS

SALT-WATER BALLADS

A CONSECRATION

Not of the princes and prelates with periwigged charioteers
Riding triumphantly laurelled to lap the fat of the years,—
Rather the scorned—the rejected—the men hemmed in with the spears;

The men of the tattered battalion which fights till it dies,
Dazed with the dust of the battle, the din and the cries,
The men with the broken heads and the blood running into their eyes.

Not the be-medalled Commander, beloved of the throne,
Riding cock-horse to parade when the bugles are blown,
But the lads who carried the koppie and cannot be known.

Not the ruler for me, but the ranker, the tramp of the road,
The slave with the sack on his shoulders pricked on with the goad,
The man with too weighty a burden, too weary a load.

The sailor, the stoker of steamers, the man with the clout,
The chantyman bent at the halliards putting a tune to the shout,
The drowsy man at the wheel and the tired lookout.

Others may sing of the wine and the wealth and the mirth,
The portly presence of potentates goodly in girth;—
Mine be the dirt and the dross, the dust and scum of the earth!

THEIRS *be the music, the colour, the glory, the gold;*
Mine be a handful of ashes, a mouthful of mould.
Of the maimed, of the halt and the blind in the rain and the cold—
Of these shall my songs be fashioned, my tales be told. AMEN

THE YARN OF THE *LOCH ACHRAY*

The *Loch Achray* was a clipper tall
With seven-and-twenty hands in all.
Twenty to hand and reef and haul,
A skipper to sail and mates to bawl
"Tally on to the tackle-fall,
Heave now 'n' start her, heave 'n' pawl!'
Hear the yarn of a sailor,
An old yarn learned at sea.

Her crew were shipped and they said "Farewell,
So-long, my Tottie, my lovely gell;
We sail to-day if we fetch to hell,
It's time we tackled the wheel a spell."
Hear the yarn of a sailor,
An old yarn learned at sea.

The dockside loafers talked on the quay
The day that she towed down to sea:
"Lord, what a handsome ship she be!
Cheer her, sonny boys, three times three!"
And the dockside loafers gave her a shout
As the red-funnelled tug-boat towed her out;
They gave her a cheer as the custom is,
And the crew yelled "Take our loves to Liz—
Three cheers, bullies, for old Pier Head
'N' the bloody stay-at-homes!" they said.
Hear the yarn of a sailor,
An old yarn learned at sea.

In the grey of the coming on of night
She dropped the tug at the Tuskar Light,
'N' the topsails went to the topmast head
To a chorus that fairly awoke the dead.

She trimmed her yards and slanted South
With her royals set and a bone in her mouth.
Hear the yarn of a sailor,
An old yarn learned at sea.

She crossed the Line and all went well,
They ate, they slept, and they struck the bell
And I give you a gospel truth when I state
The crowd didn't find any fault with the Mate,
But one night off of the River Plate.
Hear the yarn of a sailor,
An old yarn learned at sea.

It freshened up till it blew like thunder
And burrowed her deep lee-scuppers under.
The old man said, "I mean to hang on
Till her canvas busts or her sticks are gone"—
Which the blushing looney did, till at last
Overboard went her mizzen-mast.
Hear the yarn of a sailor,
An old yarn learned at sea.

Then a fierce squall struck the *Loch Achray*
And bowed her down to her water-way;
Her main-shrouds gave and her forestay,
And a green sea carried her wheel away;
Ere the watch below had time to dress
She was cluttered up in a blushing mess.
Hear the yarn of a sailor,
An old yarn learned at sea.

She couldn't lay-to nor yet pay-off,
And she got swept clean in the bloody trough;
Her masts were gone, and afore you knowed
She filled by the head and down she goed.

Her crew made seven-and-twenty dishes
For the big jack-sharks and the little fishes,
And over their bones the water swishes.
Hear the yarn of a sailor,
An old yarn learned at sea.

The wives and girls they watch in the rain
For a ship as won't come home again.
"I reckon it's them head-winds," they say,
"She'll be home to-morrow, if not to-day.
I'll just nip home 'n' I'll air the sheets
'N' buy the fixins 'n' cook the meats
As my man likes 'n' as my man eats."

So home they goes by the windy streets,
Thinking their men are homeward bound
With anchors hungry for English ground,
And the bloody fun of it is, they're drowned!
Hear the yarn of a sailor,
An old yarn learned at sea.

SING A SONG O' SHIPWRECK

He lolled on a bollard, a sun-burned son of the sea,
With ear-rings of brass and a jumper of dungaree,
"'N' many a queer lash-up have I seen," says he.

"But the toughest hooray o' the racket," he says, "I'll be sworn,
'N' the roughest traverse I worked since the day I was born,
Was a packet o' Sailor's Delight as I scoffed in the seas o' the
Horn.

"All day long in the calm she had rolled to the swell,
Rolling through fifty degrees till she clattered her bell:
'N' then came snow, 'n' a squall, 'n' a wind was colder 'n hell.

"It blew like the Bull of Barney, a beast of a breeze,
'N' over the rail come the cold green lollopin' seas,
'N' she went ashore at the dawn on the Ramirez.

"She was settlin' down by the stern when I got to the deck,
Her waist was a smother o' sea as was up to your neck,
'N' her masts were gone, 'n' her rails, 'n' she was a wreck.

"We rigged up a tackle, a purchase, a sort of a shift,
To hoist the boats off o' the deck-house and get them adrift,
When her stern gives a sickenin' settle, her bows give a lift,

"'N' comes a crash of green water as sets me afloat
With freezing fingers clutching the keel of a boat—
The bottom-up whaler—'n' that was the juice of a note.

"Well, I clambers acrost o' the keel 'n' I gets me secured,
When I sees a face in the white o' the smother to looard,
So I gives 'im a 'and, 'n' be shot if it wasn't the stooard!

"So he climbs up forrard o' me, 'n' 'thanky,' a' says,
'N' we sits 'n' shivers 'n' freeze to the bone wi' the sprays,
'N' *I* sings 'Abel Brown,' 'n' the stooard he prays.

"Wi' never a dollop to sup nor a morsel to bite,
The lips of us blue with the cold 'n' the heads of us light,
Adrift in a Cape Horn sea for a day 'n' a night.

"'N' then the stooard goes dotty 'n' puts a tune to his lip,
'N' moans about Love like a dern old hen wi' the pip—
(I sets no store upon stooards—they ain't no use on a ship).

"'N' 'mother,' the looney cackles, 'come 'n' put Willy to bed!'
So I says 'Dry up, or I'll fetch you a crack o' the head';
'The kettle's a-bilin',' he answers, ''n' I'll go butter the bread.'

"'N' he falls to singin' some slush about clinkin' a can,
'N' at last he dies, so he does, 'n' I tells you, Jan,
I was glad when he did, for he weren't no fun for a man.

"So he falls forrard, he does, 'n' he closes his eye,
'N' quiet he lays 'n' quiet I leaves him lie,
'N' I was alone with his corp, 'n' the cold green sea and the sky.

"'N' then I dithers, I guess, for the next as I knew
Was the voice of a mate as was sayin' to one of the crew,
'Easy, my son, wi' the brandy, be shot if he ain't comin'-to!'"

BURIAL PARTY

"He's deader 'n nails," the fo'c's'le said, "'n' gone to his long sleep;"
"'N' about his corp," said Tom to Dan, "d'ye think his corp'll keep
Till the day's done, 'n' the work's through, 'n' the ebb's upon the neap?"

"He's deader 'n nails," said Dan to Tom, "'n' I wish his sperrit j'y;
He spat straight 'n' he steered true, but listen to me, say I,
Take 'n' cover 'n' bury him now, 'n' I'll take 'n' tell you why.

"It's a rummy rig of a guffy's yarn, 'n' the juice of a rummy note,
But if you buries a corp at night, it takes 'n' keeps afloat,
For its bloody soul's afraid o' the dark 'n' sticks within the throat.

"'N' all the night till the grey o' the dawn the dead 'un has to swim

With a blue 'n' beastly Will o' the Wisp a-burnin' over him,
With a herring, maybe, a-scoffin' a toe or a shark a-chewin' a limb.

"'N' all the night the shiverin' corp it has to swim the sea,
With its shudderin' soul inside the throat (where a soul's no right to be),
Till the sky's grey 'n' the dawn's clear, 'n' then the sperrit's free.

"Now Joe was a man was right as rain. I'm sort of sore for Joe.
'N' if we bury him durin' the day, his soul can take 'n' go;
So we'll dump his corp when the bell strikes 'n' we can get below.

"I'd fairly hate for him to swim in a blue 'n' beastly light,
With his shudderin' soul inside of him a-feelin' the fishes bite,
So over he goes at noon, say I, 'n' he shall sleep to-night."

BILL

He lay dead on the cluttered deck and stared at the cold skies,
With never a friend to mourn for him nor a hand to close his eyes:
"Bill, he's dead," was all they said; "he's dead, 'n' there he lies."

The mate came forrard at seven bells and spat across the rail:
"Just lash him up wi' some holystone in a clout o' rotten sail,
'N', rot ye, get a gait on ye, ye're slower'n a bloody snail!"

When the rising moon was a copper disc and the sea was a strip of steel,
We dumped him down to the swaying weeds ten fathom beneath the keel.
"It's rough about Bill," the fo'c's'le said, "we'll have to stand his wheel."

FEVER SHIP

There'll be no weepin' gells ashore when *our* ship sails,
Nor no crews cheerin' us, standin' at the rails,
'N' no Blue Peter a-foul the royal stay,
For we've the Yellow Fever—Harry died to-day.—
It's cruel when a fo'c's'le gets the fever!

'N' Dick has got the fever-shakes, 'n' look what I was told
(I went to get a sack for him to keep him from the cold):
"Sir, can I have a sack?" I says, "for Dick 'e's fit to die."
"Oh, sack be shot!" the skipper says, "jest let the rotter lie!"—
It's cruel when a fo'c's'le gets the fever!

It's a cruel port is Santos, and a hungry land,
With rows o' graves already dug in yonder strip of sand,
'N' Dick is hollerin' up the hatch, 'e says 'e's goin' blue,
His pore teeth are chattering, 'n' what's a man to do?—
It's cruel when a fo'c's'le gets the fever!

FEVER-CHILLS

He tottered out of the alleyway with cheeks the colour of paste,
And shivered a spell and mopped his brow with a clout of cotton waste:
"I've a lick of fever-chills," he said, "'n' my inside it's green,
But I'd be as right as rain," he said, "if I had some quinine,—
But there ain't no quinine for us poor sailor-men.

"But them there passengers," he said, "if they gets fever-chills,
There's brimmin' buckets o' quinine for them, 'n' bulgin' crates o' pills,
'N' a doctor with Latin 'n' drugs 'n' all—enough to sink a town,
'N' they lies quiet in their blushin' bunks 'n' mops their gruel down,—
But there ain't none o' them fine ways for us poor sailor-men.

"But the Chief comes forrard 'n' he says, says he, 'I give you
a straight tip:
Come none o' your Cape Horn fever lays aboard o' this yer ship.
On wi' your rags o' duds, my son, 'n' aft, 'n' down the hole:
The best cure known for fever-chills is shovelling bloody coal.'
It's *hard*, my son, that's what it is, for us poor sailor-men."

HELL'S PAVEMENT

"When I'm discharged in Liverpool 'n' draws my bit o' pay,
I won't come to sea no more.
I'll court a pretty little lass 'n' have a weddin' day,
'N' settle somewhere down ashore.

"I'll never fare to sea again a-temptin' Davy Jones,
A-hearkening to the cruel sharks a-hungerin' for my bones;
I'll run a blushin' dairy-farm or go a-crackin' stones,
Or buy 'n' keep a little liquor store,"—
So he said.

They towed her in to Liverpool, we made the hooker fast,
And the copper-bound officials paid the crew,
And Billy drew his money, but the money didn't last,
For he painted the alongshore blue,—

It was rum for Poll, and rum for Nan, and gin for Jolly Jack.
He shipped a week later in the clothes upon his back,
He had to pinch a little straw, he had to beg a sack
  To sleep on, when his watch was through,—
                                                  So he did.

SEA-CHANGE

"Goneys and gullies an' all o' the birds o' the sea,
  They ain't no birds, not really," said Billy the Dane.
"Not mollies, nor gullies, nor goneys at all," said he,
  "But simply the sperrits of mariners livin' again.

"Them birds goin' fishin' is nothin' but souls o' the drowned,
  Souls o' the drowned an' the kicked as are never no more;
An' that there haughty old albatross cruisin' around,
  Belike he's Admiral Nelson or Admiral Noah.

"An' merry's the life they are living. They settle and dip,
  They fishes, they never stands watches, they waggle their
    wings;
When a ship comes by, they fly to look at the ship
  To see how the nowaday mariners manages things.

"When freezing aloft in a snorter, I tell you I wish
  (Though maybe it ain't like a Christian)—I wish I could be
A haughty old copper-bound albatross dipping for fish
  And coming the proud over all o' the birds o' the sea."

HARBOUR-BAR

All in the feathered palm-tree tops the bright green parrots screech,
The white line of the running surf goes booming down the beach,
But I shall never see them, though the land lies close aboard,
I've shaped the last long silent tack as takes one to the Lord.

Give me the Scripters, Jakey, 'n' my pipe atween my lips,
I'm bound for somewhere south and far beyond the track of ships;
I've run my rags of colours up and clinched them to the stay,
And God, the pilot's, come aboard to bring me up the bay.

You'll mainsail-haul my bits o' things when Christ has took my soul,
'N' you'll lay me quiet somewhere at the landward end the Mole,
Where I shall hear the steamers' sterns a-squattering from the heave,
And the topsail blocks a-piping when a rope-yarn fouls the sheave.

Give me a sup of lime-juice; Lord, I'm drifting in to port,
The landfall lies to windward and the wind comes light and short,
And I'm for signing off and out to take my watch below,
And—prop a fellow, Jakey—Lord, it's time for me to go!

THE TURN OF THE TIDE

An' Bill can have my sea-boots, Nigger Jim can have my knife,
You can divvy up the dungarees an' bed,
An' the ship can have my blessing, an' the Lord can have my life,
An' sails an' fish my body when I'm dead.

An' dreaming down below there in the tangled greens an' blues,
Where the sunlight shudders golden round about,
I shall hear the ships complainin' and the cursin' of the crews,
An' be sorry when the watch is tumbled out.

I shall hear them hilly-hollying the weather crojick brace,
And the sucking of the wash about the hull;
When they chanty up the topsail I'll be hauling in my place,
For my soul will follow seawards like a gull.

I shall hear the blocks a-grunting in the bumpkins over-side,
An' the slatting of the storm-sails on the stay,
An' the rippling of the catspaw at the making of the tide,
An' the swirl and splash of porpoises at play.

An' Bill can have my sea-boots, Nigger Jim can have my knife,
You can divvy up the whack I haven't scofft,
An' the ship can have my blessing, an' the Lord can have my life,
For it's time I quit the deck and went aloft.

ONE OF WALLY'S YARNS

The watch was up on the topsail-yard a-making fast the sail,
'N' Joe was swiggin' his gasket taut, 'n' I felt the stirrup *give*,
'N' he dropped sheer from the tops'l-yard 'n' barely cleared the
    rail,
'N' o' course, we bein' aloft, *we* couldn't do nothin'—
We couldn't lower a boat and go a-lookin' for him,
For it blew hard 'n' there was sech a sea runnin'
    That no boat wouldn't live.

I seed him rise in the white o' the wake, I seed him lift a hand
('N' him in his oilskin suit 'n' all), I heard him lift a cry;
'N' there was his place on the yard 'n' all, 'n' the stirrup's
    busted strand.
'N' the old man said, "There's a cruel old sea runnin',
A cold green Barney's Bull of a sea runnin';
It's hard, but I ain't agoin' to let a boat be lowered:"
    So we left him there to die.

He couldn't have kept afloat for long an' him lashed up 'n' all,
'N' we couldn't see him for long, for the sea was blurred with
    the sleet 'n' snow,
'N' we couldn't think of him much because o' the snortin',
    screamin' squall.
There was a hand less at the halliards 'n' the braces,
'N' a name less when the watch spoke to the muster-roll,
'N' a empty bunk 'n' a pannikin as wasn't wanted
    When the watch went below.

A VALEDICTION (LIVERPOOL DOCKS)

A CRIMP. A DRUNKEN SAILOR.

Is there anything as I can do ashore for you
When you've dropped down the tide?—

You can take 'n' tell Nan I'm goin' about the world agen,
'N' that the world's wide.
'N' tell her that there ain't no postal service
Not down on the blue sea.
'N' tell her that she'd best not keep her fires alight
Nor set up late for me.
'N' tell her I'll have forgotten all about her
Afore we cross the Line.
'N' tell her that the dollars of any other sailor-man
Is as good red gold as mine.

Is there anything as I can do aboard for you
Afore the tow-rope's taut?—

I'm new to this packet and all the ways of her,
'N' I don't know of aught;
But I knows as I'm goin' down to the seas agen
'N' the seas are salt 'n' drear;
But I knows as all the doin' as you're man enough for
Won't make them lager-beer.

'N' ain't there nothin' *as I can do ashore for you*
When you've got fair afloat?—

You can buy a farm with the dollars as you've done me of
'N' cash my advance-note.

Is there anythin' you'd fancy for your breakfastin'
When you're home across Mersey Bar?—

I wants a red herrin' 'n' a prairie oyster
'N' a bucket of Three Star,
'N' a gell with redder lips than Polly has got,
'N' prettier ways than Nan—

Well, so-long, Billy, 'n' a spankin' heavy pay-day to you!

So-long, my fancy man!

A NIGHT AT DAGO TOM'S

Oh yesterday, I t'ink it was, while cruisin' down the street,
I met with Bill.—"Hullo," he says, "let's give the girls a treat."
We'd red bandanas round our necks 'n' our shrouds new rattled down,
So we filled a couple of Santy Cruz and cleared for Sailor Town.

We scooted south with a press of sail till we fetched to a caboose,
The "Sailor's Rest," by Dago Tom, alongside "Paddy's Goose."
Red curtains to the windies, ay, 'n' white sand to the floor,
And an old blind fiddler liltin' the tune of "Lowlands no more."

He played the "Shaking of the Sheets" 'n' the couples did advance,
Bowing, stamping, curtsying, in the shuffling of the dance;
The old floor rocked and quivered, so it struck beholders dumb,
'N' arterwards there was sweet songs 'n' good Jamaikey rum.

'N' there was many a merry yarn of many a merry spree
Aboard the ships with royals set a-sailing on the sea,
Yarns of the hooker "Spindrift," her as had the clipper-bow—
"There ain't no ships," says Bill to me, "like that there hooker now."

When the old blind fiddler played the tune of "Pipe the Watch
Below,"
The skew-eyed landlord dowsed the glim and bade us "stamp
'n' go,"
'N' we linked it home, did Bill 'n' I, adown the scattered streets,
Until we fetched to Land o' Nod atween the linen sheets.

PORT OF MANY SHIPS

"It's a sunny pleasant anchorage, is Kingdom Come,
Where crews is always layin' aft for double-tots o' rum,
'N' there's dancin' 'n' fiddlin' of ev'ry kind o' sort,
It's a fine place for sailor-men is that there port.
'N' I wish—
I wish as I was there.

"The winds is never nothin' more than jest light airs,
'N' no-one gets belayin'-pinned, 'n' no-one never swears,
Yer free to loaf an' laze around, yer pipe atween yer lips,
Lollin' on the fo'c's'le, sonny, lookin' at the ships.
'N' I wish—
I wish as I was there.

"For ridin' in the anchorage the ships of all the world
Have got one anchor down 'n' all sails furled.
All the sunken hookers 'n' the crews as took 'n' died
They lays there merry, sonny, swingin' to the tide.
'N' I wish—
I wish as I was there.

"Drowned old wooden hookers green wi' drippin' wrack,
Ships as never fetched to port, as never came back,
Swingin' to the blushin' tide, dippin' to the swell,
'N' the crews all singin', sonny, beatin' on the bell.
'N' I wish—
I wish as I was there."

CAPE HORN GOSPEL—I

"I was in a hooker once," said Karlssen,
"And Bill, as was a seaman, died,
So we lashed him in an old tarpaulin
And tumbled him across the side;
And the fun of it was that all his gear was
Divided up among the crew
Before that blushing human error,
Our crawling little captain, knew.

"On the passage home one morning
(As certain as I prays for grace)
There was old Bill's shadder a-hauling
At the weather mizzen-topsail brace.
He was all grown green with sea-weed,
He was all lashed up and shored;
So I says to him, I says, 'Why, Billy!
What's a-bringin' of you back aboard?'

"'I'm a-weary of them there mermaids,'
Says old Bill's ghost to me;
'It ain't no place for a Christian
Below there—under sea.
For it's all blown sand and shipwrecks,
And old bones eaten bare,
And them cold fishy females
With long green weeds for hair.'"

A VALEDICTION

We're bound for blue water where the great winds blow,
It's time to get the tacks aboard, time for us to go;
The crowd's at the capstan and the tune's in the shout,
"A long pull, a strong pull, *and warp the hooker out.*"

The bow-wash is eddying, spreading from the bows,
Aloft and loose the topsails and some one give a rouse;
A salt Atlantic chanty shall be music to the dead,
"A long pull, a strong pull, *and the yard to the masthead.*"

Green and merry run the seas, the wind comes cold,
Salt and strong and pleasant, and worth a mint of gold;
And she's staggering, swooping, as she feels her feet,
"A long pull, a strong pull, *and aft the main-sheet.*"

Shrilly squeal the running sheaves, the weather-gear strains,
Such a clatter of chain-sheets, the devil's in the chains;
Over us the bright stars, under us the drowned,
"A long pull, a strong pull, *and we're outward bound!*"

Yonder, round and ruddy, is the mellow old moon,
The red-funneled tug has gone, and now, sonny, soon
We'll be clear of the Channel, so watch how you steer,
"Ease her when she pitches, *and so-long, my dear!*"

A PIER-HEAD CHORUS

Oh I'll be chewing salted horse and biting flinty bread,
And dancing with the stars to watch, upon the fo'c's'le head,
Hearkening to the bow-wash and the welter of the tread
Of a thousand tons of clipper running free.

For the tug has got the tow-rope and will take us to the Downs,
Her paddles churn the river-wrack to muddy greens and browns,
And I have given river-wrack and all the filth of towns
For the rolling, combing cresters of the sea.

We'll sheet the mizzen-royals home and shimmer down the Bay,
The sea-line blue with billows, the land-line blurred and grey;
The bow-wash will be piling high and thrashing into spray,
As the hooker's fore-foot tramples down the swell.

She'll log a giddy seventeen and rattle out the reel,
The weight of all the run-out line will be a thing to feel,
As the bacca-quidding shell-back shambles aft to take the wheel,
And the sea-sick little middy strikes the bell.

THE GOLDEN CITY OF ST. MARY

Out beyond the sunset, could I but find the way,
Is a sleepy blue laguna which widens to a bay,
And there's the Blessed City—so the sailors say—
The Golden City of St. Mary.

It's built of fair marble—white—without a stain,
And in the cool twilight when the sea-winds wane
The bells chime faintly, like a soft, warm rain,
In the Golden City of St. Mary.

Among the green palm-trees where the fire-flies shine,
Are the white tavern tables where the gallants dine,
Singing slow Spanish songs like old mulled wine,
In the Golden City of St. Mary.

Oh I'll be shipping sunset-wards and westward-ho
Through the green toppling combers a-shattering into snow,
Till I come to quiet moorings and a watch below,
In the Golden City of St. Mary.

TRADE WINDS

In the harbour, in the island, in the Spanish Seas,
Are the tiny white houses and the orange-trees,
And day-long, night-long, the cool and pleasant breeze
Of the steady Trade Winds blowing.

There is the red wine, the nutty Spanish ale,
The shuffle of the dancers, the old salt's tale,
The squeaking fiddle, and the soughing in the sail
Of the steady Trade Winds blowing.

And o' nights there's fire-flies and the yellow moon,
And in the ghostly palm-trees the sleepy tune
Of the quiet voice calling me, the long low croon
Of the steady Trade Winds blowing.

SEA-FEVER

I must go down to the seas again, to the lonely sea and the sky,
And all I ask is a tall ship and a star to steer her by,
And the wheel's kick and the wind's song and the white sail's shaking,
And a grey mist on the sea's face and a grey dawn breaking.

I must go down to the seas again, for the call of the running tide
Is a wild call and a clear call that may not be denied;
And all I ask is a windy day with the white clouds flying,
And the flung spray and the blown spume and the sea-gulls crying.

I must go down to the seas again to the vagrant gypsy life,
To the gull's way and the whale's way where the wind's like
a whetted knife;
And all I ask is a merry yarn from a laughing fellow-rover,
And quiet sleep and a sweet dream when the long trick's over.

A WANDERER'S SONG

A wind's in the heart of me, a fire's in my heels,
I am tired of brick and stone and rumbling wagon-wheels;
I hunger for the sea's edge, the limits of the land,
Where the wild old Atlantic is shouting on the sand.

Oh I'll be going, leaving the noises of the street,
To where a lifting foresail-foot is yanking at the sheet;
To a windy, tossing anchorage where yawls and ketches ride,
Oh I'll be going, going, until I meet the tide.

And first I'll hear the sea-wind, the mewing of the gulls,
The clucking, sucking of the sea about the rusty hulls,
The songs at the capstan in the hooker warping out,
And then the heart of me'll know I'm there or thereabout.

Oh I am tired of brick and stone, the heart of me is sick,
For windy green, unquiet sea, the realm of Moby Dick;
And I'll be going, going, from the roaring of the wheels,
For a wind's in the heart of me, a fire's in my heels.

CARDIGAN BAY

Clean, green, windy billows notching out the sky,
Grey clouds tattered into rags, sea-winds blowing high,
And the ships under topsails, beating, thrashing by,
And the mewing of the herring gulls.

Dancing, flashing green seas, shaking white locks,
Boiling in blind eddies over hidden rocks,
And the wind in the rigging, the creaking of the blocks,
  And the straining of the timber hulls.

Delicate, cool sea-weeds, green and amber-brown,
In beds where shaken sunlight slowly filters down
On many a drowned seventy-four, and many a sunken town,
  And the whitening of the dead men's skulls.

CHRISTMAS EVE AT SEA

A wind is rustling "south and soft,"
  Cooing a quiet country tune,
The calm sea sighs, and far aloft
  The sails are ghostly in the moon.

Unquiet ripples lisp and purr,
  A block there pipes and chirps i' the sheave,
The wheel-ropes jar, the reef-points stir
  Faintly—and it is Christmas Eve.

The hushed sea seems to hold her breath,
  And o'er the giddy, swaying spars,
Silent and excellent as Death,
  The dim blue skies are bright with stars.

Dear God—they shone in Palestine
  Like this, and yon pale moon serene
Looked down among the lowing kine
  On Mary and the Nazarene.

The angels called from deep to deep,
  The burning heavens felt the thrill,
Startling the flocks of silly sheep
  And lonely shepherds on the hill.

To-night beneath the dripping bows,
Where flashing bubbles burst and throng,
The bow-wash murmurs and sighs and soughs
A message from the angels' song.

The moon goes nodding down the west,
The drowsy helmsman strikes the bell;
Rex Judæorum natus est,
I charge you, brothers, sing *Nowell,*
Nowell,
Rex Judæorum natus est.

A BALLAD OF CAPE ST. VINCENT

Now, Bill, ain't it prime to be a-sailin',
Slippin' easy, splashin' up the sea,
Dossin' snug aneath the weather-railin',
Quiddin' bonded Jacky out a-lee?
English sea astern us and afore us,
Reaching out three thousand miles ahead,
God's own stars a-risin' solemn o'er us,
And—yonder's Cape St. Vincent and the Dead.

There they lie, Bill, man and mate together,
Dreamin' out the dog-watch down below,
Anchored in the Port of Pleasant Weather,
Waiting for the Bo'sun's call to blow.
Over them the tide goes lappin', swayin',
Under them's the wide bay's muddy bed,
And it's pleasant dreams—to them—to hear us sayin',
Yonder's Cape St. Vincent and the Dead.

Hear that P. and O. boat's engines dronin',
Beating out of time and out of tune,
Ripping past with every plate a-groanin',
Spitting smoke and cinders at the moon?
Ports a-lit like little stars a-settin',
See 'em glintin' yaller, green, and red,
Loggin' twenty knots, Bill,—but forgettin',
Yonder's Cape St. Vincent and the Dead.

They're "discharged" now, Billy, "left the service,"
Rough an' bitter was the watch they stood,
Drake an' Blake, an' Collingwood an' Jervis,
Nelson, Rodney, Hawke, an' Howe an' Hood.
They'd a hard time, haulin' an' directin',
There's the flag they left us, Billy—tread
Straight an' keep it flyin'—recollectin',
Yonder's Cape St. Vincent and the Dead.

THE TARRY BUCCANEER

I'm going to be a pirate with a bright brass pivot-gun,
And an island in the Spanish Main beyond the setting sun,
And a silver flagon full of red wine to drink when work is done,
Like a fine old salt-sea scavenger, like a tarry Buccaneer.

With a sandy creek to careen in, and a pig-tailed Spanish mate,
And under my main-hatches a sparkling merry freight
Of doubloons and double moidores and pieces of eight,
Like a fine old salt-sea scavenger, like a tarry Buccaneer.

With a taste for Spanish wine-shops and for spending my doubloons,
And a crew of swart mulattoes and black-eyed octoroons,
And a thoughtful way with mutineers of making them maroons,
Like a fine old salt-sea scavenger, like a tarry Buccaneer.

With a sash of crimson velvet and a diamond-hilted sword,
And a silver whistle about my neck secured to a golden cord,
And a habit of taking captives and walking them along a board,
Like a fine old salt-sea scavenger, like a tarry Buccaneer.

With a spy-glass tucked beneath my arm and a cocked hat cocked askew,
And a long low rakish schooner a-cutting of the waves in two,
And a flag of skull and cross-bones the wickedest that ever flew,
Like a fine old salt-sea scavenger, like a tarry Buccaneer.

A BALLAD OF JOHN SILVER

We were schooner-rigged and rakish, with a long and lissome hull,
And we flew the pretty colours of the cross-bones and the skull;
We'd a big black Jolly Roger flapping grimly at the fore,
And we sailed the Spanish Water in the happy days of yore.

We'd a long brass gun amidships, like a well-conducted ship,
We had each a brace of pistols and a cutlass at the hip;
It's a point which tells against us, and a fact to be deplored,
But we chased the goodly merchant-men and laid their ships aboard.

Then the dead men fouled the scuppers and the wounded filled the chains.
And the paint-work all was spatter-dashed with other people's brains,
She was boarded, she was looted, she was scuttled till she sank,
And the pale survivors left us by the medium of the plank.

O! then it was (while standing by the taffrail on the poop)
We could hear the drowning folk lament the absent chicken-coop;
Then, having washed the blood away, we'd little else to do
Than to dance a quiet hornpipe as the old salts taught us to.

O! the fiddle on the fo'c's'le, and the slapping naked soles,
And the genial "Down the middle, Jake, and curtsey when she
rolls!"
With the silver seas around us and the pale moon overhead,
And the look-out not a-looking and his pipe-bowl glowing red.

Ah! the pig-tailed, quidding pirates and the pretty pranks we
played,
All have since been put a stop to by the naughty Board of
Trade;
The schooners and the merry crews are laid away to rest,
A little south the sunset in the Islands of the Blest.

D'AVALOS' PRAYER

When the last sea is sailed, when the last shallow charted,
When the last field is reaped, and the last harvest stored,
When the last fire is out and the last guest departed,
Grant the last prayer that I shall pray, Be good to me, O Lord!

And let me pass in a night at sea, a night of storm and thunder,
In the loud crying of the wind through sail and rope and spar.
Send me a ninth great peaceful wave to drown and roll me under
To the cold tunny-fishes' home where the drowned galleons are.

And in the dim green quiet place far out of sight and hearing,
Grant I may hear at whiles the wash and thresh of the sea-foam
About the fine keen bows of the stately clippers steering
Towards the lone northern star and the fair ports of home.

THE WEST WIND

It's a warm wind, the west wind, full of birds' cries;
I never hear the west wind but tears are in my eyes.
For it comes from the west lands, the old brown hills,
And April's in the west wind, and daffodils.

It's a fine land, the west land, for hearts as tired as mine,
Apple orchards blossom there, and the air's like wine.
There is cool green grass there, where men may lie at rest,
And the thrushes are in song there, fluting from the nest.

"Will you not come home, brother? you have been long away,
It's April, and blossom time, and white is the spray;
And bright is the sun, brother, and warm is the rain,—
Will you not come home, brother, home to us again?

The young corn is green, brother, where the rabbits run,
It's blue sky, and white clouds, and warm rain and sun.
It's song to a man's soul, brother, fire to a man's brain,
To hear the wild bees and see the merry spring again.

Larks are singing in the west, brother, above the green wheat,
So will ye not come home, brother, and rest your tired feet?
I've a balm for bruised hearts, brother, sleep for aching eyes,"
Says the warm wind, the west wind, full of birds' cries.

It's the white road westwards is the road I must tread
To the green grass, the cool grass, and rest for heart and head,
To the violets and the brown brooks and the thrushes' song,
In the fine land, the west land, the land where I belong.

THE GALLEY-ROWERS

Staggering over the running combers
  The long-ship heaves her dripping flanks,
Singing together, the sea-roamers
  Drive the oars grunting in the banks.
    A long pull,
    And a long long pull to Mydath.

"Where are ye bound, ye swart sea-farers,
  Vexing the grey wind-angered brine,
Bearers of home-spun cloth, and bearers
  Of goat-skins filled with country wine?"

"We are bound sunset-wards, not knowing,
  Over the whale's way miles and miles,
Going to Vine-Land, haply going
  To the Bright Beach of the Blessed Isles.

"In the wind's teeth and the spray's stinging
  Westward and outward forth we go,
Knowing not whither nor why, but singing
  An old old oar-song as we row.
    A long pull,
    And a long long pull to Mydath."

VAGABOND

Dunno a heap about the what an' why,
  Can't say's I ever knowed.
Heaven to me's a fair blue stretch of sky,
  Earth's jest a dusty road.

Dunno the names o' things, nor what they are,
Can't say's I ever will.
Dunno about God—he's jest the noddin' star
Atop the windy hill.

Dunno about Life—it's jest a tramp alone
From wakin'-time to doss.
Dunno about Death—it's jest a quiet stone
All over-grey wi' moss.

An' why I live, an' why the old world spins,
Are things I never knowed;
My mark's the gypsy fires, the lonely inns,
An' jest the dusty road.

VISION

I have drunken the red wine and flung the dice;
Yet once in the noisy ale-house I have seen and heard
The dear pale lady with the mournful eyes,
And a voice like that of a pure grey cooing bird.

With delicate white hands—white hands that I have kist
(Oh frail white hands!)—she soothed my aching eyes;
And her hair fell about her in a dim clinging mist,
Like smoke from a golden incense burned in Paradise.

With gentle loving words, like shredded balm and myrrh,
She healed with sweet forgiveness my black bitter sins,
Then passed into the night, and I go seeking her
Down the dark, silent streets, past the warm, lighted inns.

SPUNYARN

Spunyarn, spunyarn, with one to turn the crank,
And one to slather the spunyarn, and one to knot the hank;
It's an easy job for a summer watch, and a pleasant job enough,
To twist the tarry lengths of yarn to shapely sailor stuff.

Life is nothing but spunyarn on a winch in need of oil,
Little enough is twined and spun but fever-fret and moil.
I have travelled on land and sea, and all that I have found
Are these poor songs to brace the arms that help the winches
round.

PERSONAL

Tramping at night in the cold and wet, I passed the lighted inn,
And an old tune, a sweet tune, was being played within.
It was full of the laugh of the leaves and the song the wind sings;
It brought the tears and the choked throat, and a catch to the
heart-strings.

And it brought a bitter thought of the days that now were dead
to me,
The merry days in the old home before I went to sea—
Days that were dead to me indeed. I bowed my head to the rain,
And I passed by the lighted inn to the lonely roads again.

ON MALVERN HILL

A wind is brushing down the clover,
It sweeps the tossing branches bare,
Blowing the poising kestrel over
The crumbling ramparts of the Caer.

It whirls the scattered leaves before us
  Along the dusty road to home,
Once it awakened into chorus
  The heart-strings in the ranks of Rome.

There by the gusty coppice border
  The shrilling trumpets broke the halt,
The Roman line, the Roman order,
  Swayed forwards to the blind assault.

Spearman and charioteer and bowman
  Charged and were scattered into spray,
Savage and taciturn the Roman
  Hewed upwards in the Roman way.

There—in the twilight—where the cattle
  Are lowing home across the fields,
The beaten warriors left the battle
  Dead on the clansmen's wicker shields.

The leaves whirl in the wind's riot
  Beneath the Beacon's jutting spur,
Quiet are clan and chief, and quiet
  Centurion and signifer.

ON EASTNOR KNOLL

Silent are the woods, and the dim green boughs are
Hushed in the twilight: yonder, in the path through
The apple orchard, is a tired plough-boy
Calling the cows home.

A bright white star blinks, the pale moon rounds, but
Still the red, lurid wreckage of the sunset
Smoulders in smoky fire, and burns on
The misty hill-tops.

Ghostly it grows, and darker, the burning
Fades into smoke, and now the gusty oaks are
A silent army of phantoms thronging
A land of shadows.

"REST HER SOUL, SHE'S DEAD"

She has done with the sea's sorrow and all the world's way
And the wind's grief;
Strew her with laurel, cover her with bay
And ivy-leaf.
Let the slow mournful music sound before her,
Strew the white flowers about the bier, and o'er her
The sleepy poppies red beyond belief.

On the black velvet covering her eyes
Let the dull earth be thrown;
Hers is the mightier silence of the skies,
And long, quiet rest alone.
Over the pure, dark wistful eyes of her,
O'er all the human, all that dies of her,
Gently let flowers be strown.

Lay her away in quiet old peaceful earth
(This blossom of ours),
She has done with the world's anger and the world's mirth,
Sunshine and rain-showers;
And over the poor, sad, tired face of her,
In the long grass above the place of her
(The grass which hides the glory and the grace of her),
May the Spring bring the flowers.

"ALL YE THAT PASS BY"

On the long dusty ribbon of the long city street,
The pageant of life is passing me on multitudinous feet,
With a word here of the hills, and a song there of the sea,
And—the great movement changes—the pageant passes me.

Faces—passionate faces—of men I may not know,
They haunt me, burn me to the heart, as I turn aside to go:
The king's face and the cur's face, and the face of the stuffed
swine,
They are passing, they are passing, their eyes look into mine.

I never can tire of the music of the noise of many feet,
The thrill of the blood pulsing, the tick of the heart's beat,
Of the men many as sands, of the squadrons ranked and massed
Who are passing, changing always, and never have changed
or passed.

IN MEMORY OF A. P. R.

Once in the windy wintry weather,
The road dust blowing in our eyes,
We starved or tramped or slept together
Beneath the haystacks and the skies;

Until the tiring tramp was over,
And then the call for him was blown,
He left his friend—his fellow-rover—
To tramp the dusty roads alone.

The winds wail and the woods are yellow,
The hills are blotted in the rain,
"And would he were with me," sighs his fellow,
"With me upon the roads again!"

TO-MORROW

Oh, yesterday the cutting edge drank thirstily and deep,
The upland outlaws ringed us in and herded us as sheep,
They drove us from the stricken field and bayed us into keep;
    But to-morrow,
  By the living God, we'll try the game again!

Oh, yesterday our little troop was ridden through and through,
Our swaying, tattered pennons fled, a broken, beaten few,
And all a summer afternoon they hunted us and slew;
    But to-morrow,
  By the living God, we'll try the game again!

And here upon the turret-top the bale-fire glowers red,
The wake-lights burn and drip about our hacked, disfigured dead,
And many a broken heart is here and many a broken head;
    But to-morrow,
  By the living God, we'll try the game again!

CAVALIER

All the merry kettle-drums are thudding into rhyme,
  Dust is swimming dizzily down the village street,
The scabbards are clattering, the feathers nodding time,
  To a clink of many horses' shoes, a tramp of many feet.

Seven score of Cavaliers fighting for the King,
  Trolling lusty stirrup-songs, clamouring for wine,
Riding with a loose rein, marching with a swing,
  Beneath the blue bannerol of Rupert of the Rhine.

Hey the merry company;—the loud fifes playing—
  Blue scarves and bright steel and blossom of the may,
Roses in the feathered hats, the long plumes swaying,
  A king's son ahead of them showing them the way.

GLOSSARY

Abaft the beam.—That half of a ship included between her amidship section and the taffrail. (For "taffrail," *see* below.)

Abel Brown.—An unquotable sea-song.

Advance-note.—A note for one month's wages issued to sailors on their signing a ship's articles.

Belaying-pins.—Bars of iron or hard wood to which running rigging may be secured or *belayed.*

Belaying-pins, from their handiness and peculiar club-shape, are sometimes used as bludgeons.

Bloody.—An intensive derived from the substantive "blood," a name applied to the Bucks, Scowrers, and Mohocks of the seventeenth and eighteenth centuries.

Blue Peter.—A blue and white flag hoisted at the fore-trucks of ships about to sail.

Bollard.—From *bōl* or *bōle*, the round trunk of a tree. A phallic or "sparklet"-shaped ornament of the dock-side, of assistance to mariners in warping into or out of dock.

Bonded Jacky.—Negro-head tobacco or sweet cake.

Bull of Barney.—A beast mentioned in an unquotable sea-proverb.

Bumpkin.—An iron bar (projecting out-board from the ship's side) to which the lower and topsail brace blocks are sometimes hooked.

Cape Horn fever.—The illness proper to malingerers.

Catted.—Said of an anchor when weighed and secured to the "cat-head."

Chanty.—A song sung to lighten labour at the capstan, sheets, and halliards. The soloist is known as the chanty-man, and is usually a person of some authority in the fo'c's'le. Many chanties are of great beauty and extreme antiquity.

Clipper-bow.—A bow of delicate curves and lines.

Clout.—A rag or cloth. Also a blow:—"I fetched him a clout i' the lug."

Crimp.—A sort of scoundrelly land-shark preying upon sailors.

D. B. S.—Distressed British Sailor. A term applied to those who are invalided home from foreign ports.

Dungaree.—A cheap, rough thin cloth (generally blue or brown), woven, I am told, of coco-nut fibre.

Fo'c's'le (Forecastle).—The deck-house or living-room of the crew. The word is often used to indicate the crew, or those members of it described by passengers as the "common sailors."

Fore-stay.—A powerful wire rope supporting the fore-mast forward.
Forward or *Forrard.*—Towards the bows.

Gaskets.—Ropes or plaited lines used to secure the sails in furling.
Goneys.—Albatrosses.
Guffy.—A marine or jolly.
Gullies.—Sea-gulls, Cape Horn pigeons, etc.

Heave and pawl.—A cry of encouragement at the capstan.
Hooker.—A periphrasis for ship, I suppose from a ship's carrying *hooks* or anchors.

Jack or Jackstay.—A slender iron rail running along the upper portions of the yards in some ships.

Leeward.—Pronounced "looard." That quarter to which the wind blows.

Mainsail haul.—An order in tacking ship bidding "swing the mainyards." To loot, steal, or "acquire."
Main-shrouds.—Ropes, usually wire, supporting lateral strains upon the main-mast.
Mollies.—Molly-hawks, or Fulmar petrels. Wide-winged, dusky sea-fowls, common in high latitudes, oily to taste, gluttonous. Great fishers and garbage-eaters.

Port Mahon Baboon, or *Port Mahon Soger.*—I have been unable to discover either the origin of these insulting epithets or the reasons for the peculiar bitterness with which they sting the marine recipient. They are older than Dana (*circa* 1840).

An old merchant sailor, now dead, once told me that Port Mahon was that godless city from which the Ark set sail, in which case the name may have some traditional connection with that evil "Mahoun" or "Mahu," prince of darkness, mentioned by Shakespeare and some of our older poets.

The real Port Mahon, a fine harbour in Minorca, was taken by the French, from Admiral Byng, in the year 1756.

I think that the phrases originated at the time of Byng's consequent trial and execution.
Purchase.—*See* "Tackle."

Quidding.—Tobacco-chewing.

Sails.—The sail-maker.
Santa-Cruz.—A brand of rum.

Scantling.—Planks.

Soger.—A laggard, malingerer, or hang-back. To loaf or skulk or work Tom Cox's Traverse.

Spunyarn.—A three-strand line spun out of old rope-yarns knotted together. Most sailing-ships carry a spunyarn winch, and the spinning of such yarn is a favourite occupation in fine weather.

Stirrup.—A short rope supporting the foot-rope on which the sailors stand when aloft on the yards.

Tack.—To stay or 'bout ship. A reach to windward. The weather lower corner of a course.

Tackle.—Pronounced *taykle.* A combination of pulleys for obtaining of artificial power.

Taffrail.—The rail or bulwark round the sternmost end of a ship's poop or after-deck.

Trick.—The ordinary two-hour spell at the wheel or on the look-out.

Windward or *Weather.*—That quarter from which the wind blows.

MISCELLANEOUS POEMS

MISCELLANEOUS POEMS

THE BALLAD OF SIR BORS

Would I could win some quiet and rest, and a little ease,
In the cool grey hush of the dusk, in the dim green place of the
trees,
Where the birds are singing, singing, singing, crying aloud
The song of the red, red rose that blossoms beyond the seas.

Would I could see it, the rose, when the light begins to fail,
And a lone white star in the West is glimmering on the mail;
The red, red passionate rose of the sacred blood of the Christ,
In the shining chalice of God, the cup of the Holy Grail.

The dusk comes gathering grey, and the darkness dims the
West,
The oxen low to the byre, and all bells ring to rest;
But I ride over the moors, for the dusk still bides and waits,
That brims my soul with the glow of the rose that ends the
Quest.

My horse is spavined and ribbed, and his bones come through
his hide,
My sword is rotten with rust, but I shake the reins and ride,
For the bright white birds of God that nest in the rose have
called,
And never a township now is a town where I can bide.

It will happen at last, at dusk, as my horse limps down the
fell,
A star will glow like a note God strikes on a silver bell,
And the bright white birds of God will carry my soul to Christ,
And the sight of the Rose, the Rose, will pay for the years of
hell.

SPANISH WATERS

Spanish waters, Spanish waters, you are ringing in my ears,
Like a slow sweet piece of music from the grey forgotten years;
Telling tales, and beating tunes, and bringing weary thoughts
to me
Of the sandy beach at Muertos, where I would that I could be.

There's a surf breaks on Los Muertos, and it never stops to roar,
And it's there we came to anchor, and it's there we went ashore,
Where the blue lagoon is silent amid snags of rotting trees,
Dropping like the clothes of corpses cast up by the seas.

We anchored at Los Muertos when the dipping sun was red,
We left her half-a-mile to sea, to west of Nigger Head;
And before the mist was on the Cay, before the day was done,
We were all ashore on Muertos with the gold that we had won.

We bore it through the marshes in a half-score battered chests,
Sinking, in the sucking quagmires, to the sunburn on our
breasts,
Heaving over tree-trunks, gasping, damning at the flies and heat,
Longing for a long drink, out of silver, in the ship's cool lazareet.

The moon came white and ghostly as we laid the treasure down,
There was gear there'd make a beggarman as rich as Lima Town,
Copper charms and silver trinkets from the chests of Spanish
crews,
Gold doubloons and double moydores, louis d'ors and portagues,

Clumsy yellow-metal earrings from the Indians of Brazil,
Uncut emeralds out of Rio, bezoar stones from Guayaquil;
Silver, in the crude and fashioned, pots of old Arica bronze,
Jewels from the bones of Incas desecrated by the Dons.

We smoothed the place with mattocks, and we took and blazed
 the tree,
Which marks yon where the gear is hid that none will ever see,
And we laid aboard the ship again, and south away we steers,
Through the loud surf of Los Muertos which is beating in my
 ears.

I'm the last alive that knows it. All the rest have gone their
 ways
Killed, or died, or come to anchor in the old Mulatas Cays,
And I go singing, fiddling, old and starved and in despair,
And I know where all that gold is hid, if I were only there.

It's not the way to end it all. I'm old, and nearly blind,
And an old man's past's a strange thing, for it never leaves
 his mind.
And I see in dreams, awhiles, the beach, the sun's disc dipping
 red,
And the tall ship, under topsails, swaying in past Nigger Head.

I'd be glad to step ashore there. Glad to take a pick and go
To the lone blazed coco-palm tree in the place no others know,
And lift the gold and silver that has mouldered there for years
By the loud surf of Los Muertos which is beating in my ears.

CARGOES

Quinquireme of Nineveh from distant Ophir,
Rowing home to haven in sunny Palestine,
With a cargo of ivory,
And apes and peacocks,
Sandalwood, cedarwood, and sweet white wine.

Stately Spanish galleon coming from the Isthmus,
Dipping through the Tropics by the palm-green shores,

With a cargo of diamonds,
Emeralds, amethysts,
Topazes, and cinnamon, and gold moidores.

Dirty British coaster with a salt-caked smoke stack,
Butting through the Channel in the mad March days,
With a cargo of Tyne coal,
Road-rails, pig-lead,
Firewood, iron-ware, and cheap tin trays.

CAPTAIN STRATTON'S FANCY

Oh some are fond of red wine, and some are fond of white,
And some are all for dancing by the pale moonlight;
But rum alone's the tipple, and the heart's delight
Of the old bold mate of Henry Morgan.

Oh some are fond of Spanish wine, and some are fond of French,
And some'll swallow tay and stuff fit only for a wench;
But I'm for right Jamaica till I roll beneath the bench,
Says the old bold mate of Henry Morgan.

Oh some are for the lily, and some are for the rose,
But I am for the sugar-cane that in Jamaica grows;
For it's that that makes the bonny drink to warm my copper nose,
Says the old bold mate of Henry Morgan.

Oh some are fond of fiddles, and a song well sung,
And some are all for music for to lilt upon the tongue;
But mouths were made for tankards, and for sucking at the bung,
Says the old bold mate of Henry Morgan.

Oh some are fond of dancing, and some are fond of dice,
And some are all for red lips, and pretty lasses' eyes;
But a right Jamaica puncheon is a finer prize
  To the old bold mate of Henry Morgan.

Oh some that's good and godly ones they hold that it's a sin
To troll the jolly bowl around, and let the dollars spin;
But I'm for toleration and for drinking at an inn,
  Says the old bold mate of Henry Morgan.

Oh some are sad and wretched folk that go in silken suits,
And there's a mort of wicked rogues that live in good reputes;
So I'm for drinking honestly, and dying in my boots,
  Like an old bold mate of Henry Morgan.

AN OLD SONG RE-SUNG

I saw a ship a-sailing, a-sailing, a-sailing,
With emeralds and rubies and sapphires in her hold;
And a bosun in a blue coat bawling at the railing,
Piping through a silver call that had a chain of gold;
The summer wind was failing and the tall ship rolled.

I saw a ship a-steering, a-steering, a-steering,
With roses in red thread worked upon her sails;
With sacks of purple amethysts, the spoils of buccaneering,
Skins of musky yellow wine, and silks in bales,
Her merry men were cheering, hauling on the brails.

I saw a ship a-sinking, a-sinking, a-sinking,
With glittering sea-water splashing on her decks,
With seamen in her spirit-room singing songs and drinking,
Pulling claret bottles down, and knocking off the necks,
The broken glass was chinking as she sank among the wrecks.

ST. MARY'S BELLS

It's pleasant in Holy Mary
By San Marie lagoon,
The bells they chime and jingle
From dawn to afternoon.
They rhyme and chime and mingle,
They pulse and boom and beat,
And the laughing bells are gentle
And the mournful bells are sweet.

Oh, who are the men that ring them,
The bells of San Marie,
Oh, who but sonsie seamen
Come in from over sea,
And merrily in the belfries
They rock and sway and hale,
And send the bells a-jangle,
And down the lusty ale.

It's pleasant in Holy Mary
To hear the beaten bells
Come booming into music,
Which throbs, and clangs, and swells,
From sunset till the daybreak,
From dawn to afternoon.
In port of Holy Mary
On San Marie lagoon.

LONDON TOWN

Oh London Town's a fine town, and London sights are rare,
And London ale is right ale, and brisk's the London air,
And busily goes the world there, but crafty grows the mind,
And London Town of all towns I'm glad to leave behind.

Then hey for croft and hop-yard, and hill, and field, and pond,
With Bredon Hill before me and Malvern Hill beyond.
The hawthorn white i' the hedgerow, and all the spring's attire
In the comely land of Teme and Lugg, and Clent, and Clee,
and Wyre.

Oh London girls are brave girls, in silk and cloth o' gold,
And London shops are rare shops where gallant things are sold,
And bonnily clinks the gold there, but drowsily blinks the eye,
And London Town of all towns I'm glad to hurry by.

Then, hey for covert and woodland, and ash and elm and oak,
Tewkesbury inns, and Malvern roofs, and Worcester chimney
smoke.
The apple trees in the orchard, the cattle in the byre,
And all the land from Ludlow town to Bredon church's spire.

Oh London tunes are new tunes, and London books are wise,
And London plays are rare plays, and fine to country eyes,
But wretchedly fare the most there and merrily fare the few,
And London Town of all towns I'm glad to hurry through.

So hey for the road, the west road, by mill and forge and fold,
Scent of the fern and song of the lark by brook, and field, and
wold,
To the comely folk at the hearth-stone and the talk beside the
fire,
In the hearty land, where I was bred, my land of heart's desire.

THE EMIGRANT

Going by Daly's shanty I heard the boys within
Dancing the Spanish hornpipe to Driscoll's violin,
I heard the sea-boots shaking the rough planks of the floor.
But I was going westward, I hadn't heart for more.

All down the windy village the noise rang in my ears,
Old sea boots stamping, shuffling, it brought the bitter tears,
The old tune piped and quavered, the lilts came clear and strong,
But I was going westward, I couldn't join the song.

There were the grey stone houses, the night wind blowing keen,
The hill-sides pale with moonlight, the young corn springing
 green,
The hearth nooks lit and kindly, with dear friends good to see,
But I was going westward, and the ship waited me.

PORT OF HOLY PETER

The blue laguna rocks and quivers,
 Dull gurgling eddies twist and spin,
The climate does for people's livers,
 It's a nasty place to anchor in
 Is Spanish port,
 Fever port,
 Port of Holy Peter.

The town begins on the sea-beaches,
 And the town's mad with the stinging flies,
The drinking water's mostly leeches,
 It's a far remove from Paradise
 Is Spanish port,
 Fever port,
 Port of Holy Peter.

There's sand-bagging and throat-slitting,
 And quiet graves in the sea slime,
Stabbing, of course, and rum-hitting,
 Dirt, and drink, and stink, and crime,
 In Spanish port,
 Fever port,
 Port of Holy Peter.

All the day the wind's blowing
  From the sick swamp below the hills,
All the night the plague's growing,
  And the dawn brings the fever-chills,
    In Spanish port,
    Fever port,
    Port of Holy Peter.

You get a thirst there's no slaking
  You get the chills and fever-shakes,
Tongue yellow and head aching,
  And then the sleep that never wakes.
And all the year the heat's baking,
  The sea rots and the earth quakes,
    In Spanish port,
    Fever port,
    Port of Holy Peter.

BEAUTY

I have seen dawn and sunset on moors and windy hills
Coming in solemn beauty like slow old tunes of Spain:
I have seen the lady April bringing the daffodils,
Bringing the springing grass and the soft warm April rain.

I have heard the song of the blossoms and the old chant of the
  sea,
And seen strange lands from under the arched white sails of
  ships;
But the loveliest things of beauty God ever has shown to me,
Are her voice, and her hair, and eyes, and the dear red curve
  of her lips.

THE SEEKERS

Friends and loves we have none, nor wealth nor blessed abode,
But the hope of the City of God at the other end of the road.

Not for us are content, and quiet, and peace of mind,
For we go seeking a city that we shall never find.

There is no solace on earth for us—for such as we—
Who search for a hidden city that we shall never see.

Only the road and the dawn, the sun, the wind, and the rain,
And the watch fire under stars, and sleep, and the road again.

We seek the City of God, and the haunt where beauty dwells,
And we find the noisy mart and the sound of burial bells.

Never the golden city, where radiant people meet,
But the dolorous town where mourners are going about the street.

We travel the dusty road 'till the light of the day is dim,
And sunset shows us spires away on the world's rim.

We travel from dawn to dusk, till the day is past and by,
Seeking the Holy City beyond the rim of the sky.

Friends and loves we have none, nor wealth nor blest abode,
But the hope of the City of God at the other end of the road.

DAWN

The dawn comes cold: the haystack smokes,
  The green twigs crackle in the fire,
The dew is dripping from the oaks,
And sleepy men bear milking-yokes
  Slowly towards the cattle-byre.

Down in the town a clock strikes six,
  The grey east heaven burns and glows,
The dew shines on the thatch of ricks,
A slow old crone comes gathering sticks,
  The red cock in the ox-yard crows.

Beyond the stack where we have lain
  The road runs twisted like a snake
(The white road to the land of Spain),
The road that we must foot again,
  Though the feet halt and the heart ache.

LAUGH AND BE MERRY

Laugh and be merry, remember, better the world with a song,
Better the world with a blow in the teeth of a wrong.
Laugh, for the time is brief, a thread the length of a span.
Laugh and be proud to belong to the old proud pageant of man.

Laugh and be merry: remember, in olden time
God made Heaven and Earth for joy He took in a rhyme,
Made them, and filled them full with the strong red wind of
  His mirth,
The splendid joy of the stars: the joy of the earth.

So we must laugh and drink from the deep blue cup of the sky,
Join the jubilant song of the great stars sweeping by,
Laugh, and battle, and work, and drink of the wine outpoured
In the dear green earth, the sign of the joy of the Lord.

Laugh and be merry together, like brothers akin,
Guesting awhile in the rooms of a beautiful inn,
Glad till the dancing stops, and the lilt of the music ends.
Laugh till the game is played; and be you merry, my friends.

JUNE TWILIGHT

The twilight comes; the sun
  Dips down and sets,
The boys have done
  Play at the nets.

In a warm golden glow
  The woods are steeped.
The shadows grow;
  The bat has cheeped.

Sweet smells the new-mown hay;
  The mowers pass
Home, each his way,
  Through the grass.

The night-wind stirs the fern,
  A night-jar spins;
The windows burn
  In the inns.

Dusky it grows. The moon!
The dews descend.
Love, can this beauty in our hearts
End?

ROADWAYS

One road leads to London,
One road runs to Wales,
My road leads me seawards
To the white dipping sails.

One road leads to the river,
As it goes singing slow;
My road leads to shipping,
Where the bronzed sailors go.

Leads me, lures me, calls me
To salt green tossing sea;
A road without earth's road-dust
Is the right road for me.

A wet road heaving, shining,
And wild with seagulls' cries,
A mad salt sea-wind blowing
The salt spray in my eyes.

My road calls me, lures me
West, east, south, and north;
Most roads lead men homewards,
My road leads me forth

To add more miles to the tally
Of grey miles left behind,
In quest of that one beauty
God put me here to find.

MIDSUMMER NIGHT

The perfect disc of the sacred moon
Through still blue heaven serenely swims,
And the lone bird's liquid music brims
The peace of the night with a perfect tune.

This is that holiest night of the year
When (the mowers say) may be heard and seen
The ghostly court of the English queen,
Who rides to harry and hunt the deer.

And the woodland creatures cower awake,
A strange unrest is on harts and does,
For the maiden Dian a-hunting goes,
And the trembling deer are afoot in the brake.

They start at a shaken leaf: the sound
Of a dry twig snapped by a squirrel's foot
Is a nameless dread: and to them the hoot
Of a mousing owl is the cry of a hound.

Oh soon the forest will ring with cries,
The dim green coverts will flash: the grass
Will glow as the radiant hunters pass
After the quarry with burning eyes.

The hurrying feet will range unstayed
Of questing goddess and hunted fawn,
Till the east is grey with the sacred dawn,
And the red cock wakens the milking maid.

THE HARPER'S SONG

This sweetness trembling from the strings
The music of my troublous lute
Hath timed Herodias' daughter's foot;
Setting a-clink her ankle-rings
Whenas she danced to feasted kings.

Where gemmed apparel burned and caught
The sunset 'neath the golden dome,
To the dark beauties of old Rome
My sorrowful lute hath haply brought
Sad memories sweet with tender thought.

When night had fallen and lights and fires
Were darkened in the homes of men,
Some sighing echo stirred :—and then
The old cunning wakened from the wires
The old sorrows and the old desires.

Dead Kings in long forgotten lands,
And all dead beauteous women; some
Whose pride imperial hath become
Old armour rusting in the sands
And shards of iron in dusty hands,

Have heard my lyre's soft rise and fall
  Go trembling down the paven ways,
  Till every heart was all ablaze—
Hasty each foot—to obey the call
To triumph or to funeral.

Could I begin again the slow
  Sweet mournful music filled with tears,
  Surely the old, dead, dusty ears
Would hear; the old drowsy eyes would glow,
Old memories come; old hopes and fears,
And time restore the long ago.

THE GENTLE LADY

So beautiful, so dainty-sweet,
So like a lyre's delightful touch—
A beauty perfect, ripe, complete
That art's own hand could only smutch
And nature's self not better much.

So beautiful, so purely wrought,
Like a fair missal penned with hymns,
So gentle, so surpassing thought—
A beauteous soul in lovely limbs,
A lantern that an angel trims.

So simple-sweet, without a sin,
Like gentle music gently timed,
Like rhyme-words coming aptly in,
To round a moonèd poem rhymed
To tunes the laughing bells have chimed.

THE DEAD KNIGHT

The cleanly rush of the mountain air,
And the mumbling, grumbling humble-bees,
Are the only things that wander there.
The pitiful bones are laid at ease,
The grass has grown in his tangled hair,
And a rambling bramble binds his knees.

To shrieve his soul from the pangs of hell,
The only requiem bells that rang
Were the harebell and the heather bell.
Hushed he is with the holy spell
In the gentle hymn the wind sang,
And he lies quiet, and sleeps well.

He is bleached and blanched with the summer sun;
The misty rain and the cold dew
Have altered him from the kingly one
Whom his lady loved, and his men knew,
And dwindled him to a skeleton.

The vetches have twined about his bones,
The straggling ivy twists and creeps
In his eye-sockets: the nettle keeps
Vigil about him while he sleeps.
Over his body the wind moans
With a dreary tune throughout the day,
In a chorus wistful, eerie, thin
As the gulls' cry, as the cry in the bay,
The mournful word the seas say
When tides are wandering out or in.

TWILIGHT

Twilight it is, and the far woods are dim, and the rooks cry
and call.
Down in the valley the lamps, and the mist, and a star over all,
There by the rick, where they thresh, is the drone at an end.
Twilight it is, and I travel the road with my friend.

I think of the friends who are dead, who were dear long ago
in the past,
Beautiful friends who are dead, though I know that death
cannot last;
Friends with the beautiful eyes that the dust has defiled,
Beautiful souls who were gentle when I was a child.

INVOCATION

O wanderer into many brains,
O spark the emperor's purple hides,
You sow the dusk with fiery grains
When the gold horseman rides.
O beauty on the darkness hurled,
Be it through me you shame the world.

POSTED AS MISSING

Under all her topsails she trembled like a stag,
The wind made a ripple in her bonny red flag;
They cheered her from the shore and they cheered her from the
pier,
And under all her topsails she trembled like a deer.

So she passed swaying, where the green seas run,
Her wind-steadied topsails were stately in the sun;
There was glitter on the water from her red port light,
So she passed swaying, till she was out of sight.

Long and long ago it was, a weary time it is,
The bones of her sailor-men are coral plants by this;
Coral plants, and shark-weed, and a mermaid's comb,
And if the fishers net them they never bring them home.

It's rough on sailors' women. They have to mangle hard,
And stitch at dungarees till their finger-ends are scarred,
Thinking of the sailor-men who sang among the crowd,
Hoisting of her topsails when she sailed so proud.

A CREED

I hold that when a person dies
  His soul returns again to earth;
Arrayed in some new flesh-disguise
  Another mother gives him birth.
With sturdier limbs and brighter brain
The old soul takes the roads again.

Such is my own belief and trust;
  This hand, this hand that holds the pen,
Has many a hundred times been dust
  And turned, as dust, to dust again;
These eyes of mine have blinked and shone
In Thebes, in Troy, in Babylon.

All that I rightly think or do,
  Or make, or spoil, or bless, or blast,
Is curse or blessing justly due
  For sloth or effort in the past.
My life's a statement of the sum
Of vice indulged, or overcome.

I know that in my lives to be
  My sorry heart will ache and burn,
And worship, unavailingly,
  The woman whom I used to spurn,

And shake to see another have
The love I spurned, the love she gave.

And I shall know, in angry words,
In gibes, and mocks, and many a tear,
A carrion flock of homing-birds,
The gibes and scorns I uttered here.
The brave word that I failed to speak
Will brand me dastard on the cheek.

And as I wander on the roads
I shall be helped and healed and blessed;
Dear words shall cheer and be as goads
To urge to heights before unguessed.
My road shall be the road I made;
All that I gave shall be repaid.

So shall I fight, so shall I tread,
In this long war beneath the stars;
So shall a glory wreathe my head,
So shall I faint and show the scars,
Until this case, this clogging mould,
Be smithied all to kingly gold.

WHEN BONY DEATH

When bony Death has chilled her gentle blood,
And dimmed the brightness of her wistful eyes,
And changed her glorious beauty into mud
By his old skill in hateful wizardries;

When an old lichened marble strives to tell
How sweet a grace, how red a lip was hers;
When rheumy grey-beards say, "I knew her well,"
Showing the grave to curious worshippers;

When all the roses that she sowed in me
  Have dripped their crimson petals and decayed,
Leaving no greenery on any tree
  That her dear hands in my heart's garden laid,

Then grant, old Time, to my green mouldering skull,
These songs may keep her memory beautiful.

HER HEART

Her heart is always doing lovely things,
  Filling my wintry mind with simple flowers;
Playing sweet tunes on my untunéd strings,
  Delighting all my undelightful hours.

She plays me like a lute, what tune she will,
  No string in me but trembles at her touch,
Shakes into sacred music, or is still,
  Trembles or stops, or swells, her skill is such.
And in the dusty tavern of my soul
  Where filthy lusts drink witches' brew for wine,
Her gentle hand still keeps me from the bowl,
  Still keeps me man, saves me from being swine.

All grace in me, all sweetness in my verse,
Is hers, is my dear girl's, and only hers.

BEING HER FRIEND

Being her friend, I do not care, not I,
  How gods or men may wrong me, beat me down;
Her word's sufficient star to travel by,
  I count her quiet praise sufficient crown.

Being her friend, I do not covet gold,
  Save for a royal gift to give her pleasure;
To sit with her, and have her hand to hold,
  Is wealth, I think, surpassing minted treasure.

Being her friend, I only covet art,
A white pure flame to search me as I trace
In crooked letters from a throbbing heart
The hymn to beauty written on her face.

FRAGMENTS

Troy Town is covered up with weeds,
The rabbits and the pismires brood
On broken gold, and shards, and beads
Where Priam's ancient palace stood.

The floors of many a gallant house
Are matted with the roots of grass;
The glow-worm and the nimble mouse
Among her ruins flit and pass.

And there, in orts of blackened bone,
The widowed Trojan beauties lie,
And Simois babbles over stone
And waps and gurgles to the sky.

Once there were merry days in Troy,
Her chimneys smoked with cooking meals,
The passing chariots did annoy
The sunning housewives at their wheels.

And many a lovely Trojan maid
Set Trojan lads to lovely things;
The game of life was nobly played,
They played the game like Queens and Kings.

So that, when Troy had greatly passed
In one red roaring fiery coal,
The courts the Grecians overcast
Became a city in the soul.

In some green island of the sea,
  Where now the shadowy coral grows
In pride and pomp and empery
  The courts of old Atlantis rose.

In many a glittering house of glass
  The Atlanteans wandered there;
The paleness of their faces was
  Like ivory, so pale they were.

And hushed they were, no noise of words
  In those bright cities ever rang;
Only their thoughts, like golden birds,
  About their chambers thrilled and sang.

They knew all wisdom, for they knew
  The souls of those Egyptian Kings
Who learned, in ancient Babilu,
  The beauty of immortal things.

They knew all beauty—when they thought
  The air chimed like a stricken lyre,
The elemental birds were wrought,
  The golden birds became a fire.

And straight to busy camps and marts
  The singing flames were swiftly gone,
The trembling leaves of human hearts
  Hid boughs for them to perch upon.

And men in desert places, men
  Abandoned, broken, sick with fears,
Rose singing, swung their swords agen,
  And laughed and died among the spears.

The green and greedy seas have drowned
  That city's glittering walls and towers,
Her sunken minarets are crowned
  With red and russet water-flowers.

In towers and rooms and golden courts
  The shadowy coral lifts her sprays;
The scrawl hath gorged her broken orts,
  The shark doth haunt her hidden ways.

But, at the falling of the tide,
  The golden birds still sing and gleam,
The Atlanteans have not died,
  Immortal things still give us dream.

The dream that fires man's heart to make,
  To build, to do, to sing or say,
A beauty Death can never take,
  An Adam from the crumbled clay.

BORN FOR NOUGHT ELSE

Born for nought else, for nothing but for this,
  To watch the soft blood throbbing in her throat,
To think how comely sweet her body is,
  And learn the poem of her face by rote.

Born for nought else but to attempt a rhyme
  That shall describe her womanhood aright,
And make her holy to the end of Time,
  And be my soul's acquittal in God's sight.

Born for nought else but to expressly mark
  The music of her dear delicious ways;
Born but to perish meanly in the dark,
  Yet born to be the man to sing her praise.

Born for nought else: there is a spirit tells
My lot's a King's, being born for nothing else.

TEWKESBURY ROAD

It is good to be out on the road, and going one knows not where,
Going through meadow and village, one knows not whither nor why;
Through the grey light drift of the dust, in the keen cool rush of the air,
Under the flying white clouds, and the broad blue lift of the sky.

And to halt at the chattering brook, in the tall green fern at the brink
Where the harebell grows, and the gorse, and the foxgloves purple and white;
Where the shy-eyed delicate deer troop down to the brook to drink
When the stars are mellow and large at the coming on of the night.

O, to feel the beat of the rain, and the homely smell of the earth,
Is a tune for the blood to jig to, a joy past power of words;
And the blessed green comely meadows are all a-ripple with mirth
At the noise of the lambs at play and the dear wild cry of the birds.

THE DEATH ROOMS

My soul has many an old decaying room
Hung with the ragged arras of the past,
Where startled faces flicker in the gloom,
And horrid whispers set the cheek aghast.

Those dropping rooms are haunted by a death,
A something like a worm gnawing a brain,
That bids me heed what bitter lesson saith
The blind wind beating on the window-pane.

None dwells in those old rooms: none ever can—
I pass them through at night with hidden head;
Lock'd rotting rooms her eyes must never scan,
Floors that her blessed feet must never tread.

Haunted old rooms: rooms she must never know,
Where death-ticks knock and mouldering panels glow.

IGNORANCE

Since I have learned Love's shining alphabet,
And spelled in ink what's writ in me in flame,
And borne her sacred image richly set
Here in my heart to keep me quit of shame;

Since I have learned how wise and passing wise
Is the dear friend whose beauty I extol,
And know how sweet a soul looks through the eyes,
That are so pure a window to her soul;

Since I have learned how rare a woman shows
As much in all she does as in her looks,
And seen the beauty of her shame the rose,
And dim the beauty writ about in books;

All I have learned, and can learn, shows me this—
How scant, how slight, my knowledge of her is.

THE WATCH IN THE WOOD

When Death has laid her in his quietude,
And dimmed the glow of her benignant star,
Her tired limbs shall rest within a wood,
In a green glade where oaks and beeches are,

Where the shy fawns, the pretty fawns, the deer,
  With mild brown eyes shall view her spirit's husk;
The sleeping woman of her will appear,
  The maiden Dian shining through the dusk.

And, when the stars are white as twilight fails,
  And the green leaves are hushed, and the winds swoon,
The calm pure thrilling throats of nightingales
  Shall hymn her sleeping beauty to the moon.

All the woods hushed—save for a dripping rose,
All the woods dim—save where a glow-worm glows.

Brimming the quiet woods with holiness,
  The lone brown birds will hymn her till the dawn,
The delicate, shy, dappled deer will press
Soft pitying muzzles on her swathed lawn.

The little pretty rabbits running by
  Will pause among the dewy grass to peep,
Their thudding hearts affrighted to espy
  The maiden Dian lying there asleep.

Brown, lustrous, placid eyes of sylvan things
  Will wonder at the quiet in her face,
While from the thorny branch the singer brings
  Beauty and peace to that immortal place.

Until the grey dawn sets the woods astir
The pure birds' thrilling psalm will mourn for her.

WASTE

No rose but fades: no glory but must pass:
  No hue but dims: no precious silk but frets.
Her beauty must go underneath the grass,
  Under the long roots of the violets.

O, many glowing beauties Time has hid
  In that dark, blotting box the villain sends.
He covers over with a coffin-lid
  Mothers and sons, and foes and lovely friends.

Maids that were redly-lipped and comely-skinned,
  Friends that deserved a sweeter bed than clay,
All are as blossoms blowing down the wind,
  Things the old envious villain sweeps away.

And though the mutterer laughs and church bells toll,
Death brings another April to the soul.

THIRD MATE

All the sheets are clacking, all the blocks are whining,
The sails are frozen stiff and the wetted decks are shining;
The reef's in the topsails, and it's coming on to blow,
And I think of the dear girl I left long ago.

Grey were her eyes, and her hair was long and bonny,
Golden was her hair, like the wild bees' honey.
And I was but a dog, and a mad one to despise,
The gold of her hair and the grey of her eyes.

There's the sea before me, and my home's behind me,
And beyond there the strange lands where nobody will mind me,
No one but the girls with the paint upon their cheeks,
Who sell away their beauty to whomsoever seeks.

There'll be drink and women there, and songs and laughter,
Peace from what is past and from all that follows after;
And a fellow will forget how a woman lies awake,
Lonely in the night watch crying for his sake.

Black it blows and bad and it howls like slaughter,
And the ship she shudders as she takes the water;
Hissing flies the spindrift like a wind-blown smoke,
And I think of a woman and a heart I broke.

THE WILD DUCK

Twilight. Red in the west.
Dimness. A glow on the wood.
The teams plod home to rest.
The wild duck come to glean.
O souls not understood,
What a wild cry in the pool;
What things have the farm ducks seen
That they cry so—huddle and cry?

Only the soul that goes.
Eager. Eager. Flying.
Over the globe of the moon,
Over the wood that glows.
Wings linked. Necks a-strain,
A rush and a wild crying.

* * * * *

A cry of the long pain
In the reeds of a steel lagoon,
In a land that no man knows.

CHRISTMAS, 1903

O, the sea breeze will be steady, and the tall ship's going trim,
And the dark blue skies are paling, and the white stars burning dim;
The long night watch is over, and the long sea-roving done,
And yonder light is the Start Point light, and yonder comes the sun.

O, we have been with the Spaniards, and far and long on the sea;
But there are the twisted chimneys, and the gnarled old inns on the quay.
The wind blows keen as the day breaks, the roofs are white with the rime,
And the church-bells ring as the sun comes up to call men in to Prime.

The church-bells rock and jangle, and there is peace on the earth,
Peace and good will and plenty and Christmas games and mirth.
O, the gold glints bright on the wind-vane as it shifts above the squire's house,
And the water of the bar of Salcombe is muttering about the bows.

O, the salt sea tide of Salcombe, it wrinkles into wisps of foam,
And the church-bells ring in Salcombe to ring poor sailors home.
The belfry rocks as the bells ring, the chimes are merry as a song,
They ring home wandering sailors who have been homeless long.

THE WORD

My friend, my bonny friend, when we are old,
And hand in hand go tottering down the hill,
May we be rich in love's refinèd gold,
May love's gold coin be current with us still.

May love be sweeter for the vanished days,
And your most perfect beauty still as dear
As when your troubled singer stood at gaze
In the dear March of a most sacred year.

May what we are be all we might have been,
And that potential, perfect, O my friend,
And may there still be many sheafs to glean
In our love's acre, comrade, till the end.

And may we find, when ended is the page,
Death but a tavern on our pilgrimage.

LYRICS FROM "POMPEY THE GREAT"

I
THE CHIEF CENTURIONS

Man is a sacred city, built of marvellous earth.
Life was lived nobly here to give this body birth.
Something was in this brain and in this eager hand.
Death is so dumb and blind, Death cannot understand.
Death drifts the brain with dust and soils the young limbs' glory.
Death makes women a dream and men a traveller's story.
Death drives the lovely soul to wander under the sky.
Death opens unknown doors. It is most grand to die.

II
PHILIP SINGS

Though we are ringed with spears, though the last hope is gone,
Romans stand firm, the Roman dead look on.
Before our sparks of life blow back to him who gave,
Burn clear, brave hearts, and light our pathway to the grave.

III

CHANTY

Kneel to the beautiful women who bear us this strange brave fruit.
Man with his soul so noble: man half god and half brute.
Women bear him in pain that he may bring them tears.
He is a king on earth, he rules for a term of years.
And the conqueror's prize is dust and lost endeavour.
And the beaten man becomes a story for ever.
For the gods employ strange means to bring their will to be.
We are in the wise gods' hands and more we cannot see.

EPILOGUE TO "POMPEY THE GREAT"

And all their passionate hearts are dust,
And dust the great idea that burned
In various flames of love and lust
Till the world's brain was turned.

God, moving darkly in men's brains,
Using their passions as his tool,
Brings freedom with a tyrant's chains
And wisdom with the fool.

Blindly and bloodily we drift,
Our interests clog our hearts with dreams.
God make my brooding soul a rift
Through which a meaning gleams.

Feb. 8, 1908. *July 5, 1909.*

THE EVERLASTING MERCY

THE EVERLASTING MERCY

Thy place is biggyd above the sterrys cleer,
Noon erthely paleys wrouhte in so statly wyse,
Com on my freend, my brothir moost enteer,
For the I offryd my blood in sacrifise.

JOHN LYDGATE.

THE EVERLASTING MERCY

From '41 to '51
I was my folks' contrary son;
I bit my father's hand right through
And broke my mother's heart in two.
I sometimes go without my dinner
Now that I know the times I've gi'n her.

From '51 to '61
I cut my teeth and took to fun.
I learned what not to be afraid of
And what stuff women's lips are made of.
I learned with what a rosy feeling
Good ale makes floors seem like the ceiling,
And how the moon gives shiny light
To lads as roll home singing by't.
My blood did leap, my flesh did revel,
Saul Kane was tokened to the devil.

From '61 to '67
I lived in disbelief of Heaven.
I drunk, I fought, I poached, I whored,
I did despite unto the Lord.
I cursed, 'would make a man look pale,
And nineteen times I went to gaol.

Now, friends, observe and look upon me,
Mark how the Lord took pity on me.
By Dead Man's Thorn, while setting wires,
Who should come up but Billy Myers,
A friend of mine, who used to be
As black a sprig of hell as me,
With whom I'd planned, to save encroachin',
Which fields and coverts each should poach in.
Now when he saw me set my snare,
He tells me "Get to hell from there.
This field is mine," he says, "by right;
If you poach here, there'll be a fight.
Out now," he says, "and leave your wire;
It's mine."
"It ain't."
"You put."
"You liar."
"You closhy put."
"You bloody liar."
"This is my field."
"This is my wire."
"I'm ruler here."
"You ain't."
"I am."
"I'll fight you for it."
"Right, by damn.
Not now, though, I've a-sprained my thumb,
We'll fight after the harvest hum.
And Silas Jones, that bookie wide,
Will make a purse five pounds a side."
Those were the words, that was the place
By which God brought me into grace.

On Wood Top Field the peewits go
Mewing and wheeling ever so;

And like the shaking of a timbrel
Cackles the laughter of the whimbrel.

In the old quarry-pit they say
Head-keeper Pike was made away.
He walks, head-keeper Pike, for harm,
He taps the windows of the farm;
The blood drips from his broken chin,
He taps and begs to be let in.
On Wood Top, nights, I've shaked to hark
The peewits wambling in the dark,
Lest in the dark the old man might
Creep up to me to beg a light.

But Wood Top grass is short and sweet
And springy to a boxer's feet;
At harvest hum the moon so bright
Did shine on Wood Top for the fight.

When Bill was stripped down to his bends
I thought how long we two'd been friends,
And in my mind, about that wire,
I thought "He's right, I am a liar.
As sure as skilly's made in prison
The right to poach that copse is his'n.
I'll have no luck to-night," thinks I.
"I'm fighting to defend a lie.
And this moonshiny evening's fun
Is worse than aught I've ever done."
And thinking that way my heart bled so
I almost stept to Bill and said so.
And now Bill's dead I would be glad
If I could only think I had.
But no. I put the thought away
For fear of what my friends would say.
They'd backed me, see? O Lord, the sin
Done for the things there's money in.

The stakes were drove, the ropes were hitched,
Into the ring my hat I pitched.
My corner faced the Squire's park
Just where the fir trees make it dark;
The place where I begun poor Nell
Upon the woman's road to hell.
I thought of't, sitting in my corner
After the time-keep struck his warner
(Two brandy flasks, for fear of noise,
Clinked out the time to us two boys).
And while my seconds chafed and gloved me
I thought of Nell's eyes when she loved me,
And wondered how my tot would end,
First Nell cast off and now my friend;
And in the moonlight dim and wan
I knew quite well my luck was gone;
And looking round I felt a spite
At all who'd come to see me fight;
The five and forty human faces
Inflamed by drink and going to races,
Faces of men who'd never been
Merry or true or live or clean;
Who'd never felt the boxer's trim
Of brain divinely knit to limb,
Nor felt the whole live body go
One tingling health from top to toe;
Nor took a punch nor given a swing,
But just soaked deady round the ring
Until their brains and bloods were foul
Enough to make their throttles howl,
While we whom Jesus died to teach
Fought round on round, three minutes each.

And thinking that, you'll understand
I thought, "I'll go and take Bill's hand.

I'll up and say the fault was mine,
He shan't make play for these here swine."
And then I thought that that was silly,
They'd think I was afraid of Billy;
They'd think (I thought it, God forgive me)
I funked the hiding Bill could give me.
And that thought made me mad and hot.
"Think that, will they? Well, they shall not.
They shan't think that. I will not. I'm
Damned if I will. I will not."
  Time!

From the beginning of the bout
My luck was gone, my hand was out.
Right from the start Bill called the play,
But I was quick and kept away
Till the fourth round, when work got mixed,
And then I knew Bill had me fixed.
My hand was out, why, Heaven knows;
Bill punched me when and where he chose.
Through two more rounds we quartered wide,
And all the time my hands seemed tied;
Bill punched me when and where he pleased.
The cheering from my backers eased,
But every punch I heard a yell
Of "That's the style, Bill, give him hell."
No one for me, but Jimmy's light
"Straight left! Straight left!" and "Watch his right."

I don't know how a boxer goes
When all his body hums from blows;
I know I seemed to rock and spin,
I don't know how I saved my chin;
I know I thought my only friend
Was that clinked flask at each round's end

When my two seconds, Ed and Jimmy,
Had sixty seconds help to gimme.
But in the ninth, with pain and knocks
I stopped: I couldn't fight nor box.
Bill missed his swing, the light was tricky,
But I went down, and stayed down, dicky.
"Get up," cried Jim. I said, "I will."
Then all the gang yelled, "Out him, Bill.
Out him." Bill rushed . . . and Clink, Clink, Clink.
Time! and Jim's knee, and rum to drink.
And round the ring there ran a titter:
"Saved by the call, the bloody quitter."

They drove (a dodge that never fails)
A pin beneath my finger nails.
They poured what seemed a running beck
Of cold spring water down my neck;
Jim with a lancet quick as flies
Lowered the swellings round my eyes.
They sluiced my legs and fanned my face
Through all that blessed minute's grace;
They gave my calves a thorough kneading,
They salved my cuts and stopped the bleeding.
A gulp of liquor dulled the pain,
And then the two flasks clinked again.

Time!
There was Bill as grim as death,
He rushed, I clinched, to get more breath,
And breath I got, though Billy bats
Some stinging short-arms in my slats.
And when we broke, as I foresaw,
He swung his right in for the jaw.
I stopped it on my shoulder bone,
And at the shock I heard Bill groan—

A little groan or moan or grunt
As though I'd hit his wind a bunt.
At that, I clinched, and while we clinched,
His old time right arm dig was flinched,
And when we broke he hit me light
As though he didn't trust his right,
He flapped me somehow with his wrist
As though he couldn't use his fist,
And when he hit he winced with pain.
I thought, "Your sprained thumb's crocked again."
So I got strength and Bill gave ground,
And that round was an easy round.

During the wait my Jimmy said,
"What's making Billy fight so dead?
He's all to pieces. Is he blown?"
"His thumb's out."
"No? Then it's your own.
It's all your own, but don't be rash—
He's got the goods if you've got cash,
And what one hand can do he'll do.
Be careful this next round or two."

Time. There was Bill, and I felt sick
That luck should play so mean a trick
And give me leave to knock him out
After he'd plainly won the bout.
But by the way the man came at me
He made it plain he meant to bat me;
If you'd a seen the way he come
You wouldn't think he'd crocked a thumb.
With all his skill and all his might
He clipped me dizzy left and right;
The Lord knows what the effort cost,
But he was mad to think he'd lost,

And knowing nothing else could save him
He didn't care what pain it gave him.
He called the music and the dance
For five rounds more and gave no chance.

Try to imagine if you can
The kind of manhood in the man,
And if you'd like to feel his pain
You sprain your thumb and hit the sprain.
And hit it hard, with all your power
On something hard for half-an-hour,
While someone thumps you black and blue,
And then you'll know what Billy knew.
Bill took that pain without a sound
Till halfway through the eighteenth round,
And then I sent him down and out,
And Silas said, "Kane wins the bout."

When Bill came to, you understand,
I ripped the mitten from my hand
And went across to ask Bill shake.
My limbs were all one pain and ache,
I was so weary and so sore
I don't think I'd a stood much more.
Bill in his corner bathed his thumb,
Buttoned his shirt and glowered glum.
"I'll never shake your hand," he said.
"I'd rather see my children dead.
I've been about and had some fun with you,
But you're a liar and I've done with you.
You've knocked me out, you didn't beat me;
Look out the next time that you meet me,
There'll be no friend to watch the clock for you
And no convenient thumb to crock for you,
And I'll take care, with much delight,

You'll get what you'd a got to-night;
That puts my meaning clear, I guess,
Now get to hell; I want to dress."

I dressed. My backers one and all
Said, "Well done you," or "Good old Saul."
"Saul is a wonder and a fly 'un,
What'll you have, Saul, at the Lion?"
With merry oaths they helped me down
The stony wood path to the town.

The moonlight shone on Cabbage Walk,
It made the limestone look like chalk.
It was too late for any people;
Twelve struck as we went by the steeple.
A dog barked, and an owl was calling,
The squire's brook was still a-falling,
The carved heads on the church looked down
On "Russell, Blacksmith of this Town,"
And all the graves of all the ghosts
Who rise on Christmas Eve in hosts
To dance and carol in festivity
For joy of Jesus Christ's Nativity
(Bell-ringer Dawe and his two sons
Beheld 'em from the bell-tower once),
Two and two about about
Singing the end of Advent out,
Dwindling down to windlestraws
When the glittering peacock craws,
As craw the glittering peacock should
When Christ's own star comes over the wood.
Lamb of the sky come out of fold
Wandering windy heavens cold.
So they shone and sang till twelve
When all the bells ring out of theirselve;

Rang a peal for Christmas morn,
Glory, men, for Christ is born.

All the old monks' singing places
Glimmered quick with flitting faces,
Singing anthems, singing hymns
Under carven cherubims.
Ringer Dawe aloft could mark
Faces at the window dark
Crowding, crowding, row on row,
Till all the Church began to glow.
The chapel glowed, the nave, the choir,
All the faces became fire
Below the eastern window high
To see Christ's star come up the sky.
Then they lifted hands and turned,
And all their lifted fingers burned,
Burned like the golden altar tallows,
Burned like a troop of God's own Hallows,
Bringing to mind the burning time
When all the bells will rock and chime
And burning saints on burning horses
Will sweep the planets from their courses
And loose the stars to burn up night.
Lord, give us eyes to bear the light.

We all went quiet down the Scallenge
Lest Police Inspector Drew should challenge.
But 'Spector Drew was sleeping sweet,
His head upon a charges sheet,
Under the gas jet flaring full,
Snorting and snoring like a bull,
His bull cheeks puffed, his bull lips blowing,
His ugly yellow front teeth showing.
Just as we peeped we saw him fumble
And scratch his head, and shift, and mumble.

Down in the lane so thin and dark
The tan-yards stank of bitter bark,
The curate's pigeons gave a flutter,
A cat went courting down the gutter,
And none else stirred a foot or feather.
The houses put their heads together,
Talking, perhaps, so dark and sly,
Of all the folk they'd seen go by,
Children, and men and women, merry all,
Who'd some day pass that way to burial.
It was all dark, but at the turning
The Lion had a window burning.
So in we went and up the stairs,
Treading as still as cats and hares.
The way the stairs creaked made you wonder
If dead men's bones were hidden under.
At head of stairs upon the landing
A woman with a lamp was standing;
She greet each gent at head of stairs,
With "Step in, gents, and take your chairs.
The punch'll come when kettle bubble,
But don't make noise or there'll be trouble."
'Twas Doxy Jane, a bouncing girl
With eyes all sparks and hair all curl,
And cheeks all red and lips all coal,
And thirst for men instead of soul.
She's trod her pathway to the fire.
Old Rivers had his nephew by her.

I step aside from Tom and Jimmy
To find if she'd a kiss to gimme.
I blew out lamp 'fore she could speak.
She said, "If you ain't got a cheek,"
And then beside me in the dim,
"Did he beat you or you beat him?"

"Why, I beat him" (though that was wrong).
She said, "You must be turble strong.
I'd be afraid you'd beat me, too."
"You'd not," I said, "I wouldn't do."
"Never?"
"No, never."
"Never?"
"No."
"O Saul. Here's missus. Let me go."
It wasn't missus, so I didn't,
Whether I mid do or I midn't,
Until she'd promised we should meet
Next evening, six, at top of street,
When we could have a quiet talk
On that low wall up Worcester Walk.
And while we whispered there together
I give her silver for a feather
And felt a drunkenness like wine
And shut out Christ in husks and swine.
I felt the dart strike through my liver.
God punish me for't and forgive her.

Each one could be a Jesus mild,
Each one has been a little child,
A little child with laughing look,
A lovely white unwritten book;
A book that God will take, my friend,
As each goes out at journey's end.
The Lord Who gave us Earth and Heaven
Takes that as thanks for all He's given.
The book He lent is given back
All blotted red and smutted black.

"Open the door," said Jim, "and call."
Jane gasped "They'll see me. Loose me, Saul."

She pushed me by, and ducked downstair
With half the pins out of her hair.
I went inside the lit room rollen
Her scented handkerchief I'd stolen.
"What would you fancy, Saul?" they said.
"A gin punch hot and then to bed."
"Jane, fetch the punch bowl to the gemmen;
And mind you don't put too much lemon.
Our good friend Saul has had a fight of it,
Now smoke up, boys, and make a night of it."

The room was full of men and stink
Of bad cigars and heavy drink.
Riley was nodding to the floor
And gurgling as he wanted more.
His mouth was wide, his face was pale,
His swollen face was sweating ale;
And one of those assembled Greeks
Had corked black crosses on his cheeks.
Thomas was having words with Goss,
He "wouldn't pay, the fight was cross."
And Goss told Tom that "cross or no,
The bets go as the verdicts go,
By all I've ever heard or read of.
So pay, or else I'll knock your head off."
Jim Gurvil said his smutty say
About a girl down Bye Street way,
And how the girl from Froggatt's circus
Died giving birth in Newent work'us.
And Dick told how the Dymock wench
Bore twins, poor things, on Dog Hill bench;
And how he'd owned to one in Court
And how Judge made him sorry for't.
Jack set a jew's harp twanging drily;
"Gimme another cup," said Riley.

A dozen more were in their glories
With laughs and smokes and smutty stories;
And Jimmy joked and took his sup
And sang his song of "Up, come up."
Jane brought the bowl of stewing gin
And poured the egg and lemon in,
And whisked it up and served it out
While bawdy questions went about.
Jack chucked her chin, and Jim accost her
With bits out of the "Maid of Gloster."
And fifteen arms went round her waist.
(And then men ask, Are barmaids chaste?)

O young men, pray to be kept whole
From bringing down a weaker soul.
Your minute's joy so meet in doin'
May be the woman's door to ruin;
The door to wandering up and down,
A painted whore at half a crown.
The bright mind fouled, the beauty gay
All eaten out and fallen away,
By drunken days and weary tramps
From pub to pub by city lamps,
Till men despise the game they started
Till health and beauty are departed,
And in a slum the reeking hag
Mumbles a crust with toothy jag,
Or gets the river's help to end
The life too wrecked for man to mend.
We spat and smoked and took our swipe
Till Silas up and tap his pipe,
And begged us all to pay attention
Because he'd several things to mention.
We'd seen the fight (Hear, hear. That's you);
But still one task remained to do,

That task was his, he didn't shun it,
To give the purse to him as won it.
With this remark, from start to out
He'd never seen a brisker bout.
There was the purse. At that he'd leave it.
Let Kane come forward to receive it.

I took the purse and hemmed and bowed,
And called for gin punch for the crowd;
And when the second bowl was done,
I called, "Let's have another one."
Si's wife come in and sipped and sipped
(As women will) till she was pipped.
And Si hit Dicky Twot a clouter
Because he put his arm about her;
But after Si got overtasked
She sat and kissed whoever asked.
My Doxy Jane was splashed by this,
I took her on my knee to kiss.
And Tom cried out, "O damn the gin;
Why can't we all have women in?
Bess Evans, now, or Sister Polly,
Or those two housemaids at the Folly?
Let someone nip to Biddy Price's,
They'd all come in a brace of trices.
Rose Davies, Sue, and Betsy Perks;
One man, one girl, and damn all Turks."
But, no. "More gin," they cried; "Come on.
We'll have the girls in when it's gone."
So round the gin went, hot and heady,
Hot Hollands punch on top of deady.

Hot Hollands punch on top of stout
Puts madness in and wisdom out.
From drunken man to drunken man

The drunken madness raged and ran.
"I'm climber Joe who climbed the spire."
"You're climber Joe the bloody liar."
"Who says I lie?" "I do."
"You lie,
I climbed the spire and had a fly."
"I'm French Suzanne, the Circus Dancer,
I'm going to dance a bloody Lancer."
"If I'd my rights I'm Squire's heir."
"By rights I'd be a millionaire."
"By rights I'd be the lord of you,
But Farmer Scriggins had his do,
He done me, so I've had to hoove it,
I've got it all wrote down to prove it.
And one of these dark winter nights
He'll learn I mean to have my rights;
I'll bloody him a bloody fix,
I'll bloody burn his bloody ricks."

From three long hours of gin and smokes,
And two girls' breath and fifteen blokes,
A warmish night, and windows shut,
The room stank like a fox's gut.
The heat and smell and drinking deep
Began to stun the gang to sleep.
Some fell downstairs to sleep on the mat,
Some snored it sodden where they sat.
Dick Twot had lost a tooth and wept,
But all the drunken others slept.
Jane slept beside me in the chair,
And I got up; I wanted air.

I opened window wide and leaned
Out of that pigstye of the fiend,
And felt a cool wind go like grace

About the sleeping market-place.
The clock struck three, and sweetly, slowly,
The bells chimed Holy, Holy, Holy;
And in a second's pause there fell
The cold note of the chapel bell,
And then a cock crew, flapping wings,
And summat made me think of things.
How long those ticking clocks had gone
From church and chapel, on and on,
Ticking the time out, ticking slow,
To men and girls who'd come and go,
And how they ticked in belfry dark
When half the town was bishop's park,
And how they'd rung a chime full tilt
The night after the church was built,
And how that night was Lambert's Feast,
The night I'd fought and been a beast.
And how a change had come. And then
I thought, "You tick to different men."
What with the fight and what with drinking
And being awake alone there thinking,
My mind began to carp and tetter,
"If this life's all, the beasts are better."
And then I thought, "I wish I'd seen
The many towns this town has been;
I wish I knew if they'd a got
A kind of summat we've a-not,
If them as built the church so fair
Were half the chaps folk say they were;
For they'd the skill to draw their plan,
And skill's a joy to any man;
And they'd the strength, not skill alone,
To build it beautiful in stone;
And strength and skill together thus,
O, they were happier men than us.

But if they were, they had to die
The same as every one and I.
And no one lives again, but dies,
And all the bright goes out of eyes,
And all the skill goes out of hands,
And all the wise brain understands,
And all the beauty, all the power
Is cut down like a withered flower.
In all the show from birth to rest
I give the poor dumb cattle best."

I wondered, then, why life should be,
And what would be the end of me
When youth and health and strength were gone
And cold old age came creeping on?
A keeper's gun? The Union ward?
Or that new quod at Hereford?
And looking round I felt disgust
At all the nights of drink and lust,
And all the looks of all the swine
Who'd said that they were friends of mine;
And yet I knew, when morning came,
The morning would be just the same,
For I'd have drinks and Jane would meet me
And drunken Silas Jones would greet me,
And I'd risk quod and keeper's gun
Till all the silly game was done.
"For parson chaps are mad, supposin'
A chap can change the road he's chosen."
And then the Devil whispered, "Saul,
Why should you want to live at all?
Why fret and sweat and try to mend?
It's all the same thing in the end.
But when it's done," he said, "it's ended.
Why stand it, since it can't be mended?"

And in my heart I heard him plain,
"Throw yourself down and end it, Kane."

"Why not?" said I. "Why not? But no.
I won't. I've never had my go.
I've not had all the world can give.
Death by and by, but first I'll live.
The world owes me my time of times,
And that time's coming now, by crimes."

A madness took me then. I felt
I'd like to hit the world a belt.
I felt that I could fly through air,
A screaming star with blazing hair,
A rushing comet, crackling, numbing
The folk with fear of judgment coming,
A 'Lijah in a fiery car,
Coming to tell folk what they are.
"That's what I'll do," I shouted loud,
"I'll tell this sanctimonious crowd
This town of window-peeping, prying,
Maligning, peering, hinting, lying,
Male and female human blots
Who would, but daren't be, whores and sots,
That they're so steeped in petty vice
That they're less excellent than lice,
That they're so soaked in petty virtue
That touching one of them will dirt you,
Dirt you with the stain of mean
Cheating trade and going-between,
Pinching, starving, scraping, hoarding,
Spying through the chinks of boarding
To see if Sue, the prentice lean,
Dares to touch the margarine.
Fawning, cringing, oiling boots,
Raging in the crowd's pursuits.

Flinging stones at all the Stephens,
Standing firm with all the evens,
Making hell for all the odd,
All the lonely ones of God,
Those poor lonely ones who find
Dogs more mild than human kind.
For dogs," I said, "are nobles born
To most of you, you cockled corn.
I've known dogs to leave their dinner,
Nosing a kind heart in a sinner.
Poor old Crafty wagged his tail
The day I first came home from jail.
When all my folk, so primly clad,
Glowered black and thought me mad,
And muttered how they'd been respected,
While I was what they'd all expected.
(I've thought of that old dog for years,
And of how near I come to tears.)

But you, you minds of bread and cheese,
Are less divine than that dog's fleas.
You suck blood from kindly friends,
And kill them when it serves your ends.
Double traitors, double black,
Stabbing only in the back,
Stabbing with the knives you borrow
From the friends you bring to sorrow.
You stab all that's true and strong,
Truth and strength you say are wrong.
Meek and mild, and sweet and creeping,
Repeating, canting, cadging, peeping,
That's the art and that's the life
To win a man his neighbour's wife.
All that's good and all that's true,
You kill that, so I'll kill you."

At that I tore my clothes in shreds
And hurled them on the window leads;
I flung my boots through both the winders
And knocked the glass to little flinders;
The punch bowl and the tumblers followed,
And then I seized the lamps and holloed,
And down the stairs, and tore back bolts,
As mad as twenty blooded colts;
And out into the street I pass,
As mad as two-year-olds at grass;
A naked madman waving grand
A blazing lamp in either hand.
I yelled like twenty drunken sailors,
"The devil's come among the tailors."
A blaze of flame behind me streamed,
And then I clashed the lamps and screamed
"I'm Satan, newly come from hell."
And then I spied the fire bell.

I've been a ringer, so I know
How best to make a big bell go.
So on to bell-rope swift I swoop,
And stick my one foot in the loop
And heave a down-swig till I groan
"Awake, you swine, you devil's own."
I made the fire bell awake,
I felt the bell-rope throb and shake;
I felt the air mingle and clang
And beat the walls a muffled bang,
And stifle back and boom and bay
Like muffled peals on Boxing Day,
And then surge up and gather shape,
And spread great pinions and escape;
And each great bird of clanging shrieks
O Fire! Fire, from iron beaks.

My shoulders cracked to send around
Those shrieking birds made out of sound
With news of fire in their bills.
(They heard 'em plain beyond Wall Hills.)

Up go the winders, out come heads,
I heard the springs go creak in beds;
But still I heave and sweat and tire,
And still the clang goes "Fire, Fire!"
"Where is it, then? Who is it, there?
You ringer, stop, and tell us where."
"Run round and let the Captain know."
"It must be bad, he's ringing so."
"It's in the town, I see the flame;
Look there! Look there, how red it came."
"Where is it then? O stop the bell."
I stopped and called: "It's fire of hell;
And this is Sodom and Gomorrah,
And now I'll burn you up, begorra."

By this the firemen were mustering,
The half-dressed stable men were flustering,
Backing the horses out of stalls
While this man swears and that man bawls,
"Don't take th' old mare. Back, Toby, back.
Back, Lincoln. Where's the fire, Jack?"
"Damned if I know. Out Preston way."
"No. It's at Chancey's Pitch, they say."
"It's sixteen ricks at Pauntley burnt."
"You back old Darby out, I durn't."
They ran the big red engine out,
And put 'em to with damn and shout.
And then they start to raise the shire,
"Who brought the news, and where's the fire?"
They'd moonlight, lamps, and gas to light 'em.

I give a screech-owl's screech to fright 'em,
And snatch from underneath their noses
The nozzles of the fire hoses.
"I am the fire. Back, stand back,
Or else I'll fetch your skulls a crack;
D'you see these copper nozzles here?
They weigh ten pounds apiece, my dear;
I'm fire of hell come up this minute
To burn this town, and all that's in it.
To burn you dead and burn you clean,
You cogwheels in a stopped machine,
You hearts of snakes, and brains of pigeons,
You dead devout of dead religions,
You offspring of the hen and ass,
By Pilate ruled, and Caiaphas.
Now your account is totted. Learn
Hell's flames are loose and you shall burn."

At that I leaped and screamed and ran,
I heard their cries go, "Catch him, man."
"Who was it?" "Down him." "Out him, Ern."
"Duck him at pump, we'll see who'll burn."
A policeman clutched, a fireman clutched,
A dozen others snatched and touched.
"By God, he's stripped down to his buff."
"By God, we'll make him warm enough."
"After him," "Catch him," "Out him," "Scrob him."
"We'll give him hell." "By God, we'll mob him."
"We'll duck him, scrout him, flog him, fratch him."
"All right," I said. "But first you'll catch him."

The men who don't know to the root
The joy of being swift of foot,
Have never known divine and fresh
The glory of the gift of flesh,

Nor felt the feet exult, nor gone
Along a dim road, on and on,
Knowing again the bursting glows,
The mating hare in April knows,
Who tingles to the pads with mirth
At being the swiftest thing on earth.
O, if you want to know delight,
Run naked in an autumn night,
And laugh, as I laughed then, to find
A running rabble drop behind,
And whang, on every door you pass,
Two copper nozzles, tipped with brass,
And doubly whang at every turning,
And yell, "All hell's let loose, and burning."

I beat my brass and shouted fire
At doors of parson, lawyer, squire,
At all three doors I threshed and slammed
And yelled aloud that they were damned.
I clodded squire's glass with turves
Because he spring-gunned his preserves.
Through parson's glass my nozzle swishes
Because he stood for loaves and fishes,
But parson's glass I spared a tittle.
He give me a orange once when little,
And he who gives a child a treat
Makes joy-bells ring in Heaven's street,
And he who gives a child a home
Builds palaces in Kingdom come,
And she who gives a baby birth
Brings Saviour Christ again to Earth,
For life is joy, and mind is fruit,
And body's precious earth and root.
But lawyer's glass—well, never mind,
Th' old Adam's strong in me, I find.

God pardon man, and may God's Son
Forgive the evil things I've done.

What more? By Dirty Lane I crept
Back to the Lion, where I slept.
The raging madness hot and floodin'
Boiled itself out and left me sudden,
Left me worn out and sick and cold,
Aching as though I'd all grown old;
So there I lay, and there they found me
On door-mat, with a curtain round me.
Si took my heels and Jane my head
And laughed, and carried me to bed.
And from the neighbouring street they reskied
My boots and trousers, coat and weskit;
They bath-bricked both the nozzles bright
To be mementoes of the night,
And knowing what I should awake with
They flannelled me a quart to slake with,
And sat and shook till half past two
Expecting Police Inspector Drew.
I woke and drank, and went to meat
In clothes still dirty from the street.
Down in the bar I heard 'em tell
How someone rang the fire bell,
And how th' inspector's search had thriven,
And how five pounds reward was given.
And shepherd Boyce, of Marley, glad us
By saying it was blokes from mad'us.
Or two young rips lodged at the Prince
Whom none had seen nor heard of since,
Or that young blade from Worcester Walk
(You know how country people talk).
Young Joe the ostler come in sad,
He said th'old mare had bit his dad.

He said there'd come a blazing screeching
Daft Bible-prophet chap a-preaching,
Had put th'old mare in such a taking
She'd thought the bloody earth was quaking.
And others come and spread a tale
Of cut-throats out of Gloucester jail,
And how we needed extra cops
With all them Welsh come picking hops:
With drunken Welsh in all our sheds
We might be murdered in our beds.

By all accounts, both men and wives
Had had the scare up of their lives.

I ate and drank and gathered strength,
And stretched along the bench full length,
Or crossed to window seat to pat
Black Silas Jones's little cat.
At four I called, "You devil's own,
The second trumpet shall be blown.
The second trump, the second blast;
Hell's flames are loosed, and judgment's passed.
Too late for mercy now. Take warning.
I'm death and hell and Judgment morning."
I hurled the bench into the settle,
I banged the table on the kettle,
I sent Joe's quart of cider spinning.
"Lo, here begins my second inning."
Each bottle, mug, and jug and pot
I smashed to crocks in half a tot;
And Joe, and Si, and Nick, and Percy
I rolled together topsy versy.
And as I ran I heard 'em call,
"Now damn to hell, what's gone with Saul?"

Out into street I ran uproarious
The devil dancing in me glorious.
And as I ran I yell and shriek
"Come on, now, turn the other cheek."
Across the way by almshouse pump
I see old puffing parson stump.
Old parson, red-eyed as a ferret
From nightly wrestlings with the spirit;
I ran across, and barred his path.
His turkey gills went red as wrath
And then he froze, as parsons can.
"The police will deal with you, my man."
"Not yet," said I, "not yet they won't;
And now you'll hear me, like or don't.
The English Church both is and was
A subsidy of Caiaphas.
I don't believe in Prayer nor Bible,
They're lies all through, and you're a libel,
A libel on the Devil's plan
When first he miscreated man.
You mumble through a formal code
To get which martyrs burned and glowed.

I look on martyrs as mistakes,
But still they burned for it at stakes;
Your only fire's the jolly fire
Where you can guzzle port with Squire,
And back and praise his damned opinions
About his temporal dominions.
You let him give the man who digs,
A filthy hut unfit for pigs,
Without a well, without a drain,
With mossy thatch that lets in rain,
Without a 'lotment, 'less he rent it,
And never meat, unless he scent it,

But weekly doles of 'leven shilling
To make a grown man strong and willing,
To do the hardest work on earth
And feed his wife when she gives birth,
And feed his little children's bones.
I tell you, man, the Devil groans.
With all your main and all your might
You back what is against what's right;
You let the Squire do things like these,
You back him in't and give him ease,
You take his hand, and drink his wine,
And he's a hog, but you're a swine.
For you take gold to teach God's ways,
And teach man how to sing God's praise.
And now I'll tell you what you teach
In downright honest English speech.

"You teach the ground-down starving man
That Squire's greed's Jehovah's plan.
You get his learning circumvented
Lest it should make him discontented
(Better a brutal, starving nation
Than men with thoughts above their station),
You let him neither read nor think,
You goad his wretched soul to drink
And then to jail, the drunken boor;
O, sad intemperance of the poor.
You starve his soul till it's rapscallion,
Then blame his flesh for being stallion.
You send your wife around to paint
The golden glories of "restraint;"
How moral exercise bewild'rin'
Would soon result in fewer children.
You work a day in Squire's fields
And see what sweet restraint it yields,

A woman's day at turnip picking,
Your heart's too fat for plough or ricking.

"And you whom luck taught French and Greek
Have purple flaps on either cheek,
A stately house, and time for knowledge,
And gold to send your sons to college,
That pleasant place, where getting learning
Is also key to money earning.
But quite your damndest want of grace
Is what you do to save your face;
The way you sit astride the gates
By padding wages out of rates;
Your Christmas gifts of shoddy blankets
That every working soul may thank its
Loving parson, loving squire
Through whom he can't afford a fire.
Your well-packed bench, your prison pen,
To keep them something less than men;
Your friendly clubs to help 'em bury,
Your charities of midwifery.
Your bidding children duck and cap
To them who give them workhouse pap.
O, what you are, and what you preach,
And what you do, and what you teach
Is not God's Word, nor honest schism,
But Devil's scant and pauperism."

By this time many folk had gathered
To listen to me while I blathered;
I said my piece, and when I'd said it,
I'll do old purple parson credit,
He sunk (as sometimes parsons can)
His coat's excuses in the man.
"You think that Squire and I are kings

Who made the existing state of things,
And made it ill. I answer, No,
States are not made, nor patched; they grow,
Grow slow through centuries of pain
And grow correctly in the main,
But only grow by certain laws
Of certain bits in certain jaws.
You want to doctor that. Let be.
You cannot patch a growing tree.
Put these two words beneath your hat,
These two: securus judicat.
The social states of human kinds
Are made by multitudes of minds,
And after multitudes of years
A little human growth appears
Worth having, even to the soul
Who sees most plain it's not the whole.

This state is dull and evil, both,
I keep it in the path of growth;
You think the Church an outworn fetter;
Kane, keep it, till you've built a better.
And keep the existing social state;
I quite agree it's out of date,
One does too much, another shirks,
Unjust, I grant; but still . . . it works.
To get the whole world out of bed
And washed, and dressed, and warmed, and fed,
To work, and back to bed again,
Believe me, Saul, costs worlds of pain.
Then, as to whether true or sham
That book of Christ, Whose priest I am;
The Bible is a lie, say you,
Where do you stand, suppose it true?
Good-bye. But if you've more to say,

My doors are open night and day.
Meanwhile, my friend, 'twould be no sin
To mix more water in your gin.
We're neither saints nor Philip Sidneys,
But mortal men with mortal kidneys."

He took his snuff, and wheezed a greeting,
And waddled off to mothers' meeting;
I hung my head upon my chest,
I give old purple parson best.
For while the Plough tips round the Pole
The trained mind outs the upright soul,
As Jesus said the trained mind might,
Being wiser than the sons of light,
But trained men's minds are spread so thin
They let all sorts of darkness in;
Whatever light man finds they doubt it
They love, not light, but talk about it.

But parson'd proved to people's eyes
That I was drunk, and he was wise;
And people grinned and women tittered,
And little children mocked and twittered.
So, blazing mad, I stalked to bar
To show how noble drunkards are,
And guzzled spirits like a beast,
To show contempt for Church and priest,
Until, by six, my wits went round
Like hungry pigs in parish pound.
At half past six, rememb'ring Jane,
I staggered into street again
With mind made up (or primed with gin)
To bash the cop who'd run me in;
For well I knew I'd have to cock up
My legs that night inside the lock-up,

And it was my most fixed intent
To have a fight before I went.
Our Fates are strange, and no one knows his;
Our lovely Saviour Christ disposes.

Jane wasn't where we'd planned, the jade.
She'd thought me drunk and hadn't stayed.
So I went up the Walk to look for her
And lingered by the little brook for her,
And dowsed my face, and drank at spring,
And watched two wild duck on the wing.
The moon come pale, the wind come cool,
A big pike leapt in Lower Pool,
The peacock screamed, the clouds were straking,
My cut cheek felt the weather breaking;
An orange sunset waned and thinned
Foretelling rain and western wind,
And while I watched I heard distinct
The metals on the railway clinked.
The blood-edged clouds were all in tatters,
The sky and earth seemed mad as hatters;
They had a death look, wild and odd,
Of something dark foretold by God.
And seeing it so, I felt so shaken
I wouldn't keep the road I'd taken,
But wandered back towards the inn
Resolved to brace myself with gin.
And as I walked, I said, "It's strange,
There's Death let loose to-night, and Change."

In Cabbage Walk I made a haul
Of two big pears from lawyer's wall,
And, munching one, I took the lane
Back into Market-place again.
Lamp-lighter Dick had passed the turning,

And all the Homend lamps were burning.
The windows shone, the shops were busy,
But that strange Heaven made me dizzy.
The sky had all God's warning writ
In bloody marks all over it,
And over all I thought there was
A ghastly light besides the gas.
The Devil's tasks and Devil's rages
Were giving me the Devil's wages.

In Market-place it's always light,
The big shop windows make it bright;
And in the press of people buying
I spied a little fellow crying
Because his mother'd gone inside
And left him there, and so he cried.
And mother'd beat him when she found him,
And mother's whip would curl right round him,
And mother'd say he'd done't to crost her,
Though there being crowds about he'd lost her.

Lord, give to men who are old and rougher
The things that little children suffer,
And let keep bright and undefiled
The young years of the little child.
I pat his head at edge of street
And gi'm my second pear to eat.
Right under lamp, I pat his head,
"I'll stay till mother come," I said,
And stay I did, and joked and talked,
And shoppers wondered as they walked.
"There's that Saul Kane, the drunken blaggard,
Talking to little Jimmy Jaggard.
The drunken blaggard reeks of drink."
"Whatever will his mother think?"

"Wherever has his mother gone?
Nip round to Mrs. Jaggard's, John,
And say her Jimmy's out again,
In Market-place, with boozer Kane."
"When he come out to-day he staggered.
O, Jimmy Jaggard, Jimmy Jaggard."
"His mother's gone inside to bargain,
Run in and tell her, Polly Margin,
And tell her poacher Kane is tipsy
And selling Jimmy to a gipsy."
"Run in to Mrs. Jaggard, Ellen,
Or else, dear knows, there'll be no tellin',
And don't dare leave yer till you've fount her,
You'll find her at the linen counter."
I told a tale, to Jim's delight,
Of where the tom-cats go by night,
And how when moonlight came they went
Among the chimneys black and bent,
From roof to roof, from house to house,
With little baskets full of mouse
All red and white, both joint and chop
Like meat out of a butcher's shop;
Then all along the wall they creep
And everyone is fast asleep,
And honey-hunting moths go by,
And by the bread-batch crickets cry;
Then on they hurry, never waiting
To lawyer's backyard cellar grating
Where Jaggard's cat, with clever paw,
Unhooks a broke-brick's secret door;
Then down into the cellar black,
Across the wood slug's slimy track,
Into an old cask's quiet hollow,
Where they've got seats for what's to follow;
Then each tom-cat lights little candles,

And O, the stories and the scandals,
And O, the songs and Christmas carols,
And O, the milk from little barrels.
They light a fire fit for roasting
(And how good mouse-meat smells when toasting),
Then down they sit to merry feast
While moon goes west and sun comes east.

Sometimes they make so merry there
Old lawyer come to head of stair
To 'fend with fist and poker took firm
His parchments channelled by the bookworm,
And all his deeds, and all his packs
Of withered ink and sealing wax;
And there he stands, with candle raised,
And listens like a man amazed,
Or like a ghost a man stands dumb at,
He says, "Hush! Hush! I'm sure there's summat."
He hears outside the brown owl call,
He hears the death-tick tap the wall,
The gnawing of the wainscot mouse,
The creaking up and down the house,
The unhooked window's hinges ranging,
The sounds that say the wind is changing.
At last he turns, and shakes his head,
"It's nothing, I'll go back to bed."

And just then Mrs. Jaggard came
To view and end her Jimmy's shame.

She made one rush and gi'm a bat
And shook him like a dog a rat.
"I can't turn round but what you're straying.
I'll give you tales and gipsy playing.
I'll give you wand'ring off like this

And listening to whatever 'tis.
You'll laugh the little side of the can,
You'll have the whip for this, my man;
And not a bite of meat nor bread
You'll touch before you go to bed.
Some day you'll break your mother's heart,
After God knows she's done her part,
Working her arms off day and night
Trying to keep your collars white.
Look at your face, too, in the street.
What dirty filth've you found to eat?
Now don't you blubber here, boy, or
I'll give you sum't to blubber for."
She snatched him off from where we stand
And knocked the pear-core from his hand,
And looked at me, "You Devil's limb,
How dare you talk to Jaggard's Jim;
You drunken, poaching, boozing brute, you,
If Jaggard was a man he'd shoot you."
She glared all this, but didn't speak,
She gasped, white hollows in her cheek;
Jimmy was writhing, screaming wild,
The shoppers thought I'd killed the child.

I had to speak, so I begun.
"You'd oughtn't beat your little son;
He did no harm, but seeing him there
I talked to him and gi'm a pear;
I'm sure the poor child meant no wrong,
It's all my fault he stayed so long,
He'd not have stayed, mum, I'll be bound
If I'd not chanced to come around.
It's all my fault he stayed, not his.
I kept him here, that's how it is."
"Oh! And how dare you, then?" says she,

"How dare you tempt my boy from me?
How dare you do't, you drunken swine,
Is he your child or is he mine?
A drunken sot they've had the beak to,
Has got his dirty whores to speak to,
His dirty mates with whom he drink,
Not little children, one would think.
Look on him, there," she says, "look on him
And smell the stinking gin upon him,
The lowest sot, the drunknest liar,
The dirtiest dog in all the shire:
Nice friends for any woman's son
After ten years, and all she's done.

"For I've had eight, and buried five,
And only three are left alive.
I've given them all we could afford.
I've taught them all to fear the Lord.
They've had the best we had to give,
The only three the Lord let live.

"For Minnie whom I loved the worst
Died mad in childbed with her first.
And John and Mary died of measles,
And Rob was drowned at the Teasels.
And little Nan, dear little sweet,
A cart run over in the street;
Her little shift was all one stain,
I prayed God put her out of pain.
And all the rest are gone or going
The road to hell, and there's no knowing
For all I've done and all I've made them
I'd better not have overlaid them.
For Susan went the ways of shame
The time the 'till'ry regiment came,

And t'have her child without a father
I think I'd have her buried rather.
And Dicky boozes, God forgimme,
And now't's to be the same with Jimmy.
And all I've done and all I've bore
Has made a drunkard and a whore,
A bastard boy who wasn't meant,
And Jimmy gwine where Dicky went;
For Dick began the self-same way
And my old hairs are going grey,
And my poor man's a withered knee,
And all the burden falls on me.

"I've washed eight little children's limbs,
I've taught eight little souls their hymns,
I've risen sick and lain down pinched
And borne it all and never flinched;
But to see him, the town's disgrace,
With God's commandments broke in's face,
Who never worked, not he, nor earned,
Nor will do till the seas are burned,
Who never did since he was whole
A hand's turn for a human soul,
But poached and stole and gone with women,
And swilled down gin enough to swim in,
To see him only lift one finger
To make my little Jimmy linger.
In spite of all his mother's prayers,
And all her ten long years of cares,
And all her broken spirit's cry
That drunkard's finger puts them by,
And Jimmy turns. And now I see
That just as Dick was, Jim will be,
And all my life will have been vain.
I might have spared myself the pain,
And done the world a blessed riddance

If I'd a drowned 'em all like kittens.
And he the sot, so strong and proud,
Who'd make white shirts of's mother's shroud,
He laughs now, it's a joke to him,
Though it's the gates of hell to Jim.

"I've had my heart burnt out like coal,
And drops of blood wrung from my soul
Day in, day out, in pain and tears,
For five-and-twenty wretched years;
And he, he's ate the fat and sweet,
And loafed and spat at top of street,
And drunk and leched from day till morrow,
And never known a moment's sorrow.
He come out drunk from th' inn to look
The day my little Nan was took;
He sat there drinking, glad and gay,
The night my girl was led astray;
He praised my Dick for singing well,
The night Dick took the road to hell;
And when my corpse goes stiff and blind,
Leaving four helpless souls behind,
He will be there still, drunk and strong.
It do seem hard. It do seem wrong.
But 'Woe to him by whom the offence,'
Says our Lord Jesus' Testaments.
Whatever seems, God doth not slumber,
Though he lets pass times without number.
He'll come with trump to call his own,
And this world's way'll be overthrown.
He'll come with glory and with fire
To cast great darkness on the liar,
To burn the drunkard and the treacher,
And do his judgment on the lecher,
To glorify the spirit's faces

Of those whose ways were stony places
Who chose with Ruth the better part;
O Lord, I see Thee as Thou art,
O God, the fiery four-edged sword,
The thunder of the wrath outpoured,
The fiery four-faced creatures burning,
And all the four-faced wheels all turning,
Coming with trump and fiery saint.
Jim, take me home, I'm turning faint."
They went, and some cried, "Good old sod."
"She put it to him straight, by God."

Summat she was, or looked, or said,
Went home and made me hang my head.
I slunk away into the night
Knowing deep down that she was right.
I'd often heard religious ranters,
And put them down as windy canters,
But this old mother made me see
The harm I done by being me.
Being both strong and given to sin
I 'tracted weaker vessels in.
So back to bar to get more drink,
I didn't dare begin to think,
And there were drinks and drunken singing,
As though this life were dice for flinging;
Dice to be flung, and nothing furder,
And Christ's blood just another murder.
"Come on, drinks round, salue, drink hearty,
Now, Jane, the punch-bowl for the party.
If any here won't drink with me
I'll knock his bloody eyes out. See?
Come on, cigars round, rum for mine,
Sing us a smutty song, some swine."
But though the drinks and songs went round

That thought remained, it was not drowned.
And when I'd rise to get a light
I'd think, "What's come to me to-night?"

There's always crowds when drinks are standing.
The house doors slammed along the landing,
The rising wind was gusty yet,
And those who came in late were wet;
And all my body's nerves were snappin'
With sense of summat 'bout to happen,
And music seemed to come and go
And seven lights danced in a row.
There used to be a custom then,
Miss Bourne, the Friend, went round at ten
To all the pubs in all the place,
To bring the drunkards' souls to grace;
Some sulked, of course, and some were stirred,
But none give her a dirty word.
A tall pale woman, grey and bent,
Folk said of her that she was sent.
She wore Friend's clothes, and women smiled,
But she'd a heart just like a child.
She come to us near closing time
When we were at some smutty rhyme,
And I was mad, and ripe for fun;
I wouldn't a minded what I done.
So when she come so prim and grey
I pound the bar and sing, "Hooray,
Here's Quaker come to bless and kiss us,
Come, have a gin and bitters, missus,
Or may be Quaker girls so prim
Would rather start a bloody hymn.
Now Dick, oblige. A hymn, you swine,
Pipe up the 'Officer of the Line,'
A song to make one's belly ache,

Or 'Nell and Roger at the Wake,'
Or that sweet song, the talk in town,
'The lady fair and Abel Brown.'
'O, who's that knocking at the door,'
Miss Bourne'll play the music score."
The men stood dumb as cattle are,
They grinned, but thought I'd gone too far,
There come a hush and no one break it,
They wondered how Miss Bourne would take it.
She up to me with black eyes wide,
She looked as though her spirit cried;
She took my tumbler from the bar
Beside where all the matches are
And poured it out upon the floor dust,
Among the fag-ends, spit and saw-dust.

"Saul Kane," she said, "when next you drink,
Do me the gentleness to think
That every drop of drink accursed
Makes Christ within you die of thirst,
That every dirty word you say
Is one more flint upon His way,
Another thorn about His head,
Another mock by where He tread,
Another nail, another cross.
All that you are is that Christ's loss."
The clock run down and struck a chime
And Mrs. Si said, "Closing time."

The wet was pelting on the pane
And something broke inside my brain,
I heard the rain drip from the gutters
And Silas putting up the shutters,
While one by one the drinkers went;
I got a glimpse of what it meant,

How she and I had stood before
In some old town by some old door
Waiting intent while someone knocked
Before the door for ever locked;
She was so white that I was scared,
A gas jet, turned the wrong way, flared,
And Silas snapped the bars in place.
Miss Bourne stood white and searched my face.
When Silas done, with ends of tunes
He 'gan a gathering the spittoons,
His wife primmed lips and took the till.
Miss Bourne stood still and I stood still,
And "Tick. Slow. Tick. Slow" went the clock.
She said, "He waits until you knock."
She turned at that and went out swift,
Si grinned and winked, his missus sniffed.

I heard her clang the Lion door,
I marked a drink-drop roll to floor;
It took up scraps of sawdust, furry,
And crinkled on, a half inch, blurry;
A drop from my last glass of gin;
And someone waiting to come in,
A hand upon the door latch gropen
Knocking the man inside to open.
I know the very words I said,
They bayed like bloodhounds in my head.
"The water's going out to sea
And there's a great moon calling me;
But there's a great sun calls the moon,
And all God's bells will carol soon
For joy and glory and delight
Of someone coming home to-night."
Out into darkness, out to night,
My flaring heart gave plenty light,

So wild it was there was no knowing
Whether the clouds or stars were blowing;
Blown chimney pots and folk blown blind,
And puddles glimmering like my mind,
And chinking glass from windows banging,
And inn signs swung like people hanging,
And in my heart the drink unpriced,
The burning cataracts of Christ.

I did not think, I did not strive,
The deep peace burnt my me alive;
The bolted door had broken in,
I knew that I had done with sin.
I knew that Christ had given me birth
To brother all the souls on earth,
And every bird and every beast
Should share the crumbs broke at the feast.

O glory of the lighted mind.
How dead I'd been, how dumb, how blind.
The station brook, to my new eyes,
Was babbling out of Paradise,
The waters rushing from the rain
Were singing Christ has risen again.
I thought all earthly creatures knelt
From rapture of the joy I felt.
The narrow station-wall's brick ledge,
The wild hop withering in the hedge,
The lights in huntsman's upper storey
Were parts of an eternal glory,
Were God's eternal garden flowers.
I stood in bliss at this for hours.

O glory of the lighted soul.
The dawn came up on Bradlow Knoll,

The dawn with glittering on the grasses,
The dawn which pass and never passes.

"It's dawn," I said, "And chimney's smoking,
And all the blessed fields are soaking.
It's dawn, and there's an engine shunting;
And hounds, for huntsman's going hunting.
It's dawn, and I must wander north
Along the road Christ led me forth."

So up the road I wander slow
Past where the snowdrops used to grow
With celandines in early springs,
When rainbows were triumphant things
And dew so bright and flowers so glad,
Eternal joy to lass and lad.
And past the lovely brook I paced,
The brook whose source I never traced,
The brook, the one of two which rise
In my green dream in Paradise,
In wells where heavenly buckets clink
To give God's wandering thirsty drink
By those clean cots of carven stone
Where the clear water sings alone.
Then down, past that white-blossomed pond,
And past the chestnut trees beyond,
And past the bridge the fishers knew,
Where yellow flag flowers once grew,
Where we'd go gathering cops of clover,
In sunny June times long since over.
O clover-cops half white, half red,
O beauty from beyond the dead.
O blossom, key to earth and heaven,
O souls that Christ has new forgiven.

Then down the hill to gipsies' pitch
By where the brook clucks in the ditch.
A gipsy's camp was in the copse,
Three felted tents, with beehive tops,
And round black marks where fires had been,
And one old waggon painted green,
And three ribbed horses wrenching grass,
And three wild boys to watch me pass,
And one old woman by the fire
Hulking a rabbit warm from wire.
I loved to see the horses bait.
I felt I walked at Heaven's gate,
That Heaven's gate was opened wide
Yet still the gipsies camped outside.
The waste souls will prefer the wild,
Long after life is meek and mild.
Perhaps when man has entered in
His perfect city free from sin,
The campers will come past the walls
With old lame horses full of galls,
And waggons hung about with withies,
And burning coke in tinker's stithies,
And see the golden town, and choose,
And think the wild too good to lose.
And camp outside, as these camped then,
With wonder at the entering men.
So past, and past the stone heap white
That dewberry trailers hid from sight,
And down the field so full of springs,
Where mewing peewits clap their wings,
And past the trap made for the mill
Into the field below the hill.
There was a mist along the stream,
A wet mist, dim, like in a dream;
I heard the heavy breath of cows,

And waterdrops from th'alder boughs;
And eels, or snakes, in dripping grass,
Whipping aside to let me pass.
The gate was backed against the ryme
To pass the cows at milking time.
And by the gate as I went out
A moldwarp rooted earth wi's snout.
A few steps up the Callows' Lane
Brought me above the mist again,
The two great fields arose like death
Above the mists of human breath.

All earthly things that blessèd morning
Were everlasting joy and warning.
The gate was Jesus' way made plain,
The mole was Satan foiled again,
Black blinded Satan snouting way
Along the red of Adam's clay;
The mist was error and damnation,
The lane the road unto salvation.
Out of the mist into the light,
O blessèd gift of inner sight.
The past was faded like a dream;
There come the jingling of a team,
A ploughman's voice, a clink of chain,
Slow hoofs, and harness under strain.
Up the slow slope a team came bowing,
Old Callow at his autumn ploughing,
Old Callow, stooped above the hales,
Ploughing the stubble into wales,
His grave eyes looking straight ahead,
Shearing a long straight furrow red;
His plough-foot high to give it earth
To bring new food for men to birth.
O wet red swathe of earth laid bare,

O truth, O strength, O gleaming share,
O patient eyes that watch the goal,
O ploughman of the sinner's soul.
O Jesus, drive the coulter deep
To plough my living man from sleep.

Slow up the hill the plough team plod,
Old Callow at the task of God,
Helped by man's wit, helped by the brute,
Turning a stubborn clay to fruit,
His eyes forever on some sign
To help him plough a perfect line.
At top of rise the plough team stopped,
The fore-horse bent his head and cropped.
Then the chains chack, the brasses jingle,
The lean reins gather through the cringle,
The figures move against the sky,
The clay wave breaks as they go by.
I kneeled there in the muddy fallow,
I knew that Christ was there with Callow,
That Christ was standing there with me,
That Christ had taught me what to be,
That I should plough, and as I ploughed
My Saviour Christ would sing aloud,
And as I drove the clods apart
Christ would be ploughing in my heart,
Through rest-harrow and bitter roots,
Through all my bad life's rotten fruits.

O Christ who holds the open gate,
O Christ who drives the furrow straight,
O Christ, the plough, O Christ, the laughter
Of holy white birds flying after,
Lo, all my heart's field red and torn,
And Thou wilt bring the young green corn,

The young green corn divinely springing,
The young green corn forever singing;
And when the field is fresh and fair
Thy blessèd feet shall glitter there,
And we will walk the weeded field,
And tell the golden harvest's yield,
The corn that makes the holy bread
By which the soul of man is fed,
The holy bread, the food unpriced,
Thy everlasting mercy, Christ.

The share will jar on many a stone,
Thou wilt not let me stand alone;
And I shall feel (thou wilt not fail),
Thy hand on mine upon the hale.
Near Bullen Bank, on Gloucester Road,
Thy everlasting mercy showed
The ploughman patient on the hill
Forever there, forever still,
Ploughing the hill with steady yoke
Of pine-trees lightning-struck and broke.
I've marked the May Hill ploughman stay
There on his hill, day after day
Driving his team against the sky,
While men and women live and die.
And now and then he seems to stoop
To clear the coulter with the scoop,
Or touch an ox to haw or gee
While Severn stream goes out to sea.
The sea with all her ships and sails,
And that great smoky port in Wales,
And Gloucester tower bright i' the sun,
All know that patient wandering one.
And sometimes when they burn the leaves
The bonfires' smoking trails and heaves,

And girt red flamës twink and twire
As though he ploughed the hill afire.
And in men's hearts in many lands
A spiritual ploughman stands
Forever waiting, waiting now,
The heart's "Put in, man, zook the plough."

By this the sun was all one glitter,
The little birds were all in twitter;
Out of a tuft a little lark
Went higher up than I could mark,
His little throat was all one thirst
To sing until his heart should burst,
To sing aloft in golden light
His song from blue air out of sight.
The mist drove by, and now the cows
Came plodding up to milking house.
Followed by Frank, the Callows' cowman,
Who whistled "Adam was a ploughman."
There come such cawing from the rooks,
Such running chuck from little brooks,
One thought it March, just budding green,
With hedgerows full of celandine.
An otter 'out of stream and played,
Two hares come loping up and stayed;
Wide-eyed and tender-eared but bold.
Sheep bleated up by Penny's fold.
I heard a partridge covey call.
The morning sun was bright on all.
Down the long slope the plough team drove
The tossing rooks arose and hove.
A stone struck on the share. A word
Came to the team. The red earth stirred.

I crossed the hedge by shooter's gap,
I hitched my boxer's belt a strap,

I jumped the ditch and crossed the fallow:
I took the hales from farmer Callow.

How swift the summer goes,
Forget-me-not, pink, rose.
The young grass when I started
And now the hay is carted,
And now my song is ended,
And all the summer splended;
The blackbird's second brood
Routs beech leaves in the wood;
The pink and rose have speeded,
Forget-me-not has seeded.
Only the winds that blew,
The rain that makes things new,
The earth that hides things old,
And blessings manifold.

O lovely lily clean,
O lily springing green,
O lily bursting white,
Dear lily of delight,
Spring in my heart agen
That I may flower to men.

GREAT HAMPDEN. June, 1911.

NOTE

"The Everlasting Mercy" first appeared in *The English Review* for October, 1911. I thank the Editor and Proprietors of that paper for permitting me to reprint it here. The persons and events described in the poem are entirely imaginary, and no reference is made or intended to any living person.

JOHN MASEFIELD.

THE WIDOW IN THE BYE STREET

THE WIDOW IN THE BYE STREET[1]

PART I

Down Bye Street, in a little Shropshire town,
There lived a widow with her only son:
She had no wealth nor title to renown,
Nor any joyous hours, never one.
She rose from ragged mattress before sun
And stitched all day until her eyes were red,
And had to stitch, because her man was dead.

Sometimes she fell asleep, she stitched so hard,
Letting the linen fall upon the floor;
And hungry cats would steal in from the yard,
And mangy chickens pecked about the door,
Craning their necks so ragged and so sore
To search the room for bread-crumbs, or for mouse,
But they got nothing in the widow's house.

Mostly she made her bread by hemming shrouds
For one rich undertaker in the High Street,
Who used to pray that folks might die in crowds
And that their friends might pay to let them lie sweet;
And when one died the widow in the Bye Street
Stitched night and day to give the worm his dole.
The dead were better dressed than that poor soul.

Her little son was all her life's delight,
For in his little features she could find
A glimpse of that dead husband out of sight,
Where out of sight is never out of mind.
And so she stitched till she was nearly blind,
Or till the tallow candle end was done,
To get a living for her little son.

[1] Copyright in the United Kingdom and U. S. A., 1912.

Her love for him being such she would not rest,
It was a want which ate her out and in,
Another hunger in her withered breast
Pressing her woman's bones against the skin.
To make him plump she starved her body thin.
And he, he ate the food, and never knew,
He laughed and played as little children do.

When there was little sickness in the place
She took what God would send, and what God sent
Never brought any colour to her face
Nor life into her footsteps when she went.
Going, she trembled always withered and bent,
For all went her to son, always the same,
He was first served whatever blessing came.

Sometimes she wandered out to gather sticks,
For it was bitter cold there when it snowed.
And she stole hay out of the farmer's ricks
For bands to wrap her feet in while she sewed,
And when her feet were warm and the grate glowed
She hugged her little son, her heart's desire,
With "Jimmy, ain't it snug beside the fire?"

So years went on till Jimmy was a lad
And went to work as poor lads have to do,
And then the widow's loving heart was glad
To know that all the pains she had gone through,
And all the years of putting on the screw,
Down to the sharpest turn a mortal can,
Had borne their fruit, and made her child a man.

He got a job at working on the line,
Tipping the earth down, trolley after truck,
From daylight till the evening, wet or fine,

With arms all red from wallowing in the muck,
And spitting, as the trolley tipped, for luck,
And singing "Binger" as he swung the pick,
Because the red blood ran in him so quick.

So there was bacon then, at night, for supper
In Bye Street there, where he and mother stay;
And boots they had, not leaky in the upper,
And room rent ready on the settling day;
And beer for poor old mother, worn and grey,
And fire in frost; and in the widow's eyes
It seemed the Lord had made earth Paradise.

And there they sat of evenings after dark
Singing their song of "Binger," he and she,
Her poor old cackle made the mongrels bark
And "You sing Binger, mother," carols he;
"By crimes, but that's a good song, that her be:"
And then they slept there in the room they shared,
And all the time fate had his end prepared.

One thing alone made life not perfect sweet:
The mother's daily fear of what would come
When woman and her lovely boy should meet,
When the new wife would break up the old home.
Fear of that unborn evil struck her dumb,
And when her darling and a woman met,
She shook and prayed, "Not her, O God; not yet."

"Not yet, dear God, my Jimmy took from me."
Then she would subtly question with her son.
"Not very handsome. I don't think her be?"
"God help the man who marries such an one."
Her red eyes peered to spy the mischief done.
She took great care to keep the girls away,
And all her trouble made him easier prey.

There was a woman out at Plaister's End,
Light of her body, fifty to the pound,
A copper coin for any man to spend,
Lovely to look on when the wits were drowned.
Her husband's skeleton was never found,
It lay among the rocks at Glydyr Mor
Where he drank poison finding her a whore.

She was not native there, for she belonged
Out Milford way, or Swansea; no one knew.
She had the piteous look of someone wronged,
"Anna," her name, a widow, last of Triw.
She had lived at Plaister's End a year or two;
At Callow's cottage, renting half an acre;
She was a hen-wife and a perfume-maker.

Secret she was; she lived in reputation;
But secret unseen threads went floating out:
Her smile, her voice, her face, were all temptation,
All subtle flies to trouble man the trout;
Man to entice, entrap, entangle, flout. . .
To take and spoil, and then to cast aside:
Gain without giving was the craft she plied.

And she complained, poor lonely widowed soul,
How no one cared, and men were rutters all;
While true love is an ever burning goal
Burning the brighter as the shadows fall.
And all love's dogs went hunting at the call,
Married or not she took them by the brain,
Sucked at their hearts and tossed them back again.

Like the straw fires lit on Saint John's Eve,
She burned and dwindled in her fickle heart;
For if she wept when Harry took his leave,

Her tears were lures to beckon Bob to start.
And if, while loving Bob, a tinker's cart
Came by, she opened window with a smile
And gave the tinker hints to wait a while.

She passed for pure; but, years before, in Wales,
Living at Mountain Ash with different men,
Her less discretion had inspired tales
Of certain things she did, and how, and when.
Those seven years of youth; we are frantic then.
She had been frantic in her years of youth,
The tales were not more evil than the truth.

She had two children as the fruits of trade,
Though she drank bitter herbs to kill the curse,
Both of them sons, and one she overlaid,
The other one the parish had to nurse.
Now she grew plump with money in her purse,
Passing for pure a hundred miles, I guess,
From where her little son wore workhouse dress.

There with the Union boys he came and went,
A parish bastard fed on bread and tea,
Wearing a bright tin badge in furthest Gwent,
And no one knowing who his folk could be.
His mother never knew his new name: she,—
She touched the lust of those who served her turn,
And chief among her men was Shepherd Ern.

A moody, treacherous man of bawdy mind,
Married to that mild girl from Ercall Hill,
Whose gentle goodness made him more inclined
To hotter sauces sharper on the bill.
The new lust gives the lecher the new thrill,
The new wine scratches as it slips the throat,
The new flag is so bright by the old boat.

Ern was her man to buy her bread and meat,
Half of his weekly wage was hers to spend,
She used to mock, "How is your wife, my sweet?"
Or wail, "O, Ernie, how is this to end?"
Or coo, "My Ernie is without a friend,
She cannot understand my precious life,"
And Ernie would go home and beat his wife.

So the four souls are ranged, the chess-board set,
The dark, invisible hand of secret Fate
Brought it to come to being that they met
After so many years of lying in wait.
While we least think it he prepares his Mate.
Mate, and the King's pawn played, it never ceases
Though all the earth is dust of taken pieces.

PART II

October Fair-time is the time for fun,
For all the street is hurled into rows
Of pens of heifers blinking at the sun,
And Lemster sheep which pant and seem to doze,
And stalls of hardbake and galanty shows,
And cheapjacks smashing crocks, and trumpets blowing,
And the loud organ of the horses going.

There you can buy blue ribbons for your girl
Or take her in a swing-boat tossing high,
Or hold her fast when all the horses whirl
Round to the steam pipe whanging at the sky,
Or stand her cockshies at the cocoa-shy,
Or buy her brooches with her name in red,
Or Queen Victoria done in gingerbread.

Then there are rifle shots at tossing balls,
"And if you hit you get a good cigar,"

And strength-whackers for lads to lamm with mauls,
And Cheshire cheeses on a greasy spar.
The country folk flock in from near and far,
Women and men, like blowflies, to the roast,
All love the fair; but Anna loved it most.

Anna was all agog to see the fair;
She made Ern promise to be there to meet her,
To arm her round to all the pleasures there,
And buy her ribbons for her neck, and treat her,
So that no woman at the fair should beat her
In having pleasure at a man's expense.
She planned to meet him at the chapel fence.

So Ernie went; and Jimmy took his mother,
Dressed in her finest with a Monmouth shawl,
And there was such a crowd she thought she'd smother,
And O, she loved a pep'mint above all.
Clash go the crockeries where the cheapjacks bawl,
Baa go the sheep, thud goes the waxworks' drum,
And Ernie cursed for Anna hadn't come.

He hunted for her up and down the place,
Raging and snapping like a working brew.
"If you're with someone else I'll smash his face,
And when I've done for him I'll go for you."
He bought no fairings as he'd vowed to do
For his poor little children back at home
Stuck at the glass "to see till father come."

Not finding her, he went into an inn,
Busy with ringing till and scratching matches.
Where thirsty drovers mingled stout with gin
And three or four Welsh herds were singing catches.
The swing-doors clattered, letting in in snatches
The noises of the fair, now low, now loud.
Ern called for beer and glowered at the crowd.

While he was glowering at his drinking there,
In came the gipsy Bessie, hawking toys;
A bold-eyed strapping harlot with black hair,
One of the tribe which camped at Shepherd's Bois.
She lured him out of inn into the noise
Of the steam-organ where the horses spun,
And so the end of all things was begun.

Newness in lust, always the old in love.
"Put up your toys," he said, "and come along,
We'll have a turn of swing boats up above,
And see the murder when they strike the gong."
"Don't 'ee," she giggled. "My, but ain't you strong.
And where's your proper girl? You don't know me."
"I do." "You don't." "Why, then, I will," said he.

Anna was late because the cart which drove her
Called for her late (the horse had broke a trace),
She was all dressed and scented for her lover,
Her bright blue blouse had imitation lace,
The paint was red as roses on her face,
She hummed a song, because she thought to see
How envious all the other girls would be.

When she arrived and found her Ernie gone,
Her bitter heart thought, "This is how it is.
Keeping me waiting while the sports are on:
Promising faithful, too, and then to miss.
O, Ernie, won't I give it you for this."
And looking up she saw a couple cling,
Ern with his arm round Bessie in the swing.

Ern caught her eye and spat, and cut her dead,
Bessie laughed hardly, in the gipsy way.
Anna, though blind with fury, tossed her head,

Biting her lips until the red was grey,
For bitter moments given, bitter pay,
The time for payment comes, early or late,
No earthly debtor but accounts to Fate.

She turned aside, telling with bitter oaths
What Ern should suffer if he turned agen,
And there was Jimmy stripping off his clothes
Within a little ring of farming men.
"Now, Jimmy, put the old tup into pen."
His mother, watching, thought her heart would curdle,
To see Jim drag the old ram to the hurdle.

Then the ram butted and the game began,
Till Jimmy's muscles cracked and the ram grunted.
The good old wrestling game of Ram and Man,
At which none knows the hunter from the hunted.
"Come and see Jimmy have his belly bunted."
"Good tup. Good Jim. Good Jimmy. Sick him, Rover,
By dang, but Jimmy's got him fairly over."

Then there was clap of hands and Jimmy grinned
And took five silver shillings from his backers,
And said th' old tup had put him out of wind
Or else he'd take all comers at the Whackers.
And some made rude remarks of rams and knackers,
And mother shook to get her son alone,
So's to be sure he hadn't broke a bone.

None but the lucky man deserves the fair,
For lucky men have money and success,
Things that a whore is very glad to share,
Or dip, at least, a finger in the mess.
Anne, with her raddled cheeks and Sunday dress,
Smiled upon Jimmy, seeing him succeed,
As though to say, "You are a man, indeed."

All the great things of life are swiftly done,
Creation, death, and love the double gate.
However much we dawdle in the sun
We have to hurry at the touch of Fate;
When Life knocks at the door no one can wait,
When Death makes his arrest we have to go.
And so with Love, and Jimmy found it so.

Love, the sharp spear, went pricking to the bone,
In that one look, desire and bitter aching,
Longing to have that woman all alone
For her dear beauty's sake all else forsaking;
And sudden agony that set him shaking
Lest she, whose beauty made his heart's blood cruddle,
Should be another man's to kiss and cuddle.

She was beside him when he left the ring,
Her soft dress brushed against him as he passed her;
He thought her penny scent a sweeter thing
Than precious ointment out of alabaster;
Love, the mild servant, makes a drunken master.
She smiled, half sadly, out of thoughtful eyes,
And all the strong young man was easy prize.

She spoke, to take him, seeing him a sheep,
"How beautiful you wrastled with the ram,
It made me all go tremble just to peep,
I am that fond of wrastling, that I am.
Why, here's your mother, too. Good evening, ma'am.
I was just telling Jim how well he done,
How proud you must be of so fine a son."

Old mother blinked, while Jimmy hardly knew
Whether he knew the woman there or not;
But well he knew, if not, he wanted to,

Joy of her beauty ran in him so hot,
Old trembling mother by him was forgot,
While Anna searched the mother's face, to know
Whether she took her for a whore or no.

The woman's maxim, "Win the woman first,"
Made her be gracious to the withered thing.
"This being in crowds do give one such a thirst,
I wonder if they've tea going at 'The King'?
My throat's that dry my very tongue do cling,
Perhaps you'd take my arm, we'd wander up
(If you'd agree) and try and get a cup.

Come, ma'am, a cup of tea would do you good
There's nothing like a nice hot cup of tea
After the crowd and all the time you've stood;
And 'The King's' strict, it isn't like 'The Key.'
Now, take my arm, my dear, and lean on me."
And Jimmy's mother, being nearly blind,
Took Anna's arm, and only thought her kind.

So off they set, with Anna talking to her,
How nice the tea would be after the crowd,
And mother thinking half the time she knew her,
And Jimmy's heart's blood ticking quick and loud,
And Death beside him knitting at his shroud,
And all the High Street babbling with the fair,
And white October clouds in the blue air.

So tea was made, and down they sat to drink;
O the pale beauty sitting at the board
There is more death in women than we think,
There is much danger in the soul adored,
The white hands bring the poison and the cord;
Death has a lodge in lips as red as cherries,
Death has a mansion in the yew tree berries.

They sat there talking after tea was done,
And Jimmy blushed at Anna's sparkling looks,
And Anna flattered mother on her son,
Catching both fishes on her subtle hooks.
With twilight, tea and talk in ingle-nooks,
And music coming up from the dim street,
Mother had never known a fair so sweet.

Now cow-bells clink, for milking-time is come,
The drovers stack the hurdles into carts,
New masters drive the straying cattle home,
Many a young calf from his mother parts,
Hogs straggle back to sty by fits and starts;
The farmers take a last glass at the inns,
And now the frolic of the fair begins.

All of the side shows of the fair are lighted,
Flares and bright lights, and brassy cymbals clanging
"Beginning now" and "Everyone's invited,"
Shatter the pauses of the organ's whanging,
The Oldest Show on Earth and the Last Hanging,
"The Murder in the Red Barn," with real blood,
The rifles crack, the Sally shy-sticks thud.

Anna walked slowly homeward with her prey,
Holding old tottering mother's weight upon her,
And pouring in sweet poison on the way
Of "Such a pleasure, ma'am, and such an honour,"
And "One's so safe with such a son to con her
Through all the noises and through all the press,
Boys daredn't squirt tormenters on her dress."

At mother's door they stop to say "Goodnight."
And mother must go in to set the table.
Anna pretended that she felt a fright
To go alone through all the merry babel:

"My friends are waiting at 'The Cain and Abel,'
Just down the other side of Market Square,
It'd be a mercy if you'd set me there."

So Jimmy came, while mother went inside;
Anna has got her victim in her clutch.
Jimmy, all blushing, glad to be her guide,
Thrilled by her scent, and trembling at her touch.
She was all white and dark, and said not much;
She sighed, to hint that pleasure's grave was dug,
And smiled within to see him such a mug.

They passed the doctor's house among the trees,
She sighed so deep that Jimmy asked her why.
"I'm too unhappy upon nights like these,
When everyone has happiness but I!"
"Then, aren't you happy?" She appeared to cry,
Blinked with her eyes, and turned away her head:
"Not much; but some men understand," she said.

Her voice caught lightly on a broken note,
Jimmy half-dared but dared not touch her hand,
Yet all his blood went pumping in his throat
Beside the beauty he could understand,
And Death stopped knitting at the muffling band.
"The shroud is done," he muttered, "toe to chin."
He snapped the ends, and tucked his needles in.

Jimmy, half stammering, choked, "Has any man—"
He stopped, she shook her head to answer "No."
"Then tell me." "No. Perhaps some day, if I can.
It hurts to talk of some things ever so.
But you're so different. There, come, we must go.
None but unhappy women know how good
It is to meet a soul who's understood."
"No. Wait a moment. May I call you Anna?"

"Perhaps. There must be nearness 'twixt us two."
Love in her face hung out his bloody banner,
And all love's clanging trumpets shocked and blew.
"When we got up to-day we never knew."
"I'm sure I didn't think, nor you did." "Never."
"And now this friendship's come to us forever."

"Now, Anna, take my arm, dear." "Not to-night,
That must come later when we know our minds,
We must agree to keep this evening white,
We'll eat the fruit to-night and save the rinds."
And all the folk whose shadows darked the blinds,
And all the dancers whirling in the fair,
Were wretched worms to Jim and Anna there.

"How wonderful life is," said Anna, lowly.
"But it begins again with you for friend."
In the dim lamplight Jimmy thought her holy,
A lovely fragile thing for him to tend,
Grace beyond measure, beauty without end.
"Anna," he said; "Good-night. This is the door.
I never knew what people meant before."

"Good-night, my friend. Good-bye." "But oh, my sweet,
The night's quite early yet, don't say good-bye,
Come just another short turn down the street,
The whole life's bubbling up for you and I.
Somehow I feel to-morrow we may die.
Come just as far as to the blacksmith's light."
But "No," said Anna; "not to-night. Good-night."

All the tides triumph when the white moon fills,
Down in the race the toppling waters shout,
The breakers shake the bases of the hills,
There is a thundering where the streams go out,

And the wise shipman puts his ship about
Seeing the gathering of those waters wan,
But what when love makes high tide in a man?

Jimmy walked home with all his mind on fire,
One lovely face forever set in flame.
He shivered as he went, like tautened wire,
Surge after surge of shuddering in him came
And then swept out repeating one sweet name,
"Anna, oh Anna," to the evening star.
Anna was sipping whiskey in the bar.

So back to home and mother Jimmy wandered,
Thinking of Plaister's End and Anna's lips.
He ate no supper worth the name, but pondered
On Plaister's End hedge, scarlet with ripe hips,
And of the lovely moon there in eclipse,
And how she must be shining in the house
Behind the hedge of those old dog-rose boughs.

Old mother cleared away. The clock struck eight.
"Why, boy, you've left your bacon, lawks a me,
So that's what comes of having tea so late,
Another time you'll go without your tea.
Your father liked his cup, too, didn't he,
Always 'another cup' he used to say,
He never went without on any day.

How nice the lady was and how she talked,
I've never had a nicer fair, not ever."
"She said she'd like to see us if we walked
To Plaister's End, beyond by Watersever.
Nice-looking woman, too, and that, and clever;
We might go round one evening, p'raps, we two;
Or I might go, if it's too far for you."

"No," said the mother, "we're not folk for that;
Meet at the fair and that, and there an end.
Rake out the fire and put out the cat,
These fairs are sinful, tempting folk to spend.
Of course she spoke polite and like a friend;
Of course she had to do, and so I let her,
But now it's done and past, so I forget her."

"I don't see why forget her. Why forget her?
She treat us kind. She weren't like everyone.
I never saw a woman I liked better,
And he's not easy pleased, my father's son.
So I'll go round some night when work is done."
"Now, Jim, my dear, trust mother, there's a dear."
"Well, so I do, but sometimes you're so queer."

She blinked at him out of her withered eyes
Below her lashless eyelids red and bleared.
Her months of sacrifice had won the prize,
Her Jim had come to what she always feared.
And yet she doubted, so she shook and peered
And begged her God not let a woman take
The lovely son whom she had starved to make.

Doubting, she stood the dishes in the rack,
"We'll ask her in some evening, then," she said,
"How nice her hair looked in the bit of black."
And still she peered from eyes all dim and red
To note at once if Jimmy drooped his head,
Or if his ears blushed when he heard her praised,
And Jimmy blushed and hung his head and gazed.

"This is the end," she thought. "This is the end.
I'll have to sew again for Mr. Jones,
Do hems when I can hardly see to mend,
And have the old ache in my marrow bones.

And when his wife's in child-bed, when she groans,
She'll send for me until the pains have ceased,
And give me leavings at the christening feast.

And sit aslant to eye me as I eat,
'You're only wanted here, ma'am, for to-day,
Just for the christ'ning party, for the treat,
Don't ever think I mean to let you stay;
Two's company, three's none, that's what I say.'
Life can be bitter to the very bone
When one is poor, and woman, and alone."

"Jimmy," she said, still doubting. "Come, my dear,
Let's have our 'Binger,' 'fore we go to bed."
And then "The parson's dog," she cackled clear,
"Lep over stile," she sang, nodding her head.
"His name was little Binger." "Jim," she said,
"Binger, now, chorus" . . . Jimmy kicked the hob,
The sacrament of song died in a sob.

Jimmy went out into the night to think
Under the moon so steady in the blue.
The woman's beauty ran in him like drink,
The fear that men had loved her burnt him through;
The fear that even then another knew
All the deep mystery which women make
To hide the inner nothing made him shake.

"Anna, I love you, and I always shall."
He looked towards Plaister's End beyond Cot Hills.
A white star glimmered in the long canal,
A droning from the music came in thrills.
Love is a flame to burn out human wills,
Love is a flame to set the will on fire,
Love is a flame to cheat men into mire.

One of the three, we make Love what we choose.
But Jimmy did not know, he only thought
That Anna was too beautiful to lose,
That she was all the world and he was naught,
That it was sweet, though bitter, to be caught.
"Anna, I love you." Underneath the moon,
"I shall go mad unless I see you soon."

The fair's lights threw aloft a misty glow.
The organ whangs, the giddy horses reel,
The rifles cease, the folk begin to go,
The hands unclamp the swing boats from the wheel,
There is a smell of trodden orange peel;
The organ drones and dies, the horses stop,
And then the tent collapses from the top.

The fair is over, let the people troop,
The drunkards stagger homewards down the gutters,
The showmen heave in an excited group,
The poles tilt slowly down, the canvas flutters,
The mauls knock out the pins, the last flare sputters.
"Lower away." "Go easy." "Lower, lower."
"You've dang near knock my skull in. Loose it slower."

"Back in the horses." "Are the swing boats loaded?"
"All right to start." "Bill, where's the cushion gone?
The red one for the Queen?" "I think I stowed it."
"You think, you think. Lord, where's that cushion, John?"
"It's in that ditty box you're sitting on,
What more d'you want?" A concertina plays
Far off as wandering lovers go their ways.

Up the dim Bye Street to the market-place
The dead bones of the fair are borne in carts,
Horses and swing boats at a funeral pace
After triumphant hours quickening hearts;

A policeman eyes each waggon as it starts,
The drowsy showmen stumble half asleep,
One of them catcalls, having drunken deep.

So out, over the pass, into the plain,
And the dawn finds them filling empty cans
In some sweet-smelling dusty country lane,
Where a brook chatters over rusty pans.
The iron chimneys of the caravans
Smoke as they go. And now the fair has gone
To find a new pitch somewhere further on.

But as the fair moved out two lovers came,
Ernie and Bessie loitering out together;
Bessie with wild eyes, hungry as a flame,
Ern like a stallion tugging at a tether.
It was calm moonlight, and October weather,
So still, so lovely, as they topped the ridge.
They brushed by Jimmy standing on the bridge.

And, as they passed, they gravely eyed each other,
And the blood burned in each heart beating there;
And out into the Bye Street tottered mother,
Without her shawl, in the October air.
"Jimmy," she cried, "Jimmy." And Bessie's hair
Drooped on the instant over Ernie's face,
And the two lovers clung in an embrace.

"O, Ern." "My own, my Bessie." As they kissed
Jimmy was envious of the thing unknown.
So this was Love, the something he had missed,
Woman and man athirst, aflame, alone.
Envy went knocking at his marrow bone,
And Anna's face swam up so dim, so fair,
Shining and sweet, with poppies in her hair.

PART III

After the fair, the gang began again
Tipping the trolleys down the banks of earth.
The truck of stone clanks on the endless chain,
A clever pony guides it to its berth.
"Let go." It tips, the navvies shout for mirth
To see the pony step aside, so wise,
But Jimmy sighed, thinking of Anna's eyes.

And when he stopped his shovelling he looked
Over the junipers towards Plaister way,
The beauty of his darling had him hooked,
He had no heart for wrastling with the clay.
"O Lord Almighty, I must get away;
O Lord, I must. I must just see my flower.
Why, I could run there in the dinner hour."

The whistle on the pilot engine blew,
The men knocked off, and Jimmy slipped aside
Over the fence, over the bridge, and through,
And then ahead along the water-side,
Under the red-brick rail-bridge, arching wide,
Over the hedge, across the fields, and on;
The foreman asked: "Where's Jimmy Gurney gone?"

It is a mile and more to Plaister's End,
But Jimmy ran the short way by the stream,
And there was Anna's cottage at the bend,
With blue smoke on the chimney, faint as steam.
"God, she's at home," and up his heart a gleam
Leapt like a rocket on November nights,
And shattered slowly in a burst of lights.

Anna was singing at her kitchen fire,
She was surprised, and not well pleased to see

A sweating navvy, red with heat and mire,
Come to her door, whoever he might be.
But when she saw that it was Jimmy, she
Smiled at his eyes upon her, full of pain,
And thought, "But, still, he mustn't come again.

People will talk; boys are such crazy things;
But he's a dear boy though he is so green."
So, hurriedly, she slipped her apron strings,
And dabbed her hair, and wiped her fingers clean,
And came to greet him languid as a queen,
Looking as sweet, as fair, as pure, as sad,
As when she drove her loving husband mad.

"Poor boy," she said, "Poor boy, how hot you are."
She laid a cool hand to his sweating face.
"How kind to come. Have you been running far?
I'm just going out; come up the road a pace.
O dear, these hens; they're all about the place."
So Jimmy shooed the hens at her command,
And got outside the gate as she had planned.

"Anna, my dear, I love you; love you, true;
I had to come—I don't know—I can't rest—
I lay awake all night, thinking of you.
Many must love you, but I love you best."
"Many have loved me, yes, dear," she confessed,
She smiled upon him with a tender pride,
"But my love ended when my husband died.

"Still, we'll be friends, dear friends, dear, tender friends;
Love with its fever's at an end for me.
Be by me gently now the fever ends,
Life is a lovelier thing than lovers see,
I'd like to trust a man, Jimmy," said she,
"May I trust you?" "Oh, Anna dear, my dear——"
"Don't come so close," she said, "with people near.

Dear, don't be vexed; it's very sweet to find
One who will understand; but life is life,
And those who do not know are so unkind.
But you'll be by me, Jimmy, in the strife,
I love you though I cannot be your wife;
And now be off, before the whistle goes,
Or else you'll lose your quarter, goodness knows."

"When can I see you, Anna? Tell me, dear.
To-night? To-morrow? Shall I come to-night?"
"Jimmy, my friend, I cannot have you here;
But when I come to town perhaps we might.
Dear, you must go; no kissing; you can write,
And I'll arrange a meeting when I learn
What friends are doing" (meaning Shepherd Ern).

"Good-bye, my own." "Dear Jim, you understand.
If we were only free, dear, free to meet,
Dear, I would take you by your big, strong hand
And kiss your dear boy eyes so blue and sweet;
But my dead husband lies under the sheet,
Dead in my heart, dear, lovely, lonely one,
So, Jim, my dear, my loving days are done.

But though my heart is buried in his grave
Something might be—friendship and utter trust—
And you, my dear starved little Jim shall have
Flowers of friendship from my dead heart's dust;
Life would be sweet if men would never lust.
Why do you, Jimmy? Tell me sometime, dear,
Why men are always what we women fear.

Not now. Good-bye; we understand, we two,
And life, oh, Jim, how glorious life is;
This sunshine in my heart is due to you;
I was so sad, and life has given this.

I think 'I wish I had something of his,'
Do give me something, will you be so kind?
Something to keep you always in my mind."

"I will," he said. "Now go, or you'll be late."
He broke from her and ran, and never dreamt
That as she stood to watch him from the gate
Her heart was half amusement, half contempt,
Comparing Jim the squab, red and unkempt,
In sweaty corduroys, with Shepherd Ern.
She blew him kisses till he passed the turn.

The whistle blew before he reached the line;
The foreman asked him what the hell he meant,
Whether a duke had asked him out to dine,
Or if he thought the bag would pay his rent?
And Jim was fined before the foreman went.
But still his spirit glowed from Anna's words,
Cooed in the voice so like a singing bird's.

"O Anna, darling, you shall have a present;
I'd give you golden gems if I were rich,
And everything that's sweet and all that's pleasant."
He dropped his pick as though he had a stitch,
And stared tow'rds Plaister's End, past Bushe's Pitch.
"O beauty, what I have to give I'll give,
All mine is yours, beloved, while I live."

All through the afternoon his pick was slacking,
His eyes were always turning west and south,
The foreman was inclined to send him packing,
But put it down to after fair-day drouth;
He looked at Jimmy with an ugly mouth,
And Jimmy slacked, and muttered in a moan,
"My love, my beautiful, my very own."

So she had loved. Another man had had her;
She had been his with passion in the night;
An agony of envy made him sadder,
Yet stabbed a pang of bitter-sweet delight—
O he would keep his image of her white.
The foreman cursed, stepped up, and asked him flat
What kind of gum tree he was gaping at.

It was Jim's custom, when the pay day came,
To take his weekly five and twenty shilling
Back in the little packet to his dame:
Not taking out a farthing for a filling,
Nor twopence for a pot, for he was willing
That she should have it all to save or spend.
But love makes many lovely customs end.

Next pay day came, and Jimmy took the money,
But not to mother, for he meant to buy
A thirteen shilling locket for his honey,
Whatever bellies hungered and went dry,
A silver heart-shape with a ruby eye
He bought the thing and paid the shopman's price
And hurried off to make the sacrifice.

"Is it for me? You dear, dear generous boy.
How sweet of you. I'll wear it in my dress.
When you're beside me life is such a joy,
You bring the sun to solitariness."
She brushed his jacket with a light caress,
His arms went round her fast, she yielded meek;
He had the happiness to kiss her cheek.

"My dear, my dear." "My very dear, my Jim,
How very kind my Jimmy is to me;
I ache to think that some are harsh to him;
Not like my Jimmy, beautiful and free.

My darling boy, how lovely it would be
If all would trust as we two trust each other."
And Jimmy's heart grew hard against his mother.

She, poor old soul, was waiting in the gloom
For Jimmy's pay, that she could do the shopping.
The clock ticked out a solemn tale of doom;
Clogs on the bricks outside went clippa-clopping,
The owls were coming out and dew was dropping.
The bacon burnt, and Jimmy not yet home.
The clock was ticking dooms out like a gnome.

"What can have kept him that he doesn't come?
O God, they'd tell me if he'd come to hurt."
The unknown, unseen evil struck her numb,
She saw his body bloody in the dirt,
She saw the life blood pumping through the shirt,
She saw him tipsy in the navvies' booth,
She saw all forms of evil but the truth.

At last she hurried up the line to ask
If Jim were hurt or why he wasn't back.
She found the watchman wearing through his task;
Over the fire basket in his shack;
Behind, the new embankment rose up black.
"Gurney?" he said. "He'd got to see a friend."
"Where?" "I dunno. I think out Plaister's End."

Thanking the man, she tottered down the hill,
The long-feared fang had bitten to the bone.
The brook beside her talked as water will
That it was lonely singing all alone,
The night was lonely with the water's tone,
And she was lonely to the very marrow.
Love puts such bitter poison on Fate's arrow.

She went the long way to them by the mills,
She told herself that she must find her son.
The night was ominous of many ills;
The soughing larch-clump almost made her run,
Her boots hurt (she had got a stone in one)
And bitter beaks were tearing at her liver
That her boy's heart was turned from her forever.

She kept the lane, past Spindle's past the Callows',
Her lips still muttering prayers against the worst,
And there were people coming from the sallows,
Along the wild duck patch by Beggar's Hurst.
Being in moonlight mother saw them first,
She saw them moving in the moonlight dim,
A woman with a sweet voice saying "Jim."

Trembling she grovelled down into the ditch,
They wandered past her pressing side to side.
"O Anna, my belov'd, if I were rich."
It was her son, and Anna's voice replied,
"Dear boy, dear beauty boy, my love and pride."
And he: "It's but a silver thing, but I
Will earn you better lockets by and by."

"Dear boy, you mustn't." "But I mean to do."
"What was that funny sort of noise I heard?"
"Where?"
"In the hedge; a sort of sob or coo.
Listen. It's gone." "It may have been a bird."
Jim tossed a stone but mother never stirred.
She hugged the hedgerow, choking down her pain,
While the hot tears were blinding in her brain.

The two passed on, the withered woman rose,
For many minutes she could only shake,

Staring ahead with trembling little "Oh's,"
The noise a very frightened child might make.
"O God, dear God, don't let the woman take
My little son, God, not my little Jim.
O God, I'll have to starve if I lose him."

So back she trembled, nodding with her head,
Laughing and trembling in the bursts of tears,
Her ditch-filled boots both squelching in the tread,
Her shopping-bonnet sagging to her ears,
Her heart too dumb with brokenness for fears.
The nightmare whickering with the laugh of death
Could not have added terror to her breath.

She reached the house, and: "I'm all right," said she,
"I'll just take off my things; but I'm all right,
I'd be all right with just a cup of tea,
If I could only get this grate to light,
The paper's damp and Jimmy's late to-night;
'Belov'd, if I was rich,' was what he said,
Oh, Jim, I wish that God would kill me dead."

While she was blinking at the unlit grate,
Scratching the moistened match-heads off the wood,
She heard Jim coming, so she reached his plate,
And forked the over-frizzled scraps of food.
"You're late," she said, "and this yer isn't good,
Whatever makes you come in late like this?"
"I've been to Plaister's End, that's how it is."

M. "You've been to Plaister's End?"
J. "Yes."
M. "I've been staying
For money for the shopping ever so.
Down here we can't get victuals without paying.

There's no trust down the Bye Street, as you know,
And now it's dark and it's too late to go.
You've been to Plaister's End. What took you there?"
J. "The lady who was with us at the fair."

M. "The lady, eh? The lady?"
J. "Yes, the lady."
M. "You've been to see her?"
J. "Yes."

M. "What happened then?"
J. "I saw her."
M. "Yes. And what filth did she trade ye?
Or d'you expect your locket back agen?
I know the rotten ways of whores with men.
What did it cost ye?"
J. "What did what cost?"
M. "It.
Your devil's penny for the devil's bit."
J. "I don't know what you mean."
M. "Jimmy, my own.
Don't lie to mother, boy, for mother knows.
I know you and that lady to the bone,
And she's a whore, that thing you call a rose,
A whore who takes whatever male thing goes;
A harlot with the devil's skill to tell
The special key of each man's door to hell."

J. "She's not. She's nothing of the kind, I tell 'ee."
M. "You can't tell women like a woman can;
A beggar tells a lie to fill his belly,
A strumpet tells a lie to win a man,
Women were liars since the world began;
And she's a liar, branded in the eyes,
A rotten liar, who inspires lies."

J. "I say she's not."
M. "No, don't 'ee, Jim, my dearie,
You've seen her often in the last few days,
She's given a love as makes you come in weary
To lie to me before going out to laze.
She's tempted you into the devil's ways,
She's robbing you, full fist, of what you earn,
In God's Name, what's she giving in return?"

J. "Her faith, my dear, and that's enough for me."
M. "Her faith. Her faith. Oh, Jimmy, listen, dear;
Love doesn't ask for faith, my son, not he;
He asks for life throughout the live-long year,
And life's a test for any plough to ere.
Life tests a plough in meadows made of stones,
Love takes a toll of spirit, mind and bones.

I know a woman's portion when she loves,
It's hers to give, my darling, not to take;
It isn't lockets, dear, nor pairs of gloves,
It isn't marriage bells nor wedding cake,
It's up and cook, although the belly ache;
And bear the child, and up and work again,
And count a sick man's grumble worth the pain.

Will she do this, and fifty times as much?"
J. "No. I don't ask her."
M. "No. I warrant, no.
She's one to get a young fool in her clutch,
And you're a fool to let her trap you so.
She love you? She? O Jimmy, let her go;
I was so happy, dear, before she came,
And now I'm going to the grave in shame.

I bore you, Jimmy, in this very room.
For fifteen years I got you all you had,

You were my little son, made in my womb,
Left all to me, for God had took your dad,
You were a good son, doing all I bade,
Until this strumpet came from God knows where,
And now you lie, and I am in despair.

Jimmy, I won't say more. I know you think
That I don't know, being just a withered old,
With chaps all fallen in and eyes that blink,
And hands that tremble so they cannot hold.
A bag of bones to put in churchyard mould,
A red-eyed hag beside your evening star."
And Jimmy gulped, and thought, "By God, you are."

"Well, if I am, my dear, I don't pretend.
I got my eyes red, Jimmy, making you.
My dear, before our love time's at an end
Think just a minute what it is you do.
If this were right, my dear, you'd tell me true;
You don't, and so it's wrong; you lie; and she
Lies too, or else you wouldn't lie to me.

Women and men have only got one way
And that way's marriage; other ways are lust.
If you must marry this one, then you may
If you'll not drop her."
J. "No."
M. "I say you must.
Or bring my hairs with sorrow to the dust.
Marry your whore, you'll pay, and there an end.
My God, you shall not have a whore for friend.

By God, you shall not, not while I'm alive.
Never, so help me God, shall that thing be.
If she's a woman fit to touch she'll wive,
If not she's whore, and she shall deal with me.

And may God's blessed mercy help us see
And may He make my Jimmy count the cost,
My little boy who's lost, as I am lost."

People in love cannot be won by kindness,
And opposition makes them feel like martyrs.
When folk are crazy with drunken blindness
It's best to flog them with each other's garters,
And have the flogging done by Shropshire carters,
Born under Ercall where the white stones lie;
Ercall that smells of honey in July.

Jimmy said nothing in reply, but thought
That mother was an old, hard, jealous thing.
"I'll love my girl through good and ill report,
I shall be true whatever grief it bring."
And in his heart he heard the death-bell ring
For mother's death, and thought what it would be
To bury her in churchyard and be free.

He saw the narrow grave under the wall,
Home without mother nagging at his dear,
And Anna there with him at evenfall,
Bidding him dry his eyes and be of cheer.
"The death that took poor mother brings me near,
Nearer than we have ever been before,
Near as the dead one came, but dearer, more."

"Good-night, my son," said mother. "Night," he said.
He dabbed her brow wi's lips and blew the light,
She lay quite silent crying on the bed,
Stirring no limb, but crying through the night,
He slept, convinced that he was Anna's knight.
And when he went to work he left behind
Money for mother crying herself blind.

After that night he came to Anna's call,
He was a fly in Anna's subtle weavings,
Mother had no more share in him at all;
All that the mother had was Anna's leavings.
There were more lies, more lockets, more deceivings,
Taunts from the proud old woman, lies from him,
And Anna's coo of "Cruel. Leave her, Jim."

Also the foreman spoke: "You make me sick,
You come-day-go-day-God-send-plenty-beer.
You put less mizzle on your bit of Dick,
Or get your time, I'll have no slackers here,
I've had my eye on you too long, my dear."
And Jimmy pondered while the man attacked,
"I'd see her all day long if I were sacked."

And trembling mother thought, "I'll go to see'r.
She'd give me back my boy if she were told
Just what he is to me, my pretty dear:
She wouldn't leave me starving in the cold,
Like what I am." But she was weak and old.
She thought, "But if I ast her, I'm afraid
He'd hate me ever after," so she stayed.

PART IV

Bessie, the gipsy, got with child by Ern,
She joined her tribe again at Shepherd's Meen,
In that old quarry overgrown with fern,
Where goats are tethered on the patch of green.
There she reflected on the fool she'd been,
And plaited kipes and waited for the bastard,
And thought that love was glorious while it lasted.

And Ern, the moody man, went moody home,
To that most gentle girl from Ercall Hill,

And bade her take a heed now he had come,
Or else, by cripes, he'd put her through the mill.
He didn't want her love, he'd had his fill,
Thank you, of her, the bread and butter sack.
And Anna heard that Shepherd Ern was back.

"Back. And I'll have him back to me," she muttered,
"This lovesick boy of twenty, green as grass,
Has made me wonder if my brains are buttered,
He, and his lockets, and his love, the ass.
I don't know why he comes. Alas! alas!
God knows I want no love; but every sun
I bolt my doors on some poor loving one.

It breaks my heart to turn them out of doors,
I hear them crying to me in the rain;
One, with a white face, curses, one implores,
'Anna, for God's sake, let me in again,
Anna, belov'd, I cannot bear the pain.'
Like hoovey sheep bleating outside a fold,
'Anna, belov'd, I'm in the wind and cold.'"

I want no men. I'm weary to the soul
Of men like moths about a candle flame,
Of men like flies about a sugar bowl,
Acting alike, and all wanting the same,
My dreamed-of swirl of passion never came,
No man has given me the love I dreamed,
But in the best of each one something gleamed.

If my dear darling were alive, but he. . .
He was the same; he didn't understand.
The eyes of that dead child are haunting me,
I only turned the blanket with my hand.
It didn't hurt, he died as I had planned.
A little skinny creature, weak and red;
It looked so peaceful after it was dead.

I have been all alone, in spite of all.
Never a light to help me place my feet:
I have had many a pain and many a fall.
Life's a long headache in a noisy street,
Love at the budding looks so very sweet,
Men put such bright disguises on their lust,
And then it all goes crumble into dust.

Jimmy the same, dear, lovely Jimmy, too,
He goes the self-same way the others went:
I shall bring sorrow to those eyes of blue.
He asks the love I'm sure I never meant.
Am I to blame? And all his money spent!
Men make this shutting doors such cruel pain.
O, Ern, I want you in my life again."

On Sunday afternoons the lovers walk
Arm within arm, dressed in their Sunday best,
The man with the blue necktie sucks a stalk,
The woman answers when she is addressed,
On quiet country stiles they sit to rest,
And after fifty years of wear and tear
They think how beautiful their courtships were.

Jimmy and Anna met to walk together
The Sunday after Shepherd Ern returned;
And Anna's hat was lovely with a feather
Bought and dyed blue with money Jimmy earned.
They walked towards Callows' Farm, and Anna yearned:
"Dear boy," she said, "This road is dull to-day,
Suppose we turn and walk the other way."

They turned, she sighed. "What makes you sigh?" he asked.
"Thinking," she said, "thinking and grieving, too.
Perhaps some wicked woman will come masked
Into your life, my dear, to ruin you.

And trusting every woman as you do
It might mean death to love and be deceived;
You'd take it hard, I thought, and so I grieved."

"Dear one, dear Anna." "O my lovely boy,
Life is all golden to the fingers tips.
What will be must be: but to-day's a joy.
Reach me that lovely branch of scarlet hips."
He reached and gave; she put it to her lips.
"And here," she said, "we come to Plaister Turns,"
And then she chose the road to Shepherd Ern's.

As the deft angler, when the fishes rise,
Flicks on the broadening circle over each
The delicatest touch of dropping flies,
Then pulls more line and whips a longer reach,
Longing to feel the rod bend, the reel screech,
And the quick comrade net the monster out,
So Anna played the fly over her trout.

Twice she passed, thrice, she with the boy beside her,
A lovely fly, hooked for a human heart,
She passed his little gate, while Jimmy eyed her,
Feeling her beauty tear his soul apart:
Then did the great trout rise, the great pike dart,
The gate went clack, a man came up the hill,
The lucky strike had hooked him through the gill.

Her breath comes quick, her tired beauty glows,
She would not look behind, she looked ahead,
It seemed to Jimmy she was like a rose,
A golden white rose faintly flushed with red.
Her eyes danced quicker at the approaching tread,
Her finger nails dug sharp into her palm.
She yearned to Jimmy's shoulder, and kept calm.

"Evening," said Shepherd Ern. She turned and eyed him,
Cold and surprised, but interested too,
To see how much he felt the hook inside him,
And how much he surmised, and Jimmy knew,
And if her beauty still could make him do
The love tricks he had gambolled in the past.
A glow shot through her that her fish was grassed.

"Evening," she said. "Good evening." Jimmy felt
Jealous and angry at the shepherd's tone;
He longed to hit the fellow's nose a belt,
He wanted his beloved his alone.
A fellow's girl should be a fellow's own.
Ern gave the lad a glance and turned to Anna,
Jim might have been in China by his manner.

"Still walking out?" "As you are." "I'll be bound."
"Can you talk gipsy yet, or plait a kipe?"
"I'll teach you if I can when I come round."
"And when will that be?" "When the time is ripe."
And Jimmy longed to hit the man a swipe
Under the chin to knock him out of time,
But Anna stayed: she still had twigs to lime.

"Come, Anna, come, my dear," he muttered low.
She frowned, and blinked and spoke again to Ern.
"I hear the gipsy has a row to hoe."
"The more you hear," he said, "the less you'll learn."
"We've come out," she said, "to take a turn;
Suppose you come along: the more the merrier."
"All right," he said, "but how about the terrier?"

He cocked an eye at Jimmy. "Does he bite?"
Jimmy blushed scarlet. "He's a dear," said she.
Ern walked a step, "Will you be in tonight?"
She shook her head, "I doubt if that may be.

Jim, here's a friend who wants to talk to me,
So will you go and come another day?"
"By crimes, I won't!" said Jimmy, "I shall stay."

"I thought he bit," said Ern, and Anna smiled,
And Jimmy saw the smile and watched her face,
While all the jealous devils made him wild;
A third in love is always out of place;
And then her gentle body full of grace
Leaned to him sweetly as she tossed her head,
"Perhaps we two'll be getting on," she said.

They walked, but Jimmy turned to watch the third.
"I'm here, not you," he said; the shepherd grinned:
Anna was smiling sweet without a word;
She got the scarlet berry branch unpinned.
"It's cold," she said, "this evening, in the wind."
A quick glance showed that Jimmy didn't mind her,
She beckoned with the berry branch behind her.

Then dropped it gently on the broken stones,
Preoccupied, unheeding, walking straight,
Saying "You jealous boy," in even tones,
Looking so beautiful, so delicate,
Being so very sweet: but at her gate
She felt her shoe unlaced and looked to know
If Ern had taken up the sprig or no.

He had, she smiled. "Anna," said Jimmy sadly,
"That man's not fit to be a friend of yourn,
He's nobbut just an oaf; I love you madly,
And hearing you speak kind to'm made me burn.
Who is he, then?" She answered "Shepherd Ern,
A pleasant man, an old, old friend of mine."
"By cripes, then, Anna, drop him, he's a swine."

"Jimmy," she said, "you must have faith in me,
Faith's all the battle in a love like ours.
You must believe, my darling, don't you see,
That life to have its sweets must have its sours.
Love isn't always two souls picking flowers.
You must have faith. I give you all I can.
What, can't I say 'Good evening' to a man?"

"Yes," he replied, "but not a man like him."
"Why not a man like him?" she said, "What next?"
By this they'd reached her cottage in the dim,
Among the daisies that the cold had kexed.
"Because I say. Now, Anna, don't be vexed."
"I'm more than vexed," she said, "with words like these.
'You say,' indeed. How dare you. Leave me, please."

"Anna, my Anna." "Leave me." She was cold,
Proud and imperious with a lifting lip,
Blazing within, but outwardly controlled;
He had a colt's first instance of the whip.
The long lash curled to cut a second strip.
"You to presume to teach. Of course, I know
You're mother's Sunday scholar, aren't you? Go."

She slammed the door behind her, clutching skirts.
"Anna." He heard her bedroom latches thud.
He learned at last how bitterly love hurts;
He longed to cut her throat and see her blood,
To stamp her blinking eyeballs into mud.
"Anna, by God!" Love's many torments make
That tune soon change to "Dear, for Jesus' sake."

He beat the door for her. She never stirred,
But primming bitter lips before her glass;
Admired her hat as though she hadn't heard,
And tried her front hair parted, and in mass.

She heard her lover's hasty footsteps pass.
"He's gone," she thought. She crouched below the pane,
And heard him cursing as he tramped the lane.

Rage ran in Jimmy as he tramped the night;
Rage, strongly mingled with a youth's disgust
At finding a beloved woman light,
And all her precious beauty dirty dust;
A tinsel-varnish gilded over lust.
Nothing but that. He sat him down to rage,
Beside the stream whose waters never age.

Plashing, it slithered down the tiny fall
To eddy wrinkles in the trembling pool
With that light voice whose music cannot pall,
Always the note of solace, flute-like, cool.
And when hot-headed man has been a fool,
He could not do a wiser thing than go
To that dim pool where purple teazels grow.

He glowered there until suspicion came,
Suspicion, anger's bastard, with mean tongue,
To mutter to him till his heart was flame,
And every fibre of his soul was wrung,
That even then Ern and his Anna clung
Mouth against mouth in passionate embrace.
There was no peace for Jimmy in the place.

Raging he hurried back to learn the truth.
The little swinging wicket glimmered white,
The chimney jagged the skyline like a tooth,
Bells came in swoons, for it was Sunday night.
The garden was all dark, but there was light
Up in the little room where Anna slept:
The hot blood beat his brain; he crept, he crept

Clutching himself to hear, clutching to know,
Along the path, rustling with withered leaves,
Up to the apple, too decayed to blow,
Which crooked a palsied finger at the eaves.
And up the lichened trunk his body heaves.
Dust blinded him, twigs snapped, the branches shook,
He leaned along a mossy bough to look.

Nothing at first, except a guttering candle
Shaking amazing shadows on the ceiling.
Then Anna's voice upon a bar of "Randal,
Where have you been?" and voice and music reeling,
Trembling, as though she sang with flooding feeling.
The singing stopped midway upon the stair,
Then Anna showed in white with loosened hair.

Her back was towards him, and she stood awhile,
Like a wild creature tossing back her mane,
And then her head went back, he saw a smile
On the half face half turned towards the pane;
Her eyes closed, and her arms went out again.
Jim gritted teeth, and called upon his Maker,
She dropped into a man's arms there to take her.

Agony first, sharp, sudden, like a knife,
Then down the tree to batter at the door;
"Open there. Let me in. I'll have your life.
You Jezebel of hell, you painted whore.
Talk about faith, I'll give you faith galore."
The window creaked, a jug of water came
Over his head and neck with certain aim.

"Clear out," said Ern; "I'm here, not you, to-night,
Clear out. We whip young puppies when they yap."
"If you're a man," said Jim, "come down and fight,
I'll put a stopper on your ugly chap."

"Go home," said Ern; "go home and get your pap.
To kennel, pup, and bid your mother bake
Some soothing syrup in your puppy-cake."

There was a dibble sticking in the bed,
Jim wrenched it out and swung it swiftly round,
And sent it flying at the shepherd's head:
"I'll give you puppy-cake. Take that, you hound."
The broken glass went clinking to the ground,
The dibble balanced, checked, and followed flat.
"My God," said Ern, "I'll give you hell for that."

He flung the door ajar with "Now, my pup—
Hold up the candle, Anna—now, we'll see."
"By crimes, come on," said Jimmy; "put them up.
Come, put them up, you coward, here I be."
And Jim, eleven stone, what chance had he
Against fourteen? but what he could he did;
Ern swung his right: "That settles you, my kid."

Jimmy went down and out: "The kid," said Ern.
"A kid, a sucking puppy; hold the light."
And Anna smiled: "It gave me such a turn.
You look so splendid, Ernie, when you fight."
She looked at Jim with: "Ern, is he all right?"
"He's coming to." She shuddered, "Pah, the brute,
What things he said;" she stirred him with her foot.

"You go inside," said Ern, "and bolt the door,
I'll deal with him." She went and Jimmy stood.
"Now, pup," said Ern, "don't come round here no more.
I'm here, not you, let that be understood.
I tell you frankly, pup, for your own good."
"Give me my hat," said Jim. He passed the gate,
And as he tottered off he called, "You wait."

"Thanks, I don't have to," Shepherd Ern replied;
"You'll do whatever waiting's being done."
The door closed gently as he went inside,
The bolts jarred in the channels one by one.
"I'll give you throwing bats about, my son.
Anna." "My dear?" "Where are you?" "Come and find."
The light went out, the windows stared out blind,

Blind as blind eyes forever seeing dark.
And in the dim the lovers went upstairs,
Her eyes fast closed, the shepherd's burning stark,
His lips entangled in her straying hairs,
Breath coming short as in a convert's prayers,
Her stealthy face all drowsy in the dim
And full of shudders as she yearned to him.

Jim crossed the water, cursing in his tears,
"By cripes, you wait. My God, he's with her now,
And all her hair pulled down over her ears;
Loving the blaggard like a filthy sow.
I saw her kiss him from the apple bough.
They say a whore is always full of wiles.
O God, how sweet her eyes are when she smiles.

Curse her and curse her. No, my God, she's sweet.
It's all a helly nightmare. I shall wake.
If it were all a dream I'd kiss her feet,
I wish it were a dream for Jesus' sake.
One thing: I bet I made his guzzle ache,
I cop it fair before he sent me down,
I'll cop him yet some evening on the crown.

O God, O God, what pretty ways she had.
He's kissing all her skin, so white and soft.
She's kissing back. I think I'm going mad.

Like rutting rattens in the apple loft.
She held that light she carried high aloft
Full in my eyes for him to hit me by,
I had the light all dazzling in my eye.

She had her dress all clutched up to her shoulder,
And all her naked arm was all one gleam.
It's going to freeze to-night, it's turning colder.
I wish there was more water in the stream,
I'd drownd myself. Perhaps it's all a dream,
And by and by I'll wake and find it stuff.
By crimes, the pain I suffer's real enough."

About two hundred yards from Gunder Loss
He stopped to shudder, leaning on the gate,
He bit the touchwood underneath the moss;
"Rotten, like her," he muttered in his hate;
He spat it out again with "But, you wait,
We'll see again, before to-morrow's past,
In this life he laughs longest who laughs last."

All through the night the stream ran to the sea,
The different water always saying the same,
Cat-like, and then a tinkle, never glee,
A lonely little child alone in shame.
An otter snapped a thorn twig when he came,
It drifted down, it passed the Hazel Mill,
It passed the Springs; but Jimmy stayed there still.

Over the pointed hill-top came the light,
Out of the mists on Ercall came the sun,
Red like a huntsman hallowing after night,
Blowing a horn to rouse up everyone;
Through many glittering cities he had run,
Splashing the wind vanes on the dewy roofs
With golden sparks struck by his horse's hoofs.

The watchman rose, rubbing his rusty eyes,
He stirred the pot of cocoa for his mate;
The fireman watched his head of power rise.
"What time?" he asked.
"You haven't long to wait."
"Now, is it time?"
"Yes. Let her ripple." Straight
The whistle shrieked its message, "Up to work!
Up, or be fined a quarter if you shirk."

Hearing the whistle, Jimmy raised his head,
"The warning call, and me in Sunday clo'es;
I'd better go; I've time. The sun looks red,
I feel so stiff I'm very nearly froze."
So over brook and through the fields he goes,
And up the line among the navvies' smiles,
"Young Jimmy Gurney's been upon the tiles."

The second whistle blew and work began,
Jimmy worked too, not knowing what he did,
He tripped and stumbled like a drunken man;
He muddled all, whatever he was bid,
The foreman cursed, "Good God, what ails the kid?
Hi! Gurney. You. We'll have you crocking soon,
You take a lie down till the afternoon."

"I won't," he answered. "Why the devil should I?
I'm here, I mean to work. I do my piece,
Or would do if a man could, but how could I
When you come nagging round and never cease?
Well, take the job and give me my release,
I want the sack, now give it, there's my pick;
Give me the sack." The sack was given quick.

PART V

Dully he got his time-check from the keeper.
"Curse her," he said; "and that's the end of whores"—
He stumbled drunkenly across a sleeper—
"Give all you have and get kicked out—a-door."
He cashed his time-check at the station stores.
"Bett'ring yourself, I hope, Jim," said the master;
"That's it," said Jim; "and so I will do, blast her."

Beyond the bridge, a sharp turn to the right
Leads to "The Bull and Boar," the carters' rest;
An inn so hidden it is out of sight
To anyone not coming from the west,
The high embankment hides it with its crest.
Far up above, the Chester trains go by,
The drinkers see them sweep against the sky.

Canal men used it when the bargers came,
The navvies used it when the line was making;
The pigeons strut and sidle, ruffling, tame,
The chuckling brook in front sets shadows shaking.
Cider and beer for thirsty workers' slaking,
A quiet house; like all that God controls,
It is Fate's instrument on human souls.

Thither Jim turned. "And now I'll drink," he said.
"I'll drink and drink—I never did before—
I'll drink and drink until I'm mad or dead,
For that's what comes of meddling with a whore."
He called for liquor at "The Bull and Boar";
Moody he drank; the woman asked him why:
"Have you had trouble?" "No," he said, "I'm dry.

Dry and burnt up, so give's another drink;
That's better, that's much better, that's the sort,"

And then he sang, so that he should not think,
His Binger-Bopper song, but cut it short.
His wits were working like a brewer's wort,
Until among them came the vision gleaming
Of Ern with bloody nose and Anna screaming.

"That's what I'll do," he muttered; "knock him out,
And kick his face in with a running jump.
I'll not have dazzled eyes this second bout,
And she can wash the fragments under pump."
It was his ace; but Death had played a trump.
Death the blind beggar chuckled, nodding dumb,
"My game; the shroud is ready, Jimmy—come."

Meanwhile, the mother, waiting for her child,
Had tottered out a dozen times to search.
"Jimmy," she said, "you'll drive your mother wild;
Your father's name's too good a name to smirch,
Come home, my dear, she'll leave you in the lurch;
He was so good, my little Jim, so clever;
He never stop a night, away, not ever.

"He never slept a night away till now,
Never, not once, in all the time he's been.
It's the Lord's will, they say, and we must bow,
But O, it's like a knife, it cuts so keen!
He'll work in's Sunday clothes, it'll be seen,
And then they'll laugh, and say 'It isn't strange;
He slept with her, and so he couldn't change.'

"Perhaps," she thought, "I'm wrong; perhaps he's dead;
Killed himself like; folk do in love, they say.
He never tells what passes in his head,
And he's been looking late so old and grey.
A railway train has cut his head away,
Like the poor hare we found at Maylow's shack.
O God, have pity, bring my darling back!"

All the high stars went sweeping through the sky,
The sun made all the orient clean, clear gold.
"O blessed God," she prayed, "do let me die,
Or bring my wand'ring lamb back into fold.
The whistle's gone, and all the bacon's cold;
I must know somehow if he's on the line,
He could have bacon sandwich when he dine."

She cut the bread, and started, short of breath,
Up the canal now draining for the rail;
A poor old woman pitted against death,
Bringing her pennyworth of love for bail.
Wisdom, beauty, and love may not avail.
She was too late. "Yes, he was here; oh, yes.
He chucked his job and went." "Where?" "Home, I guess."

"Home, but he hasn't been home." "Well, he went.
Perhaps you missed him, mother." "Or perhaps
He took the field path yonder through the bent.
He very likely done that, don't he, chaps?"
The speaker tested both his trouser straps
And took his pick. "He's in the town," he said.
"He'll be all right, after a bit in bed."

She trembled down the high embankment's ridge,
Glad, though too late; not yet too late, indeed.
For forty yards away, beyond the bridge,
Jimmy still drank, the devil still sowed seed.
"A bit in bed," she thought, "is what I need.
I'll go to 'Bull and Boar' and rest a bit,
They've got a bench outside; they'd let me sit."

Even as two soldiers on a fortress wall
See the bright fire streak of a coming shell,
Catch breath, and wonder "Which way will it fall?
To you? to me? or will it all be well?"

Ev'n so stood life and death, and could not tell
Whether she'd go to th' inn and find her son,
Or take the field and let the doom be done.

"No, not the inn," she thought. "People would talk.
I couldn't in the open daytime; no.
I'll just sit here upon the timber balk,
I'll rest for just a minute and then go."
Resting, her old tired heart began to glow,
Glowed and gave thanks, and thought itself in clover,
"He's lost his job, so now she'll throw him over."

Sitting, she saw the rustling thistle-kex,
The picks flash bright above, the trolleys tip.
The bridge-stone shining, full of silver specks,
And three swift children running down the dip.
A Stoke Saint Michael carter cracked his whip,
The water in the runway made its din.
She half heard singing coming from the inn.

She turned, and left the inn, and took the path
And "Brother Life, you lose," said Brother Death,
"Even as the Lord of all appointed hath
In this great miracle of blood and breath."
He doeth all things well, as the Book saith,
He bids the changing stars fulfil their turn,
His hand is on us when we least discern.

Slowly she tottered, stopping with the stitch,
Catching her breath, "O lawks, a dear, a dear.
How the poor tubings in my heart do twitch,
It hurts like the rheumatics very near."
And every painful footstep drew her clear
From that young life she bore with so much pain.
She never had him to herself again.

Out of the inn came Jimmy, red with drink,
Crying: "I'll show her. Wait a bit. I'll show her.
You wait a bit. I'm not the kid you think.
I'm Jimmy Gurney, champion tupper-thrower,
When I get done with her you'll never know her,
Nor him you won't. Out of my way, you fowls,
Or else I'll rip the red things off your jowls."

He went across the fields to Plaister's End.
There was a lot of water in the brook,
Sun and white cloud and weather on the mend
For any man with any eyes to look.
He found old Callow's plough-bat, which he took.
"My innings now, my pretty dear," said he.
"You wait a bit. I'll show you. Now you'll see."

Her chimney smoke was blowing blue and faint,
The wise duck shook a tail across the pool,
The blacksmith's shanty smelt of burning paint,
Four newly tired cartwheels hung to cool.
He had loved the place when under Anna's rule.
Now he clenched teeth and flung aside the gate,
There at the door they stood. He grinned "Now wait."

Ern had just brought her in a wired hare,
She stood beside him stroking down the fur.
"O, Ern, poor thing, look how its eyes do stare."
"It isn't *it*," he answered. "It's a her."
She stroked the breast and plucked away a bur,
She kissed the pads, and leapt back with a shout,
"My God, he's got the spudder. Ern. Look out."

Ern clenched his fists. Too late. He felt no pain,
Only incredible haste in something swift,
A shock that made the sky black on his brain,
Then stillness, while a little cloud went drift.

The weight upon his thigh bones wouldn't lift;
Then poultry in a long procession came,
Grey-legged, doing the goose-step, eyes like flame.

Grey-legged old cocks and hens sedate in age,
Marching with jerks as though they moved on springs,
With sidelong hate in round eyes red with rage,
And shouldered muskets clipped by jealous wings,
Then an array of horns and stupid things:
Sheep on a hill with harebells, hare for dinner.
"Hare." A slow darkness covered up the sinner.

"But little time is right hand fain of blow."
Only a second changes life to death;
Hate ends before the pulses cease to go,
There is great power in the stop of breath.
There's too great truth in what the dumb thing saith,
Hate never goes so far as that, nor can.
"I am what life becomes. D'you hate me, man?"

Hate with his babbling instant, red and damning,
Passed with his instant, having drunken red.
"You've killed him."
"No, I've not, he's only shamming.
Get up."
"He can't."
"O God, he isn't dead."
"O God."
"Here. Get a basin. Bathe his head.
Ernie, for God's sake, what are you playing at?
I only give him one, like, with the bat."

Man cannot call the brimming instant back;
Time's an affair of instants spun to days;
If man must make an instant gold, or black,
Let him, he may, but Time must go his ways.

Life may be duller for an instant's blaze.
Life's an affair of instants spun to years,
Instants are only cause of all these tears.

Then Anna screamed aloud. "Help. Murder. Murder."
"By God, it is," he said. "Through you, you slut."
Backing, she screamed, until the blacksmith heard her.
"Hurry," they cried, "the woman's throat's being cut."
Jim had his coat off by the water butt.
"He might come to," he said, "with wine or soup.
I only hit him once, like, with the scoop."

"Splash water on him, chaps. I only meant
To hit him just a clip, like, nothing more.
There. Look. He isn't dead, his eyelids went.
And he went down. O God, his head's all tore.
I've washed and washed: it's all one gob of gore.
He don't look dead to you? What? Nor to you?
Not kill, the clip I give him, couldn't do."

"God send; he looks damn bad," the blacksmith said.
"Py Cot," his mate said, "she wass altogether;
She hass an illness look of peing ted."
"Here. Get a glass," the smith said, "and a feather."
"Wass you at fightings or at playings whether?"
"Here, get a glass and feather. Quick's the word."
The glass was clear. The feather never stirred.

"By God, I'm sorry, Jim. That settles it."
"By God. I've killed him, then."
"The doctor might."
"Try, if you like; but that's a nasty hit."
"Doctor's gone by. He won't be back till night."
"Py Cot, the feather was not looking right."
"By Jesus, chaps, I never meant to kill 'un.
Only to bat. I'll go p'leece and tell 'un.

O Ern, for God's sake speak, for God's sake speak."
No answer followed: Ern had done with dust,
"The p'leece is best," the smith said, "or a beak.
I'll come along; and so the lady must.
Evans, you bring the lady, will you just?
Tell 'em just how it come, lad. Come your ways;
And Joe, you watch the body where it lays."

They walked to town, Jim on the blacksmith's arm.
Jimmy was crying like a child, and saying,
"I never meant to do him any harm."
His teeth went clack, like bones at mummers playing,
And then he trembled hard and broke out praying,
"God help my poor old mother. If he's dead,
I've brought her my last wages home," he said.

He trod his last free journey down the street;
Treading the middle road, and seeing both sides,
The school, the inns, the butchers selling meat,
The busy market where the town divides.
Then past the tanpits full of stinking hides,
And up the lane to death, as weak as pith.
"By God, I hate this, Jimmy," said the smith.

PART VI

Anna in black, the judge in scarlet robes,
A fuss of lawyers' people coming, going,
The windows shut, the gas alight in globes,
Evening outside, and pleasant weather blowing.
"They'll hang him?" "I suppose so; there's no knowing."
"A pretty piece, the woman, ain't she, John?
He killed the fellow just for carrying on."

"She give her piece to counsel pretty clear."
"Ah, that she did, and when she stop she smiled."

"She's had a-many men, that pretty dear;
She's drove a-many fellow pretty wild."
"More silly idiots they to be beguiled."
"Well, I don't know." "Well, I do. See her eyes?
Mystery, eh? A woman's mystery's lies."

"Perhaps." "No p'raps about it, that's the truth.
I know these women; they're a rotten lot."
"You didn't use to think so in your youth."
"No; but I'm wiser now, and not so hot.
Married or buried, *I* say, wives or shot,
These unmanned, unattached Maries and Susans
Make life no better than a proper nuisance."

"Well, I don't know." "Well, if you don't you will."
"I look on women as as good as men."
"Now, that's the kind of talk that makes me ill.
When have they been as good? I ask you when?"
"Always they have." "They haven't. Now and then
P'raps one or two was neither hen nor fury."
"One for your mother, that. Here comes the jury."

Guilty. Thumbs down. No hope. The judge passed sentence:
"A frantic passionate youth, unfit for life,
A fitting time afforded for repentance,
Then certain justice with a pitiless knife.
For her, his wretched victim's widowed wife,
Pity. For her who bore him, pity. (Cheers.)
The jury were exempt for seven years."

All bowed; the Judge passed to the robing-room,
Dismissed his clerks, disrobed, and knelt and prayed
As was his custom after passing doom,
Doom upon life, upon the thing not made.
"O God, who made us out of dust, and laid
Thee in us bright, to lead us to the truth,
O God, have pity upon this poor youth.

Show him Thy grace, O God, before he die;
Shine in his heart; have mercy upon me
Who deal the laws men make to travel by
Under the sun upon the path to Thee;
O God, Thou knowest I'm as blind as he,
As blind, as frantic, not so single, worse,
Only Thy pity spared me from the curse.

"Thy pity, and Thy mercy, God, did save,
Thy bounteous gifts, not any grace of mine,
From all the pitfalls leading to the grave,
From all the death-feasts with the husks and swine.
God, who hast given me all things, now make shine
Bright in this sinner's heart that he may see.
God, take this poor boy's spirit back to Thee."

Then trembling with his hands, for he was old,
He went to meet his college friend, the Dean,
The loiterers watched him as his carriage rolled.
"There goes the Judge," said one, and one was keen:
"Hanging that wretched boy, that's where he's been."
A policeman spat, two lawyers talked statistics,
"'Crime passionel' in Agricultural Districts."

"They'd oughn't hang a boy:" but one said "Stuff.
This sentimental talk is rotten, rotten.
The law's the law and not half strict enough,
Forgers and murderers are misbegotten,
Let them be hanged and let them be forgotten.
A rotten fool should have a rotten end;
Mend them, you say? The rotten never mend."

And one "Not mend? The rotten not, perhaps.
The rotting would; so would the just infected.
A week in quod has ruined lots of chaps
Who'd all got good in them till prison wrecked it."

And one, "Society must be protected."
"He's just a kid. She trapped him." "No, she didden."
"He'll be reprieved." "He mid be and he midden."

So the talk went; and Anna took the train,
Too sad for tears, and pale; a lady spoke
Asking if she were ill or suffering pain?
"Neither," she said; but sorrow made her choke,
"I'm only sick because my heart is broke.
My friend, a man, my oldest friend here, died.
I had to see the man who killed him, tried.

"He's to be hanged. Only a boy. My friend.
I thought him just a boy; I didn't know.
And Ern was killed, and now the boy's to end,
And all because he thought he loved me so."
"My dear," the lady said; and Anna, "Oh,
It's very hard to bear the ills men make,
He thought he loved, and it was all mistake."

"My dear," the lady said; "you poor, poor woman,
"Have you no friends to go to?" "I'm alone.
I've parents living, but they're both inhuman,
And none can cure what pierces to the bone.
I'll have to leave and go where I'm not known.
Begin my life again." Her friend said "Yes.
Certainly that. But leave me your address:

"For I might hear of something; I'll enquire,
Perhaps the boy might be reprieved or pardoned.
Couldn't we ask the rector or the squire
To write and ask the Judge? He can't be hardened.
What do you do? Is it housework? Have you gardened?
Your hands are very white and soft to touch."
"Lately I've not had heart for doing much."

So the talk passes as the train descends
Into the vale, and halts, and starts to climb
To where the apple-bearing country ends
And pleasant-pastured hills rise sweet with thyme,
Where clinking sheepbells make a broken chime
And sunwarm gorses rich the air with scent
And kestrels poise for mice, there Anna went.

There, in the April, in the garden-close,
One heard her in the morning singing sweet,
Calling the birds from the unbudded rose,
Offering her lips with grains for them to eat.
The redbreasts come with little wiry feet,
Sparrows and tits and all wild feathery things,
Brushing her lifted face with quivering wings.

Jimmy was taken down into a cell,
He did not need a hand, he made no fuss.
The men were kind: "For what the kid done . . . well—
The same might come to any one of us."
They brought him bits of cake at tea time: thus
The love that fashioned all in human ken,
Works in the marvellous hearts of simple men.

And in the nights (they watched him night and day)
They told him bits of stories through the grating,
Of how the game went at the football play,
And how the rooks outside had started mating.
And all the time they knew the rope was waiting,
And every evening friend would say to friend,
"I hope we've not to drag him at the end."

And poor old mother came to see her son,
"The Lord has gave," she said, "The Lord has took;
I loved you very dear, my darling one,
And now there's none but God where we can look.

"We've got God's promise written in His Book,
He will not fail; but oh, it do seem hard."
She hired a room outside the prison yard.

"Where did you get the money for the room?
And how are you living, mother; how'll you live?"
"It's what I'd saved to put me in the tomb,
I'll want no tomb but what the parish give."
"Mother, I lied to you that time, O forgive,
I brought home half my wages, half I spent,
And you went short that week to pay the rent.

"I went to see'r, I spent my money on her,
And you who bore me paid the cost in pain.
You went without to buy the clothes upon her:
A hat, a locket, and a silver chain.
O mother dear, if all might be again,
Only from last October, you and me;
O mother dear, how different it would be.

"We were so happy in the room together,
Singing at 'Binger-Bopper,' weren't us, just?
And going a-hopping in the summer weather,
And all the hedges covered white with dust,
And blackberries, and that, and traveller's trust.
I thought her wronged, and true, and sweet, and wise,
The devil takes sweet shapes when he tells lies.

"Mother, my dear, will you forgive your son?"
"God knows I do, Jim, I forgive you, dear;
You didn't know, and couldn't, what you done.
God pity all poor people suffering here,
And may His mercy shine upon us clear,
And may we have His Holy Word for mark,
To lead us to His Kingdom through the dark."

"Amen. Amen," said Jimmy; then they kissed.
The warders watched, the little larks were singing,
A plough team jangled, turning at the rist;
Beyond, the mild cathedral bells were ringing,
The elm-tree rooks were cawing at the springing:
O beauty of the time when winter's done,
And all the fields are laughing at the sun!

"I s'pose they've brought the line beyond the Knapp?"
"Ah, and beyond the Barcle, so they say."
"Hearing the rooks begin reminds a chap.
Look queer, the street will, with the lock away;
O God, I'll never see it." "Let us pray.
Don't think of that, but think," the mother said,
"Of men going on long after we are dead.

"Red helpless little things will come to birth,
And hear the whistles going down the line,
And grow up strong and go about the earth,
And have much happier times than yours and mine;
And some day one of them will get a sign,
And talk to folk, and put an end to sin,
And then God's blessed kingdom will begin.

"God dropped a spark down into everyone,
And if we find and fan it to a blaze
It'll spring up and glow, like—like the sun,
And light the wandering out of stony ways.
God warms His hands at man's heart when he prays,
And light of prayer is spreading heart to heart;
It'll light all where now it lights a part.

"And God who gave His mercies takes His mercies,
And God who gives beginning gives the end.
I dread my death; but it's the end of curses,
A rest for broken things too broke to mend.

O Captain Christ, our blessed Lord and Friend,
We are two wandered sinners in the mire,
Burn our dead hearts with love out of Thy fire.

"And when thy death comes, Master, let us bear it
As of Thy will, however hard to go;
Thy Cross is infinite for us to share it,
Thy help is infinite for us to know.
And when the long trumpets of the Judgment blow
May our poor souls be glad and meet agen,
And rest in Thee." "Say, 'Amen,' Jim." "Amen."

* * * * * *

There was a group outside the prison gate,
Waiting to hear them ring the passing bell,
Waiting as empty people always wait
For the strong toxic of another's hell.
And mother stood there, too, not seeing well,
Praying through tears to let His will be done,
And not to hide His mercy from her son.

Talk in the little group was passing quick.
"It's nothing now to what it was, to watch."
"Poor wretched kid, I bet he's feeling sick."
"Eh? What d'you say, chaps? Someone got a match?"
"They draw a bolt and drop you down a hatch
And break your neck, whereas they used to strangle
In the old times, when you could see them dangle."

Someone said, "Off hats," when the bell began.
Mother was whimpering now upon her knees.
A broken ringing like a beaten pan,
It sent the sparrows wavering to the trees.
The wall-top grasses whickered in the breeze,
The broken ringing clanged, clattered and clanged,
As though men's bees were swarming, not men hanged.

Now certain Justice with the pitiless knife.
The white, sick chaplain snuffling at the nose,
"I am the resurrection and the life."
The bell still clangs, the small procession goes,
The prison warders ready ranged in rows.
"Now, Gurney, come, my dear; it's time," they said.
And ninety seconds later he was dead.

Some of life's sad ones are too strong to die,
Grief doesn't kill them as it kills the weak,
Sorrow is not for those who sit and cry
Lapped in the love of turning t'other cheek,
But for the noble souls austere and bleak
Who have had the bitter dose and drained the cup
And wait for Death face fronted, standing up.

As the last man upon the sinking ship,
Seeing the brine creep brightly on the deck,
Hearing aloft the slatting topsails rip,
Ripping to rags among the topmast's wreck,
Yet hoists the new red ensign without speck,
That she, so fair, may sink with colours flying,
So the old widowed mother kept from dying.

She tottered home, back to the little room,
It was all over for her, but for life;
She drew the blinds, and trembled in the gloom;
"I sat here thus when I was wedded wife;
Sorrow sometimes, and joy; but always strife.
Struggle to live except just at the last,
O God, I thank Thee for the mercies past.

"Harry, my man, when we were courting; eh . . .
The April morning up the Cony-gree.
How grand he looked upon our wedding day.

'I wish we'd had the bells,' he said to me;
And we'd the moon that evening, I and he,
And dew come wet, oh, I remember how,
And we come home to where I'm sitting now.

"And he lay dead here, and his son was born here;
He never saw his son, his little Jim.
And now I'm all alone here, left to mourn here,
And there are all his clothes, but never him.
He's down under the prison in the dim,
With quicklime working on him to the bone,
The flesh I made with many and many a groan.

"Oh, how his little face come, with bright hair.
Dear little face. We made this room so snug;
He sit beside me in his little chair,
I give him real tea sometimes in his mug.
He liked the velvet in the patchwork rug.
He used to stroke it, did my pretty son,
He called it Bunny, little Jimmy done.

"And then he ran so, he was strong at running,
Always a strong one, like his dad at that.
In summertimes I done my sewing sunning,
And he'd be sprawling, playing with the cat.
And neighbours brought their knitting out to chat
Till five o'clock; he had his tea at five;
How sweet life was when Jimmy was alive."

* * * * *

Darkness and midnight, and the midnight chimes.
Another four-and-twenty hours begin.
Darkness again, and many, many times,
The alternating light and darkness spin
Until the face so thin is still more thin,
Gazing each earthly evening, wet or fine,
For Jimmy coming from work along the line.

Over her head the Chester wires hum,
Under the bridge the rocking engines flash.
"He's very late this evening, but he'll come
And bring his little packet full of cash
(Always he does), and supper's cracker hash,
That is his favourite food excepting bacon.
They say my boy was hanged; but they're mistaken."

And sometimes she will walk the cindery mile,
Singing, as she and Jimmy used to do,
Singing "The parson's dog lep over a stile,"
Along the path where water lilies grew.
The stars are placid on the evening's blue,
Burning like eyes so calm, so unafraid,
On all that God has given and man has made.

Burning they watch, and mothlike owls come out,
The redbreast warbles shrilly once and stops;
The homing cowman gives his dog a shout,
The lamps are lighted in the village shops.
Silence; the last bird passes; in the copse
The hazels cross the moon, a nightjar spins,
Dew wets the grass, the nightingale begins.

Singing her crazy song the mother goes,
Singing as though her heart were full of peace,
Moths knock the petals from the dropping rose,
Stars make the glimmering pool a golden fleece,
The moon droops west, but still she does not cease,
The little mice peep out to hear her sing,
Until the inn-man's cockerel shakes his wing.

And in the sunny dawns of hot Julys,
The labourers going to meadow see her there.
Rubbing the sleep out of their heavy eyes,

They lean upon the parapet to stare;
They see her plaiting basil in her hair,
Basil, the dark red wound-wort, cops of clover,
The blue self-heal and golden Jacks of Dover.

Dully they watch her, then they turn to go
To that high Shropshire upland of late hay;
Her singing lingers with them as they mow,
And many times they try it, now grave, now gay,
Till, with full throat, over the hills away,
They lift it clear; oh, very clear it towers
Mixed with the swish of many falling flowers.

BIOGRAPHY

When I am buried, all my thoughts and acts
Will be reduced to lists of dates and facts,
And long before this wandering flesh is rotten
The dates which made me will be all forgotten;
And none will know the gleam there used to be
About the feast days freshly kept by me,
But men will call the golden hour of bliss
"About this time," or "shortly after this."

Men do not heed the rungs by which men climb
Those glittering steps, those milestones upon Time,
Those tombstones of dead selves, those hours of birth,
Those moments of the soul in years of earth
They mark the height achieved, the main result,
The power of freedom in the perished cult,
The power of boredom in the dead man's deeds,
Not the bright moments of the sprinkled seeds.

By many waters and on many ways
I have known golden instants and bright days;
The day on which, beneath an arching sail,
I saw the Cordilleras and gave hail;
The summer day on which in heart's delight
I saw the Swansea Mumbles bursting white,
The glittering day when all the waves wore flags
And the ship *Wanderer* came with sails in rags;
That curlew-calling time in Irish dusk
When life became more splendid than its husk,

When the rent chapel on the brae at Slains
Shone with a doorway opening beyond brains;

The dawn when, with a brace-block's creaking cry,
Out of the mist a little barque slipped by,
Spilling the mist with changing gleams of red,
Then gone, with one raised hand and one turned head;
The howling evening when the spindrift's mists
Broke to display the four Evangelists,
Snow-capped, divinely granite, lashed by breakers,
Wind-beaten bones of long since buried acres;
The night alone near water when I heard
All the sea's spirit spoken by a bird;
The English dusk when I beheld once more
(With eyes so changed) the ship, the citied shore,
The lines of masts, the streets so cheerly trod
(In happier seasons) and gave thanks to God.
All had their beauty, their bright moments' gift,
Their something caught from Time, the ever-swift.

All of those gleams were golden; but life's hands
Have given more constant gifts in changing lands,
And when I count those gifts, I think them such
As no man's bounty could have bettered much:
The gift of country life, near hills and woods
Where happy waters sing in solitudes,
The gift of being near ships, of seeing each day
A city of ships with great ships under weigh,
The great street paved with water, filled with shipping,
And all the world's flags flying and seagulls dipping.

Yet when I am dust my penman may not know
Those water-trampling ships which made me glow,
But think my wonder mad and fail to find
Their glory, even dimly, from my mind,
And yet they made me:
not alone the ships
But men hard-palmed from tallying-on to whips,

The two close friends of nearly twenty years,
Sea-followers both, sea-wrestlers and sea-peers,
Whose feet with mine wore many a bolt-head bright
Treading the decks beneath the riding light.
Yet death will make that warmth of friendship cold
And who'll know what one said and what one told,
Our hearts' communion and the broken spells
When the loud call blew at the strike of bells?
No one, I know, yet let me be believed,
A soul entirely known is life achieved.

Years blank with hardship never speak a word
Live in the soul to make the being stirred,
Towns can be prisons where the spirit dulls
Away from mates and ocean-wandering hulls,
Away from all bright water and great hills
And sheep-walks where the curlews cry their fills,
Away in towns, where eyes have nought to see
But dead museums and miles of misery
And floating life unrooted from man's need
And miles of fish-hooks baited to catch greed
And life made wretched out of human ken
And miles of shopping women served by men.
So, if the penman sums my London days
Let him but say that there were holy ways,
Dull Bloomsbury streets of dull brick mansions old
With stinking doors where women stood to scold
And drunken waits at Christmas with their horn
Droning the news, in snow, that Christ was born;
And windy gas lamps and the wet roads shining
And that old carol of the midnight whining,
And that old room (above the noisy slum)
Where there was wine and fire and talk with some
Under strange pictures of the wakened soul
To whom this earth was but a burnt-out coal.

O Time, bring back those midnights and those friends,
Those glittering moments that a spirit lends
That all may be imagined from the flash
The cloud-hid god-game through the lightning gash
Those hours of stricken sparks from which men took
Light to send out to men in song or book.
Those friends who heard St. Pancras' bells strike two
Yet stayed until the barber's cockerel crew.
Talking of noble styles, the Frenchman's best,
The thought beyond great poets not expressed,
The glory of mood where human frailty failed,
The forts of human light not yet assailed,
Till the dim room had mind and seemed to brood
Binding our wills to mental brotherhood,
Till we become a college, and each night
Was discipline and manhood and delight,
Till our farewells and winding down the stairs
At each grey dawn had meaning that Time spares
That we, so linked, should roam the whole world round
Teaching the ways our brooding minds had found,
Making that room our Chapter, our one mind
Where all that this world soiled should be refined.

Often at night I tread those streets again
And see the alley glimmering in the rain,
Yet now I miss that sigh of earlier tramps
A house with shadows of plane-boughs under lamps,
The secret house where once a beggar stood
Trembling and blind to show his woe for food.
And now I miss that friend who used to walk
Home to my lodgings with me, deep in talk,
Wearing the last of night out in still streets
Trodden by us and policemen on their beats
And cats, but else deserted; now I miss
That lively mind and guttural laugh of his

And that strange way he had of making gleam,
Like something real, the art we used to dream.
London has been my prison; but my books
Hills and great waters, labouring men and brooks,
Ships and deep friendships and remembered days
Which even now set all my mind ablaze
As that June day when, in the red bricks' chinks,
I saw the old Roman ruins white with pinks
And felt the hillside haunted even then
By not dead memory of the Roman men,
And felt the hillside thronged by souls unseen
Who knew the interest in me and were keen
That man alive should understand man dead
So many centuries since the blood was shed,
And quickened with strange hush because this comer
Sensed a strange soul alive behind the summer.
That other day on Ercall when the stones
Were sunbleached white, like long unburied bones,
While the bees droned and all the air was sweet
From honey buried underneath my feet,
Honey of purple heather and white clover
Sealed in its gummy bags till summer's over.
Then other days by water, by bright sea,
Clear as clean glass and my bright friend with me,
The cove clean bottomed where we saw the brown
Red spotted plaice go skimming six feet down
And saw the long fronds waving, white with shells,
Waving, unfolding, drooping, to the swells;
That sadder day when we beheld the great
And terrible beauty of a Lammas spate
Roaring white-mouthed in all the great cliff's gaps
Headlong, tree-tumbling fury of collapse,
While drenching clouds drove by and every sense
Was water roaring or rushing or in offence,
And mountain sheep stood huddled and blown gaps gleamed

Where torn white hair of torrents shook and streamed.
That sadder day when we beheld again
A spate going down in sunshine after rain,
When the blue reach of water leaping bright
Was one long ripple and clatter, flecked with white.
And that far day, that never blotted page,
When youth was bright like flowers about old age
Fair generations bringing thanks for life
To that old kindly man and trembling wife
After their sixty years: Time never made
A better beauty since the Earth was laid
Than that thanksgiving given to grey hair
For the great gift of life which brought them there.

Days of endeavour have been good: the days
Racing in cutters for the comrades' praise,
The day they led my cutter at the turn
Yet could not keep the lead and dropped astern,
The moment in the spurt when both boats' oars
Dipped in each other's wash and throats grew hoarse
And teeth ground into teeth and both strokes quickened
Lashing the sea, and gasps came, and hearts sickened
And coxswains damned us, dancing, banking stroke,
To put our weights on, though our hearts were broke
And both boats seemed to stick and sea seemed glue,
The tide a mill race we were struggling through
And every quick recover gave us squints
Of them still there, and oar tossed water-glints;
And cheering came, our friends, our foemen cheering,
A long, wild, rallying murmur on the hearing—
"Port Fore!" and "Starboard Fore!" "Port Fore!" "Port
Fore!"
"Up with her, Starboard," and at that each oar
Lightened, though arms were bursting, and eyes shut
And the oak stretchers grunted in the strut

And the curse quickened from the cox, our bows
Crashed, and drove talking water, we made vows
Chastity vows and temperance; in our pain
We numbered things we'd never eat again
If we could only win; then came the yell
"Starboard," "Port Fore," and then a beaten bell
Rung as for fire to cheer us. "Now." Oars bent
Soul took the looms now body's bolt was spent,
"Damn it, come on now," "On now," "On now," "Starboard."
"Port Fore." "Up with her, Port"; each cutter harboured
Ten eye-shut painsick strugglers, "Heave, oh, heave,"
Catcalls waked echoes like a shrieking sheave.
"Heave," and I saw a back, then two. "Port Fore."
"Starboard." "Come on." I saw the midship oar
And knew we had done them. "Port Fore." "Starboard."
"Now."
I saw bright water spurting at their bow
Their cox' full face an instant. They were done.
The watcher's cheering almost drowned the gun.
We had hardly strength to toss our oars; our cry
Cheering the losing cutter was a sigh.
Other bright days of action have seemed great:
Wild days in a pampero off the Plate;
Good swimming days, at Hog Back or the Coves
Which the young gannet and the corbie loves;
Surf-swimming between rollers, catching breath
Between the advancing grave and breaking death,
Then shooting up into the sunbright smooth
To watch the advancing roller bare her tooth,
And days of labour also, loading, hauling;
Long days at winch or capstan, heaving, pawling;
The days with oxen, dragging stone from blasting,
And dusty days in mills, and hot days masting.
Trucking on dust-dry deckings smooth like ice,
And hunts in mighty wool-racks after mice;

Mornings with buckwheat when the fields did blanch
With White Leghorns come from the chicken ranch.
Days near the spring upon the sunburnt hill,
Plying the maul or gripping tight the drill.
Delights of work most real, delights that change
The headache life of towns to rapture strange
Not known by townsmen, nor imagined; health
That puts new glory upon mental wealth
And makes the poor man rich.
But that ends, too,
Health with its thoughts of life; and that bright view,
That sunny landscape from life's peak, that glory,
And all a glad man's comments on life's story
And thoughts of marvellous towns and living men
And what pens tell and all beyond the pen
End, and are summed in words so truly dead
They raise no image of the heart and head,
The life, the man alive, the friend we knew,
The mind ours argued with or listened to,
None; but are dead, and all life's keenness, all,
Is dead as print before the funeral,
Even deader after, when the dates are sought,
And cold minds disagree with what we thought.
This many pictured world of many passions
Wears out the nations as a woman fashions,
And what life is is much to very few,
Men being so strange, so mad, and what men do
So good to watch or share; but when men count
Those hours of life that were a bursting fount,
Sparkling the dusty heart with living springs,
There seems a world, beyond our earthly things,
Gated by golden moments, each bright time
Opening to show the city white like lime,
High towered and many peopled. This made sure,
Work that obscures those moments seems impure,

Making our not-returning time of breath
Dull with the ritual and records of death,
That frost of fact by which our wisdom gives
Correctly stated death to all that lives.

Best trust the happy moments. What they gave
Makes man less fearful of the certain grave,
And gives his work compassion and new eyes.
The days that make us happy make us wise.

SHIPS

I cannot tell their wonder nor make known
Magic that once thrilled through me to the bone,
But all men praise some beauty, tell some tale,
Vent a high mood which makes the rest seem pale,
Pour their heart's blood to flourish one green leaf,
Follow some Helen for her gift of grief,
And fail in what they mean, whate'er they do:
You should have seen, man cannot tell to you
The beauty of the ships of that my city.
That beauty now is spoiled by the sea's pity;
For one may haunt the pier a score of times,
Hearing St. Nicholas' bells ring out the chimes,
Yet never see those proud ones swaying home
With mainyards backed and bows a cream of foam,
Those bows so lovely-curving, cut so fine,
Those coulters of the many-bubbled brine,
As once, long since, when all the docks were filled
With that sea-beauty man has ceased to build.

Yet, though their splendour may have ceased to be,
Each played her sovereign part in making me;
Now I return my thanks with heart and lips
For the great queenliness of all those ships.

And first the first bright memory, still so clear,
An autumn evening in a golden year,
When in the last lit moments before dark
The *Chepica*, a steel-grey lovely barque,
Came to an anchor near us on the flood,
Her trucks aloft in sun-glow red as blood.

Then come so many ships that I could fill
Three docks with their fair hulls remembered still,
Each with her special memory's special grace,
Riding the sea, making the waves give place
To delicate high beauty; man's best strength,
Noble in every line in all their length.
Ailsa, *Genista*, ships with long jibbooms,
The *Wanderer* with great beauty and strange dooms,
Liverpool (mightiest then) superb, sublime,
The *California* huge, as slow as time.
The *Copley* swift, the perfect *J. T. North*,
The loveliest barque my city has sent forth,
Dainty *John Lockett* well remembered yet,
The splendid *Argus* with her skysail set,
Stalwart *Drumcliff*, white-blocked, majestic *Sierras*,
Divine bright ships, the water's standard-bearers;
Melpomene, *Euphrosyne*, and their sweet
Sea-troubling sisters of the Fernie fleet;
Corunna (in whom my friend died) and the old
Long since loved *Esmeralda*, long since sold.
Centurion passed in Rio, *Glaucus* spoken,
Aladdin burnt, the *Bidston* water-broken,
Yola, in whom my friend sailed, *Dawpool* trim,
Fierce-bowed *Egeria* plunging to the swim,
Stanmore wide-sterned, sweet *Cupica*, tall *Bard*,
Queen in all harbours with her moon sail yard.

Though I tell many, there must still be others,
McVickar Marshall's ships and Fernie Brothers',

Lochs, *Counties*, *Shires*, *Drums*, the countless lines
Whose house-flags all were once familiar signs
At high main-trucks on Mersey's windy ways
When sunlight made the wind-white water blaze.
Their names bring back old mornings, when the docks
Shone with their house-flags and their painted blocks,
Their raking masts below the Custom House
And all the marvellous beauty of their bows.

Familiar steamers, too, majestic steamers,
Shearing Atlantic roller-tops to streamers,
Umbria, *Etruria*, noble, still at sea,
The grandest, then, that man had brought to be.
Majestic, *City of Paris*, *City of Rome*,
Forever jealous racers, out and home.
The *Alfred Holt's* blue smoke-stacks down the stream,
The fair *Loanda* with her bows a-cream.
Booth liners, Anchor liners, Red Star liners,
The marks and styles of countless ship-designers,
The *Magdelena*, *Puno*, *Potosi*,
Lost *Cotopaxi*, all well-known to me.

These splendid ships, each with her grace, her glory,
Her memory of old song or comrade's story,
Still in my mind the image of life's need,
Beauty in hardest action, beauty indeed.
"They built great ships and sailed them" sounds most brave
Whatever arts we have or fail to have;
I touch my country's mind, I come to grips
With half her purpose, thinking of these ships
That art untouched by softness, all that line
Drawn ringing hard to stand the test of brine,
That nobleness and grandeur, all that beauty
Born of a manly life and bitter duty,
That splendour of fine bows which yet could stand

The shock of rollers never checked by land.
That art of masts, sail-crowded, fit to break,
Yet stayed to strength and backstayed into rake,
The life demanded by that art, the keen,
Eye-puckered, hard-case seamen, silent, lean,—
They are grander things than all the art of towns,
Their tests are tempests and the sea that drowns,
They are my country's line, her great art done
By strong brains labouring on the thought unwon,
They mark our passage as a race of men,
Earth will not see such ships as those again.

TRUTH

Man with his burning soul
Has but an hour of breath
To build a ship of Truth
In which his soul may sail,
Sail on the sea of death.
For death takes toll
Of beauty, courage, youth,
Of all but Truth.

Life's city ways are dark,
Men mutter by; the wells
Of the great waters moan.
O death, O sea, O tide,
The waters moan like bells.
No light, no mark,
The soul goes out alone
On seas unknown.

Stripped of all purple robes,
Stripped of all golden lies,
I will not be afraid.
Truth will preserve through death;

Perhaps the stars will rise,
The stars like globes.
The ship my striving made
May see night fade.

THEY CLOSED HER EYES

FROM THE SPANISH OF DON GUSTAVO A. BÉCQUER

They closed her eyes,
They were still open;
They hid her face
With a white linen,
And, some sobbing,
Others in silence,
From the sad bedroom
All came away.

The night-light in a dish
Burned on the floor,
It flung on the wall
The bed's shadow,
And in that shadow
One saw sometimes
Drawn in sharp line
The body's shape.

The day awakened
At its first whiteness
With its thousand noises;
The town awoke
Before that contrast
Of life and strangeness,
Of light and darkness.
I thought a moment,
My God, how lonely
The dead are!

From the house, shoulder-high
To church they bore her,
And in a chapel
They left her bier.
There they surrounded
Her pale body
With yellow candles
And black stuffs.

At the last stroke
Of the ringing for the souls
An old crone finished
Her last prayers.
She crossed the narrow nave;
The doors moaned,
And the holy place
Remained deserted.

From a clock one heard
The measured ticking,
And from some candles
The guttering.
All things there
Were so grim and sad,
So dark and rigid,
That I thought a moment,
My God, how lonely
The dead are!

From the high belfry
The tongue of iron
Clanged, giving out
His sad farewell.
Crape on their clothes,
Her friends and kindred

Passed in a row,
Making procession.

In the last vault,
Dark and narrow,
The pickaxe opened
A niche at one end;
There they laid her down.
Soon they bricked the place up,
And with a gesture
Bade grief farewell.

Pickaxe on shoulder
The grave-digger,
Singing between his teeth,
Passed out of sight.
The night came down;
It was all silent,
Lost in the shadows
I thought a moment,
My God, how lonely
The dead are!

In the long nights
Of bitter winter,
When the wind makes
The rafters creak,
When the violent rain
Lashes the windows,
Lonely, I remember
That poor girl.

There falls the rain
With its noise eternal.
There the north wind
Fights with the rain.

Stretched in the hollow
Of the damp bricks
Perhaps her bones
Freeze with the cold.

Does the dust return to dust?
Does the soul fly to heaven?
Is all vile matter,
Rottenness, filthiness?
I know not. But
There is something—something
That I cannot explain,
Something that gives us
Loathing, terror,
To leave the dead
So alone, so wretched.

THE HARP

FROM THE SPANISH OF DON GUSTAVO A. BÉCQUER

In a dark corner of the room,
Perhaps forgotten by its owner,
Silent and dim with dust,
I saw the harp.

How many musics slumbered in its strings,
As the bird sleeps in the branches,
Waiting the snowy hand
That could awaken them.

Ah me, I thought, how many, many times
Genius thus slumbers in a human soul,
Waiting, as Lazarus waited, for a voice
To bid him "Rise and walk."

SONNET

FROM THE SPANISH OF DON FRANCISCO DE QUEVEDO

I saw the ramparts of my native land,
One time so strong, now dropping in decay,
Their strength destroyed by this new age's way
That has worn out and rotted what was grand.
I went into the fields: there I could see
The sun drink up the waters newly thawed,
And on the hills the moaning cattle pawed;
Their miseries robbed the day of light for me.

I went into my house: I saw how spotted,
Decaying things made that old home their prize.
My withered walking-staff had come to bend;
I felt the age had won; my sword was rotted,
And there was nothing on which I set my eyes
That was not a reminder of the end.

SONNET ON THE DEATH OF HIS WIFE

FROM THE PORTUGUESE OF ANTONIO DE FERREIRO

That blessed sunlight that once showed to me
My way to heaven more plain more certainly,
And with her bright beam banished utterly
All trace of mortal sorrow far from me,
Has gone from me, has left her prison sad,
And I am blind and alone and gone astray,
Like a lost pilgrim in a desert way
Wanting the blessed guide that once he had.

Thus with a spirit bowed and mind a blur
I trace the holy steps where she has gone,
By valleys and by meadows and by mountains,
And everywhere I catch a glimpse of her.
She takes me by the hand and leads me on,
And my eyes follow her, my eyes made fountains.

SONG

One sunny time in May
When lambs were sporting,
The sap ran in the spray
And I went courting,
And all the apple boughs
Were bright with blossom,
I picked an early rose
For my love's bosom.

And then I met her friend,
Down by the water,
Who cried "She's met her end,
That grey-eyed daughter;
That voice of hers is stilled,
Her beauty broken."
O me, my love is killed,
My love unspoken.

She was too sweet, too dear,
To die so cruel.
O Death, why leave me here
And take my jewel?
Her voice went to the bone,
So true, so ringing,
And now I go alone,
Winter or springing.

C. L. M.

In the dark womb where I began
My mother's life made me a man.
Through all the months of human birth
Her beauty fed my common earth.
I cannot see, nor breathe, nor stir,
But through the death of some of her.

Down in the darkness of the grave
She cannot see the life she gave.
For all her love, she cannot tell
Whether I use it ill or well,
Nor knock at dusty doors to find
Her beauty dusty in the mind.

If the grave's gates could be undone,
She would not know her little son,
I am so grown. If we should meet
She would pass by me in the street,
Unless my soul's face let her see
My sense of what she did for me.

What have I done to keep in mind
My debt to her and womankind?
What woman's happier life repays
Her for those months of wretched days?
For all my mouthless body leeched
Ere Birth's releasing hell was reached?

What have I done, or tried, or said
In thanks to that dear woman dead?
Men triumph over women still,
Men trample women's rights at will,
And man's lust roves the world untamed.

* * * * * *

O grave, keep shut lest I be shamed.

DAUBER

DAUBER

I

Four bells were struck, the watch was called on deck,
All work aboard was over for the hour,
And some men sang and others played at check,
Or mended clothes or watched the sunset glower.
The bursting west was like an opening flower,
And one man watched it till the light was dim,
But no one went across to talk to him.

He was the painter in that swift ship's crew,
Lampman and painter—tall, a slight-built man,
Young for his years, and not yet twenty-two;
Sickly, and not yet brown with the sea's tan.
Bullied and damned at since the voyage began,
"Being neither man nor seaman by his tally,"
He bunked with the idlers just abaft the galley.

His work began at five; he worked all day,
Keeping no watch and having all night in.
His work was what the mate might care to say;
He mixed red lead in many a bouilli tin;
His dungarees were smeared with paraffin.
"Go drown himself" his round-house mates advised him,
And all hands called him "Dauber" and despised him.

Si, the apprentice, stood beside the spar,
Stripped to the waist, a basin at his side,
Slushing his hands to get away the tar,
And then he washed himself and rinsed and dried;
Towelling his face, hair-towzelled, eager-eyed,
He crossed the spar to Dauber, and there stood
Watching the gold of heaven turn to blood.

They stood there by the rail while the swift ship
Tore on out of the tropics, straining her sheets,
Whitening her trackway to a milky strip,
Dim with green bubbles and twisted water meets,
Her clacking tackle tugged at pins and cleats,
Her great sails bellied stiff, her great masts leaned:
They watched how the seas struck and burst and greened.

Si talked with Dauber, standing by the side.
"Why did you come to sea, painter?" he said.
"I want to be a painter," he replied,
"And know the sea and ships from A to Z,
And paint great ships at sea before I'm dead;
Ships under skysails running down the Trade—
Ships and the sea; there's nothing finer made.

"But there's so much to learn, with sails and ropes,
And how the sails look, full or being furled,
And how the lights change in the troughs and slopes,
And the sea's colours up and down the world,
And how a storm looks when the sprays are hurled
High as the yard (they say) I want to see;
There's none ashore can teach such things to me.

"And then the men and rigging, and the way
Ships move, running or beating, and the poise
At the roll's end, the checking in the sway—
I want to paint them perfect, short of the noise;
And then the life, the half-decks full of boys,
The fo'c's'les with the men there, dripping wet:
I know the subjects that I want to get.

"It's not been done, the sea, not yet been done,
From the inside, by one who really knows;
I'd give up all if I could be the one,
But art comes dear the way the money goes.

So I have come to sea, and I suppose
Three years will teach me all I want to learn
And make enough to keep me till I earn."

Even as he spoke his busy pencil moved,
Drawing the leap of water off the side
Where the great clipper trampled iron-hooved,
Making the blue hills of the sea divide,
Shearing a glittering scatter in her stride,
And leaping on full tilt with all sails drawing,
Proud as a war-horse, snuffing battle, pawing.

"I cannot get it yet—not yet," he said;
"That leap and light, and sudden change to green,
And all the glittering from the sunset's red,
And the milky colours where the bursts have been,
And then the clipper striding like a queen
Over it all, all beauty to the crown.
I see it all, I cannot put it down.

"It's hard not to be able. There, look there!
I cannot get the movement nor the light;
Sometimes it almost makes a man despair
To try and try and never get it right.
Oh, if I could—oh, if I only might,
I wouldn't mind what hells I'd have to pass,
Not if the whole world called me fool and ass."

Down sank the crimson sun into the sea,
The wind cut chill at once, the west grew dun.
"Out sidelights!" called the mate. "Hi, where is he?"
The Boatswain called, "Out sidelights, damn you! Run!"
"He's always late or lazing," murmured one—
"The Dauber, with his sketching." Soon the tints
Of red and green passed on dark waterglints.

Darker it grew, still darker, and the stars
Burned golden, and the fiery fishes came.
The wire-note loudened from the straining spars;
The sheet-blocks clacked together always the same;
The rushing fishes streaked the seas with flame,
Racing the one speed noble as their own:
What unknown joy was in those fish unknown!

Just by the round-house door, as it grew dark,
The Boatswain caught the Dauber with, "Now, you;
Till now I've spared you, damn you! now you hark:
I've just had hell for what you didn't do;
I'll have you broke and sent among the crew
If you get me more trouble by a particle.
Don't you forget, you daubing, useless article!

"You thing, you twice-laid thing from Port Mahon!"
Then came the Cook's "Is that the Dauber there?
Why don't you leave them stinking paints alone?
They stink the house out, poisoning all the air.
Just take them out." "Where to?" "I don't care where.
I won't have stinking paint here." From their plates:
"That's right; wet paint breeds fever," growled his mates.

He took his still wet drawings from the berth
And climbed the ladder to the deck-house top;
Beneath, the noisy half-deck rang with mirth,
For two ship's boys were putting on the strop:
One, clambering up to let the skylight drop,
Saw him bend down beneath a boat and lay
His drawings there, till all were hid away.

And stand there silent, leaning on the boat,
Watching the constellations rise and burn,
Until the beauty took him by the throat,
So stately is their glittering overturn;

Armies of marching eyes, armies that yearn
With banners rising and falling, and passing by
Over the empty silence of the sky.

The Dauber sighed there looking at the sails,
Wind-steadied arches leaning on the night,
The high trucks traced on heaven and left no trails;
The moonlight made the topsails almost white,
The passing sidelight seemed to drip green light.
And on the clipper rushed with fire-bright bows;
He sighed, "I'll never do't," and left the house.

"Now," said the reefer, "up! Come, Sam; come, Si,
Dauber's been hiding something." Up they slid,
Treading on naked tiptoes stealthily
To grope for treasure at the long-boat skid.
"Drawings!" said Sam. "Is this what Dauber hid?
Lord! I expected pudding, not this rot.
Still, come, we'll have some fun with what we've got."

They smeared the paint with turpentine until
They could remove with mess-clouts every trace
Of quick perception caught by patient skill,
And lines that had brought blood into his face.
They wiped the pigments off and did erase,
With knives, all sticking clots. When they had done
Under the boat they laid them every one.

All he had drawn since first he came to sea,
His six weeks' leisure fruits, they laid them there.
They chuckled then to think how mad he'd be
Finding his paintings vanished into air.
Eight bells were struck, and feet from everywhere
Went shuffling aft to muster in the dark;
The mate's pipe glowed above, a dim red spark.

Names in the darkness passed and voices cried;
The red spark glowed and died, the faces seemed
As things remembered when a brain has died,
To all but high intenseness deeply dreamed.
Like hissing spears the fishes' fire streamed,
And on the clipper rushed with tossing mast,
A bath of flame broke round her as she passed.

The watch was set, the night came, and the men
Hid from the moon in shadowed nooks to sleep,
Bunched like the dead; still, like the dead, as when
Plague in a city leaves none even to weep.
The ship's track brightened to a mile-broad sweep;
The mate there felt her pulse, and eyed the spars:
South-west by south she staggered under the stars.

Down in his bunk the Dauber lay awake
Thinking of his unfitness for the sea.
Each failure, each derision, each mistake,
There in the life not made for such as he;
A morning grim with trouble sure to be,
A noon of pain from failure, and a night
Bitter with men's contemning and despite.

This is the first beginning, the green leaf,
Still in the Trades before bad weather fell;
What harvest would he reap of hate and grief
When the loud Horn made every life a hell?
When the sick ship lay over, clanging her bell,
And no time came for painting or for drawing,
But all hands fought, and icy death came clawing?

Hell, he expected,—hell. His eyes grew blind;
The snoring from his messmates droned and snuffled,
And then a gush of pity calmed his mind.
The cruel torment of his thought was muffled,

Without, on deck, an old, old, seaman shuffled,
Humming his song, and through the open door
A moonbeam moved and thrust along the floor.

The green bunk curtains moved, the brass rings clicked,
The Cook cursed in his sleep, turning and turning,
The moonbeam's moving finger touched and picked,
And all the stars in all the sky were burning.
"This is the art I've come for, and am learning,
The sea and ships and men and travelling things.
It is most proud, whatever pain it brings."

He leaned upon his arm and watched the light
Sliding and fading to the steady roll;
This he would some day paint, the ship at night,
And sleeping seamen tired to the soul;
The space below the bunks as black as coal,
Gleams upon chests, upon the unlit lamp,
The ranging door hook, and the locker clamp.

This he would paint, and that, and all these scenes,
And proud ships carrying on, and men their minds,
And blues of rollers toppling into greens,
And shattering into white that bursts and blinds,
And scattering ships running erect like hinds,
And men in oilskins beating down a sail
High on the yellow yard, in snow, in hail.

With faces ducked down from the slanting drive
Of half-thawed hail mixed with half-frozen spray,
The roaring canvas like a thing alive,
Shaking the mast, knocking their hands away,
The foot-ropes jerking to the tug and sway,
The savage eyes salt-reddened at the rims,
And icicles on the south-wester brims.

And sunnier scenes would grow under his brush,
The tropic dawn with all things dropping dew,
The darkness and the wonder and the hush,
The insensate grey before the marvel grew;
Then the veil lifted from the trembling blue,
The walls of sky burst in, the flower, the rose,
All the expanse of heaven a mind that glows.

He turned out of his bunk; the Cook still tossed,
One of the other two spoke in his sleep.
A cockroach scuttled where the moonbeam crossed;
Outside there was the ship, the night, the deep.
"It is worth while," the youth said; "I will keep
To my resolve, I'll learn to paint all this.
My Lord, my God, how beautiful it is!"

Outside was the ship's rush to the wind's hurry,
A resonant wire-hum from every rope,
The broadening bow-wash in a fiery flurry,
The leaning masts in their majestic slope,
And all things strange with moonlight: filled with hope
By all that beauty going as man bade,
He turned and slept in peace. Eight bells were made.

II

Next day was Sunday, his free painting day,
While the fine weather held, from eight till eight.
He rose when called at five, and did array
The round-house gear, and set the kit-bags straight;
Then kneeling down, like housemaid at a grate,
He scrubbed the deck with sand until his knees
Were blue with dye from his wet dungarees.

Soon all was clean, his Sunday tasks were done;
His day was clear for painting as he chose.

The wetted decks were drying in the sun,
The men coiled up, or swabbed, or sought repose.
The drifts of silver arrows fell and rose
As flying fish took wing; the breakfast passed,
Wasting good time, but he was free at last.

Free for two hours and more to tingle deep,
Catching a likeness in a line or tint,
The canvas running up in a proud sweep,
Wind-wrinkled at the clews, and white like lint,
The glittering of the blue waves into glint;
Free to attempt it all, the proud ship's pawings,
The sea, the sky—he went to fetch his drawings.

Up to the deck-house top he quickly climbed,
He stooped to find them underneath the boat.
He found them all obliterated, slimed,
Blotted, erased, gone from him line and note.
They were all spoiled: a lump came in his throat,
Being vain of his attempts, and tender skinned—
Beneath the skylight watching reefers grinned.

He clambered down, holding the ruined things.
"Bosun," he called, "look here, did you do these:
Wipe off my paints and cut them into strings,
And smear them till you can't tell chalk from cheese?
Don't stare, but did you do it? Answer, please."
The Bosun turned: "I'll give you a thick ear!
Do it! I didn't. Get to hell from here!

"I touch your stinking daubs? The Dauber's daft."
A crowd was gathering now to hear the fun;
The reefers tumbled out, the men laid aft,
The Cook blinked, cleaning a mess kid in the sun.
"What's up with Dauber now?" said everyone.

"Someone has spoiled my drawings—look at this!"
"Well, that's a dirty trick, by God, it is!"

"It is," said Sam, "a low-down dirty trick,
To spoil a fellow's work in such a way,
And if you catch him, Dauber, punch him sick,
For he deserves it, be he who he may."
A seaman shook his old head wise and grey.
"It seems to me," he said, "who ain't no judge,
Them drawings look much better now they're smudge."

"Where were they, Dauber? On the deck-house? Where?"
"Under the long-boat, in a secret place."
"The blackguard must have seen you put them there.
He is a swine! I tell him to his face:
I didn't think we'd anyone so base."
"Nor I," said Dauber. "There was six weeks' time
Just wasted in these drawings: it's a crime!"

"Well, don't you say we did it," growled his mates,
"And as for crime, be damned! the things were smears—
Best overboard, like you, with shot for weights;
Thank God they're gone, and now go shake your ears."
The Dauber listened, very near to tears.
"Dauber, if I were you," said Sam again,
"I'd aft, and see the Captain and complain."

A sigh came from the assembled seamen there.
Would he be such a fool for their delight
As go to tell the Captain? Would he dare?
And would the thunder roar, the lightning smite?
There was the Captain come to take a sight,
Handling his sextant by the chart-house aft.
The Dauber turned, the seamen thought him daft.

The Captain took his sights—a mate below
Noted the times; they shouted to each other,

The Captain quick with "Stop," the answer slow,
Repeating slowly one height then another.
The swooping clipper stumbled through the smother,
The ladder brasses in the sunlight burned,
The Dauber waited till the Captain turned.

There stood the Dauber, humbled to the bone,
Waiting to speak. The Captain let him wait,
Glanced at the course, and called in even tone,
"What is the man there wanting, Mr. Mate?"
The logship clattered on the grating straight,
The reel rolled to the scuppers with a clatter,
The Mate came grim: "Well, Dauber, what's the matter?"

"Please, sir, they spoiled my drawings." "Who did?" "They."
"Who's they?" "I don't quite know, sir." "Don't quite know,
sir?
Then why are you aft to talk about it, hey?
Whom d'you complain of?" "No one." "No one?" "No, sir."
"Well, then, go forward till you've found them. Go, sir.
If you complain of someone, then I'll see.
Now get to hell! and don't come bothering me."

"But, sir, they washed them off, and some they cut.
Look here, sir, how they spoiled them." "Never mind.
Go shove your head inside the scuttle butt,
And that will make you cooler. You will find
Nothing like water when you're mad and blind.
Where were the drawings? in your chest, or where?"
"Under the long-boat, sir; I put them there."

"Under the long-boat, hey? Now mind your tip.
I'll have the skids kept clear with nothing round them;
The long-boat ain't a store in this here ship.
Lucky for you it wasn't I who found them.

If I had seen them, Dauber, I'd have drowned them.
Now you be warned by this. I tell you plain—
Don't stow your brass-rags under boats again.

"Go forward to your berth." The Dauber turned.
The listeners down below them winked and smiled,
Knowing how red the Dauber's temples burned,
Having lost the case about his only child.
His work was done to nothing and defiled,
And there was no redress: the Captain's voice
Spoke, and called "Painter," making him rejoice.

The Captain and the Mate conversed together.
"Drawings, you tell me, Mister?" "Yes, sir; views:
Wiped off with turps, I gather that's his blether.
He says they're things he can't afford to lose.
He's Dick, who came to sea in dancing shoes,
And found the dance a bear dance. They were hidden
Under the long-boat's chocks, which I've forbidden."

"Wiped off with turps?" The Captain sucked his lip.
"Who did it, Mister?" "Reefers, I suppose;
Them devils do the most pranks in a ship;
The round-house might have done it, Cook or Bose."
"I can't take notice of it till he knows.
How does he do his work?" "Well, no offence;
He tries; he does his best. He's got no sense."

"Painter," the Captain called; the Dauber came.
"What's all this talk of drawings? What's the matter?"
"They spoiled my drawings, sir." "Well, who's to blame?
The long-boat's there for no one to get at her;
You broke the rules, and if you choose to scatter
Gear up and down where it's no right to be,
And suffer as result, don't come to me.

"Your place is in the round-house, and your gear
Belongs where you belong. Who spoiled your things?
Find out who spoiled your things and fetch him here."
"But, sir, they cut the canvas into strings."
"I want no argument nor questionings.
Go back where you belong and say no more,
And please remember that you're not on shore."

The Dauber touched his brow and slunk away—
They eyed his going with a bitter eye.
"Dauber," said Sam, "what did the Captain say?"
The Dauber drooped his head without reply.
"Go forward, Dauber, and enjoy your cry."
The Mate limped to the rail; like little feet
Over his head the drumming reef-points beat.

The Dauber reached the berth and entered in,
Much mockery followed after as he went,
And each face seemed to greet him with the grin
Of hounds hot following on a creature spent.
"Aren't you a fool?" each mocking visage meant.
"Who did it, Dauber? What did Captain say?
It is a crime, and there'll be hell to pay."

He bowed his head, the house was full of smoke;
The Sails was pointing shackles on his chest.
"Lord, Dauber, be a man and take a joke"—
He puffed his pipe—"and let the matter rest.
Spit brown, my son, and get a hairy breast;
Get shoulders on you at the crojick braces,
And let this painting business go to blazes.

"What good can painting do to anyone?
I don't say never do it; far from that—
No harm in sometimes painting just for fun.
Keep it for fun, and stick to what you're at.

Your job's to fill your bones up and get fat;
Rib up like Barney's bull, and thick your neck.
Throw paints to hell, boy; you belong on deck."

"That's right," said Chips; "It's down-right good advice.
Painting's no good; what good can painting do
Up on a lower topsail stiff with ice,
With all your little fish-hooks frozen blue?
Painting won't help you at the weather clew,
Nor pass your gaskets for you, nor make sail.
Painting's a balmy job not worth a nail."

The Dauber did not answer; time was passing.
He pulled his easel out, his paints, his stool.
The wind was dropping, and the sea was glassing—
New realms of beauty waited for his rule;
The draught out of the crojick kept him cool.
He sat to paint, alone and melancholy.
"No turning fools," the Chips said, "from their folly."

He dipped his brush and tried to fix a line
And then came peace, and gentle beauty came,
Turning his spirit's water into wine,
Lightening his darkness with a touch of flame:
O, joy of trying for beauty, ever the same,
You never fail, your comforts never end;
O, balm of this world's way; O, perfect friend!

III

They lost the Trades soon after; then came calm,
Light little gusts and rain, which soon increased
To glorious northers shouting out a psalm
At seeing the bright blue water silver fleeced;
Hornwards she rushed, trampling the seas to yeast.
There fell a rain-squall in a blind day's end
When for an hour the Dauber found a friend.

Out of the rain the voices called and passed,
The stay-sails flogged, the tackle yanked and shook.
Inside the harness-room a lantern cast
Light and wild shadows as it ranged its hook.
The watch on deck was gathered in the nook,
They had taken shelter in that secret place,
Wild light gave wild emotions to each face.

One beat the beef-cask, and the others sang
A song that had brought anchors out of seas
In ports where bells of Christians never rang,
Nor any sea mark blazed among the trees.
By forlorn swamps, in ice, by windy keys,
That song had sounded; now it shook the air
From these eight wanderers brought together there.

Under the poop-break, sheltering from the rain,
The Dauber sketched some likeness of the room,
A note to be a prompting to his brain,
A spark to make old memory reillume.
"Dauber," said someone near him in the gloom,
"How goes it, Dauber?" It was reefer Si.
"There's not much use in trying to keep dry."

They sat upon the sail-room doorway coaming,
The lad held forth like youth, the Dauber listened
To how the boy had had a taste for roaming,
And what the sea is said to be and isn't.
Where the dim lamplight fell the wet deck glistened.
Si said the Horn was still some weeks away,
"But tell me, Dauber, where d'you hail from? Eh?"

The rain blew past and let the stars appear;
The seas grew larger as the moonlight grew;
For half an hour the ring of heaven was clear,
Dusty with moonlight, grey rather than blue;

In that great moon the showing stars were few.
The sleepy time-boy's feet passed overhead.
"I come from out past Gloucester," Dauber said;

"Not far from Pauntley, if you know those parts;
The place is Spital Farm, near Silver Hill,
Above a trap-hatch where a mill-stream starts.
We had the mill once, but we've stopped the mill;
My dad and sister keep the farm on still.
We're only tenants, but we've rented there,
Father and son, for over eighty year.

"Father has worked the farm since grandfer went;
It means the world to him; I can't think why.
They bleed him to the last half-crown for rent,
And this and that have almost milked him dry.
The land's all starved; if he'd put money by,
And corn was up, and rent was down two-thirds. . . .
But then they aren't, so what's the use of words.

"Yet still he couldn't bear to see it pass
To strangers, or to think a time would come
When other men than us would mow the grass,
And other names than ours have the home.
Some sorrows come from evil thought, but some
Come when two men are near, and both are blind
To what is generous in the other's mind.

"I was the only boy, and father thought
I'd farm the Spital after he was dead,
And many a time he took me out and taught
About manures and seed-corn white and red,
And soils and hops, but I'd an empty head;
Harvest or seed, I would not do a turn—
I loathed the farm, I didn't want to learn.

"He did not mind at first, he thought it youth
Feeling the collar, and that I should change.
Then time gave him some inklings of the truth,
And that I loathed the farm, and wished to range.
Truth to a man of fifty's always strange;
It was most strange and terrible to him
That I, his heir, should be the devil's limb.

"Yet still he hoped the Lord might change my mind.
I'd see him bridle-in his wrath and hate,
And almost break my heart he was so kind,
Biting his lips sore with resolve to wait.
And then I'd try awhile; but it was Fate:
I didn't want to learn; the farm to me
Was mire and hopeless work and misery.

"Though there were things I loved about it, too—
The beasts, the apple-trees, and going haying.
And then I tried; but no, it wouldn't do,
The farm was prison, and my thoughts were straying.
And there'd come father, with his grey head, praying,
'O, my dear son, don't let the Spital pass;
It's my old home, boy, where your grandfer was.

"'And now you won't learn farming; you don't care
The old home's nought to you. I've tried to teach you;
I've begged Almighty God, boy, all I dare,
To use His hand if word of mine won't reach you.
Boy, for your granfer's sake I do beseech you,
Don't let the Spital pass to strangers. Squire
Has said he'd give it you if we require.

"'Your mother used to walk here, boy, with me;
It was her favourite walk down to the mill;
And there we'd talk how little death would be,
Knowing our work was going on here still.

You've got the brains, you only want the will—
Don't disappoint your mother and your father.
I'll give you time to travel, if you'd rather.'

"But, no, I'd wander up the brooks to read.
Then sister Jane would start with nagging tongue,
Saying my sin made father's heart to bleed,
And how she feared she'd live to see me hung.
And then she'd read me bits from Dr. Young.
And when we three would sit to supper, Jane
Would fillip dad till dad began again.

"'I've been here all my life, boy. I was born
Up in the room above—looks on the mead.
I never thought you'd cockle my clean corn,
And leave the old home to a stranger's seed.
Father and I have made here 'thout a weed:
We've give our lives to make that. Eighty years.
And now I go down to the grave in tears.'

"And then I'd get ashamed and take off coat,
And work maybe a week, ploughing and sowing
And then I'd creep away and sail my boat,
Or watch the water when the mill was going.
That's my delight—to be near water flowing,
Dabbling or sailing boats or jumping stanks,
Or finding moorhens' nests along the banks.

"And one day father found a ship I'd built;
He took the cart-whip to me over that,
And I, half mad with pain, and sick with guilt,
Went up and hid in what we called the flat,
A dusty hole given over to the cat.
She kittened there; the kittens had worn paths
Among the cobwebs, dust, and broken laths.

"And putting down my hand between the beams
I felt a leathery thing, and pulled it clear:
A book with white cocoons stuck in the seams.
Where spiders had had nests for many a year.
It was my mother's sketch-book; hid, I fear,
Lest dad should ever see it. Mother's life
Was not her own while she was father's wife.

"There were her drawings dated, pencilled faint.
March was the last one, eighteen eighty-three,
Unfinished that, for tears had smeared the paint.
The rest was landscape, not yet brought to be.
That was a holy afternoon to me;
That book a sacred book; the flat a place
Where I could meet my mother face to face.

"She had found peace of spirit, mother had,
Drawing the landscape from the attic there—
Heart-broken, often, after rows with dad,
Hid like a wild thing in a secret lair.
That rotting sketch-book showed me how and where
I, too, could get away; and then I knew
That drawing was the work I longed to do.

"Drawing became my life. I drew, I toiled,
And every penny I could get I spent
On paints and artist's matters, which I spoiled
Up in the attic to my heart's content,
Till one day father asked me what I meant;
The time had come, he said, to make an end.
Now it must finish: what did I intend?

"Either I took to farming, like his son,
In which case he would teach me, early and late
(Provided that my daubing mood was done),
Or I must go: it must be settled straight.

If I refused to farm, there was the gate.
I was to choose, his patience was all gone,
The present state of things could not go on.

"Sister was there; she eyed me while he spoke.
The kitchen clock ran down and struck the hour,
And something told me father's heart was broke,
For all he stood so set and looked so sour.
Jane took a duster, and began to scour
A pewter on the dresser; she was crying.
I stood stock still a long time, not replying.

"Dad waited, then he snorted and turned round.
'Well, think of it,' he said. He left the room,
His boots went clop along the stony ground
Out to the orchard and the apple-bloom.
A cloud came past the sun and made a gloom;
I swallowed with dry lips, then sister turned.
She was dead white but for her eyes that burned.

"'You're breaking father's heart, Joe,' she began;
'It's not as if——' she checked, in too much pain.
'O, Joe, don't help to kill so fine a man;
You're giving him our mother over again.
It's wearing him to death, Joe, heart and brain;
You know what store he sets on leaving this
To (it's too cruel)—to a son of his.

"'Yet you go painting all the day. O, Joe,
Couldn't you make an effort? Can't you see
What folly it is of yours? It's not as though
You are a genius or could ever be.
O, Joe, for father's sake, if not for me,
Give up this craze for painting, and be wise
And work with father, where your duty lies.'

"'It goes too deep,' I said; 'I loathe the farm;
I couldn't help, even if I'd the mind.
Even if I helped, I'd only do him harm;
Father would see it, if he were not blind.
I was not built to farm, as he would find.
O, Jane, its bitter hard to stand alone
And spoil my father's life or spoil my own.'

"'Spoil both', she said, 'the way you're shaping now.
You're only a boy not knowing your own good.
Where will you go, suppose you leave here? How
Do you propose to earn your daily food?
Draw? Daub the pavements? There's a feckless brood
Goes to the devil daily, Joe, in cities
Only from thinking how divine their wit is.

"'Clouds are they, without water, carried away.
And you'll be one of them, the way you're going,
Daubing at silly pictures all the day,
And praised by silly fools who're always blowing.
And you choose this when you might go a-sowing,
Casting the good corn into chosen mould
That shall in time bring forth a hundred-fold.'

"So we went on, but in the end it ended.
I felt I'd done a murder; I felt sick.
There's much in human minds cannot be mended,
And that, not I, played dad a cruel trick.
There was one mercy: that it ended quick.
I went to join my mother's brother: he
Lived down the Severn. He was kind to me.

"And there I learned house-painting for a living.
I'd have been happy there, but that I knew
I'd sinned before my father past forgiving,
And that they sat at home, that silent two,

Wearing the fire out and the evening through,
Silent, defeated, broken, in despair,
My plate unset, my name gone, and my chair.

"I saw all that; and sister Jane came white—
White as a ghost, with fiery, weeping eyes.
I saw her all day long and half the night,
Bitter as gall, and passionate and wise.
'Joe, you have killed your father: there he lies.
You have done your work—you with our mother's ways.'
She said it plain, and then her eyes would blaze.

"And then one day I had a job to do
Down below bridge, by where the docks begin,
And there I saw a clipper towing through,
Up from the sea that morning, entering in.
Raked to the nines she was, lofty and thin,
Her ensign ruffling red, her bunts in pile,
Beauty and strength together, wonder, style.

"She docked close to the gates, and there she lay
Over the water from me, well in sight;
And as I worked I watched her all the day,
Finding her beauty ever fresh delight.
Her house-flag was bright green with strips of white;
High in the sunny air it rose to shake
Above the skysail poles' most splendid rake.

"And when I felt unhappy I would look
Over the river at her; and her pride,
So calm, so quiet, came as a rebuke
To half the passionate pathways which I tried;
And though the autumn ran its term and died,
And winter fell and cold December came,
She was still splendid there, and still the same.

"Then on a day shc sailed; but when she went
My mind was clear on what I had to try:
To see the sea and ships, and what they meant,
That was the thing I longed to do; so I
Drew and worked hard, and studied and put by,
And thought of nothing else but that one end,
But let all else go hang—love, money, friend.

"And now I've shipped as Dauber I've begun.
It was hard work to find a dauber's berth;
I hadn't any friends to find me one,
Only my skill, for what it may be worth;
But I'm at sea now, going about the earth,
And when the ship's paid off, when we return,
I'll join some Paris studio and learn."

He stopped, the air came moist, Si did not speak;
The Dauber turned his eyes to where he sat,
Pressing the sail-room hinges with his cheek,
His face half covered with a dropping hat.
Huge dewdrops from the stay-sails dropped and spat.
Si did not stir, the Dauber touched his sleeve;
A little birdlike noise came from a sheave.

Si was asleep, sleeping a calm deep sleep,
Still as a warden of the Egyptian dead
In some old haunted temple buried deep
Under the desert sand, sterile and red.
The Dauber shook his arm; Si jumped and said,
"Good yarn, I swear! I say, you have a brain—
Was that eight bells that went?" He slept again.

Then waking up, "I've had a nap," he cried.
"Was that one bell? What, Dauber, you still here?"
"Si there?" the Mate's voice called. "Sir," he replied.

The order made the lad's thick vision clear;
A something in the Mate's voice made him fear.
"Si," said the Mate, "I hear you've made a friend—
Dauber, in short. That friendship's got to end.

"You're a young gentleman. Your place aboard
Is with the gentlemen abaft the mast.
You're learning to command; you can't afford
To yarn with any man. But there . . . it's past.
You've done it once; let this time be the last.
The Dauber's place is forward. Do it again,
I'll put you bunking forward with the men.

"Dismiss." Si went, but Sam, beside the Mate,
Timekeeper there, walked with him to the rail
And whispered him the menace of "You wait"—
Words which have turned full many a reefer pale.
The watch was changed; the watch on deck trimmed sail.
Sam, going below, called all the reefers down,
Sat in his bunk and eyed them with a frown.

"Si here," he said, "has soiled the half-deck's name
Talking to Dauber—Dauber, the ship's clout.
A reefer takes the Dauber for a flame,
The half-deck take the round-house walking out.
He's soiled the half-deck's honour; now, no doubt,
The Bosun and his mates will come here sneaking,
Asking for smokes, or blocking gangways speaking.

"I'm not a vain man, given to blow or boast;
I'm not a proud man, but I truly feel
That while I've bossed this mess and ruled this roost
I've kept this hooker's half-deck damned genteel.
Si must ask pardon, or be made to squeal.
Down on your knees, dog; them we love we chasten.
Jao, pasea, my son—in English, Hasten"

Si begged for pardon, meekly kneeling down
Before the reefer's mess assembled grim.
The lamp above them smoked the glass all brown;
Beyond the door the dripping sails were dim.
The Dauber passed the door; none spoke to him.
He sought his berth and slept, or, waking, heard
Rain on the deck-house—rain, no other word.

IV

Out of the air a time of quiet came,
Calm fell upon the heaven like a drouth;
The brass sky watched the brassy water flame.
Drowsed as a snail the clipper loitered south
Slowly, with no white bone across her mouth;
No rushing glory, like a queen made bold,
The Dauber strove to draw her as she rolled.

There the four leaning spires of canvas rose,
Royals and skysails lifting, gently lifting,
White like the brightness that a great fish blows
When billows are at peace and ships are drifting;
With mighty jerks that set the shadows shifting,
The courses tugged their tethers: a blue haze
Drifted like ghosts of flocks come down to graze.

There the great skyline made her perfect round,
Notched now and then by the sea's deeper blue;
A smoke-smutch marked a steamer homeward bound,
The haze wrought all things to intenser hue.
In tingling impotence the Dauber drew
As all men draw keen to the shaken soul
To give a hint that might suggest the whole.

A naked seaman washing a red shirt
Sat at a tub whistling between his teeth;
Complaining blocks quavered like something hurt.

A sailor cut an old boot for a sheath,
The ship bowed to her shadow-ship beneath,
And little splash of spray came at the roll
On to the deck-planks from the scupper-hole.

He watched it, painting patiently, as paints,
With eyes that pierce behind the blue sky's veil,
The Benedictine in a Book of Saints
Watching the passing of the Holy Grail;
The green dish dripping blood, the trump, the hail,
The spears that pass, the memory and the passion,
The beauty moving under this world's fashion.

But as he painted, slowly, man by man,
The seamen gathered near; the Bosun stood
Behind him, jeering; then the Sails began
Sniggering with comment that it was not good.
Chips flicked his sketch with little scraps of wood,
Saying, "That hit the top-knot," every time.
Cook mocked, "My lovely drawings; it's a crime."

Slowly the men came nearer, till a crowd
Stood at his elbow, muttering as he drew;
The Bosun, turning to them, spoke aloud,
"This is the ship that never got there. You
Look at her here, what Dauber's trying to do.
Look at her! lummy, like a Christmas-tree.
That thing's a ship; he calls this painting. See?"

Seeing the crowd, the Mate came forward; then
"Sir," said the Bosun, "come and see the sight!
Here's Dauber makes a circus for the men.
He calls this thing a ship—this hell's delight!"
"Man," said the Mate, "you'll never get her right
Daubing like that. Look here!" He took a brush.
"Now Dauber, watch; I'll put you to the blush.

"Look here. Look there. Now watch this ship of mine."
He drew her swiftly from a memory stored.
"God, sir," the Bosun said, "you do her fine!"
"Ay," said the Mate, "I do so, by the Lord!
I'll paint a ship with any man aboard."
They hung about his sketch like beasts at bait.
"There now, I taught him painting," said the Mate.

When he had gone, the gathered men dispersed;
Yet two or three still lingered to dispute
What errors made the Dauber's work the worst.
They probed his want of knowledge to the root.
"Bei Gott!" they swore, "der Dauber cannot do 't;
He haf no knolich how to put der pense.
Der Mate's is goot. Der Dauber haf no sense."

"You hear?" the Bosun cried, "you cannot do it!"
"A gospel truth," the Cook said, "true as hell!
And wisdom, Dauber, if you only knew it;
A five year boy would do a ship as well."
"If that's the kind of thing you hope to sell,
God help you," echoed Chips. "I tell you true,
The job's beyond you, Dauber; drop it, do.

"Drop it, in God's name drop it, and have done!
You see you cannot do it. Here's the Mate
Paints you to frazzles before everyone;
Paints you a dandy clipper while you wait.
While you, Lord love us, daub. I tell you straight,
We've had enough of daubing; drop it; quit.
You cannot paint, so make an end of it."

"That's sense," said all; "you cannot, why pretend?"
The Dauber rose and put his easel by.
"You've said enough," he said, "now let it end.

Who cares how bad my painting may be? I
Mean to go on, and, if I fail, to try.
However much I miss of my intent,
If I have done my best I'll be content.

"You cannot understand that. Let it be.
You cannot understand, nor know, nor share.
This is a matter touching only me;
My sketch may be a daub, for aught I care.
You may be right. But even if you were,
Your mocking should not stop this work of mine;
Rot though it be, its prompting is divine.

"You cannot understand that—you, and you,
And you, you Bosun. You can stand and jeer,
That is the task your spirit fits you to,
That you can understand and hold most dear.
Grin, then, like collars, ear to donkey ear,
But let me daub. Try, you, to understand
Which task will bear the light best on God's hand."

V

The wester came as steady as the Trades;
Brightly it blew, and still the ship did shoulder
The brilliance of the water's white cockades
Into the milky green of smoky smoulder.
The sky grew bluer and the air grew colder.
Southward she thundered while the westers held,
Proud, with taut bridles, pawing, but compelled.

And still the Dauber strove, though all men mocked,
To draw the splendour of the passing thing,
And deep inside his heart a something locked,
Long pricking in him, now began to sting—

A fear of the disasters storm might bring;
His rank as painter would be ended then—
He would keep watch and watch like other men.

And go aloft with them to man the yard
When the great ship was rolling scuppers under,
Burying her snout all round the compass card,
While the green water struck at her and stunned her;
When the lee-rigging slacked, when one long thunder
Boomed from the black to windward, when the sail
Booted and spurred the devil in the gale.

For him to ride on men: that was the time
The Dauber dreaded; then lest the test would come,
When seas, half-frozen, slushed the decks with slime,
And all the air was blind with flying scum;
When the drenched sails were furled, when the fierce hum
In weather riggings died into the roar
Of God's eternal never tamed by shore.

Once in the passage he had worked aloft,
Shifting her suits one summer afternoon,
In the bright Trade wind, when the wind was soft,
Shaking the points, making the tackle croon.
But that was child's play to the future: soon
He would be ordered up when sails and spars
Were flying and going mad among the stars.

He had been scared that first time, daunted, thrilled,
Not by the height so much as by the size,
And then the danger to the man unskilled
In standing on a rope that runs through eyes.
"But in a storm," he thought, "the yards will rise
And roll together down, and snap their gear!"
The sweat came cold upon his palms for fear.

Sometimes in Gloucester he had felt a pang
Swinging below the house-eaves on a stage.
But stages carry rails; here he would hang
Upon a jerking rope in a storm's rage,
Ducked that the sheltering oilskin might assuage
The beating of the storm, clutching the jack,
Beating the sail, and being beaten back.

Drenched, frozen, gasping, blinded, beaten dumb,
High in the night, reeling great blinding arcs
As the ship rolled, his chappy fingers numb,
The deck below a narrow blur of marks,
The sea a welter of whiteness shot with sparks,
Now snapping up in bursts, now dying away,
Salting the horizontal snow with spray.

A hundred and fifty feet above the deck,
And there, while the ship rolls, boldly to sit
Upon a foot-rope moving, jerk and check,
While half-a-dozen seamen work on it;
Held by one hand, straining, by strength and wit
To toss a gasket's coil around the yard,
How could he compass that when blowing hard?

And if he failed in any least degree,
Or faltered for an instant, or showed slack,
He might go drown himself within the sea,
And add a bubble to the clipper's track.
He had signed his name, there was no turning back,
No pardon for default—this must be done.
One iron rule at sea binds everyone.

Till now he had been treated with contempt
As neither man nor thing, a creature borne
On the ship's articles, but left exempt
From all the seamen's life except their scorn.

But he would rank as seaman off the Horn,
Work as a seaman, and be kept or cast
By standards set for men before the mast.

Even now they shifted suits of sails; they bent
The storm-suit ready for the expected time;
The mighty wester that the Plate had lent
Had brought them far into the wintry clime.
At dawn, out of the shadow, there was rime,
The dim Magellan Clouds were frosty clear,
The wind had edge, the testing-time was near.

And then he wondered if the tales were lies
Told by old hands to terrify the new,
For, since the ship left England, only twice
Had there been need to start a sheet or clew,
Then only royals, for an hour or two,
And no seas broke aboard, nor was it cold.
What were these gales of which the stories told?

The thought went by. He had heard the Bosun tell
Too often, and too fiercely, not to know
That being off the Horn in June is Hell:
Hell of continual toil in ice and snow,
Frostbitten hell in which the westers blow
Shrieking for days on end, in which the seas
Gulf the starved seamen till their marrows freeze.

Such was the weather he might look to find,
Such was the work expected: there remained
Firmly to set his teeth, resolve his mind,
And be the first, however much it pained,
And bring his honour round the Horn unstained,
And win his mates' respect; and thence, untainted,
Be ranked as man however much he painted.

He drew deep breath; a gantline swayed aloft
A lower topsail, hard with rope and leather,
Such as men's frozen fingers fight with oft
Below the Ramirez in Cape Horn weather.
The arms upon the yard hove all together,
Lighting the head along; a thought occurred
Within the painter's brain like a bright bird:

That this, and so much like it, of man's toil,
Compassed by naked manhood in strange places,
Was all heroic, but outside the coil
Within which modern art gleams or grimaces;
That if he drew that line of sailor's faces
Sweating the sail, their passionate play and change,
It would be new, and wonderful, and strange.

That that was what his work meant; it would be
A training in new vision—a revealing
Of passionate men in battle with the sea,
High on an unseen stage, shaking and reeling;
And men through him would understand their feeling,
Their might, their misery, their tragic power,
And all by suffering pain a little hour;

High on the yard with them, feeling their pain,
Battling with them; and it had not been done.
He was a door to new worlds in the brain,
A window opening letting in the sun,
A voice saying, "Thus is bread fetched and ports won,
And life lived out at sea where men exist
Solely by man's strong brain and sturdy wrist."

So he decided, as he cleaned his brasses,
Hearing without, aloft, the curse, the shout
Where the taut gantline passes and repasses,
Heaving new topsails to be lighted out.

It was most proud, however self might doubt,
To share man's tragic toil and paint it true.
He took the offered Fate: this he would do.

That night the snow fell between six and seven,
A little feathery fall so light, so dry—
An aimless dust out of a confused heaven,
Upon an air no steadier than a sigh;
The powder dusted down and wandered by
So purposeless, so many, and so cold,
Then died, and the wind ceased and the ship rolled.

Rolled till she clanged—rolled till the brain was tired,
Marking the acme of the heaves, the pause
While the sea-beauty rested and respired,
Drinking great draughts of roller at her hawse.
Flutters of snow came aimless upon flaws.
"Lock up your paints," the Mate said, speaking light:
"This is the Horn; you'll join my watch to-night!"

VI

All through the windless night the clipper rolled
In a great swell with oily gradual heaves
Which rolled her down until her time-bells tolled,
Clang, and the weltering water moaned like beeves.
The thundering rattle of slatting shook the sheaves,
Startles of water made the swing ports gush,
The sea was moaning and sighing and saying "Hush!"

It was all black and starless. Peering down
Into the water, trying to pierce the gloom,
One saw a dim, smooth, oily glitter of brown
Heaving and dying away and leaving room
For yet another. Like the march of doom
Came those great powers of marching silences;
Then fog came down, dead-cold, and hid the seas.

They set the Dauber to the foghorn. There
He stood upon the poop, making to sound
Out of the pump the sailor's nasal blare,
Listening lest ice should make the note resound.
She bayed there like a solitary hound
Lost in a covert; all the watch she bayed.
The fog, come closelier down, no answer made.

Denser it grew, until the ship was lost.
The elemental hid her; she was merged
In mufflings of dark death, like a man's ghost,
New to the change of death, yet thither urged.
Then from the hidden waters something surged—
Mournful, despairing, great, greater than speech,
A noise like one slow wave on a still beach.

Mournful, and then again mournful, and still
Out of the night that mighty voice arose;
The Dauber at his foghorn felt the thrill.
Who rode that desolate sea? What forms were those?
Mournful, from things defeated, in the throes
Of memory of some conquered hunting-ground,
Out of the night of death arose the sound.

"Whales!" said the Mate. They stayed there all night long
Answering the horn. Out of the night they spoke,
Defeated creatures who had suffered wrong,
But were still noble underneath the stroke.
They filled the darkness when the Dauber woke;
The men came peering to the rail to hear,
And the sea sighed, and the fog rose up sheer.

A wall of nothing at the world's last edge,
Where no life came except defeated life.
The Dauber felt shut in within a hedge,

Behind which form was hidden and thought was rife,
And that a blinding flash, a thrust, a knife
Would sweep the hedge away and make all plain,
Brilliant beyond all words, blinding the brain.

So the night passed, but then no morning broke—
Only a something showed that night was dead.
A sea-bird, cackling like a devil, spoke,
And the fog drew away and hung like lead.
Like mighty cliffs it shaped, sullen and red;
Like glowering gods at watch it did appear,
And sometimes drew away, and then drew near.

Like islands, and like chasms, and like hell,
But always mighty and red, gloomy and ruddy,
Shutting the visible sea in like a well;
Slow heaving in vast ripples, blank and muddy,
Where the sun should have risen it streaked bloody.
The day was still-born; all the sea-fowl scattering
Splashed the still water, mewing, hovering, clattering.

Then Polar snow came down little and light,
Till all the sky was hidden by the small,
Most multitudinous drift of dirty white
Tumbling and wavering down and covering all—
Covering the sky, the sea, the clipper tall,
Furring the ropes with white, casing the mast,
Coming on no known air, but blowing past.

And all the air seemed full of gradual moan,
As though in those cloud-chasms the horns were blowing
The mort for gods cast out and overthrown,
Or for the eyeless sun plucked out and going.
Slow the low gradual moan came in the snowing;
The Dauber felt the prelude had begun.
The snowstorm fluttered by; he saw the sun

Show and pass by, gleam from one towering prison
Into another, vaster and more grim,
Which in dull crags of darkness had arisen
To muffle-to a final door on him.
The gods upon the dull crags lowered dim,
The pigeons chattered, quarrelling in the track.
In the south-west the dimness dulled to black.

Then came the cry of "Call all hands on deck!"
The Dauber knew its meaning; it was come:
Cape Horn, that tramples beauty into wreck,
And crumples steel and smites the strong man dumb.
Down clattered flying kites and staysails: some
Sang out in quick, high calls: the fair-leads skirled,
And from the south-west came the end of the world.

"Caught in her ball-dress," said the Bosun, hauling;
"Lee-ay, lee-ay!" quick, high, come the men's call;
It was all wallop of sails and startled calling.
"Let fly!" "Let go!" "Clew up!" and "Let go all!"
"Now up and make them fast!" "Here, give us a haul!"
"Now up and stow them! Quick! By God! we're done!"
The blackness crunched all memory of the sun.

"Up!" said the Mate. "Mizen top-gallants. Hurry!"
The Dauber ran, the others ran, the sails
Slatted and shook; out of the black a flurry
Whirled in fine lines, tattering the edge to trails.
Painting and art and England were old tales
Told in some other life to that pale man,
Who struggled with white fear and gulped and ran.

He struck a ringbolt in his haste and fell—
Rose, sick with pain, half-lamed in his left knee;
He reached the shrouds where clambering men pell-mell

Hustled each other up and cursed him; he
Hurried aloft with them: then from the sea
Came a cold, sudden breath that made the hair
Stiff on the neck, as though Death whispered there.

A man below him punched him in the side.
"Get up, you Dauber, or let me get past."
He saw the belly of the skysail skied,
Gulped, and clutched tight, and tried to go more fast.
Sometimes he missed his ratline and was grassed,
Scraped his shin raw against the rigid line
The clamberers reached the futtock-shrouds' incline.

Cursing they came; one, kicking out behind,
Kicked Dauber in the mouth, and one below
Punched at his calves; the futtock-shrouds inclined
It was a perilous path for one to go.
"Up, Dauber, up!" A curse followed a blow.
He reached the top and gasped, then on, then on.
And one voice yelled "Let go!" and one "All gone!"

Fierce clamberers, some in oilskins, some in rags,
Hustling and hurrying up, up the steep stairs.
Before the windless sails were blown to flags,
And whirled like dirty birds athwart great airs,
Ten men in all, to get this mast of theirs
Snugged to the gale in time. "Up! Damn you, run!"
The mizen topmast head was safely won.

"Lay out!" the Bosun yelled. The Dauber laid
Out on the yard, gripping the yard and feeling
Sick at the mighty space of air displayed
Below his feet, where mewing birds were wheeling.
A giddy fear was on him; he was reeling.
He bit his lip half through, clutching the jack.
A cold sweat glued the shirt upon his back.

The yard was shaking, for a brace was loose.
He felt that he would fall; he clutched, he bent,
Clammy with natural terror to the shoes
While idiotic promptings came and went.
Snow fluttered on a wind-flaw and was spent;
He saw the water darken. Someone yelled,
"Frap it; don't stay to furl! Hold on!" He held.

Darkness came down—half darkness—in a whirl;
The sky went out, the waters disappeared.
He felt a shocking pressure of blowing hurl
The ship upon her side. The darkness speared
At her with wind; she staggered, she careered,
Then down she lay. The Dauber felt her go;
He saw his yard tilt downwards. Then the snow

Whirled all about—dense, multitudinous, cold—
Mixed with the wind's one devilish thrust and shriek,
Which whiffled out men's tears, deafened, took hold,
Flattening the flying drift against the cheek.
The yards buckled and bent, man could not speak.
The ship lay on her broadside; the wind's sound
Had devilish malice at having got her downed.

* * * * *

How long the gale had blown he could not tell,
Only the world had changed, his life had died.
A moment now was everlasting hell,
Nature an onslaught from the weather side,
A withering rush of death, a frost that cried,
Shrieked, till he withered at the heart; a hail
Plastered his oilskins with an icy mail.

"Cut!" yelled his mate. He looked—the sail was gone,
Blown into rags in the first furious squall;
The tatters drummed the devil's tattoo. On

The buckling yard a block thumped like a mall.
The ship lay—the sea smote her, the wind's bawl
Came, "loo, loo, loo!" The devil cried his hounds
On to the poor spent stag strayed in his bounds.

"Cut! Ease her!" yelled his mate; the Dauber heard.
His mate wormed up the tilted yard and slashed,
A rag of canvas skimmed like a darting bird.
The snow whirled, the ship bowed to it, the gear lashed,
The sea-tops were cut off and flung down smashed;
Tatters of shouts were flung, the rags of yells—
And clang, clang, clang, below beat the two bells.

"O God!" the Dauber moaned. A roaring rang,
Blasting the royals like a cannonade;
The backstays parted with a crackling clang,
The upper spars were snapped like twigs decayed—
Snapped at their heels, their jagged splinters splayed,
Like white and ghastly hairs erect with fear.
The Mate yelled, "Gone, by God, and pitched them clear!"

"Up!" yelled the Bosun; "up and clear the wreck!"
The Dauber followed where he led: below
He caught one giddy glimpsing of the deck
Filled with white water, as though heaped with snow.
He saw the streamers of the rigging blow
Straight out like pennons from the splintered mast,
Then, all sense dimmed, all was an icy blast

Roaring from nether hell and filled with ice,
Roaring and crashing on the jerking stage,
An utter bridle given to utter vice,
Limitless power mad with endless rage
Withering the soul; a minute seemed an age.
He clutched and hacked at ropes, at rags of sail.
Thinking that comfort was a fairy-tale

Told long ago—long, long ago—long since
Heard of in other lives—imagined, dreamed—
There where the basest beggar was a prince
To him in torment where the tempest screamed,
Comfort and warmth and ease no longer seemed
Things that a man could know: soul, body, brain,
Knew nothing but the wind, the cold, the pain.

"Leave that!" the Bosun shouted; "Crojick save!"
The splitting crojick, not yet gone to rags,
Thundered below, beating till something gave,
Bellying between its buntlines into bags.
Some birds were blown past, shrieking: dark, like shags,
Their backs seemed, looking down. "Leu, leu!" they cried.
The ship lay, the seas thumped her; she had died.

They reached the crojick yard, which buckled, buckled
Like a thin whalebone to the topsail's strain.
They laid upon the yard and heaved and knuckled,
Pounding the sail, which jangled and leapt again.
It was quite hard with ice, its rope like chain,
Its strength like seven devils; it shook the mast.
They cursed and toiled and froze: a long time passed.

Two hours passed, then a dim lightening came.
Those frozen ones upon the yard could see
The mainsail and the foresail still the same,
Still battling with the hands and blowing free,
Rags tattered where the staysails used to be.
The lower topsails stood; the ship's lee deck
Seethed with four feet of water filled with wreck.

An hour more went by; the Dauber lost
All sense of hands and feet, all sense of all
But of a wind that cut him to the ghost,
And of a frozen fold he had to haul,

Of heavens that fell and never ceased to fall,
And ran in smoky snatches along the sea,
Leaping from crest to wave-crest, yelling. He

Lost sense of time; no bells went, but he felt
Ages go over him. At last, at last
They frapped the cringled crojick's icy pelt;
In frozen bulge and bunt they made it fast.
Then, scarcely live, they laid in to the mast.
The Captain's speaking trumpet gave a blare,
"Make fast the topsail, Mister, while you're there."

Some seamen cursed, but up they had to go—
Up to the topsail yard to spend an hour
Stowing a topsail in a blinding snow,
Which made the strongest man among them cower.
More men came up, the fresh hands gave them power,
They stowed the sail; then with a rattle of chain
One half the crojick burst its bonds again.

* * * * *

They stowed the sail, frapping it round with rope,
Leaving no surface for the wind, no fold,
Then down the weather shrouds, half dead, they grope;
That struggle with the sail had made them old.
They wondered if the crojick furl would hold.
"Lucky," said one, "it didn't spring the spar."
"Lucky!" the Bosun said, "Lucky! We are!"

She came within two shakes of turning top
Or stripping all her shroud-screws, that first quiff.
Now fish those wash-deck buckets out of the slop.
Here's Dauber says he doesn't like Cape Stiff.
This isn't wind, man, this is only a whiff.
Hold on, all hands, hold on!" a sea, half seen,
Paused, mounted, burst, and filled the main-deck green.

The Dauber felt a mountain of water fall.
It covered him deep, deep, he felt it fill,
Over his head, the deck, the fife-rails, all,
Quieting the ship, she trembled and lay still.
Then with a rush and shatter and clanging shrill
Over she went; he saw the water cream
Over the bitts; he saw the half-deck stream.

Then in the rush he swirled, over she went;
Her lee-rail dipped, he struck, and something gave;
His legs went through a port as the roll spent;
She paused, then rolled, and back the water drave.
He drifted with it as a part of the wave,
Drowning, half-stunned, exhausted, partly frozen,
He struck the booby hatchway; then the Bosun

Leaped, seeing his chance, before the next sea burst,
And caught him as he drifted, seized him, held,
Up-ended him against the bitts, and cursed.
"This ain't the George's Swimming Baths," he yelled;
"Keep on your feet!" Another grey-back felled
The two together, and the Bose, half-blind,
Spat: "One's a joke," he cursed, "but two's unkind."

"Now, damn it, Dauber!" said the Mate. "Look out,
Or you'll be over the side!" The water freed;
Each clanging freeing-port became a spout.
The men cleared up the decks as there was need.
The Dauber's head was cut, he felt it bleed
Into his oilskins as he clutched and coiled.
Water and sky were devil's brews which boiled,

Boiled, shrieked, and glowered; but the ship was saved.
Snugged safely down, though fourteen sails were split.
Out of the dark a fiercer fury raved.

The grey-backs died and mounted, each crest lit
With a white toppling gleam that hissed from it
And slid, or leaped, or ran with whirls of cloud,
Mad with inhuman life that shrieked aloud.

The watch was called; Dauber might go below.
"Splice the main brace!" the Mate called. All laid aft
To get a gulp of momentary glow
As some reward for having saved the craft.
The steward ladled mugs, from which each quaff'd
Whisky, with water, sugar, and lime-juice, hot,
A quarter of a pint each made the tot.

Beside the lamp-room door the steward stood
Ladling it out, and each man came in turn,
Tipped his sou'-wester, drank it, grunted "Good!"
And shambled forward, letting it slowly burn:
When all were gone the Dauber lagged astern,
Torn by his frozen body's lust for heat,
The liquor's pleasant smell, so warm, so sweet,

And by a promise long since made at home
Never to taste strong liquor. Now he knew
The worth of liquor; now he wanted some.
His frozen body urged him to the brew;
Yet it seemed wrong, an evil thing to do
To break that promise. "Dauber," said the Mate,
"Drink, and turn in, man; why the hell d'ye wait?"

"Please, sir, I'm temperance." "Temperance are you, hey?
That's all the more for me! So you're for slops?
I thought you'd had enough slops for to-day.
Go to your bunk and ease her when she drops.
And—damme, steward! you brew with too much hops!
Stir up the sugar, man!—and tell your girl
How kind the Mate was teaching you to furl."

Then the Mate drank the remnants, six men's share,
And ramped into his cabin, where he stripped
And danced unclad, and was uproarious there.
In waltzes with the cabin cat he tripped.
Singing in tenor clear that he was pipped—
That "he who strove the tempest to disarm,
Must never first embrail the lee yard-arm."

And that his name was Ginger. Dauber crept
Back to the round-house, gripping by the rail.
The wind howled by; the passionate water leapt;
The night was all one roaring with the gale.
Then at the door he stopped, uttering a wail;
His hands were perished numb and blue as veins,
He could not turn the knob for both the Spains.

A hand came shuffling aft, dodging the seas,
Singing "her nut-brown hair" between his teeth;
Taking the ocean's tumult at his ease
Even when the wash about his thighs did seethe.
His soul was happy in its happy sheath;
"What, Dauber, won't it open? Fingers cold?
You'll talk of this time, Dauber, when you're old."

He flung the door half open, and a sea
Washed them both in, over the splashboard, down;
"You silly, salt miscarriage!" sputtered he.
"Dauber, pull out the plug before we drown!
That's spoiled my laces and my velvet gown.
Where is the plug?" Groping in pitch dark water,
He sang between his teeth "The Farmer's Daughter."

It was pitch dark within there; at each roll
The chests slid to the slant; the water rushed,
Making full many a clanging tin pan bowl
Into the black below-bunks as it gushed.

The dog-tired men slept through it; they were hushed.
The water drained, and then with matches damp
The man struck heads off till he lit the lamp.

"Thank you," the Dauber said; the seaman grinned.
"This is your first foul weather?" "Yes." "I thought
Up on the yard you hadn't seen much wind.
Them's rotten sea-boots, Dauber, that you brought.
Now I must cut on deck before I'm caught."
He went; the lamp-flame smoked; he slammed the door;
A film of water loitered across the floor.

The Dauber watched it come and watched it go;
He had had revelation of the lies
Cloaking the truth men never choose to know;
He could bear witness now and cleanse their eyes.
He had beheld in suffering; he was wise;
This was the sea, this searcher of the soul—
This never-dying shriek fresh from the Pole.

He shook with cold; his hands could not undo
His oilskin buttons, so he shook and sat,
Watching his dirty fingers, dirty blue,
Hearing without the hammering tackle slat,
Within, the drops from dripping clothes went pat,
Running in little patters, gentle, sweet,
And "Ai, ai!" went the wind, and the seas beat.

His bunk was sopping wet; he clambered in,
None of his clothes were dry; his fear recurred.
Cramps bunched the muscles underneath his skin.
The great ship rolled until the lamp was blurred.
He took his Bible and tried to read a word;
Trembled at going aloft again, and then
Resolved to fight it out and show it to men.

Faces recurred, fierce memories of the yard,
The frozen sail, the savage eyes, the jests,
The oaths of one great seaman, syphilis-scarred,
The tug of leeches jammed beneath their chests,
The buntlines bellying bunts out into breasts.
The deck so desolate-grey, the sky so wild,
He fell asleep, and slept like a young child.

But not for long; the cold awoke him soon,
The hot-ache and the skin-cracks and the cramp,
The seas thundering without, the gale's wild tune,
The sopping misery of the blankets damp.
A speaking-trumpet roared; a sea-boot's stamp
Clogged at the door. A man entered to shout:
"All hands on deck! Arouse here! Tumble out!"

The caller raised the lamp; his oilskins clicked
As the thin ice upon them cracked and fell.
"Rouse out!" he said. "This lamp is frozen wick'd.
Rouse out!" His accent deepened to a yell.
"We're among ice; it's blowing up like hell.
We're going to hand both topsails. Time, I guess,
We're sheeted up. Rouse out! Don't stay to dress!"

"Is it cold on deck?" said Dauber. "Is it cold?
We're sheeted up, I tell you, inches thick!
The fo'c'sle's like a wedding-cake, I'm told.
Now tumble out, my sons; on deck here, quick!
Rouse out, away, and come and climb the stick.
I'm going to call the half-deck. Bosun! Hey!
Both topsails coming in. Heave out! Away!"

He went; the Dauber tumbled from his bunk,
Clutching the side. He heard the wind go past,
Making the great ship wallow as if drunk.

There was a shocking tumult up the mast.
"This is the end," he muttered, "come at last!
I've got to go aloft, facing this cold.
I can't. I can't. I'll never keep my hold.

"I cannot face the topsail yard again.
I never guessed what misery it would be."
The cramps and hot-ache made him sick with pain.
The ship stopped suddenly from a devilish sea,
Then, with a triumph of wash, a rush of glee,
The door burst in, and in the water rolled,
Filling the lower bunks, black, creaming, cold.

The lamp sucked out. "Wash!" went the water back,
Then in again, flooding; the Bosun swore.
"You useless thing! You Dauber! You lee slack!
Get out, you heekapoota! Shut the door!
You coo-ilyaira, what are you waiting for?
Out of my way, you thing—you useless thing!"
He slammed the door indignant, clanging the ring.

And then he lit the lamp, drowned to the waist;
"Here's a fine house! Get at the scupper-holes"—
He bent against it as the water raced—
"And pull them out to leeward when she rolls.
They say some kinds of landsmen don't have souls.
I well believe. A Port Mahon baboon
Would make more soul than you got with a spoon."

Down in the icy water Dauber groped
To find the plug; the racing water sluiced
Over his head and shoulders as she sloped.
Without, judged by the sound, all hell was loosed.
He felt cold Death about him tightly noosed.
That Death was better than the misery there
Iced on the quaking foothold high in air.

And then the thought came: "I'm a failure. All
My life has been a failure. They were right.
It will not matter if I go and fall;
I should be free then from this hell's delight.
I'll never paint. Best let it end to-night.
I'll slip over the side. I've tried and failed."
So in the ice-cold in the night he quailed.

Death would be better, death, than this long hell
Of mockery and surrender and dismay—
This long defeat of doing nothing well,
Playing the part too high for him to play.
"O Death! who hides the sorry thing away,
Take me; I've failed. I cannot play these cards."
There came a thundering from the topsail yards.

And then he bit his lips, clenching his mind,
And staggered out to muster, beating back
The coward frozen self of him that whined.
Come what cards might he meant to play the pack.
"Ai!" screamed the wind; the topsail sheet went clack;
Ice filled the air with spikes; the grey-backs burst.
"Here's Dauber," said the Mate, "on deck the first.

"Why, holy sailor, Dauber, you're a man!
I took you for a soldier. Up now, come!"
Up on the yards already they began
That battle with a gale which strikes men dumb.
The leaping topsail thundered like a drum.
The frozen snow beat in the face like shots.
The wind spun whipping wave-crests into clots.

So up upon the topsail yard again,
In the great tempest's fiercest hour, began
Probation to the Dauber's soul, of pain
Which crowds a century's torment in a span.

For the next month the ocean taught this man,
And he, in that month's torment, while she wested,
Was never warm nor dry, nor full nor rested

But still it blew, or, if it lulled, it rose
Within the hour and blew again; and still
The water as it burst aboard her froze.
The wind blew off an ice-field, raw and chill,
Daunting man's body, tampering with his will;
But after thirty days a ghostly sun
Gave sickly promise that the storms were done.

VII

A great grey sea was running up the sky,
Desolate birds flew past; their mewings came
As that lone water's spiritual cry,
Its forlorn voice, its essence, its soul's name.
The ship limped in the water as if lame.
Then in the forenoon watch to a great shout
More sail was made, the reefs were shaken out.

A slant came from the south; the singers stood
Clapped to the halliards, hauling to a tune,
Old as the sea, a fillip to the blood.
The upper topsail rose like a balloon.
"So long, Cape Stiff. In Valparaiso soon,"
Said one to other, as the ship lay over,
Making her course again—again a rover.

Slowly the sea went down as the wind fell.
Clear rang the songs, "Hurrah! Cape Horn is bet!"
The combless seas were lumping into swell;
The leaking fo'c'sles were no longer wet.
More sail was made; the watch on deck was set
To cleaning up the ruin broken bare
Below, aloft, about her, everywhere.

The Dauber, scrubbing out the roundhouse, found
Old pantiles pulped among the mouldy gear,
Washed underneath the bunks and long since drowned
During the agony of the Cape Horn year.
He sang in scrubbing, for he had done with fear—
Fronted the worst and looked it in the face;
He had got manhood at the testing-place.

Singing he scrubbed, passing his watch below,
Making the round-house fair; the Bosun watched,
Bringing his knitting slowly to the toe.
Sails stretched a mizen skysail which he patched;
They thought the Dauber was a bad egg hatched.
"Daubs," said the Bosun cheerly, "can you knit?
I've made a Barney's bull of this last bit."

Then, while the Dauber counted, Bosun took
Some marline from his pocket. "Here," he said,
"You want to know square sennit? So fash. Look!
Eight foxes take, and stop the ends with thread.
I've known an engineer would give his head
To know square sennit." As the Bose began,
The Dauber felt promoted into man.

It was his warrant that he had not failed—
That the most hard part in his difficult climb
Had not been past attainment; it was scaled:
Safe footing showed above the slippery slime.
He had emerged out of the iron time,
And knew that he could compass his life's scheme;
He had the power sufficient to his dream.

Then dinner came, and now the sky was blue.
The ship was standing north, the Horn was rounded;
She made a thundering as she weltered through.

The mighty grey-backs glittered as she bounded.
More sail was piled upon her; she was hounded
North, while the wind came; like a stag she ran
Over grey hills and hollows of seas wan.

She had a white bone in her mouth: she sped;
Those in the round-house watched her as they ate
Their meal of pork-fat fried with broken bread.
"Good old!" they cried. "She's off; she's gathering gait!"
Her track was whitening like a Lammas spate.
"Good old!" they cried. "Oh, give her cloth! Hurray!
For three weeks more to Valparaiso Bay!

"She smells old Vallipo," the Bosun cried.
"We'll be inside the tier in three weeks more,
Lying at double-moorings where they ride
Off of the market, half a mile from shore,
And bumboat pan, my sons, and figs galore,
And girls in black mantillas fit to make a
Poor seaman frantic when they dance the cueca."

Eight bells were made, the watch was changed, and now
The Mate spoke to the Dauber: "This is better.
We'll soon be getting mudhooks over the bow.
She'll make her passage still if this'll let her.
Oh, run, you drogher! dip your fo'c'sle wetter.
Well, Dauber, this is better than Cape Horn.
Them topsails made you wish you'd not been born."

"Yes, sir," the Dauber said. "Now," said the Mate,
"We've got to smart her up. Them Cape Horn seas
Have made her paint-work like a rusty grate.
Oh, didn't them topsails make your fishhooks freeze?
A topsail don't pay heed to 'Won't you, please?'
Well, you have seen Cape Horn, my son; you've learned,
You've dipped your hand and had your fingers burned.

"And now you'll stow that folly, trying to paint.
You've had your lesson; you're a sailor now.
You come on board a female ripe to faint.
All sorts of slush you'd learned, the Lord knows how.
Cape Horn has sent you wisdom over the bow
If you've got sense to take it. You're a sailor.
My God! before you were a woman's tailor.

"So throw your paints to blazes and have done.
Words can't describe the silly things you did
Sitting before your easel in the sun,
With all your colours on the paint-box lid.
I blushed for you . . . and then the daubs you hid.
My God! you'll have more sense now, eh? You've quit?"
"No sir." "You've not?" "No, sir." "God give you wit

"I thought you'd come to wisdom." Thus they talked,
While the great clipper took her bit and rushed
Like a skin-glistening stallion not yet baulked,
Till fire-bright water at her swing ports gushed;
Poising and bowing down her fore-foot crushed
Bubble on glittering bubble; on she went
The Dauber watched her, wondering what it meant.

To come, after long months, at rosy dawn,
Into the placid blue of some great bay.
Treading the quiet waters like a fawn
Ere yet the morning haze was blown away.
A rose-flushed figure putting by the grey,
And anchoring there before the city smoke
Rose, or the church-bells rang, or men awoke.

And then, in the first light, to see grow clear
That long-expected haven filled with strangers—
Alive with men and women; see and hear

Its clattering market and its money-changers;
And hear the surf beat, and be free from dangers,
And watch the crinkled ocean blue with calm
Drowsing beneath the Trade, beneath the palm.

Hungry for that he worked; the hour went by,
And still the wind grew, still the clipper strode,
And now a darkness hid the western sky,
And sprays came flicking off at the wind's goad.
She stumbled now, feeling her sail a load.
The Mate gazed hard to windward, eyed his sail,
And said the Horn was going to flick her tail.

Boldly he kept it on her till she staggered,
But still the wind increased; it grew, it grew,
Darkening the sky, making the water haggard;
Full of small snow the mighty wester blew.
"More fun for little fish-hooks," sighed the crew.
They eyed the taut topgallants stiff like steel;
A second hand was ordered to the wheel.

The Captain eyed her aft, sucking his lip,
Feeling the sail too much, but yet refraining
From putting hobbles on the leaping ship,
The glad sea-shattering stallion, halter-straining,
Wing-musical, uproarious, and complaining;
But, in a gust, he cocked his finger, so:
"You'd better take them off, before they go."

All saw. They ran at once without the word,
"Lee-ay! Lee-ay!" Loud rang the clewline cries;
Sam in his bunk within the half-deck heard,
Stirred in his sleep, and rubbed his drowsy eyes.
"There go the lower to'gallants." Against the skies
Rose the thin bellying strips of leaping sail.
The Dauber was the first man over the rail.

Three to a mast they ran; it was a race.
"God!" said the Mate; "that Dauber, he can go."
He watched the runners with an upturned face
Over the futtocks, struggling heel to toe,
Up to the topmast cross-trees into the blow
Where the three sails were leaping. "Dauber wins!"
The yards were reached, and now the race begins.

Which three will furl their sail first and come down?
Out to the yard-arm for the leech goes one,
His hair blown flagwise from a hatless crown,
His hands at work like fever to be done.
Out of the gale a fiercer fury spun.
The three sails leaped together, yanking high,
Like talons darting up to clutch the sky.

The Dauber on the fore-topgallant yard
Out at the weather yard-arm was the first
To lay his hand upon the buntline-barred
Topgallant yanking to the wester's burst;
He craned to catch the leech; his comrades cursed;
One at the buntlines, one with oaths observed,
"The eye of the outer jib-stay isn't served."

"No," said the Dauber. "No," the man replied.
They heaved, stowing the sail, not looking round,
Panting, but full of life and eager-eyed;
The gale roared at them with its iron sound.
"That's you," the Dauber said. His gasket wound
Swift round the yard, binding the sail in bands;
There came a gust, the sail leaped from his hands,

So that he saw it high above him, grey,
And there his mate was falling; quick he clutched
An arm in oilskins swiftly snatched away.

A voice said "Christ!" a quick shape stooped and touched,
Chain struck his hands, ropes shot, the sky was smutched
With vast black fires that ran, that fell, that furled,
And then he saw the mast, the small snow hurled,

The fore-topgallant yard far, far aloft,
And blankness settling on him and great pain;
And snow beneath his fingers wet and soft,
And topsail sheet-blocks shaking at the chain.
He knew it was he who had fallen; then his brain
Swirled in a circle while he watched the sky.
Infinite multitudes of snow blew by.

"I thought it was Tom who fell," his brain's voice said.
"Down on the bloody deck!" the Captain screamed.
The multitudinous little snow-flakes sped.
His pain was real enough, but all else seemed.
Si with a bucket ran, the water gleamed
Tilting upon him; others came, the Mate . . .
They knelt with eager eyes like things that wait

For other things to come. He saw them there.
"It will go on," he murmured, watching Si.
Colours and sounds seemed mixing in the air,
The pain was stunning him, and the wind went by.
"More water," said the Mate. "Here, Bosun, try.
Ask if he's got a message. Hell, he's gone!
Here, Dauber, paints." He said, "It will go on."

Not knowing his meaning rightly, but he spoke
With the intenseness of a fading soul
Whose share of Nature's fire turns to smoke,
Whose hand on Nature's wheel loses control.
The eager faces glowered red like coal.
They glowed, the great storm glowed, the sails, the mast.
"It will go on," he cried aloud, and passed.

Those from the yard came down to tell the tale.
"He almost had me off," said Tom. "He slipped.
There come one hell of a jump-like from the sail. .
He clutched at me and almost had me pipped.
He caught my 'ris'band, but the oilskin ripped. . .
It tore clean off. Look here. I was near gone.
I made a grab to catch him; so did John.

"I caught his arm. My God! I was near done.
He almost had me over; it was near.
He hit the ropes and grabbed at every one."
"Well," said the Mate, "we cannot leave him here.
Run, Si, and get the half-deck table clear.
We'll lay him there. Catch hold there, you, and you
He's dead, poor son; there's nothing more to do."

Night fell, and all night long the Dauber lay
Covered upon the table; all night long
The pitiless storm exulted at her prey,
Huddling the waters with her icy thong.
But to the covered shape she did no wrong.
He lay beneath the sailcloth. Bell by bell
The night wore through; the stars rose, the stars fell.

Blowing most pitiless cold out of clear sky
The wind roared all night long; and all night through
The green seas on the deck went washing by,
Flooding the half-deck; bitter hard it blew.
But little of it all the Dauber knew—
The sopping bunks, the floating chests, the wet,
The darkness, and the misery, and the sweat.

He was off duty. So it blew all night,
And when the watches changed the men would come
Dripping within the door to strike a light
And stare upon the Dauber lying dumb,

And say, "He come a cruel thump, poor chum."
Or, "He'd a-been a fine big man;" or, "He . . .
A smart young seaman he was getting to be."

Or, "Damn it all, it's what we've all to face! . . .
I knew another fellow one time . . ." then
Came a strange tale of death in a strange place
Out on the sea, in ships, with wandering men.
In many ways Death puts us into pen.
The reefers came down tired and looked and slept.
Below the skylight little dribbles crept

Along the painted woodwork, glistening, slow,
Following the roll and dripping, never fast,
But dripping on the quiet form below,
Like passing time talking to time long past.
And all night long "Ai, ai!" went the wind's blast,
And creaming water swished below the pale,
Unheeding body stretched beneath the sail.

At dawn they sewed him up, and at eight bells
They bore him to the gangway, wading deep,
Through the green-clutching, white-toothed water-hells
That flung his carriers over in their sweep.
They laid an old red ensign on the heap,
And all hands stood bare-headed, stooping, swaying,
Washed by the sea while the old man was praying

Out of a borrowed prayer-book. At a sign
They twitched the ensign back and tipped the grating
A creamier bubbling broke the bubbling brine.
The muffled figure tilted to the weighting;
It dwindled slowly down, slowly gyrating.
Some craned to see; it dimmed, it disappeared;
The last green milky bubble blinked and cleared.

"Mister, shake out your reefs," the Captain called.
"Out topsail reefs!" the Mate cried; then all hands
Hurried, the great sails shook, and all hands hauled,
Singing that desolate song of lonely lands,
Of how a lover came in dripping bands,
Green with the wet and cold, to tell his lover
That Death was in the sea, and all was over.

Fair came the falling wind; a seaman said
The Dauber was a Jonah; once again
The clipper held her course, showing red lead,
Shattering the sea-tops into golden rain.
The waves bowed down before her like blown grain;
Onwards she thundered, on; her voyage was short,
Before the tier's bells rang her into port.

Cheerly they rang her in, those beating bells,
The new-come beauty stately from the sea,
Whitening the blue heave of the drowsy swells,
Treading the bubbles down. With three times three
They cheered her moving beauty in, and she
Came to her berth so noble, so superb;
Swayed like a queen, and answered to the curb.

Then in the sunset's flush they went aloft,
And unbent sails in that most lovely hour,
When the light gentles and the wind is soft,
And beauty in the heart breaks like a flower.
Working aloft they saw the mountain tower,
Snow to the peak; they heard the launch-men shout;
And bright along the bay the lights came out.

And then the night fell dark, and all night long
The pointed mountain pointed at the stars,
Frozen, alert, austere; the eagle's song

Screamed from her desolate screes and splintered scars.
On her intense crags where the air is sparse
The stars looked down; their many golden eyes
Watched her and burned, burned out, and came to rise.

Silent the finger of the summit stood,
Icy in pure, thin air, glittering with snows.
Then the sun's coming turned the peak to blood,
And in the rest-house the muleteers arose.
And all day long, where only the eagle goes,
Stones, loosened by the sun, fall; the stones falling
Fill empty gorge on gorge with echoes calling.

GLOSSARY

EXPLANATIONS OF SOME OF THE SEA TERMS USED IN THE POEM

Backstays.—Wire ropes which support the masts against lateral and after strains.

Barney's bull.—A figure in marine proverb. A jewel in marine repartee.

Bells.—Two bells (one forward, one aft) which are struck every half-hour in a certain manner to mark the passage of the watches.

Bitts.—Strong wooden structures (built round each mast) upon which running rigging is secured.

Block.—A sheaved pulley.

Boatswain.—A supernumerary or idler, generally attached to the mate's watch, and holding considerable authority over the crew.

Bouilli tin.—Any tin that contains, or has contained, preserved meat.

Bows.—The forward extremity of a ship.

Brace-blocks.—Pulleys through which the braces travel.

Braces.—Ropes by which the yards are inclined forward or aft.

Bumboat pan.—Soft bread sold by the bumboat man, a kind of sea costermonger who trades with ships in port.

Bunt.—Those cloths of a square sail which are nearest to the mast when the sail is set. The central portion of a furled square sail. The human abdomen (figuratively).

Buntlines.—Ropes which help to confine square sails to the yards in the operation of furling.

Chocks.—Wooden stands on which the boats rest.

Cleats.—Iron or wooden contrivances to which ropes may be secured.

Clew-lines.—Ropes by which the lower corners of square sails are lifted.

Clews.—The lower corners of square sails.

Clipper.—A title of honour given to ships of more than usual speed and beauty.

Coaming.—The raised rim of a hatchway; a barrier at a doorway to keep water from entering.

Courses.—The large square sails set upon the lower yards of sailing ships. The mizen course is called the "crojick."

Cringled.—Fitted with iron rings or cringles, many of which are let into sails or sail-roping for various purposes.

Crojick (or cross-jack).—A square sail set upon the lower yard of the mizen mast.

Dungarees.—Thin blue or khaki-coloured overalls made from cocoanut fibre.

Fairleads.—Rings of wood or iron by means of which running rigging is led in any direction.

Fife-rails.—Strong wooden shelves fitted with iron pins, to which ropes may be secured.

Fish-hooks.—*I. e.*, fingers.

Foot-ropes.—Ropes on which men stand when working aloft.

Fo'c'sle.—The cabin or cabins in which the men are berthed. It is usually an iron deck-house divided through the middle into two compartments for the two watches, and fitted with wooden bunks. Sometimes it is even fitted with lockers and an iron water-tank.

Foxes.—Strands, yarns, or arrangements of yarns of rope.

Freeing-ports.—Iron doors in the ship's side which open outwards to free the decks of water.

Frap.—To wrap round with rope.

Futtock-shrouds.—Iron bars to which the topmast rigging is secured. As they project outward and upward from the masts they are difficult to clamber over.

Galley.—The ship's kitchen.

Gantline (girtline).—A rope used for the sending of sails up and down from aloft.

Gaskets.—Ropes by which the sails are secured in furling.

Half-deck.—A cabin or apartment in which the apprentices are berthed. Its situation is usually the ship's waist; but it is sometimes further aft, and occasionally it is under the poop or even right forward under the top-gallant fo'c'sle.

Halliards.—Ropes by which sails are hoisted.

Harness-room.—An office or room from which the salt meat is issued, and in which it is sometimes stored.

Hawse.—The bows or forward end of a ship.

Head.—The forward part of a ship. That upper edge of a square sail which is attached to the yard.

House-flag.—The special flag of the firm to which a ship belongs.

Idlers.—The members of the round-house mess, generally consisting of the carpenter, cook, sailmaker, boatswain, painter, etc., are known as the idlers.

Jack (or jackstay).—An iron bar (fitted along all yards in sailing ships) to which the head of a square sail is secured when bent.

Kites.—Light upper sails.

Leeches.—The outer edges of square sails. In furling some square sails the leech is dragged inwards till it lies level with the head upon the surface of the yard. This is done by the first man who gets upon the yard, beginning at the weather side.

Logship.—A contrivance by which a ship's speed is measured.

Lower topsail.—The second sail from the deck on square rigged masts. It is a very strong, important sail.

Marline.—Tarry line or coarse string made of rope-yarns twisted together.

Mate.—The First or Chief Mate is generally called the Mate.

Mizen-topmast-head.—The summit of the second of the three or four spars which make the complete mizen-mast.

Mudhooks.—Anchors.

Pins.—Iron or wooden bars to which running rigging is secured.

Pointing.—A kind of neat plait with which ropes are sometimes ended off or decorated.

Poop-break.—The forward end of the after superstructure.

Ratlines.—The rope steps placed across the shrouds to enable the seamen to go aloft.

Reefers.—Apprentices.

Reef-points.—Ropes by which the area of some sails may be reduced in the operation of reefing. Reef-points are securely fixed to the sails fitted with them, and when not in use their ends patter continually upon the canvas with a gentle drumming noise.

Reel.—A part of the machinery used with a logship.

Round-house.—A cabin (of all shapes except round) in which the idlers are berthed.

Royals.—Light upper square sails; the fourth, fifth, or sixth sails from the deck according to the mast's rig.

Sail-room.—A large room or compartment in which the ship's sails are stored.

"*Sails.*"—The sailmaker is meant.

Scuttle-butt.—A cask containing fresh water.

Shackles.—Rope handles for a sea-chest.

Sheet-blocks.—Iron blocks, by means of which sails are sheeted home. In any violent wind they beat upon the mast with great rapidity and force.

Sheets.—Ropes or chains which extend the lower corners of square sails in the operation of sheeting home.

Shifting suits (of sails).—The operation of removing a ship's sails, and replacing them with others.

Shrouds.—Wire ropes of great strength, which support lateral strains on masts.
Shroud-screws.—Iron contrivances by which shrouds are hove taut.
Sidelights.—A sailing ship carries two of these between sunset and sunrise: one green, to starboard; one red, to port.
Sights.—Observations to help in the finding of a ship's position.
Skid.—A wooden contrivance on which ship's boats rest.
Skysails.—The uppermost square sails; the fifth, sixth, or seventh sails from the deck according to the mast's rig.
Slatting.—The noise made by sails flogging in the wind.
Slush.—Grease, melted fat.
South-wester.—A kind of oilskin hat. A gale from the south-west.
Spit-brown.—To chew tobacco.
Square sennit.—A cunning plait which makes a four-square bar.
Staysails.—Fore and aft sails set upon the stays between the masts.
Stow.—To furl.
Strop (the, putting on).—A strop is a grument or rope ring. The two players kneel down facing each other, the strop is placed over their heads, and the men then try to pull each other over by the strength of their neck-muscles.
Swing-ports.—Iron doors in the ship's side which open outwards to free the decks from water.

Tackle (pronounced "taykel").—Blocks, ropes, pulleys, etc.
Take a caulk.—To sleep upon the deck.
Topsails.—The second and third sails from the deck on the masts of a modern square-rigged ship are known as the lower and upper topsails.
Trucks.—The summits of the masts.

Upper topsail.—The third square sail from the deck on the masts of square-rigged ships.

Yards.—The steel or wooden spars (placed across masts) from which square sails are set.

THE DAFFODIL FIELDS

THE DAFFODIL FIELDS

I

Between the barren pasture and the wood
There is a patch of poultry-stricken grass,
Where, in old time, Ryemeadows' Farmhouse stood,
And human fate brought tragic things to pass.
A spring comes bubbling up there, cold as glass,
It bubbles down, crusting the leaves with lime,
Babbling the self-same song that it has sung through time.

Ducks gobble at the selvage of the brook,
But still it slips away, the cold hill-spring,
Past the Ryemeadows' lonely woodland nook
Where many a stubble grey-goose preens her wing,
On, by the woodland side. You hear it sing
Past the lone copse where poachers set their wires,
Past the green hill once grim with sacrificial fires.

Another water joins it; then it turns,
Runs through the Ponton Wood, still turning west,
Past foxgloves, Canterbury bells, and ferns,
And many a blackbird's, many a thrush's nest;
The cattle tread it there; then, with a zest
It sparkles out, babbling its pretty chatter
Through Foxholes Farm, where it gives white-faced cattle water.

Under the road it runs, and now it slips
Past the great ploughland, babbling, drop and linn,
To the moss'd stumps of elm trees which it lips,
And blackberry-bramble-trails where eddies spin.
Then, on its left, some short-grassed fields begin,
Red-clayed and pleasant, which the young spring fills
With the never-quiet joy of dancing daffodils.

There are three fields where daffodils are found;
Thc grass is dotted blue-grey with their leaves;
Their nodding beauty shakes along the ground
Up to a fir-clump shutting out the eaves
Of an old farm where always the wind grieves
High in the fir boughs, moaning; people call
This farm The Roughs, but some call it the Poor Maid's Hall.

There, when the first green shoots of tender corn
Show on the plough; when the first drift of white
Stars the black branches of the spiky thorn,
And afternoons are warm and evenings light,
The shivering daffodils do take delight,
Shaking beside the brook, and grass comes green,
And blue dog-violets come and glistening celandine.

And there the pickers come, picking for town
Those dancing daffodils; all day they pick;
Hard-featured women, weather-beaten brown,
Or swarthy-red, the colour of old brick.
At noon they break their meats under the rick.
The smoke of all three farms lifts blue in air
As though man's passionate mind had never suffered there.

And sometimes as they rest an old man comes,
Shepherd or carter, to the hedgerow-side,
And looks upon their gangrel tribe, and hums,
And thinks all gone to wreck since master died;
And sighs over a passionate harvest-tide
Which Death's red sickle reaped under those hills,
There, in the quiet fields among the daffodils.

When this most tragic fate had time and place,
And human hearts and minds to show it by,
Ryemeadows' Farmhouse was in evil case:
Its master, Nicholas Gray, was like to die.

He lay in bed, watching the windy sky,
Where all the rooks were homing on slow wings,
Cawing, or blackly circling in enormous rings.

With a sick brain he watched them; then he took
Paper and pen, and wrote in straggling hand
(Like spiders' legs, so much his fingers shook)
Word to the friends who held the adjoining land,
Bidding them come; no more he could command
His fingers twitching to the feebling blood;
He watched his last day's sun dip down behind the wood,

While all his life's thoughts surged about his brain.
Memories and pictures clear, and faces known—
Long dead, perhaps; he was a child again,
Treading a threshold in the dark alone.
Then back the present surged, making him moan.
He asked if Keir had come yet. "No," they said.
"Nor Occleve?" "No." He moaned: "Come soon or I'll be dead."

The names like live things wandered in his mind:
"Charles Occleve of The Roughs," and "Rowland Keir—
Keir of the Foxholes"; but his brain was blind,
A blind old alley in the storm of the year,
Baffling the traveller life with "No way here,"
For all his lantern raised; life would not tread
Within that brain again, along those pathways red.

Soon all was dimmed but in the heaven one star.
"I'll hold to that," he said then footsteps stirred.
Down in the court a voice said, "Here they are,"
And one, "He's almost gone." The sick man heard.
"Oh God, be quick," he moaned. "Only one word.
Keir! Occleve! Let them come. Why don't they come?
Why stop to tell them that?—the devil strike you dumb.

"I'm neither doll nor dead; come in, come in.
Curse you, you women, quick," the sick man flamed.
"I shall be dead before I can begin.
A sick man's womaned-mad, and nursed and damed."
Death had him by the throat; his wrath was tamed.
"Come in," he fumed; "stop muttering at the door."
The friends came in; a creaking ran across the floor.

"Now, Nick, how goes it, man?" said Occleve. "Oh."
The dying man replied, "I am dying; past;
Mercy of God, I die, I'm going to go.
But I have much to tell you if I last.
Come near me, Occleve, Keir. I am sinking fast,
And all my kin are coming; there, look there.
All the old, long dead Grays are moving in the air.

"It is my Michael that I called you for:
My son, abroad, at school still, over sea.
See if that hag is listening at the door.
No? Shut the door; don't lock it, let it be.
No faith is kept to dying men like me.
I am dipped deep and dying, bankrupt, done;
I leave not even a farthing to my lovely son.

"Neighbours, these many years our children played.
Down in the fields together, down the brook;
Your Mary, Keir, the girl, the bonny maid,
And Occleve's Lion, always at his book;
Them and my Michael: dear, what joy they took
Picking the daffodils; such friends they've been—
My boy and Occleve's boy and Mary Keir for queen.

"I had made plans; but I am done with, I.
Give me the wine. I have to ask you this:
I can leave Michael nothing, and I die.

By all our friendship used to be and is,
Help him, old friends. Don't let my Michael miss
The schooling I've begun. Give him his chance.
He does not know I am ill; I kept him there in France.

"Saving expense; each penny counts. Oh, friends,
Help him another year; help him to take
His full diploma when the training ends,
So that my ruin won't be his. Oh, make
This sacrifice for our old friendship's sake,
And God will pay you; for I see God's hand
Pass in most marvellous ways on souls: I understand

"How just rewards are given for man's deeds
And judgment strikes the soul. The wine there, wine.
Life is the daily thing man never heeds.
It is ablaze with sign and countersign.
Michael will not forget: that son of mine
Is a rare son, my friends; he will go far.
I shall behold his course from where the blessed are."

"Why, Nick," said Occleve, "come, man. Gather hold.
Rouse up. You've given way. If times are bad,
Times must be bettering, master; so be bold;
Lift up your spirit, Nicholas, and be glad.
Michael's as much to me as my dear lad.
I'll see he takes his school." "And I," said Keir.
"Set you no keep by that, but be at rest, my dear.

"We'll see your Michael started on the road."
"But there," said Occleve, "Nick's not going to die.
Out of the ruts, good nag, now; zook the load.
Pull up, man. Death! Death and the fiend defy.
We'll bring the farm round for you, Keir and I.
Put heart at rest and get your health." "Ah, no,"
The sick man faintly answered. "I have got to go."

Still troubled in his mind, the sick man tossed.
"Old friends," he said, "I once had hoped to see
Mary and Michael wed, but fates are crossed,
And Michael starts with nothing left by me.
Still, if he loves her, will you let it be?
So in the grave, maybe, when I am gone,
I'll know my hope fulfilled, and see the plan go on."

"I judge by hearts, not money," answered Keir.
"If Michael suits in that and suits my maid,
I promise you, let Occleve witness here,
He shall be free for me to drive his trade.
Free, ay, and welcome, too. Be not afraid,
I'll stand by Michael as I hope some friend
Will stand beside my girl in case my own life end."

"And I," said Occleve; but the sick man seemed
Still ill at ease. "My friends," he said, "my friends,
Michael may come to all that I have dreamed,
But he's a wild yarn full of broken ends.
So far his life in France has made amends.
God grant he steady so; but girls and drink
Once brought him near to hell, aye, to the very brink.

"There is a running vein of wildness in him:
Wildness and looseness both, which vices make
That woman's task a hard one who would win him:
His life depends upon the course you take.
He is a fiery-mettled colt to break,
And one to curb, one to be curbed, remember."
The dying voice died down, the fire left the ember.

But once again it flamed. "Ah me," he cried;
"Our secret sins take body in our sons,
To haunt our age with what we put aside.
I was a devil for the women once.

He is as I was. Beauty like the sun's;
Within, all water; minded like the moon.
Go now. I sinned. I die. I shall be punished soon."

The two friends tiptoed to the room below.
There, till the woman came to them, they told
Of brave adventures in the long ago,
Ere Nick and they had thought of growing old;
Snipe-shooting in the marshlands in the cold,
Old soldiering days as yeomen, days at fairs,
Days that had sent Nick tired to those self-same chairs.

They vowed to pay the schooling for his son.
They talked of Michael, testing men's report,
How the young student was a lively one,
Handsome and passionate both, and fond of sport,
Eager for fun, quick-witted in retort.
The girls' hearts quick to see him cocking by,
Young April on a blood horse, with a roving eye.

And, as they talked about the lad, Keir asked
If Occleve's son had not, at one time, been
Heartsick for Mary, though with passion masked.
"Ay," Occleve said: "Time was. At seventeen.
It took him hard, it ran his ribs all lean,
All of a summer; but it passed, it died.
Her fancying Michael better touched my Lion's pride."

Mice flickered from the wainscot to the press,
Nibbling at crumbs, rattling to shelter, squeaking.
Each ticking in the clock's womb made life less;
Oil slowly dropped from where the lamp was leaking.
At times the old nurse set the staircase creaking,
Harked to the sleeper's breath, made sure, returned,
Answered the questioning eyes, then wept. The great stars burned.

"Listen," said Occleve, "listen, Rowland. Hark."
"It's Mary, come with Lion," answered Keir:
"They said they'd come together after dark."
He went to door and called "Come in, my dear."
The burning wood log blazed with sudden cheer,
So that a glowing lighted all the room.
His daughter Mary entered from the outer gloom.

The wind had brought the blood into her cheek,
Heightening her beauty, but her great grey eyes
Were troubled with a fear she could not speak.
Firm, scarlet lips she had, not made for lies.
Gentle she seemed, pure-natured, thoughtful, wise,
And when she asked what turn the sickness took,
Her voice's passing pureness on a low note shook.

Young Lion Occleve entered at her side,
A well-built, clever man, unduly grave,
One whose repute already travelled wide
For skill in breeding beasts. His features gave
Promise of brilliant mind, far-seeing, brave,
One who would travel far. His manly grace
Grew wistful when his eyes were turned on Mary's face.

"Tell me," said Mary, "what did doctor say?
How ill is he? What chance of life has he?
The cowman said he couldn't last the day,
And only yesterday he joked with me."
"We must be meek," the nurse said; "such things be."
"There's little hope," said Keir; "He's dying, sinking."
"Dying without his son," the young girl's heart was thinking.

"Does Michael know?" she asked. "Has he been called?"
A slow confusion reddened on the faces,
As when one light neglect leaves friends appalled.

"No time to think," said nurse, "in such like cases."
Old Occleve stooped and fumbled with his laces.
"Let be," he said; "there's always time for sorrow.
He could not come in time; he shall be called to-morrow."

"There is a chance," she cried, "there always is.
Poor Mr. Gray might rally, might live on.
Oh, I must telegraph to tell him this.
Would it were day still and the message gone."
She rose, her breath came fast, her grey eyes shone.
She said, "Come Lion; see me through the wood.
Michael must know." Keir sighed. "Girl, it will do no good.

"Our friend is on the brink and almost passed."
"All the more need," she said, "for word to go;
Michael could well arrive before the last.
He'd see his father's face at least. I know
The office may be closed; but even so,
Father, I must. Come, Lion." Out they went,
Into the roaring woodland where the saplings bent.

Like breakers of the sea the leafless branches
Swished, bowing down, rolling like water, roaring
Like the sea's welcome when the clipper launches
And full affronted tideways call to warring.
Daffodils glimmered underfoot, the flooring
Of the earthy woodland smelt like torn-up moss;
Stones in the path showed white, and rabbits ran across.

They climbed the rise and struck into the ride,
Talking of death, while Lion, sick at heart,
Thought of the woman walking at his side,
And as he talked his spirit stood apart,
Old passion for her made his being smart,
Rankling within. Her thought for Michael ran
Like glory and like poison through his inner man.

"This will break Michael's heart," he said at length.
"Poor Michael," she replied; "they wasted hours.
He loved his father so. God give him strength.
This is a cruel thing this life of ours."
The windy woodland glimmered with shut flowers,
White wood anemones that the wind blew down.
The valley opened wide beyond the starry town.

"Ten," clanged out of the belfry. Lion stayed
One hand upon a many-carven bole.
"Mary," he said. "Dear, my beloved maid,
I love you, dear one, from my very soul."
Her beauty in the dusk destroyed control.
"Mary, my dear, I've loved you all these years."
"Oh, Lion, no," she murmured, choking back her tears.

"I love you," he repeated. "Five years since
This thing began between us: every day
Oh sweet, the thought of you has made me wince;
The thought of you, my sweet, the look, the way.
It's only you, whether I work or play,
You and the hope of you, sweet you, dear you.
I never spoke before; now it has broken through.

"Oh, my belovéd, can you care for me?"
She shook her head. "O, hush, oh, Lion dear,
Don't speak of love, for it can never be
Between us two, never, however near.
Come on, my friend, we must not linger here."
White to the lips she spoke; he saw her face
White in the darkness by him in the windy place.

"Mary, in time you could, perhaps," he pleaded.
"No," she replied, "no, Lion; never, no."
Over the stars the boughs burst and receded.

The nobleness of Love comes in Love's woe.
"God bless you then, belovéd, let us go.
Come on," he said, "and if I gave you pain,
Forget it, dear; be sure I never will again."

They stepped together down the ride, their feet
Slipped on loose stones. Little was said; his fate,
Staked on a kingly cast, had met defeat.
Nothing remained but to endure and wait.
She was still wonderful, and life still great.
Great in that bitter instant side by side,
Hallowed by thoughts of death there in the blinded ride.

He heard her breathing by him, saw her face
Dim, looking straight ahead; her feet by his
Kept time beside him, giving life a grace;
Night made the moment full of mysteries.
"You are beautiful," he thought; "and life is this:
Walking a windy night while men are dying,
To cry for one to come, and none to heed our crying."

"Mary," he said, "are you in love with him,
With Michael? Tell me. We are friends, we three."
They paused to face each other in the dim.
"Tell me," he urged. "Yes, Lion," answered she;
"I love him, but he does not care for me.
I trust your generous mind, dear; now you know,
You, who have been my brother, how our fortunes go.

"Now come; the message waits." The heavens cleared,
Cleared, and were starry as they trod the ride.
Chequered by tossing boughs the moon appeared;
A whistling reached them from the Hall House side;
Climbing, the whistler came. A brown owl cried.
The whistler paused to answer, sending far
That haunting, hunting note. The echoes laughed Aha!

Something about the calling made them start.
Again the owl note laughed; the ringing cry
Made the blood quicken within Mary's heart.
Like a dead leaf a brown owl floated by.
"Michael?" said Lion. "Hush." An owl's reply
Came down the wind; they waited; then the man,
Content, resumed his walk, a merry song began.

"Michael," they cried together. "Michael, you?"
"Who calls?" the singer answered. "Where away?
Is that you, Mary?" Then with glad halloo
The singer ran to meet them on the way.
It was their Michael; in the moonlight grey,
They made warm welcome; under tossing boughs,
They met and told the fate darkening Ryemeadows' House.

As they returned at speed their comrade spoke
Strangely and lightly of his coming home,
Saying that leaving France had been a joke,
But that events now proved him wise to come.
Down the steep 'scarpment to the house they clomb,
And Michael faltered in his pace; they heard
How dumb rebellion in the much-wronged cattle stirred.

And as they came, high, from the sick man's room,
Old Gray burst out a-singing of the light
Streaming upon him from the outer gloom,
As his eyes dying gave him mental sight.
"Triumphing swords," he carolled, "in the bright;
Oh fire, Oh beauty fire," and fell back dead.
Occleve took Michael up to kneel beside the bed.

So the night passed; the noisy wind went down;
The half-burnt moon her starry trackway rode.
Then the first fire was lighted in the town,

And the first carter stacked his early load.
Upon the farm's drawn blinds the morning glowed;
And down the valley, with little clucks and trills,
The dancing waters danced by dancing daffodils.

II

They buried Gray; his gear was sold; his farm
Passed to another tenant. Thus men go;
The dropped sword passes to another arm,
And different waters in the river flow.
His two old faithful friends let Michael know
His father's ruin and their promise. Keir
Brought him to stay at Foxholes till a path was clear.

There, when the sale was over, all three met
To talk about the future, and to find
Upon what project Michael's heart was set.
Gentle the two old men were, thoughtful, kind.
They urged the youth to speak his inmost mind,
For they would compass what he chose; they told
How he might end his training; they would find the gold.

"Thanks, but I cannot," Michael said. He smiled.
"Cannot. They've kicked me out. I've been expelled;
Kicked out for good and all for being wild.
They stopped our evening leave, and I rebelled.
I am a gentle soul until compelled,
And then I put my ears back. The old fool
Said that my longer presence might inflame the school.

"And I am glad, for I have had my fill
Of farming by the book with those old fools,
Exhausted talkatives whose blood is still,
Who strive to bind a living man with rules.

This fettered kind of life, these laws, these schools,
These codes, these checks, what are they but the clogs
Made by collected sheep to mortify the dogs?

"And I have had enough of them; and now
I make an end of them. I want to go
Somewhere where man has never used a plough,
Nor ever read a book; where clean winds blow,
And passionate blood is not its owner's foe,
And land is for the asking for it. There
Man can create a life and have the open air.

"The River Plate's the country. There, I know,
A man like me can thrive. There, on the range,
The cattle pass like tides; they ebb and flow,
And life is changeless in unending change,
And one can ride all day, and all day strange,
Strange, never trodden, fenceless, waiting there,
To feed unending cattle for the men who dare.

"There I should have a chance; this land's too old."
Old Occleve grunted at the young man's mood;
Keir, who was losing money, thought him bold,
And thought the scheme for emigration good.
He said that, if he wished to go, he should.
South to the pampas, there to learn the trade.
Old Occleve thought it mad, but no objection made.

So it was settled that the lad should start,
A place was found for him, a berth was taken;
And Michael's beauty plucked at Mary's heart,
And now the fabric of their lives was shaken:
For now the hour's nearness made love waken
In Michael's heart for Mary. Now Time's guile
Granted her passionate prayer, nor let her see his smile:

Granted his greatest gifts; a night-time came
When the two walking down the water learned
That life till then had only been a name.
Love had unsealed their spirits: they discerned.
Mutely, at moth-time there, their spirits yearned.
"I shall be gone three years, dear soul," he said.
"Dear, will you wait for me?" "I will," replied the maid.

So troth was pledged between them. Keir received
Michael as Mary's suitor, feeling sure
That the lad's fortunes would be soon retrieved,
Having a woman's promise as a lure.
The three years' wait would teach them to endure.
He bade them love and prosper and be glad.
And fast the day drew near that was to take the lad.

Cowslips had come along the bubbling brook,
Cowslips and oxlips rare, and in the wood
The many-blossomed stalks of bluebells shook;
The outward beauty fed their mental mood.
Thought of the parting stabbed her as he wooed,
Walking the brook with her, and day by day,
The precious fortnight's grace dropped, wasted, slipped away.

Till only one clear day remained to her:
One whole clear, precious day, before he sailed.
Some forty hours, no more, to minister
To months of bleakness before which she quailed.
Mist rose along the brook; the corncrake railed;
Dim red the sunset burned. He bade her come
Into the wood with him; they went, the night came dumb.

Still as high June, the very water's noise
Seemed but a breathing of the earth; the flowers
Stood in the dim like souls without a voice.

The wood's conspiracy of occult powers
Drew all about them, and for hours on hours
No murmur shook the oaks, the stars did house
Their lights like lamps upon those never-moving boughs.

Under their feet the woodland sloped away
Down to the valley, where the farmhouse lights
Were sparks in the expanse the moon made grey.
June's very breast was bare this night of nights.
Moths blundered up against them, greys and whites
Moved on the darkness where the moths were out,
Nosing for sticky sweet with trembling uncurled snout.

But all this beauty was but music played,
While the high pageant of their hearts prepared.
A spirit thrilled between them, man to maid,
Mind flowed in mind, the inner heart was bared,
They needed not to tell how much each cared;
All the soul's strength was at the other's soul.
Flesh was away awhile, a glory made them whole.

Nothing was said by them; they understood,
They searched each other's eyes without a sound.
Alone with moonlight in the heart of the wood,
Knowing the stars and all the soul of the ground.
"Mary," he murmured. "Come." His arms went round.
A white moth glimmered by, the woods were hushed;
The rose at Mary's bosom dropped its petals, crushed.

No word profaned the peace of that glad giving,
But the warm dimness of the night stood still,
Drawing all beauty to the point of living,
There in the beech-tree's shadow on the hill.
Spirit to spirit murmured; mingling will
Made them one being; Time's decaying thought
Fell from them like a rag; it was the soul they sought.

The moonlight found an opening in the boughs;
It entered in, it filled that sacred place
With consecration on the throbbing brows;
It came with benediction and with grace.
A whispering came from face to yearning face:
"Beloved, will you wait for me?" "My own."
"I shall be gone three years, you will be left alone;

"You'll trust and wait for me?" "Yes, yes," she sighed;
She would wait any term of years, all time—
So faithful to first love these souls abide,
Carrying a man's soul with them as they climb.
Life was all flower to them; the church bells' chime
Rang out the burning hour ere they had sealed
Love's charter there below the June sky's starry field.

Sweetly the church bells' music reached the wood,
Chiming an old slow tune of some old hymn,
Calling them back to life from where they stood
Under the moonlit beech-tree grey and dim.
"Mary," he murmured; pressing close to him,
Her kiss came on the gift he gave her there,
A silken scarf that bore her name worked in his hair.

But still the two affixed their hands and seals
To a life compact witnessed by the sky,
Where the great planets drove their glittering wheels,
Bringing conflicting fate, making men die.
They loved, and she would wait, and he would try.
"Oh, beauty of my love," "My lovely man."
So beauty made them noble for their little span.

Time cannot pause, however dear the wooer;
The moon declined, the sunrise came, the hours,
Left to the lovers, dwindled swiftly fewer,

Even as the seeds from dandelion-flowers
Blow, one by one, until the bare stalk cowers,
And the June grass grows over; even so
Daffodil-picker Time took from their lives the glow,

Stole their last walk along the three green fields,
Their latest hour together; he took, he stole
The white contentment that a true love yields;
He took the triumph out of Mary's soul.
Now she must lie awake and blow the coal
Of sorrow of heart. The parting hour came;
They kissed their last good-bye, murmuring the other's name.

Then the flag waved, the engine snorted, then
Slowly the couplings tautened, and the train
Moved, bearing off from her her man of men;
She looked towards it going blind with pain.
Her father turned and drove her home again.
It was a different home. Awhile she tried
To cook the dinner there, but flung her down and cried.

Then in the dusk she wandered down the brook,
Treading again the trackway trod of old,
When she could hold her loved-one in a look.
The night was all unlike those nights of gold.
Michael was gone, and all the April old,
Withered and hidden. Life was full of ills;
She flung her down and cried i' the withered daffodils.

III

The steaming river loitered like old blood
On which the tugboat bearing Michael beat,
Past whitened horse bones sticking in the mud.
The reed stems looked like metal in the heat.

Then the banks fell away, and there were neat,
Red herds of sullen cattle drifting slow.
A fish leaped, making rings, making the dead blood flow.

Wormed hard-wood piles were driv'n in the river bank,
The steamer threshed alongside with sick screws
Churning the mud below her till it stank;
Big gassy butcher-bubbles burst on the ooze.
There Michael went ashore; as glad to lose
One not a native there, the Gauchos flung
His broken gear ashore, one waved, a bell was rung.

The bowfast was cast off, the screw revolved,
Making a bloodier bubbling; rattling rope
Fell to the hatch, the engine's tune resolved
Into its steadier beat of rise and slope;
The steamer went her way; and Michael's hope
Died as she lessened; he was there alone.
The lowing of the cattle made a gradual moan.

He thought of Mary, but the thought was dim;
That was another life, lived long before.
His mind was in new worlds which altered him.
The startling present left no room for more.
The sullen river lipped, the sky, the shore
Were vaster than of old, and lonely, lonely.
Sky and low hills of grass and moaning cattle only.

But for a hut bestrewn with skulls of beeves,
Round which the flies danced, where an Indian girl
Bleared at him from her eyes' ophthalmic eaves,
Grinning a welcome; with a throaty skirl,
She offered him herself; but he, the churl,
Stared till she thought him fool; she turned, she sat,
Scratched in her short, black hair, chewed a cigar-end, spat.

Up, on the rise, the cattle bunched; the bulls
Drew to the front with menace, pawing bold,
Snatching the grass-roots out with sudden pulls,
The distant cattle raised their heads; the wold
Grew dusty at the top; a waggon rolled,
Drawn by a bickering team of mules whose eyes
Were yellow like their teeth and bared and full of vice.

Down to the jetty came the jingling team,
An Irish cowboy driving, while a Greek
Beside him urged the mules with blow and scream.
They cheered the Indian girl and stopped to speak.
Then lifting her aloft they kissed her cheek,
Calling to Michael to be quick aboard,
Or they (they said) would fall from virtue, by the Lord.

So Michael climbed aboard, and all day long
He drove the cattle range, rise after rise,
Dotted with limber shorthorns grazing strong,
Cropping sweet-tasted pasture, switching flies;
Dull trouble brooded in their smoky eyes.
Some horsemen watched them. As the sun went down,
The waggon reached the estancia builded like a town.

With wide corràles where the horses squealed,
Biting and lashing out; some half-wild hounds
Gnawed at the cowbones littered on the field,
Or made the stallions stretch their picket bounds.
Some hides were drying; horsemen came from rounds,
Unsaddled stiff, and turned their mounts to feed,
And then brewed bitter drink and sucked it through a reed.

The Irishman removed his pipe and spoke:
"You take a fool's advice," he said. "Return.
Go back where you belong before you're broke:

The riot with the cowboys seemed unkind
To that far faithful heart; he could not find
Peace in the thought of her; he found no spur
To instant upright action in his love for her.

She faded to the memory of a kiss,
There in the rough life among foreign faces;
Love cannot live where leisure never is;
He could not write to her from savage places,
Where drunken mates were betting on the aces,
And rum went round and smutty songs were lifted.
He would not raise her banner against that; he drifted,

Ceasing, in time, to write, ceasing to think,
But happy in the wild life to the bone;
The riding in vast space, the songs, the drink,
Some careless heart beside him like his own,
The racing and the fights, the ease unknown
In older, soberer lands; his young blood thrilled.
The pampas seemed his own, his cup of joy was filled.

And one day, riding far after strayed horses,
He rode beyond the ranges to a land
Broken and made most green by watercourses,
Which served as strayline to the neighbouring brand.
A house stood near the brook; he stayed his hand,
Seeing a woman there, whose great eyes burned,
So that he could not choose but follow when she turned

After that day he often rode to see
That woman at the peach farm near the brook,
And passionate love between them came to be
Ere many days. Their fill of love they took;
And even as the blank leaves of a book
The days went over Mary, day by day,
Blank as the last, was turned, endured, passed, turned away.

Spring came again greening the hawthorn buds;
The shaking flowers, new-blossomed, seemed the same,
And April put her riot in young bloods;
The jays flapped in the larch clump like blue flame.
She did not care; his letter never came.
Silent she went, nursing the grief that kills,
And Lion watched her pass among the daffodils.

IV

Time passed, but still no letter came; she ceased,
Almost, to hope, but never to expect.
The June moon came which had beheld love's feast,
Then waned, like it; the meadow-grass was flecked
With moon-daisies, which died; little she recked
Of change in outward things, she did not change;
Her heart still knew one star, one hope, it did not range,

Like to the watery hearts of tidal men,
Swayed by all moons of beauty; she was firm,
When most convinced of misery firmest then.
She held a light not subject to the worm.
The pageant of the summer ran its term,
The last stack came to staddle from the wain;
The snow fell, the snow thawed, the year began again.

With the wet glistening gold of celandines,
And snowdrops pushing from the withered grass,
Before the bud upon the hawthorn greens,
Or blackbirds go to building; but, alas!
No spring within her bosom came to pass.
"You're going like a ghost," her father said.
"Now put him out of mind, and be my prudent maid."

It was an April morning brisk with wind,
She wandered out along the brook sick-hearted,
Picking the daffodils where the water dinned,

While overhead the first-come swallow darted.
There, at the place where all the passion started,
Where love first knocked about her maiden heart,
Young Lion Occleve hailed her, calling her apart

To see his tulips at the Roughs, and take
A spray of flowering currant; so she went.
It is a bitter moment, when hearts ache,
To see the loved unhappy; his intent
Was but to try comfort her; he meant
To show her that he knew her heart's despair,
And that his own heart bled to see her wretched there.

So, as they talked, he asked her, had she heard
From Michael lately? No, she had not; she
Had been a great while now, without a word.
"No news is always good news," answered he.
"You know," he said, "how much you mean to me;
You've always been the queen. Oh, if I could
Do anything to help, my dear, you know I would."

"Nothing," she said, much touched. "But you believe—
You still believe in him?" "Why, yes," he said.
Lie though it was he did not dare deceive
The all too cruel faith within the maid.
"That ranching is a wild and lonely trade,
Far from all posts; it may be hard to send;
All puzzling things like this prove simple in the end.

"We should have heard if he were ill or dead.
Keep a good heart. Now come"; he led the way
Beyond the barton to the calving-shed,
Where, on a strawy litter topped with hay,
A double-pedigree prize bull-calf lay.
"Near three weeks old," he said, "the Wrekin's pet;
Come up, now, son, come up; you haven't seen him yet.

"We have done well," he added, "with the stock,
But this one, if he lives, will make a name."
The bull-calf gambolled with his tail acock,
Then shyly nosed towards them, scared but tame;
His troublous eyes were sulky with blue flame.
Softly he tip-toed, shying at a touch;
He nosed, his breath came sweet, his pale tongue curled to clutch.

They rubbed his head, and Mary went her way,
Counting the dreary time, the dreary beat
Of dreary minutes dragging through the day;
Time crawled across her life with leaden feet;
There still remained a year before her sweet
Would come to claim her; surely he would come;
Meanwhile there was the year, her weakening father, home.

Home with its deadly round, with all its setting,
Things, rooms, and fields and flowers to sting, to burn
With memories of the love time past forgetting
Ere absence made her very being yearn.
"My love, be quick," she moaned, "return, return;
Come when the three years end, oh, my dear soul,
It's bitter, wanting you." The lonely nights took toll,

Putting a sadness where the beauty was,
Taking a lustre from the hair; the days
Saw each a sadder image in the glass.
And when December came, fouling the ways,
And ashless beech-logs made a Christmas blaze,
Some talk of Michael came; a rumour ran,
Someone had called him "wild" to some returning man,

Who, travelling through that cattle-range, had heard
Nothing more sure than this; but this he told
At second-hand upon a cowboy's word.

It struck on Mary's heart and turned her cold.
That winter was an age which made her old.
"But soon," she thought, "soon the third year will end;
March, April, May, and June, then I shall see my friend.

"He promised he would come; he will not fail.
Oh, Michael, my beloved man, come soon;
Stray not to make a home for me, but sail.
Love and the hour will put the world in tune.
You in my life for always is the boon
I ask from life—we two, together, lovers."
So leaden time went by who eats things and discovers.

Then, in the winds of March, her father rode,
Hunting the Welland country on Black Ned;
The tenor cry gave tongue past Clencher's Lode,
And on he galloped, giving the nag his head;
Then, at the brook, he fell, was picked up dead.
Hounds were whipped off; men muttered with one breath,
"We knew that hard-mouthed brute would some day be his death."

They bore his body on a hurdle home;
Then came the burial, then the sadder day
When the peaked lawyer entered like a gnome,
With word to quit and lists of debts to pay.
There was a sale; the Foxholes passed away
To strangers, who discussed the points of cows,
Where love had put such glory on the lovers' brows.

Kind Lion Occleve helped the maid's affairs.
Her sorrow brought him much beside her; he
Caused her to settle, having stilled her cares,
In the long cottage under Spital Gree.
He had no hope that she would love him; she
Still waited for her lover, but her eyes
Thanked Lion to the soul; he made the look suffice.

By this the yearling bull-calf had so grown
That all men talked of him; mighty he grew,
Huge-shouldered, scaled above a hundred stone,
With deep chest many-wrinkled with great thew,
Plain-loined and playful-eyed; the Occleves knew
That he surpassed his pasture; breeders came
From far to see this bull; he brought the Occleves fame.

Till a meat-breeding rancher on the plains
Where Michael wasted, sent to buy the beast,
Meaning to cross his cows with heavier strains
Until his yield of meat and bone increased.
He paid a mighty price; the yearling ceased
To be the wonder of the countryside.
He sailed in Lion's charge, south, to the Plate's red tide.

There Lion landed with the bull, and there
The great beast raised his head and bellowed loud,
Challenging that expanse and that new air;
Trembling, but full of wrath and thunder-browed,
Far from the daffodil fields and friends, but proud,
His wild eye kindled at the great expanse.
Two scraps of Shropshire life they stood there; their advance

Was slow along the well-grassed cattle land,
But at the last an end was made; the brute
Ate his last bread crust from his master's hand,
And snuffed the foreign herd and stamped his foot;
Steers on the swelling ranges gave salute.
The great bull bellowed back and Lion turned;
His task was now to find where Michael lived; he learned

The farm's direction, and with heavy mind,
Thinking of Mary and her sorrow, rode,
Leaving the offspring of his fields behind.

A last time in his ears the great bull lowed.
Then, shaking up his horse, the young man glowed
To see the unfenced pampas opening out
Grass that makes old earth sing and all the valleys shout.

At sunset on the second day he came
To that white cabin in the peach-tree plot
Where Michael lived; they met, the Shropshire name
Rang trebly dear in that outlandish spot.
Old memories swam up dear, old joys forgot,
Old friends were real again; but Mary's woe
Came into Lion's mind, and Michael vexed him so,

Talking with careless freshness, side by side
With that dark Spanish beauty who had won,
As though no heart-broke woman, heavy-eyed,
Mourned for him over sea, as though the sun
Shone but to light his steps to love and fun,
While she, that golden and beloved soul,
Worth ten of him, lay wasting like an unlit coal.

So supper passed; the meat in Lion's gorge
Stuck at the last, he could not bide that face.
The idle laughter on it plied the forge
Where hate was smithying tools; the jokes, the place,
Wrought him to wrath; he could not stay for grace.
The tin mug full of red wine spilled and fell,
He kicked his stool aside with "Michael, this is hell.

"Come out into the night and talk to me."
The young man lit a cigarette and followed;
The stars seemed trembling at a brink to see;
A little ghostly white-owl stooped and hollowed.
Beside the stake-fence Lion stopped and swallowed,
While all the wrath within him made him grey.
Michael stood still and smoked, and flicked his ash away.

"Well, Lion," Michael said, "men make mistakes,
And then regret them; and an early flame
Is frequently the worst mistake man makes.
I did not seek this passion, but it came.
Love happens so in life. Well? Who's to blame?
You'll say I've broken Mary's heart; the heart
Is not the whole of life, but an inferior part,

"Useful for some few years and then a curse.
Nerves should be stronger. You have come to say
The three-year term is up; so much the worse.
I cannot meet the bill; I cannot pay.
I would not if I could. Men change. To-day
I know that that first choice, however sweet,
Was wrong and a mistake; it would have meant defeat,

"Ruin and misery to us both. Let be.
You say I should have told her this? Perhaps.
You try to make a loving woman see
That the warm link which holds you to her snaps.
Neglect is deadlier than the thunder-claps.
Yet she is bright and I am water. Well,
I did not make myself; this life is often hell.

"Judge if you must, but understand it first.
We are old friends, and townsmen, Shropshire born,
Under the Wrekin. You believe the worst.
You have no knowledge how the heart is torn,
Trying for duty up against the thorn.
Now say I've broken Mary's heart: begin.
Break hers, or hers and mine, which were the greater sin?"

"Michael," said Lion, "I have heard you. Now
Listen to me. Three years ago you made
With a most noble soul a certain vow.

Now you reject it, saying that you played.
She did not think so, Michael, she has stayed,
Eating her heart out for a line, a word,
News that you were not dead; news that she never heard.

"Not once, after the first. She has held firm
To what you counted pastime; she has wept
Life, day by weary day throughout the term,
While her heart sickened, and the clock-hand crept.
While you, you with your woman here, have kept
Holiday, feasting; you are fat; you smile.
You have had love and laughter all the ghastly while.

"I shall be back in England six weeks hence,
Standing with your poor Mary face to face;
Far from a pleasant moment, but intense.
I shall be asked to tell her of this place.
And she will eye me hard and hope for grace,
Some little crumb of comfort while I tell;
And every word will burn like a red spark from hell.

"That you have done with her, that you are living
Here with another woman; that you care
Nought for the pain you've given and are giving;
That all your lover's vows were empty air.
This I must tell: thus I shall burn her bare,
Burn out all hope, all comfort, every crumb,
End it, and watch her whiten, hopeless, tearless, dumb.

"Or do I judge you wrongly?" He was still.
The cigarette-end glowed and dimmed with ash;
A preying night bird whimpered on the hill.
Michael said "Ah!" and fingered with his sash,
Then stilled. The night was still; there came no flash
Of sudden passion bursting. All was still;
A lonely water gurgled like a whip-poor-will.

"Now I must go," said Lion; "where's the horse?"
"There," said his friend; "I'll set you on your way."
They caught and rode, both silent, while remorse
Worked in each heart, though neither would betray
What he was feeling, and the moon came grey,
Then burned into an opal white and great,
Silvering the downs of grass where these two travelled late,

Thinking of English fields which that moon saw,
Fields full of quiet beauty lying hushed
At midnight in the moment full of awe,
When the red fox comes creeping, dewy-brushed.
But neither spoke; they rode; the horses rushed,
Scattering the great clods skywards with such thrills
As colts in April feel there in the daffodils.

V

The river brimming full was silvered over
By moonlight at the ford; the river bank
Smelt of bruised clote buds and of yellow clover.
Nosing the gleaming dark the horses drank,
Drooping and dripping as the reins fell lank;
The men drooped too; the stars in heaven drooped;
Rank after hurrying rank the silver water trooped

In ceaseless bright procession past the shallows,
Talking its quick inconsequence. The friends,
Warmed by the gallop on the unfenced fallows,
Felt it a kindlier thing to make amends.
"A jolly burst," said Michael; "here it ends.
Your way lies straight beyond the water. There.
Watch for the lights, and keep those two stars as they bear."

Something august was quick in all that sky,
Wheeling in multitudinous march with fire;
The falling of the wind brought it more nigh,

They felt the earth take solace and respire;
The horses shifted foothold in the mire,
Splashing and making eddies. Lion spoke:
"Do you remember riding past the haunted oak

"That Christmas Eve, when all the bells were ringing,
So that we picked out seven churches' bells,
Ringing the night, and people carol-singing?
It hummed and died away and rose in swells
Like a sea breaking. We have been through hells
Since then, we two, and now this being here
Brings all that Christmas back, and makes it strangely near."

"Yes," Michael answered, "they were happy times,
Riding beyond there; but a man needs a change;
I know what they connote, those Christmas chimes,
Fudge in the heart, and pudding in the grange.
It stifles me all that; I need the range,
Like this before us, open to the sky;
There every wing is clipped, but here a man can fly."

"Ah," said his friend, "man only flies in youth,
A few short years at most, until he finds
That even quiet is a form of truth,
And all the rest a coloured rag that blinds.
Life offers nothing but contented minds.
Some day you'll know it, Michael. I am grieved
That Mary's heart will pay until I am believed."

There was a silence while the water dripped
From the raised muzzles champing on the steel.
Flogging the crannied banks the water lipped.
Night up above them turned her starry wheel;
And each man feared to let the other feel
How much he felt; they fenced; they put up bars.
The moon made heaven pale among the withering stars.

"Michael," said Lion, "why should we two part?
Ride on with me; or shall we both return,
Make preparation, and to-morrow start,
And travel home together? You would learn
How much the people long to see you; turn.
We will ride back and say good-bye, and then
Sail, and see home again, and see the Shropshire men,

"And see the old Shropshire mountain and the fair,
Full of drunk Welshmen bringing mountain ewes;
And partridge shooting would be starting there."
Michael hung down his head and seemed to choose.
The horses churned fresh footing in the ooze.
Then Michael asked if Tom were still alive,
Old Tom, who fought the Welshman under Upton Drive,

For nineteen rounds, on grass, with the bare hands?
"Shaky," said Lion, "living still, but weak;
Almost past speaking, but he understands."
"And old Shon Shones we teased so with the leek?"
"Dead." "When?" "December." Michael did not speak,
But muttered "Old Jones dead." A minute passed.
"What came to little Sue, his girl?" he said at last.

"Got into trouble with a man and died;
Her sister keeps the child." His hearer stirred.
"Dead, too? She was a pretty girl," he sighed,
"A graceful pretty creature, like a bird.
What is the child?" "A boy. Her sister heard
Too late to help; poor Susan died; the man
None knew who he could be, but many rumours ran."

"Ah," Michael said. The horses tossed their heads;
A little wind arising struck in chill;
"Time," he began, "that we were in our beds."

A distant heifer challenged from the hill,
Scraped at the earth with 's forefoot and was still.
"Come with me," Lion pleaded. Michael grinned;
He turned his splashing horse, and prophesied a wind.

"So long," he said, and "Kind of you to call.
Straight on, and watch the stars"; his horse's feet
Trampled the firmer foothold, ending all.
He flung behind no message to his sweet,
No other word to Lion; the dull beat
Of his horse's trample drummed upon the trail;
Lion could watch him drooping in the moonlight pale,

Drooping and lessening; half expectant still
That he would turn and greet him; but no sound
Came, save the lonely water's whip-poor-will
And the going horse-hoofs dying on the ground.
"Michael," he cried, "Michael!" A lonely mound
Beyond the water gave him back the cry.
"That's at an end," he said, "and I have failed her—I."

Soon the far hoof-beats died, save for a stir
Half heard, then lost, then still, then heard again.
A quickening rhythm showed he plied the spur.
Then a vast breathing silence took the plain.
The moon was like a soul within the brain
Of the great sleeping world; silent she rode
The water talked, talked, talked; it trembled as it flowed.

A moment Lion thought to ride in chase.
He turned, then turned again, knowing his friend.
He forded through with death upon his face,
And rode the plain that seemed never to end.
Clumps of pale cattle nosed the thing unkenned,
Riding the night; out of the night they rose,
Snuffing with outstretched heads, stamping with surly lows,

Till he was threading through a crowd, a sea
Of curious shorthorns backing as he came,
Barring his path, but shifting warily;
He slapped the hairy flanks of the more tame.
Unreal the ghostly cattle lumbered lame.
His horse kept at an even pace; the cows
Broke right and left like waves before advancing bows.

Lonely the pampas seemed amid that herd.
The thought of Mary's sorrow pricked him sore;
He brought no comfort for her, not a word;
He would not ease her pain, but bring her more.
The long miles dropped behind; lights rose before,
Lights and the seaport and the briny air;
And so he sailed for home to comfort Mary there.

* * * * * *

When Mary knew the worst she only sighed,
Looked hard at Lion's face, and sat quite still,
White to the lips, but stern and stony-eyed,
Beaten by life in all things but the will.
Though the blow struck her hard it did not kill.
She rallied on herself, a new life bloomed
Out of the ashy heart where Michael lay entombed.

And more than this: for Lion touched a sense
That he, the honest humdrum man, was more
Than he by whom the glory and the offence
Came to her life three bitter years before.
This was a treason in her being's core;
It smouldered there; meanwhile as two good friends
They met at autumn dusks and winter daylight-ends.

And once, after long twilight talk, he broke
His strong restraint upon his passion for her,
And burningly, most like a man he spoke,

Until her pity almost overbore her.
It could not be, she said; her pity tore her;
But still it could not be, though this was pain.
Then on a frosty night they met and spoke again.

And then he wooed again, clutching her hands,
Calling the maid his mind, his heart, his soul,
Saying that God had linked their lives in bands
When the worm Life first started from the goal;
That they were linked together, past control,
Linked from all time, could she but pity; she
Pitied from the soul, but said it could not be.

"Mary," he asked, "you cannot love me? No?"
"No," she replied; "would God I could, my dear."
"God bless you, then," he answered, "I must go,
Go over sea to get away from here,
I cannot think of work when you are near;
My whole life falls to pieces; it must end.
This meeting now must be 'good-bye,' beloved friend."

White-lipped she listened, then with failing breath,
She asked for yet a little time; her face
Was even as that of one condemned to death.
She asked for yet another three months' grace,
Asked it, as Lion inly knew, in case
Michael should still return; and "Yes" said he,
"I'll wait three months for you, beloved; let it be."

Slowly the three months dragged: no Michael came.
March brought the daffodils and set them shaking.
April was quick in Nature like green flame;
May came with dog-rose buds, and corncrakes craking,
Then dwindled like her blossom; June was breaking.
"Mary," said Lion, "can you answer now?"
White like a ghost she stood, he long remembered how.

Wild-eyed and white, and trembling like a leaf,
She gave her answer, "Yes"; she gave her lips,
Cold as a corpse's to the kiss of grief,
Shuddering at him as if his touch were whips.
Then her best nature, struggling to eclipse
This shrinking self, made speech; she jested there;
They searched each other's eyes, and both souls saw despair.

So the first passed, and after that began
A happier time: she could not choose but praise
That recognition of her in the man
Striving to salve her pride in myriad ways;
He was a gentle lover: gentle days
Passed like a music after tragic scenes;
Her heart gave thanks for that, but still the might-have-beens

Haunted her inner spirit day and night,
And often in his kiss the memory came
Of Michael's face above her, passionate, white,
His lips at her lips murmuring her name,
Then she would suffer sleepless, sick with shame,
And struggle with her weakness. She had vowed
To give herself to Lion; she was true and proud.

He should not have a woman sick with ghosts,
But one firm-minded to be his; so time
Passed one by one the summer's marking posts,
The dog-rose and the fox-glove and the lime.
Then on a day the church-bells rang a chime.
Men fired the bells till all the valley filled
With bell-noise from the belfry where the jackdaws build.

Lion and she were married; home they went,
Home to The Roughs as man and wife; the news
Was printed in the paper. Mary sent
A copy out to Michael. Now we lose

Sight of her for a time, and the great dews
Fall, and the harvest-moon grows red and fills
Over the barren fields where March brings daffodils.

VI

The rider lingered at the fence a moment,
Tossed out the pack to Michael, whistling low,
Then rode, waving his hand, without more comment,
Down the vast grey-green pampas sloping slow.
Michael's last news had come so long ago,
He wondered who had written now; the hand
Thrilled him with vague alarm, it brought him to a stand.

He opened it with one eye on the hut,
Lest she within were watching him, but she
Was combing out her hair, the door was shut,
The green sun-shutters closed, she could not see.
Out fell the love-tryst handkerchief which he
Had had embroidered with his name for her;
It had been dearly kept, it smelt of lavender.

Something remained: a paper, crossed with blue,
Where he should read; he stood there in the sun,
Reading of Mary's wedding till he knew
What he had cast away, what he had done.
He was rejected, Lion was the one.
Lion, the godly and the upright, he.
The black lines in the paper showed how it could be.

He pocketed the love-gift and took horse,
And rode out to the pay-shed for his savings.
Then turned, and rode a lonely water-course,
Alone with bitter thoughts and bitter cravings.
Sun-shadows on the reeds made twinkling wavings;
An orange-bellied turtle scooped the mud;
Mary had married Lion, and the news drew blood.

And with the bitterness, the outcast felt
A passion for those old kind Shropshire places.
The ruined chancel where the nuns had knelt;
High Ercall and the Chase End and the Chases,
The glimmering mere, the burr, the well-known faces,
By Wrekin and by Zine and country town.
The orange-bellied turtle burrowed further down.

He could remember Mary now; her crying
Night after night alone through weary years,
Had touched him now and set the cords replying;
He knew her misery now, her ache, her tears,
The lonely nights, the ceaseless hope, the fears,
The arm stretched out for one not there, the slow
Loss of the lover's faith, the letting comfort go.

"Now I will ride," he said. Beyond the ford
He caught a fresh horse and rode on. The night
Found him a guest at Pepe Blanco's board,
Moody and drinking rum and ripe for fight;
Drawing his gun, he shot away the light,
And parried Pepe's knife and caught his horse,
And all night long he rode bedevilled by remorse.

At dawn he caught an eastward-going ferry,
And all day long he steamed between great banks
Which smelt of yellow thorn and loganberry.
Then wharves appeared, and chimneys rose in ranks,
Mast upon mast arose; the river's flanks
Were filled with English ships, and one he found
Needing another stoker, being homeward bound.

And all the time the trouble in his head
Ran like a whirlwind moving him; he knew
Since she was lost that he was better dead.
He had no project outlined, what to do,

Beyond go home; he joined the steamer's crew.
She sailed that night: he dulled his maddened soul,
Plying the iron coal-slice on the bunker coal.

Work did not clear the turmoil in his mind;
Passion takes colour from the nature's core;
His misery was as his nature, blind.
Life was still turmoil when he went ashore.
To see his old love married lay before;
To see another have her, drink the gall,
Kicked like a dog without, while he within had all.

* * * * *

Soon he was at the Foxholes, at the place
Whither, from over sea, his heart had turned
Often at evening-ends in times of grace.
But little outward change his eye discerned;
A red rose at her bedroom window burned,
Just as before. Even as of old the wasps
Poised at the yellow plums: the gate creaked on its hasps,

And the white fantails sidled on the roof
Just as before; their pink feet, even as of old,
Printed the frosty morning's rime with proof.
Still the zew-tallat's thatch was green with mould;
The apples on the withered boughs were gold.
Men and the times were changed: "And I," said he,
"Will go and not return, since she is not for me.

"I'll go, for it would be a scurvy thing
To spoil her marriage, and besides, she cares
For that half-priest she married with the ring.
Small joy for me in seeing how she wears,
Or seeing what he takes and what she shares.
That beauty and those ways: she had such ways,
There in the daffodils in those old April days."

So with an impulse of good will he turned,
Leaving that place of daffodils; the road
Was paven sharp with memories which burned;
He trod them strongly under as he strode.
At the Green Turning's forge the furnace glowed;
Red dithying sparks flew from the crumpled soft
Fold from the fire's heart; down clanged the hammers oft.

That was a bitter place to pass, for there
Mary and he had often, often stayed
To watch the horseshoe growing in the glare.
It was a tryst in childhood when they strayed.
There was a stile beside the forge; he laid
His elbows on it, leaning, looking down
The river-valley stretched with great trees turning brown.

Infinite, too, because it reached the sky,
And distant spires arose and distant smoke;
The whiteness on the blue went stilly by;
Only the clinking forge the stillness broke.
Ryemeadows brook was there; The Roughs, the oak
Where the White Woman walked; the black firs showed
Around the Occleve homestead, Mary's new abode.

A long, long time he gazed at that fair place,
So well remembered from of old; he sighed.
"I will go down and look upon her face,
See her again, whatever may betide.
Hell is my future; I shall soon have died,
But I will take to hell one memory more;
She shall not see nor know; I shall be gone before;

"Before they turn the dogs upon me, even.
I do not mean to speak; but only see.
Even the devil gets a peep at heaven;
One peep at her shall come to hell with me:

One peep at her, no matter what may be."
He crossed the stile and hurried down the slope.
Remembered trees and hedges gave a zest to hope.

* * * * * *

A low brick wall with privet shrubs beyond
Ringed in The Roughs upon the side he neared.
Eastward some bramble bushes cloaked the pond;
Westward was barley-stubble not yet cleared.
He thrust aside the privet boughs and peered.
The drooping fir trees let their darkness trail
Black like a pirate's masts bound under easy sail.

The garden with its autumn flowers was there;
Few that his wayward memory linked with her:
Summer had burnt the summer flowers bare,
But honey-hunting bees still made a stir.
Sprigs were still bluish on the lavender,
And bluish daisies budded, bright flies poised;
The wren upon the tree-stump carolled cheery-voiced.

He could not see her there. Windows were wide,
Late wasps were cruising, and the curtains shook.
Smoke, like the house's breathing, floated, sighed,
Among the trembling firs strange ways it took.
But still no Mary's presence blessed his look;
The house was still as if deserted, hushed.
Faint fragrance hung about it as if herbs were crushed,

Fragrance that gave his memory's guard a hint
Of times long past, of reapers in the corn,
Bruising with heavy boots the stalks of mint,
When first the berry reddens on the thorn.
Memories of her that fragrance brought. Forlorn
That vigil of the watching outcast grew;
He crept towards the kitchen, sheltered by a yew.

The windows of the kitchen opened wide.
Again the fragrance came; a woman spoke;
Old Mrs. Occleve talked to one inside.
A smell of cooking filled a gust of smoke.
Then fragrance once again, for herbs were broke;
Pourri was being made; the listener heard
Things lifted and laid down, bruised into sweetness, stirred.

While an old woman made remarks to one
Who was not the beloved: Michael learned
That Roger's wife at Upton had a son,
And that the red geraniums should be turned;
A hen was missing, and a rick was burned;
Our Lord commanded patience; here it broke;
The window closed, it made the kitchen chimney smoke.

Steps clacked on flagstones to the outer door;
A dairy-maid, whom he remembered well,
Lined, now, with age, and greyer than before,
Rang a cracked cow-bell for the dinner-bell.
He saw the dining-room; he could not tell
If Mary were within: inly he knew
That she was coming now, that she would be in blue,

Blue with a silver locket at the throat,
And that she would be there, within there, near,
With the little blushes that he knew by rote,
And the grey eyes so steadfast and so dear,
The voice, pure like the nature, true and clear,
Speaking to her belov'd within the room.
The gate clicked, Lion came: the outcast hugged the gloom,

Watching intently from below the boughs,
While Lion cleared his riding-boots of clay,
Eyed the high clouds and went within the house.

His eyes looked troubled, and his hair looked grey.
Dinner began within with much to say.
Old Occleve roared aloud at his own joke.
Mary, it seemed, was gone; the loved voice never spoke.

Nor could her lover see her from the yew;
She was not there at table; she was ill,
Ill, or away perhaps—he wished he knew.
Away, perhaps, for Occleve bellowed still.
"If sick," he thought, "the maid or Lion will
Take food to her." He watched; the dinner ended.
The staircase was not used; none climbed it, none descended.

"Not here," he thought; but wishing to be sure,
He waited till the Occleves went to field,
Then followed, round the house, another lure,
Using the well-known privet as his shield.
He meant to run a risk; his heart was steeled.
He knew of old which bedroom would be hers;
He crouched upon the north front in among the firs.

The house stared at him with its red-brick blank,
Its vacant window-eyes; its open door,
With old wrought bridle ring-hooks at each flank,
Swayed on a creaking hinge as the wind bore.
Nothing had changed; the house was as before,
The dull red brick, the windows sealed or wide:
"I will go in," he said. He rose and stepped inside.

None could have seen him coming; all was still;
He listened in the doorway for a sign.
Above, a rafter creaked, a stir, a thrill
Moved, till the frames clacked on the picture line.
"Old Mother Occleve sleeps, the servants dine,"
He muttered, listening. "Hush." A silence brooded.
Far off the kitchen dinner clattered; he intruded.

Still, to his right, the best room door was *l*ocked.
Another door was at his left; he stayed.
Within, a stately timepiece ticked and tocked,
To one who slumbered breathing deep; it made
An image of Time's going and man's trade.
He looked: Old Mother Occleve lay asleep,
Hands crossed upon her knitting, rosy, breathing deep.

He tiptoed up the stairs which creaked and cracked.
The landing creaked; the shut doors, painted grey,
Loomed, as if shutting in some dreadful act.
The nodding frames seemed ready to betray.
The east room had been closed in Michael's day,
Being the best; but now he guessed it hers;
The fields of daffodils lay next it, past the firs.

Just as he reached the landing, Lion cried,
Somewhere below, "I'll get it." Lion's feet
Struck on the flagstones with a hasty stride.
"He's coming up," thought Michael, "we shall meet."
He snatched the nearest door for his retreat,
Opened with thieves' swift silence, dared not close,
But stood within, behind it. Lion's footsteps rose,

Running two steps at once, while Michael stood,
Not breathing, only knowing that the room
Was someone's bedroom smelling of old wood,
Hung with engravings of the day of doom.
The footsteps stopped; and Lion called, to whom?
A gentle question, tapping at a door,
And Michael shifted feet, and creakings took the floor.

The footsteps recommenced, a door-catch clacked;
Within an eastern room the footsteps passed.
Drawers were pulled loudly open and ransacked,

Chattels were thrust aside and overcast.
What could the thing be that he sought? At last
His voice said, "Here it is." The worméd floor
Creaked with returning footsteps down the corridor.

The footsteps came as though the walker read,
Or added rows of figures by the way;
There was much hesitation in the tread;
Lion seemed pondering which, to go or stay;
Then, seeing the door, which covered Michael, sway,
He swiftly crossed and shut it. "Always one
For order," Michael muttered. "Now be swift, my son."

The action seemed to break the walker's mood;
The footsteps passed downstairs, along the hall,
Out at the door and off towards the wood.
"Gone," Michael muttered. "Now to hazard all."
Outside, the frames still nodded on the wall.
Michael stepped swiftly up the floor to try
The door where Lion tapped and waited for reply.

It was the eastmost of the rooms which look
Over the fields of daffodils; the bound
Scanned from its windows is Ryemeadows brook,
Banked by gnarled apple trees and rising ground.
Most gently Michael tapped; he heard no sound,
Only the blind-pull tapping with the wind;
The kitchen-door was opened; kitchen-clatter dinned.

A woman walked along the hall below,
Humming; a maid, he judged; the footsteps died,
Listening intently still, he heard them go,
Then swiftly turned the knob and went inside.
The blind-pull at the window volleyed wide;
The curtains streamed out like a waterfall;
The pictures of the fox-hunt clacked along the wall.

No one was there; no one; the room was hers.
A book of praise lay open on the bed;
The clothes-press smelt of many lavenders,
Her spirit stamped the room; herself was fled.
Here she found peace of soul like daily bread,
Here, with her lover Lion; Michael gazed;
He would have been the sharer had he not been crazed.

He took the love-gift handkerchief again;
He laid it on her table, near the glass,
So opened that the broidered name was plain;
"Plain," he exclaimed, "she cannot let it pass.
It stands and speaks for me as bold as brass.
My answer, my heart's cry, to tell her this,
That she is still my darling: all she was she is.

"So she will know at least that she was wrong,
That underneath the blindness I was true.
Fate is the strongest thing, though men are strong;
Out from beyond life I was sealed to you.
But my blind ways destroyed the cords that drew;
And now, the evil done, I know my need;
Fate has his way with those who mar what is decreed.

"And now, goodbye." He closed the door behind him,
Then stept, with firm swift footstep down the stair,
Meaning to go where she would never find him;
He would go down through darkness to despair.
Out at the door he stept; the autumn air
Came fresh upon his face; none saw him go.
"Goodbye, my love," he muttered; "it is better so."

Soon he was on the high road, out of sight
Of valley and farm; soon he could see no more
The oast-house pointing finger take the light

As tumbling pigeons glittered over; nor
Could he behold the wind-vane gilded o'er,
Swinging above the church; the road swung round.
"Now, the last look," he cried: he saw that holy ground.

"Goodbye," he cried; he could behold it all,
Spread out as in a picture; but so clear
That the gold apple stood out from the wall;
Like a red jewel stood the grazing steer.
Precise, intensely coloured, all brought near,
As in a vision, lay that holy ground.
"Mary is there," he moaned, "and I am outward bound.

"I never saw this place so beautiful,
Never like this. I never saw it glow.
Spirit is on this place; it fills it full.
So let the die be cast; I will not go.
But I will see her face to face and know
From her own lips what thoughts she has of me;
And if disaster come: right; let disaster be."

Back, by another way, he turned. The sun
Fired the yew-tops in the Roman woods.
Lights in the valley twinkled one by one,
The starlings whirled in dropping multitudes.
Dusk fingered into one earth's many moods,
Back to The Roughs he walked; he neared the brook;
A lamp burned in the farm; he saw; his fingers shook.

He had to cross the brook, to cross a field,
Where daffodils were thick when years were young.
Then, were she there, his fortunes should be sealed.
Down the mud trackway to the brook he swung;
Then while the passion trembled on his tongue,
Dim, by the dim bridge-stile, he seemed to see
A figure standing mute; a woman—it was she.

She stood quite stilly, waiting for him there.
She did not seem surprised; the meeting seemed
Planned from all time by powers in the air
To change their human fates; he even deemed
That in another life this thing had gleamed,
This meeting by the bridge. He said, "It's you."
"Yes, I," she said, "who else? You must have known; you knew

"That I should come here to the brook to see,
After your message." "You were out," he said.
"Gone, and I did not know where you could be.
Where were you, Mary, when the thing was laid?"
"Old Mrs. Cale is dying, and I stayed
Longer than usual, while I read the Word.
You could have hardly gone." She paused, her bosom stirred.

"Mary, I sinned," he said. "Not that, dear, no,"
She said; "but, oh, you were unkind, unkind,
Never to write a word and leave me so,
But out of sight with you is out of mind."
"Mary, I sinned," he said, "and I was blind.
Oh, my beloved, are you Lion's wife?"
"Belov'd sounds strange," she answered, "in my present life.

"But it is sweet to hear it, all the same.
It is a language little heard by me
Alone, in that man's keeping, with my shame.
I never thought such miseries could be.
I was so happy in you, Michael. He
Came when I felt you changed from what I thought you.
Even now it is not love, but jealousy that brought you."

"That is untrue," he said. "I am in hell.
You are my heart's beloved, Mary, you.
By God, I know your beauty now too well.
We are each other's, flesh and soul, we two."

"That was sweet knowledge once," she said; "we knew
That truth of old. Now, in a strange man's bed,
I read it in my soul, and find it written red."

"Is he a brute?" he asked. "No," she replied.
"I did not understand what it would mean.
And now that you are back, would I had died;
Died, and the misery of it not have been.
Lion would not be wrecked, nor I unclean.
I was a proud one once, and now I'm tame;
Oh, Michael, say some word to take away my shame."

She sobbed; his arms went round her; the night heard
Intense fierce whispering passing, soul to soul,
Love running hot on many a murmured word,
Love's passionate giving into new control.
Their present misery did but blow the coal,
Did but entangle deeper their two wills,
While the brown brook ran on by buried daffodils.

VII

Upon a light gust came a waft of bells,
Ringing the chimes for nine; a broken sweet,
Like waters bubbling out of hidden wells,
Dully upon those lovers' ears it beat,
Their time was at an end. Her tottering feet
Trod the dim field for home; he sought an inn.
"Oh, I have sinned," she cried, "but not a secret sin."

Inside The Roughs they waited for her coming;
Eyeing the ticking clock the household sat.
"Nine," the clock struck; the clock-weights ran down drumming;
Old Mother Occleve stretched her sewing flat.
"It's nine," she said. Old Occleve stroked the cat.
"Ah, cat," he said, "hast had good go at mouse?"
Lion sat listening tense to all within the house.

"Mary is late to-night," the gammer said.
"The times have changed," her merry husband roared.
"Young married couples now like lonely trade,
Don't think of bed at all, they think of board.
No multiplying left in people. Lord!
When I was Lion's age I'd had my five.
There was some go in folk when us two took to wive."

Lion arose and stalked and bit his lip.
"Or was it six?" the old man muttered, "six.
Us had so many I've alost the tip.
Us were two right good souls at getting chicks.
Two births of twins, then Johnny's birth, then Dick's"...
"Now give a young man time," the mother cried.
Mary came swiftly in and flung the room door wide.

Lion was by the window when she came,
Old Occleve and his wife were by the fire;
Big shadows leapt the ceiling from the flame.
She fronted the three figures and came nigher.
"Lion," she whispered, "I return my hire."
She dropped her marriage-ring upon the table.
Then, in a louder voice, "I bore what I was able,

"And Time and marriage might have worn me down,
Perhaps, to be a good wife and a blest,
With little children clinging to my gown,
And little blind mouths fumbling for my breast,
And this place would have been a place of rest
For you and me; we could have come to know
The depth; but that is over; I have got to go.

"He has come back, and I have got to go.
Our marriage ends." She stood there white and breathed.
Old Occleve got upon his feet with "So."

Blazing with wrath upon the hearth he seethed.
A log fell from the bars; blue spirals wreathed
Across the still old woman's startled face;
The cat arose and yawned. Lion was still a space.

Old Occleve turned to Lion. Lion moved
Nearer to Mary, picking up the ring.
His was grim physic from the soul beloved;
His face was white and twitching with the sting.
"You are my wife, you cannot do this thing,"
He said at last. "I can respect your pride.
This thing affects your soul; my judgment must decide.

"You are unsettled, shaken from the shock."
"Not so," she said. She stretched a hand to him,
White, large and noble, steady as a rock,
Cunning with many powers, curving, slim.
The smoke, drawn by the door-draught, made it dim.
"Right," Lion answered. "You are steady. Then
There is but one world, Mary; this, the world of men.

"And there's another world, without its bounds,
Peopled by streaked and spotted souls who prize
The flashiness that comes from marshy grounds
Above plain daylight. In their blinkered eyes
Nothing is bright but sentimental lies,
Such as are offered you, dear, here and now;
Lies which betray the strongest, God alone knows how.

"You, in your beauty and your whiteness, turn
Your strong, white mind, your faith, your fearless truth,
All for these rotten fires that so burn.
A sentimental clutch at perished youth.
I am too sick for wisdom, sick with ruth,
And this comes suddenly; the unripe man
Misses the hour, oh God. But you, what is your plan?

"What do you mean to do, how act, how live?
What warrant have you for your life? What trust?
You are for going sailing in a sieve.
This brightness is too mortal not to rust.
So our beginning marriage ends in dust.
I have not failed you, Mary. Let me know
What you intend to do, and whither you will go."

"Go from this place; it chokes me," she replied.
"This place has branded me; I must regain
My truth that I have soiled, my faith, my pride,
It is all poison and it leaves a stain.
I cannot stay nor be your wife again.
Never. You did your best, though; you were kind.
I have grown old to-night and left all that behind.

"Goodbye." She turned. Old Occleve faced his son.
Wrath at the woman's impudence was blent,
Upon his face, with wrath that such an one
Should stand unthrashed until her words were spent.
He stayed for Lion's wrath; but Mary went
Unchecked; he did not stir. Her footsteps ground
The gravel to the gate; the gate-hinge made a sound

Like to a cry of pain after a shot.
Swinging, it clicked, it clicked again, it swung
Until the iron latch bar hit the slot.
Mary had gone, and Lion held his tongue.
Old Mother Occleve sobbed; her white head hung
Over her sewing while the tears ran down
Her worn, blood-threaded cheeks and splashed upon her gown.

"Yes, it is true," said Lion, "she must go.
Michael is back. Michael was always first,
I did but take his place. You did not know.
Now it has happened, and you know the worst.

So passion makes the passionate soul accurst
And crucifies his darling. Michael comes
And the savage truth appears and rips my life to thrums."

Upon old Occleve's face the fury changed
First to contempt, and then to terror lest
Lion, beneath the shock, should be deranged.
But Lion's eyes were steady, though distressed.
"Father, good-night," he said, "I'm going to rest.
Good-night, I cannot talk. Mother, good-night."
He kissed her brow and went; they heard him strike a light,

And go with slow depressed step up the stairs,
Up to the door of her deserted bower;
They heard him up above them, moving chairs;
The memory of his paleness made them cower.
They did not know their son; they had no power
To help, they only saw the new-won bride
Defy their child, and faith and custom put aside.

* * * * * *

After a time men learned where Mary was:
Over the hills, not many miles away,
Renting a cottage and a patch of grass
Where Michael came to see her. Every day
Taught her what fevers can inhabit clay,
Shaking this body that so soon must die.
The time made Lion old: the winter dwindled by.

Till the long misery had to end or kill:
And "I must go to see her," Lion cried;
"I am her standby, and she needs me still;
If not to love she needs me to decide.
Dear, I will set you free. Oh, my bright bride,
Lost in such piteous ways, come back." He rode
Over the wintry hills to Mary's new abode.

And as he topped the pass between the hills,
Towards him, up the swerving road, there came
Michael, the happy cause of all his ills;
Walking as though repentance were the shame,
Sucking a grass, unbuttoned, still the same,
Humming a tune; his careless beauty wild
Drawing the woman's eyes; he wandered with a child

Who heard, wide-eyed, the scraps of tales which fell
Between the fragments of the tune; they seemed
A cherub bringing up a soul from hell.
Meeting unlike the meeting long since dreamed.
Lion dismounted; the great valley gleamed
With waters far below; his teeth were set
His heart thumped at his throat; he stopped; the two men met

The child well knew that fatal issues joined;
He stood round-eyed to watch them, even as Fate
Stood with his pennypiece of causes coined
Ready to throw for issue; the bright hate
Throbbed, that the heavy reckoning need not wait.
Lion stepped forward, watching Michael's eyes.
"We are old friends," he said. "Now, Michael, you be wise,

"And let the harm already done suffice;
Go, before Mary's name is wholly gone.
Spare her the misery of desertion twice,
There's only ruin in the road you're on—
Ruin for both, whatever promise shone
In sentimental shrinkings from the fact.
So, Michael, play the man, and do the generous act.

"And go; if not for my sake, go for hers.
You only want her with your sentiment.
You are water roughed by every wind that stirs,

One little gust will alter your intent
All ways, to every wind, and nothing meant,
Is your life's habit. Man, one takes a wife,
Not for a three months' fancy, but the whole of life.

"We have been friends, and so I speak you fair.
How will you bear her ill, or cross, or tired?
Sentiment sighing will not help you there.
You call a half life's volume not desired.
I know your love for her. I saw it mired,
Mired, past going, by your first sharp taste
Of life and work; it stopped; you let her whole life waste,

"Rather than have the trouble of such love,
You will again; but if you do it now,
It will mean death, not sorrow. But enough.
You know too well you cannot keep a vow.
There are grey hairs already on her brow.
You brought them there. Death is the next step. Go,
Before you take the step." "No," Michael answered, "No.

"As for my past, I was a dog, a cur,
And I have paid blood-money, and still pay.
But all my being is ablaze with her;
There is no talk of giving up to-day.
I will not give her up. You used to say
Bodies are earth. I heard you say it. Liar!
You never loved her, you. She turned the earth to fire."

"Michael," said Lion, "you have said such things
Of other women; less than six miles hence
You and another woman felt love's wings
Rosy and fair, and so took leave of sense.
She's dead, that other woman, dead, with pence
Pressed on her big brown eyes, under the ground;
She that was merry once, feeling the world go round.

"Her child (and yours) is with her sister now,
Out there, behind us, living as they can;
Pinched by the poverty that you allow.
All a long autumn many rumours ran
About Sue Jones that was: you were the man.
The lad is like you. Think about his mother,
Before you turn the earth to fire with another."

"That is enough," said Michael, "you shall know
Soon, to your marrow, what my answer is;
Know to your lying heart; now kindly go.
The neighbours smell that something is amiss.
We two will keep a dignity in this,
Such as we can. No quarrelling with me here.
Mary might see; now go; but recollect, my dear,

"That if you twit me with your wife, you lie;
And that your further insult waits a day
When God permits that Mary is not by;
I keep the record of it, and shall pay.
And as for Mary; listen: we betray
No one. We keep our troth-plight as we meant.
Now go, the neighbours gather." Lion bowed and went.

Home to his memories for a month of pain,
Each moment like a devil with a tongue,
Urging him, "Set her free," or "Try again,"
Or "Kill that man and stamp him into dung."
"See her," he cried. He took his horse and swung
Out on the road to her; the rain was falling;
Her dropping house-eaves splashed him when he knocked there, calling.

Drowned yellow jasmine dripped; his horse's flanks
Steamed, and dark runnels on his yellow hair
Streaked the groomed surface into blotchy ranks.

The noise of water dropping filled the air.
He knocked again; but there was no one there;
No one within, the door was locked, no smoke
Came from the chimney stacks, no clock ticked, no one spoke.

Only the water dripped and dribble-dripped,
And gurgled through the rain-pipe to the butt;
Drops, trickling down the windows paused or slipped;
A wet twig scråked as though the glass were cut.
The blinds were all drawn down, the windows shut.
No one was there. Across the road a shawl
Showed at a door a space; a woman gave a call.

"They're gone away," she cried. "They're gone away.
Been gone a matter of a week." Where to?
The woman thought to Wales, but could not say,
Nor if she planned returning; no one knew.
She looked at Lion sharply; then she drew
The half-door to its place and passed within,
Saying she hoped the rain would stop and spring begin.

Lion rode home. A month went by, and now
Winter was gone; the myriad shoots of green
Bent to the wind, like hair, upon the plough,
And up from withered leaves came celandine.
And sunlight came, though still the air was keen,
So that the first March market was most fair,
And Lion rode to market, having business there.

And in the afternoon, when all was done,
While Lion waited idly near the inn,
Watching the pigeons sidling in the sun,
As Jim the ostler put his gelding in,
He heard a noise of rioting begin
Outside the yard, with catcalls; there were shouts
Of "Occleve. Lion Occleve," from a pack of louts,

Who hung about the courtyard-arch, and cried,
"Yah, Occleve, of The Roughs, the married man,
Occleve, who had the bed and not the bride."
At first without the arch; but some began
To sidle in, still calling; children ran
To watch the baiting; they were farmers' leavings
Who shouted thus, men cast for drunkenness and thievings.

Lion knew most of them of old; he paid
No heed to them, but turned his back and talked
To Jim, of through-pin in his master's jade,
And how no horse-wounds should be stuped or caulked.
The rabble in the archway, not yet baulked,
Came crowding nearer, and the boys began,
"Who was it took your mistress, master married man?"

"Who was it, master, took your wife away?"
"I wouldn't let another man take mine."
"She had two husbands on her wedding day."
"See at a blush: he blushed as red as wine."
"She'd ought a had a cart-whip laid on fine."
The farmers in the courtyard watched the baiting,
Grinning, the barmaids grinned above the window grating.

Then through the mob of brawlers Michael stepped
Straight to where Lion stood. "I come," he said,
"To give you back some words which I have kept
Safe in my heart till I could see them paid.
You lied about Sue Jones; she died a maid
As far as I'm concerned, and there's your lie,
Full in your throat, and there, and there, and in your eye.

"And there's for stealing Mary". . . as he struck,
He slipped upon a piece of peel and dropped
Souse in a puddle of the courtyard muck;
Loud laughter followed when he rose up sopped.

Friends rushed to intervene, the fight was stopped.
The two were hurried out by different ways.
Men said, "'Tis stopped for now, but not for many days."

* * * * * *

April appeared, the green earth's impulse came,
Pushing the singing sap until each bud
Trembled with delicate life as soft as flame,
Filled by the mighty heart-beat as with blood;
Death was at ebb, and Life in brimming flood.
But little joy in life could Lion see,
Striving to gird his will to set his loved one free,

While in his heart a hope still struggled dim
That the mad hour would pass, the darkness break,
The fever die, and she return to him,
The routed nightmare let the sleeper wake.
"Then we could go abroad," he cried "and make
A new life, soul to soul; oh, love! return."
"Too late," his heart replied. At last he rode to learn.

Bowed, but alive with hope, he topped the pass,
And saw, below, her cottage by the way,
White, in a garden green with springing grass,
And smoke against the blue sky going grey.
"God make us all the happier for to-day,"
He muttered humbly; then, below, he spied,
Mary and Michael entering, walking side by side.

Arm within arm, like lovers, like dear lovers
Matched by the happy stars and newly wed,
Over whose lives a rosy presence hovers.
Lion dismounted, seeing hope was dead.
A child was by the road, he stroked his head,
And "Little one," he said, "who lives below
There, in the cottage there, where those two people go?"

"They do," the child said, pointing: "Mrs. Gray
Lives in the cottage there, and he does, too.
They've been back near a week since being away."
It was but seal to what he inly knew.
He thanked the child and rode. The Spring was blue,
Bluer than ever, and the birds were glad;
Such rapture in the hedges all the blackbirds had.

He was not dancing to that pipe of the Spring.
He reached The Roughs, and there, within her room,
Bowed for a time above her wedding ring,
Which had so changed him to unhappy doom;
All his dead marriage haunted in the gloom
Of that deserted chamber; all her things
Lay still as she had left them when her love took wings.

He kept a bitter vigil through the night,
Knowing his loss, his ten years' passion wasted,
His life all blasted, even at its height,
His cup of life's fulfilment hardly tasted.
Grey on the budding woods the morning hasted,
And looking out he saw the dawn come chill
Over the shaking acre pale with daffodil.

Birds were beginning in the meadows; soon
The blackbirds and the thrushes with their singing
Piped down the withered husk that was the moon,
And up the sky the ruddy sun came winging.
Cows plodded past, yokes clanked, the men were bringing
Milk from the barton. Someone shouted "Hup.
Dog, drive them dangy red ones down away on up."

Some heavy hours went by before he rose.
He went out of the house into the grass,
Down which the wind flowed much as water flows;
The daffodils bowed down to let it pass.

At the brook's edge a boggy bit there was,
Right at the field's north corner, near the bridge,
Fenced by a ridge of earth; he sat upon the ridge,

Watching the water running to the sea,
Watching the bridge, the stile, the path beyond,
Where the white violet's sweetness brought the bee.
He paid the price of being overfond.
The water babbled always from the pond
Over the pretty shallows, chattering, tinkling,
With trembles from the sunlight in its clearness wrinkling.

So gazing, like one stunned, it reached his mind,
That the hedge-brambles overhung the brook
More than was right, making the selvage blind;
The dragging brambles too much flotsam took.
Dully he thought to mend. He fetched a hook,
And standing in the shallow stream he slashed,
For hours, it seemed; the thorns, the twigs, the dead leaves
splashed,

Splashed and were bobbed away across the shallows;
Pale grasses with the sap gone from them fell,
Sank, or were carried down beyond the sallows.
The bruised ground-ivy gave out earthy smell.
"I must be dead," he thought "and this is hell."
Fiercely he slashed, till, glancing at the stile,
He saw that Michael stood there, watching, with a smile,

His old contemptuous smile of careless ease,
As though the world with all its myriad pain
Sufficed, but only just sufficed, to please.
Michael was there, the robber come again.
A tumult ran like flame in Lion's brain;
Then, looking down, he saw the flowers shake:
Gold, trembling daffodils; he turned, he plucked a stake

Out of the hedge that he had come to mend,
And flung his hook to Michael, crying, "Take;
We two will settle our accounts, my friend,
Once and for ever. May the Lord God make
You see your sins in time." He whirled his stake
And struck at Michael's head; again he struck;
While Michael dodged and laughed, "Why, man, I bring you
luck.

"Don't kill a bringer of good news. You fool,
Stop it and listen. I have come to say:
Lion, for God's sake, listen and be cool.
You silly hothead, put that stake away.
Listen, I tell you." But he could not stay
The anger flaming in that passionate soul.
Blows rained upon him thick; they stung; he lost control.

Till, "If you want to fight," he cried, "let be.
Let me get off the bridge and we will fight.
That firm bit by the quag will do for me.
So. Be on guard, and God defend the right.
You foaming madman, with your hell's delight,
Smashing a man with stakes before he speaks:
On guard. I'll make you humbler for the next few weeks."

The ground was level there; the daffodils
Glimmered and danced beneath their cautious feet
Quartering for openings for the blow that kills.
Beyond the bubbling brook a thrush was sweet.
Quickly the footsteps slid; with feint and cheat,
The weapons poised and darted and withdrew.
"Now stop it," Michael said, "I want to talk to you."

"We do not stop till one of us is dead,"
Said Lion, rushing in. A short blow fell
Dizzily, through all guard, on Michael's head.

His hedging-hook slashed blindly but too well:
It struck in Lion's side. Then, for a spell,
Both, sorely stricken, staggered, while their eyes
Dimmed under mists of blood; they fell, they tried to rise,—

Tried hard to rise, but could not, so they lay,
Watching the clouds go sailing on the sky,
Touched with a redness from the end of day.
There was all April in the blackbird's cry.
And lying there they felt they had to die,
Die and go under mould and feel no more
April's green fire of life go running in earth's core.

"There was no need to hit me," Michael said;
"You quiet thinking fellows lose control.
This fighting business is a foolish trade.
And now we join the grave-worm and the mole.
I tried to stop you. You're a crazy soul;
You always were hot-headed. Well, let be:
You deep and passionate souls have always puzzled me.

"I'm sorry that I struck you. I was hit,
And lashed out blindly at you; you were mad.
It would be different if you'd stopped a bit.
You are too blind when you are angry, lad.
Oh, I am giddy, Lion; dying, bad.
Dying." He raised himself, he sat, his look
Grew greedy for the water bubbling in the brook.

And as he watched it, Lion raised his head
Out of a bloodied clump of daffodil.
"Michael," he moaned, "I, too, am dying: dead.
You're nearer to the water. Could you fill
Your hat and give me drink? Or would it spill?
Spill, I expect." "I'll try," said Michael, "try—
I may as well die trying, since I have to die."

Slowly he forced his body's failing life
Down to the water; there he stooped and filled;
And as his back turned Lion drew his knife,
And hid it close, while all his being thrilled
To see, as Michael came, the water spilled,
Nearer and ever nearer, bright, so bright.
"Drink," muttered Michael, "drink. We two shall sleep to-
night."

He tilted up the hat, and Lion drank.
Lion lay still a moment, gathering power,
Then rose, as Michael gave him more, and sank.
Then, like a dying bird whom death makes tower,
He raised himself above the bloodied flower
And struck with all his force in Michael's side.
"You should not have done that," his stricken comrade cried.

"No; for I meant to tell you, Lion; meant
To tell you; but I cannot now; I die.
That hit me to the heart and I am spent.
Mary and I have parted; she and I
Agreed she must return, lad. That is why
I came to see you. She is coming here,
Back to your home to-night. Oh, my beloved dear,

"You come to tread a bloody path of flowers.
All the gold flowers are covered up with blood,
And the bright bugles blow along the towers;
The bugles triumph like the Plate in flood."
His spilled life trickled down upon the mud
Between weak, clutching fingers. "Oh," he cried,
"This isn't what we planned here years ago." He died.

Lion lay still while the cold tides of death
Came brimming up his channels. With one hand
He groped to know if Michael still drew breath.

His little hour was running out its sand.
Then, in a mist, he saw his Mary stand
Above. He cried aloud, "He was my brother.
I was his comrade sworn, and we have killed each other.

"Oh desolate grief, belovéd, and through me.
We wise who try to change. Oh, you wild birds,
Help my unhappy spirit to the sea.
The golden bowl is scattered into sherds."
And Mary knelt and murmured passionate words
To that poor body on the dabbled flowers:
"Oh, beauty, oh, sweet soul, oh, little love of ours—

"Michael, my own heart's darling, speak; it's me,
Mary. You know my voice. I'm here, dear, here.
Oh, little golden-haired one, listen. See,
It's Mary, Michael. Speak to Mary, dear.
Oh, Michael, little love, he cannot hear;
And you have killed him, Lion; he is dead.
My little friend, my love, my Michael, golden head.

"We had such fun together, such sweet fun,
My love and I, my merry love and I.
Oh, love, you shone upon me like the sun.
Oh, Michael, say some little last good-bye."
Then in a great voice Lion called, "I die.
Go home and tell my people. Mary. Hear
Though I have wrought this ruin, I have loved you, dear.

"Better than he; not better, dear, as well.
If you could kiss me, dearest, at this last.
We have made bloody doorways from our hell,
Cutting our tangle. Now, the murder past,
We are but pitiful poor souls; and fast
The darkness and the cold come. Kiss me, sweet;
I loved you all my life; but some lives never meet

"Though they go wandering side by side through Time.
Kiss me," he cried. She bent, she kissed his brow:
"Oh, friend," she said, "you're lying in the slime."
"Three blind ones, dear," he murmured, "in the slough,
Caught fast for death; but never mind that now;
Go home and tell my people. I am dying,
Dying, dear, dying now." He died; she left him lying,

And kissed her dead one's head and crossed the field.
"They have been killed," she called, in a great crying.
"Killed, and our spirits' eyes are all unsealed.
The blood is scattered on the flowers drying."
It was the hush of dusk, and owls were flying;
They hooted as the Occleves ran to bring
That sorry harvest home from Death's red harvesting.

They laid the bodies on the bed together.
And "You were beautiful," she said, "and you
Were my own darling in the April weather.
You knew my very soul, you knew, you knew.
Oh, my sweet, piteous love, I was not true.
Fetch me fair water and the flowers of spring;
My love is dead, and I must deck his burying."

They left her with her dead; they could not choose
But grant the spirit burning in her face
Rights that their pity urged them to refuse.
They did her sorrow and the dead a grace.
All night they heard her passing footsteps trace
Down to the garden from the room of death.
They heard her singing there, lowly, with gentle breath,

To the cool darkness full of sleeping flowers,
Then back, still singing soft, with quiet tread,
But at the dawn her singing gathered powers
Like to the dying swan who lifts his head

On Eastnor, lifts it, singing, dabbled red,
Singing the glory in his tumbling mind,
Before the doors burst in, before death strikes him blind.

So triumphing her song of love began,
Ringing across the meadows like old woe
Sweetened by poets to the help of man
Unconquered in eternal overthrow;
Like a great trumpet from the long ago
Her singing towered; all the valley heard.
Men jingling down to meadow stopped their teams and stirred.

And they, the Occleves, hurried to the door,
And burst it, fearing; there the singer lay
Drooped at her lover's bedside on the floor,
Singing her passionate last of life away.
White flowers had fallen from a blackthorn spray
Over her loosened hair. Pale flowers of spring
Filled the white room of death; they covered everything.

Primroses, daffodils, and cuckoo-flowers.
She bowed her singing head on Michael's breast.
"Oh, it was sweet," she cried, "that love of ours.
You were the dearest, sweet; I loved you best.
Beloved, my beloved, let me rest
By you forever, little Michael mine.
Now the great hour is stricken, and the bread and wine

"Broken and spilt; and now the homing birds
Draw to a covert, Michael; I to you.
Bury us two together," came her words.
The dropping petals fell about the two.
Her heart had broken; she was dead. They drew
Her gentle head aside; they found it pressed
Against the broidered 'kerchief spread on Michael's breast,

The one that bore her name in Michael's hair,
Given so long before. They let her lie,
While the dim moon died out upon the air,
And happy sunlight coloured all the sky.
The last cock crowed for morning; carts went by;
Smoke rose from cottage chimneys; from the byre
The yokes went clanking by, to dairy, through the mire.

In the day's noise the water's noise was stilled,
But still it slipped along, the cold hill-spring,
Dropping from leafy hollows, which it filled,
On to the pebbly shelves which made it sing;
Glints glittered on it from the 'fisher's wing;
It saw the moorhen nesting; then it stayed
In a great space of reeds where merry otters played.

Slowly it loitered past the shivering reeds
Into a mightier water; thence its course
Becomes a pasture where the salmon feeds,
Wherein no bubble tells its humble source;
But the great waves go rolling, and the horse
Snorts at the bursting waves and will not drink,
And the great ships go outward, bubbling to the brink,

Outward, with men upon them, stretched in line,
Handling the halliards to the ocean's gates,
Where flicking windflaws fill the air with brine,
And all the ocean opens. Then the mates
Cry, and the sunburnt crew no longer waits,
But sings triumphant and the topsail fills
To this old tale of woe among the daffodils.

SONNETS AND OTHER POEMS

SONNETS AND OTHER POEMS

SONNETS

Long long ago, when all the glittering earth
Was heaven itself, when drunkards in the street
Were like mazed kings shaking at giving birth
To acts of war that sickle men like wheat,
When the white clover opened Paradise
And God lived in a cottage up the brook,
Beauty, you lifted up my sleeping eyes
And filled my heart with longing with a look;
And all the day I searched but could not find
The beautiful dark-eyed who touched me there,
Delight in her made trouble in my mind,
She was within all Nature, everywhere,
The breath I breathed, the brook, the flower, the grass,
Were her, her word, her beauty, all she was.

Night came again, but now I could not sleep.
The owls were watching in the yew, the mice
Gnawed at the wainscot; the mid-dark was deep,
The death-watch knocked the dead man's summons thrice.
The cats upon the pointed housetops peered
About the chimneys, with lit eyes which saw
Things in the darkness, moving, which they feared.
The midnight filled the quiet house with awe.
So, creeping down the stair, I drew the bolt
And passed into the darkness, and I knew
That Beauty was brought near by my revolt.
Beauty was in the moonlight, in the dew,
But more within myself whose venturous tread
Walked the dark house where death-ticks called the dead.

Even after all these years there comes the dream
Of lovelier life than this in some new earth,
In the full summer of that unearthly gleam
Which lights the spirit when the brain gives birth,
Of a perfected I, in happy hours,
Treading above the sea that trembles there,
A path through thickets of immortal flowers
That only grow where sorrows never were.
And, at a turn, of coming face to face
With Beauty's self, that Beauty I have sought
In women's hearts, in friends, in many a place,
In barren hours passed at grips with thought,
Beauty of woman, comrade, earth and sea,
Incarnate thought come face to face with me.

If I could come again to that dear place
Where once I came, where Beauty lived and moved,
Where, by the sea, I saw her face to face,
That soul alive by which the world has loved;
If, as I stood at gaze among the leaves,
She would appear again, as once before,
While the red herdsman gathered up his sheaves
And brimming waters trembled up the shore;
If, as I gazed, her Beauty that was dumb,
In that old time, before I learned to speak,
Would lean to me and revelation come,
Words to the lips and color to the cheek,
Joy with its searing-iron would burn me wise,
I should know all; all powers, all mysteries.

Men are made human by the mighty fall
The mighty passion led to, these remain.
The despot, at the last assaulted wall,
By long disaster is made man again,
The faithful fool who follows the torn flag,
The woman marching by the beaten man,
Make with their truth atonement for the brag,
And earn a pity for the too proud plan.
For in disaster, in the ruined will,
In the soiled shreds of what the brain conceived,
Something above the wreck is steady still,
Bright above all that cannot be retrieved,
Grandeur of soul, a touching of the star
That good days cover but by which we are.

Here in the self is all that man can know
Of Beauty, all the wonder, all the power,
All the unearthly color, all the glow,
Here in the self which withers like a flower;
Here in the self which fades as hours pass,
And droops and dies and rots and is forgotten,
Sooner, by ages, than the mirroring glass
In which it sees its glory still unrotten.
Here in the flesh, within the flesh, behind,
Swift in the blood and throbbing on the bone,
Beauty herself, the universal mind,
Eternal April wandering alone.
The god, the holy ghost, the atoning lord,
Here in the flesh, the never yet explored.

Flesh, I have knocked at many a dusty door,
Gone down full many a windy midnight lane,
Probed in old walls and felt along the floor,
Pressed in blind hope the lighted window-pane.
But useless all, though sometimes, when the moon
Was full in heaven and the sea was full,
Along my body's alleys came a tune
Played in the tavern by the Beautiful.
Then for an instant I have felt at point
To find and seize her, whosoe'er she be,
Whether some saint whose glory doth anoint
Those whom she loves, or but a part of me,
Or something that the things not understood
Make for their uses out of flesh and blood.

But all has passed, the tune has died away,
The glamour gone, the glory; is it chance?
Is the unfeeling mud stabbed by a ray
Cast by an unseen splendor's great advance?
Or does the glory gather crumb by crumb
Unseen, within, as coral islands rise,
Till suddenly the apparitions come
Above the surface, looking at the skies?
Or does sweet Beauty dwell in lovely things,
Scattering the holy hintings of her name
In women, in dear friends, in flowers, in springs,
In the brook's voice, for us to catch the same?
Or is it we who are Beauty, we who ask,
We by whose gleams the world fulfils its task?

These myriad days, these many thousand hours,
A man's long life, so choked with dusty things,
How little perfect poise with perfect powers,
Joy at the heart and Beauty at the springs.
One hour, or two, or three, in long years scattered,
Sparks from a smithy that have fired a thatch,
Are all that life has iven and all that mattered,
The rest, all heaving at a moveless latch.
For these, so many years of useless toil,
Despair, endeavor, and again despair,
Sweat, that the base machine may have its oil,
Idle delight to tempt one everywhere.
A life upon the cross. To make amends
Three flaming memories that the deathbed ends.

There, on the darkened deathbed, dies the brain
That flared three several times in seventy years;
It cannot lift the silly hand gain,
Nor speak, nor sing, it neither sees nor hears.
And muffled mourners put it in the ground
And then go home, and in the earth it lies,
Too dark for vision and too deep for sound,
The million cells that made a good man wise.
Yet for a few short years an influence stirs
A sense or wraith or essence of him dead,
Which makes insensate things its ministers
To those beloved, his spirit's daily bread;
Then that, too, fades; in book or deed a spark
Lingers, then that, too, fades; then all is dark.

So in the empty sky the stars appear,
Are bright in heaven marching through the sky,
Spinning their planets, each one to his year,
Tossing their fiery hair until they die;
Then in the tower afar the watcher sees
The sun, that burned, less noble than it was,
Less noble still, until by dim degrees,
No spark of him is specklike in his glass.
Then blind and dark in heaven the sun proceeds,
Vast, dead and hideous, knocking on his moons,
Till crashing on his like creation breeds,
Striking such life a constellation swoons.
From dead things striking fire a new sun springs,
New fire, new life, new planets with new wings.

It may be so with us, that in the dark,
When we have done with Time and wander Space,
Some meeting of the blind may strike a spark,
And to Death's empty mansion give a grace.
It may be, that the loosened soul may find
Some new delight of living without limbs,
Bodiless joy of flesh-untrammelled mind,
Peace like a sky where starlike spirit swims.
It may be, that the million cells of sense,
Loosed from their seventy years' adhesion, pass
Each to some joy of changed experience,
Weight in the earth or glory in the grass;
It may be that we cease; we cannot tell.
Even if we cease, life is a miracle.

Man has his unseen friend, his unseen twin,
His straitened spirit's possibility,
The palace unexplored he thinks an inn,
The glorious garden which he wanders by.
It is beside us while we clutch at clay
To daub ourselves that we may never see.
Like the lame donkey lured by moving hay
We chase the shade but let the real be.
Yet, when confusion in our heaven brings stress,
We thrust on that unseen, get stature from it,
Cast to the devil's challenge the man's yes,
And stream our fiery hour like a comet,
And know for that fierce hour a friend behind,
With sword and shield, the second to the mind.

What am I, Life? A thing of watery salt
Held in cohesion by unresting cells,
Which work they know not why, which never halt,
Myself unwitting where their Master dwells.
I do not bid them, yet they toil, they spin;
A world which uses me as I use them,
Nor do I know which end or which begin
Nor which to praise, which pamper, which condemn.
So, like a marvel in a marvel set,
I answer to the vast, as wave by wave
The sea of air goes over, dry or wet,
Or the full moon comes swimming from her cave,
Or the great sun comes north, this myriad I
Tingles, not knowing how, yet wondering why.

If I could get within this changing I,
This ever altering thing which yet persists,
Keeping the features it is reckoned by,
While each component atom breaks or twists,
If, wandering past strange groups of shifting forms,
Cells at their hidden marvels hard at work,
Pale from much toil, or red from sudden storms,
I might attain to where the Rulers lurk.
If, pressing past the guards in those grey gates,
The brain's most folded intertwisted shell,
I might attain to that which alters fates,
The King, the supreme self, the Master Cell,
Then, in Man's earthly peak, I might behold
The unearthly self beyond, unguessed, untold.

What is this atom which contains the whole,
This miracle which needs adjuncts so strange,
This, which imagined God and is the soul,
The steady star persisting amid change?
What waste, that smallness of such power should need
Such clumsy tools so easy to destroy,
Such wasteful servants difficult to feed,
Such indirect dark avenues to joy.
Why, if its business is not mainly earth,
Should it demand such heavy chains to sense?
A heavenly thing demands a swifter birth,
A quicker hand to act intelligence.
An earthly thing were better like the rose
At peace with clay from which its beauty grows.

Ah, we are neither heaven nor earth, but men;
Something that uses and despises both,
That takes its earth's contentment in the pen,
Then sees the world's injustice and is wroth,
And flinging off youth's happy promise, flies
Up to some breach, despising earthly things,
And, in contempt of hell and heaven, dies,
Rather than bear some yoke of priests or kings.
Our joys are not of heaven nor earth, but man's,
A woman's beauty or a child's delight,
The trembling blood when the discoverer scans
The sought-for world, the guessed-at satellite;
The ringing scene, the stone at point to blush
For unborn men to look at and say "Hush."

Roses are beauty, but I never see
Those blood drops from the burning heart of June
Glowing like thought upon the living tree,
Without a pity that they die so soon,
Die into petals, like those roses old,
Those women, who were summer in men's hearts
Before the smile upon the Sphinx was cold,
Or sand had hid the Syrian and his arts.
O myriad dust of beauty that lies thick
Under our feet that not a single grain
But stirred and moved in beauty and was quick
For one brief moon and died nor lived again;
But when the moon rose lay upon the grass
Pasture to living beauty, life that was.

Over the church's door they moved a stone
And there, unguessed, forgotten, mortared up,
Lay the priest's cell where he had lived alone;
There was his ashy hearth, his drinking cup;
There was the window whence he saw the host,
The god whose beauty quickened bread and wine,
The skeleton of a religion lost,
The ghostless bones of what had been divine.
O many a time the dusty masons come,
Knocking their trowels in the stony brain,
To cells where perished priests had once a home,
Or where devout brows pressed the window pane,
Watching the thing made God, the god whose bones
Bind underground our soul's foundation stones.

I never see the red rose crown the year,
Nor feel the young grass underneath my tread,
Without the thought "This living beauty here
Is earth's remembrance of a beauty dead.
Surely where all this glory is displayed
Love has been quick, like fire, to high ends,
Here, in this grass, an altar has been made
For some white joy, some sacrifice of friends;
Here, where I stand, some leap of human brains
Has touched immortal things and left its trace,
The earth is happy here, the gleam remains;
Beauty is here, the spirit of the place,
I touch the faith which nothing can destroy,
The earth, the living church of ancient joy."

Out of the clouds come torrents, from the earth
Fire and quakings, from the shrieking air
Tempests that harry half the planet's girth.
Death's unseen seeds are scattered everywhere.
Yet in his iron cage the mind of man
Measures and braves the terrors of all these,
The blindest fury and the subtlest plan
He turns, or tames, or shows in their degrees.
Yet in himself are forces of like power,
Untamed, unreckoned; seeds that brain to brain
Pass across oceans bringing thought to flower,
New worlds, new selves, where he can live again,
Eternal beauty's everlasting rose
Which casts this world as shadow as it goes.

O little self, within whose smallness lies
All that man was, and is, and will become,
Atom unseen that comprehends the skies
And tells the tracks by which the planets roam.
That, without moving, knows the joys of wings,
The tiger's strength, the eagle's secrecy,
And in the hovel can consort with kings,
Or clothe a god with his own mystery.
O with what darkness do we cloak thy light,
What dusty folly gather thee for food,
Thou who alone art knowledge and delight,
The heavenly bread, the beautiful, the good
O living self, O god, O morning star,
Give us thy light, forgive us what we are.

I went into the fields, but you were there
Waiting for me, so all the summer flowers
Were only glimpses of your starry powers,
Beautiful and inspired dust they were.
I went down by the waters, and a bird
Sang with your voice in all the unknown tones
Of all that self of you I have not heard,
So that my being felt you to the bones.
I went into my house, and shut the door
To be alone, but you were there with me;
All beauty in a little room may be
Though the roof lean and muddy be the floor.
Then in my bed I bound my tired eyes
To make a darkness for my weary brain,
But like a presence you were there again,
Being and real, beautiful and wise,
So that I could not sleep and cried aloud,
"You strange grave thing, what is it you would say?"
The redness of your dear lips dimmed to grey,
The waters ebbed, the moon hid in a cloud.

There are two forms of life, of which one moves,
Seeking its meat in many forms of Death,
On scales, on wings, on all the myriad hooves
Which stamp earth's exultation in quick breath.
It rustles through the reeds in shivering fowl,
Cries over moors in curlew, glitters green
In the lynx' eye, is fearful in the howl
Of winter-bitten wolves whose flanks are lean.
It takes dumb joy in cattle, it is fierce,
It torts the tiger's loin, the eagle's wings,
Its tools are claws to smite and teeth to pierce,
Arms to destroy, and coils, and poison stings;
Wherever earth is quick and life runs red
Its mark is death, its meat is something dead.

Restless and hungry, still it moves and slays,
Feeding its beauty on dead beauty's bones,
Most merciless in all its million ways,
Its breath for singing bought by dying groans,
Roving so far with such a zest to kill
(Its strongness adding hunger) that at last
Its cells attain beyond the cruel skill
To where life's earliest impulses are past.
Then this creation of the linkéd lusts,
To move and eat, still under their control,
Hunts for his prey in thought, his thinking thrusts
Through the untrodden jungle of the soul,
Through slip and quag, morasses dripping green,
Seeking the thing supposed but never seen.

How many ways, how many different times
The tiger Mind has clutched at what it sought,
Only to prove supposéd virtues crimes,
The imagined godhead but a form of thought.
How many restless brains have wrought and schemed,
Padding their cage, or built, or brought to law,
Made in outlasting brass the something dreamed,
Only to prove themselves the things of awe,
Yet, in the happy moment's lightning blink,
Comes scent, or track, or trace, the game goes by,
Some leopard thought is pawing at the brink,
Chaos below, and, up above, the sky.
Then the keen nostrils scent, about, about,
To prove the Thing Within a Thing Without.

The other form of Living does not stir;
Where the seed chances there it roots and grows,
To suck what makes the lily or the fir
Out of the earth and from the air that blows.
Great power of Will that little thing the seed
Has, all alone in earth, to plan the tree,
And, though the mud oppresses, to succeed,
And put out branches where the birds may be.
Then the wind blows it, but the bending boughs
Exult like billows, and their million green
Drink the all-living sunlight in carouse,
Like dainty harts where forest wells are clean.
While it, the central plant, which looks o'er miles,
Draws milk from the earth's breast, and sways, and smiles.

Is there a great green commonwealth of Thought
Which ranks the yearly pageant, and decides
How Summer's royal progress shall be wrought,
By secret stir which in each plant abides?
Does rocking daffodil consent that she,
The snowdrop of wet winters, shall be first?
Does spotted cowslip with the grass agree
To hold her pride before the rattle burst?
And in the hedge what quick agreement goes,
When hawthorn blossoms redden to decay,
That Summer's pride shall come, the Summer's rose,
Before the flower be on the bramble spray?
Or is it, as with us, unresting strife,
And each consent a lucky gasp for life?

Beauty, let be; I cannot see your face,
I shall not know you now, nor touch your feet,
Only within me tremble to your grace
Tasting this crumb vouchsafed which is so sweet.
Even when the full-leaved Summer bore no fruit,
You give me this, this apple of man's tree;
This planet sings when other spheres were mute,
This light begins when darkness covered me.
Now, though I know that I shall never know
All, through my fault, nor blazon with my pen
That path prepared where only I could go,
Still, I have this, not given to other men.
Beauty, this grace, this spring, this given bread.
This life, this dawn, this wakening from the dead.

Here, where we stood together, we three men,
Before the war had swept us to the East
Three thousand miles away, I stand again
And hear the bells, and breathe, and go to feast.
We trod the same path, to the self-same place,
Yet here I stand, having beheld their graves,
Skyros whose shadows the great seas erase,
And Seddul Bahr that ever more blood craves.
So, since we command here, our bones have been
Nearer, perhaps, than they again will be,
Earth and the world-wide battle lie between,
Death lies between, and friend-destroying sea.
Yet here, a year ago, we talked and stood
As I stand now, with pulses beating blood.

I saw her like a shadow on the sky
In the last light, a blur upon the sea,
Then the gale's darkness put the shadow by,
But from one grave that island talked to me;
And, in the midnight, in the breaking storm,
I saw its blackness and a blinking light,
And thought, "So death obscures your gentle form,
So memory strives to make the darkness bright;
And, in that heap of rocks, your body lies,
Part of the island till the planet ends,
My gentle comrade, beautiful and wise,
Part of this crag this bitter surge offends,
While I, who pass, a little obscure thing,
War with this force, and breathe, and am its king."

Not that the stars are all gone mad in heaven
Plucking the unseen reins upon men's souls,
Not that the law that bound the planets seven
Is discord now; man probes for new controls.
He bends no longer to the circling stars,
New moon and full moon and the living sun,
Love-making Venus, Jove and bloody Mars
Pass from their thrones, their rule of him is done.
And paler gods, made liker men, are past,
Like their sick eras to their funeral urns,
They cannot stand the fire blown by the blast
In which man's soul that measures heaven burns.
Man in his cage of many millioned pain
Burns all to ash to prove if God remain.

There is no God, as I was taught in youth,
Though each, according to his stature, builds
Some covered shrine for what he thinks the truth,
Which day by day his reddest heart-blood gilds.
There is no God; but death, the clasping sea,
In which we move like fish, deep over deep
Made of men's souls that bodies have set free,
Floods to a Justice though it seems asleep.
There is no God, but still, behind the veil,
The hurt thing works, out of its agony.
Still, like a touching of a brimming Grail,
Return the pennies given to passers by.
There is no God, but we, who breathe the air,
Are God ourselves and touch God everywhere.

Beauty retires; the blood out of the earth
Shrinks, the stalk dries, lifeless November still
Drops the brown husk of April's greenest birth.
Through the thinned beech clump I can see the hill.
So withers man, and though his life renews
In Aprils of the soul, an autumn comes
Which gives an end, not respite, to the thews
That bore his soul through the world's martyrdoms.
Then all the beauty will be out of mind,
Part of man's store, that lies outside his brain,
Touch to the dead and vision to the blind,
Drink in the desert, bread, eternal grain;
Part of the untilled field that beauty sows
With flowers untold, where quickened spirit goes.

Wherever beauty has been quick in clay
Some effluence of it lives, a spirit dwells,
Beauty that death can never take away,
Mixed with the air that shakes the flower bells;
So that by waters where the apples fall,
Or in lone glens, or valleys full of flowers,
Or in the streets where bloody tidings call,
The haunting waits the mood that makes it ours.
Then at a turn, a word, an act, a thought,
Such difference comes, the spirit apprehends
That place's glory, for where beauty fought
Under the veil the glory never ends,
But the still grass, the leaves, the trembling flower,
Keep, through dead time, that everlasting hour.

You are more beautiful than women are,
Wiser than men, stronger than ribbéd death,
Juster than Time, more constant than the star,
Dearer than love, more intimate than breath;
Having all art, all science, all control
Over the still unsmithied, even as Time
Cradles the generations of man's soul,
You are the light to guide, the way to climb.
So, having followed beauty, having bowed
To wisdom and to death, to law, to power,
I like a blind man stumble from the crowd
Into the darkness of a deeper hour,
Where in the lonely silence I may wait
The prayed-for gleam—your hand upon the gate.

Not for the anguish suffered is the slur,
Not for the woman's mocks, the taunts of men,
No, but because you never welcomed her,
Her of whose beauty I am only the pen.
There was a dog, dog-minded, with dog's eyes,
Damned by a dog's brute-nature to be true,
Something within her made his spirit wise,
He licked her hand, he knew her, not so you.
When all adulterate beauty has gone by,
When all inanimate matter has gone down,
We will arise and walk, that dog and I,
The only two who knew her in the town,
We'll range the pleasant mountains side by side,
Seeking the blood-stained flowers where Christs have died.

Beauty was with me once, but now, grown old,
I cannot hear nor see her: thus a king
In the high turret kept him from the cold
Over the fire with his magic ring
Which, as he wrought, made pictures come and go
Of men and times, past, present, and to be,
Now like a smoke, now flame-like, now a glow,
Now dead, now bright, but always fantasy.
While, on the stair without, a faithful slave,
Stabbed to the death, crawled bleeding, whispering "Sir,
They come to kill you, fly: I come to save;
O you great gods, have pity, let him hear."
Then, with his last strength tapped and muttered, "Sire,"
While the king smiled and drowsed above the fire.

So beauty comes, so with a failing hand
She knocks and cries, and fails to make me hear,
She who tells futures in the falling sand
And still, by signs, makes hidden meanings clear;
She, who behind this many-peopled smoke,
Moves in the light and struggles to direct,
Through the deaf ear and by the baffled stroke,
The wicked man, the honored architect.
Yet at a dawn before the birds begin,
In dreams, as the horse stamps and the hound stirs,
Sleep slips the bolt and beauty enters in
Crying aloud those hurried words of hers,
And I awake and, in the birded dawn,
Know her for Queen and own myself a pawn.

If Beauty be at all, if, beyond sense,
There be a wisdom piercing into brains,
Why should the glory wait in impotence,
Biding its time till blood is in the veins?
There is no beauty, but when thought is quick,
Out of the noisy sickroom of ourselves,
Some flattery comes to try to cheat the sick,
Some drowsy drug is groped for on the shelves,
And, for the rest, we play upon a scene
Beautiful with the blood of living things;
We move and speak and wonder and have been,
Upon the dust as dust, not queens and kings;
We know no beauty, nor does beauty care
For us, this dust, that men make everywhere.

Each greedy self, by consecrating lust,
Desire pricking into sacrifice,
Adds, in his way, some glory to the dust,
Brings, to the light, some haze of Paradise,
Hungers and thirsts for beauty; like the hound
Snaps it, to eat alone; in secret keeps
His miser's patch of consecrated ground
Where beauty's coins are dug down to the deeps.
So when disturbing death digs up our lives,
Some little gleam among the broken soil
May witness for us as the shovel rives
The dirty heap of all our tiny toil;
Some gleam of you may make the digger hold,
Touched for an instant with the thought of gold.

Time being an instant in eternity,
Beauty above man's million years must see
The heaped corrupted mass that had to die,
The husk of man that set the glitter free;
Now from those million bodies in the dark,
Forgotten, rotten, part of fields or roads,
The million gleam united makes a spark
Which Beauty sees among her star abodes.
And, from the bodies, comes a sigh, "Alas,
We hated, fought and killed, as separate men;
Now all is merged and we are in the grass,
Our efforts merged, would we had known it then.
All our lives' battle, all our spirits' dream,
Nought in themselves, a clash which made a gleam."

You will remember me in days to come
With love, or pride, or pity, or contempt:
So will my friends (not many friends, yet some)
When this my life will be a dream out-dreamt;
And one, remembering friendship by the fire,
And one, remembering love-time in the dark,
And one, remembering unfulfilled desire,
Will sigh, perhaps, yet be beside the mark;
For this my body with its wandering ghost
Is nothing solely but an empty grange,
Dark in a night that owls inhabit most,
Yet when the king rides by there comes a change;
The windows gleam, the cresset's fiery hair
Blasts the blown branch and beauty lodges there.

Out of the barracks to the castle yard
Those Roman soldiers came, buckling their gear;
The word was passed that they were prison guard;
The sergeant proved their dressing with his spear.
Then, as the prisoner came, a wretch who bled
Holding a cross, those nearest cursed his soul:
He might have died some other time, they said,
Not at high noon: the sergeant called the roll.
Then, sloping spears, the files passed from the court
Into the alleys, thrusting back the crowd,
They cursed the bleeding man for stepping short;
The drums beat time: the sergeant hummed aloud;
The rabble closed behind: the soldiers cursed
The prisoner's soul, the flies, their packs, their thirst.

They took the bloody body from the cross,
They laid it in its niche and rolled the stone.
One said, "Our blessed Master," one "His loss
Ends us companions, we are left alone."
And one, "I thought that Pilate would acquit
Right to the last;" and one, "The sergeant took
The trenching mall and drove the nails with it."
One who was weeping went apart and shook.
Then one, "He promised that in three short days
He would return, oh God; but He is dead."
And one, "What was it that He meant to raise?
The Temple? No? What was it that He said?
He said that He would build? that He would rise?"
"No," answered one, "but come from Paradise.

"Come to us fiery with the saints of God
To judge the world and take His power and reign."
Then one, "This was the very road we trod
That April day, would it could come again;
The day they flung the flowers." "Let be," said one,
"He was a lovely soul, but what He meant
Passes our wit, for none among us, none,
Had brains enough to fathom His intent.
His mother did not, nor could one of us,
But while He spoke I felt I understood."
And one, "He knew that it would finish thus.
Let His thought be, I know that He was good.
There is the orchard, see, the very same
Where we were sleeping when the soldiers came."

So from the cruel cross they buried God;
So, in their desolation, as they went
They dug him deeper with each step they trod,
Their lightless minds distorting what He meant.
Lamenting Him, their leader, who had died,
They heaped the stones, they rolled the heavy door;
They said, "Our glory has been crucified,
Unless He rise our glory will be o'er."
While in the grave the spirit left the corpse
Broken by torture, slowly, line by line,
And saw the dawn come on the eastern thorpes,
And shook his wings and sang in the divine,
Crying "I told the truth, even unto death,
Though I was earth and now am only breath."

If all be governed by the moving stars,
If passing planets bring events to be,
Searing the face of Time with bloody scars,
Drawing men's souls even as the moon the sea;
If as they pass they make a current pass
Across man's life and heap it to a tide,
We are but pawns, ignobler than the grass
Cropped by the beast and crunched and tossed aside.
Is all this beauty that does inhabit heaven
Trail of a planet's fire? Is all this lust
A chymic means by warring stars contriven
To bring the violets out of Cæsar's dust?
Better be grass, or in some hedge unknown
The spilling rose whose beauty is its own.

In emptiest furthest heaven where no stars are
Perhaps some planet of our master sun
Still rolls an unguessed orbit round its star
Unthought, unseen, unknown of any one.
Roving dead space according to its law
Casting our light on burnt-out suns and blind
Singing in the frozen void its word of awe
One wandering thought in all that idiot mind.
And, in some span of many a thousand year,
Passing through heaven, its influence may arouse
Beauty unguessed in those who habit here,
And men may rise with glory on their brows,
And feel new life like fire, and see the old
Fall from them dead, the bronze's broken mould.

Perhaps in chasms of the wasted past,
That planet wandered within hail of ours,
And plucked men's souls to loveliness and cast
The old, that was, away, like husks of flowers;
And made them stand erect and bade them build
Nobler than hovels plaited in the mire,
Gave them an altar and a god to gild,
Bridled the brooks for them and fettered fire;
And, in another coming, forged the steel
Which, on life's scarlet wax, forever set
Longing for beauty bitten as a seal
That blood not clogs nor centuries forget,
That built Atlantis, and, in time will raise
That grander thing whose image haunts our days.

For, like an outcast from the city, I
Wander the desert strewn with travellers' bones,
Having no comrade but the starry sky
Where the tuned planets ride their floating thrones.
I pass old ruins where the kings caroused
In cups long shards from vines long since decayed,
I tread the broken brick where queens were housed
In beauty's time ere beauty was betrayed;
And in the ceaseless pitting of the sand
On monolith and pyle, I see the dawn,
Making those skeletons of beauty grand
By fire that comes as darkness is withdrawn;
And in that fire the art of men to come
Shines with such glow I bless my martyrdom.

Death lies in wait for you, you wild thing in the wood,
Shy-footed beauty dear, half-seen, half-understood,
Glimpsed in the beech wood dim, and in the dropping fir,
Shy like a fawn and sweet and beauty's minister.
Glimpsed as in flying clouds by night the little moon,
A wonder, a delight, a paleness passing soon.
Only a moment held, only an hour seen,
Only an instant known in all that life has been,
One instant in the sand to drink that gush of grace,
The beauty of your way, the marvel of your face.
Death lies in wait for you, but few short hours he gives,
I perish even as you by whom all spirit lives,
Come to me, spirit, come, and fill my hour of breath
With hours of life in life that pay no toll to death.

What are we given, what do we take away?
Five little senses, startling with delight,
That dull to death and perish into clay
And pass from human memory as from sight.
So the new penny glittering from the mint,
Bears the king's head awhile, but Time effaces
The head, the date, the seated queen, the print
Even as a brook the stone in pebbly places.
We bear the stamp, are current, and are prized,
Hoarded or spent, the while the mintage passes,
Then, like light money, challenged or despised,
We join the heap of dross which Time amasses,
Erased, uncurrent discs no more to range
The clanging counters in the great exchange.

They called that broken hedge The Haunted Gate.
Strange fires (they said) burnt there at moonless times.
Evil was there, men never went there late,
The darkness there was quick with threatened crimes.
And then one digging in that bloodied clay
Found, but a foot below, a rotted chest.
Coins of the Romans, tray on rusted tray,
Hurriedly heaped there by a digger prest.
So that one knew how, centuries before,
Some Roman flying from the sack by night,
Digging in terror there to hide his store,
Sweating his pick, by windy lantern light,
Had stamped his anguish on that place's soul,
So that it knew and could rehearse the whole.

There was an evil in the nodding wood
Above the quarry long since overgrown,
Something which stamped it as a place of blood
Where tortured spirit cried from murdered bone.
Then, after years, I saw a rusty knife
Stuck in a woman's skull, just as 'twas found,
Blackt with a centuried crust of clotted life,
In the red clay of that unholy ground.
So that I knew the unhappy thing had spoken,
That tongueless thing for whom the quarry spoke,
The evil seals of murder had been broken
By the red earth, the grass, the rooted oak,
The inarticulate dead had forced the spade,
The hand, the mind, till murder was displayed.

Go, spend your penny, Beauty, when you will,
In the grave's darkness let the stamp be lost.
The water still will bubble from the hill,
And April quick the meadows with her ghost;
Over the grass the daffodils will shiver,
The primroses with their pale beauty abound,
The blackbird be a lover and make quiver
With his glad singing the great soul of the ground;
So that if the body rot, it will not matter;
Up in the earth the great game will go on,
The coming of Spring and the running of the water,
And the young things glad of the womb's darkness gone;
And the joy we felt will be a part of the glory
In the lover's kiss that makes the old couple's story.

Not for your human beauty nor the power
To shake me by your voice or by your touch,
Summer must have its rose, the rose must flower,
Beauty burn deep, I do not yield to such.
No, but because your beauty where it falls
Lays bare the spirits in the crowded streets,
Shatters the lock, destroys the castle walls,
Breaks down the bars till friend with comrade meets,
So that I wander brains where beauty dwelled
In long dead time, and see again the rose
By long dead men for living beauty held,
That Death's knife spares, and Winter with his snows,
And know it bloodied by that pulse of birth
Which greens the grass in Aprils upon earth.

The little robin hopping in the wood
Draws friendship from you, the rapt nightingale
Making the night a marvellous solitude,
Only of you to darkness tells the tale.
Kingfishers are but jewels on your dress,
Dun deer that rove and timid rabbits shy
Are but the hintings of your gentleness.
Upon your wings the eagle climbs the sky.
Fish that are shadows in the water pass
With mystery from you, the purpled moth
Dust from your kirtle on his broidery has,
Out of your bounty every beauty flowth.
For you are all, all fire, all living form,
Marvel in man and glory in the worm.

Though in life's streets the tempting shops have lured,
Because all beauty, howsoever base,
Is vision of you, marred, I have endured
Tempted or fall'n, to look upon your face.
Now through the grinning death's-head in the paint,
Within the tavern-song, hid in the wine,
In many kinded man, emperor and saint,
I see you pass, you breath of the divine.
I see you pass, as centuries ago
The long dead men with passionate spirit saw,
O brother man, whom spirit habits so,
Through your red sorrows Beauty keeps her law,
Beauty herself, who takes your dying hand,
To leave through Time the Memnon in the sand.

When all these million cells that are my slaves
Fall from my pourried ribs and leave me alone,
A living speck among a world of graves,
What shall I be, that spot in the unknown?
A glow-worm in a night that floats the sun?
Or deathless dust feeling the passer's foot?
An eye undying mourning things undone?
Or seed for quickening free from prisoning ruit?
Or an eternal jewel on your robe,
Caught to your heart, one with the April fire
That made me yours as man upon the globe,
One with the Spring, a breath in all desire,
One with the primrose, present in all joy?
Or pash that rots, which pismires can destroy?

Let that which is to come be as it may,
Darkness, extinction, justice, life intense.
The flies are happy in the summer day,
Flies will be happy many summers hence.
Time with his antique breeds that built the Sphynx,
Time with her men to come whose wings will tower,
Poured and will pour, not as the wise man thinks,
But with blind force, to each his little hour.
And when the hour has struck, comes death or change,
Which, whether good or ill, we cannot tell,
But the blind planet will wander through her range,
Bearing men like us who will serve as well.
The sun will rise, the winds that ever move
Will blow our dust that once were men in love.

THE *WANDERER*

All day they loitered by the resting ships,
Telling their beauties over, taking stock;
At night the verdict left my messmates' lips,
"The *Wanderer* is the finest ship in dock."

I had not seen her, but a friend, since drowned,
Drew her, with painted ports, low, lovely, lean,
Saying, "The *Wanderer*, clipper, outward bound,
The loveliest ship my eyes have ever seen—

"Perhaps to-morrow you will see her sail.
She sails at sunrise": but the morrow showed
No *Wanderer* setting forth for me to hail;
Far down the stream men pointed where she rode,

Rode the great trackway to the sea, dim, dim,
Already gone before the stars were gone.
I saw her at the sea-line's smoky rim
Grow swiftly vaguer as they towed her on.

Soon even her masts were hidden in the haze
Beyond the city; she was on her course
To trample billows for a hundred days;
That afternoon the norther gathered force,

Blowing a small snow from a point of east.
"Oh, fair for her," we said, "to take her south."
And in our spirits, as the wind increased,
We saw her there, beyond the river mouth,

Setting her side-lights in the wildering dark,
To glint upon mad water, while the gale
Roared like a battle, snapping like a shark,
And drunken seamen struggled with the sail.

While with sick hearts her mates put out of mind
Their little children left astern, ashore,
And the gale's gathering made the darkness blind,
Water and air one intermingled roar.

Then we forgot her, for the fiddlers played,
Dancing and singing held our merry crew;
The old ship moaned a little as she swayed.
It blew all night, oh, bitter hard it blew!

So that at midnight I was called on deck
To keep an anchor-watch: I heard the sea
Roar past in white procession filled with wreck;
Intense bright frosty stars burned over me,

And the Greek brig beside us dipped and dipped,
White to the muzzle like a half-tide rock,
Drowned to the mainmast with the seas she shipped;
Her cable-swivels clanged at every shock.

And like a never-dying force, the wind
Roared till we shouted with it, roared until
Its vast vitality of wrath was thinned,
Had beat its fury breathless and was still.

By dawn the gale had dwindled into flaw,
A glorious morning followed: with my friend
I climbed the fo'c's'le-head to see; we saw
The waters hurrying shorewards without end.

Haze blotted out the river's lowest reach;
Out of the gloom the steamers, passing by,
Called with their sirens, hooting their sea-speech;
Out of the dimness others made reply.

And as we watched, there came a rush of feet
Charging the fo'c's'le till the hatchway shook.
Men all about us thrust their way, or beat,
Crying, "The *Wanderer!* Down the river! Look!"

I looked with them towards the dimness; there
Gleamed like a spirit striding out of night,
A full-rigged ship unutterably fair,
Her masts like trees in winter, frosty-bright.

Foam trembled at her bows like wisps of wool;
She trembled as she towed. I had not dreamed
The work of man could be so beautiful,
In its own presence and in what it seemed.

"So, she is putting back again," I said.
"How white with frost her yards are on the fore."
One of the men about me answer made,
"That is not frost, but all her sails are tore,

"Torn into tatters, youngster, in the gale;
Her best foul-weather suit gone." It was true,
Her masts were white with rags of tattered sail
Many as gannets when the fish are due.

Beauty in desolation was her pride,
Her crowned array a glory that had been;
She faltered tow'rds us like a swan that died,
But although ruined she was still a queen.

"Put back with all her sails gone," went the word;
Then, from her signals flying, rumour ran,
"The sea that stove her boats in killed her third;
She has been gutted and has lost a man."

So, as though stepping to a funeral march,
She passed defeated homewards whence she came,
Ragged with tattered canvas white as starch,
A wild bird that misfortune had made tame.

She was refitted soon: another took
The dead man's office; then the singers hove
Her capstan till the snapping hawsers shook;
Out, with a bubble at her bows, she drove.

Again they towed her seawards, and again
We, watching, praised her beauty, praised her trim,
Saw her fair house-flag flutter at the main,
And slowly saunter seawards, dwindling dim;

And wished her well, and wondered, as she died,
How, when her canvas had been sheeted home,
Her quivering length would sweep into her stride,
Making the greenness milky with her foam.

But when we rose next morning, we discerned
Her beauty once again a shattered thing;
Towing to dock the *Wanderer* returned,
A wounded sea-bird with a broken wing.

A spar was gone, her rigging's disarray
Told of a worse disaster than the last;
Like draggled hair dishevelled hung the stay,
Drooping and beating on the broken mast.

Half-mast upon her flagstaff hung her flag;
Word went among us how the broken spar
Had gored her captain like an angry stag,
And killed her mate a half-day from the bar.

She passed to dock upon the top of flood.
An old man near me shook his head and swore:
"Like a bad woman, she has tasted blood—
There'll be no trusting in her any more."

We thought it truth, and when we saw her there
Lying in dock, beyond, across the stream,
We would forget that we had called her fair,
We thought her murderess and the past a dream.

And when she sailed again, we watched in awe,
Wondering what bloody act her beauty planned,
What evil lurked behind the thing we saw,
What strength was there that thus annulled man's hand,

How next its triumph would compel man's will
Into compliance with external Fate,
How next the powers would use her to work ill
On suffering men; we had not long to wait

For soon the outcry of derision rose,
"Here comes the *Wanderer!*" the expected cry.
Guessing the cause, our mockings joined with those
Yelled from the shipping as they towed her by.

She passed us close, her seamen paid no heed
To what was called: they stood, a sullen group,
Smoking and spitting, careless of her need,
Mocking the orders given from the poop.

Her mates and boys were working her; we stared.
What was the reason of this strange return,
This third annulling of the thing prepared?
No outward evil could our eyes discern.

Only like one who having formed a plan
Beyond the pitch of common minds, she sailed,
Mocked and deserted by the common man,
Made half divine to me for having failed.

We learned the reason soon; below the town
A stay had parted like a snapping reed,
"Warning," the men thought, "not to take her down."
They took the omen, they would not proceed.

Days passed before another crew would sign.
The *Wanderer* lay in dock alone, unmanned,
Feared as a thing possessed by powers malign,
Bound under curses not to leave the land.

But under passing Time fear passes too;
That terror passed, the sailors' hearts grew bold.
We learned in time that she had found a crew
And was bound out and southwards as of old.

And in contempt we thought, "A little while
Will bring her back again, dismantled, spoiled.
It is herself; she cannot change her style;
She has the habit now of being foiled."

So when a ship appeared among the haze,
We thought, "The *Wanderer* back again"; but no,
No *Wanderer* showed for many, many days,
Her passing lights made other waters glow.

But we would often think and talk of her,
Tell newer hands her story, wondering, then,
Upon what ocean she was *Wanderer*,
Bound to the cities built by foreign men.

And one by one our little conclave thinned,
Passed into ships and sailed and so away,
To drown in some great roaring of the wind,
Wanderers themselves, unhappy fortune's prey.

And Time went by me making memory dim,
Yet still I wondered if the *Wanderer* fared
Still pointing to the unreached ocean's rim,
Brightening the water where her breast was bared.

And much in ports abroad I eyed the ships,
Hoping to see her well-remembered form
Come with a curl of bubbles at her lips
Bright to her berth, the sovereign of the storm.

I never did, and many years went by,
Then, near a Southern port, one Christmas Eve,
I watched a gale go roaring through the sky,
Making the caldrons of the clouds upheave.

Then the wrack tattered and the stars appeared,
Millions of stars that seemed to speak in fire;
A byre cock cried aloud that morning neared,
The swinging wind-vane flashed upon the spire.

And soon men looked upon a glittering earth,
Intensely sparkling like a world new-born;
Only to look was spiritual birth,
So bright the raindrops ran along the thorn.

So bright they were, that one could almost pass
Beyond their twinkling to the source, and know
The glory pushing in the blade of grass,
That hidden soul which makes the flowers grow.

That soul was there apparent, not revealed,
Unearthly meanings covered every tree,
That wet grass grew in an immortal field,
Those waters fed some never-wrinkled sea.

The scarlet berries in the hedge stood out
Like revelations but the tongue unknown;
Even in the brooks a joy was quick: the trout
Rushed in a dumbness dumb to me alone.

All of the valley was aloud with brooks;
I walked the morning, breasting up the fells,
Taking again lost childhood from the rooks,
Whose cawing came above the Christmas bells.

I had not walked that glittering world before,
But up the hill a prompting came to me,
"This line of upland runs along the shore:
Beyond the hedgerow I shall see the sea."

And on the instant from beyond away
That long familiar sound, a ship's bell, broke
The hush below me in the unseen bay.
Old memories came: that inner prompting spoke.

And bright above the hedge a seagull's wings
Flashed and were steady upon empty air.
"A Power unseen," I cried, "prepares these things;
Those are her bells, the *Wanderer* is there."

So, hurrying to the hedge and looking down,
I saw a mighty bay's wind-crinkled blue
Ruffling the image of a tranquil town,
With lapsing waters glittering as they grew.

And near me in the road the shipping swung,
So stately and so still in such great peace
That like to drooping crests their colours hung,
Only their shadows trembled without cease.

I did but glance upon those anchored ships.
Even as my thought had told, I saw her plain;
Tense, like a supple athlete with lean hips,
Swiftness at pause, the *Wanderer* come again—

Come as of old a queen, untouched by Time,
Resting the beauty that no seas could tire,
Sparkling, as though the midnight's rain were rime,
Like a man's thought transfigured into fire.

And as I looked, one of her men began
To sing some simple tune of Christmas day;

Among her crew the song spread, man to man,
Until the singing rang across the bay;

And soon in other anchored ships the men
Joined in the singing with clear throats, until
The farm-boy heard it up the windy glen,
Above the noise of sheep-bells on the hill.

Over the water came the lifted song—
Blind pieces in a mighty game we swing;
Life's battle is a conquest for the strong;
The meaning shows in the defeated thing.

AUGUST, 1914

How still this quiet cornfield is to-night!
By an intenser glow the evening falls,
Bringing, not darkness, but a deeper light;
Among the stooks a partridge covey calls.

The windows glitter on the distant hill;
Beyond the hedge the sheep-bells in the fold
Stumble on sudden music and are still;
The forlorn pinewoods droop above the wold.

An endless quiet valley reaches out
Past the blue hills into the evening sky;
Over the stubble, cawing goes a rout
Of rooks from harvest, flagging as they fly.

So beautiful it is, I never saw
So great a beauty on these English fields,
Touched by the twilight's coming into awe,
Ripe to the soul and rich with summer's yields.

* * * * * *

These homes, this valley spread below me here,
The rooks, the tilted stacks, the beasts in pen,
Have been the heartfelt things, past-speaking dear
To unknown generations of dead men,

Who, century after century, held these farms,
And, looking out to watch the changing sky,
Heard, as we hear, the rumours and alarms
Of war at hand and danger pressing nigh.

And knew, as we know, that the message meant
The breaking off of ties, the loss of friends,
Death, like a miser getting in his rent,
And no new stones laid where the trackway ends.

The harvest not yet won, the empty bin,
The friendly horses taken from the stalls,
The fallow on the hill not yet brought in,
The cracks unplastered in the leaking walls.

Yet heard the news, and went discouraged home,
And brooded by the fire with heavy mind,
With such dumb loving of the Berkshire loam
As breaks the dumb hearts of the English kind,

Then sadly rose and left the well-loved Downs,
And so by ship to sea, and knew no more
The fields of home, the byres, the market towns,
Nor the dear outline of the English shore,

But knew the misery of the soaking trench,
The freezing in the rigging, the despair
In the revolting second of the wrench
When the blind soul is flung upon the air,

And died (uncouthly, most) in foreign lands
For some idea but dimly understood

Of an English city never built by hands
Which love of England prompted and made good.

* * * * * *

If there be any life beyond the grave,
It must be near the men and things we love,
Some power of quick suggestion how to save,
Touching the living soul as from above.

An influence from the Earth from those dead hearts
So passionate once, so deep, so truly kind,
That in the living child the spirit starts,
Feeling companioned still, not left behind.

Surely above these fields a spirit broods,
A sense of many watchers muttering near
Of the lone Downland with the forlorn woods
Loved to the death, inestimably dear.

A muttering from beyond the veils of Death
From long-dead men, to whom this quiet scene
Came among blinding tears with the last breath,
The dying soldier's vision of his queen.

All the unspoken worship of those lives
Spent in forgotten wars at other calls
Glimmers upon these fields where evening drives
Beauty like breath, so gently darkness falls.

Darkness that makes the meadows holier still,
The elm-trees sadden in the hedge, a sigh
Moves in the beech-clump on the haunted hill,
The rising planets deepen in the sky,

And silence broods like spirit on the brae,
A glimmering moon begins, the moonlight runs
Over the grasses of the ancient way
Rutted this morning by the passing guns.

THE RIVER

All other waters have their time of peace,
Calm, or the turn of tide or summer drought;
But on these bars the tumults never cease,
In violent death this river passes out.

Brimming she goes, a bloody-coloured rush
Hurrying her heaped disorder, rank on rank,
Bubbleless speed so still that in the hush
One hears the mined earth dropping from the bank,

Slipping in little falls whose tingeings drown,
Sunk by the waves for ever pressing on.
Till with a stripping crash the tree goes down,
Its washing branches flounder and are gone.

Then, roaring out aloud, her water spreads,
Making a desolation where her waves
Shriek and give battle, tossing up their heads,
Tearing the shifting sandbanks into graves,

Changing the raddled ruin of her course
So swiftly, that the pilgrim on the shore
Hears the loud whirlpool laughing like a horse
Where the scurfed sand was parched an hour before.

And always underneath that heaving tide
The changing bottom runs, or piles, or quakes
Flinging immense heaps up to wallow wide,
Sucking the surface into whirls like snakes,

If anything should touch that shifting sand,
All the blind bottom sucks it till it sinks;
It takes the clipper ere she comes to land,
It takes the thirsting tiger as he drinks.

And on the river pours—it never tires;
Blind, hungry, screaming, day and night the same
Purposeless hurry of a million ires,
Mad as the wind, as merciless as flame.

* * * * * *

There was a full-rigged ship, the *Travancore*,
Towing to port against that river's rage—
A glittering ship made sparkling for the shore,
Taut to the pins in all her equipage.

Clanging, she topped the tide; her sails were furled,
Her men came loitering downwards from the yards;
They who had brought her half across the world,
Trampling so many billows into shards,

Now looking up, beheld their duty done,
The ship approaching port, the great masts bare,
Gaunt as three giants striding in the sun,
Proud, with the colours tailing out like hair.

So, having coiled their gear, they left the deck;
Within the fo'c's'le's gloom of banded steel,
Mottled like wood with many a painted speck,
They brought their plates and sat about a meal.

Then pushing back the tins, they lit their pipes,
Or slept, or played at cards, or gently spoke,
Light from the portholes shot in dusty stripes
Tranquilly moving, sometimes blue with smoke.

These sunbeams sidled when the vessel rolled,
Their lazy dust-strips crossed the floor,
Lighting a man-hole leading to the hold,
A man-hole leaded down the day before.

Like gold the solder on the man-hole shone;
A few flies threading in a drowsy dance
Slept in their pattern, darted, and were gone.
The river roared against the ship's advance.

And quietly sleep came upon the crew,
Man by man drooped upon his arms and slept;
Without, the tugboat dragged the vessel through,
The rigging whined, the yelling water leapt,

Till blindly a careering wave's collapse
Rose from beneath her bows and spouted high,
Spirting the fo'c'sle floor with noisy slaps;
A sleeper at the table heaved a sigh,

And lurched, half-drunk with sleep, across the floor,
Muttering and blinking like a man insane,
Cursed at the river's tumult, shut the door,
Blinked, and lurched back and fell asleep again.

Then there was greater silence in the room,
Ship's creakings ran along the beams and died,
The lazy sunbeams loitered up the gloom,
Stretching and touching till they reached the side.

* * * * * *

Yet something jerking in the vessel's course
Told that the tug was getting her in hand
As, at a fence, one steadies down a horse,
To rush the whirlpool on Magellan Sand;

And in the uneasy water just below
Her Mate inquired "if the men should stir
And come on deck?" Her Captain answered "No,
Let them alone, the tug can manage her."

Then, as she settled down and gathered speed,
Her Mate inquired again "if they should come
Just to be ready there in case of need,
Since, on such godless bars, there might be some."

But "No," the Captain said, "the men have been
Boxing about since midnight, let them be.
The pilot's able and the ship's a queen,
The hands can rest until we come to quay."

They ceased, they took their stations; right ahead
The whirlpool heaped and sucked; in tenor tone
The steady leadsman chanted at the lead,
The ship crept forward trembling to the bone.

And just above the worst a passing wave
Brought to the line such unexpected stress
That as she tossed her bows her towrope gave,
Snapped at the collar like a stalk of cress.

Then, for a ghastly moment, she was loose,
Blind in the whirlpool, groping for a guide,
Swinging adrift without a moment's truce,
She struck the sand and fell upon her side.

And instantly the sand beneath her gave
So that she righted and again was flung,
Grinding the quicksand open for a grave,
Straining her masts until the steel was sprung.

The foremast broke; its mighty bulk of steel
Fell on the fo'c'sle door and jammed it tight;
The sand-rush heaped her to an even keel,
She settled down, resigned, she made no fight,

But, like an overladen beast, she lay
Dumb in the mud with billows at her lips,

Broken, where she had fallen in the way,
Grinding her grave among the bones of ships.

* * * * * *

At the first crashing of the mast, the men
Sprang from their sleep to hurry to the deck;
They found that Fate had caught them in a pen,
The door that opened out was jammed with wreck.

Then, as, with shoulders down, their gathered strength
Hove on the door, but could not make it stir,
They felt the vessel tremble through her length;
The tug, made fast again, was plucking her.

Plucking, and causing motion, till it seemed
That she would get her off; they heard her screw
Mumble the bubbled rip-rap as she steamed;
"Please God, the tug will shift her!" said the crew.

"She's off!" the seamen said; they felt her glide,
Scraping the bottom with her bilge, until
Something collapsing clanged along her side;
The scraping stopped, the tugboat's screw was still.

"She's holed!" a voice without cried; "holed and jammed—
Holed on the old *Magellan*, sunk last June.
I lose my ticket and the men are damned;
They'll drown like rats unless we free them soon.

"My God, they shall not!" and the speaker beat
Blows with a crow upon the foremast's wreck;
Minute steel splinters fell about his feet,
No tremour stirred the ruin on the deck.

And as their natures bade, the seamen learned
That they were doomed within that buried door;

Some cursed, some raved, but one among them turned
Straight to the manhole leaded in the floor,

And sitting down astride it, drew his knife,
And staidly dug to pick away the lead,
While at the ports his fellows cried for life:
"Burst in the door, or we shall all be dead!"

For like a brook the leak below them clucked.
They felt the vessel settling; they could feel
How the blind bog beneath her gripped and sucked.
Their fingers beat their prison walls of steel.

And then the gurgling stopped—the ship was still.
She stayed; she sank no deeper—an arrest
Fothered the pouring leak; she ceased to fill.
She trod the mud, drowned only to the breast.

And probing at the well, the captain found
The leak no longer rising, so he cried:
"She is not sinking—you will not be drowned;
The shifting sand has silted up her side.

"Now there is time. The tug shall put ashore
And fetch explosives to us from the town;
I'll burst the house or blow away the door
(It will not kill you if you all lie down).

"Be easy in your minds, for you'll be free
As soon as we've the blast." The seamen heard
The tug go townwards, butting at the sea;
Some lit their pipes, the youngest of them cheered.

But still the digger bent above the lid,
Gouging the solder from it as at first,
Pecking the lead, intent on what he did;
The other seamen mocked at him or cursed.

And some among them nudged him as he picked.
He cursed them, grinning, but resumed his game;
His knife-point sometimes struck the lid and clicked.
The solder-pellets shone like silver flame.

And still his knife-blade clicked like ticking time
Counting the hour till the tug's return,
And still the ship stood steady on the slime,
While Fate above her fingered with her urn.

* * * * *

Then from the tug beside them came the hail:
"They have none at the stores, nor at the dock,
Nor at the quarry, so I tried the gaol.
They thought they had, but it was out of stock.

"So then I telephoned to town; they say
They've sent an engine with some to the pier;
I did not leave till it was on its way,
A tug is waiting there to bring it here:

"It can't be here, though, for an hour or more;
I've lost an hour in trying, as it is.
For want of thought commend me to the shore.
You'd think they'd know their river's ways by this."

"So there is nothing for it but to wait,"
The Captain answered, fuming. "Until then,
We'd better go to dinner, Mr. Mate."
The cook brought dinner forward to the men.

* * * * *

Another hour of prison loitered by;
The strips of sunlight stiffened at the port,
But still the digger made the pellets fly,
Paying no heed to his companions' sport,

While they, about him, spooning at their tins,
Asked if he dug because he found it cold,
Or whether it was penance for his sins,
Or hope of treasure in the forward hold.

He grinned and cursed, but did not cease to pick,
His sweat dropped from him when he bent his head,
His knife-blade quarried down, till with a click
Its grinded thinness snapped against the lead.

Then, duly rising, brushing back his sweat,
He asked his fellows for another knife.
"Never," they said; "man, what d'ye hope to get?"
"Nothing," he said, "except a chance for life."

"Havers," they said, and one among them growled,
"You'll get no knife from any here to break.
You've dug the manhole since the door was fouled,
And now your knife's broke, quit, for Jesus' sake."

But one, who smelt a bargain, changed his tone,
Offering a sheath-knife for the task in hand
At twenty times its value, as a loan
To be repaid him when they reached the land.

And there was jesting at the lender's greed
And mockery at the digger's want of sense,
Closing with such a bargain without need,
Since in an hour the tug would take them thence.

But "Right," the digger said. The deal was made
He took the borrowed knife, and sitting down
Gouged at the channelled solder with the blade,
Saying, "Let be, it's better dig than drown."

And nothing happened for a while; the heat
Grew in the stuffy room, the sunlight slid,

Flies buzzed about and jostled at the meat,
The knife-blade clicked upon the manhole lid:

And one man said ,"She takes a hell of time
Bringing the blaster," and another snorted;
One, between pipe-puffs, hummed a smutty rhyme,
One, who was weaving, thudded with his sword.

It was as though the ship were in a dream,
Caught in a magic ocean, calm like death,
Tranced, till a presence should arise and gleam,
Making the waters conscious with her breath.

It was so drowsy that the river's cries,
Roaring aloud their ever-changing tune,
Came to those sailors like a drone of flies,
Filling with sleep the summer afternoon.

So that they slept, or, if they spoke, it was
Only to worry lest the tug should come:
Such power upon the body labour has
That prison seemed a blessed rest to some,

Till one man leaning at the port-hole, stared,
Checking his yawning at the widest stretch,
Then blinked and swallowed, while he muttered, scared,
"That blasting-cotton takes an age to fetch."

Then swiftly passing from the port he went
Up and then down the fo'c'sle till he stayed,
Fixed at the port-hole with his eyes intent,
Round-eyed and white, as if he were afraid,

And muttered as he stared, "My God! she is.
She's deeper than she was, she's settling down,
That palm-tree top was steady against this,
And now I see the quay below the town.

"Look here at her. She's sinking in her tracks.
She's going down by inches as she stands;
The water's darker and it stinks like flax,
Her going down is churning up the sands."

And instantly a panic took the crew,
Even the digger blenched; his knife-blade's haste
Cutting the solder witnessed that he knew
Time on the brink with not a breath to waste.

While far away the tugboat at the quay
Under her drooping pennon waited still
For that explosive which would set them free,
Free, with the world a servant to their will.

Then from a boat beside them came a blare,
Urging that tugboat to be quick; and men
Shouted to stir her from her waiting there,
"Hurry the blast, and get us out of pen.

"She's going down. She's going down, man! Quick!"
The tugboat did not stir, no answer came;
They saw her tongue-like pennon idly lick
Clear for an instant, lettered with her name.

Then droop again. The engine had not come,
The blast had not arrived. The prisoned hands
Saw her still waiting though their time had come,
Their ship was going down among the sands,

Going so swiftly now, that they could see
The banks arising as she made her bed;
Full of sick sound she settled deathward, she
Gurgled and shook, the digger picked the lead.

And, as she paused to take a final plunge,
Prone like a half-tide rock, the men on deck

Jumped to their boats and left, ere like a sponge
The river's rotten heart absorbed the wreck;

And on the perilous instant ere Time struck
The digger's work was done, the lead was cleared,
He cast the manhole up; below it muck
Floated, the hold was full, the water leered.

All of his labour had but made a hole
By which to leap to death; he saw black dust
Float on the bubbles of that brimming bowl,
He drew a breath and took his life in thrust,

And plunged head foremost into that black pit,
Where floating cargo bumped against the beams.
He groped a choking passage blind with grit,
The roaring in his ears was shot with screams.

So, with a bursting heart and roaring ears
He floundered in that sunk ship's inky womb,
Drowned in deep water for what seemed like years,
Buried alive and groping through the tomb,

Till suddenly the beams against his back
Gave, and the water on his eyes was bright;
He shot up through a hatchway foul with wrack
Into clean air and life and dazzling light,

And striking out, he saw the fo'c'sle gone,
Vanished, below the water, and the mast
Standing columnar from the sea; it shone
Proud, with its colours flying to the last.

And all about, a many-wrinkled tide
Smoothed and erased its eddies, wandering chilled,
Like glutted purpose, trying to decide
If its achievement had been what it willed.

And men in boats were there; they helped him in.
He gulped for breath and watched that patch of smooth,
Shaped like the vessel, wrinkle into grin,
Furrow to waves and bare a yellow tooth.

Then the masts leaned until the shroud-screws gave.
All disappeared—her masts, her colours, all.
He saw the yardarms tilting to the grave;
He heard the siren of a tugboat call,

And saw her speeding, foaming at the bow,
Bringing the blast-charge that had come too late.
He heard one shout, "It isn't wanted now."
Time's minute-hand had been the hand of Fate.

Then the boats turned; they brought him to the shore.
Men crowded round him, touched him, and were kind;
The Mate walked with him, silent, to the store.
He said, "We've left the best of us behind."

Then, as he wrung his sodden clothes, the Mate
Gave him a drink of rum, and talked awhile
Of men and ships and unexpected Fate;
And darkness came and cloaked the river's guile,

So that its huddled hurry was not seen,
Only made louder, till the full moon climbed
Over the forest, floated, and was queen.
Within the town a temple-belfry chimed.

Then, upon silent pads, a tiger crept
Down to the river-brink, and crouching there
Watched it intently, till you thought he slept
But for his ghastly eye and stiffened hair.

Then, trembling at a lust more fell than his,
He roared and bounded back to coverts lone,
Where, among mooonlit beauty, slaughter is,
Filling the marvellous night with myriad groan.

WATCHING BY A SICK-BED

I heard the wind all day,
And what it was trying to say.
I heard the wind all night
Rave as it ran to fight;
After the wind the rain,
And then the wind again
Running across the hill
As it runs still.

And all day long the sea
Would not let the land be,
But all night heaped her sand
On to the land;
I saw her glimmer white
All through the night,
Tossing the horrid hair
Still tossing there.

And all day long the stone
Felt how the wind was blown;
And all night long the rock
Stood the sea's shock;
While, from the window, I
Looked out, and wondered why,
Why at such length
Such force should fight such strength.

LOLLINGDON DOWNS AND OTHER POEMS

LOLLINGDON DOWNS, AND OTHER POEMS

LOLLINGDON DOWNS

I

So I have known this life,
These beads of coloured days,
This self the string.
What is this thing?

Not beauty; no; not greed,
O, not indeed;
Not all, though much;
Its colour is not such.

It has no eyes to see,
It has no ears,
It is a red hour's war
Followed by tears.

It is an hour of time,
An hour of road,
Flesh is its goad,
Yet, in the sorrowing lands,
Women and men take hands.

O earth, give us the corn,
Come rain, come sun,
We men who have been born
Have tasks undone.
Out of this earth
Comes the thing birth,
The things unguessed, unwon.

II

O wretched man, that, for a little mile
Crawls beneath heaven for his brother's blood,
Whose days the planets number with their style,
To whom all earth is slave, all living, food;

O withering man, within whose folded shell
Lies yet the seed, the spirit's quickening corn,
That Time and Sun will change out of the cell
Into green meadows, in the world unborn;

If Beauty be a dream, do but resolve
And fire shall come, that in the stubborn clay
Works to make perfect till the rocks dissolve,
The barriers burst and Beauty takes her way,

Beauty herself, within whose blossoming Spring
Even wretched man shall clap his hands and sing.

III

Out of the special cell's most special sense
  Came the suggestion when the light was sweet;
All skill, all beauty, all magnificence
  Are hints so caught, man's glimpse of the complete.

And, though the body rots, that sense survives,
  Being of life's own essence it endures
(Fruit of the spirit's tillage in men's lives)
  Round all this ghost that wandering flesh immures.

That is our friend, who, when the iron brain
  Assails, or the earth clogs, or the sun hides,
Is the good God to whom none calls in vain,
  Man's Achieved Good, which, being Life, abides,

The man-made God, that man in happy breath
Makes in despite of Time and dusty death.

IV

You are the link which binds us each to each.
Passion, or too much thought, alone can end
Beauty, the ghost, the spirit's common speech,
Which man's red longing left us for our friend.

Even in the blinding war I have known this,
That flesh is but the carrier of a ghost
Who, through his longing, touches that which is
Even as the sailor knows the foreign coast.

So, by the bedside of the dying black
I felt our uncouth souls subtly made one,
Forgiven, the meanness of each other's lack,
Forgiven, the petty tale of ill things done.

We were but Man, who for a tale of days
Seeks the one city by a million ways.

V

I could not sleep for thinking of the sky,
The unending sky, with all its million suns
Which turn their planets everlastingly
In nothing, where the fire-haired comet runs.

If I could sail that nothing, I should cross
Silence and emptiness with dark stars passing,
Then, in the darkness, see a point of gloss
Burn to a glow, and glare, and keep amassing,

And rage into a sun with wandering planets
And drop behind, and then, as I proceed,
See his last light upon his last moon's granites
Die to a dark that would be night indeed.

Night where my soul might sail a million years
In nothing, not even Death, not even tears.

VI

How did the nothing come, how did these fires,
These million-leagues of fires, first toss their hair,
Licking the moons from heaven in their ires
Flinging them forth for them to wander there?

What was the Mind? Was it a mind which thought?
Or chance? Or law? Or conscious law? Or Power?
Or a vast balance by vast clashes wrought?
Or Time at trial with Matter for an hour?

Or is it all a body where the cells
Are living things supporting something strange
Whose mighty heart the singing planet swells
As it shoulders nothing in unending change?

Is this green earth of many-peopled pain
Part of a life, a cell within a brain?

VII

It may be so; but let the unknown be.
We, on this earth, are servants of the sun.
Out of the sun comes all the quick in me,
His golden touch is life to everyone.

His power it is that makes us spin through space,
His youth is April and his manhood bread,
Beauty is but a looking on his face,
He clears the mind, he makes the roses red.

What he may be, who knows? But we are his,
We roll through nothing round him, year by year,
The withering leaves upon a tree which is
Each with his greed, his little power, his fear.

What we may be, who knows? But everyone
Is dust on dust a servant of the sun.

VIII

The Kings go by with jewelled crowns,
Their horses gleam, their banners shake, their spears are many.
The sack of many-peopled towns
Is all their dream:
The way they take
Leaves but a ruin in the brake
And, in the furrow that the ploughmen make,
A stampless penny; a tale, a dream.

The merchants reckon up their gold,
Their letters come, their ships arrive, their freights are glories:
The profits of their treasures sold
They tell and sum;
Their foremen drive
The servants starved to half-alive
Whose labours do not make the earth a hive
Of stinking stories; a tale, a dream.

The priests are singing in their stalls,
Their singing lifts, their incense burns, their praying clamours;
Yet God is as the sparrow falls;
The ivy drifts,
The votive urns
Are all left void when Fortune turns,
The god is but a marble for the kerns
To break with hammers: a tale, a dream.

O Beauty, let me know again
The green earth cold, the April rain,
The quiet waters figuring sky,
The one star risen.
So shall I pass into the feast
Not touched by King, merchant or priest,
Know the red spirit of the beast,
Be the green grain;
Escape from prison.

IX

What is this life which uses living cells
It knows not how nor why, for no known end,
This soul of man upon whose fragile shells
Of blood and brain his very powers depend?
Pour out its little blood or touch its brain
The thing is helpless, gone, no longer known,
The carrion cells are never man again,
No hand relights the little candle blown.
It comes not from Without, but from the sperm
Fed in the womb, it is a man-made thing,
That takes from man its power to live a term
Served by live cells of which it is the King.
Can it be blood and brain? It is most great,
Through blood and brain alone it wrestles Fate.

X

Can it be blood and brain, this transient force
Which, by an impulse, seizes flesh and grows
To man, the thing less splendid than the horse,
More blind than owls, less lovely than the rose?
O, by a power unknown it works the cells
Of blood and brain; it has the power to see
Beyond the apparent thing the something else
Which it inspires dust to bring to be.
O, blood and brain are its imperfect tools,
Easily wrecked, soon worn, slow to attain,
Only by years of toil the master rules
To lovely ends, those servants blood and brain.
And Death, a touch, a germ, has still the force
To make him ev'n as the rose, the owl, the horse.

XI

Not only blood and brain its servants are,
There is a finer power that needs no slaves
Whose lovely service distance cannot bar
Nor the green sea with all her hell of waves,
Nor snowy mountains, nor the desert sand,
Nor heat, nor storm, it bends to no control,
It is a stretching of the spirit's hand
To touch the brother's or the sister's soul;
So that from darkness in the narrow room
I can step forth and be about her heart,
Needing no star, no lantern in the gloom,
No word from her, no pointing on the chart,
Only red knowledge of a window flung
Wide to the night, and calling without tongue.

XII

Drop me the seed, that I, even in my brain
May be its nourishing earth. No mortal knows
From what immortal granary comes the grain,
Nor how the earth conspires to make the rose;

But from the dust and from the wetted mud
Comes help, given or taken; so with me
Deep in my brain the essence of my blood
Shall give it stature until Beauty be.

It will look down, even as the burning flower
Smiles upon June, long after I am gone.
Dust-footed Time will never tell its hour,
Through dusty Time its rose will draw men on,

Through dusty Time its beauty shall make plain
Man, and, Without, a spirit scattering grain.

XIII

Ah, but Without there is no spirit scattering;
Nothing but Life, most fertile but unwise,
Passing through change in the sun's heat and cloud's watering,
Pregnant with self, unlit by inner eyes.

There is no Sower, nor seed for any tillage;
Nothing but the grey brain's pash, and the tense will
And that poor fool of the Being's little village
Feeling for the truth in the little veins that thrill.

There is no Sowing, but digging, year by year,
In a hill's heart, now one way, now another,
Till the rock breaks and the valley is made clear
And the poor Fool stands, and knows the sun for his brother,

And the Soul shakes wings like a bird escaped from cage
And the tribe moves on to camp in its heritage.

XIV

You are too beautiful for mortal eyes,
You the divine unapprehended soul;
The red worm in the marrow of the wise
Stirs as you pass, but never sees you whole.

Even as the watcher in the midnight tower
Knows from a change in heaven an unseen star,
So from your beauty, so from the summer flower,
So from the light, one guesses what you are.

So in the darkness does the traveller come
To some lit chink, through which he cannot see,
More than a light, nor hear, more than a hum,
Of the great hall where Kings in council be.

So, in the grave, the red and mouthless worm
Knows of the soul that held his body firm.

XV

Is it a sea on which the souls embark
Out of the body, as men put to sea?
Or do we come like candles in the dark
In the rooms in cities in eternity?

Is it a darkness that our powers can light?
Is this, our little lantern of man's love,
A help to find friends wandering in the night
In the unknown country with no star above?

Or is it sleep, unknowing, outlasting clocks
That outlast men, that, though the cockcrow ring,
Is but one peace, of the substance of the rocks,
Is but one space in the now unquickened thing,

Is but one joy, that, though the million tire,
Is one, always the same, one life, one fire?

THE BLACKSMITH

XVI

The blacksmith in his sparky forge
Beat on the white-hot softness there;
Even as he beat he sang an air
To keep the sparks out of his gorge.

So many shoes the blacksmith beat,
So many shares and links for traces,
So many builders' struts and braces,
Such tackling for the chain-fore-sheet,

That, in his pride, big words he spake;
"I am the master of my trade,

What iron is good for I have made,
I make what is in iron to make."

Daily he sang thus by his fire,
Till one day, as he poised his stroke
Above his bar, the iron spoke,
"You boaster, drop your hammer, liar."

The hammer dropped out of his hand,
The iron rose, it gathered shape,
It took the blacksmith by the nape,
It pressed him to the furnace, and

Heaped fire upon him till his form
Was molten, flinging sparks aloft,
Until his bones were melted soft,
His hairs crisped in a fiery storm.

The iron drew him from the blaze
To place him on the anvil, then
It beat him from the shape of men,
Like drugs the apothecary brays;

Beat him to ploughing-coulters, beat
Body and blood to links of chain,
With endless hammerings of pain,
Unending torment of white heat;

And did not stop the work, but still
Beat on him while the furnace roared;
The blacksmith suffered and implored,
With iron bonds upon his will.

And, though he could not die nor shrink,
He felt his being beat by force
To horse shoes stamped on by the horse,
And into troughs whence cattle drink.

He felt his blood, his dear delight,
Beat into shares, he felt it rive
The green earth red; he was alive,
Dragged through the earth by horses' might.

He felt his brain, that once had planned
His daily life, changed to a chain
Which curbed a sail or dragged a wain,
Or hoisted ship-loads to the land.

He felt his heart, that once had thrilled
With love of wife and little ones,
Cut out and mingled with his bones
To pin the bricks where men rebuilt.

He felt his very self impelled
To common uses, till he cried,
"There's more within me than is tried,
More than you ever think to weld.

"For all my pain I am only used
To make the props for daily labour;
I burn, I am beaten like a tabor
To make men tools; I am abused.

"Deep in the white heat where I gasp
I see the unmastered finer powers,
Iron by cunning wrought to flowers,
File-worked, not tortured by the rasp.

"Deep in this fire-tortured mind
Thought bends the bar in subtler ways,
It glows into the mass, its rays
Purge, till the iron is refined.

"Then, as the full moon draws the tide
Out of the vague uncaptained sea,

Some moon power there ought to be
To work on ore; it should be tried.

"By this fierce fire in which I ache
I see new fires not yet begun,
A blacksmith smithying with the sun,
At unmade things man ought to make.

"Life is not fire and blows, but thought,
Attention kindling into joy,
Those who make nothing new destroy,
O me, what evil I have wrought.

"O me," and as he moaned he saw
His iron master shake, he felt
No blow, nor did the fire melt
His flesh, he was released from law.

He sat upon the anvil top
Dazed, as the iron was dazed, he took
Strength, seeing that the iron shook,
He said, "This cruel time must stop."

He seized the iron and held him fast
With pincers, in the midmost blaze,
A million sparks went million ways,
The cowhorn handle plied the blast.

"Burn, then," he cried; the fire was white,
The iron was whiter than the fire.
The fireblast made the embers twire,
The blacksmith's arm began to smite.

First vengeance for old pain, and then
Beginning hope of better things,
Then swordblades for the sides of Kings
And corselets for the breasts of men.

And crowns and such like joys and gems.
And stars of honour for the pure,
Jewel of honour to endure,
Beautiful women's diadems.

And coulters, sevenfold-twinned, to rend,
And girders to uphold the tower,
Harness for unimagined power,
New ships to make the billows bend,

And stores of fire-compelling things
By which men dominate and pierce
The iron-imprisoned universe
Where angels lie with banded wings.

THE FRONTIER
XVII

PERSONS { COTTA, LUCIUS, THEIR CHIEF }

COTTA

Would God the route would come for home.
My God, this place, day after day,
A month of heavy march from Rome.
This camp, the troopers' huts of clay,
The horses tugging at their pins,
The roaring brook and then the whins
And nothing new to do or say.

LUCIUS

They say the tribes are up.

COTTA

Who knows?

LUCIUS

Our scouts say that they saw their fires.

COTTA

Well, if we fight it's only blows
And bogging horses in the mires.

LUCIUS

Their raiders crossed the line last night,
Eastward from this, to raid the stud,
They stole our old chief's stallion, Kite.
He's in pursuit.

COTTA

That looks like blood.

LUCIUS

Well, better that than dicing here
Beside this everlasting stream.

COTTA

My God, I was in Rome last year,
Under the sun, it seems a dream.

LUCIUS

Things are not going well in Rome,
This frontier war is wasting men
Like water, and the Tartars come
In hordes.

COTTA

We beat them back again.

LUCIUS

So far we have, and yet I feel
The Empire is too wide a bow
For one land's strength.

COTTA

The stuff's good steel.

LUCIUS

Too great a strain may snap it though.
If we were ordered home. . . .

COTTA

Good Lord . . .

LUCIUS

If . . . Then our friends, the tribesmen there,
Would have glad days.

COTTA

This town would flare
To warm old Foxfoot and his horde.

LUCIUS

We have not been forethoughtful here,
Pressing the men to fill the ranks
Centurions sweep the province clear.

COTTA

Rightly.

LUCIUS

Perhaps.

COTTA

We get no thanks.

LUCIUS

We strip the men for troops abroad
And leave the women and the slaves
For merchants and their kind. The graves
Of half each province line the road.
These people could not stand a day
Against the tribes, with us away.

COTTA

Rightly.

LUCIUS

Perhaps.

COTTA

Here comes the Chief.

LUCIUS

Sir, did your riders catch the thief?

CHIEF

No, he got clear and keeps the horse
But bad news always comes with worse.
The frontier's fallen, we're recalled,
Our army's broken, Rome's appalled.
My God, the whole world's in a blaze.
So now, we've done with idle days
Fooling on frontiers. Boot and start.
It gives a strange feel in the heart
To think that this, that Rome has made,
Is done with. Yes, the stock's decayed.
We march at once. You mark my words,
We're done, we're crumbled into sherds,
We shall not see this place again
When once we go.

LUCIUS

Do none remain?

CHIEF

No, none, all march. Here ends the play.
March, and burn camp. The order's gone,
Your men have sent your baggage on.

COTTA

My God, hark how the trumpets bray.

CHIEF

They do. You see the end of things.
The power of a thousand kings
Helped us to this, and now the power
Is so much hay that was a flower.

LUCIUS

We have been very great and strong.

CHIEF

That's over now.

LUCIUS

It will be long
Before the world will see our like.

CHIEF

We've kept these thieves beyond the dyke
A good long time, here on the Wall.

LUCIUS

Colonel, we ought to sound a call
To mark the end of this.

CHIEF

We ought.
Look. There's the hill top where we fought
Old Foxfoot. Look, there in the whin.
Old ruffian knave. Come on. Fall in.

THE DOWNLAND

XVIII

Night is on the downland, on the lonely moorland,
On the hills where the wind goes over sheep-bitten turf,
Where the bent grass beats upon the unploughed poorland
And the pine woods roar like the surf.

Here the Roman lived on the wind-barren lonely,
Dark now and haunted by the moorland fowl;
None comes here now but the peewit only,
And moth-like death in the owl.

Beauty was here, on this beetle-droning downland;
The thought of a Cæsar in the purple came
From the palace by the Tiber in the Roman townland
To this wind-swept hill with no name.

Lonely Beauty came here and was here in sadness,
Brave as a thought on the frontier of the mind,
In the camp of the wild upon the march of madness,
The bright-eyed Queen of the blind.

Now where Beauty was are the wind-withered gorses
Moaning like old men in the hill-wind's blast;
The flying sky is dark with running horses
And the night is full of the past.

MIDNIGHT

XIX

The fox came up by Stringer's Pound,
He smelt the south west warm on the ground,
From west to east a feathery smell
Of blood on the wing-quills tasting well.
A buck's hind feet thumped on the sod,
The whip-like grass snake went to clod,
The dog-fox put his nose in the air
To taste what food was wandering there.
Under the clover down the hill
A hare in form that knew his will.
Up the hill, the warren awake
And the badger shewing teeth like a rake.

Down the hill the two twin thropes
Where the crying night owl waked the corpse,
And the moon on the stilly windows bright
Instead of a dead man's waking light.
The cock on his perch that shook his wing
When the clock struck for the chimes to ring,
A duck that muttered, a rat that ran
And a horse that stamped, remembering man.

ON THE DOWNS

XX

Up on the downs the red-eyed kestrels hover
Eyeing the grass.
The field mouse flits like a shadow into cover
As their shadows pass.

Men are burning the gorse on the down's shoulder;
A drift of smoke
Glitters with fire and hangs, and the skies smoulder,
And the lungs choke.

Once the tribe did thus on the downs, on these downs, burning
Men in the frame,
Crying to the gods of the downs till their brains were turning
And the gods came.

And to-day on the downs, in the wind, the hawks, the grasses,
In blood and air,
Something passes me and cries as it passes,
On the chalk downland bare.

THE COLD COTSWOLDS

XXI

No man takes the farm,
Nothing grows there,
The ivy's arm
Strangles the rose there.

Old Farmer Kyrle
Farmed there the last;
He beat his girl
(It's seven years past).

After market it was
He beat his girl;
He liked his glass,
Old Farmer Kyrle.

Old Kyrle's son
Said to his father,
"Now, dad, you ha' done,
I'll kill you rather.

"Stop beating sister
Or by God I'll kill you."
Kyrle was full of liquor.
Old Kyrle said, "Will you?"

Kyrle took his cobb'd stick
And beat his daughter.
He said, "Ill teach my chick
As a father oughter."

Young Will, the son,
Heard his sister shriek,
He took his gun
Quick as a streak.

He said, "Now, dad,
Stop, once for all."
He was a good lad,
Good at kicking the ball.

His father clubbed
The girl on the head.
Young Will upped
And shot him dead.

"Now, sister," said Will,
"I've a-killed father,
As I said I'd kill.
O my love, I'd rather

"A kill him again
Than see you suffer.
O my little Jane,
Kiss goodbye to your brother.

"I won't see you again,
Nor the cows homing,
Nor the mice in the grain,
Nor the primrose coming,

"Nor the fair, nor folk,
Nor the summer flowers

Growing on the wold
Nor aught that's ours.

"Not Tib the cat,
Not Stub the mare,
Nor old dog Pat
Never anywhere.

"For I'll be hung
In Gloucester prison
When the bell's rung
And the sun's risen."

* * * *

They hanged Will
As Will said,
With one thrill
They choked him dead.

Jane walked the wold
Like a grey gander;
All grown old
She would wander.

She died soon.
At high tide,
At full moon
Jane died.

The brook chatters
As at first,
The farm it waters
Is accurst;

No man takes it,
Nothing grows there,
Blood straiks it,
A ghost goes there.

A HUNDRED YEARS AGO

XXII

A hundred years ago, they quarried for the stone here;
The carts came through the wood by the track still plain;
The drills shew in the rock where the blasts were blown here,
They shew up dark after rain.

Then the last cart of stone went away through the wood,
To build the great house for some April of a woman,
Till her beauty stood in stone, as the man's thought made it good,
And the dumb rock was made human.

The house still stands, but the April of its glory
Is gone, long since, with the beauty that has gone,
She wandered away west, it is an old sad story,
It is best not talked upon.

And the man has gone, too, but the quarry that he made,
Whenever April comes as it came in old time,
Is a dear delight to the man who loves a maid,
For the primrose comes from the lime. . . .

And the blackbird builds below the catkin shaking
And the sweet white violets are beauty in the blood,
And daffodils are there, and the blackthorn blossom breaking
Is a wild white beauty in bud.

HERE THE LEGION HALTED

XXIII

Here the legion halted, here the ranks were broken,
And the men fell out to gather wood,
And the green wood smoked, and bitter words were spoken,
And the trumpets called to food.

And the sentry on the rampart saw the distance dying
In the smoke of distance blue and far,
And heard the curlew calling and the owl replying
As the night came cold with one star;

And thought of home beyond, over moorland, over marshes,
Over hills, over the sea, across the plains, across the pass,
By a bright sea trodden by the ships of Tarshis,
The farm, with cicadæ in the grass.

And thought, as I, "Perhaps I may be done with living
To-morrow, when we fight. I shall see those souls no more.
O, beloved souls, be beloved in forgiving
The deeds and the words that make me sore."

WE DANCED

XXIV

We danced away care till the fiddler's eyes blinked,
And at supper, at midnight, our wine-glasses chinked,
Then we danced till the roses that hung round the wall
Were broken red petals that did rise and did fall
To the ever-turning couples of the bright-eyed and gay,
Singing in the midnight to dance care away.

Then the dancing died out and the carriages came,
And the beauties took their cloaks and the men did the same,
And the wheels crunched the gravel and the lights were turned
down,
And the tired beauties dozed through the cold drive to town.

Nan was the belle and she married her beau,
Who drank, and then beat her, and she died long ago,
And Mary, her sister, is married and gone
To a tea planter's lodge, in the plains, in Ceylon.

And Dorothy's sons have been killed out in France,
And Mary lost her man in the August advance,
And Em, the man jilted, and she lives all alone
In the house of this dance which seems burnt in my bone.

Margaret and Susan and Marion and Phyllis
With red lips laughing and the beauty of lilies
And the grace of wild swans and a wonder of bright hair,
Dancing among roses with petals in the air.

All, all are gone, and Hetty's little maid
Is so like her mother that it makes me afraid.
And Rosalind's son, whom I passed in the street,
Clinked on the pavement with the spurs on his feet.

PART TWO

REYNARD THE FOX; OR, THE GHOST HEATH RUN

PART I

The meet was at "The Cock and Pye"
By Charles and Martha Enderby,
The grey, three-hundred-year-old inn
Long since the haunt of Benjamin
The highwayman, who rode the bay.
The tavern fronts the coaching way,
The mail changed horses there of old.
It has a strip of grassy mould
In front of it, a broad green strip.
A trough, where horses' muzzles dip,
Stands opposite the tavern front,
And there that morning came the hunt,
To fill that quiet width of road
As full of men as Framilode
Is full of sea when tide is in.

The stables were alive with din
From dawn until the time of meeting.
A pad-groom gave a cloth a beating,
Knocking the dust out with a stake.
Two men cleaned stalls with fork and rake,
And one went whistling to the pump,
The handle whined, ker-lump ker-lump,
The water splashed into the pail,
And, as he went, it left a trail,
Lipped over on the yard's bricked paving.
Two grooms (sent on before) were shaving
There in the yard, at glasses propped

On jutting bricks; they scraped and stropped,
And felt their chins and leaned and peered,
A woodland day was what they feared
(As second horsemen), shaving there.
Then, in the stalls where hunters were,
Straw rustled as the horses shifted,
The hayseeds ticked and haystraws drifted
From racks as horses tugged their feed.
Slow gulping sounds of steady greed
Came from each stall, and sometimes stampings,
Whinnies (at well-known steps) and rampings
To see the horse in the next stall.

Outside, the spangled cock did call
To scattering grain that Martha flung.
And many a time a mop was wrung
By Susan ere the floor was clean.
The harness room, that busy scene,
Clinked and chinked from ostlers brightening
Rings and bits with dips of whitening,
Rubbing fox-flecks out of stirrups,
Dumbing buckles of their chirrups
By the touch of oily feathers.
Some, with stag's bones rubbed at leathers,
Brushed at saddle-flaps or hove
Saddle linings to the stove.
Blue smoke from strong tobacco drifted
Out of the yard, the passers snifft it,
Mixed with the strong ammonia flavor
Of horses' stables and the savour
Of saddle-paste and polish spirit
Which put the gleam on flap and tirrit.
The grooms in shirts with rolled-up sleeves,
Belted by girths of coloured weaves,
Groomed the clipped hunters in their stalls.

One said "My dad cured saddle galls,
He called it Doctor Barton's cure;
Hog's lard and borax, laid on pure."
And others said, "Ge' back, my son,"
"Stand over, girl; now, girl, ha' done."
"Now, boy, no snapping; gently. Crikes
He gives a rare pinch when he likes."
"Drawn blood? I thought he looked a biter."
"I give 'em all sweet spit of nitre
For that, myself: that sometimes cures."
"Now, Beauty, mind them feet of yours."
They groomed, and sissed with hissing notes
To keep the dust out of their throats.

There came again and yet again
The feed-box lid, the swish of grain,
Or Joe's boots stamping in the loft,
The hay-fork's stab and then the soft
Hay's scratching slither down the shoot.
Then with a thud some horse's foot
Stamped, and the gulping munch again
Resumed its lippings at the grain.

The road outside the inn was quiet
Save for the poor, mad, restless pyat
Hopping his hanging wicker-cage.
No calmative of sleep or sage
Will cure the fever to be free.
He shook the wicker ceaselessly
Now up, now down, but never out
On wind-waves, being blown about,
Looking for dead things good to eat.
His cage was strewn with scattered wheat.

At ten o'clock, the Doctor's lad
Brought up his master's hunting pad

And put him in a stall, and leaned
Against the stall, and sissed, and cleaned
The port and cannons of his curb.
He chewed a sprig of smelling herb.
He sometimes stopped, and spat, and chid
The silly things his master did.

At twenty past, old Baldock strode
His ploughman's straddle down the road.
An old man with a gaunt, burnt face;
His eyes rapt back on some far place,
Like some starved, half-mad saint in bliss
In God's world through the rags of this.
He leaned upon a stake of ash
Cut from a sapling: many a gash
Was in his old, full-skirted coat.
The twisted muscles in his throat
Moved, as he swallowed, like taut cord.
His oaken face was seamed and gored.
He halted by the inn and stared
On that far bliss, that place prepared
Beyond his eyes, beyond his mind.

Then Thomas Copp, of Cowfoot's Wynd,
Drove up; and stopped to take a glass.
"I hope they'll gallop on my grass,"
He said, "My little girl does sing
To see the red coats galloping.
It's good for grass, too, to be trodden
Except they poach it, where it's sodden."
Then Billy Waldrist, from the Lynn,
With Jockey Hill, from Pitts, came in
And had a sip of gin and stout
To help the jockey's sweatings out.
"Rare day for scent," the jockey said.

A pony like a feather bed
On four short sticks, took place aside.
The little girl who rode astride
Watched everything with eyes that glowed
With glory in the horse she rode.

At half-past ten, some lads on foot
Came to be beaters to a shoot
Of rabbits at the Warren Hill.
Rough sticks they had, and Hob and Jill,
Their ferrets, in a bag, and netting.
They talked of dinner-beer and betting;
And jeered at those who stood around.
They rolled their dogs upon the ground
And teased them: "Rats", they cried, "go fetch."
"Go seek, good Roxer; 'z bite, good betch.
What dinner-beer'll they give us, lad?
Sex quarts the lot last year we had.
They'd ought to give us seven this.
Seek, Susan; what a betch it is."

A pommle cob came trotting up
Round-bellied like a drinking-cup
Bearing on back a pommle man
Round-bellied like a drinking-can.
The clergyman from Condicote.
His face was scarlet from his trot,
His white hair bobbed about his head
As halos do round clergy dead.
He asked Tom Copp, "How long to wait?"
His loose mouth opened like a gate,
To pass the wagons of his speech,
He had a mighty voice to preach.
Though indolent in other matters
He let his children go in tatters.

His daughter Madge on foot, flush-cheekt,
In broken hat and boots that leakt,
With bits of hay all over her,
Her plain face grinning at the stir
(A broad pale face, snub-nosed, with speckles
Of sandy eyebrows sprinkt with freckles)
Came after him and stood apart
Beside the darling of her heart,
Miss Hattie Dyce from Baydon Dean;
A big young fair one, chiselled clean,
Brow, chin and nose, with great blue eyes,
All innocence and sweet surprise,
And golden hair piled coil on coil
Too beautiful for time to spoil.
They talked in undertones together
Not of the hunting, nor the weather.
Old Steven from Scratch Steven Place,
(A white beard and a rosy face),
Came next on his stringhalty grey,
"I've come to see the hounds away,"
He said, "And ride a field or two.
We old have better things to do
Than breaking all our necks for fun."
He shone on people like the sun,
And on himself for shining so.

Three men came riding in a row:—
John Pym, a bull-man, quick to strike,
Gross and blunt-headed like a shrike
Yet sweet-voiced as a piping flute;
Tom See, the trainer, from the Toot,
Red, with an angry, puzzled face
And mouth twitched upward out of place,
Sucking cheap grapes and spitting seeds;
And Stone, of Bartle's Cattle Feeds,

A man whose bulk of flesh and bone
Made people call him Twenty Stone.
He was the man who stood a pull
At Tencombe with the Jersey bull
And brought the bull back to his stall.

Some children ranged the tavern-wall.
Sucking their thumbs and staring hard;
Some grooms brought horses from the yard.
Jane Selbie said to Ellen Tranter,
"A lot on 'em come doggin', ant her?"
"A lot on 'em," said Ellen, "look
There'm Mr. Gaunt of Water's Hook.
They say he" . . . (whispered). "Law," said Jane.
Gaunt flung his heel across the mane,
And slithered from his horse and stamped.
"Boots tight," he said, "my feet are cramped."

A loose-shod horse came clicking clack;
Nick Wolvesey on a hired hack
Come tittup, like a cup and ball.
One saw the sun, moon, stars and all
The great green earth twixt him and saddle;
Then Molly Wolvesey riding straddle
Red as a rose, with eyes like sparks,
Two boys from college out for larks
Hunted bright Molly for a smile
But were not worth their quarry's while.

Two eyeglassed gunners dressed in tweed
Came with a spaniel on a lead
And waited for a fellow gunner.
The parson's son, the famous runner,
Came dressed to follow hounds on foot.
His knees were red as yew tree root

From being bare, day in day out;
He wore a blazer, and a clout
(His sweater's arms) tied round his neck.
His football shorts had many a speck
And splash of mud from many a fall
Got as he picked the slippery ball
Heeled out behind a breaking scrum.
He grinned at people, but was dumb,
Not like these lousy foreigners.
The otter-hounds and harriers
From Godstow to the Wye all knew him.

And with him came the stock which grew him
The parson and his sporting wife,
She was a stout one, full of life
With red, quick, kindly, manly face.
She held the knave, queen, king and ace,
In every hand she played with men.
She was no sister to the hen,
But fierce and minded to be queen.
She wore a coat and skirt of green,
A waistcoat cut of hunting red,
Her tie pin was a fox's head.

The parson was a manly one
His jolly eyes were bright with fun.
His jolly mouth was well inclined
To cry aloud his jolly mind
To everyone, in jolly terms.
He did not talk of churchyard worms,
But of our privilege as dust
To box a lively bout with lust
Ere going to Heaven to rejoice.
He loved the sound of his own voice.
His talk was like a charge of horse;

His build was all compact, for force,
Well-knit, well-made, well-coloured, eager,
He kept no Lent to make him meagre.
He loved his God, himself and man.
He never said "life's wretched span;
This wicked world," in any sermon.
This body that we feed the worm on,
To him, was jovial stuff that thrilled.
He liked to see the foxes killed;
But most he felt himself in clover
To hear "Hen left, hare right, cock over,"
At woodside, when the leaves are brown.
Some grey cathedral in a town
Where drowsy bells toll out the time
To shaven closes sweet with lime,
And wall-flower roots drive out of the mortar
All summer on the Norman Dortar,
Was certain some day to be his.
Nor would a mitre go amiss
To him, because he governed well.
His voice was like the tenor bell
When services were said and sung.
And he had read in many a tongue,
Arabic, Hebrew, Spanish, Greek.

Two bright young women, nothing meek,
Rode up on bicycles and propped
Their wheels in such wise that they dropped
To bring the parson's son to aid.
Their cycling suits were tailor-made,
Smart, mannish, pert, but feminine.
The colour and the zest of wine
Were in their presence and their bearing;
Like spring, they brought the thought of pairing.
The parson's lady thought them pert.

And they could mock a man and flirt,
Do billiard tricks with corks and pennies,
Sing ragtime songs and win at tennis
The silver cigarette-case prize.
They had good colour and bright eyes,
Bright hair, bright teeth and pretty skin,
Which many lads had longed to win
On darkened stairways after dances.
Their reading was the last romances,
And they were dashing hockey players,
Men called them, "Jill and Joan, the slayers."
They were as bright as fresh sweet-peas.
Old Farmer Bennett followed these
Upon his big-boned savage black
Whose mule-teeth yellowed to bite back
Whatever came within his reach.
Old Bennett sat him like a leech
The grim old rider seemed to be
As hard about the mouth as he.

The beaters nudged each other's ribs
With "There he goes, his bloody Nibs.
He come on Joe and Anty Cop,
And beat 'em with his hunting crop
Like tho' they'd bin a sack of beans.
His pickers were a pack of queans,
And Joe and Anty took a couple
He caught 'em there, and banged 'em supple.
Women and men, he didn't care
(He'd kill 'em some day, if he dare)
He beat the whole four nearly dead.
'I'll learn 'ee rabbit in my shed,
That's how my ricks get set afire.'
That's what he said, the bloody liar;
Old oaf, I'd like to burn his ricks,

Th' old swine's too free with fists and sticks.
He keeps that Mrs. Jones himselve."

Just like an axehead on its helve
Old Bennett sat and watched the gathering.
He'd given many a man a lathering
In field or barn, and women, too.
His cold eye reached the women through
With comment, and the men with scorn.
He hated women gently born;
He hated all beyond his grasp;
For he was minded like the asp
That strikes whatever is not dust.

Charles Copse, of Copse Hold Manor, thrust
Next into view. In face and limb
The beauty and the grace of him
Were like the golden age returned.
His grave eyes steadily discerned
The good in men and what was wise.
He had deep blue, mild-coloured eyes,
And shocks of harvest-coloured hair,
Still beautiful with youth. An air
Or power of kindness went about him;
No heart of youth could ever doubt him
Or fail to follow where he led.
He was a genius, simply bred,
And quite unconscious of his power.
He was the very red rose flower
Of all that coloured countryside.
Gauchos had taught him how to ride.
He knew all arts, but practised most
The art of bettering flesh and ghost
In men and lads down in the mud.
He knew no class in flesh and blood.

He loved his kind. He spent some pith
Long since, relieving Ladysmith.
Many a horse he trotted tame,
Heading commandos from their aim,
In those old days upon the veldt.
An old bear in a scarlet pelt
Came next, old Squire Harridew,
His eyebrows gave a man the grue
So bushy and so fierce they were;
He had a bitter tongue to swear.
A fierce, hot, hard, old, stupid squire,
With all his liver made of fire,
Small brain, great courage, mulish will.
The hearts in all his house stood still
When someone crossed the squire's path.
For he was terrible in wrath,
And smashed whatever came to hand.
Two things he failed to understand,
The foreigner and what was new.

His daughters, Carrie, Jane and Lu
Rode with him, Carrie at his side.
His son, the ne'er-do-weel, had died
In Arizona, long before.
The Squire set the greatest store
By Carrie, youngest of the three,
And lovely to the blood was she;
Blonde, with a face of blush and cream,
And eyes deep violet in their gleam,
Bright blue when quiet in repose.
She was a very golden rose.
And many a man when sunset came
Would see the manor windows flame,
And think, "My beauty's home is there."
Queen Helen had less golden hair,

Queen Cleopatra paler lips,
Queen Blanche's eyes were in eclipse,
By golden Carrie's glancing by.
She had a wit for mockery
And sang mild, pretty senseless songs
Of sunsets, Heav'n and lover's wrongs,
Sweet to the Squire when he had dined.
A rosebud need not have a mind.
A lily is not sweet from learning.
Jane looked like a dark lantern, burning.
Outwardly dark, unkempt, uncouth,
But minded like the living truth,
A friend that nothing shook nor wearied.
She was not "Darling Jane'd," nor "dearie'd,"
She was all prickles to the touch,
So sharp, that many feared to clutch,
So keen, that many thought her bitter.
She let the little sparrows twitter.
She had a hard ungracious way.
Her storm of hair was iron-grey,
And she was passionate in her heart
For women's souls that burn apart,
Just as her mother's had, with Squire.
She gave the sense of smouldering fire.
She was not happy being a maid,
At home, with Squire, but she stayed
Enduring life, however bleak,
To guard her sisters who were weak,
And force a life for them from Squire.
And she had roused and stood his fire
A hundred times, and earned his hate,
To win those two a better state.
Long years before the Canon's son
Had cared for her, but he had gone
To Klondyke, to the mines, for gold,

To find, in some strange way untold
A foreign grave that no men knew.

No depth, nor beauty, was in Lu,
But charm and fun, for she was merry,
Round, sweet and little like a cherry,
With laughter like a robin's singing;
She was not kittenlike and clinging,
But pert and arch and fond of flirting,
In mocking ways that were not hurting,
And merry ways that women pardoned.
Not being married yet she gardened.
She loved sweet music; she would sing
Songs made before the German King
Made England German in her mind.
She sang "My lady is unkind,"
"The Hunt is up," and those sweet things
Which Thomas Campion set to strings
"Thrice toss," and "What," and "Where are now?"

The next to come was Major Howe
Driv'n in a dog-cart by a groom.
The testy major was in fume
To find no hunter standing waiting;
The groom who drove him caught a rating,
The groom who had the horse in stable,
Was damned in half the tongues of Babel.
The Major being hot and heady
When horse or dinner was not ready.
He was a lean, tough, liverish fellow,
With pale blue eyes (the whites pale yellow),
Moustache clipped toothbrush-wise, and jaws
Shaved bluish like old partridge claws.
When he had stripped his coat he made
A speckless presence for parade,

New pink, white cords, and glossy tops,
New gloves, the newest thing in crops,
Worn with an air that well expressed
His sense that no one else was dressed.

Quick trotting after Major Howe
Came Doctor Frome of Quickemshow,
A smiling silent man whose brain
Knew all of every secret pain
In every man and woman there.
Their inmost lives were all laid bare
To him, because he touched their lives
When strong emotions sharp as knives
Brought out what sort of soul each was.
As secret as the graveyard grass
He was, as he had need to be.
At some time he had had to see
Each person there, sans clothes, sans mask,
Sans lying even, when to ask
Probed a tamed spirit into truth.

Richard, his son, a jolly youth
Rode with him, fresh from Thomas's,
As merry as a yearling is
In maytime in a clover patch.
He was a gallant chick to hatch
Big, brown and smiling, blithe and kind,
With all his father's love of mind
And greater force to give it act.
To see him when the scrum was packt,
Heave, playing forward, was a sight.
His tackling was the crowd's delight
In many a danger close to goal.
The pride in the three quarter's soul
Dropped, like a wet rag, when he collared.
He was as steady as a bollard,

And gallant as a skysail yard.
He rode a chestnut mare which sparred.
In good St. Thomas' Hospital,
He was the crown imperial
Of all the scholars of his year.

The Harold lads, from Tencombe Weir,
Came all on foot in corduroys,
Poor widowed Mrs. Harold's boys,
Dick, Hal and Charles, whose father died.
(Will Masemore shot him in the side
By accident at Masemore Farm,
A hazel knocked Will Masemore's arm
In getting through a hedge; his gun
Was not half-cocked, so it was done
And those three boys left fatherless.)
Their gaitered legs were in a mess
With good red mud from twenty ditches.
Hal's face was plastered like his breeches,
Dick chewed a twig of juniper.
They kept at distance from the stir
Their loss had made them lads apart.
Next came the Colways' pony cart
From Coln St. Evelyn's with the party,
Hugh Colway jovial, bold and hearty
And Polly Colway's brother, John
(Their horses had been both sent on)
And Polly Colway drove them there.
Poor pretty Polly Colway's hair.
The grey mare killed her at the brook
Down Seven Springs Mead at Water Hook
Just one month later, poor sweet woman.
Her brother was a rat-faced Roman
Lean, puckered, tight-skinned from the sea
Commander in the *Canace*

Able to drive a horse, or ship,
Or crew of men, without a whip
By will, as long as they could go.
His face would wrinkle, row on row,
From mouth to hair-roots when he laught
He looked ahead as though his craft
Were with him still, in dangerous channels.
He and Hugh Colway tossed their flannels
Into the pony-cart and mounted.
Six foiled attempts the watchers counted,
The horses being bickering things,
That so much scarlet made like kings,
Such sidling and such pawing and shifting.

When Hugh was up his mare went drifting
Sidelong and feeling with her heels
For horses' legs and poshay wheels,
While lather creamed her neat clipt skin.
Hugh guessed her foibles with a grin.
He was a rich town-merchant's son,
A wise and kind man fond of fun,
Who loved to have a troop of friends
At Coln St. Eves for all week-ends,
And troops of children in for tea
He gloried in a Christmas Tree.
And Polly was his heart's best treasure,
And Polly was a golden pleasure
To everyone, to see or hear.

Poor Polly's dying struck him queer,
He was a darkened man thereafter,
Cowed silent, he would wince at laughter
And be so gentle it was strange
Even to see. Life loves to change.

Now Coln St. Evelyn's hearths are cold
The shutters up, the hunters sold,

And green mould damps the locked front door.
But this was still a month before,
And Polly, golden in the chaise,
Still smiled, and there were golden days,
Still thirty days, for those dear lovers.

The Riddens came, from Ocle Covers,
Bill Ridden riding Stormalong,
(By Tempest out of Love-me-long)
A proper handful of a horse,
That nothing but the Aintree course
Could bring to terms, save Bill perhaps.
All sport, from bloody war to craps,
Came well to Bill, that big-mouthed smiler;
They nick-named him "the mug-beguiler",
For Billy lived too much with horses
In coper's yards and sharper's courses,
To lack the sharper-coper streak.
He did not turn the other cheek,
When struck (as English Christians do),
He boxed like a Whitechapel Jew,
And many a time his knuckles bled
Against a race-course-gipsy's head.
For "hit him first and argue later,"
Was truth at Billy's alma mater,
Not love, not any bosh of love.
His hand was like a chamois glove
And riding was his chief delight.
He bred the 'chaser Chinese-white,
From Lilybud by Mandarin.
And when his mouth tucked corners in,
And scent was high and hounds were going,
He went across a field like snowing
And tackled anything that came.

His wife, Sal Ridden, was the same,
A loud, bold, blonde, abundant mare,
With white, horse teeth and stooks of hair,
(Like polished brass) and such a manner
It flaunted from her like a banner.
Her father was Tom See the trainer;
She rode a lovely earth-disdainer
Which she and Billy wished to sell.

Behind them rode her daughter Bell,
A strange, shy, lovely girl whose face
Was sweet with thought, and proud with race,
And bright with joy at riding there.
She was as good as blowing air
But shy and difficult to know;
The kittens in the barley-mow,
The setter's toothless puppies sprawling,
The blackbird in the apple calling,
All knew her spirit more than we
So delicate these maidens be
In loving lovely, helpless things.

The Manor set, from Tencombe Rings,
Came, with two friends, a set of six.
Ed Manor with his cockerel chicks,
Nob, Cob and Bunny as they called them,
(God help the school or rule which galled them;
They carried head) and friends from town.

Ed Manor trained on Tencombe Down.
He once had been a famous bat,
He had that stroke, "the Manor-pat,"
Which snicked the ball for three, past cover.
He once scored twenty in an over,
But now he cricketed no more.
He purpled in the face and swore

At all three sons, and trained, and told
Long tales of cricketing of old,
When he alone had saved his side.
Drink made it doubtful if he lied,
Drink purpled him, he could not face
The fences now, nor go the pace
He brought his friends to meet; no more.

His big son Nob, at whom he swore,
Swore back at him, for Nob was surly,
Tall, shifty, sullen-smiling, burly,
Quite fearless, built with such a jaw
That no man's rule could be his law
Nor any woman's son his master.
Boxing he relished. He could plaster
All those who boxed out Tencombe way.
A front tooth had been knocked away
Two days before, which put his mouth
A little to the east of south.
And put a venom in his laughter.

Cob was a lighter lad, but dafter;
Just past eighteen, while Nob was twenty.
Nob had no nerves but Cob had plenty
So Cobby went where Nobby led.
He had no brains inside his head,
Was fearless, just like Nob, but put
Some clog of folly round his foot,
Where Nob put will of force or fraud;
He spat aside and muttered "Gawd"
When vext; he took to whiskey kindly
And loved and followed Nobby blindly,
And rode as in the saddle born.

Bun looked upon the two with scorn
He was the youngest, and was wise.

He, too, was fair, with sullen eyes,
He too (a year before) had had
A zest for going to the bad,
With Cob and Nob. He knew the joys
Of drinking with the stable-boys,
Or smoking while he filled his skin
With pints of Guinness dashed with gin
And Cobby yelled a bawdy ditty,
Or cutting Nobby for the kitty,
And damning peoples' eyes and guts,
Or drawing evening-church for sluts
He knew them all and now was quit.

Sweet Polly Colway managed it.
And Bunny changed. He dropped his drink,
(The pleasant pit's seductive brink),
He started working in the stable,
And well, for he was shrewd and able.
He left the doubtful female friends
Picked up at Evening-Service ends,
He gave up cards and swore no more.
Nob called him "the Reforming Whore,"
"The Soul's Awakening," or "The Text,"
Nob being always coarse when vext.

Ed Manor's friends were Hawke and Sladd,
Old college friends, the last he had,
Rare horsemen, but their nerves were shaken
By all the whiskey they had taken.
Hawke's hand was trembling on his rein.
His eyes were dead-blue like a vein,
His peaked, sad face was touched with breeding,
His querulous mind was quaint from reading,
His piping voice still quirked with fun.
Many a mad thing he had done,
Riding to hounds and going to races.

A glimmer of the gambler's graces,
Wit, courage, devil, touched his talk.

Sladd's big fat face was white as chalk,
His mind went wandering, swift yet solemn,
'Twixt winning-post and betting column,
The weights and forms and likely colts.
He said "This road is full of jolts.
I shall be seasick riding here.
O, damn last night with that liqueur."

Len Stokes rode up on Peterkin;
He owned the Downs by Baydon Whin;
And grazed some thousand sheep; the boy
Grinned round at men with jolly joy
At being alive and being there.
His big round face and mop of hair
Shone, his great teeth shone in his grin,
The clean blood in his clear tanned skin
Ran merry, and his great voice mocked
His young friends present till they rocked.

Steer Harpit came from Rowell Hill,
A small, frail man, all heart and will,
A sailor as his voice betrayed.
He let his whip-thong droop and played
At snicking off the grass-blades with it.
John Hankerton, from Compton Lythitt,
Was there with Pity Hankerton,
And Mike, their good-for-little son,
Back, smiling, from his seventh job.
Joan Urch was there upon her cob.
Tom Sparsholt on his lanky grey.
John Restrop from Hope Goneaway.
And Vaughan, the big, black handsome devil,
Loose-lipped with song, and wine, and revel,
All rosy from his morning tub.

The Godsdown tigress with her cub
(Lady and Tommy Crowmarsh) came.
The great eyes smouldered in the dame,
Wit glittered, too, which few men saw.
There was more beauty there than claw.
Tommy in bearing, horse and dress
Was black, fastidious handsomeness,
Choice to his trimmed soul's fingertips.
Heredia's sonnets on his lips.
A line undrawn, a plate not bitten,
A stone uncut, a phrase unwritten,
That would be perfect, made his mind.
A choice pull, from a rare print, signed,
Was Tommy. He collected plate,
(Old Sheffield) and he owned each state
Of all the Meryon Paris etchings.
Colonel Sir Button Budd of Fletchings
Was there; Long Robert Thrupp was there,
(Three yards of him men said there were),
Long as the King of Prussia's fancy.
He rode the longlegged Necromancy,
A useless racehorse that could canter.
George Childrey with his jolly banter
Was there; Nick Childrey, too, come down
The night before from London town,
To hunt and have his lungs blown clean.
The Ilsley set from Tuttocks Green
Was there (old Henry Ilsley drove),
Carlotta Ilsely brought her love
A flop-jowled broker from the city.
Men pitied her, for she was pretty.

Some grooms and second horsemen mustered.
A lot of men on foot were clustered
Round the inn-door, all busy drinking,

One heard the kissing glasses clinking
In passage as the tray was brought.
Two terriers (which they had there) fought
There on the green, a loud, wild whirl.
Bell stopped them like a gallant girl.
The hens behind the tavern clucked.

Then on a horse which bit and bucked
(The half-broke four-year-old Marauder)
Came Minton-Price of th' Afghan border
Lean, puckered, yellowed, knotted, scarred,
Tough as a hide-rope twisted hard,
Tense tiger-sinew knit to bone.
Strange-wayed from having lived alone
With Kafir, Afghan and Beloosh
In stations frozen in the Koosh
Where nothing but the bullet sings.
His mind had conquered many things
Painting, mechanics, physics, law,
White-hot, hand-beaten things to draw
Self-hammered from his own soul's stithy,
His speech was blacksmith-sparked and pithy.
Danger had been his brother bred;
The stones had often been his bed
In bickers with the border-thieves.

A chestnut mare, with swerves and heaves,
Came plunging, scattering all the crowd,
She tossed her head and laughed aloud
And bickered sideways past the meet.
From pricking ears to mincing feet
She was all tense with blood and quiver;
You saw her clipt hide twitch and shiver
Over her netted cords of veins.
She carried Cothill, of the Sleins;

A tall, black, bright-eyed handsome lad.
Great power and great grace he had.
Men hoped the greatest things of him,
His grace made people think him slim,
But he was muscled like a horse
A sculptor would have wrought his torse
In bronze or marble for Apollo.
He loved to hurry like a swallow
For miles on miles of short-grassed, sweet
Blue-harebelled downs, where dewy feet
Of pure winds hurry ceaselessly.
He loved the downland like a sea,
The downland where the kestrels hover;
The downland had him for a lover.
And every other thing he loved
In which a clean free spirit moved.

So beautiful, he was, so bright.
He looked to men like young delight
Gone courting April maidenhood,
That has the primrose in her blood,
He on his mincing lady mare.

Ock Gurney and old Pete were there,
Riding their bonny cobs and swearing.
Ock's wife had giv'n them both a fairing,
A horse-rosette, red, white and blue.
Their cheeks were brown as any brew,
And every comer to the meet
Said "Hello, Ock" or "Morning, Pete;
Be you a going to a wedding?"
"Why, noa," they said, "we'm going a bedding;
Now ben't us, uncle, ben't us, Ock?"
Pete Gurney was a lusty cock
Turned sixty-three, but bright and hale,
A dairy-farmer in the vale,

Much like a robin in the face,
Much character in little space,
With little eyes like burning coal.
His mouth was like a slit or hole
In leather that was seamed and lined.
He had the russet-apple mind
That betters as the weather worsen.
He was a manly English person,
Kind to the core, brave, merry, true;
One grief he had, a grief still new,
That former Parson joined with Squire
In putting down the Playing Quire,
In church, and putting organ in.
"Ah, boys, that was a pious din
That Quire was; a pious praise
The noise was that we used to raise;
I and my serpent, George with his'n,
On Easter Day in 'He is Risen,'
Or blessed Christmas in 'Venite';
And how the trombone came in mighty,
In Alleluias from the heart.
Pious, for each man played his part,
Not like 'tis now." Thus he, still sore
For changes forty years before,
When all (that could) in time and tune,
Blew trumpets to the newë moon.
He was a bachelor, from choice.
He and his nephew farmed the Boyce
Prime pasture land for thirty cows.
Ock's wife, Selina Jane, kept house,
And jolly were the three together.

Ock had a face like summer weather
A broad red sun, split by a smile.
He mopped his forehead all the while,

And said "By damn," and "Ben't us, Unk?"
His eyes were close and deeply sunk.
He cursed his hunter like a lover,
"Now blast your soul, my dear, give over.
Woa, now, my pretty, damn your eyes."
Like Pete he was of middle size,
Dean-oak-like, stuggy, strong in shoulder,
He stood a wrestle like a boulder,
He had a back for pitching hay,
His singing voice was like a bay.
In talk he had a sideways spit,
Each minute, to refresh his wit.
He cracked Brazil nuts with his teeth.
He challenged Cobbett of the Heath
(Weight-lifting champion) once, but lost.
Hunting was what he loved the most,
Next to his wife and Uncle Pete.
With beer to drink and cheese to eat,
And rain in May to fill the grasses,
This life was not a dream that passes
To Ock, but like the summer flower.
But now the clock had struck the hour,
And round the corner, down the road
The bob-bob-bobbing serpent flowed
With three black knobs upon its spine;
Three bobbing black-caps in a line.
A glimpse of scarlet at the gap
Showed underneath each bobbing cap,
And at the corner by the gate,
One heard Tom Dansey give a rate,
"Hep, Drop it, Jumper; have a care."
There came a growl, half-rate, half-swear,
A spitting crack, a tuneful whimper
And sweet religion entered Jumper.

There was a general turn of faces,
The men and horses shifted places,
And round the corner came the hunt,
Those feathery things, the hounds, in front,
Intent, wise, dipping, trotting, straying,
Smiling at people, shoving, playing,
Nosing to children's faces, waving
Their feathery sterns, and all behaving,
One eye to Dansey on Maroon.
Their padding cat-feet beat a tune,
And though they trotted up so quiet
Their noses brought them news of riot,
Wild smells of things with living blood,
Hot smells, against the grippers good,
Of weasel, rabbit, cat and hare,
Whose feet had been before them there,
Whose taint still tingled every breath;
But Dansey on Maroon was death,
So, though their noses roved, their feet
Larked and trit-trotted to the meet.

Bill Tall and Ell and Mirtie Key
(Aged fourteen years between the three)
Were flooded by them at the bend,
They thought their little lives would end,
For grave sweet eyes looked into theirs,
Cold noses came, and clean short hairs
And tails all crumpled up like ferns,
A sea of moving heads and sterns,
All round them, brushing coat and dress:
One paused, expecting a caress.
The children shrank into each other,
Shut eyes, clutched tight, and shouted "Mother"
With mouths wide open, catching tears.

Sharp Mrs. Tall allayed their fears,
"Err out the road, the dogs won't hurt 'ee.
There now, you've cried your faces dirty.
More cleaning up for me to do.
What? Cry at dogs, great lumps like you?"
She licked her handkerchief and smeared
Their faces where the dirt appeared.

The hunt trit-trotted to the meeting,
Tom Dansey touching cap to greeting,
Slow-lifting crop-thong to the rim,
No hunter there got more from him
Except some brightening of the eye.
He halted at the "Cock and Pye,"
The hounds drew round him on the green,
Arrogant, Daffodil and Queen,
Closest, but all in little space.
Some lolled their tongues, some made grimace,
Yawning, or tilting nose in quest,
All stood and looked about with zest,
They were uneasy as they waited.
Their sires and dams had been well-mated,
They were a lovely pack for looks;
Their forelegs drumsticked without crooks,
Straight, without overtread or bend,
Muscled to gallop to the end,
With neat feet round as any cat's.
Great chested, muscled in the slats,
Bright, clean, short-coated, broad in shoulder,
With stag-like eyes that seemed to smoulder.
The heads well-cocked, the clean necks strong;
Brows broad, ears close, the muzzles long;
And all like racers in the thighs;
Their noses exquisitely wise,
Their minds being memories of smells;

Their voices like a ring of bells;
Their sterns all spirit, cock and feather;
Their colours like the English weather,
Magpie and hare, and badger-pye,
Like minglings in a double dye,
Some smutty-nosed, some tan, none bald;
Their manners were to come when called,
Their flesh was sinew knit to bone,
Their courage like a banner blown.
Their joy, to push him out of cover,
And hunt him till they rolled him over.
They were as game as Robert Dover.
Tom Dansey was a famous whip
Trained as a child in horsemanship
Entered, as soon as he was able
As boy at Caunter's racing stable;
There, like the other boys, he slept
In stall beside the horse he kept,
Snug in the straw; and Caunter's stick
Brought morning to him all too quick.
He learned the high quick gingery ways
Of thoroughbreds; his stable days
Made him a rider, groom and vet.
He promised to be too thickset
For jockeying, so left it soon.
Now he was whip and rode Maroon.

He was a small, lean, wiry man
With sunk cheeks weathered to a tan
Scarred by the spikes of hawthorn sprays
Dashed thro', head down, on going days,
In haste to see the line they took.
There was a beauty in his look
It was intent. His speech was plain.
Maroon's head, reaching to the rein,

Had half his thought before he spoke.
His "gone away," when foxes broke,
Was like a bell. His chief delight
Was hunting fox from noon to night.
His pleasure lay in hounds and horses,
He loved the Seven Springs water-courses,
Those flashing brooks (in good sound grass,
Where scent would hang like breath on glass).
He loved the English countryside;
The wine-leaved bramble in the ride,
The lichen on the apple-trees,
The poultry ranging on the lees,
The farms, the moist earth-smelling cover,
His wife's green grave at Mitcheldover,
Where snowdrops pushed at the first thaw.
Under his hide his heart was raw
With joy and pity of these things.
The second whip was Kitty Myngs
Still but a lad but keen and quick
(Son of old Myngs who farmed the Wick)
A horse-mouthed lad who knew his work.
He rode the big black horse, the Turk,
And longed to be a huntsman bold.
He had the horse-look, sharp and old,
With much good-nature in his face.
His passion was to go the pace
His blood was crying for a taming.
He was the Devil's chick for gaming,
He was a rare good lad to box.
He sometimes had a main of cocks
Down at the Flags. His job with hounds
At present kept his blood in bounds
From rioting and running hare.
Tom Dansey made him have a care
He worshipped Dansey heart and soul.

To be a huntsman was his goal;
To be with hounds, to charge full tilt
Blackthorns that made the gentry wilt
Was his ambition and his hope.
He was a hot colt needing rope
He was too quick to speak his passion
To suit his present huntsman's fashion.

The huntsman, Robin Dawe, looked round,
He sometimes called a favourite hound,
Gently, to see the creature turn,
Look happy, up and wag his stern.
He smiled, and nodded, and saluted,
To those who hailed him, as it suited.
And patted Pip's, his hunter's neck.
His new pink was without a speck;
He was a red-faced smiling fellow,
His voice clear tenor, full and mellow,
His eyes, all fire, were black and small.
He had been smashed in many a fall.
His eyebrow had a white curved mark
Left by the bright shoe of The Lark,
Down in a ditch by Seven Springs.
His coat had all been trod to strings,
His ribs laid bare and shoulder broken
Being jumped on, down at Water's Oaken,
The time his horse came down and rolled.
His face was of the country mould
Such as the mason sometimes cutted
On English moulding-ends which jutted
Out of the church walls, centuries since.
And as you never know the quince,
How good he is, until you try,
So, in Dawe's face, what met the eye
Was only part, what lay behind

Was English character and mind.
Great kindness, delicate sweet feeling,
(Most shy, most clever in concealing
Its depth) for beauty of all sorts,
Great manliness and love of sports,
A grave wise thoughtfulness and truth,
A merry fun, outlasting youth,
A courage terrible to see
And mercy for his enemy.

He had a clean-shaved face, but kept
A hedge of whisker neatly clipt,
A narrow strip or picture frame
(Old Dawe, the woodman, did the same),
Under his chin from ear to ear.

But now the resting hounds gave cheer,
Joyful and Arrogant and Catch-him,
Smelt the glad news and ran to snatch him,
The Master's dogcart turned the bend.
Damsel and Skylark knew their friend;
A thrill ran through the pack like fire,
And little whimpers ran in quire.
The horses cocked and pawed and whickered,
Young Cothill's chaser kicked and bickered,
And stood on end and struck out sparks.
Joyful and Catch-him sang like larks,
There was the Master in the trap,
Clutching old Roman in his lap,
Old Roman, crazy for his brothers,
And putting frenzy in the others,
To set them at the dogcart wheels,
With thrusting heads and little squeals.

The Master put old Roman by,
And eyed the thrusters heedfully,

He called a few pet hounds and fed
Three special friends with scraps of bread,
Then peeled his wraps, climbed down and strode
Through all those clamourers in the road,
Saluted friends, looked round the crowd,
Saw Harridew's three girls and bowed,
Then took White Rabbit from the groom.

He was Sir Peter Bynd, of Coombe;
Past sixty now, though hearty still,
A living picture of good-will,
An old, grave soldier, sweet and kind,
A courtier with a knightly mind,
Who felt whatever thing he thought.
His face was scarred, for he had fought
Five wars for us. Within his face
Courage and power had their place,
Rough energy, decision, force.
He smiled about him from his horse.
He had a welcome and salute
For all, on horse or wheel or foot,
Whatever kind of life each followed.
His tanned, drawn cheeks looked old and hollowed,
But still his bright blue eyes were young,
And when the pack crashed into tongue,
And staunch White Rabbit shook like fire,
He sent him at it like a flier,
And lived with hounds while horses could.
"They'm lying in the Ghost Heath Wood,
Sir Peter," said an earth-stopper,
(Old Baldy Hill), "You'll find 'em there.
'Z I come'd across I smell 'em plain.
There's one up back, down Tuttock's drain,
But, Lord, it's just a bog, the Tuttocks,
Hounds would be swallered to the buttocks.

Heath Wood, Sir Peter's best to draw."
Sir Peter gave two minutes' law
For Kingston Challow and his daughter;
He said. "They're late. We'll start the slaughter.
Ghost Heath, then, Dansey. We'll be going."

Now, at his word, the tide was flowing
Off went Maroon, off went the hounds,
Down road, then off, to Chols Elm Grounds,
Across soft turf with dead leaves cleaving
And hillocks that the mole was heaving,
Mild going to those trotting feet.
After the scarlet coats, the meet
Came clopping up the grass in spate
They poached the trickle at the gate;
Their horses' feet sucked at the mud;
Excitement in the horses' blood,
Cocked forward every ear and eye;
They quivered as the hounds went by,
They trembled when they first trod grass;
They would not let another pass,
They scattered wide up Chols Elm Hill.

The wind was westerly but still;
The sky a high fair-weather cloud,
Like meadows ridge-and-furrow ploughed,
Just glinting sun but scarcely moving.
Blackbirds and thrushes thought of loving,
Catkins were out; the day seemed tense
It was so still. At every fence
Cow-parsley pushed its thin green fern.
White-violet-leaves shewed at the burn.

Young Cothill let his 'chaser go
Round Chols Elm Field a turn or so
To soothe his edge. The riders went

Chatting and laughing and content
In groups of two or three together.
The hounds, a flock of shaking feather,
Bobbed on ahead, past Chols Elm Cop.
The horses' shoes went clip-a-clop,
Along the stony cart-track there.
The little spinney was all bare,
But in the earth-moist winter day
The scarlet coats twixt tree and spray,
The glistening horses pressing on,
The brown faced lads, Bill, Dick and John,
And all the hurry to arrive,
Were beautiful like spring alive.
The hounds melted away with Master
The tanned lads ran, the field rode faster,
The chatter joggled in the throats
Of riders bumping by like boats,
"We really ought to hunt a bye day."
"Fine day for scent," "A fly or die day."
"They chopped a bagman in the check,
He had a collar round his neck."
"Old Ridden's girl's a pretty flapper."
"That Vaughan's a cad, the whipper-snapper."
"I tell 'ee, lads, I seed 'em plain,
Down in the Rough at Shifford's Main,
Old Squire stamping like a duke,
So red with blood I thought he'd puke,
In appleplexie, as they do.

Miss Jane stood just as white as dew,
And heard him out in just white heat,
And then she trimmed him down a treat,
About Miss Lu it was, or Carrie
(She'd be a pretty peach to marry)."

"Her'll draw up-wind, so us'll go
Down by the furze, we'll see 'em so."

"Look, there they go, lad."

There they went,
Across the brook and up the bent,
Past Primrose Wood, past Brady Ride,
Along Ghost Heath to cover side.
The bobbing scarlet, trotting pack,
Turf scatters tossed behind each back,
Some horses blowing with a whinny,
A jam of horses in the spinney,
Close to the ride-gate; leather straining,
Saddles all creaking; men complaining,
Chaffing each other as they pass't,
On Ghost Heath turf as they trotted fast.
Now as they neared the Ghost Heath Wood,
Some riders grumbled, "What's the good:
It's shot all day and poached all night.
We shall draw blank and lose the light,
And lose the scent, and lose the day.
Why can't he draw Hope Goneaway,
Or Tuttocks Wood, instead of this?
There's no fox here, there never is."

But as he trotted up to cover,
Robin was watching to discover
What chance there was, and many a token
Told him, that though no hound had spoken,
Most of them stirred to something there.
The old hounds' muzzles searched the air,
Thin ghosts of scents were in their teeth,
From foxes which had crossed the Heath
Not very many hours before.

"We'll find," he said, "I'll bet a score."
Along Ghost Heath they trotted well,
The hoof-cuts made the bruised earth smell,
The shaken brambles scattered drops,
Stray pheasants kukkered out of copse,
Cracking the twigs down with their knockings
And planing out of sight with cockings;
A scut or two lopped white to bramble.

And now they gathered to the gamble
At Ghost Heath Wood on Ghost Heath Down,
The hounds went crackling through the brown
Dry stalks of bracken killed by frost.
The wood stood silent in its host
Of halted trees all winter bare.
The boughs, like veins that suck the air,
Stretched tense, the last leaf scarcely stirred.
There came no song from any bird;
The darkness of the wood stood still
Waiting for fate on Ghost Heath Hill.
The whips crept to the sides to view;
The Master gave the nod, and "Leu,
Leu in, Ed-hoick, Ed-hoick, Leu in,"
Went Robin, cracking through the whin
And through the hedge-gap into cover.
The binders crashed as hounds went over,
And cock-cock-cock the pheasants rose.
Then up went stern and down went nose,
And Robin's cheerful tenor cried,
Through hazel-scrub and stub and ride,
"O wind him beauties, push him out,
Yooi, onto him, Yahout, Yahout,
O push him out, Yooi, wind him, wind him."
The beauties burst the scrub to find him,
They nosed the warren's clipped green lawn,

The bramble and the broom were drawn,
The covert's northern end was blank.

They turned to draw along the bank
Through thicker cover than the Rough
Through three-and-four-year understuff
Where Robin's forearm screened his eyes.
"Yooi, find him, beauties," came his cries.
"Hark, hark to Daffodil," the laughter
Faln from his horn, brought whimpers after,
For ends of scents were everywhere.
He said, "This Hope's a likely lair.
And there's his billets, grey and furred.
And George, he's moving, there's a bird."

A blue uneasy jay was chacking.
(A swearing screech, like tearing sacking)
From tree to tree, as in pursuit,
He said "That's it. There's fox afoot.
And there, they're feathering, there she speaks.
Good Daffodil, good Tarrybreeks,
Hark there, to Daffodil, hark, hark."
The mild horn's note, the soft flaked spark
Of music, fell on that rank scent.
From heart to wild heart magic went.
The whimpering quivered, quavered, rose.
"Daffodil has it. There she goes.
O hark to her." With wild high crying
From frantic hearts, the hounds went flying
To Daffodil for that rank taint.
A waft of it came warm but faint,
In Robin's mouth, and faded so.
"First find a fox, then let him go,"
Cried Robin Dawe. "For any sake.
Ring, Charley, till you're fit to break."

He cheered his beauties like a lover
And charged beside them into cover.

PART II

On old Cold Crendon's windy tops
Grows wintrily Blown Hilcote Copse,
Wind-bitten beech with badger barrows,
Where brocks eat wasp-grubs with their marrows,
And foxes lie on short-grassed turf,
Nose between paws, to hear the surf
Of wind in the beeches drowsily.
There was our fox bred lustily
Three years before, and there he berthed
Under the beech-roots snugly earthed,
With a roof of flint and a floor of chalk
And ten bitten hens' heads each on its stalk,
Some rabbits' paws, some fur from scuts,
A badger's corpse and a smell of guts.
And there on the night before my tale
He trotted out for a point in the vale.
He saw, from the cover edge, the valley
Go trooping down with its droops of sally
To the brimming river's lipping bend,
And a light in the inn at Water's End.
He heard the owl go hunting by
And the shriek of the mouse the owl made die,
And the purr of the owl as he tore the red
Strings from between his claws and fed;
The smack of joy of the horny lips
Marbled green with the blobby strips.
He saw the farms where the dogs were barking,
Cold Crendon Court and Copsecote Larking;
The fault with the spring as bright as gleed,
Green-slash-laced with water weed.

A glare in the sky still marked the town,
Though all folk slept and the blinds were down,
The street lamps watched the empty square,
The night-cat sang his evil there.
The fox's nose tipped up and round
Since smell is a part of sight and sound.
Delicate smells were drifting by,
The sharp nose flaired them heedfully;
Partridges in the clover stubble,
Crouched in a ring for the stoat to nubble.
Rabbit bucks beginning to box;

A scratching place for the pheasant cocks;
A hare in the dead grass near the drain,
And another smell like the spring again.

A faint rank taint like April coming,
It cocked his ears and his blood went drumming,
For somewhere out by Ghost Heath Stubs
Was a roving vixen wanting cubs.
Over the valley, floating faint
On a warmth of windflaw came the taint,
He cocked his ears, he upped his brush,
And he went up wind like an April thrush.
By the Roman Road to Braiches Ridge
Where the fallen willow makes a bridge,
Over the brook by White Hart's Thorn,
To the acres thin with pricking corn.
Over the sparse green hair of the wheat,
By the Clench Brook Mill at Clench Brook Leat,
Through Cowfoot Pastures to Nonely Stevens,
And away to Poltrewood St. Jevons.
Past Tott Hill Down all snaked with meuses,
Past Clench St. Michael and Naunton Crucis,
Past Howle's Oak Farm where the raving brain

Of a dog who heard him foamed his chain,
Then off, as the farmer's window opened,
Past Stonepits Farm to Upton Hope End;
Over short sweet grass and worn flint arrows,
And the three dumb hows of Tencombe Barrows;
And away and away with a rolling scramble,
Through the blackthorn and up the bramble,
With a nose for the smells the night wind carried,
And his red fell clean for being married.
For clicketting time and Ghost Heath Wood
Had put the violet in his blood.

At Tencombe Rings near the Manor Linney,
His foot made the great black stallion whinny,
And the stallion's whinny aroused the stable,
And the bloodhound bitches stretched their cable,
And the clink of the bloodhound's chain aroused
The sweet-breathed kye as they chewed and drowsed,
And the stir of the cattle changed the dream
Of the cat in the loft to tense green gleam.
The red-wattled black cock hot from Spain
Crowed from his perch for dawn again,
His breast-pufft hens, one-legged on perch,
Gurgled, beak-down, like men in church,
They crooned in the dark, lifting one red eye
In the raftered roost as the fox went by.

By Tencombe Regis and Slaughters Court,
Through the great grass square of Roman Fort,
By Nun's Wood Yews and the Hungry Hill,
And the Corpse Way Stones all standing still,
By Seven Springs Mead to Deerlip Brook,
And a lolloping leap to Water Hook.
Then with eyes like sparks and his blood awoken
Over the grass to Water's Oaken,

And over the hedge and into ride
In Ghost Heath Wood for his roving bride.

Before the dawn he had loved and fed
And found a kennel and gone to bed
On a shelf of grass in a thick of gorse
That would bleed a hound and blind a horse.
There he slept in the mild west weather
With his nose and brush well tucked together,
He slept like a child, who sleeps yet hears
With the self who needs neither eyes nor ears.

He slept while the pheasant cock untucked
His head from his wing, flew down and kukked,
While the drove of the starlings whirred and wheeled
Out of the ash-trees into field.
While with great black flags that flogged and paddled
The rooks went out to the plough and straddled,
Straddled wide on the moist red cheese,
Of the furrows driven at Uppat's Leas.
Down in the village, men awoke,
The chimneys breathed with a faint blue smoke,
The fox slept on, though tweaks and twitches
Due to his dreams, ran down his flitches.

The cows were milked and the yards were sluict,
And the cocks and hens let out of roost,
Windows were opened, mats were beaten,
All men's breakfasts were cooked and eaten,
But out in the gorse on the grassy shelf,
The sleeping fox looked after himself.

Deep in his dream he heard the life
Of the woodland seek for food or wife,
The hop of a stoat, a buck that thumped,

The squeal of a rat as a weasel jumped,
The blackbird's chackering scattering crying,
The rustling bents from the rabbits flying,
Cows in a byre, and distant men,
And Condicote church-clock striking ten.

At eleven o'clock a boy went past,
With a rough-haired terrier following fast,
The boy's sweet whistle and dog's quick yap
Woke the fox from out of his nap.

He rose and stretched till the claws in his pads
Stuck hornily out like long black gads,
He listened a while, and his nose went round
To catch the smell of the distant sound.

The windward smells came free from taint
They were rabbit, strongly, with lime-kiln, faint,
A wild-duck, likely, at Sars Holt Pond,
And sheep on the Sars Holt Down beyond.
The lee-ward smells were much less certain
For the Ghost Heath Hill was like a curtain,
Yet vague, from the lee-ward, now and then,
Came muffled sounds like the sound of men.

He moved to his right to a clearer space,
And all his soul came into his face,
Into his eyes and into his nose,
As over the hill a murmur rose.

His ears were cocked and his keen nose flaired,
He sneered with his lips till his teeth were bared,
He trotted right and lifted a pad
Trying to test what foes he had.

On Ghost Heath turf was a steady drumming
Which sounded like horses quickly coming,

It died as the hunt went down the dip,
Then Malapert yelped at Myngs's whip.
A bright iron horseshoe clinkt on stone,
Then a man's voice spoke, not one alone,
Then a burst of laughter, swiftly still,
Muffled away by Ghost Heath Hill.
Then, indistinctly, the clop, clip, clep,
On Brady Ride, of a horse's step.
Then silence, then, in a burst, much clearer,
Voices and horses coming nearer,
And another noise, of a pit-pat beat
On the Ghost Hill grass, of foxhound feet.

He sat on his haunches listening hard,
While his mind went over the compass card,
Men were coming and rest was done,
But he still had time to get fit to run;
He could outlast horse and outrace hound,
But men were devils from Lobs's Pound.
Scent was burning, the going good,
The world one lust for a fox's blood,
The main earths stopped and the drains put-to,
And fifteen miles to the land he knew.
But of all the ills, the ill least pleasant
Was to run in the light when men were present.
Men in the fields to shout and sign
For a lift of hounds to a fox's line.
Men at the earth at the long point's end,
Men at each check and none his friend,
Guessing each shift that a fox contrives,
But still, needs must when the devil drives.

He readied himself, then a soft horn blew,
Then a clear voice carolled "Ed-hoick. Eleu."
Then the wood-end rang with the clear voice crying

And the crackle of scrub where hounds were trying.
Then, the horn blew nearer, a hound's voice quivered,
Then another, then more, till his body shivered,
He left his kennel and trotted thence
With his ears flexed back and his nerves all tense.

He trotted down with his nose intent
For a fox's line to cross his scent,
It was only fair (he being a stranger)
That the native fox should have the danger.
Danger was coming, so swift, so swift,
That the pace of his trot began to lift
The blue-winged Judas, a jay, began
Swearing, hounds whimpered, air stank of man.

He hurried his trotting, he now felt frighted,
It was his poor body made hounds excited;
He felt as he ringed the great wood through
That he ought to make for the land he knew.

Then the hounds' excitement quivered and quickened,
Then a horn blew death till his marrow sickened,
Then the wood behind was a crash of cry
For the blood in his veins; it made him fly.

They were on his line; it was death to stay,
He must make for home by the shortest way.
But with all this yelling and all this wrath
And all these devils, how find a path?

He ran like a stag to the wood's north corner,
Where the hedge was thick and the ditch a yawner,
But the scarlet glimpse of Myngs on Turk,
Watching the woodside, made him shirk.
He ringed the wood and looked at the south.
What wind there was blew into his mouth.

But close to the woodland's blackthorn thicket
Was Dansey, still as a stone, on picket.
At Dansey's back were a twenty more
Watching the cover and pressing fore.

The fox drew in and flaired with his muzzle.
Death was there if he messed the puzzle.
There were men without and hounds within,
A crying that stiffened the hair on skin,
Teeth in cover and death without,
Both deaths coming, and no way out.

His nose ranged swiftly, his heart beat fast,
Then a crashing cry rose up in a blast,
Then horse hooves trampled, then horses' flitches
Burst their way through the hazel switches.
Then the horn again made the hounds like mad,
And a man, quite near, said "Found, by Gad,"
And a man, quite near, said "Now he'll break.
Lark's Leybourne Copse is the line he'll take."
And the men moved up with their talk and stink
And the traplike noise of the horseshoe clink.
Men whose coming meant death from teeth
In a worrying wrench with him beneath.

The fox sneaked down by the cover side,
(With his ears flexed back) as a snake would glide,
He took the ditch at the cover-end,
He hugged the ditch as his only friend.
The blackbird cock with the golden beak
Got out of his way with a jabbering shriek
And the shriek told Tom on the raking bay
That for eighteen pence he was gone away.

He ran in the hedge in the triple growth
Of bramble and hawthorn, glad of both,

Till a couple of fields were past, and then
Came the living death of the dread of men.

Then, as he listened, he heard a "Hoy,"
Tom Dansey's horn and "Awa-wa-woy."
Then all hounds crying with all their forces,
Then a thundering down of seventy horses.
Robin Dawe's horn and halloos of "Hey
Hark Hollar, Hoik" and "Gone away,"
"Hark Hollar Hoick," and the smack of a whip
A yelp as a tail hound caught the clip.
"Hark Hollar, Hark Hollar"; then Robin made
Pip go crash through the cut-and-laid,
Hounds were over and on his line
With a head like bees upon Tipple Tine.
The sound of the nearness sent a flood
Of terror of death through the fox's blood.
He upped his brush and he cocked his nose,
And he went up wind as a racer goes.

Bold Robin Dawe was over first,
Cheering his hounds on at the burst;
The field were spurring to be in it
"Hold hard, sirs, give them half a minute,"
Came from Sir Peter on his white.
The hounds went romping with delight
Over the grass and got together;
The tail hounds galloped hell-for-leather
After the pack at Myngs's yell;
A cry like every kind of bell
Rang from these rompers as they raced.

The riders thrusting to be placed,
Jammed down their hats and shook their horses,
The hounds romped past with all their forces,

They crashed into the blackthorn fence;
The scent was heavy on their sense,
So hot it seemed the living thing,
It made the blood within them sing,
Gusts of it made their hackles rise,
Hot gulps of it were agonies
Of joy, and thirst for blood, and passion.
"Forrard," cried Robin, "that's the fashion."
He raced beside his pack to cheer.
The field's noise died upon his ear,
A faint horn, far behind, blew thin
In cover, lest some hound were in.
Then instantly the great grass rise
Shut field and cover from his eyes,
He and his racers were alone.
"A dead fox or a broken bone,"
Said Robin, peering for his prey.
The rise, which shut his field away,
Shewed him the vale's great map spread out,
The downs' lean flank and thrusting snout,
Pale pastures, red-brown plough, dark wood,
Blue distance, still as solitude,
Glitter of water here and there,
The trees so delicately bare.
The dark green gorse and bright green holly.
"O glorious God," he said, "how jolly."
And there, down hill, two fields ahead,
The lolloping red dog-fox sped
Over Poor Pastures to the brook.
He grasped these things in one swift look
Then dived into the bulfinch heart
Through thorns that ripped his sleeves apart
And skutched new blood upon his brow.
"His point's Lark's Leybourne Covers now,"
Said Robin, landing with a grunt,

"Forrard, my beautifuls."
The hunt
Followed down hill to race with him,
White Rabbit with his swallow's skim,
Drew within hail, "Quick burst, Sir Peter."
"A traveller. Nothing could be neater.
Making for Godsdown clumps I take it?"
"Lark's Leybourne, sir, if he can make it.
Forrard."

Bill Ridden thundered down;
His big mouth grinned beneath his frown,
The hounds were going away from horses.
He saw the glint of water-courses,
Yell Brook and Wittold's Dyke ahead,
His horse shoes sliced the green turf red.
Young Cothill's chaser rushed and passt him,
Nob Manor, running next, said "Blast him,
That poet chap who thinks he rides."
Hugh Colway's mare made straking strides
Across the grass, the Colonel next:
Then Squire volleying oaths and vext,
Fighting his hunter for refusing:
Bell Ridden like a cutter cruising
Sailing the grass, then Cob on Warder
Then Minton Price upon Marauder;
Ock Gurney with his eyes intense,
Burning as with a different sense,
His big mouth muttering glad "by damns";
Then Pete crouched down from head to hams,
Rapt like a saint, bright focussed flame.
Bennett with devils in his wame
Chewing black cud and spitting slanting;
Copse scattering jests and Stukely ranting;
Sal Ridden taking line from Dansey;

Long Robert forcing Necromancy;
A dozen more with bad beginnings;
Myngs riding hard to snatch an innings;
A wild last hound with high shrill yelps;
Smacked forrard with some whip-thong skelps.
Then last of all, at top of rise,
The crowd on foot all gasps and eyes
The run up hill had winded them.

They saw the Yell Brook, like a gem
Blue in the grass, a short mile on;
They heard faint cries, but hounds were gone
A good eight fields and out of sight
Except a rippled glimmer white
Going away with dying cheering,
And scarlet flappings disappearing,
And scattering horses going, going,
Going like mad, White Rabbit snowing
Far on ahead, a loose horse taking,
Fence after fence with stirrups shaking,
And scarlet specks and dark specks dwindling.

Nearer, were twigs knocked into kindling,
A much bashed fence still dropping stick,
Flung clods, still quivering from the kick,
Cut hoof-marks pale in cheesy clay,
The horse-smell blowing clean away.
Birds flitting back into the cover.
One last faint cry, then all was over.
The hunt had been, and found, and gone.

At Neakings Farm, three furlongs on,
Hounds raced across the Waysmore Road,
Where many of the riders slowed

To tittup down a grassy lane,
Which led as hounds led in the main
And gave no danger of a fall.
There, as they tittupped one and all,
Big Twenty Stone came scattering by,
His great mare made the hoof-casts fly.
"By leave," he cried. "Come on. Come up,
This fox is running like a tup;
Let's leave this lane and get to terms.
No sense in crawling here like worms.
Come let me past and let me start,
This fox is running like a hart,
And this is going to be a run.
Come on. I want to see the fun.
Thanky. By leave. Now, Maiden; do it."
He faced the fence and put her through it
Shielding his eyes lest spikes should blind him,
The crashing blackthorn closed behind him.
Mud-scatters chased him as he scudded.
His mare's ears cocked, her neat feet thudded.

The kestrel cruising over meadow
Watched the hunt gallop on his shadow,
Wee figures, almost at a stand,
Crossing the multi-coloured land,
Slow as a shadow on a dial.

Some horses, swerving at a trial,
Baulked at a fence: at gates they bunched.
The mud about the gates was dunched
Like German cheese; men pushed for places,
And kicked the mud into the faces
Of those who made them room to pass.
The half-mile's gallop on the grass,
Had tailed them out, and warmed their blood.

"His point's the Banner Barton Wood."
"That, or Goat's Gorse." "A stinger, this."
"You're right in that; by Jove it is."
"An up-wind travelling fox, by George."
"They say Tom viewed him at the forge."
"Well, let me pass and let's be on."

They crossed the lane to Tolderton,
The hill-marl died to valley clay,
And there before them ran the grey
Yell Water, swirling as it ran,
The Yell Brook of the hunting man.
The hunters eyed it and were grim.
They saw the water snaking slim
Ahead, like silver; they could see
(Each man) his pollard willow tree
Firming the bank, they felt their horses
Catch the gleam's hint and gather forces;
They heard the men behind draw near.
Each horse was trembling as a spear
Trembles in hand when tense to hurl,
They saw the brimmed brook's eddies curl.
The willow-roots like water-snakes;
The beaten holes the ratten makes,
They heard the water's rush; they heard
Hugh Colway's mare come like a bird;
A faint cry from the hounds ahead,
Then saddle-strain, the bright hooves' tread,
Quick words, the splash of mud, the launch,
The sick hope that the bank be staunch,
Then Souse, with Souse to left and right.
Maroon across, Sir Peter's white
Down but pulled up, Tom over, Hugh
Mud to the hat but over, too,
Well splashed by Squire who was in.

With draggled pink stuck close to skin,
The Squire leaned from bank and hauled
His mired horse's rein; he bawled
For help from each man racing by.
"What, help you pull him out? Not I.
What made you pull him in?" they said.
Nob Manor cleared and turned his head,
And cried "Wade up. The ford's upstream."
Ock Gurney in a cloud of steam
Stood by his dripping cob and wrung
The taste of brook mud from his tongue
And scraped his poor cob's pasterns clean.
"Lord, what a crowner we've a been,
This jumping brook's a mucky job."
He muttered, grinning, "Lord, poor cob.
Now sir, let me." He turned to Squire
And cleared his hunter from the mire
By skill and sense and strength of arm.

Meanwhile the fox passed Nonesuch Farm,
Keeping the spinney on his right.
Hounds raced him here with all their might
Along the short firm grass, like fire.
The cowman viewed him from the byre
Lolloping on, six fields ahead,
Then hounds, still carrying such a head,
It made him stare, then Rob on Pip,
Sailing the great grass like a ship,
Then grand Maroon in all his glory
Sweeping his strides, his great chest hoary
With foam fleck and the pale hill-marl.
They strode the Leet, they flew the Snarl,
They knocked the nuts at Nonesuch Mill,
Raced up the spur of Gallows Hill
And viewed him there. The line he took

Was Tineton and the Pantry Brook,
Going like fun and hounds like mad.
Tom glanced to see what friends he had
Still within sight, before he turned
The ridge's shoulder; he discerned,
One field away, young Cothill sailing
Easily up. Pete Gurney failing,
Hugh Colway quartering on Sir Peter,
Bill waiting on the mare to beat her,
Sal Ridden skirting to the right.
A horse, with stirrups flashing bright
Over his head at every stride,
Looked like the Major's; Tom espied
Far back, a scarlet speck of man
Running, and straddling as he ran.
Charles Copse was up, Nob Manor followed,
Then Bennett's big-boned black that wallowed
Clumsy, but with the strength of ten.
Then black, and brown, and scarlet men,
Brown horses, white, and black, and grey
Scattered a dozen fields away.

The shoulder shut the scene away.
From the Gallows Hill to the Tineton Copse
There were ten ploughed fields like ten full stops,
All wet red clay where a horse's foot
Would be swathed, feet thick, like an ash-tree root.
The fox raced on, on the headlands firm,
Where his swift feet scared the coupling worm,
The rooks rose raving to curse him raw
He snarled a sneer at their swoop and caw.
Then on, then on, down a half ploughed field
Where a ship-like plough drave glitter-keeled,
With a bay horse near and a white horse leading,
And a man saying "Zook" and the red earth bleeding

He gasped as he saw the ploughman drop
The stilts and swear at the team to stop.
The ploughman ran in his red clay clogs
Crying "Zick un Towzer; zick, good dogs."
A couple of wire-haired lurchers lean
Arose from his wallet, nosing keen;
With a rushing swoop they were on his track,
Putting chest to stubble to bite his back.
He swerved from his line with the curs at heel,
The teeth as they missed him clicked like steel,
With a worrying snarl, they quartered on him,
While the ploughman shouted "Zick; upon him."

The lurcher dogs soon shot their bolt,
And the fox raced on by the Hazel Holt,
Down the dead grass tilt to the sandstone gash
Of the Pantry Brook at Tineton Ash.
The loitering water, flooded full,
Had yeast on its lip like raddled wool,
It was wrinkled over with Arab script
Of eddies that twisted up and slipt.
The stepping stones had a rush about them
So the fox plunged in and swam without them.

He crossed to the cattle's drinking shallow
Firmed up with rush and the roots of mallow,
He wrung his coat from his draggled bones
And romped away for the Sarsen Stones.

A sneaking glance with his ears flexed back,
Made sure that his scent had failed the pack,
For the red clay, good for corn and roses,
Was cold for scent and brought hounds to noses.
He slackened pace by the Tineton Tree,
(A vast hollow ash-tree grown in three),

He wriggled a shake and padded slow,
Not sure if the hounds were on or no.

A horn blew faint, then he heard the sounds
Of a cantering huntsman, lifting hounds,
The ploughman had raised his hat for sign,
And the hounds were lifted and on his line.
He heard the splash in the Pantry Brook,
And a man's voice: "Thiccy's the line he took,"
And a clear "Yoi doit" and a whimpering quaver,
Though the lurcher dogs had dulled the savour.

The fox went off while the hounds made halt,
And the horses breathed and the field found fault,
But the whimpering rose to a crying crash
By the hollow ruin of Tineton Ash.
Then again the kettle drum horse hooves beat,
And the green blades bent to the fox's feet,
And the cry rose keen not far behind
Of the "Blood, blood, blood" in the fox-hounds' mind.

The fox was strong, he was full of running,
He could run for an hour and then be cunning,
But the cry behind him made him chill,
They were nearer now and they meant to kill.
They meant to run him until his blood
Clogged on his heart as his brush with mud,
Till his back bent up and his tongue hung flagging,
And his belly and brush were filthed from dragging.
Till he crouched stone still, dead-beat and dirty,
With nothing but teeth against the thirty.
And all the way to that blinding end
He would meet with men and have none his friend.
Men to holloa and men to run him,
With stones to stagger and yells to stun him,

Men to head him, with whips to beat him,
Teeth to mangle and mouths to eat him.
And all the way, that wild high crying,
To cold his blood with the thought of dying,
The horn and the cheer, and the drum-like thunder,
Of the horse hooves stamping the meadows under.
He upped his brush and went with a will
For the Sarsen Stones on Wan Dyke Hill.

As he ran the meadow by Tineton Church,
A christening party left the porch,
They stood stock still as he pounded by,
They wished him luck but they thought he'd die.
The toothless babe in his long white coat
Looked delicate meat, the fox took note;
But the sight of them grinning there, pointing finger,
Made him put on steam till he went a stinger.

Past Tineton Church over Tineton Waste,
With the lolloping ease of a fox's haste,
The fur on his chest blown dry with the air,
His brush still up and his cheek-teeth bare.
Over the Waste where the ganders grazed,
The long swift lilt of his loping lazed,
His ears cocked up as his blood ran higher,
He saw his point, and his eyes took fire.
The Wan Dyke Hill with its fir tree barren,
Its dark of gorse and its rabbit warren.
The Dyke on its heave like a tightened girth,
And holes in the Dyke where a fox might earth.
He had rabbitted there long months before,
The earths were deep and his need was sore,
The way was new, but he took a bearing,
And rushed like a blown ship billow-sharing.

Off Tineton Common to Tineton Dean,
Where the wind-hid elders pushed with green:
Through the Dean's thin cover across the lane,
And up Midwinter to King of Spain.
Old Joe at digging his garden grounds,
Said "A fox, being hunted; where be hounds?
O lord, my back, to be young again,
'Stead a zellin zider in King of Spain.
O hark, I hear 'em, O sweet, O sweet.
Why there be redcoat in Gearge's wheat.
And there be redcoat, and there they gallop.
Thur go a browncoat down a wallop.
Quick, Ellen, quick, come Susan, fly.
Here'm hounds. I zeed the fox go by,
Go by like thunder, go by like blasting,
With his girt white teeth all looking ghasting.
Look there come hounds. Hark, hear 'em crying,
Lord, belly to stubble, ain't they flying.
There's huntsmen, there. The fox come past,
(As I was digging) as fast as fast.
He's only been gone a minute by;
A girt dark dog as pert as pye."

Ellen and Susan came out scattering
Brooms and dustpans till all was clattering;
They saw the pack come head to foot
Running like racers nearly mute;
Robin and Dansey quartering near,
All going gallop like startled deer.
A half dozen flitting scarlets shewing
In the thin green Dean where the pines were growing.
Black coats and brown coats thrusting, and spurring,
Sending the partridge coveys whirring,
Then a rattle up hill and a clop up lane,
It emptied the bar of the King of Spain.

Tom left his cider, Dick left his bitter,
Granfer James left his pipe and spitter,
Out they came from the sawdust floor,
They said, "They'm going." They said "O Lor."

The fox raced on, up the Barton Balks,
With a crackle of kex in the nettle stalks,
Over Hammond's grass to the dark green line
Of the larch-wood smelling of turpentine.
Scratch Steven Larches, black to the sky,
A sadness breathing with one long sigh,
Grey ghosts of trees under funeral plumes,
A mist of twig over soft brown glooms.
As he entered the wood he heard the smacks,
Chip-jar, of the fir pole feller's axe,
He swerved to the left to a broad green ride,
Where a boy made him rush for the further side.
He swerved to the left, to the Barton Road,
But there were the timberers come to load.
Two timber carts and a couple of carters
With straps round their knees instead of garters.
He swerved to the right, straight down the wood,
The carters watched him, the boy hallooed.
He leaped from the larch-wood into tillage,
The cobbler's garden of Barton village.

The cobbler bent at his wooden foot,
Beating sprigs in a broken boot;
He wore old glasses with thick horn rim,
He scowled at his work for his sight was dim.
His face was dingy, his lips were grey,
From primming sparrowbills day by day;
As he turned his boot he heard a noise
At his garden-end and he thought, "It's boys."

He saw his cat nip up on the shed,
Where her back arched up till it touched her head,
He saw his rabbit race round and round
Its little black box three feet from ground.
His six hens cluckered and flucked to perch,
"That's boys," said cobbler, "so I'll go search."
He reached his stick and blinked in his wrath,
When he saw a fox in his garden path.
The fox swerved left and scrambled out
Knocking crinked green shells from the Brussels Sprout,
He scrambled out through the cobbler's paling,
And up Pill's orchard to Purton's Tailing,
Across the plough at the top of bent,
Through the heaped manure to kill his scent,
Over to Aldams, up to Cappells,
Past Nursery Lot with its white-washed apples,
Past Colston's Broom, past Gaunts, past Sheres,
Past Foxwhelps Oasts with their hooded ears,
Past Monk's Ash Clerewell, past Beggars Oak,
Past the great elms blue with the Hinton smoke,
Along Long Hinton to Hinton Green,
Where the wind-washed steeple stood serene
With its golden bird still sailing air,
Past Banner Barton, past Chipping Bare,
Past Maddings Hollow, down Dundry Dip,
And up Goose Grass to the Sailing Ship.

The three black firs of the Ship stood still
On the bare chalk heave of the Dundry Hill,
The fox looked back as he slackened past
The scaled red-bole of the mizzen-mast.

There they were coming, mute but swift,
A scarlet smear in the blackthorn rift,
A white horse rising, a dark horse flying,

And the hungry hounds too tense for crying.
Stormcock leading, his stern spear-straight,
Racing as though for a piece of plate,
Little speck horsemen field on field;
Then Dansey viewed him and Robin squealed.

At the View Halloo the hounds went frantic,
Back went Stormcock and up went Antic,
Up went Skylark as Antic sped
It was zest to blood how they carried head.
Skylark drooped as Maroon drew by,
Their hackles lifted, they scored to cry.

The fox knew well, that before they tore him,
They should try their speed on the downs before him,
There were three more miles to the Wan Dyke Hill,
But his heart was high, that he beat them still.
The wind of the downland charmed his bones
So off he went for the Sarsen Stones.

The moan of the three great firs in the wind,
And the Ai of the foxhounds died behind,
Wind-dapples followed the hill-wind's breath
On the Kill Down gorge where the Danes found death;
Larks scattered up; the peewits feeding
Rose in a flock from the Kill Down Steeding.
The hare leaped up from her form and swerved
Swift left for the Starveall harebell-turved.
On the wind-bare thorn some longtails prinking
Cried sweet, as though wind blown glass were chinking.
Behind came thudding and loud halloo
Or a cry from hounds as they came to view.

The pure clean air came sweet to his lungs,
Till he thought foul scorn of those crying tongues,

In a three mile more he would reach the haven
In the Wan Dyke croaked on by the raven,
In a three mile more he would make his berth
On the hard cool floor of a Wan Dyke earth,
Too deep for spade, too curved for terrier,
With the pride of the race to make rest the merrier.
In a three mile more he would reach his dream,
So his game heart gulped and he put on steam.

Like a rocket shot to a ship ashore,
The lean red bolt of his body tore,
Like a ripple of wind running swift on grass,
Like a shadow on wheat when a cloud blows past,
Like a turn at the buoy in a cutter sailing,
When the bright green gleam lips white at the railing,
Like the April snake whipping back to sheath,
Like the gannet's hurtle on fish beneath,
Like a kestrel chasing, like a sickle reaping,
Like all things swooping, like all things sweeping,
Like a hound for stay, like a stag for swift,
With his shadow beside like spinning drift.

Past the gibbet-stock all stuck with nails,
Where they hanged in chains what had hung at jails,
Past Ashmundshowe where Ashmund sleeps,
And none but the tumbling peewit weeps,
Past Curlew Calling, the gaunt grey corner
Where the curlew comes as a summer mourner,
Past Blowbury Beacon shaking his fleece,
Where all winds hurry and none brings peace,
Then down, on the mile-long green decline
Where the turf's like spring and the air's like wine,
Where the sweeping spurs of the downland spill
Into Wan Brook Valley and Wan Dyke Hill.
On he went with a galloping rally

Past Maesbury Clump for Wan Brook Valley,
The blood in his veins went romping high
"Get on, on, on to the earth or die."
The air of the downs went purely past,
Till he felt the glory of going fast,
Till the terror of death, though there indeed,
Was lulled for a while by his pride of speed;
He was romping away from hounds and hunt,
He had Wan Dyke Hill and his earth in front,
In a one mile more when his point was made,
He would rest in safety from dog or spade;
Nose between paws he would hear the shout
Of the "gone to earth" to the hounds without,
The whine of the hounds, and their cat feet gadding,
Scratching the earth, and their breath pad-padding,
He would hear the horn call hounds away,
And rest in peace till another day.
In one mile more he would lie at rest
So for one mile more he would go his best.
He reached the dip at the long droop's end
And he took what speed he had still to spend.

So down past Maesbury beech clump grey,
That would not be green till the end of May,
Past Arthur's Table, the white chalk boulder,
Where pasque flowers purple the down's grey shoulder
Past Quichelm's Keeping, past Harry's Thorn
To Thirty Acre all thin with corn.
As he raced the corn towards Wan Dyke Brook,
The pack had view of the way he took,
Robin hallooed from the downland's crest,
He capped them on till they did their best.
The quarter mile to the Wan Brook's brink
Was raced as quick as a man can think.
And here, as he ran to the huntsman's yelling,

The fox first felt that the pace was telling,
His body and lungs seemed all grown old,
His legs less certain, his heart less bold,
The hound-noise nearer, the hill slope steeper,
The thud in the blood of his body deeper,
His pride in his speed, his joy in the race
Were withered away, for what use was pace?
He had run his best, and the hounds ran better.
Then the going worsened, the earth was wetter.
Then his brush drooped down till it sometimes dragged,
And his fur felt sick and his chest was tagged
With taggles of mud, and his pads seemed lead,
It was well for him he'd an earth ahead.
Down he went to the brook and over,
Out of the corn and into the clover,
Over the slope that the Wan Brook drains,
Past Battle Tump where they earthed the Danes,
Then up the hill that the Wan Dyke rings
Where the Sarsen Stones stand grand like kings.

Seven Sarsens of granite grim,
As he ran them by they looked at him;
As he leaped the lip of their earthen paling
The hounds were gaining and he was failing.

He passed the Sarsens, he left the spur,
He pressed up hill to the blasted fir,
He slipped as he leaped the hedge; he slithered;
"He's mine," thought Robin. "He's done; he's dithered."
At the second attempt he cleared the fence,
He turned half right where the gorse was dense,
He was leading hounds by a furlong clear.
He was past his best, but his earth was near.
He ran up gorse, to the spring of the ramp,
The steep green wall of the dead men's camp,

He sidled up it and scampered down
To the deep green ditch of the dead men's town.

Within, as he reached that soft green turf,
The wind, blowing lonely, moaned like surf,
Desolate ramparts rose up steep,
On either side, for the ghosts to keep.
He raced the trench, past the rabbit warren,
Close grown with moss which the wind made barren,
He passed the spring where the rushes spread,
And there in the stones was his earth ahead.
One last short burst upon failing feet,
There life lay waiting, so sweet, so sweet,
Rest in a darkness, balm for aches.

The earth was stopped. It was barred with stakes.

With the hounds at head so close behind
He had to run as he changed his mind.
This earth, as he saw, was stopped, but still
There was one earth more on the Wan Dyke Hill.
A rabbit burrow a furlong on,
He could kennel there till the hounds were gone.
Though his death seemed near he did not blench
He upped his brush and ran the trench.

He ran the trench while the wind moaned treble,
Earth trickled down, there were falls of pebble.
Down in the valley of that dark gash
The wind-withered grasses looked like ash.
Trickles of stones and earth fell down
In that dark valley of dead men's town.
A hawk arose from a fluff of feathers,
From a distant fold came a bleat of wethers.

He heard no noise from the hounds behind
But the hill-wind moaning like something blind.

He turned the bend in the hill and there
Was his rabbit-hole with its mouth worn bare,
But there with a gun tucked under his arm
Was young Sid Kissop of Purlpits Farm,
With a white hob ferret to drive the rabbit
Into a net which was set to nab it.
And young Jack Cole peered over the wall
And loosed a pup with a "Z'bite en, Saul,"
The terrier pup attacked with a will,
So the fox swerved right and away down hill.

Down from the ramp of the Dyke he ran
To the brackeny patch where the gorse began,
Into the gorse, where the hill's heave hid
The line he took from the eyes of Sid
He swerved down wind and ran like a hare
For the wind-blown spinney below him there.

He slipped from the gorse to the spinney dark
(There were curled grey growths on the oak tree bark)
He saw no more of the terrier pup.
But he heard men speak and the hounds come up.

He crossed the spinney with ears intent
For the cry of hounds on the way he went
His heart was thumping, the hounds were near now
He could make no sprint at a cry and cheer now,
He was past his perfect, his strength was failing,
His brush sag-sagged and his legs were ailing.
He felt as he skirted Dead Men's Town,
That in one mile more they would have him down.

Through the withered oak's wind-crouching tops
He saw men's scarlet above the copse,
He heard men's oaths, yet he felt hounds slacken
In the frondless stalks of the brittle bracken.
He felt that the unseen link which bound
His spine to the nose of the leading hound,
Was snapped, that the hounds no longer knew
Which way to follow nor what to do;
That the threat of the hound's teeth left his neck,
They had ceased to run, they had come to check,
They were quartering wide on the Wan Hill's bent.

The terrier's chase had killed his scent.

He heard bits chink as the horses shifted,
He heard hounds cast, then he heard hounds lifted,
But there came no cry from a new attack,
His heart grew steady, his breath came back.

He left the spinney and ran its edge,
By the deep dry ditch of the blackthorn hedge,
Then out of the ditch and down the meadow,
Trotting at ease in the blackthorn shadow
Over the track called Godsdown Road,
To the great grass heave of the gods' abode,
He was moving now upon land he knew
Up Clench Royal and Morton Tew
The Pol Brook, Cheddesdon and East Stoke Church,
High Clench St. Lawrence and Tinker's Birch,
Land he had roved on night by night,
For hot blood suckage or furry bite,
The threat of the hounds behind was gone;
He breathed deep pleasure and trotted on.

While young Sid Kissop thrashed the pup,
Robin on Pip came heaving up,

And found his pack spread out at check.
"I'd like to wring your terrier's neck,"
He said, "You see? He's spoiled our sport.
He's killed the scent." He broke off short,
And stared at hounds and at the valley.
No jay or magpie gave a rally
Down in the copse, no circling rooks
Rose over fields; old Joyful's looks
Were doubtful in the gorse, the pack
Quested both up and down and back.
He watched each hound for each small sign.
They tried, but could not hit the line,
The scent was gone. The field took place
Out of the way of hounds. The pace
Had tailed them out; though four remained:
Sir Peter, on White Rabbit stained
Red from the brooks, Bill Ridden cheery,
Hugh Colway with his mare dead weary.
The Colonel with Marauder beat.
They turned towards a thud of feet;
Dansey, and then young Cothill came
(His chestnut mare was galloped tame).
"There's Copse, a field behind," he said.
"Those last miles put them all to bed.
They're strung along the downs like flies."
Copse and Nob Manor topped the rise.
"Thank God, a check," they said, "at last."

"They cannot own it; you must cast,"
Sir Peter said. The soft horn blew
Tom turned the hounds up wind; they drew
Up wind, down hill, by spinney side.
They tried the brambled ditch; they tried
The swamp, all choked with bright green grass
And clumps of rush and pools like glass,

Long since, the dead men's drinking pond.
They tried the White Leaved Oak beyond,
But no hound spoke to it or feathered.
The horse heads drooped like horses tethered,
The men mopped brows. "An hour's hard run.
Ten miles," they said, "we must have done.
It's all of six from Colston's Gorses."
The lucky got their second horses.

The time ticked by. "He's lost," they muttered
A pheasant rose. A rabbit scuttered.
Men mopped their scarlet cheeks and drank.

They drew down wind along the bank,
(The Wan Way) on the hill's south spur,
Grown with dwarf oak and juniper
Like dwarves alive, but no hound spoke.
The seepings made the ground one soak.
They turned the spur; the hounds were beat.
Then Robin shifted in his seat
Watching for signs, but no signs shewed.
"I'll lift across the Godsdown Road,
Beyond the spinney," Robin said.
Tom turned them; Robin went ahead.

Beyond the copse a great grass fallow
Stretched towards Stoke and Cheddesdon Mallow.
A rolling grass where hounds grew keen.
"Yoi doit, then; this is where he's been,"
Said Robin, eager at their joy.
"Yooi, Joyful, lad, yooi, Cornerboy.
They're on to him."
At his reminders
The keen hounds hurried to the finders.
The finding hounds began to hurry,

Men jammed their hats prepared to skurry,
The Ai Ai of the cry began.
Its spirit passed to horse and man,
The skirting hounds romped to the cry.
Hound after hound cried Ai Ai Ai,
Till all were crying, running, closing,
Their heads well up and no heads nosing,
Joyful ahead with spear-straight stern.
They raced the great slope to the burn.
Robin beside them, Tom behind,
Pointing past Robin down the wind.

For there, two furlongs on, he viewed
On Holy Hill or Cheddesdon Rood
Just where the ploughland joined the grass,
A speck down the first furrow pass,
A speck the colour of the plough.
"Yonder he goes. We'll have him now,"
He cried. The speck passed slowly on,
It reached the ditch, paused, and was gone.

Then down the slope and up the Rood,
Went the hunt's gallop. Godsdown Wood
Dropped its last oak-leaves at the rally.
Over the Rood to High Clench Valley
The gallop led; the red-coats scattered,
The fragments of the hunt were tattered
Over five fields, ev'n since the check.
"A dead fox or a broken neck,"
Said Robin Dawe, "Come up, the Dane."
The hunter leant against the rein,
Cocking his ears, he loved to see
The hounds at cry. The hounds and he
The chiefs in all that feast of pace.

The speck in front began to race.

The fox heard hounds get on to his line,
And again the terror went down his spine,
Again the back of his neck felt cold,
From the sense of the hound's teeth taking hold.
But his legs were rested, his heart was good,
He had breath to gallop to Mourne End Wood,
It was four miles more, but an earth at end,
So he put on pace down the Rood Hill Bend.

Down the great grass slope which the oak trees dot
With a swerve to the right from the keeper's cot,
Over High Clench brook in its channel deep,
To the grass beyond, where he ran to sheep.
The sheep formed line like a troop of horse,
They swerved, as he passed, to front his course
From behind, as he ran, a cry arose,
"See the sheep, there. Watch them. There he goes."

He ran the sheep that their smell might check
The hounds from his scent and save his neck,
But in two fields more he was made aware
That the hounds still ran; Tom had viewed him there.

Tom had held them on through the taint of sheep,
They had kept his line, as they meant to keep,
They were running hard with a burning scent,
And Robin could see which way he went.
The pace that he went brought strain to breath,
He knew as he ran that the grass was death.
He ran the slope towards Morton Tew
That the heave of the hill might stop the view,
Then he doubled down to the Blood Brook red,
And swerved upstream in the brook's deep bed.
He splashed the shallows, he swam the deeps,
He crept by banks as a moorhen creeps,

He heard the hounds shoot over his line,
And go on, on, on towards Cheddesdon Zine.

In the minute's peace he could slacken speed,
The ease from the strain was sweet indeed.
Cool to the pads the water flowed,
He reached the bridge on the Cheddesdon road.

As he came to light from the culvert dim,
Two boys on the bridge looked down on him;
They were young Bill Ripple and Harry Meun,
"Look, there be squirrel, a-swimmin', see 'un."
"Noa, ben't a squirrel, be fox, be fox.
Now, Hal, get pebble, we'll give en socks."
"Get pebble, Billy, dub un a plaster;
There's for thy belly, I'll learn ee, master."

The stones splashed spray in the fox's eyes,
He raced from brook in a burst of shies,
He ran for the reeds in the withy car,
Where the dead flags shake and the wild-duck are.

He pushed through the reeds which cracked at his passing,
To the High Clench Water, a grey pool glassing,
He heard Bill Ripple in Cheddesdon road,
Shout, "This way, huntsman, it's here he goed."

The Leu Leu Leu went the soft horn's laughter,
The hounds (they had checked) came romping after,
The clop of the hooves on the road was plain,
Then the crackle of reeds, then cries again.

A whimpering first, then Robin's cheer,
Then the Ai Ai Ai; they were all too near;

His swerve had brought but a minute's rest
Now he ran again, and he ran his best.

With a crackle of dead dry stalks of reed
The hounds came romping at topmost speed
The redcoats ducked as the great hooves skittered
The Blood Brook's shallows to sheets that glittered;
With a cracking whip and a "Hoik, Hoik, Hoik,
Forrard," Tom galloped. Bob shouted "Yoick."
Like a running fire the dead reeds crackled,
The hounds' heads lifted, their necks were hackled.
Tom cried to Bob as they thundered through,
"He is running short, we shall kill at Tew."
Bob cried to Tom as they rode in team,
"I was sure, that time, that he turned upstream.
As the hounds went over the brook in stride,
I saw old Daffodil fling to side,
So I guessed at once, when they checked beyond."
The ducks flew up from the Morton Pond.
The fox looked up at their tailing strings,
He wished (perhaps) that a fox had wings.
Wings with his friends in a great V straining
The autumn sky when the moon is gaining;
For better the grey sky's solitude,
Than to be two miles from the Mourne End Wood
With the hounds behind, clean-trained to run,
And your strength half spent and your breath half done.
Better the reeds and the sky and water
Than that hopeless pad from a certain slaughter.
At the Morton Pond the fields began,
Long Tew's green meadows; he ran; he ran.

First the six green fields that make a mile,
With the lip-full Clench at the side the while,
With the rooks above, slow-circling, shewing

The world of men where a fox was going;
The fields all empty, dead grass, bare hedges,
And the brook's bright gleam in the dark of sedges.
To all things else he was dumb and blind,
He ran, with the hounds a field behind.

At the sixth green field came the long slow climb,
To the Mourne End Wood as old as time
Yew woods dark, where they cut for bows,
Oak woods green with the mistletoes,
Dark woods evil, but burrowed deep
With a brock's earth strong, where a fox might sleep.
He saw his point on the heaving hill,
He had failing flesh and a reeling will,
He felt the heave of the hill grow stiff,
He saw black woods, which would shelter—If—
Nothing else, but the steepening slope,
And a black line nodding, a line of hope
The line of the yews on the long slope's brow,
A mile, three-quarters, a half-mile now.
A quarter-mile, but the hounds had viewed
They yelled to have him this side the wood,
Robin capped them, Tom Dansey steered them
With a "Yooi, Yooi, Yooi," Bill Ridden cheered them.
Then up went hackles as Shatterer led,
"Mob him," cried Ridden, "the wood's ahead.
Turn him, damn it; Yooi, beauties, beat him,
O God, let them get him; let them eat him.
O God," said Ridden, "I'll eat him stewed,
If you'll let us get him this side the wood."

But the pace, uphill, made a horse like stone,
The pack went wild up the hill alone.
Three hundred yards, and the worst was past,
The slope was gentler and shorter-grassed,

The fox saw the bulk of the woods grow tall
On the brae ahead like a barrier-wall
He saw the skeleton trees show sky,
And the yew trees darken to see him die,
And the line of the woods go reeling black,
There was hope in the woods, and behind, the pack.

Two hundred yards, and the trees grew taller,
Blacker, blinder, as hope grew smaller,
Cry seemed nearer, the teeth seemed gripping
Pulling him back, his pads seemed slipping.
He was all one ache, one gasp, one thirsting,
Heart on his chest-bones, beating, bursting,
The hounds were gaining like spotted pards
And the wood-hedge still was a hundred yards.
The wood-hedge black was a two year, quick
Cut-and-laid that had sprouted thick
Thorns all over, and strongly plied,
With a clean red ditch on the take-off side.

He saw it now as a redness, topped
With a wattle of thorn-work spiky cropped,
Spiky to leap on, stiff to force,
No safe jump for a failing horse,
But beyond it, darkness of yews together,
Dark green plumes over soft brown feather,
Darkness of woods where scents were blowing
Strange scents, hot scents, of wild things going,
Scents that might draw these hounds away.
So he ran, ran, ran to that clean red clay.

Still, as he ran, his pads slipped back,
All his strength seemed to draw the pack,
The trees drew over him dark like Norns,
He was over the ditch and at the thorns.

He thrust at the thorns, which would not yield,
He leaped, but fell, in sight of the field,
The hounds went wild as they saw him fall,
The fence stood stiff like a Bucks flint wall.

He gathered himself for a new attempt,
His life before was an old dream dreamt,
All that he was was a blown fox quaking,
Jumping at thorns too stiff for breaking,
While over the grass in crowd, in cry,
Came the grip teeth grinning to make him die,
The eyes intense, dull, smouldering red,
The fell like a ruff round each keen head
The pace like fire, and scarlet men
Galloping, yelling, "Yooi, eat him, then."
He gathered himself, he leaped, he reached
The top of the hedge like a fish-boat beached,
He steadied a second and then leaped down
To the dark of the wood where bright things drown.

He swerved, sharp right, under young green firs.
Robin called on the Dane with spurs,
He cried "Come, Dansey: if God's not good,
We shall change our fox in this Mourne End Wood."
Tom cried back as he charged like spate,
"Mine can't jump that, I must ride to gate."
Robin answered, "I'm going at him.
I'll kill that fox, if he kills me, drat him.
We'll kill in covert. Gerr on, now, Dane."
He gripped him tight and he made it plain,
He slowed him down till he almost stood
While his hounds went crash into Mourne End Wood.

Like a dainty dancer with footing nice,
The Dane turned side for a leap in twice.

He cleared the ditch to the red clay bank,
He rose at the fence as his quarters sank,
He barged the fence as the bank gave way
And down he came in a fall of clay.

Robin jumped off him and gasped for breath;
He said "That's lost him as sure as death.
They've over-run him. Come up, the Dane,
But I'll kill him yet, if we ride to Spain."

He scrambled up to his horse's back,
He thrust through cover, he called his pack,
He cheered them on till they made it good,
Where the fox had swerved inside the wood.

The fox knew well as he ran the dark,
That the headlong hounds were past their mark
They had missed his swerve and had overrun.
But their devilish play was not yet done.

For a minute he ran and heard no sound,
Then a whimper came from a questing hound,
Then a "This way, beauties," and then "Leu Leu,"
The floating laugh of the horn that blew.
Then the cry again and the crash and rattle
Of the shrubs burst back as they ran to battle.
Till the wood behind seemed risen from root,
Crying and crashing to give pursuit,
Till the trees seemed hounds and the air seemed cry,
And the earth so far that he needs but die,
Die where he reeled in the woodland dim
With a hound's white grips in the spine of him;
For one more burst he could spurt, and then
Wait for the teeth, and the wrench, and men.

He made his spurt for the Mourne End rocks,
The air blew rank with the taint of fox;
The yews gave way to a greener space
Of great stones strewn in a grassy place.
And there was his earth at the great grey shoulder,
Sunk in the ground, of a granite boulder
A dry deep burrow with rocky roof,
Proof against crowbars, terrier-proof,
Life to the dying, rest for bones.

The earth was stopped; it was filled with stones.

Then, for a moment, his courage failed,
His eyes looked up as his body quailed,
Then the coming of death, which all things dread,
Made him run for the wood ahead.

The taint of fox was rank on the air,
He knew, as he ran, there were foxes there.
His strength was broken, his heart was bursting
His bones were rotten, his throat was thirsting
His feet were reeling, his brush was thick
From dragging the mud, and his brain was sick.

He thought as he ran of his old delight
In the wood in the moon in an April night,
His happy hunting, his winter loving,
The smells of things in the midnight roving;
The look of his dainty-nosing, red,
Clean-felled dam with her footpad's tread,
Of his sire, so swift, so game, so cunning
With craft in his brain and power of running,
Their fights of old when his teeth drew blood.
Now he was sick, with his coat all mud.

He crossed the covert, he crawled the bank,
To a meuse in the thorns and there he sank,
With his ears flexed back and his teeth shown white,
In a rat's resolve for a dying bite.

And there, as he lay, he saw the vale,
That a struggling sunlight silvered pale,
The Deerlip Brook like a strip of steel,
The Nun's Wood Yews where the rabbits squeal,
The great grass square of the Roman Fort,
And the smoke in the elms at Crendon Court.

And above the smoke in the elm-tree tops,
Was the beech-clump's blue, Blown Hilcote Copse,
Where he and his mates had long made merry
In the bloody joys of the rabbit-herry.

And there as he lay and looked, the cry
Of the hounds at head came rousing by;
He bent his bones in the blackthorn dim.

But the cry of the hounds was not for him
Over the fence with a crash they went,
Belly to grass, with a burning scent,
Then came Dansey, yelling to Bob,
"They've changed, O damn it, now here's a job."
And Bob yelled back, "Well, we cannot turn 'em,
It's Jumper and Antic, Tom; we'll learn 'em.
We must just go on, and I hope we kill."
They followed hounds down the Mourne End Hill.
The fox lay still in the rabbit-meuse,
On the dry brown dust of the plumes of yews.
In the bottom below a brook went by,
Blue, in a patch, like a streak of sky.
There, one by one, with a clink of stone

Came a red or dark coat on a horse half blown.
And man to man with a gasp for breath
Said, "Lord, what a run. I'm fagged to death."

After an hour, no riders came,
The day drew by like an ending game;
A robin sang from a pufft red breast,
The fox lay quiet and took his rest.
A wren on a tree-stump carolled clear,
Then the starlings wheeled in a sudden sheer,
The rooks came home to the twiggy hive
In the elm-tree tops which the winds do drive.
Then the noise of the rooks fell slowly still,
And the lights came out in the Clench Brook Mill
Then a pheasant cocked, then an owl began
With the cry that curdles the blood of man.

The stars grew bright as the yews grew black,
The fox rose stiffly and stretched his back.
He flaired the air, then he padded out
To the valley below him dark as doubt,
Winter-thin with the young green crops,
For Old Cold Crendon and Hilcote Copse.

As he crossed the meadows at Naunton Larking,
The dogs in the town all started barking,
For with feet all bloody and flanks all foam,
The hounds and the hunt were limping home;
Limping home in the dark, dead-beaten,
The hounds all rank from a fox they'd eaten,
Dansey saying to Robin Dawe,
"The fastest and longest I ever saw."
And Robin answered, "O Tom, 'twas good,
I thought they'd changed in the Mourne End Wood,
But now I feel that they did not change.

We've had a run that was great and strange;
And to kill in the end, at dusk, on grass.
We'll turn to the Cock and take a glass,
For the hounds, poor souls, are past their forces.
And a gallon of ale for our poor horses,
And some bits of bread for the hounds, poor things,
After all they've done (for they've done like kings),
Would keep them going till we get in.
We had it alone from Nun's Wood Whin."
Then Tom replied, "If they changed or not,
There've been few runs longer and none more hot,
We shall talk of to-day until we die."

The stars grew bright in the winter sky,
The wind came keen with a tang of frost,
The brook was troubled for new things lost,
The copse was happy for old things found,
The fox came home and he went to ground.

And the hunt came home and the hounds were fed,
They climbed to their bench and went to bed,
The horses in stable loved their straw.
"Good-night, my beauties," said Robin Dawe.

Then the moon came quiet and flooded full
Light and beauty on clouds like wool,
On a feasted fox at rest from hunting,
In the beech wood grey where the brocks were grunting.

The beech wood grey rose dim in the night
With moonlight fallen in pools of light,
The long dead leaves on the ground were rimed.
A clock struck twelve and the church-bells chimed.

ENSLAVED

All early in the April when daylight comes at five
I went into the garden most glad to be alive
The thrushes and the blackbirds were singing in the thorn
The April flowers were singing for joy of being born.

I smelt the dewy morning come blowing through the woods
Where all the wilding cherries do toss their snowy snoods,
I thought of the running water where sweet white violets grow
I said, "I'll pick them for her, because she loves them so."

So in the dewy morning I turned to climb the hill
Beside the running water whose tongue is never still,
O delicate green and dewy were all the budding trees
The blue dog-violets grew there and many primroses.

Out of the wood I wandered, but paused upon the heath
To watch, beyond the tree tops, the wrinkled sea beneath,
Its blueness and its stillness were trembling as it lay
In the old un-autumned beauty that never goes away.

And the beauty of the water brought my love into my mind
Because all sweet love is beauty and the loved thing turns
to kind,
And I thought, "It is a beauty spread, for setting of your grace,
O white violet of a woman with the April in your face."

So I gathered the white violets where young men pick them
still,
And I turned to cross the woodland to her house beneath the
hill,

And I thought of her delight in the flowers that I brought her,
Bright like sunlight, sweet like singing, cool like running of the
water.

Now I noticed as I crossed the wood towards my lady's house,
That wisps of smoke were blowing blue in the young green of the
boughs:
But I thought, "They're burning weeds," and I felt the green
and blue
To be lovely, so, together, while the green was in its dew.

Then I smelt the smell of burning; but I thought, "The bonfire
takes,
And the tongues of flame are licking up below the lifting flakes."
Though, I thought, "The fire must be big, to raise a smoke so
thick."
And I wondered for a moment if the fire were a rick.

But the love that sang within me made me put the thought
away,
What do young men care for trouble if they see their love to-day,
And my thought kept running forward till it knelt before my
sweet,
Laying thought and joy and service in a love-gift at her feet.

And I thought of life beside her, and of all our days together,
Stormy days, perhaps, of courage, with our faces to the weather,
Never any days, but happy, so I thought, if passed with her.
Then the smoke came blowing thickly till it made the wood a
blur.

Still, I did not think of evil, for one could not, living there.
But I said, "The rooks are startled," for their crying filled the
air,

And I wondered, in the meadow, why the cows were not at grass,
Only smoke, down-blowing, bitter, that the birds were loath to
pass.

So I quickened through the meadow to the close that hid the
home
And the smoke drove down in volleys, lifted up, and wreathed
and clomb,
And I could not see, because of it, and what one cannot see
Holds the fear that lives in darkness, so that fear began in me.

And the place was like a death-house save for cawings overhead,
All the cocks and hens were silent and the dogs were like the
dead,
Nothing but the smoke seemed living, thick, and hiding whence
it came,
Bitter with the change of burning, hot upon the cheek from
flame.

Then my fear became a terror, and I knew that ill had fallen
From the fate that comes unthought of when the unheard word
is callen,
So I flung the little gate astray and burst the bushes through
Little red-white blossoms flecked me and my face was dashed
with dew.

Then I saw what ill had fallen, for the house had burned to
death,
Though it gleamed with running fire when a falling gave a
breath,
All the roof was sky, the lead dripped, all the empty windows
wide
Spouted smoke, and all was silent, save the volleying rooks that
cried.

This I saw. I rocked with anguish at the flicking heap that glowed.
She was dead among the ashes that the lead drops did corrode.
She was dead, that gave a meaning to the beauty of the spring,
Yet the daffodils still nodded and the blackbirds still did sing.

When the stunning passed, I stumbled to the house's westward side
Thinking there to find some neighbour that could tell me how she died;
Fearing, too, lest Death the devil who had dealt such murder there
Should be hiding there behind me for to clutch me unaware.

There was no one there alive, but my leaping heart was stilled
By the sight of bodies lying in the grass where they were killed.
Drooped into the grass they lay there, pressing close into the ground
As the dead do, in the grasses; all my world went spinning round.

Then I saw, that with the bodies, all the ground was heaped and strown
With the litter of a house that had been gutted to the bone;
Split and hingeless coffers yawning, linen drooped like people dead,
Trinkets broken for their jewels, barrels staved, and crusts of bread.

Then a mess of feathers blowing, then the cattle's heads, and then
Stunned at all this wreck I hurried to the bodies of the men.
Five were workers of the household, lying dead in her defence;
Roused from sleep, perhaps, in darkness so that death might dash them thence.

But the other three were strangers, swarthy, bearded, hook-nosed, lean,
Wearing white (for night surprisal) over seamen's coats of green;
Moorish-coloured men, still greedy for the prize they died to snatch;
Clutching broken knives, or grass-blades, or some tatters of their catch.

Then I moaned aloud, for then I knew the truth, that these
Were the Moorish pirate raiders who had come there from the seas,
Come upon my love defenceless, by surprise, and I not there.
Come to burn or kill her beauty or to drag her to their lair.

"Dragged away to be a slave," I thought. I saw what she had seen,
All the good friends lying slaughtered in the young grass dewy green;
All the cattle killed for provant and the gutted homestead burning,
And the skinny Moors to drag her to the death of no returning.

Minutes passed, yet still I stood there, when I heard one call my name,
Amys, once my darling's woman, from her hiding-corner came,
"O," she cried, "They came upon us when the light was growing gray
And they sacked and burned and slaughtered, and they've carried her away.

"I was sleeping in the cottage when I heard the noise of men,
And the shots; and I could see them, for the house was blazing then.
They were like to devils, killing, so I hid, and then I heard
Rollo moaning in the bushes with a face as white as curd.

"He was dying from a bullet, but he said 'Saffee. Saffee
Pirates, Amys; they were burning and they shot and murdered
me.
Amys, look where I was murdered, look, they blew away my
side,
And they burnt the cows in stable.' Then he moaned until he
died.

"It was terrible to hear them kill the beasts and pack their prey.
Then they shouldered up their plunder and they sang and
marched away;
And they took my lady with them as a slave-girl to be sold.
I saw them kill Paloma, they said that she was old.

"Then they went on board their cruiser and she sailed away at
once.
Look there, beyond the beaches, you see her where she
runs—"

* * * * * * *

I saw a peaked sail pointing and feathering oars that flasht
In the blueness of the water that was whitened where they
gasht.

* * * * * * *

There they carried my beloved in a pirate ship at sea
To be sold like meat for killing in the markets of Saffee.
Some fire-shrivelled oak-leaves blew lightly past my face,
A beam fell in ruins, the fire roared a space.

I walked down to the water, my heart was torn in two
For the anguish of her future and the nothing I could do.
The ship had leaned a little as she snouted to the spray;
The feathering oars flashed steadily at taking her away.

I took a fisher's boat there was and dragged her down the sand,
I set her sail and took an oar and thrust her from the land,

I headed for the pirate, and the brown weed waved beneath
And the boat trod down the bubbles of the bone between her
teeth.

I brought them down the land-wind so from the first I gained;
I set a tiny topsail that bowed her till she strained.
My mind was with my darling aboard that ship of fear
In cabin close with curtains where Moormen watched my dear.

Now when they saw me coming they wondered what it meant,
This young man in a fish-boat who followed where they went.
They judged that I was coming to buy the woman free;
So suddenly the oars stopped, they waited on the sea.

I dropped my sail close to them and ranged to easy hail,
Her plunges shivered wrinklings along her spilling sail,
The water running by her had made her shine like gold,
The oar blades poised in order kissed water when she rolled.

A hundred naked rowers stared down their oars at me
With all the bitter hatred the slave has for the free.
The boatswain walked above them, he mocked me, so did they:
The sun had burnt their bodies and yet their look was gray.

So there we rocked together, while she, at every roll,
Moaned from her guns with creakings that shook her to the
soul;
I did not see my darling; she lay in ward below
Down in the green hung cabin she first joined hands with woe.

The galley plowtered, troubling; the mockings of the slaves
Passed from bench to bench, like bird's cries, her bow-beak
slapt the waves,

Then her captain came on deck, quick and hard, with snapping force,
And a kind of cringe of terror stiffened down those banks of oars.

The captain walked the deck; he eyed me for a moment,
He called some Turkish words with a muttered added comment,
Then he called, "Well. What d'ye want?" in the lingua of the sea.
The boatswain leaned and spoke, then they sneered and looked at me.

So I stood upon the thwart, and I called, "I want to come
To be comrade to the woman whom you've dragged away from home.
Since I cannot set her free, I want only to be near her."
"Ah," he said, "Men buy love dear, but by God you buy it dearer.

"Well; you shall;" he spoke in Moorish and a seaman tossed a cord,
So I hove myself alongside, scrambled up and climbed aboard.
All were silent, but they watched me; all those eyes above the oars
Stared, and all their bitter tushes gnashed beneath them like a boar's!

At an order, all the oars clanked aft, and checked, and sliced the sea,
The rowers' lips twitched upward, the sheets tugged to be free,
The wrinklings in the sail ran up as it rounded to a breast,
The ship bowed to a billow and snouted through the crest.

My boat was tossed behind us, she bowed and swung away.
The captain stood and mocked me, "Well, since you would, you may.

You shall be near your lady, until we fetch to port."
They chained me to the oar-loom upon the after-thwart.

All day, until the twilight, I swung upon the oar;
Above the dropping taffrail I sometimes saw the shore,
Behind me swung the rowers, again and yet again
A gasp, a clank of rollocks and then a cry of pain.

The boatswain walked above us to lash us if we slackened;
With blood of many beatings the rowers' backs were blackened,
Again and yet again came the lash and then the cry,
Then a mutter for revenge would run round the ship and die.

But twilight with her planet that brings quiet to the tired,
Bringing dusk upon the water brought the gift that I desired
For they brought my well-beloved to the deck to breathe the
air,
Not a half an oar's length from me, so we spoke together there.

"You," she said; "Yes, I, beloved, to be near you over sea.
I have come to be beside you and to help to set you free.
Keep your courage and be certain that the God who took will
give.
God will dawn and we shall prosper for the living soul will live."

Then they bade me stop my talking and to use my breath to row.
Darkness came upon the water and they took my love below.
Fire in the oar-stirred water swirled in streaks that raced away;
Toppling up and down the taffrail touched the red sky and the
gray.

Then the wind began to freshen till the shrouds were twanging
sharp,
Thrilling an unchanging honing like a madman with a harp,
Thrilling on a rising water that was hissing as it rose
To be foamed asunder by us as we struck it down with blows.

Soon we could not row, but rested with the oar blades triced above,
Then my soul went from my body to give comfort to my love,
Though indeed the only comfort that my mind could find to say
Was, that God, who makes to-morrow makes it better than to-day.

So I yearned towards my darling while I drooped upon my bench.
All the galley's length was shaken when the mainsail gave a wrench;
Always when I roused, the taffrail toppled up to touch the stars,
And the roaring seas ran hissing, and the planks whined, and the spars.

Day by day I rowed the galley, night by night I saw the Pole
Sinking lower in the northward to the sorrow of my soul,
Yet at night I saw my darling when she came on deck to walk,
And our thoughts passt to each other though they would not let us talk.

Till early on a morning before the dawn had come
Some foreign birds came crying with strong wings wagging home.
Then on the wind a warmness, a sweetness as of cloves,
Blew faintly in the darkness from spice and orange groves.

Then, as they set us rowing, the sun rose over land
That seemed a mist of forest above a gleam of sand.
White houses glittered on it, the pirates cheered to see.
By noon we reached the haven, we anchored in Saffee.

They cloaked my well-beloved and carried her ashore
She slipped a paper to me while brushing past my oar.
I took it, muttering "Courage"; I read it when I dared:
"They mean me for the Khalif. I have to be prepared."

They led her up the jetty, she passed out of my sight.
Then they knocked away our irons and worked us till the night,
Unbending sails, unstepping masts, clean-scraping banks, unshipping oars
Rousing casks and loot and cables from the orlop into stores.

When all the gear was warehoused, they marched us up the street,
All sand it was, where dogs lay, that sprang and snapped our feet,
Then lancers came at gallop, they knocked us to the side,
They struck us with their lance-staves to make them room to ride.

Then, as we cleared the roadway, with clatter, riding hard,
With foam flung from the bit-cups, there came the body-guard,
Then splendid in his scarlet the Khalif's self went by
A grand young bird of rapine with a hawk-look in his eye.

A slave said, "There's the Khalif. He's riding north to-night,
To Marrakesh, the vineyard, his garden of delight.
That means a night of quiet to us poor dogs who row,
The guards will take their pleasure and we shall rest below."

Then, in the dusk, they marched us to the quarries of the slaves
Which were dripping shafts in limestone giving passage into caves.
There they left us with our rations to the night that prisoners know
Longing after what was happy far away and long ago.

* * * * * * *

Now often, as I rowed upon the bench,
In tugging back the oar-loom in the stroke,
A rower opposite whose face was French

Had signalled to me, with a cheer or joke,
Grinning askant, and tossing back his hair
To shew his white, keen features debonair.

And now that I was sitting on the stone,
He came to where I sat, and sat beside.
"So," he exclaimed, "you eat your heart alone.
I did, at first; but prison kills the pride.
It kills the heart, and all it has to give
Is hatred, daunted by the will to live.

"I was a courtier in the French King's court
Three years ago; you would not think it now,
To see me rower in a pirate port
Rusting my chain with sweatings from my brow.
But I was once Duhamel, over sea,
And should be still, if they would ransom me.

"I honour you for coming as you did
To save your lady. It was nobly done.
They took her for the Khalif; she is hid
There in the woman's palace; but, my son,
You will not look upon her face again.
Best face the fact, whatever be the pain.

"No, do not speak, for she is lost forever,
Hidden in that dark palace of the King.
Not all the loving in the world would ever
Bring word to her, or help, or anything.
She will be pasture to the King's desires,
Then sold, or given in barter, when he tires.

"A woman in the Khalif's house is dead
To all the world forever; that is truth:
And you (most gallantly) have put your head

Into the trap. Till you have done with youth,
You will be slave, in prison or at sea.
Sickness or death alone will set you free."

"Surely," I said, "since people have escaped
From worser hells than this, I, too, might try.
Fate, that is given to all men partly shaped,
Is man's, to alter daily till he die.
I mean to try to save her. Things which men
Mean with their might, succeed, as this will then."

I saw him look about him with alarm.
"O, not so loud," he said, "for there are spies."
His look of tension passed, he caught my arm,
"I think none heard," he said, "but, oh, be wise
Slaves have been ganched upon the hooks for less.
This place has devilries men cannot guess.

"But no man, ever, has escaped from here.
To talk of it is death; your friend and you
Are slaves for life, and after many a year,
(At best) when you are both too old to do
The work of slaves, you may be flung abroad,
To beg for broken victuals in the road."

I saw that what he said was certainty.
I knew it, even then, but answered, "Well.
I will at least be near her till I die,
And Life is change, and no man can foretell.
Even if thirty years hence we may meet
It is worth while, and prison shall be sweet."

He looked at me with pleasure, then he sighed
And said, "Well, you deserve her." Then he stared
Across the quarry, trying to decide

If I were fit to see his spirit bared.
Quick glances of suspicion and distrust
Searched at my face, and then he said, "I must.

"I must not doubt you, lad, so listen now.
I have a plan, myself, for leaving this.
I meant to try to-night; I'll shew you how
To save your lady. And to-night there is
Hope, for the Kaliph sleeps at Marrakesh.
When knots are loosened fish can burst the mesh."

So eagerly I plighted faith to try
That very night to help him. "If we fail"
He said, "It will be Fate, who flings the die
Against which nothing mortal can avail.
But we are desperate men whose throws succeed,
Being one with Fate, or Change from Passionate Need."

So we agreed, that when the cave was still,
We would attempt, and having broken prison,
Would raid the women's palace on the hill,
And save my lady ere the sun was risen,
Then put to sea towards some hiding-place
North, in the shoals, where galleys could not chase.

Even as we made an end, another slave,
(They called him English Gerard) joined us there.
Often, upon the toppling of a wave
I'd seen him rowing and had heard him swear.
Forceful he was, with promise in his eye
Of rough capacity and liberty.

"Still talking of escape, I'll bet a crown,"
He said to me; "But you are young, my friend,
We oldsters know we cannot leave the town,
We shall be here until the bitter end.

Give up the hope, lad, better let it be,
No slave has ever broken from Saffee.

"Inland, there's desert, westward, there's the sea,
Northward, the Moorish towns, and in the south,
Swamps and the forest to eternity.
The young colt jibs at iron in his mouth
But has to take it, and the fact for us
Is, that we're slaves, and have to linger thus."

"Just what I told him," said Duhamel, "Just
My very words. It's bitter, but the truth.
We shall be slaves until we turn to dust
Your lady, too, until she loses youth.
Put hope aside, and make what life you can
Being a slave, for slave you are, young man."

"Perhaps," said Gerard, "you were told what comes
Of trying to escape, for men have tried.
They only added to their martyrdoms,
Two got away at Christmas, but they died.
The one they skinned and stuffed, the other hangs
Still, near the gate, upon the ganches' fangs."

"How were they caught?" I asked. "They were betrayed,"
Said Gerard. "How? By whom? I cannot tell.
They trusted someone with the plans they made
And he betrayed them, like a fiend from hell.
How do I know it? Well. They left no trace,
And yet the lancers knew their hiding place.

"They went straight to it, straight, and caught them there
As soon as daylight came, when they had gone.
(As you'll be taken if you don't beware)

They keep great hooks to hang the bodies on
Of those who run away, or try, for none
Succeeds, nor can, so you be warned, my son."

He nodded to me, gripped my arm, and went
Back to his place, the other side the cave.
"That was a spy," Duhamel whispered, "sent
To test your spirit as a new-come slave.
I know the man, and if report speaks true
He helped in that betrayal of the two.

"Now seem to sleep and when the cave is quiet
We two will try; they say God helps the mad.
To be a slave to Moors is bitter diet
That poisons men; two bitter years I've had
But before dawn we two will end it, lad.
Now seem to sleep."
I cuddled to the stone;
Yet Gerard's voice seemed calling to my bone.

And opening my eyes, I saw him there
Looking intently at me, and he shook
His head at me, as though to say "Beware",
And frowned a passionate warning in a look.
A wind-flaw, blowing through the window, took
The flame within the lantern, that it shed
Bright light on him. Again he shook his head.

The wind blowing in from the sea made the flame like a plume;
The slaves, huddled close, cursed in whispers, with chattering teeth,
The wolves of their spirits came stealthy to snarl in the gloom
Over bones of their pleasures long-perished: the sea moaned beneath.

And my heart glowed with joy that that night I might rescue
my love,
Glowed with joy in Duhamel whose cunning would conquer
the guards.
The wind blew in fresher; a sentry went shuffling above,
Some gamblers crouched tense, while a lean hand flickered the
cards.

Then one by one the gamblers left their game
The shadows shaken by the blowing flame
Winked on the wall until the lamp blew out.
Wrapping his ankle irons in a clout
(To save his skin) each branded slave prepared
To take his sleep his only comfort spared.

A kind of clearness blowing from the night
Made sleepers' faces bonelike with its light.
A sleeper moaning, twisted with his shoulder
Close to the limestone as the wind grew colder.
Trickles of water glistened down and splashed
Pools on the limestone into rings that flashed.
Often a stirring sleeper struck the bell
Of chain-links upon stones. Deep breathing fell
Like sighing, out of all that misery
Of vermined men who dreamed of being free.
Heavily on the beaches fell the sea.

Then, as the tide came in, the waters seething
Under the quarries, mingled with the breathing,
Until the prison in the rock y-hewen
Seemed like a ship that trod the water's ruin
Trampling the toppling sea, while water creeping,
Splashed from the seams in darkness on men sleeping.
Far in the city all the dogs were howling
At that white bird the moon in heaven owling.

Out in the guardhouse soldiers made a dither
About the wiry titter of a zither,
Their long-drawn songs were timed with clapping hands.

The water hissed its life out on the sands.
The wheel of heaven with all her glittering turned,
The city window-lights no longer burned.
Then one by one the soldiers left their clatter,
The moon arose and walked upon the water
The sleepers turned to screen her from their eyes.
A fishing boat sailed past; the fishers' cries
Rang in the darkness of the bay without.
Her sail flapped as she creaked and stood about,
Then eased, then leaned, then strained and stood away.
Deep silence followed, save where breathers lay.

So, lying there, with all my being tense
Prepared to strike, to take my lady thence,
A prompting bade me not to trust too far
This man Duhamel as a guiding star.
Some little thing in him had jarred on me
A touch (the flesh being raw) hurts cruelly.
And something in his speech or in his bearing
Made me mistrust his steadiness in daring
Or his endurance, or his faith to us.
Some smile or word made me distrustful thus.
Who knows the hidden things within our being
That prompt our brain to safety without seeing,
Hear the unheard and save us without sense?
What fingers touch our strings when we are tense?

Even at that point, Duhamel crept to me,
And whispered, "Come, by morning we'll be free.
Creep down the passage there towards the entry,
See what the guards do while I time the sentry.

I think that all the guards are sleeping sound
But, there's his foot, one sentry goes his round.
And I must time him till I know his beat."
Loitering upon the rampart came the feet
Of some loose-slippered soldier. I could hear
Him halt, humming a tune, grounding his spear.

I listened, while Duhamel urged me on.
"Hurry," he said, "the night will soon be gone;
Watch from the passage what the guards are doing:
I'll time the sentry. There'll be no pursuing
If we can pass the guards with him away.
Beyond the bend he cannot see the bay."

"No," I replied, "yet even if the guard
Be all asleep, it cannot but be hard
For us to pick the lock of that steel grille
Without their waking. We cannot be still
Crouched in the puddle, scraping at the lock.
The guards will wake and kill us at a knock."

"Hush," said Duhamel, "Let me whisper close.
I did not dare before for fear of those,
(The rowers and the spies), I have a key
That will unlock the grating silently,
Making no noise at all in catch or ward.
Now creep along and spy upon the guard."

"A key?" said I. My first suspicions died.
"Yes," said the man, "I slipped it from his side,
While he was checking us this afternoon.
Courage, my son, she'll be in safety soon."
He shewed a key, and urged me to be gone
Down the gaunt gashway carven in the stone,
A darkness in the else half-glimmering lime,

Where drops, each minute splashing, told the time.
There, in the darkness somewhere, lay the gate
Where courage and the moment might make Fate.

I rose, half-doubting, upon hands and knees;
The blood within my temples sang like bees;
I heard my heart. I saw Duhamel's face,
Dark eyes in focus in a whitish space,
Watching me close. I doubted, even then.
Then with the impulse which transfigures men,
Doubt, hesitation, terror passed. I crawled
Into the dripping tunnel limestone-walled.

A cold drop spattered on my neck; the wet
Struck chilly where my hands and knees were set.
I crawled into a darkness like a vault
Glimmering and sweating like a rock of salt.

I crept most thief-like till the passage turned.
There, in a barrèd greyness, I discerned
The world without, shut from me by the grille.
I stopped, most thief-like, listening.

All was still;

The quarry I had left was still as stone.
The melancholy water-drip alone
Broke silence near me, and ahead the night
Was silent in the beauty of its light,
Across which fell the black of prison bars.

I crawled ten paces more and saw the stars
Above the guard-hut in the quarry pit:
The hut was still, it had no lantern lit.
I crawled again with every nerve intent.

The cleanly sea-wind bringing pleasant scent
Blew through the grille with little specks of sand.
Each second I expected the word "Stand."
That, or a shot, but still, no challenge came.
The twilight of the moon's unearthly flame
Burned steadily; the palm-leaves on the hut
Rustled in gusts, the crazy door was shut.
The guards were either sleeping or not there.

I peered out through the grille and drank the air
For any scent that might betray a guard
Hidden in ambush near me keeping ward;
But no scent, save the cleanness of the sea,
Blew on the night wind blowing in on me.
There was no trace of man.

I watched and listened.
The water dropped, the trickling passage glistened,
The coldness of the iron pressed my brow.
Then, as I listened, (I can hear it now),
A strangled cry such as a dreamer cries
When the dream binds him that he cannot rise,
Gurgled behind me in the sleepers' cave.
A failing hand that struggled with the grave
Beat on the floor, then fluttered, then relaxed,
Limp as an altar ox a priest has axed.
No need to say that someone had been killed
That was no dream.

Yet all the cave was stilled.
Nobody spoke, or called, or ran to aid.
The fingers of the palm leaves ticked and played
On the hut-roof, but yet no guard appeared.
I started to crawl back, because I feared.
I knew that someone must have heard that calling

Of the killed blood upon the midnight falling.
"I shall be judged the killer," so I thought.

So crawling swiftly back like one distraught,
I groped that tunnel where the blackness made
Me feel each inch before my hand was laid.
There was no gleam, save wetness on the wall,
No noise but heart beat or the droppings' fall.
Blackness and silence tense with murder done,
Tense with a soul that had not yet begun
To know the world without the help of clay.
I was in terror in that inky way.

Then suddenly, while stretching out my hand
The terror brought my heart's blood to a stand.
I touched a man.
His face was turned to me.
He whispered, "To the grille. I have the key."
So, without speech I turned; he followed after.
I trembled at the droppings from the rafter.
Each noise without seemed footsteps in pursuit.
The palm-leaves fluttered like a running foot.
The moonlight held her lantern to betray us.
A stricken stone was as a sword to slay us.
Then at the grille we paused that I could see
That it was not Duhamel there with me
But English Gerard.

"Do not speak," he said;
"Don't think about Duhamel; he is dead.
This key, that should unlock, is sticking: try."
With shaking hands I took the clicket, I.
A lean cogged bolt of iron jangled bright
By shaking in the key-ring, day and night;
It stuck in the knobbed latch and would not lift.

All kinds of terror urged me to be swift,
Fear of the guards and of the darkness dying,
And of Duhamel's body mutely crying
The thin red cry of murdered blood and bone
Piping in darkness to make murder known.
But there the clicket jammed the iron socket
Nor could my hand withdraw it or unlock it.
"Let me," said Gerard; then with guile and skill
He coaxed the knobbed iron from the grille
"It does not fit," he muttered; "after all."
Outside, within his roost, a cock did call
His warning to the ghosts, and slept again,
The stars that glittered in the sky like grain
Seemed paler, and the ticking time sped on
To the guard's waking and the darkness gone
With nothing done.

Then Gerard turned to me
"Though this is wrong, Duhamel had the key,
And has it still about him as I guess
Tied to his flesh or hidden in his dress.
Wait here, while I go rummage through his clothes."

A sleeper, tossing, jabbered broken oaths
Then slept, while Gerard crawled.

I was alone
Afraid no more, but anxious to the bone.

And looking out I saw a sentry come
Slowly towards the grille. I cowered numb
Back into blackness pressed against the wall.
I heard the measure of his footsteps fall
Along the quarry to me. I could see
The tenseness of his eyes turned full on me
I felt that he must see me and give speech.

His hand, that shook the grille, was in my reach.
He peered within to see if all were well.
Wet as though spat a drop of water fell.
He peered into the blackness where I stood,
Then, having tried the lock, he tossed his hood,
Crouched at the grille and struck a light, and lit
Tinder, and blew the glowing end of it
Till all his face was fierce in the strong glow;
He sucked the rank tobacco lighted so,
And stood a moment blowing bitter smoke.
I hardly dared to breathe lest I should choke.
I longed to move, but dared not. Had I stirred
Even a finger's breadth, he must have heard.
He must have touched me had he thrust his hand
Within the grille to touch the wall he scanned.

Then, slowly, muttering to himself, he took
Three steps away, then turned for one more look
Straight at the grille and me. I counted ten.
Something within the passage moved him then
Because he leaned and peered as though unsure.
Then, stepping to the grille-work's embrasure,
He thrust his face against the iron grid,
And stared into the blackness where I hid,
And softly breathed, "Duhamel."

As he spoke

A passing cloud put dimness as of smoke
Over the moon's face. No-one answered him,
A drip-drop spat its wetness in the dim.
He paused to call again, then turned away.
He wandered slowly up the quarry way
But at the bend he stopped to rest his bones.
He sat upon the bank and juggled stones
For long, long minutes. Gerard joined me there.

We watched the sentry tossing stones in air
To catch them on his hand's back as they fell.
We wished him in the bottom pit of hell.
At last he rose and sauntered round the bend.
The falling of his footsteps had an end
At last, and Gerard spoke, "I have the key."

The cogs caught in the locket clickily,
The catch fell back, the heavy iron gave.
We pushed the grille and stept out of the grave
Into the moonlight where the wind was blowing.
"Hurry," I whispered, for the cocks were crowing
In unseen roosts, the morning being near.
We climbed the bank.
"This way," said Gerard, "here.

Now, down the slope. We dodge the sentry so.
Now through the water where the withies grow.
Now we are out of sight; now we can talk."
We changed our crouching running to a walk.

He led me up a slope where rats carousing
Squealed or showed teeth among the tumbled housing,
Half-ruined wooden huts, or lime-washed clay.
We turned from this into a trodden way
Pale in the moonlight, where the dogs that prowled
Snarled as we passed, then eyed the moon and howled.
Below us, to our right, the harbour gleamed,
In front, pale with the moon, the city dreamed,
Roof upon roof, with pointing fingers white,
The minarets, frost-fretted with the light,
With many a bubbled dome-top like a shell
Covering the hillside to the citadel.

"There, to the left," said Gerard, "where the trees are,
That whiteness is the palace of the Cæsar,

His gardens and his fishpools. That long building
Flanked by the domes that glitter so with gilding
Is where the women are. She will be there.
But courage, comrade, never yield to care,
We'll set her free, before the morning breaks,
But oh, my son, no more of your mistakes.
What made you trust Duhamel as you did?
Well, he is dead. The world is better rid
Of men like him. He tempted and betrayed
Those two poor souls last year.
Ah, when he bade
You go to watch the guard I studied him.
He was a bitter viper, supple—slim.
When he had judged that you had reached the entry,
He stole towards the grate and called the sentry,
'Hussein, Hussein—' but Hussein never heard.
He called him twice, but never called the third
I stopped his calling, luckily for you."
"Yes, but" (I said), "what did he mean to do,
Calling the sentry? What could that have done?"
"Caught you in trying to escape, my son,
The thing they love to do from time to time.
They reckon that examples stop the crime.
One caught and skinned makes many fear to try.
They would have flayed your skin off cruelly
In face of all these slaves, to daunt them down.
Then you'd have hung a dying in the town
Nailed to some post, two days, perhaps, or three,
With thirst and flies.
But let Duhamel be,
Bad though he was, misfortune tempts a soul
Worse than we think, and few men can control
Their virtue, being slave; and he had been
A Knight of France, a courtier of the Queen.

He must have suffered to have fallen so,
A slave, a spy on slaves; we cannot know
Thank God, what power of sinking lies in us.
God keep us all."

So talking to me thus,
He turned me leftward from the citadel
Uphill. He said, "I know this city well,
There is the Khalif's palace straight ahead.
How many days I've staggered nearly dead
From thirst, and from the sun, and from the load,
Up to the palace-gates along this road,
Bearing the plunder of the cruise to store,
After a month of tugging at the oar,
But now, please God, I shall not come again."

Our talking stopped; we turned into a lane.
High, white-washed walls rose up on either side,
The narrow gash between was four feet wide,
And there at sprawl within the narrow way
With head in hood a sleeping beggar lay.
We stepped across his body heedfully
Deep in his dream he muttered drowsily.

We tip-toed on. The wall-tops, high above,
White in the quiet moonlight, hid my love.
We crept like worms in darkness yard by yard,
Still as the dead, but that our hearts beat hard.
And, spite of self, my teeth clickt from the flood
Of quick excitement running in my blood.
We were so near her, and the peril came
Close, with the moment that would prove the same.

The lane turned sharply twice. In shadow dark,
With shiverings of singing like a lark,

A fountain sprang, relented, sprinkled, bubbled,
In some cool garden that the moonlight troubled,
Unseen by us, although a smell of roses
Warm on the wind, stole to us from its closes.
Then came a wood-smoke smell, and mixed therewith
Gums from the heart's blood of the sinnam's pith.
And Gerard touched me. We had reached the place.
The woman's palace-wall was there in face
The garden-wall merged with it, moonlight-topped,
Just where the two together merged we stopped.
Then, as we stood there, breathing, we could hear,
Beyond the wall, some footsteps loitering near,
Some garden sentry slowly paced his watch
Crooning a love song; I could smell the match
That smouldered in the linstock at his hand.

His footsteps passed away upon the sand
Slowly, with pauses, for he stopped to eat
The green buds of the staric on his beat.
When he had gone, a cock crowed in the lane.
"It will be morning when he crows again."
Was in our thoughts: we had full little time.

Some joist-holes gave us foothold, we could climb
Without much trouble to the wall's flat top,
There we lay still, to let the plaster drop,
And see what dangers lay below us there.

The garden of the palace breathed sweet air
Under our perch, the fountain's leaping glitter
Shone; a bird started with a frightened twitter.
Alleys of blossomed fruit trees girt a cool
White marble screen about a bathing pool,
The palace rose beyond among its trees,
Splay-fronded figs and dates and cypresses.

Close to our left hands was the Woman's House.
We crept along our wall-top perilous
Till we could touch the roof that hid my love
A teaken joist-end jutted out above.
We swung ourselves upon the roof thereby.
The dewy wet flat house-top faced the sky.
We crouched together there.
Sweet smoke was wreathing
Out of a trap-door near us; heavy breathing
Came from a woman sleeping near the trap.
I crept to her, not knowing what might hap.
She was an old Moor woman with primmed lips,
And foul white hair, and hennaed finger tips
That clutched a dark hair blanket to her chin.

I crept to the trap-door and peered within.
A ladder led within. A lantern burning
Shewed us a passage leading to a turning
But open to the garden at one end.

Even as we peered, a man came round the bend,
Walked slowly down that lamp-lit corridor,
And stood to watch the garden at the door.
We saw his back within that moonlit square.
He had a curving sword which glittered bare.
He stood three minutes still, watching the night,
Each beating second made the east more light.
He cracked and relished nuts or melon seeds.

The hoof-sparks of the morning's running steeds
Made a pale dust now in the distant east
But still the man stood cracking at his feast
Nut after nut; then flinging broken shell
Into the rose-walk, clicking as it fell,
He turned towards us up the passage dim.

There at the trap we crouched right over him,
And as he passed beneath, his fingers tried
A door below us in the passage-side.
Then, slowly loitering on, he reached and passed
The passage turning; he was gone at last
His footsteps died away; they struck on stone
In some far cloister; we were left alone.

Then, while our leaping hearts beat like to drums
We took the gambler's way, that takes what comes.
We slid into the trap and down the stair,
Steep, like a loft's; eleven rungs there were.
We stood within the passage at the door
Tried by the guard that little while before.

Within, there was a rustling and a chinking,
(Like the glass dangles that the wind sets clinking)
And something tense there was within; the throbbing
Of hearts in a despair too deep for sobbing
We felt it there before we pressed the latch.

The teaken bar rose stiffly from its catch.
We slipt within and closed the door again.
We were within the dwelling place of pain,
Among the women whom the Moors had taken,
The broken-hearts, despairing and forsaken,
The desolate that cried where no man heard.

Nobody challenged, but some women stirred.
It was so dark at first, after the moon.
A smoking censer, swinging, creaked a croon,
There was a hanging lamp of beaten brass
That gave dim light through scraps of coloured glass
I saw a long low room with many a heap
Dark, on the floor, where women lay asleep

On silken cushions. Round the wall there ran
(Dark, too, with cushioned women) a divan,
And women stirred and little chains were shaken.

What horror 'tis, to prisoners, to waken
Out of the dreams of home back to the chain,
Back to the iron and the mill again,
In some far land among one's enemies.
I knew that then; those women made me wise.

We stared into the twilight till our eyes
Could see more clearly: no one challenged us.
But standing back against the doorway thus,
I saw the warden of the room, asleep,
Close to me, on the cushions, breathing deep,
Her hard face made like iron by the gloom.
An old grim Moor that warden of the room,
A human iron fettered on the poor.
Far down the room a fetter touched the floor.

Even in the gloom I knew that she was there,
My April of a woman with bright hair;
She sat upright against the wall alone
By burning meditation turned to stone,
Staring ahead and when I touched her shoulder
Her body (stiffened like a corpse and colder)
Seemed not herself, her mind seemed far away.

There was no need to talk, but to essay
The light steel chain that linked her to the wall,
We gripped it, heaving, till its links were gall
Biting across our hands, but still we drave
She, I and Gerard heaving till it gave
The leaded staple snapped across the shank.

The loosed chain struck the flooring with a clank.
We all lay still, my arm about my own.
"Who's moving there? Be silent," snapped the crone.

Cross with the slave who had awakened her
She stared towards us. We could hear her stir,
Craning towards us, but she could not see
More than the cushions tumbled there with me.
She thought, perhaps, "That fair one shook her chain."
She growled, "I'll beat you, if you stir again.
A Moorish whip upon your Christian skin."

I saw her clutch her blanket to her chin
Turn to her side and settle to her rest.
The dawn, that brings the skylark from her nest
Was flying with bright feet that ever hasted.
Each moment there meant happy chances wasted,
Yet still we had to stay until she slept.

When she had fallen to a doze we crept
Stealthily to the door on hands and knees.
All of those women came from over seas.
We could not waken them to share our chance.
Not Peru's silver nor the fields of France
Could buy a place in our society.
One tender feeling might have made us die
All three, and been no kindness to the fourth:
Compassions perish when the wind is north.

Close to the door, a woman leaned and caught
My darling's hand and kissed it swift as thought
And whispered, "O, good luck," and then was still.
She had no luck, but O she had good will.
We blest her in our hearts.

The warder stirred
Growling but dozing lightly, then we heard
Outside the door, within three feet of us,
The footsteps of the sentry perilous,
The clinking of his scabbard lightly touching
Some metal button, then his fingers clutching
The teaken catch to try if it were home.

We stood stone-still expecting him to come.
He did not come, he pushed the door and passed,
Treading this beat exactly like the last,
To loiter at the door to crack and spit.

The time dragged by till he had done with it.
Then back he came, and once again he shook
The catch upon its socket, then he took
His way along the passage out of hearing.

The room 'gan glimmer from the dawning nearing
The warder struggled with a dream and cried
The lamp-flame purred from want of oil and died.
And she, the woman who had kissed her hand,
Whispered, "O go, for God's sake, do not stand
One moment more, but go. God help you free."

We crept out of the prison silently,
Gerard the last, who closed the door behind us,
The crowing of a cock came to remind us
That it was morning now with daylight breaking
The leaves all shivering and birds awaking.
We climbed the ladder.

Its eleven rungs
Called to the Moors of us with all their tongues.
"Wake," "Wake;" "They fly." "The three of them are
flying."

"O broken house," "O sleepers, thieves are trying
To take the Khalif's treasure." "Guards," "Awake."
"They rob the women." "For the prophet's sake."
"Slaughter these Christians." Thus the ladder spoke
Three times aloud yet nobody awoke
Even the hag upon the roof was still.

Now the red cock of dawning triumphed shrill
And little ends of landwind shook the leaves.
White through the cypress gleamed the palace eaves.
The dim and dewy beauty of the blossom,
Shy with the daybreak, trembled in its bosom,
Some snowy petals loitered to the ground.
The city houses had a wakening sound
Some smoke was rising, and we heard the stirs
Made at the gates by country marketers;
Only a moment's twilight yet remained.

The supple links that held my darling chained
Served as a rope to help her down the wall.
Our hearts stood still to hear the plaster fall
But down we scrambled safely to the lane.
We heard the hag upon the roof complain
She called strange names and listened for reply.
We heard her tread the ladder heavily
It was her rising time, perhaps, we thought.

And now the dangers that the daylight brought
Came thick upon us; for our foreign dress
Betrayed us at each step beyond a guess,
Even to be seen was certain death to us.
We hid my darling's face, and hasting thus
Kept up the narrow lane as Gerard bade.
He said, "Beyond, the city wall is laid
Heaped in the ditch and we can cross it there.

It fell from rottenness and dis-repair.
They set no guard there—or they did not set.
They will not notice us, and we can get
Out to the tombs and hide inside a vault."

In overbrimming beauty without fault
The sun brought colour to that dingy hive.
It made the black tree green, the sea alive,
The huts like palaces, but us who fled
Like ghosts at cockcrow hasting to the dead.

The lane had ceased. We reached an open space,
The greenish slope, the horses' baiting place,
Between the city and the palace wall.
The hill dipped sharply in a steepish fall
Down to the houses, and the grass was worn
With hoofs, and littered with the husks of corn.
"Now, slowly," Gerard said, "for Moors go slowly."

There trembling in its blueness dim and holy
Lay the great water bursting on the Mole
Her tremblings came as thoughts come in a soul.
There was our peace, there was the road to home,
That never trodden trembling bright with foam.
"There lies the road," said Gerard, "now, come on."

The high leaves in the trees above us shone,
For now the sun had climbed the eastern hill,
The coldness of the dawn was with us still.
We walked along the grass towards an alley
Between high walls beyond a tiny valley.

Fronting this alley's mouth our sloping grass
Dipped down and up, a little gut there was
Down which we slithered and from which we climbed.

And just as we emerged, exactly timed,
Just as we drew my darling to the top,
There came a noise that made our pulses stop.

For down towards us, blocking all the road,
Their horses striking sparks out as they strode,
Came lancers clattering with their hands held high,
Their knees bent up, and many a sharp quick cry;
The pennons in their lance heads flapped like flame.

Three ranks in twos and then a swordsman came,
Then one who held a scarlet banner; then
One in a scarlet cloak, a King of men.

It was the Khalif's self, returning home,
His rein had smeared his stallion's crest with foam,
I noticed that. He was not twenty yards
From us. He saw us.

At a sign his guards
Rode round us; bade us stand; there was no hope.

"Our luck," said Gerard. Then they took a rope
And hitched our wrists together. Then they led
The three of us down-hearted like the dead
Before the Khalif's self. The swordsman bared
His right arm to the shoulder and prepared.

The Khalif stared at us, and we at him
We were defiant at him, he was grim.
A hawk-like fellow, like a bird of prey,
A hawk to strike, a swift to get away.
His clean brown face (with blood beneath the brown),
Puckered, his thin lips tightened in a frown,
He knew without our telling, what we were.

The swordsman looked for word to kill us there.

I saw the lancers' glances at their chief.
Death on the instant would have seemed relief
To that not knowing what her fate would be
After the sword had made an end of me.

The Khalif's face grew grimmer; then he said
"Bring them with us." The swordsman sheathed his blade.

They took us to the palace, to a chamber
Smelling of bruisèd spice and burning amber,
There slaves were sent to fetch the newly risen
Servants and warders of the woman's prison.
The white of death was on them when they came.

The Khalif lightened on them with quick flame.
Harsh though she was, I sorrowed for the crone,
For she was old, a woman, and alone,
And came, in age, upon disgrace through me;
I know not what disgrace, I did not see
Those crones again, I doubt not they were whipt
For letting us escape them while they slept.
Perhaps they killed the sentry. Who can tell?
The devil ever keeps the laws in hell.
They dragged them out to justice one by one.
However bitter was the justice done
I doubt not they were thankful to be quit
(At cost of some few pangs) the fear of it.
Then our turn came.

The Khalif's fury raged
Because our eyes had seen those women caged,
Because our Christian presence had defiled
The Woman's House and somehow had beguiled

A woman-slave, his victim, out of it,
Against all Moorish law and Holy Writ
If we had killed his son it had been less.

He rose up in his place and rent his dress
"Let them be ganched upon the hooks," he cried,
"Throughout to-day, but not till they have died.
Then gather all the slaves, and flay these three
Alive, before them, that the slaves may see
What comes to dogs who try to get away.
So, ganch the three."

Then Gerard answered, "Stay
Before you fling us to the hooks, hear this.
There are two laws, and men may go amiss
Either by breaking or by keeping one.
There is man's law by which man's work is done.
Your galleys rowed, your palace kept in state,
Your victims ganched or headed on the gate
And accident has bent us to its yoke.
We break it: death: but it is better broke.

"You know, you Khalif, by what death you reign,
What force of fraud, what cruelty of pain,
What spies and prostitutes support your power,
And help your law to run its little hour,
We, who are but ourselves, defy it all.

"We were free people till you made us thrall
I was a sailor whom you took at sea
While sailing home. This woman that you see
You broke upon with murder in the night
To drag her here to die for your delight,
This young man is her lover.

When he knew
That she was taken by your pirate crew

He followed her to save her, or at least
Be near her in her grief. Man is a beast
And women are his pasture by your law.
This young man was in safety, but he saw
His darling taken to the slave-girls' pen
Of weeping in the night and beasts of men.
He gave up everything, risked everything,
Came to your galley, took the iron ring,
Rowed at the bitter oar-loom as a slave,
Only for love of her, for hope to save
Her from one bruise of all the many bruises
That fall upon a woman when she loses
Those whom your gang of bloodhounds made her lose.

"Knowing another law we could not choose
But stamp your law beneath our feet as dust,
Its bloodshed and its rapine and its lust,
For one clean hour of struggle to be free;
She for her passionate pride of chastity,
He for his love of her, and I because
I'm not too old to glory in the cause
Of generous souls who have harsh measure meted.

"We did the generous thing and are defeated.
Boast, then, to-night when you have drunken deep,
Between the singing woman's song and sleep,
That you have tortured to the death three slaves
Who spat upon your law and found their graves
Helping each other in the generous thing.
No mighty triumph for a boast, O King."

Then he was silent while the Khalif stared.
Never before had any being dared
To speak thus to him. All the courtiers paled.
We, who had died, expected to be haled

To torture there and then before the crowd.
It was so silent that the wind seemed loud
Clicking a lose slat in the open shutter.
I heard the distant breakers at their mutter
Upon the Mole, I saw my darling's face
Steady and proud; a breathing filled the place,
Men drawing breath until the Khalif spoke.
His torn dress hung upon him like a cloak
He spoke at last. "You speak of law," he said.
"By climates and by soils the laws are made.
Ours is a hawk-law suited to the land,
This rock of hawks or eyrie among sand,
I am a hawk, the hawk law pleases me.

"But I am man, and, being man, can be
Moved, sometimes, Christian, by the law which makes
Men who are suffering from man's mistakes,
Brothers sometimes.
I had not heard this tale
Of you, the lover, following to jail
The woman whom you loved. You bowed your neck
Into the iron fettered to the deck,
And followed her to prison, all for love?

"Allah, who gives men courage from above,
Has surely blessed you, boy.
"And you, his queen;
Without your love his courage had not been.
Your beauty and your truth prevailed on him.
Allah has blessed you, too.
"And you, the grim
Killer of men at midnight, you who speak
To Kings as peers with colour in your cheek,

Allah made you a man who helps his friends.
God made you all. I will not thwart his ends.
You shall be free.
Hear all. These folk are free.
You Emir, fit a xebec for the sea
To let them sail at noon.
Go where you will.
And lest my rovers should molest you still,
Here is my seal that they shall let you pass."

Throughout the room a sudden murmur was
A gasp of indrawn breath and shifting feet.
So life was given back, the thing so sweet
The undrunk cup that we were longing for.

My darling spoke, "O Khalif, one gift more.
After this bounty that our hearts shall praise
At all our praying-times by nights and days
I ask yet more, O raiser from the dead.
There in your woman's prison as we fled
A hopeless woman blessed us. It is said
That blessings from the broken truly bless.
Khalif, we would not leave in hopelessness
One whose great heart could bless us even then
Even as we left her in the prison pen.
She wished us fortune from a broken heart.
Let her come with us, Khalif, when we start."
"Go, you," the Khalif said, "and choose her forth."

At noon the wind was blowing to the north,
A swift felucca with a scarlet sail
Was ready for us, deep with many a bale,
Of gold and spice and silk, the great King's gifts.
The banners of the King were on her lifts.
The King and all his court rode down to see
Us four glad souls put seawards from Saffee.

In the last glowing of the sunset's gold
We looked our last upon that pirate hold;
The palace gilding shone awhile like fire,
We were at sea with all our heart's desire
Beauty and friendship and the dream fulfilled.
The golden answer to the deeply willed.
The purely longed for, hardly tried for thing.
Into the dark our sea boat dipped her wing
Polaris climbed out of the dark and shone,
Then came the moon, and now Saffee was gone
With all hell's darkness hidden by the sea.

O beautiful is love and to be free
Is beautiful, and beautiful are friends.
Love, freedom, comrades, surely make amends
For all these thorns through which we walk to death.
God let us breathe your beauty with our breath.

All early in the Maytime when daylight comes at four,
We blessed the hawthorn blossom that welcomed us ashore,
O beautiful in this living that passes like the foam
It is to go with sorrow yet come with beauty home.

THE HOUNDS OF HELL

ABOUT the crowing of the cock,
When the shepherds feel the cold,
A horse's hoofs went clip-a-clock
Along the Hangman's wold.

The horse-hoofs trotted on the stone,
The hoof-sparks glittered by,
And then a hunting horn was blown
And hounds broke into cry.

There was a strangeness in the horn,
A wildness in the cry,
A power of devilry forlorn
Exulting bloodily.

A power of night that ran a prey
Along the Hangman's hill.
The shepherds heard the spent buck bray
And the horn blow for the kill.

They heard the worrying of the hounds
About the dead beast's bones;
Then came the horn, and then the sounds
Of horse-hoofs treading stones.

"What hounds are these, that hunt the night?"
The shepherds asked in fear:
"Look, there are calkins clinking bright;
They must be coming here."

The calkins clinkered to a spark,
  The hunter called the pack;
The sheep-dogs' fells all bristled stark
  And all their lips went back.

"Lord God," the shepherds said, "they come;
  And see what hounds he has;
All dripping bluish fire, and dumb,
  And nosing to the grass.

"And trotting scatheless through the gorse,
  And bristling in the fell:
Lord, it is death upon the horse,
  And they're the hounds of hell!"

They shook to watch them as they sped,
  All black against the sky;
A horseman with a hooded head
  And great hounds padding by.

When daylight drove away the dark
  And larks went up and thrilled,
The shepherds climbed the wold to mark
  What beast the hounds had killed.

They came to where the hounds had fed,
  And in that trampled place
They found a pedlar lying dead
  With horror in his face.

There was a farmer on the wold
  Where all the brooks begin,
He had a thousand sheep from fold
  Out grazing on the whin.

The next night, as he lay in bed
He heard a canterer come
Trampling the wold-top with a tread
That sounded like a drum.

He thought it was a post that rode,
So turned him to his sleep,
But the canterer in his dreams abode
Like horse-hoofs running sheep.

And in his dreams a horn was blown
And feathering hounds replied,
And all his wethers stood like stone
In rank on the hillside.

Then, while he struggled still with dreams,
He saw his wethers run
Before a pack cheered on with screams,
The thousand sheep as one.

So, leaping from his bed in fear,
He flung the window back,
And he heard a death-horn blowing clear
And the crying of a pack.

And the thundering of a thousand sheep,
All mad and running wild
To the stone-pit seven fathoms deep,
Whence all the town is tiled.

After them came the hounds of hell
With hell's own fury filled;
Into the pit the wethers fell
And all but three were killed.

The hunter blew his horn a note
  And laughed against the moon;
The farmer's breath caught in his throat,
  He fell into a swoon.

The next night when the watch was set
  A heavy rain came down,
The leaden gutters dripped with wet
  Into the shuttered town.

So close the shutters were, the chink
  Of lamplight scarcely showed;
The men at fireside heard no clink
  Of horse-hoofs on the road.

They heard the creaking hinge complain
  And the mouse that gnawed the floor,
And the limping footsteps of the rain
  On the stone outside the door.

And on the wold the rain came down
  Till trickles streakt the grass:
A traveller riding to the town
  Drew rein to let it pass.

The wind sighed in the fir-tree tops,
  The trickles sobb'd in the grass,
The branches ran with showers of drops;
  No other noise there was.

Till up the wold the traveller heard
  A horn blow faint and thin;
He thought it was the curlew bird
  Lamenting to the whin;

And when the far horn blew again,
He thought an owl hallooed,
Or a rabbit gave a shriek of pain
As the stoat leapt in the wood.

But when the horn blew next, it blew
A trump that split the air,
And hounds gave cry to an Halloo—
The hunt of hell was there.

"Black," (said the traveller), "black and swift,
Those running devils came;
Scoring to cry with hackles stifft,
And grin-jowls dripping flame."

They settled to the sightless scent,
And up the hill a cry
Told where the frightened quarry went,
Well knowing it would die.

Then presently a cry rang out,
And a mort blew for the kill;
A shepherd with his throat torn out
Lay dead upon the hill.

When this was known, the shepherds drove
Their flocks into the town;
No man, for money or for love,
Would watch them on the down.

But night by night the terror ran,
The townsmen heard them still;
Nightly the hell-hounds hunted man
And the hunter whooped the kill.

The men who lived upon the moor
  Would waken to the scratch
Of hounds' claws digging at the door.
  Or scraping at the latch.

And presently no man would go
  Without doors after dark,
Lest hell's black hunting horn should blow,
  And hell's black bloodhounds mark.

They shivered round the fire at home,
  While out upon the bent
The hounds with black jowls dropping foam
  Went nosing to the scent.

Men let the hay crop run to seed,
  And the corn crop sprout in ear,
And the root crop choke itself in weed
  That hell-hound hunting year.

Empty to heaven lay the wold,
  Village and church grew green,
The courtyard flagstones spread with mould,
  And weeds sprang up between.

And sometimes when the cock had crowed,
  And the hillside stood out grey,
Men saw them slinking up the road,
  All sullen from their prey.

A hooded horseman on a black,
  With nine black hounds at heel,
After the hell-hunt going back
  All bloody from their meal.

And in men's minds a fear began
  That hell had over-hurled
The guardians of the soul of man
  And come to rule the world.

With bitterness of heart by day,
  And terror in the night,
And the blindness of a barren way
  And withering of delight.

St. Withiel lived upon the moor,
  Where the peat-men live in holes;
He worked among the peat-men poor,
  Who only have their souls.

He brought them nothing but his love
  And the will to do them good,
But power filled him from above,
  His very touch was food.

Men told St. Withiel of the hounds
  And how they killed their prey.
He thought them far beyond his bounds,
  So many miles away.

Then one whose son the hounds had killed
  Told him the tale at length;
St. Withiel pondered why God willed
  That hell should have such strength.

Then one, a passing traveller, told
  How, since the hounds had come,
The church was empty on the wold,
  And all the priests were dumb.

St. Withiel rose at this, and said,
"This priest will not be dumb;
My spirit will not be afraid
Though all hell's devils come."

He took his stick and out he went,
The long way to the wold,
Where the sheep-bells clink upon the bent
And every wind is cold.

He past the rivers running red
And the mountains standing bare;
At last the wold-land lay ahead,
Un-yellowed by the share.

All in the brown October time
He clambered to the weald;
The plum lay purpled into slime,
The harvest lay in field.

Trampled by many-footed rain,
The sun-burnt corn lay dead;
The myriad finches in the grain
Rose bothering at his tread.

The myriad finches took a sheer
And settled back to food:
A man was not a thing to fear
In such a solitude.

The hurrying of their wings died out,
A silence took the hill;
There was no dog, no bell, no shout,
The windmill's sails were still.

The gate swung creaking on its hasp,
  The pear splashed from the tree,
In the rotting apple's heart the wasp
  Was drunken drowsily.

The grass upon the cart-wheel ruts
  Had made the trackways dim,
The rabbits ate and hopped their scuts,
  They had no fear of him.

The sunset reddened in the west;
  The distant depth of blue
Stretched out and dimmed; to twiggy nest
  The rooks in clamour drew.

The oakwood in his mail of brass
  Bowed his great crest and stood;
The pine-tree saw St. Withiel pass,
  His great bole blushed like blood.

Then tree and wood alike were dim,
  Yet still St. Withiel strode;
The only noise to comfort him
  Were his footsteps on the road.

The crimson in the west was smoked,
  The west-wind heaped the wrack,
Each tree seemed like a murderer cloaked
  To stab him in the back.

Darkness and desolation came
  To dog his footsteps there;
The dead leaves rustling called his name,
  The death-moth brushed his hair.

The murmurings of the wind fell still;
He stood and stared around:
He was alone upon the hill,
On devil-haunted ground.

What was the whitish thing which stood
In front, with one arm raised,
Like death a-grinning in a hood?
The saint stood still and gazed.

"What are you?" said St. Withiel. "Speak!"
Not any answer came
But the night-wind making darkness bleak,
And the leaves that called his name.

A glow shone on the whitish thing,
It neither stirred nor spoke:
In spite of faith, a shuddering
Made the good saint to choke.

He struck the whiteness with his staff—
It was a withered tree:
An owl flew from it with a laugh,
The darkness shook with glee.

The darkness came all round him close
And cackled in his ear:
The midnight, full of life none knows,
Was very full of fear.

The darkness cackled in his heart,
That things of hell were there,
That the startled rabbit played a part
And the stoat's leap did prepare—

Prepare the stage of night for blood
  And the mind of night for death,
For a spirit trembling in the mud,
  In an agony for breath.

A terror came upon the saint,
  It stripped his spirit bare;
He was sick body standing faint,
  Cold sweat and stiffened hair.

He took his terror by the throat
  And stamped it underfoot;
Then, far away, the death-horn's note
  Quailed like a screech-owl's hoot.

Still far away that devil's horn
  Its quavering death-note blew,
But the saint could hear the crackling thorn
  That the hounds trod as they drew.

"Lord, it is true," St. Withiel moaned,
  "And the hunt is drawing near;
Devils that Paradise disowned;
  They know that I am here.

"And there, O God, a hound gives tongue
  And great hounds quarter dim."—
The saint's hands to his body clung,
  He knew they came for him.

Then close at hand the horn was loud,
  Like Peter's cock of old,
For joy that Peter's soul was cowed,
  And Jesus' body sold.

Then terribly the hounds in cry
  Gave answer to the horn;
The saint in terror turned to fly
  Before his flesh was torn.

After his body came the hounds,
  After the hounds the horse;
Their running crackled with the sounds
  Of fire that runs in gorse.

The saint's breath failed, but still they came:
  The hunter cheered them on;
Even as a wind that blows a flame
  In the vigil of St. John.

And as St. Withiel's terror grew
  The crying of the pack
Bayed nearer, as though terror drew
  Those grip teeth to his back.

No hope was in his soul, no stay,
  Nothing but screaming will
To save his terror-stricken clay
  Before the hounds could kill.

The laid corn tripped, the bramble caught,
  He stumbled on the stones,
The thorn that scratched him, to his thought,
  Was hell's teeth at his bones.

His legs seemed bound as in a dream,
  The wet earth held his feet,
He screamed aloud as rabbits scream
  Before the stoat's teeth meet.

A black thing struck him on the brow,
  A blackness loomed and waved;
It was a tree. He caught a bough
  And scrambled up it, saved.

Saved for the moment, as he thought,
  He pressed against the bark:
The hell-hounds missed the thing they sought,
  They quartered in the dark.

They panted underneath the tree,
  They quartered to the call,
The hunter cried, "Yoi doit, go see!"
  His death-horn blew a fall.

Now up, now down, the hell-hounds went
  With soft feet padding wide;
They tried, but could not hit the scent,
  However hard they tried.

Then presently the horn was blown,
  The hounds were called away,
The hoof-beats glittered on the stone
  And trotted on the brae.

The saint gat strength, but with it came
  A horror of his fear,
Anguish at having failed, and shame,
  And sense of judgment near.

Anguish at having left his charge
  And having failed his trust,
At having flung his sword and targe
  To save his body's dust.

He clambered down the saving tree;
"I am unclean," he cried.
"Christ died upon a tree for me,
I used a tree to hide.

"The hell-hounds bayed about the cross,
And tore his clothes apart,
But Christ was gold and I am dross,
And mud is in my heart."

He stood in anguish in the field;
A little wind blew by,
The dead leaves dropped, the great stars wheeled
Their squadrons in the sky.

"Lord, I will try again," he said,
"Though all hell's devils tear.
This time I will not be afraid
And what is sent I'll dare."

He set his face against the slope
Until he topped the brae;
Courage had healed his fear, and hope
Had put his shame away.

And then, far off, a quest-note ran,
A feathering hound replied:
The hounds still drew the night for man
Along that countryside.

Then one by one the hell-hounds spoke
And still the horn made cheer;
Then the full devil-chorus woke
To fill the saint with fear.

He knew that they were after him
 To hunt him till he fell;
He turned and fled into the dim,
 And after him came hell.

Over the stony wold he went,
 Through thorns and over quags;
The bloodhounds cried upon the scent,
 They ran like rutting stags.

And when the saint looked round, he saw
 Red eyes intently strained,
The bright teeth in the grinning jaw,
 And running shapes that gained.

Uphill, downhill, with failing breath,
 He ran to save his skin,
Like one who knocked the door of death,
 Yet dared not enter in.

Then water gurgled in the night,
 Dark water lay in front,
The saint saw bubbles running bright;
 The huntsman cheered his hunt.

The saint leaped far into the stream
 And struggled to the shore.
The hunt died like an evil dream,
 A strange land lay before.

He waded to a glittering land,
 With brighter light than ours,
The water ran on silver sand
 By yellow water-flowers.

The fishes nosed the stream to rings
As petals floated by,
The apples were like orbs of kings
Against a glow of sky.

On cool and steady stalks of green
The outland flowers grew,
The ghost-flower, silver like a queen,
The queen-flower streakt with blue.

The king-flower, crimson on his stalk,
With frettings in his crown,
The peace-flower purple, from the chalk,
The flower that loves the down.

Lilies like thoughts, roses like words
In the sweet brain of June;
The bees there, like the stock-dove birds,
Breathed all the air with croon.

Purple and golden hung the plums.
Like slaves bowed down with gems
The peach-trees were; sweet-scented gums
Oozed clammy from their stems.

And birds of every land were there,
Like flowers that sang and flew;
All beauty that makes singing fair
That sunny garden knew.

For all together sang with throats
So tuned, that the intense
Colour and odour pearled the notes
And passed into the sense.

And as the saint drew near, he heard
  The birds talk, each to each,
The fire-bird to the glory-bird;
  He understood their speech.

One said, "The saint was terrified
  Because the hunters came."
Another said, "The bloodhounds cried
  And all their eyes were flame."

Another said, "No shame to him,
  For mortal men are blind,
They cannot see beyond the grim
  Into the peace behind."

Another sang, "They cannot know,
  Unless we give the clue,
The power that waits in them below
  The thing they are to do."

Another sang: "They never guess
  That deep within them stand
Courage and peace and loveliness,
  Wisdom and skill of hand."

Another sang, "Sing, brothers; come,
  Make beauty in the air;
The saint is shamed with martyrdom
  Beyond his strength to bear.

"Sing, brothers, every bird that flies!"
  They stretcht their throats to sing,
With the sweetness known in Paradise
  When the bells of heaven ring.

"Open the doors, good saint," they cried,
"Pass deeper to your soul;
There is a spirit in your side
That hell cannot control.

"Open the doors to let him in,
That beauty with the sword.
The hounds are silly shapes of sin;
They shrivel at a word.

"Come, saint!" and as they sang, the air
Shone with the shapes of flame,
Bird after bright bird glittered there,
Crying aloud they came.

A rush of brightness and delight,
White as the snow in drift,
The fire-bird and the glory-bright,
Most beautiful, most swift.

Sweeping aloft to show the way
And singing as they flew,
Many and glittering as the spray
When windy seas are blue.

So cheerily they rushed, so strong
Their sweep was through the flowers,
The saint was swept into their song
And gloried in their powers.

He sang, and leaped into the stream
And struggled to the shore;
The garden faded like a dream,
A darkness lay before.

Darkness with glimmery light forlorn
And quavering hounds in quest,
A huntsman blowing on a horn,
And lost things not at rest.

He saw the huntsman's hood show black
Against the greying east,
He heard him hollo to the pack
And horn them to the feast.

He heard the bloodhounds come to cry
And settle to the scent,
The black horse made the hoof-casts fly,
The sparks flashed up the bent.

The saint stood still until they came
Baying to ring him round;
A horse whose flecking foam was flame,
And hound on yelling hound.

And jaws that dripped with bitter fire
Snarled at the saint to tear.
Pilled hell-hounds, balder than the geier,
Leaped round him everywhere.

St. Withiel let the hell-hounds rave.
He cried, "Now, in this place,
Climb down, you huntsman of the grave,
And let me see your face.

"Climb down, you huntsman out of hell,
And show me what you are.
The judge has stricken on the bell,
Now answer at the bar."

The baying of the hounds fell still,
Their jaws' salt fire died.
The wind of morning struck in chill
Along that countryside.

The blackness of the horse was shrunk,
His sides seemed ribbed and old.
The rider, hooded like a monk,
Was trembling with the cold.

The rider bowed as though with pain;
Then clambered down and stood,
The thin thing that the frightened brain
Had fed with living blood.

"Show me. What are you?" said the saint.
A hollow murmur spoke.
"This, Lord," it said; a hand moved faint
And drew aside the cloak.

A Woman Death that palsy shook
Stood sick and dwindling there;
Her fingers were a bony crook
And blood was on her hair.

"Stretch out your hands and sign the Cross,"
Was all St. Withiel said.
The bloodhounds moaned upon the moss,
The Woman Death obeyed.

Whimpering with pain, she made the sign.
"Go, devil-hag," said he,
"Beyond all help of bread and wine,
Beyond all land and sea,

"Into the ice, into the snow,
Where Death himself is stark.
Out, with your hounds about you, go,
And perish in the dark."

They dwindled as the mist that fades
At coming of the sun,
Like rags of stuff that fire abrades,
They withered and were done.

The cock, that scares the ghost from earth,
Crowed as they dwindled down;
The red sun, happy in his girth,
Strode up above the town.

Sweetly above the sunny wold
The bells of churches rang;
The sheep-bells clinked within the fold,
And the larks went up and sang.

Sang for the setting free of men
From devils that destroyed.
The lark, the robin and the wren,
They joyed and over-joyed.

The chats, that harbour in the whin,
Their little sweet throats swelled,
The blackbird and the thrush joined in,
The missel-thrush excelled.

Till round the saint the singing made
A beauty in the air,
An ecstasy that cannot fade
But is forever there.

CAP ON HEAD
A TALE OF THE O'NEILL

O'NEILL took ship, O'Neill set sail,
And left his wife ashore
In the foursquare castle like a jail
Between the Mull and the Gore.

Many a month he stayed away,
His lady sorrowed long;
She heard the tide come twice a day
And the sea-lark at his song;

She watched the sun go down in the west,
And another day begin,
At nights she made her mate a nest
But no mate came therein.

One night, a red light burned at sea,
A ship came in to port,
A foot stirred and the horn was blown
Within the outer court.

It was all dark, save up the brae,
The dead moon wore her heel,
The watchman called, "Who's there the day?"
A voice said, " The O'Neill."

The watchman flung the great gate back,
"Come in, Lord, to your own."
O'Neill stood huddled up in black,
Upon the threshold stone.

White as a riser from the dead
  He passed the lintel post.
"God spare us, Lord," the watchman said,
  "I thought you were a ghost.

"I never heard you come ashore,
  And, look your ship is gone.
Are all our fellows dead, my lord,
  That you should come alone?"

O'Neill stood grinning in the porch
  A little breathing space;
The redness blowing from the torch
  Put colour in his face.

"I've left my ship behind," he said,
  "To join the Scotch King's fleet.
I've left my men behind," he said,
  "To haul on her fore-sheet.

"I have come home all alone," he said,
  "In a country ship from sea.
Let my lady know the news," he said,
  "Then open here to me."

Then lights were lit and men gave hail
  And welcomed him ashore;
The wife was glad within that jail
  Between the Mull and the Gore.

O'Neill went swimming in the sea
  And hunting up the glen;
No one could swim or ride as he
  Of all the sons of men.

His wife went happy in the lane,
  And singing in the tower;
The sweet of having him again
  Had ended all the sour.

But Kate, an old crone muttering dark
  About that windy place,
Did not rejoice: she said, "I mark
  O'Neill has fal'n from grace.

"He has been under the dark star
  Since when he went away.
Men think that when they wander far
  The black thing becomes grey.

"He has been dipped in the strange vat
  And dyed with the strange dye,
And then the black thing, what is that
  That dogs him, going by?

"A dog thing, black, goes padding past
  Forever at his heel:
God help us all to peace at last,
  I fear for the O'Neill.

"His teeth show when the Host does come
  To comfort dying men,
And in the chapel he is dumb,
  He never says Amen."

She would not speak with the O'Neill,
  But when he crossed her path
She prayed, as tremblers do that feel
  The devil in his wrath.

And so the Time went by, whose hand
  Upheaves the lives of men,
The cuckoo left his burning land
  To toll along the glen.

So loud the thrushes sang that spring,
  So rich the hawthorn was,
The air was like a living thing
  Between the sky and the grass.

O'Neill's wife bore a little son
  And set him on her knee;
He grew apace to romp and run
  And dabble in the sea.

But one thing strange about the child
  The neighbors noted there:
That, even if the winds were mild,
  His head was never bare.

His father made him wear a cap
  At all times, night and day,
Bound round his forehead with a strap
  To keep the cold away.

And up and down the little lad
  Went singing at his game:
Men marvelled at the grace he had
  To make the wild birds tame.

Men marvelled at the joy he took
  And at the things he said,
And at the beauty of his look,
  This little Cap on Head.

And when the nights were dark between
The new moon and the old,
And fires were lit, and winds blew keen,
And old wives' tales were told,

This little son would scramble near
Beside his mother's place,
To listen to the tale and peer
With firelight on his face.

O'Neill would gather to the glow
With great eyes glittering fierce;
Old Kate would shake to see him so
And cross herself from curse.

It fell about hay-harvest time,
When the Lammas floods were out,
A ship all green with water-slime
Stood in and went about,

And anchored off the bight of sand,
And swam there like a seal,
With a banner of the bloody hand,
The flag of the O'Neill.

Then there was cheering in the court
And hurrying to the beach:
"A ship!" they cried, "A ship in port,
Brought up in Castle Reach.

"It is our ship. They are our men
There, coiling up the sheet;
It is our ship come home agen
From out the Scotch King's fleet.

"And who's the noble in the boat
  Comes rowing through the sea?
His colours are the O'Neill coat,
  But what O'Neill is he?"

O'Neill was in his turret tower,
  With writings red and black;
Kate crossed herself to see him glower
  That tide the ship came back.

He looked long at the anchored ship,
  And at the coming boat;
The devil writhelled up his lip,
  And snickered in his throat.

He strode the room and bit his nails,
  He bit his flesh with rage,
As maddened felons do in jails,
  And rats do in a cage.

He looked at Kate, who crossed her breast,
  He heard them cheer below:
He said, "The wicked cannot rest,
  And now I have to go."

They saw him hurry up the green
  And on into the rain;
Beyond the brae he was not seen:
  He was not seen again.

O'Neill's wife went to watch the boat
  Come driving to the sand:
The noble in the O'Neill coat
  Stood up and waved his hand.

"That is O'Neill!" the clansmen cried,
"Or else his very twin.
How came he to the ship?" they cried.
"Just now he was within."

"It is O'Neill," the lady said,
"And that's his ship returned.
A woman's life's a school," she said,
"Where bitter things are learned."

O'Neill called to her through his tears,
"The bitter days are past.
I've prayed for this for seven years,
Now here I am at last."

Then, as the boat's bows cut the strand,
Among the slipping foam,
He sprang to take his lady's hand,
He said, "I have come home."

His lady fainted like the dead,
Beside the slipping sea.
"This is O'Neill," the servants said,
"What is that other he?"

"Master," they said, "where have you been
These seven years and more?"
"I've served the Scottish King and Queen,
Along the Scottish shore."

"Master," they said, "Another came
So like in voice and face
To you, we thought it was the same,
And so he took your place.

"These seven years he's ruled us here,
While you were still at sea,
And that's his son that's coming here:
Look, Master, that is he."

O'Neill took off the wee boy's cap
And ruffled through his hair;
He said, "A young tree full of sap,
A good shoot growing fair."

He turned the hair for men to see
And swallowed down his tears;
He said, "The gods be good to me,
The boy has devil's ears."

He took the young child by the heels
And broke him, head and breast:
The red hand ridded the O'Neills
That cuckoo in the nest.

O'Neill flung out the little limbs
To drift about the bay:
"Watch, fellows, if he sinks or swims,"
Was all they heard him say.

He said, "The wicked cannot rest
And now I have to go."
He set his ship's head north and west
And stood into the flow.

The ship went shining like a seal
And dimmed into the rain—
And no man saw the great O'Neill,
Nor heard of him again.

SONNETS

Like bones the ruins of the cities stand,
Like skeletons and skulls with ribs and eyes
Strewn in the saltness of the desert sand
Carved with the unread record of Kings' lies.
Once they were strong with soldiers, loud with voices,
The markets clattered as the carts drove through,
Where now the jackal in the moon rejoices
And the still asp draws death along the dew.
There at the gates the market men paid toll
In bronze and silver pennies long worn thin,
Wine was a silver penny for a bowl,
Women they had there, and the moon and sin.
And looking from his tower the watchman saw
Green fields for miles, the roads, the great king's law.

Now they are gone with all their songs and sins,
Women and men, to dust; their copper penny,
Of living, spent, among these dusty inns;
The glittering One made level with the many.
Their speech is gone, none speaks it, none can read
The pictured writing of their conqueror's march.
The dropping plaster of a fading screed
Ceils with its mildews he decaying arch.
The fields are sand, the streets are fallen stones,
Nothing is bought or sold there, nothing spoken,
The sand hides all, the wind that blows it moans,
Blowing more sand until the plinth is broken.
Day in, day out, no other utterance falls;
Only the sand, pit-pitting on the walls.

None knows what overthrew that city's pride.
Some say, the spotted pestilence arose
And smote them to the marrow, that they died
Till every pulse was dusty; no man knows.
Some say, that foreign Kings with all their hosts,
Sieged it with mine and tower till it fell
So that the sword shred shrieking flesh from ghosts
Till every street was empty; who can tell?
Some think, that in the fields, or in the pit,
Out of the light, in filth, among the rotten,
Insects like sands in number, swift as wit,
Famined the city dead; it is forgotten.
Only the city's bones stand, gaunt in air,
Pocked by the pitting sandspecks everywhere.

So shall we be; so will our cities lie,
Unknown beneath the grasses of the summer,
Walls without roofs, naves open to the sky,
Doors open to the wind, the only comer.
And men will grub the ruins, eyes will peer,
Fingers will grope for pennies, brains will tire
To chronicle the skills we practised here,
While still we breathed the wind and trod the mire.
O, like the ghost at dawn, scared by the cock,
Let us make haste, to let the spirit dive
Deep in self's sea, until the deeps unlock
The depths and sunken gold of being alive,
Till, though our Many pass, a Something stands
Aloft through Time that covers all with sands.

THE PASSING STRANGE

Out of the earth to rest or range
Perpetual in perpetual change
The unknown passing through the strange.

Water and saltness held together
To tread the dust and stand the weather
And plough the field and stretch the tether.

To pass the wine cup and be witty,
Water the sands and build the city,
Slaughter like devils and have pity;

Be red with rage and pale with lust,
Make beauty come, make peace, make trust,
Water and saltness mixed with dust;

Drive over earth, swim under sea,
Fly in the eagle's secrecy,
Guess where the hidden comets be;

Know all the deathy seeds that still
Queen Helen's beauty, Cæsar's will,
And slay them even as they kill;

Fashion an altar for a rood,
Defile a continent with blood,
And watch a brother starve for food;

Love like a madman, shaking, blind,
Till self is burnt into a kind
Possession of another mind;

Brood upon beauty till the grace
Of beauty with the holy face
Brings peace into the bitter place;

Probe in the lifeless granites, scan
The stars for hope, for guide, for plan,
Live as a woman or a man;

Fasten to lover or to friend
Until the heart break at the end
The break of death that cannot mend.

Then to lie useless, helpless, still
Down in the earth, in dark, to fill
The roots of grass or daffodil.

Down in the earth, in dark, alone,
A mockery of the ghost in bone,
The strangeness, passing the unknown.

Time will go by, that outlasts clocks,
Dawn in the thorps will rouse the cocks
Sunset be glory on the rocks.

But it, the thing, will never heed
Even the rootling from the seed
Thrusting to suck it for its need.

Since moons decay and suns decline
How else should end this life of mine?
Water and saltness are not wine.

But in the darkest hour of night
When even the foxes peer for sight
The byre-cock crows; he feels the light.

So, in this water mixed with dust,
The byre-cock spirit crows from trust
That death will change because it must,

For all things change, the darkness changes,
The wandering spirits change their ranges,
The corn is gathered to the granges.

The corn is sown again, it grows;
The stars burn out, the darkness goes.
The rhythms change, they do not close.

They change, and we, who pass like foam,
Like dust blown through the streets of Rome,
Change ever, too; we have no home,

Only a beauty, only a power,
Sad in the fruit, bright in the flower,
Endlessly erring for its hour

But gathering, as we stray, a sense
Of Life, so lovely and intense,
It lingers when we wander hence.

That those who follow feel behind
Their backs, when all before is blind,
Our joy, a rampart to the mind.

ANIMULA

This is the place, this house beside the sea,
This was the setting where they played their parts.
Two men, who knew them all, have talked to me.
Beauty she had, and all had passionate hearts.
I write this in the window where she sat.
Two fields, all green with summer, lie below,
Then the grey sea, at thought, cloud-coloured, flat,
Wind-dappled from the glen, the tide at flow.
Her portrait and her husband's hang together
One on each side the fire; it is close:
The tree-tops toss; it is a change of weather;
They were most lovely and unhappy, those,
That married pair and he who loved too well;
This was the door by which they entered hell.

This, is a drawing of her as a child;
This, is she wed; the faces are the same,
Only, the beauty of the babe is wild;
The woman's beauty has been broken tame.
Witty, bright, gentle, earnest, with great eyes,
Dark hair in heaps, pure colour, lips that smile;
Beauty that is more wisdom than the wise
Lived in this woman for a little while.
Dressed in that beauty that our mothers wore
(So touching now), she looks out of the frame
With stag-like eyes, that wept till they were sore
Many's the time, till she was broken tame.
Witty, bright, gentle, earnest, even so:
Destiny calls and spirits come and go.

This, is her husband in his youth; and this,
Is he in manhood; this, is he in age:
There is a devil in those eyes of his,
A glittering devil, restless in his cage.
A grand man, with a beauty and a pride,
A manner and a power and a fire
With beaks of vultures eating at his side,
The great brain mad with unfulfilled desire.
"With grand ideas," they say; tall, wicked, proud,
Cold, cruel, bitter, clever, dainty, skilled;
Splendid to see, a head above the crowd,
Splendid with every strength, yet unfulfilled.
Cutting himself (and all those near) with hate
From that sharp mind which should have shaped a state.

And many years ago I saw the third
Bowed in old age and mad with misery,
Mad with the bright eyes of the eagle bird;
Burning his heart at fires of memory.
He stood behind a chair and bent and muttered,
Grand still, grey, sunburnt, bright with mad eyes brown,
Burning, though dying, like a torch that guttered
That once had lit Queen Helen through the town.
I only saw him once: I saw him go
Leaning uphill his body to the rain,
Too good a man for life to punish so,
Theirs were the pride and passion, his the pain.
His old coat flapped: the little children turned
To see him pass, that passionate age that burned.

"I knew them well, all three," the old man said;
"He was an unused force and she a child.
She caught him with her beauty, being a maid.
The thought that she had trapped him drove him wild.
He would not work with others, could not rest,
And nothing here could use him or engage him,
Yet here he stayed with devils in his breast
To blast the woman who had dared to cage him.
Then, when the scholar came, it made the three,
She turned to him and he, he turned to her.
They both were saints: elopement could not be:
So here they stayed, and passion plied the spur.
Then the men fought, and later she was found
In that green pool beyond the headland, drowned.

"They carried her drowned body up the grass
Here to the house, they laid it on the bed
(This very bed, where I have slept, it was),
The scholar begged to see her, being dead.
The husband walked downstairs to see him there
Begging to see her as one asks an alms;
He spat at him and cut his cheek-bone bare,
'There's pay,' he said, 'my poet, for your psalms.'
And then they fought together at the door
Biting each other, like two dogs, while she
Lay dead, poor woman, dripping on the floor
Out of her hair the death-drops of the sea.
Later, they fought whenever they might meet
In church, or in the fields, or in the street."

Up, on the hill, another aged man
Remembered them. He said, "They were afraid.
They feared to end the passions they began.
They held the cards and yet they never played.
He should have broken from her at all cost.
She should have loved her lover and gone free.
They all held winning cards and yet they lost,
So two were wrecked and one drowned in the sea.
Some harshness or some law, or else some fear
Stifled their souls: God help us, when we know
Certainly, certain things, the way is clear.
And yet, they paid, and one respects them, so.
Perhaps they were too fine. I know not, I.
Men must have mercy, being ripe to die."

So this old house of mourning was the stage
(This house and those green fields) for all that woe.
There are her books, her writing on the page,
In those chocked beds she made the flowers grow.
Most desolate it is, the rain is pouring,
The trees all toss and drip and scatter evil,
The floods are out, the waterfall is roaring,
The bar is mad with many a leaping devil.
And in this house the wind goes whining wild,
The door blows open, till I think to see
That delicate sweet woman like a child
Standing with great dark stag's eyes watching me;
Watching as though her sorrow might make plain
(Had I but wit) the meaning of such pain.

I wonder if she sang in this old room.
Ah, never; no; they tell me that she stood
For hours together staring into gloom
Out of the pri on bars of flesh and blood.
So, when the ninth wave drowned her, haply she
Wakened, with merging senses, till she blent
Into the joy and colour of the sea
One with the purpose of the element.
And there, perhaps, she cannot feel the woe
Passed in this rotting house, but runs like light
Over the billows where the clippers go,
One with the blue sea's pureness of delight.
Laughing, perhaps, at that old woe of hers
Chained in the cage with fellow prisoners.

He died in that lone cottage near the sea.
In the grey morning when the tide was turning,
The wards of life slipt back and set him free
From cares of meat and dress, from joys and yearning.
Then, like an old man gathering strength, he strayed
Over the beach, and strength came into him.
Beauty that never threatened nor betrayed
Made bright the eyes that sorrow had made dim.
So that upon that stretch of barren sand
He knew his dreams; he saw her beauty run
With Sorrowful Beauty, laughing, hand in hand.
He heard the trumpets blow in Avalon.
He saw the golden statue stretching down
The wreath, for him, of roses, in a crown.

They say that as her husband lay a-dying
He clamoured for a chain to beat the hound.
They say that all the garden rang with crying
That came out of the air, out of the ground,
Out of the waste that was his soul, may be,
Out of the running wolf-hound of his soul,
That had been kennelled in and now broke free
Out to the moors where stags go, past control.
All through his life his will had kennelled him,
Now he was free, and with a hackling fell
He snarled out of the body to the dim
To run the spirits with the hounds of hell.
To run forever at the quarry gone,
The uncaught thing a little further on.

So, one by one, Time took them to his keeping,
Those broken lanterns that had held his fire,
Dust went to dust and flesh had time for sleeping,
And soul, the stag, escaped the hound desire.
And now, perhaps, the memory of their hate
Has passed from them and they are friends again,
Laughing at all the troubles of this state
Where men and women work each other pain.
And in that wind that runs along the glen
Beating at cottage doors, they may go by,
Exulting now, and helping sorrowing men
To do some little good before they die.
For from these ploughed-up souls the spirit brings
Harvest at last, and sweet from bitter things.

THE LEMMINGS

Once in a hundred years the Lemmings come
Westward, in search of food, over the snow,
Westward, until the salt sea drowns them dumb,
Westward, till all are drowned, those Lemmings go.
Once, it is thought, there was a westward land
(Now drowned) where there was food for those starved things,
And memory of the place has burnt its brand
In the little brains of all the Lemming Kings.
Perhaps, long since, there was a land beyond
Westward from death, some city, some calm place,
Where one could taste God's quiet and be fond
With the little beauty of a human face;
But now the land is drowned, yet still we press
Westward, in search, to death, to nothingness.

FORGET

Forget all these, the barren fool in power,
The madman in command, the jealous O,
The bitter world biting its bitter hour,
The cruel now, the happy long ago.
Forget all these, for, though they truly hurt,
Even to the soul, they are not lasting things,
Men are no gods; we tread the city dirt,
But in our souls we can be queens and kings.
And I, O Beauty, O divine white wonder,
On whom my dull eyes, blind to all else, peer,
Have you for peace, that not the whole war's thunder
Nor the world's wreck, can threat or take from here.
So you remain, though all man's passionate seas
Roar their blind tides, I can forget all these.

ON GROWING OLD

Be with me, Beauty, for the fire is dying,
My dog and I are old, too old for roving.
Man, whose young passion sets the spindrift flying,
Is soon too lame to march, too cold for loving.
I take the book and gather to the fire,
Turning old yellow leaves; minute by minute,
The clock ticks to my heart; a withered wire
Moves a thin ghost of music in the spinet.
I cannot sail your seas, I cannot wander,
Your cornland, nor your hill-land nor your valleys,
Ever again, nor share the battle yonder
Where the young knight the broken squadron rallies.
Only stay quiet while my mind remembers
The beauty of fire from the beauty of embers.

Beauty, have pity, for the strong have power,
The rich their wealth, the beautiful their grace,
Summer of man its sunlight and its flower,
Spring-time of man all April in a face.
Only, as in the jostling in the Strand,
Where the mob thrusts or loiters or is loud,
The beggar with the saucer in his hand
Asks only a penny from the passing crowd,
So, from this glittering world with all its fashion,
Its fire and play of men, its stir, its march,
Let me have wisdom, Beauty, wisdom and passion,
Bread to the soul, rain where the summers parch.
Give me but these, and though the darkness close
Even the night will blossom as the rose.

LYRIC

Give me a light that I may see her,
Give me a grace that I may be her,
Give me a clue that I may find her,
Whose beauty shews the brain behind her.
Stars and women and running rivers
And sunny water where a shadow shivers,
And the little brooks that lift the grasses
And April flowers are where she passes.
And all things good and all things kind
Are glimmerings coming from her mind
And in the May a blackbird sings
Against her very heartë springs.

RIGHT ROYAL

PART I

An hour before the race they talked together,
A pair of lovers, in the mild March weather,
Charles Cothill and the golden lady, Em.
Beautiful England's hands had fashioned them.

He was from Sleins, that manor up the Lithe.
Riding the Downs had made his body blithe;
Stalwart he was, and springy, hardened, swift,
Able for perfect speed with perfect thrift,
Man to the core yet moving like a lad.
Dark honest eyes with merry gaze he had,
A fine firm mouth, and wind-tan on his skin.
He was to ride and ready to begin.
He was to ride Right Royal, his own horse,
In the English 'Chasers' Cup on Compton Course.

Under the pale coat reaching to his spurs
One saw his colours, which were also hers,
Narrow alternate bars of blue and white,
Blue as the speedwell's eye and silver bright.

What with hard work and waiting for the race,
Trouble and strain were marked upon his face;
Men would have said that something worried him.

She was a golden lady, dainty, trim,
As like the love time as laburnum blossom.
Mirth, truth and goodness harboured in her bosom.

Pure colour and pure contour and pure grace
Made the sweet marvel of her singing face;

She was the very may-time that comes in
When hawthorns bud and nightingales begin.
To see her tread the red-tippet daisies white
In the green fields all golden with delight
Was to believe Queen Venus come again,
She was as dear as sunshine after rain;
Such loveliness this golden lady had.

All lovely things and pure things made her glad,
But most she loved the things her lover loved,
The windy Downlands where the kestrels roved,
The sea of grasses that the wind runs over
Where blundering beetles drunken from the clover
Stumble about the startled passer-by.

There on the great grass underneath the sky
She loved to ride with him for hours on hours,
Smelling the seasoned grass and those small flowers,
Milkworts and thymes, that grow upon the Downs.
There from a chalk edge they would see the towns:
Smoke above trees, by day, or spires of churches
Gleaming with swinging wind-cocks on their perches,
Or windows flashing in the light, or trains
Burrowing below white smoke across the plains.
By night, the darkness of the valley set
With scattered lights to where the ridges met
And three great glares making the heaven dun,
Oxford and Wallingford and Abingdon.
"Dear, in an hour," said Charles, "the race begins.
Before I start I must confess my sins.
For I have sinned, and now it troubles me."

"I saw that you were sad," said Emily.

"Before I speak," said Charles, "I must premise.
You were not here to help me to be wise,

And something happened, difficult to tell.
Even if I sinned, I feel I acted well,
From inspiration, mad as that may seem.
Just at the grey of dawn I had a dream.

It was the strangest dream I ever had.
It was the dream that drove me to be mad.

I dreamed I stood upon the race-course hére,
Watching a blinding rainstorm blowing clear,
And as it blew away, I said aloud,
'That rain will make soft going on the ploughed.'
And instantly I saw the whole great course,
The grass, the brooks, the fences toppt with gorse,
Gleam in the sun; and all the ploughland shone
Blue, like a marsh, though now the rain had gone.
And in my dream I said, 'That plough will be
Terrible work for some, but not for me.
Not for Right Royal.'
                And a voice said, 'No
Not for Right Royal.'
                And I looked, and, lo!
There was Right Royal, speaking, at my side.
The horse's very self, and yet his hide
Was like, what shall I say? like pearl on fire,
A white soft glow of burning that did twire
Like soft white-heat with every breath he drew.
A glow, with utter brightness running through;
Most splendid, though I cannot make you see.

His great crest glittered as he looked at me
Criniered with spitting sparks; he stamped the ground
All cock and fire, trembling like a hound,
And glad of me, and eager to declare
His horse's mind.

And I was made aware
That, being a horse, his mind could only say
Few things to me. He said, 'It is my day,
My day, to-day; I shall not have another.'

And as he spoke he seemed a younger brother
Most near, and yet a horse, and then he grinned
And tossed his crest and crinier to the wind,
And looked down to the Water with an eye
All fire of soul to gallop dreadfully.

All this was strange, but then a stranger thing
Came afterwards. I woke all shivering
With wonder and excitement, yet with dread
Lest the dream meant that Royal should be dead,
Lest he had died and come to tell me so.
I hurried out; no need to hurry, though;
There he was shining like a morning star.
Now hark. You know how cold his manners are,
Never a whinny for his dearest friend.
To-day he heard me at the courtyard end,
He left his breakfast with a shattering call,
A View Halloo, and, swinging in his stall,
Ran up to nuzzle me with signs of joy.
It staggered Harding and the stable-boy,
And Harding said, 'What's come to him to-day?
He must have had a dream he beat the bay.'

Now that was strange; and, what was stranger, this.
I know he tried to say those words of his,
'It is my day'; and Harding turned to me:
'It is his day to-day, that's plain to see.'
Right Royal nuzzled at me as he spoke.
That staggered me. I felt that I should choke

It came so pat upon my unsaid thought,
I asked him what he meant.
He answered 'Naught.
It only came into my head to say.
But there it is. To-day's Right Royal's day.'

That was the dream. I cannot put the glory
With which it filled my being in a story.
No one can tell a dream.
Now to confess.
The dream made daily life a nothingness,
Merely a mould which white-hot beauty fills,
Pure from some source of passionate joys and skills.
And being flooded with my vision thus,
Certain of winning, puffed and glorious,
Walking upon this earth-top like a king,
My judgment went. I did a foolish thing,
I backed myself to win with all I had.

Now that it's done I see that it was mad,
But still, I had to do it, feeling so.
That is the full confession; now you know."

SHE
The thing is done, and being done, must be.
You cannot hedge. Would you had talked with me
Before you plunged. But there, the thing is done.

HE
Do not exaggerate the risks I run.
Right Royal was a bad horse in the past,
A rogue, a cur, but he is cured at last;
For I was right, his former owner wrong,
He is a game good 'chaser, going strong.
He and my lucky star may pull me through.

She
O grant they may; but think what's racing you,
Think for a moment what his chances are
Against Sir Lopez, Soyland, Kubbadar.

He
You said you thought Sir Lopez past his best.
I do, myself.

She
But there are all the rest.
Peterkinooks, Red Ember, Counter Vair,
And then Grey Glory and the Irish mare.

He
She's scratched. The rest are giving me a stone.
Unless the field hides something quite unknown
I stand a chance. The going favours me.
The ploughland will be bogland certainly,
After this rain. If Royal keeps his nerve,
If no one cannons me at jump or swerve,
I stand a chance. And though I dread to fail,
This passionate dream that drives me like a sail
Runs in my blood, and cries, that I shall win.

She
Please Heaven you may; but now (for me) begin
Again the horrors that I cannot tell,
Horrors that made my childhood such a hell,
Watching my Father near the gambler's grave
Step after step, yet impotent to save.

You do not know, I never let you know,
The horror of those days of long ago
When Father raced to ruin. Every night

After my Mother took away the light,
For weeks before each meeting, I would see
Horrible horses looking down on me,
Laughing and saying, "We shall beat your Father."
Then when the meetings came I used to gather
Close up to Mother, and we used to pray,
"O God, for Christ's sake, let him win to-day."

And then we had to watch for his return,
Craning our necks to see if we could learn,
Before he entered, what the week had been.

Now I shall look on such another scene
Of waiting on the race-chance. For to-day,
Just as I did with Father, I shall say,
"Yes, he'll be beaten by a head, or break
A stirrup leather at the wall, or take
The brook too slow, and, then, all will be lost."

Daily, in mind, I saw the Winning Post,
The Straight, and all the horses' glimmering forms
Rushing between the railings' yelling swarms,
My Father's colours leading. Every day,
Closing my eyes, I saw them die away,
In the last strides, and lose, lose by a neck,
Lose by an inch, but lose, and bring the wreck
A day's march nearer. Now begins again
The agony of waiting for the pain.
The agony of watching ruin come
Out of man's dreams to overwhelm a home.

Go now, my dear. Before the race is due,
We'll meet again, and then I'll speak with you.

In a race-course box behind the Stand
Right Royal shone from a strapper's hand.

A big dark bay with a restless tread,
Fetlock deep in a wheat-straw bed;
A noble horse of a nervy blood,
By O Mon Roi out of Rectitude.
Something quick in his eye and ear
Gave a hint that he might be queer.
In front, he was all to a horseman's mind;
Some thought him a trifle light behind.
By two good points might his rank be known,
A beautiful head and a Jumping Bone.
He had been the hope of Sir Button Budd,
Who bred him there at the Fletchings stud,
But the Fletchings jockey had flogged him cold
In a narrow thing as a two-year-old.
After that, with his sulks and swerves,
Dread of the crowd and fits of nerves,
Like a wastrel bee who makes no honey,
He had hardly earned his entry money.

Liking him still, though he failed at racing,
Sir Button trained him for steeple-chasing.
He jumped like a stag, but his heart was cowed;
Nothing would make him face the crowd.
When he reached the Straight where the crowds began
He would make no effort for any man.

Sir Button sold him, Charles Cothill bought him,
Rode him to hounds and soothed and taught him.
After two years' care Charles felt assured
That his horse's broken heart was cured,
And the jangled nerves in tune again.
And now, as proud as a King of Spain,
He moved in his box with a restless tread,
His eyes like sparks in his lovely head,
Ready to run between the roar

Of the stands that face the Straight once more;
Ready to race, though blown, though beat,
As long as his will could lift his feet;
Ready to burst his heart to pass
Each gasping horse in that street of grass.

John Harding said to his stable-boy:
"Would looks were deeds, for he looks a joy.
He's come on well in the last ten days."
The horse looked up at the note of praise,
He fixed his eye upon Harding's eye,
Then he put all thought of Harding by,
Then his ears went back and he clipped all clean
The manger's well where his oats had been.

John Harding walked to the stable-yard,
His brow was worried with thinking hard.
He thought, "His sire was a Derby winner,
His legs are steel, and he loves his dinner,
And yet of old when they made him race,
He sulked or funked like a real disgrace;
Now for man or horse, I say, it's plain,
That what once he's been, he'll be again.

For all his looks, I'll take my oath
That horse is a cur, and slack as sloth.

He'll funk at a great big field like this,
And the lad won't cure that sloth of his,
He stands no chance, and yet Bungay says
He's been backed all morning a hundred ways.
He was twenty to one, last night, by Heaven:
Twenty to one, and now he's seven.
Well, one of these fools whom fortune loves
Has made up his mind to go for the gloves;
But here's Dick Cappell to bring me news."

Dick Cappell came from a London Mews,
His fleshless face was a stretcht skin sheath
For the narrow pear of the skull beneath.
He had cold blue eyes, and a mouth like a slit,
With yellow teeth sticking out from it.
There was no red blood in his lips or skin,
He'd a sinister, hard, sharp soul within.
Perhaps, the thing that he most enjoyed
Was being rude when he felt annoyed.
He sucked his cane, he nodded to John,
He asked, "What's brought your lambkin on?"

John said, "I had meant to ask of you,
Who's backing him, Dick, I hoped you knew."
Dick said, "Pill Stewart has placed the money.
I don't know whose."
John said, "That's funny."

"Why funny?" said Dick; but John said naught;
He looked at the horse's legs and thought.
Yet at last he said, "It beats me clean,
But whoever he is, he must be green.
There are eight in this could give him a stone,
And twelve should beat him on form alone.
The lad can ride, but it's more than riding
That will give the bay and the grey a hiding."

Dick sucked his cane and looked at the horse
With "Nothing's certain on Compton Course.
He looks a peach. Have you tried him high?"
John said, "You know him as well as I;
What he has done and what he can do.
He's been ridden to hounds this year or two.
When last he was raced, he made the running,
For a stable companion twice at Sunning.

He was placed, bad third, in the Blowbury Cup
And second at Tew with Kingston up.
He sulked at Folkestone, he funked at Speen,
He baulked at the ditch at Hampton Green,
Nick Kingston thought him a slug and cur,
'You must cut his heart out to make him stir.'
But his legs are iron; he's fine and fit."

Dick said, "Maybe; but he's got no grit.
With to-day's big field, on a course like this,
He will come to grief with that funk of his.
Well, it's queer, to me, that they've brought him on.
It's Kubbadar's race. Good morning, John."

When Dick had gone from the stable-yard,
John wrote a note on a racing card.
He said, "Since Stewart has placed the com.,
It's Mr. Cothill he got it from.
Now why should that nice young man go blind
And back his horse? Has he lost his mind?
Such a nice young fellow, so civil-spoken,
Should have more sense than to get him broken,
For broken he'll be as sure as eggs
If he puts his money on horses' legs.
And to trust to this, who's a nice old thing,
But can no more win than a cow can sing.
Well, they say that wisdom is dearly bought,
A world of pain for a want of thought;
But why should he back what stands no chance,
No more than the Rowley Mile's in France?
Why didn't he talk of it first with me?

Well, Lord, we trainers can let it be,
Why can't these owners abstain the same?
It can't be aught but a losing game.

He'll finish ninth; he'll be forced to sell
His horse, his stud, and his home as well;
He'll lose his lady, and all for this—
A daft belief in that horse of his.

It's nothing to me, a man might say,
That a rich young fool should be cast away,
Though what he does with his own, in fine,
Is certainly no concern of mine.
I'm paid to see that his horse is fit,
I can't engage for an owner's wit.
For the heart of a man may love his brother,
But who can be wise to save another?
Souls are our own to save from burning,
We must all learn how, and pay for learning.

And now, by the clock, that bell that went
Was the Saddling Bell for the first event.

Since the time comes close, it will save some swearing
If we get beforehand, and start preparing."

The roads were filled with a drifting crowd,
Many mouth-organs droned aloud,
A couple of lads in scarlet hats,
Yellow trousers and purple spats,
Dragged their banjos, wearily eyeing
Passing brakes full of sportsmen Hi-ing.

Then with a long horn blowing a glory
Came the four-in-hand of the young Lord Tory,
The young Lord's eyes on his leader's ears
And the blood-like team going by to cheers.
Then in a brake came cheerers and hooters
Peppering folk from tin peashooters;

The Green Man's Friendly in bright mauve caps
Followed fast in the Green Man's traps.
The crowd made way for the traps to pass
Then a drum beat up with a blare of brass,
Medical students smart as paint
Sang gay songs of a sad complaint.

A wolf-eyed man who carried a kipe
Whistled as shrill as a man could pipe,
Then paused and grinned with his gaps of teeth
Crying "Here's your colours for Compton Heath,
All the colours of all the starters,
For gentlemen's ties and ladies' garters;
Here you have them, penny a pin,
Buy your colours and see them win.
Here you have them, the favourites' own,
Sir Lopez' colours, the blue-white-roan,
For all the races and what'll win 'em
Real jockey's silk with a pin to pin 'em."

Out of his kipe he sold to many
Bright silk buttons and charged a penny.

A bookie walked with his clerk beside him,
His stool on his shoulders seemed to ride him,
His white top-hat bore a sign which ran
"Your old pal Bunkie the working man."
His clothes were a check of three-inch squares,
"Bright brown and fawn with the pearls in pairs."
Double pearl buttons ran down the side,
The knees were tight and the ankles wide,
A bright, thick chain made of discs of tin
Secured a board from his waist to chin.

The men in the brakes that passed at trot
Read "First past Post" and "Run or Not."

The bookie's face was an angry red,
His eyes seemed rolling inside his head.
His clerk was a lean man, secret, spare,
With thin lips knowing and damp black hair.
A big black bag much weathered with rain
Hung round his neck by a leathered chain.

Seven linked dancers singing a song
Bowed and kicked as they danced along,
The middleman thrust and pulled and squeezed
A concertina to tunes that pleased.
After them, honking, with Hey, Hey, Hey,
Came drivers thrusting to clear the way,
Drivers vexed by the concertina,
Saying "Go bury that d——d hyena."
Drivers dusty with wind-red faces
Leaning out of their driving-places.
The dancers mocked them and called them names:
"Look at our butler," "Drive on, James."
The cars drove past and the dust rose after,
Little boys chased them yelling with laughter,
Clambering on them when they slowed
For a dirty ride down a perch of road.
A dark green car with a smart drab lining
Passed with a stately pair reclining;
Peering walkers standing aside
Saw Soyland's owner pass with his bride,
Young Sir Eustace, biting his lip,
Pressing his chin with his finger-tip,
Nerves on edge, as he could not choose,
From thought of the bets he stood to lose.
His lady, a beauty whom thought made pale,
Prayed from fear that the horse might fail.
A bright brass rod on the motor's bonnet
Carried her husband's colours on it,

Scarlet spots on a field of cream:
She stared ahead in a kind of dream.

Then came cabs from the railway stations,
Carrying men from all the nations,
Olive-skinned French with clipped moustaches,
Almond-eyed like Paris apaches.
Rosy French with their faces shining
From joy of living and love of dining.
Silent Spaniards, merry Italians,
Nobles, commoners, saints, rapscallions;
Russians tense with the quest of truth
That maddens manhood and saddens youth;
Learned Norwegians hale and limber,
Brown from the barques new in with timber.
Oregon men of six feet seven
With backs from Atlas and hearts from Heaven.
Orleans Creoles, ready for duels,
Their delicate ears with scarlet jewels,
Green silk handkerchiefs round their throats,
In from sea with the cotton boats.
Portuguese and Brazilianos,
Men from the mountains, men from the Llanos,
Men from the Pampas, men from the Sierras,
Men from the mines of the Cordilleras,
Men from the flats of the tropic mud
Where the butterfly glints his mail with blood;
Men from the pass where day by day
The sun's heat scales the rocks away;
Men from the hills where night by night
The sheep-bells give the heart delight;
Indians, Lascars and Bengalese.
Greeks from the mainland, Greeks from the seas;
All kinds of bodies, all kinds of faces,
All were coming to see the races,

Coming to see Sir Lopez run
And watch the English having their fun.

The Carib boxer from Hispaniola
Wore a rose in his tilted bowler;
He drove a car with a yellow panel,
He went full speed and he drove a channel.

Then came dog-carts and traps and wagons
With hampers of lunches, pies and flagons,
Bucks from city and flash young bloods
With vests "cut saucy" to show their studs,
Hawbuck Towler and Spicey Random
Tooled in style in a rakish tandem.
Blood Dick Haggit and Bertie Askins
Had dancers' skirts on their horses' gaskins;
Crash Pete Snounce with that girl of Dowser's
Drove a horse that was wearing trousers;
The waggonette from The Old Pier Head
Drove to the tune "My Monkey's Dead."

The costermongers as smart as sparrows
Brought their wives in their donkey barrows.
The clean-legged donkeys, clever and cunning,
Their ears cocked forward, their neat feet running,
Their carts and harness flapping with flags,
Were bright as heralds and proud as stags.
And there in pride in the flapping banners
Were the costers' selves in blue bandannas,
And the costers' wives in feathers curling,
And their sons, with their sweet mouth-organs skirling.

And from midst of the road to the roadside shifting
The crowd of the world on foot went drifting,
Standing aside on the trodden grass

To chaff as they let the traffic pass.
Then back they flooded, singing and cheering,
Plodding forward and disappearing,
Up to the course to take their places,
To lunch and gamble and see the races.

The great grand stand, made grey by the weather,
Flaunted colours that tugged their tether;
Tier upon tier the wooden seats
Were packed as full as the London streets
When the King and Queen go by in state.

Click, click, clack, went the turnstile gate;
The orange-sellers cried "Fat and fine
Seville oranges, sweet, like wine:
Twopence apiece, all juice, all juice."
The pea and the thimble caught their goose.

Two white-faced lurchers, not over-clean,
Urged the passers to "spot the Queen."
They flicked three cards that the world might choose,
They cried "All prizes. You cannot lose.
Come, pick the lady. Only a shilling."
One of their friends cried out, "I'm willing."
He "picked the lady" and took his pay,
And he cried, "It's giving money away."

Men came yelling "Cards of the races";
Men hawked matches and studs and laces;
Gipsy-women in green shawls dizened
Read girls' fortunes with eyes that glistened;
Negro minstrels on banjos strumming
Sang at the stiles to people coming.

Like glistening beetles clustered close,
The myriad motors parked in rows,

The bonnets flashed, and the brass did clink,
As the drivers poured their motors drink.
The March wind blew the smell of the crowd,
All men there seemed crying aloud,
But over the noise a louder roar
Broke, as the wave that bursts on shore,
Drowns the roar of the wave that comes,
So this roar rose on the lesser hums,
"I back the Field. I back the Field."

Man who lives under sentence sealed,
Tragical man, who has but breath
For few brief years as he goes to death,
Tragical man by strange winds blown
To live in crowds ere he die alone,
Came in his jovial thousands massing,
To see Life moving and Beauty passing.

They sucked their fruit in the wooden tiers
And flung the skins at the passers' ears;
Drumming their heels on the planks below,
They sang of Dolly of Idaho.
Past, like a flash, the first race went.
The time drew by to the great event.

At a quarter to three the big bell pealed;
The horses trooped to the Saddling Field.
Covered in clothing, horse and mare
Pricked their ears at the people there;
Some showed devil, and some, composure,
As they trod their way to the great enclosure.

When the clock struck three and the men weighed out,
Charles Cothill shook, though his heart was stout.

The thought of his bets, so gaily laid,
Seemed a stone the more when he sat and weighed.

As he swung in the scales and nursed his saddle,
It seemed to him that his brains would addle;
For now that the plunger reached the brink,
The risk was more than he liked to think.

In ten more minutes his future life,
His hopes of home with his chosen wife,
Would all depend on a doubtful horse
In a crowded field over Compton Course.

He had backed Right Royal for all he owned.
At thought of his want of sense he groaned.
"All for a dream of the night," he thought.
He was right for weight at eleven naught.

Then Em's sweet face rose up in his brain,
He cursed his will that had dealt her pain:
To hurt sweet Emmy and lose her love
Was madman's folly by all above.
He saw too well as he crossed the yard
That his madman's plunge had borne her hard.
"To wring sweet Em like her drunken father,

I'd fall at the Pitch and end it rather.
Oh I hope, hope, hope, that her golden heart
Will give me a word before I start.
If I thought our love should have come to wreck,
I'd pull Right Royal and break my neck,
And Monkery's shoe might kick my brains out
That my own heart's blood might wash my stains out.

But even if Emmy, my sweet, forgive,
I'm a ruined man, so I need not live,

For I've backed my horse with my all, by Heaven,
To be first in a field of thirty-seven,
And good as he is, the dream's a lie."

He saw no hope, but to fall and die.

As he left the room for the Saddling Paddock
He looked as white as the flesh of haddock.
But Love, all seeing, though painted blind,
Makes wisdom live in a woman's mind:
His love knew well from her own heart's bleeding
The word of help that her man was needing;
And there she stood with her eyes most bright,
Ready to cheer her heart's delight.

She said, "My darling, I feel so proud
To see you followed by all the crowd;
And I shall be proud as I see you win.

Right Royal, Soyland and Peterkin
Are the three I pick, first, second, third.
And oh, now listen to what I heard.
Just now in the park Sir Norman Cooking
Said, 'Harding, how well Right Royal's looking.
They've brought him on in the ring, they say.'
John said, 'Sir Norman, to-day's his day.'
And Sir Norman said, 'If I had a monkey
I'd put it on yours, for he looks so spunky.'

So you see that the experts think as you.
Now, my own, own, own, may your dream come true,
As I know it will, as I know it must;
You have all my prayer and my love and trust.

Oh, one thing more that Sir Norman said,
'A lot of money has just been laid

On the mare Gavotte that no one knows.'
He said 'She's small, but, my word, she goes.
Since she bears no weight, if she only jumps,
She'll put these cracks to their ace of trumps.
But,' he said, 'she's slight for a course like this.'

That's all my gossip, so there it is.

Dear, reckon the words I spoke unspoken,
I failed in love and my heart is broken.
Now I go to my place to blush with pride
As the people talk of how well you ride;
I mean to shout like a bosun's mate
When I see you lead coming up the Straight.
Now may all God's help be with you, dear."

"Well, bless you, Em, for your words of cheer.
And now is the woodcock near the gin.
Good-bye.
Now, Harding, we'd best begin."

At buckle and billet their fingers wrought,
Till the sheets were home and the bowlines taut.
As he knotted the reins and took his stand
The horse's soul came into his hand
And up from the mouth that held the steel
Came an innermost word, half thought, half feel,
"My day to-day, O master, O master;
None shall jump cleaner, none shall go faster,
Call till you kill me, for I'll obey,
It's my day to-day, it's my day to-day."

In a second more he had found his seat,
And the standers-by jumped clear of feet,
For the big dark bay all fire and fettle

Had his blood in a dance to show his mettle.
Charles soothed him down till his tricks were gone;
Then he leaned for a final word from John.

John Harding's face was alert and grim,
From under his hand he talked to him.
"It's none of my business, sir," he said,
"What you stand to win or the bets you've made,
But the rumour goes that you've backed your horse.

Now you need no telling of Compton Course.
It's a dangerous course at the best of times,
But on days like this some jumps are crimes;
With a field like this, nigh forty starting,
After one time round it'll need re-charting.

Now think it a hunt, the first time round;
Don't think too much about losing ground,
Lie out of your ground, for sure as trumps
There'll be people killed in the first three jumps.
The second time round, pipe hands for boarding,
You can see what's doing and act according.

Now your horse is a slug and a sulker too,
Your way with the horse I leave to you;
But, sir, you watch for these joker's tricks
And watch that devil on number six;
There's nothing he likes like playing it low,
What a horse mayn't like or a man mayn't know,
And what they love when they race a toff
Is to flurry his horse at taking off.
The ways of the crook are hard to learn.

Now watch that fence at the outer turn;
It looks so slight but it's highly like

That it's killed more men than the Dyers' Dyke.
It's down in a dip and you turn to take it,
And men in a bunch, just there, mistake it.
But well to the right, it's firmer ground,
And the quick way there is the long way round.
In Cannibal's year, in just this weather,
There were five came down at that fence together.
I called it murder, not riding races.
You've nothing to fear from the other places,
Your horse can jump.
Now I'll say no more.
They say you're on, as I said before.
It's none of my business, sir, but still
I would like to say that I hope you will.
Sir, I wish you luck. When we two next meet
I hope to hear how you had them beat."

Charles Cothill nodded with, "Thank you, John.
We'll try; and, oh, you're a thousand on."

He heard John's thanks, but knew at a glance
That John was sure that he stood no chance.

He turned Right Royal, he drew deep breath
With the thought "Now for it; a ride to death."
"Now come, my beauty, for dear Em's sake,
And if come you can't, may our necks both break."

And there to his front, with their riders stooping
For the final word, were the racers trooping.

Out at the gate to cheers and banter
They paced in pride to begin their canter.

Muscatel with the big white star,
The roan Red Ember, and Kubbadar,

Kubbadar with his teeth bared yellow
At the Dakkanese, his stable fellow.
Then Forward-Ho, then a chestnut weed,
Skysail, slight, with a turn of speed.
The neat Gavotte under black and coral,
Then the Mutineer, Lord Leybourne's sorrel,
Natuna mincing, Syringa sidling,
Stormalong fighting to break his bridling,
Thunderbolt dancing with raw nerves quick,
Trying a savage at Bitter Dick.
The Ranger (winner three years before),
Now old, but ready for one try more;
Hadrian; Thankful; the stable-cronies,
Peterkinooks and Dear Adonis;
The flashing Rocket, with taking action;
Exception, backed by the Tencombe faction;
Old Sir Francis and young King Tony,
Culverin striding from great hips bony.

At this, he rode through the open gate
Into the course to try his fate.

He heard a roar from a moving crowd;
Right Royal kindled and cried aloud.
There was the course, stand, rail and pen,
Peopled with seventy thousand men;
Seventy thousand faces staring,
Carriages parked, a brass band blaring:
Over the stand the flags in billows
Bent their poles like the wands of willows.
All men there seemed trying to bawl,
Yet a few great voices topped them all:
"I back the Field! I back the Field!"

Right Royal trembled with pride and squealed.

Charles Cothill smiled with relief to find
This roaring crowd to his horse's mind.

He passed the stand where his lady stood,
His nerves were tense to the multitude;
His blood beat hard and his eyes grew dim
As he knew that some were cheering him.
Then, as he turned, at his pace's end
There came a roar as when floods descend.
All down the Straight from the crowded stands
Came the yells of voices and clap of hands,
For with bright bay beauty that shone like flame
The favorite horse, Sir Lopez, came.

His beautiful hips and splendid shoulders
And power of stride moved all beholders,
Moved non-bettors to try to bet
On that favourite horse not beaten yet.
With glory of power and speed he strode
To a sea of cheering that moved and flowed
And followed and heaped and burst like storm
From the joy of men in the perfect form;
Cheers followed his path both sides the course.

Charles Cothill sighed when he saw that horse.

The cheering died, then a burst of clapping
Met Soyland's coming all bright from strapping,
A big dark brown who was booted thick
Lest one of the jumps should make him click.
He moved very big, he'd a head like a fiddle,
He seemed all ends without any middle,
But ill as he looked, that outcast racer
Was a rare good horse and a perfect 'chaser.
Then The Ghost came on, then Meringue, the bay,

Then proud Grey Glory, the dapple-grey;
The splendid grey brought a burst of cheers.
Then Cimmeroon, who had tried for years
And had thrice been placed and had once been fourth,
Came trying again the proverb's worth.

Then again, like a wave as it runs a pier,
On and on, unbroken, there came a cheer
As Monkery, black as a collier-barge,
Trod sideways, bickering, taking charge.
Cross-Molin, from the Blowbury, followed,
Lucky Shot skipped, Coranto wallowed,
Then Counter Vair, the declared-to-win,
Stable-fellow of Cross-Molin;
Culverin last, with Cannonade,
Formed rearguard to the grand parade.

And now, as they turned to go to post,
The Skysail calfishly barged The Ghost,
The Ghost lashed out with a bitter knock
On the tender muscle of Skysail's hock,
And Skysail's hope of that splendid hour
Was cut off short like a summer flower.
From the cantering crowd he limped apart
Back to the Paddock and did not start.

As they cantered down, Charles Cothill's mind
Was filled with joy that his horse went kind;
He showed no sulks, no sloth, no fear,
But leant on his rein and pricked his ear.
They lined themselves at the Post to start,
Charles took his place with a thumping heart.

Excitement running in waves took hold,
His teeth were chattered, his hands were cold,

His joy to be there was mixed with dread
To be left at post when they shot ahead.
The horses sparred as though drunk with wine,
They bickered and snatched at taking line.

Then a grey-haired man with a hawklike face
Read from a list each rider's place.
Sitting astride his pommely hack,
He ordered them up or sent them back;
He bade them heed that they jump their nags
Over every jump between the flags.
Here Kubbadar, who was pulling double,
Went sideways, kicking and raising trouble,
Monkery seconded, kicking and biting,
Thunderbolt followed by starting fighting.

The starter eyed them and gave the order
That the three wild horses keep the border,
With men to hold them to keep them quiet.
Boys from the stables stopped their riot.
Out of the line to the edge of the field,
The three wild biters and kickers wheeled;
Then the rest edged up and pawed and bickered,
Reached at their reins and snatched and snickered,
Flung white foam as they stamped their hate
Of passionate blood compelled to wait.

Then the starter shouted to Charles, "Good heaven,
This isn't a circus, you on Seven."
For Royal squirmed like a box of tricks
And Coranto's rider, the number Six,
Cursed at Charles for a green young fool
Who ought to be at a riding school.

After a minute of swerves and shoving,
A line like a half-moon started moving,

Then Rocket and Soyland leaped to stride,
To be pulled up short and wheeled to side.

Then the trickier riders started thrusting,
Judging the starter's mind too trusting;
But the starter said, "You know quite clearly
That isn't allowed; though you'd like it dearly."

Then Cannonade made a sideways bolt
That gave Exception an ugly jolt.
Then the line, reformed, broke all to pieces.
Then the line reforms, and the tumult ceases.
Each man sits tense though his racer dances;
In a slow, jerked walk the line advances.

And then in a flash, more felt than seen,
The flag shot down and the course showed green,
And the line surged forwards and all that glory
Of speed was sweeping to make a story.

One second before, Charles Cothill's mind
Had been filled with fear to be left behind,
But now with a rush, as when hounds leave cover,
The line broke up and his fear was over.
A glimmer of bay behind The Ghost
Showed Dear Adonis still there at post.
Out to the left, a joy to his backer,

Kubbadar led the field a cracker,
The thunder of horses, all fit and foaming,
Made the blood not care whether death were coming.
A glimmer of silks, blue, white, green, red,
Flashed into his eye and went ahead;
Then hoof-casts scattered, then rushing horses
Passed at his side with all their forces.

His blood leapt up but his mind said "No,
Steady, my darling, slow, go slow.
In the first time round this ride's a hunt."

The Turk's Grave Fence made a line in front.

Long years before, when the race began,
That first of the jumps had maimed a man;
His horse, the Turk, had been killed and buried
There in the ditch by horse-hoofs herried;
And over the poor Turk's bones at pace
Now, every year, there goes the race,
And many a man makes doctor's work
At the thorn-bound ditch that hides the Turk,
And every man as he rides that course
Thinks, there, of the Turk, that good old horse.

The thick thorn-fence stands five feet high,
With a ditch beyond unseen by eye,
Which a horse must guess from his urgent rider
Pressing him there to jump it wider.

And being so near both Stand and Post,
Out of all the jumps men haunt it most,
And there, with the crowd, and the undulled nerves,
The old horse balks and the young horse swerves,
And the good horse falls with the bad on top
And beautiful boldness comes to stop.

Charles saw the rush of the leading black,
And the forehands lift and the men sway back;
He steadied his horse, then with crash and crying
The top of the Turk's Grave Fence went flying.
Round in a flash, refusing danger,
Came the Lucky Shot right into Ranger;

Ranger swerving knocked Bitter Dick,
Who blundered at it and leaped too quick;
Then crash went blackthorn as Bitter Dick fell,
Meringue jumped on him and rolled as well.
As Charles got over he splashed the dirt
Of the poor Turk's grave on two men hurt.

Right Royal landed. With cheers and laughter
Some horses passed him and some came after;
A fine brown horse strode up beside him,
It was Thankful running with none to ride him;
Thankful's rider, dizzy and sick,
Lay in the mud by Bitter Dick.

In front, was the curving street of Course,
Barred black by the leaps unsmashed by horse.
A cloud blew by and the sun shone bright,
Showing the guard-rails gleaming white.
Little red flags, that gusts blew tense,
Streamed to the wind at each black fence.

And smiting the turf to clods that scattered
Was the rush of the race, the thing that mattered,
A tide of horses in fury flowing,
Beauty of speed in glory going,
Kubbadar pulling, romping first,
Like a big black fox that had made his burst.
And away and away and away they went,
A visible song of what life meant.
Living in houses, sleeping in bed,
Going to business, all seemed dead,
Dead as death to that rush in strife
Pulse for pulse with the heart of life.

"For to all," Charles thought, "when the blood beats high
Comes the glimpse of that which may not die;

When the world is stilled, when the wanting dwindles,
When the mind takes light and the spirit kindles,
One stands on a peak of this old earth."

Charles eyed his horses and sang with mirth.
What of this world that spins through space?
With red blood running he rode a race,
The beast's red spirit was one with his,
Emulous and in ecstasies;
Joy that from heart to wild heart passes
In the wild things going through the grasses;

In the hares in the corn, in shy gazelles
Running the sand where no man dwells;
In horses scared at the prairie spring;
In the dun deer noiseless, hurrying;
In fish in the dimness scarcely seen,
Save as shadows shooting in a shaking green;
In birds in the air, neck-straining, swift,
Wing touching wing while no wings shift,
Seen by none, but when stars appear
A reaper wandering home may hear
A sigh aloft where the stars are dim,
Then a great rush going over him:
This was his; it had linked him close
To the force by which the comet goes,
With the rein none sees, with the lash none feels,
But with fire-mane tossing and flashing heels.

The roar of the race-course died behind them,
In front were their Fates, they rode to find them,
With the wills of men, with the strengths of horses,
They dared the minute with all their forces.

PART II

Still pulling double, black Kubbadar led,
Pulling his rider half over his head;
Soyland's cream jacket was spotted with red,
Spotted with dirt from the rush of their tread.

Bright bay Sir Lopez, the loveliest there,
Galloped at ease as though taking the air,
Well in his compass with plenty to spare.
Gavotte and The Ghost and the brown Counter Vair,
Followed him close with Syringa the mare,
And the roan horse Red Ember, who went like a hare,
And Forward-Ho bolting, though his rider did swear.

Keeping this order, they reached the next fence,
Which was living plashed blackthorn with gorse-toppings dense;
In the gloom of its darkness it loomed up immense.
And Forward-Ho's glory had conquered his sense
And he rushed it, not rising, and never went thence.

And down in the ditch where the gorse-spikes were scattered,
That bright chestnut's soul from his body was shattered,
And his rider shed tears on the dear head all spattered.

King Tony came down, but got up with a stumble,
His rider went sideways, but knew how to tumble,
And got up and remounted, though the pain made him humble,
And rode fifty yards and then stopped in a fumble.

With a rush and a crashing Right Royal went over
With the stride of a stalwart and the blood of a lover,
He landed on stubble now pushing with clover.

And just as he landed, the March sun shone bright
And the blue sky showed flamelike and the dun clouds turned white;
The little larks panted aloft their delight,
Trembling and singing as though one with the light.

And Charles, as he rode, felt the joy of their singing,
While over the clover the horses went stringing,
And up from Right Royal the message came winging,
"It is my day to-day, though the pace may be stinging,
Though the jumps be all danger and the going all clinging."

The white, square church-tower with its weather-cocks swinging,
Rose up on the right above grass and dark plough
Where the elm trees' black branches had bud on the bough.

Riderless Thankful strode on at his side,
His bright stirrup-irons flew up at each stride,
Being free, in this gallop, had filled him with pride.
Charles thought, "What would come, if he ran out or shied?
I wish from my heart that the brute would keep wide."
Coranto drew up on Right Royal's near quarter,
Beyond lay a hurdle and ditch full of water.
And now as they neared it, Right Royal took heed
Of the distance to go and the steps he would need;
He cocked to the effort with eyes bright as gleed,
Then Coranto's wide wallow shot past him at speed:
His rider's "Hup, hup, now!" called out quick and cheerly,
Sent him over in style, but Right Royal jumped early.

Just a second too soon, and from some feet too far,
Charles learned the mistake as he struck the top bar;
Then the water flashed skywards, the earth gave a jar,
And the man on Coranto looked back with "Aha!

That'll teach you, my son." Then with straining of leather,
Grey Glory and Monkery landed together.

For a second the stunning kept Charles from his pain,
Then his sense flooded back, making everything plain.
He was down on the mud, but he still held the rein;
Right Royal was heaving his haunch from the drain.
The field was ahead of him, going like rain,
And though the plough held them, they went like the wind
To the eyes of a man left so badly behind.

Charles climbed to his feet as Right Royal crawled out,
He said, "That's extinction beyond any doubt."
On the plough, on and on, went the rush of the rout.
Charles mounted and rode, for his courage was stout,
And he would not give in till the end of the bout,
But plastered with poachings he rode on forsaken:
He had lost thirty lengths and his horse had been shaken.

Across the wet ploughland he took a good pull,
With the thought that the cup of his sorrow was full,
For the speed of a stag and the strength of a bull
Could hardly recover the ground he had lost.

Right Royal went dully, then snorted and tost,
Tost his head, with a whicker, went on, and went kind,
And the horse's great spirit touched Charles in the mind.
Though his bruise made him dizzy and tears made him blind,
He would try to the finish, and so they should find.
He was last, thirty lengths. Here he took in his sails,
For the field had come crash at the white post and rails.

Here Sir Francis ran out, scaring all who stood near,
Going crash through the rail like a runaway deer.
Then the riderless Thankful upset Mutineer.

Dakkanese, in refusing, wheeled round like a top
Into Culverin's shoulder which made them both stop.
They reeled from the shock, slithered sideways, and crashed,
Dakkanese on the guard-rail which gave, and then smashed.
As he rolled, the near shoes of the Culverin flashed
High in air for a moment, bright iron in strain:
Then he rose with no rider and tripped in his rein.

Right Royal came up as the Dakkanese rose
All trembling and cowed as though beaten with blows;
The Culverin stumbled with the reins in his toes;
On the far side the leap stood the Mutineer grazing
His man was a heap which some fellows were raising.
Right Royal strode on, through a second wet plough,
With the field far ahead (Kubbadar in the bow).
Charles thought, "Kubbadar's got away from him now.
Well, it's little to me, for they're so far ahead
That they'll never come back, though I ride myself dead."

Right Royal bored forward and leaned on his hand,
"Good boy," said his master. "He must understand.
You're the one friend I'll have when I've sold all my land.
God pity my Em as we come past the Stand,
Last of all, and all muddy; but now for Jim's Pitch."
Four feet of gorse fence, then a fifteen foot ditch.
And the fifteen foot ditch glittered bright to the brim
With the brook that ran through it where the grayling did swim;
In the shallows it sparkled, in the deeps it was dim,
When the race was first run it had nearly drowned Jim.
And now the bright irons of twenty-four horses
Were to flicker its ripples with knockings of gorses.

From far in the rear Charles could watch them take hold
Of their horses and push them across the light mould;

How their ears all cocked forward, how the drumming hoofs
rolled!
Kubbadar, far ahead, flew across like a bird,
Then Soyland, bad second, with Muscatel third.
Then Sir Lopez, and Path Finder, striding alone,
Then the good horse, Red Ember, the flea-bitten roan.
Then the little Gavotte bearing less than ten stone.
Then a crowd of all colours with Peterkinooks
Going strong as a whale goes, head up and out flukes.

And then as Charles watched, as the shoulders went back,
The riderless Thankful swerved left off the track,
Crossing just to the front of the Cimmeroon black.
Ere the rider could see what his horse was about,
Cimmeroon swerved, like Thankful, and followed him out.
Across the great grass in the midst of the course
Cimmeroon ran a match race with the riderless horse,
Then the rider took charge, part by skill part by force;
He turned Cimmeroon to re-enter the race
Seven lengths behind Charles in the post of disgrace.

Beyond the next fence, at the top of a slope,
Charles saw his field fading and gave up all hope.
Yet he said, "Any error will knot me my rope.
I wish that some power would help me to see
What would give the best chance for Right Royal and me.
Shall I hurry downhill, to catch up when I can?
Being last is the devil for horse and for man,
For it makes the horse slack and it makes the man sick.
Well, I've got to decide and I've got to be quick.

I had better catch up, for if I should be last,
It would kill my poor Emmy to see me come past.
I cannot leave Emmy to suffer like that,
So I'll hurry downhill and then pull on the flat."

So he thought, so he settled, but then, as he stirred,
Right Royal's ears moved like a vicious man's word;
So he thought, "If I try it, the horse will refuse."
So he gave up the project and shook in his shoes.
Then he thought, "Since the horse will not stand interference,
I must even sit quiet and sink the appearance,
Since his nerves have been touched, it's as well we're alone."
He turned down the hill with his heart like a stone.

"But," he cried, "they'll come back, for they've gone such a
bust
That they'll all soon be panting, in need to be nursed,
They will surely come back, but to wait till they do,
Lord, it's hell to the waiter, it cuts a man through."

Then into his mind came the Avalon case,
When a man, left at post, without hope of a place,
First had suffered in patience, then had wormed his way up,
Then had come with fine judgment, and just won the Cup.

Hoofs thundered behind him, the Cimmeroon caught him,
His man cursing Thankful and the sire who wrought him.
"Did you see that brown devil?" he cried as he passed;
"He carried me out, but I'll never be last.

Just the wrong side the water the brute gave a swerve,
And he carried me out, half across the course-curve.
Look, he's cut right across now, we'll meet him again.
Well, I hope someone knocks him and kicks out his brain.

Well, I'll never be last, though I can't win the Cup.
No sense lolling here, man, you'd better pull up."
Then he roused Cimmeroon, and was off like a swallow.

Charles watched, sick at heart, with a longing to follow.

"Better follow," he thought, "for he knows more than I,
Since he rode here before, and it's wiser to try:
Would my horse had but wings, would his feet would but lift;
Would we spun on this speedway as wind spins the drift.

There they go out of sight, over fence, to the Turn;
They are going still harder, they leave me astern.
They will never come back, I am lost past recall."
So he cried for a comfort, and only gat gall.

In the glittering branches of the world without end
Were the spirits, Em's Helper and Charles Cothill's Friend,
And the Force of Right Royal with a crinier of flame;
There they breathed the bright glory till the summoning came.

From the Stand where Em watched, from the field where
Charles rode,
From the mud where Right Royal in solitude strode,
Came the call of three spirits to the spirits that guard,
Crying, "Up now, and help him, for the danger bears hard."

There they looked, those immortals, from the boughs dropping
balm,
But their powers were stirred not, and their grave brows were
calm,
For they said, "He's despairing and the horse is still vext."
Charles cleared Channing's Blackthorn and strode to the next.

The next was the Turn in a bogland of rushes;
There the springs of still water were trampled to slushes;
The peewits lamented, flapping down, flagging far,
The riders dared deathwards each trusting his star.

The mud made them slither, the turn made them close,
The stirrup steels clinked as they thrust in their toes,

The brown horse Exception was struck as he rose,
Struck to earth by the Rocket, then kicked by the grey,
Then Thunderbolt smote him and rolled him astray.

The man on Exception, Bun Manor, fell clear
With Monkery's shoes half an inch from his ear,
A drench of wet mud from the hoofs struck his cheek,
But the race was gone from him before he could speak.

There Exception and Thunderbolt ended their race,
Their bright flanks all smeared with the mud of the place;
In the green fields of Tencombe and the grey downs of Churn
Their names had been glories till they fell at the Turn.

Em prayed in her place that her lover might know
Not to hurry Right Royal but let him go slow;
White-lipped from her praying, she sat, with shut eyes,
Begging help from her Helper, the deathless, the wise.

From the gold of his branches her Helper took heed,
He sent forth a thought to help Charles in his need.
As the white, gleaming gannet eyes fish in the sea,
So the thought sought a mortal to bring this to be.

By the side of Exception Bun Manor now stood,
Sopping rags on a hock that was dripping bright blood.
He had known Charles of old and defeat made him kind,
The thought from the Helper came into his mind.

So he cried to Charles Cothill, "Go easy," he cried,
"Don't hurry; don't worry; sit still and keep wide.
They flowed like the Severn, they'll ebb like the tide.
They'll come back and you'll catch them." His voice died away.
In front lay the Dyke, deep as drowning, steel grey.

Charles felt his horse see it and stir at the sight.
Again his heart lifted to the dream of the night;
Once again in his heart's blood the horse seemed to say,
"I'll die or I'll do it. It's my day to-day."

He saw the grey water in shade from its fence,
The rows of white faces all staring intense;
All the heads straining forward, all the shoulders packt dense.
Beyond, he saw Thankful, the riderless brown,
Snatching grass, dodging capture, with reins hanging down.

Then Thankful stopped eating and cocked up his head,
He eyed the swift horses that Kubbadar led,
His eye filled with fire at the roll of their tread;
Then he tore down the course with a flash of bright shoes,
As the race's bright herald on fire with news.

As Charles neared the water, the Rocket ran out
By jumping the railings and kicking a clout
Of rotten white woodwork to startle the trout.
When Charles cleared the water, the grass stretcht before
And the glory of going burned in to the core.

Far over his head with a whicker of wings
Came a wisp of five snipe from a field full of springs;
The gleam on their feathers went wavering past—
And then some men booed him for being the last.

But last though he was, all his blood was on fire
With the rush of the wind and the gleam of the mire,
And the leap of his heart to the skylarks in quire,
And the feel of his horse going onward, on, on,
Under sky with white banners and bright sun that shone.

Like a star in the night, like a spring in the waste,
The image of Emmy rose up as he raced,

Till his mind was made calm, and his spirit was braced.
For the prize was bright Emmy; his blood beat and beat
As her beauty made music in that thunder of feet.

The wind was whirled past him, it hummed in his ears,
Right Royal's excitement had banished his fears,
For his leap was like singing, his stride was like cheers,
All his blood was in glory, all his soul was blown bare,
They were one, blood and purpose, they strode through the air.

"What is life if I lose her, what is death if I win?
At the end of this living the new lives begin.
Whatever life may be, whatever death is,
I am spirit eternal, I am this, I am this!"

Girls waved, and men shouted, like flashes, like shots,
Out of pale blurs of faces whose features were dots;
Two fences with toppings were cleared without hitch,
Then they ran for Lost Lady's, a fence and dry ditch.

Here Monkery's rider, on seeing a chance,
Shot out beyond Soyland to lead the advance.
Then he steadied and summed up his field with a glance.
All crossed the Lost Lady's, that dry ditch of fear,
Then a roar broke about them, the racecourse was near.

Right and left were the swing-boats and merry-go-rounds,
Yellow varnish that wavered, machines making sounds,
Rifles cracking like cork-pops, fifes whining with steam,
"All hot," from a pieman; all blurred as in dream.

Then the motors, then cheering, then the brass of a band,
Then the white rails all crowded with a mob on each hand.
Then they swerved to the left over gorsebush and hurdle
And they rushed for the Water where a man's blood might
curdle.

Charles entered the race-course and prayed in his mind
That love for the moment might make Emmy blind,
Not see him come past half a distance behind;
For an instant he thought, "I must shove on ahead,
For to pass her like this, Lord, I'd rather be dead."

Then, in crossing the hurdle the Stand arose plain,
All the flags, horns and cheers beat like blows on his brain,
And he thought, "Time to race when I come here again,
If I once lose my head, I'll be lost past appeal."
All the crowd flickered past like a film on a reel,

Like a ribbon, whirled past him, all painted with eyes.
All the real, as he rode, was the horse at his thighs,
And the thought "They'll come back, if I've luck, if I'm wise."
Some banners uncrumpled on the blue of the skies,
The cheers became frantic, the blur of men shook,
As Thankful and Kubbadar went at the brook.

Neck and neck, stride for stride, they increased as they neared
    it,
Though the danger gleamed greyly, they galloped to beard it;
And Kubbadar dwelt on his jump as he cleared it,
While Thankful went on with a half a length lead.
Charles thought, "Kubbadar, there, is going to seed."

Then Monkery took it, then Soyland, then two,
Muscatel and Sir Lopez, who leaped not but flew,
Like a pair of June swallows going over the dew,
Like a flight of bright fishes from a field of seas blue,
Like a wisp of snipe wavering in the dusk out of view.
Then Red Ember, Path Finder, Gavotte and Coranto,
Then The Ghost going level by Syringa a-taunto,

Then Peterkinooks, then the Cimmeroon black,
Who had gone to his horses, not let them come back;

Then Stormalong rousing, then the Blowbury crack,
Counter Vair, going grandly beside Cross-Molin,
All charged the bright brook and Coranto went in.

Natuna, Grey Glory and Hadrian followed,
Flying clear of the water where Coranto now wallowed;
Cannonade leaped so big that the lookers-on holloed.
Ere the splash from Coranto was bright on the grass,
The face of the water had seen them all pass.
But Coranto half scrambled, then slipped on his side,
Then churned in the mud till the brook was all dyed;
As Charles reached the water Coranto's man cried,
"Put him at it like blazes and give him a switch;
Jump big, man, for God's sake, I'm down in the ditch."

Right Royal went at it and streamed like a comet,
And the next thing Charles knew, he was twenty yards from it;
And he thought about Em as he rushed past her place,
With a prayer for God's peace on her beautiful face.

Then he tried to keep steady. "O steady," he said,
"I'm riding with judgment, not leading a raid,
And I'm getting excited, and there's Cannonade.
What's the matter?" he shouted, as Royal swept past.
"Sprained!" shouted the man, "Over-jumped, at the last."

"Rough luck," shouted Charles. Then the crowd dropped away,
Then the sun shone behind him, the bright turned to grey;
They were round, the first time, they were streaming away
For the second time round. There the starting-post shone.
Then they swung round the curve and went galloping on.

All the noise died behind, Fate was waiting in front,
Now the racing began, they had done with the hunt.

With the sunlight behind him Charles saw how they went;
No nearer, but further, and only one spent.

Only Kubbadar dwelling, the rest going strong,
Taking jump after jump as a bird takes a song,
Their thirty lengths' lead seemed a weary way long,
It seemed to grow longer, it seemed to increase:
"This is bitter," he said. "May it be for my peace.

My dream was a glimpse of the world beyond sense,
All beauty and wisdom are messages thence.
There the difference of bodies and the strain of control
Are removed; beast with man speaks, and spirit with soul.

My vision was Wisdom, or the World as it Is.
Fate rules us, not Wisdom, whose ways are not his,
Fate, weaponed with all things, has willed that I fall;
So be it, Fate orders, and we go to the wall.

Go down to the beaten, who have come to the truth
That is deeper than sorrow and stronger than youth,
That is God, the foundation, who sees and is just
To the beauty within us who are nothing but dust.

Yet, Royal, my comrade, before Fate decides,
His hand stays, uncertain, like the sea between tides,
Then a man has a moment, if he strike not too late,
When his soul shakes the world-soul, and can even change Fate.

So you and I, Royal, before we give in
Will spend blood and soul in our effort to win,
And if all be proved vain when our effort is sped,
May the hoofs of our conquerors trample us dead."

Then the soul of Right Royal thrilled up through each hand,
"We are one, for this gallop; we both understand.

If my lungs give me breathing, if my loins stand the strain,
You may lash me to strips and it shan't be in vain.

For to-day, in this hour, my Power will come
From my Past to my Present (and a Spirit gives some).
We have gone many gallops, we two, in the past,
When I go with my Power you will know me at last.

You remember the morning when the red leaf hung still,
When they found in the beech-clump on Lollingdon Hill,
When we led past the Sheep Fold and along the Fair Mile?
When I go with my Power, that will not seem worth while.

Then the day in the valley when we found in the wood,
When we led all the gallop to the river in flood,
And the sun burst out shining as the fox took the stream,
When I go with my Power, that will all seem a dream.

Then the day on the Downland when we went like the light
From the spring by Hurst Compton till the Clump was in sight,
Till we killed by The Romans, where Blowbury is,
All the best of that gallop shall be nothing to this.

If I failed in the past with my Power away,
I was only my shadow, it was not my day,
So I sulked like my sire, or shrank, like my dam;
Now I come to my Power you will know what I am.

I've the strength, you've the brain, we are running as one
And nothing on earth can be lost till it's won.
If I live to the end, naught shall put you to shame."
So he thrilled, going flame-like, with a crinier of flame.

"Yet," he thrilled, "It may be, that before the end come
Death will touch me, the Changer, and carry me home.

For we know not, O master, when our life shall have rest,
But the Life is near change that has uttered its best.
If we grow like the grasses, we fall like the flower,
And I know, I touch Death when I come to my Power."

Now over the course flew invisible birds,
All the Wants of the Watchers, all the thoughts and winged
words,
Swift as floatings of fire from a bonfire's crest
When they burn leaves on Kimble and the fire streams west,

Bright an instant, then dying, but renewed and renewed,
So the thoughts chased the racers like hounds that pursued,
Bringing cheer to their darlings, bringing curse to their foes,
Searching into men's spirits till their Powers arose.

Red and rigid the Powers of the riding men were,
And as sea birds on Ailsa, in the nesting time there,
Rise like leaves in a whirlwind and float like leaves blown,
So the wants chased the riders and fought for their own.

Unseen by the riders, from the myriad tense brains
Came the living thoughts flying to clutch at men's reins,
Clearing paths for their darlings by running in cry
At the heads of their rivals till the darlings gat by.

As in football, when forwards heave all in a pack,
With their arms round each other and their heels heeling back,
And their bodies all straining, as they heave, and men fall,
And the halves hover hawklike to pounce on the ball,

And the runners poise ready, while the mass of hot men
Heaves and slips, like rough bullocks making play in a pen,
And the crowd sees the heaving, and is still, till it break,
So the riders endeavoured as they strained for the stake.

They skimmed through the grassland, they came to the plough,
The wind rushed behind them like the waves from a prow,
The clods rose behind them with speckles of gold
From the iron-crusht coltsfoot flung up from the mould.

All green was the plough with the thrusts of young corn,
Pools gleamed in the ruts that the cartwheels had worn,
And Kubbadar's man wished he had not been born.
Natuna was weary and dwelt on her stride,
Grey Glory's grey tail rolled about, side to side.

Then swish, came a shower, from a driving grey cloud,
Though the blue sky shone brightly and the larks sang aloud
As the squall of rain pelted, the coloured caps bowed,
With Thankful still leading and Monkery close,
The hoofs smacked the clayland, the flying clods rose.

They slowed on the clayland, the rain pelted by,
The end of a rainbow gleamed out in the sky;
Natuna dropped back till Charles heard her complain,
Grey Glory's forequarters seemed hung on his rein,
Cimmeroon clearly was feeling the strain.
But the little Gavotte skimmed the clay like a witch,
Charles saw her coquet as she went at Jim's Pitch.

They went at Jim's Pitch, through the deeply dug gaps
Where the hoofs of great horses had kicked off the scraps,
And there at the water they met with mishaps,
For Natuna stopped dead and Grey Glory went in
And a cannon on landing upset Cross-Molin.

As swallows bound northward when apple-bloom blows,
See laggards drop spent from their flight as it goes,
Yet can pause not in Heaven as they scythe the thin air
But go on to the house-eaves and the nests clinging bare,

So Charles flashed beyond them, those three men the less
Who had gone to get glory and met with distress.

He rode to the rise-top, and saw, down the slope,
The race far ahead at a steady strong lope
Going over the grassland, too well for his peace,
They were steady as oxen and strong as wild geese.

As a man by a cornfield on a windy wild day
Sees the corn bow in shadows ever hurrying away,
And wonders, in watching, when the light with bright feet
Will harry those shadows from the ears of the wheat,
So Charles, as he watched, wondered when the bright face
Of the finish would blaze on that smouldering race.

On the last of the grass, ere the going was dead,
Counter Vair's man shot out with his horse by the head,
Like a partridge put up from the stubble he sped,
He dropped Kubbadar and he flew by Red Ember
Up to Monkery's girth like a leaf in November.

Then Stormalong followed, and went to the front,
And just as the find puts a flame to a hunt,
So the rush of those horses put flame to the race.
Charles saw them all shaken to quickening pace.
And Monkery moved, not to let them go by,
And the steadiest rider made ready to fly;
Well into the wet land they leaped from the dry,
They scattered the rain-pools that mirrored the sky,
They crushed down the rushes that pushed from the plough
And Charles longed to follow, but muttered "Not now."

"Not now," so he thought, "Yet if not" (he said) "when
Shall I come to those horses and scupper their men?
Will they never come back? Shall I never get up?"
So he drank bitter gall from a very cold cup.

But he nursed his horse gently and prayed for the best,
And he caught Cimmeroon, who was sadly distrest,
And he passed Cimmeroon, with the thought that the black
Was as nearly dead beat as the man on his back.
Then he gained on his field who were galled by the Churn,
The plough searched them out as they came to the Turn.
But Gavotte, black and coral, went strong as a spate
Charles thought "She's a flier and she carries no weight."

And now, beyond question the field began tailing,
For all had been tested and many were ailing,
The riders were weary, the horses were failing,
The blur of bright colours rolled over the railing.
With the grunts of urged horses, and the oaths of hot men,
"Gerr on, you," "Come on, now," agen and agen;
They spattered the mud on the willow tree's bole
And they charged at the danger; and the danger took toll.

For Monkery landed, but dwelt on the fence
So that Counter Vair passed him in galloping thence.
Then Stormalong blundered, then bright Muscatel
Slipped badly on landing and stumbled and fell,

Then rose in the morrish, with his man on his neck
Like a nearly dead sailor afloat on a wreck,
With his whip in the mud and his stirrups both gone,
Yet he kept in the saddle and made him go on.

As Charles leaped the Turn, all the field was tailed out
Like petals of roses that wind blows about,
Like petals of colour blown back and brought near,
Like poppies in wind-flaws when corn is in ear,
Fate held them or sped them, the race was beginning.
Charles said, "I must ride, or I've no chance of winning,"

So gently he quickened, yet making no call;
Right Royal replied as though knowing it all,
He passed Kubbadar who was ready to fall,
Then he strode up to Hadrian, up to his girth,
They eyed the Dyke's glitter and picked out a berth.
Now the race reached the water and over it flew
In a sweep of great muscle strained taut and guyed true.
There Muscatel floundered and came to a halt,
Muscatel, the bay chaser without any fault.

Right Royal's head lifted, Right Royal took charge,
On the left near the railings, ears cocked, going large,
Leaving Hadrian behind as a yacht leaves a barge.
Though Hadrian's rider called something unheard,
He was past him at speed like the albatross bird,
Running up to Path Finder, they leaped, side by side,
And the foam from Path Finder flecked white on his hide.
And on landing, he lifted, while Path Finder dwelt,
And his noble eye brightened from the glory he felt,
And the mud flung behind him flicked Path Finder's chest,
As he left him behind and went on to the rest.

Charles cast a glance back, but he could not divine
Why the man on Path Finder should make him a sign,
Nor why Hadrian's rider should shout, and then point,
With his head nodded forward and a jerked elbow joint.

But he looked as he pointed, both forward and down,
And he saw that Right Royal was smeared like a clown,
Smeared red and bespattered with flecks of bright blood,
From a blood-vessel burst, as he well understood.

And just as he saw it, Right Royal went strange
As one whom Death's finger has touched to a change;

He went with a stagger that sickened the soul,
As a force stricken feeble and out of control.

Charles thought, "He is dying, and this is the end,
I am losing my Emmy and killing my friend;
He was hurt when we fell, as I thought at the first,
And I've forced him three miles with a blood-vessel burst.

And his game heart went on." Here a rush close behind
Made him cast a glance back with despair in his mind.
It was Cimmeroon rushing, his lips twitcht apart,
His eyes rolled back sightless, and death in his heart.
He reached to Right Royal, then fell, and was dead,
Nevermore to stretch reins with his beautiful head.

A gush of bright blood filled his mouth as he sank,
And he reached out his hoofs to the heave of his flank,
And Charles, leaning forward, made certain, and cried,
"This is Cimmeroon's blood, blown in passing beside,
And Roy's going strangely was just that he felt
Death coming behind him, or blood that he smelt."

So Charles's heart lightened and Royal went steady
As a water bound seaward set free from an eddy,
As a water sucked downward to leap at a weir
Sucked swifter and swifter till it shoot like a spear.

There, a mile on ahead, was the Stand like a cliff,
Grey wood, packed with faces, under banners blown stiff,
Where, in two minutes more, they would cheer for him—if—
If he came to those horses still twelve lengths ahead.
"O Royal, you do it, or kill me!" he said.

They went at the hurdle as though it weren't there,
White splinters of hurdle flew up in the air,

And down, like a rabbit, went Syringa the mare;
Her man somersaulted right under Gavotte,
And Syringa went on but her rider did not.

But the little Gavotte tucked her feet away clear,
Just an inch to one side of the fallen man's ear,
With a flash of horse wisdom as she went on the wing
Not to tread on man's body, that marvellous thing.

As in mill-streams in summer the dark water drifts
Petals mown in the hayfield skimmed over by swifts,
Petals blue from the speedwell or sweet from the lime,
And the fish rise to test them, as they float, for a time,
Yet they all loiter sluicewards and are whirled, and then
    drowned,
So the race swept the horses till they glimmered the ground.

Charles looked at those horses, and speedily guesst
That the roan horse, Red Ember, was one of the best;
He was level and easy, not turning a hair,
But with power all ready when his rider should care,
And he leaped like a lover and his coat still did shine.
Charles thought, "He's a wonder, and he's twelve lengths from
    mine."

There were others still in it, according to looks:—
Sir Lopez, and Soyland, and Peterkinooks,
Counter Vair and Gavotte, all with plenty to spend;
Then Monkery worn, and The Ghost at his end.
But the roan horse, Red Ember, seemed playing a game.
Charles thought, "He's the winner; he can run us all tame."
The wind brought a tune and a faint noise of cheers,
Right Royal coquetted and cocked up his ears.

Charles saw his horse gaining; the going increased;
His touch on the mouth felt the soul of the beast,

And the heave of each muscle and the look of his eye
Said, "I'll come to those horses, and pass them, or die."

Like a thing in a dream the grey buildings drew nearer,
The babble rose louder and the organ's whine clearer,
The hurdle came closer, he rushed through its top
Like a comet in heaven that nothing can stop.

Then they strode the green grass for the Lost Lady's grave,
And Charles felt Right Royal rise up like a wave,
Like a wave far to seaward that lifts in a line
And advances to shoreward in a slipping incline,

And climbs, and comes toppling, and advances in glory,
Mounting inwards, marching onwards, with his shoulders all
hoary,
Sweeping shorewards with a shouting to burst on the sand,
So Right Royal sent meaning through the rein in each hand.

Charles felt like a captain whose ship has long chased
Some ship better handled, better manned, better placed,
And has all day beheld her, that ship of his dream,
Bowing swanlike beyond him up a blue hill of gleam,

Yet, at dark, the wind rising makes his rival strike sail
While his own ship crowds canvas and comes within hail;
Till he see her, his rival, snouting into the grey,
Like a sea-rock in winter that stands and breaks spray,
And by lamplight goes past her in a roaring of song
Shouting, "Let fall your royals: stretch the halliards along!"

Now The Ghost dropped behind him, now his horses drew close.
Charles watched them, in praying, while his hopes rose and rose,
"O God, give me patience, give me luck, give me skill,
For he's going so grandly I think that he will."

They went at Lost Lady's like Severn at flood,
With an urging of horses and a squelching of mud;
By the hot flanks of horses the toppings were bruised,
And Syringa the manless swerved right and refused.

Swerved right on a sudden, as none could expect,
Straight into Right Royal, who slithered and pecked,
Though Charles held him up and got safely across,
He was round his nag's neck within touch of a toss

He gat to his saddle, he never knew how;
What hope he had had was knocked out of him now,
But his courage came back as his terror declined,
He spoke to Right Royal and made up his mind.
He judged the lengths lost and the chance that remained,
And he followed his field, and he gained, and he gained.

He watched them, those horses, so splendid, so swift,
Whirled down the green roadway like leaves in the lift:
Now he measured their mettle, and said with a moan,
"They can beat me, Lord help me, though they give me a stone.
Red Ember's a wonder, and Soyland's the same,
And Gavotte there's a beauty, and she goes like a flame;
But Peterkinooks, that I used to despise,
Is the horse that must win if his looks are not lies."

Their bright colours flitted as at dusk in Brazil
Bright birds reach the tree-tops when the land wind falls still,
When the sky is all scarlet on the tops of the treen
Comes a whirl of birds flying, blue and orange and green.

As a whirl of notes running in a fugue that men play,
And the thundering follows as the pipe flits away,
And the laughter comes after and the hautboys begin,
So they ran at the hurdle and scattered the whin.

As they leaped to the race-course the sun burst from cloud
And like tumult in dream came the roar of the crowd.

For to right and to left, now, were crowded men yelling,
And a great cry boomed backward like muffled bells knelling,
And a surge of men running seemed to follow the race,
The horses all trembled and quickened their pace.

As the porpoise, grown weary of his rush through the dim
Of the unlitten silence where the swiftnesses swim,
Learns at sudden the tumult of a clipper bound home
And exults with this playmate and leaps in her foam,

Or as nightingales coming into England in May,
Coming songless at sunset, being worn with the way,
Settle spent in the twilight, drooping head under wing,
Yet are glad when the dark comes, while at moonrise they sing;

Or as fire on a hillside, by happy boys kindled,
That has burnt black a heath-tuft, scorcht a bramble, and
    dwindled,
Blown by wind yet arises in a wave of flogged flame,
So the souls of those horses to the testing time came.

Now they closed on their leaders, and the running increased,
They rushed down the arc curving round to the east;
All the air rang with roaring, all the peopled loud stands
Roared aloud from tense faces, shook with hats and waved
    hands.

So they cleared the green gorse-bush by bursting it through,
There was no time for thinking, there was scarce time to do.
Charles gritted his spirit as he charged through the gorse:
"You must just grin and suffer: sit still on your horse."

There in front was a hurdle and the Distance Post white,
And the long, green, broad Straight washed with wind and blown bright;
Now the roaring had screaming, bringing names to their ears:
"Come, Soyland!" "Sir Lopez!" Then catcalls; then cheers.

"Sir Lopez! Sir Lopez!" then the jigging brass laughter
From the yellow tost swing-boats swooping rafter to rafter.
Then the blare of all organs, then the roar of all throats,
And they shot past the side shows, the horses and boats.

Now the Wants of the Watchers whirled into the race
Like flames in their fury, like men in the face,
Mad-red from the Wanting that made them alive,
They fought with those horses or helped them to strive.

Like leaves blown on Hudson when maples turn gold,
They whirled in their colour, they clutched to catch hold,
They sang to the riders, they smote at their hearts
Like flakes of live fire, like castings of darts.

As a snow in Wisconsin when the darkness comes down,
Running white on the prairie, making all the air brown,
Blinding men with the hurry of its millions of feet,
So the Wants pelted on them, so they blinded and beat.

And like spirits calm shining upon horses of flame,
Came the Friends of those riders to shield them from shame,
White as fire white-burning, rushing each by his friend,
Singing songs of the glory of the world without end;

And as men in Wisconsin driving cars in the snow
Butt against its impulsion and face to the blow,
Tossing snow from their bonnets as a ship tosses foam,
So the Friends tossed the Wantings as they brought their friends home.

Now they charged the last hurdle that led to the Straight,
Charles longing to ride, though his spirit said "Wait."
He came to his horses as they came to the leap,
Eight hard-driven horses, eight men breathing deep.

On the left, as he leaped it, a flashing of brown
Kicking white on the grass, showed that Thankful was down;
Then a glance right and left showed, that barring all flukes,
It was Soyland's, Sir Lopez', or Peterkinooks'.

For Stormalong blundered and dwelt as he landed,
Counter Vair's man was beaten and Monkery stranded.
As he reached to Red Ember the man on the red
Cried, "Lord, Charlie Cothill, I thought you were dead!"

He passed the Red Ember, he came to the flank
Of Peterkinooks, whom he reached and then sank.
There were only two others, going level alone,
First the spotted cream jacket, then the blue, white and roan.

Up the street of green race-course they strained for the prize,
While the stands blurred with waving and the air shook with
cries:
"Now, Sir Lopez!" "Come, Soyland!" "Now, Sir Lopez!
Now, now!"
Then Charles judged his second, but he could not tell how.

But a glory of sureness leaped from horse into man,
And the man said, "Now, beauty," and the horse said, "I can."
And the long weary Royal made an effort the more,
Though his heart thumped like drum-beats as he went to the
fore.

Neck and neck went Sir Lopez and Soyland together,
Soyland first, a short head, with his neck all in lather;

Both were ridden their hardest, both were doing their best,
Right Royal reached Soyland and came to his chest.

There Soyland's man saw him with the heel of his eye,
A horse with an effort that could beat him or tie;
Then he glanced at Sir Lopez, and he bit through his lip,
And he drove in his spurs and he took up his whip.

There he lashed the game Soyland who had given his all,
And he gave three strides more, and then failed at the call,
And he dropped behind Royal like a leaf in a tide:
Then Sir Lopez and Royal ran on side by side.

There they looked at each other, and they rode, and were grim;
Charles thought, "That's Sir Lopez. I shall never beat him."
All the yells for Sir Lopez seemed to darken the air,
They were rushing past Emmy and the White Post was there.

He drew to Sir Lopez; but Sir Lopez drew clear;
Right Royal clung to him and crept to his ear.
Then the man on Sir Lopez judged the moment had come
For the last ounce of effort that would bring his horse home.

So he picked up his whip for three swift slashing blows,
And Sir Lopez drew clear, but Right Royal stuck close.
Charles sat still as stone, for he dared not to stir—
There was that in Right Royal that needed no spur.

In the trembling of an instant power leaped up within,
Royal's pride of high spirit not to let the bay win.
Up he went, past his withers, past his neck, to his head,
With Sir Lopez' man lashing, Charles still, seeing red.

So they rushed for one second, then Sir Lopez shot out:
Charles thought, "There, he's done me, without any doubt.

O come now, Right Royal!"
And Sir Lopez changed feet
And his ears went back level; Sir Lopez was beat.

Right Royal went past him, half an inch, half a head,
Half a neck, he was leading, for an instant he led;
Then a hooped black and coral flew up like a shot,
With a lightning-like effort from little Gavotte.

The little bright mare, made of nerves and steel springs,
Shot level beside him, shot ahead as with wings.
Charles felt his horse quicken, felt the desperate beat
Of the blood in his body from his knees to his feet.

Three terrible strides brought him up to the mare,
Then they rushed to wild shouting through a whirl of blown air;
Then Gavotte died to nothing; Soyland came once again
Till his muzzle just reached to the knot on his rein.

Then a whirl of urged horses thundered up, whipped and blown,
Soyland, Peterkinooks, and Red Ember the roan.
For an instant they challenged, then they drooped and were done;
Then the White Post shot backwards, Right Royal had won.

Won a half length from Soyland, Red Ember close third;
Fourth, Peterkinooks; fifth, Gavotte harshly spurred;
Sixth, Sir Lopez, whose rider said "Just at the Straight
He swerved at the hurdle and twisted a plate."

Then the numbers went up; then John Harding appeared
To lead in the Winner while the bookmakers cheered.
Then the riders weighed-in, and the meeting was over,
And bright Emmy Crowthorne could go with her lover.

For the bets on Right Royal which Cothill had made
The taker defaulted, they never were paid;
The taker went West, whence he sent Charles's bride
Silver bit-cups and beadwork on antelope hide.

Charles married his lady, but he rode no more races;
He lives on the Downland on the blown grassy places,
Where he and Right Royal can canter for hours
On the flock-bitten turf full of tiny blue flowers.

There the Roman pitcht camp, there the Saxon kept sheep,
There he lives out this Living that no man can keep,
That is manful but a moment before it must pass,
Like the stars sweeping westward, like the wind on the grass.

KING COLE

King Cole was King before the troubles came,
The land was happy while he held the helm,
The valley-land from Condicote to Thame,
Watered by Thames and green with many an elm.
For many a year he governed well his realm,
So well-beloved, that, when at last he died,
It was bereavement to the countryside.

So good, so well-beloved, had he been
In life, that when he reached the judging-place
(There where the scales are even, the sword keen),
The Acquitting Judges granted him a grace,
Aught he might choose, red, black, from king to ace,
Beneath the bright arch of the heaven's span;
He chose, to wander earth, the friend of man.

So, since that time, he wanders shore and shire,
An old, poor, wandering man, with glittering eyes
Helping distressful folk to their desire
By power of spirit that within him lies.
Gentle he is, and quiet, and most wise,
He wears a ragged grey, he sings sweet words,
And where he walks there flutter little birds.

And when the planets glow as dusk begins
He pipes a wooden flute to music old.
Men hear him on the downs, in lonely inns,
In valley woods, or up the Chiltern wold;
His piping feeds the starved and warms the cold,
It gives the beaten courage; to the lost
It brings back faith, that lodestar of the ghost.

And most he haunts the beech-tree-pasturing chalk,
The Downs and Chilterns with the Thames between.
There still the Berkshire shepherds see him walk,
Searching the unhelped woe with instinct keen,
His old hat stuck with never-withering green,
His flute in poke, and little singings sweet
Coming from birds that flutter at his feet.

Not long ago a circus wandered there,
Where good King Cole most haunts the public way,
Coming from Reading for St. Giles's Fair
Through rain unceasing since Augustine's Day;
The horses spent, the waggons splashed with clay,
The men with heads bowed to the wester roaring,
Heaving the van-wheels up the hill at Goring.

Wearily plodding up the hill they went,
Broken by bitter weather and the luck;
Six vans, and one long waggon with the tent,
And piebald horses following in the muck,
Dragging their tired hooves out with a suck,
And heaving on, like some defeated tribe
Bound for Despair with Death upon their kibe.

All through the morn the circus floundered thus,
The nooning found them at the Crossing Roads,
Stopped by an axle splitting in its truss.
The horses drooped and stared before their loads.
Dark with the wet they were, and cold as toads.
The men were busy with the foundered van,
The showman stood apart, a beaten man.

He did not heed the dripping of the rain,
Nor the wood's roaring, nor the blotted hill,
He stood apart and bit upon his pain,

Biting the bitter meal with bitter will.
Focussed upon himself, he stood, stock still,
Staring unseeing, while his mind repeated,
"This is the end; I'm ruined; I'm defeated."

From time to time a haggard woman's face
Peered at him from a van, and then withdrew;
Seeds from the hayrack blew about the place,
The smoke out of the waggon chimneys blew,
From wicker creel the skinny cockerel crew.
The men who set the floundered axle straight
Glanced at their chief, and each man nudged his mate.

And one, the second clown, a snub-nosed youth,
Fair-haired, with broken teeth, discolored black,
Muttered, "He looks a treat, and that's the truth.
I've had enough: I've given him the sack."
He took his wrench, arose, and stretched his back,
Swore at a piebald pony trying to bite,
And rolled a cigarette and begged a light.

Within, the second's wife, who leaped the hoops,
Nursed sour twins, her son and jealousy,
Thinking of love, in luckier, happier troupes
Known on the roads in summers now gone by
Before her husband had a roving eye,
Before the rat-eyed baggage with red hair
Came to do tight-rope and make trouble there.

Beside the vans, the clown, old Circus John,
Growled to the juggler as he sucked his briar,
"How all the marrow of a show was gone
Since women came, to sing and walk the wire,
Killing the clown his act for half his hire,

Killing the circus trade: because," said he,
"Horses and us are what men want to see."

The juggler was a young man shaven clean,
Even in the mud his dainty way he had,
Red-cheeked, with eyes like boxer's, quick and keen,
A jockey-looking youth with legs besprad,
Humming in baritone a ditty sad,
And tapping on his teeth his finger-nails,
The while the clown suckt pipe and spat his tales.

Molly, the singer, watched him wearily
With big black eyes that love had brimmed with tears,
Her mop of short cut hair was blown awry,
Her firm mouth shewed her wiser than her years.
She stroked a piebald horse and pulled his ears,
And kissed his muzzle, while her eyes betrayed
This, that she loved the juggler, not the jade.

And growling in a group the music stood
Sucking short pipes, their backs against the rain,
Plotting rebellion in a bitter mood,
"A shilling more, or never play again."
Their old greatcoats were foul with many a stain,
Weather and living rough had stamped their faces,
They were cast clerks, old sailors, old hard cases.

Within the cowboy's van the rat-eyed wife,
Her reddish hair in papers twisted close,
Turned wet potatoes round against the knife,
And in a bucket dropped the peelèd Oes.
Her little girl was howling from her blows.
The cowboy smoked and with a spanner whackt
The metal target of his shooting act.

And in another van more children cried
From being beaten or for being chid
By fathers cross or mothers haggard-eyed,
Made savage by the fortunes that betide.
The rain dripped from the waggons: the drops glid
Along the pony's flanks; the thick boots stamped
The running muck for warmth, and hope was damped.

Yet all of that small troupe in misery stuck,
Were there by virtue of their nature's choosing
To be themselves and take the season's luck,
Counting the being artists worth the bruising.
To be themselves, as artists, even if losing
Wealth, comfort, health, in doing as they chose,
Alone of all life's ways brought peace to those.

So there below the forlorn woods, they grumbled,
Stamping for warmth and shaking off the rain.
Under the foundered van the tinkers fumbled,
Fishing the splitted truss with wedge and chain.
Soon, all was done, the van could go again,
Men cracked their whips, the horses' shoulders forged
Up to the collar while the mud disgorged.

So with a jangling of their chains they went,
Lean horses, swaying vans and creaking wheels,
Bright raindrops tilting off the van roof pent
And reedy cockerels crying in the creels,
Smoke driving down, men's shouts and children's squeals,
Whips cracking, and the hayrack sheddings blowing;
The Showman stood aside to watch them going.

What with the rain and misery making mad,
The Showman never saw a stranger come

Till there he stood, a stranger roughly clad
In ragged grey of woolen spun at home.
Green sprigs were in his hat, and other some
Stuck in his coat; he bore a wooden flute,
And redbreasts hopped and carolled at his foot.

It was King Cole, who smiled and spoke to him.

KING COLE: The mend will hold until you reach a wright.
Where do you play?
THE SHOWMAN: In Wallingford to-night.
KING COLE: There are great doings there.
THE SHOWMAN: I know of none.
KING COLE: The Prince will lay the Hall's foundation stone
This afternoon: he and the Queen are there.
THE SHOWMAN: Lord, keep this showman patient, lest he swear.
KING COLE: Why should you swear? Be glad; your town is filled.
THE SHOWMAN: What use are crowds to me with business killed?
KING COLE: I see no cause for business to be crosst.
THE SHOWMAN: Counter-attractions, man, at public cost.
Fireworks, dancing, bonfires, soldiers, speeches.
In all my tour along the river's reaches
I've had ill-luck: I've clashed with public feasts.
At Wycombe fair, we met performing beasts,
At Henley, waxworks, and at Maidenhead
The Psyche woman talking with the dead.
At Bray, we met the rain, at Reading, flood,
At Pangbourne, politics, at Goring, mud.
Now here, at Wallingford, the Royal Pair.
Counter-attraction killing everywhere,
Killing a circus dead: God give me peace;

If this be living, death will be release.
By God, it brims the cup; it fills the can.
What trade are you?

KING COLE: I am a wandering man.

THE SHOWMAN: You mean, a tramp who flutes for bread and pence?

KING COLE: I come, and flute, and then I wander thence.

THE SHOWMAN: Quicksilver Tom, who couldn't keep his place.

KING COLE: My race being run, I love to watch the race.

THE SHOWMAN: You ought to seek your rest.

KING COLE: My rest is this,
The world of men, wherever trouble is.

THE SHOWMAN: If trouble rests you, God! your life is rest.

KING COLE: Even the sun keeps moving, east to west.

THE SHOWMAN: Little he gets by moving; less than I.

KING COLE: He sees the great green world go floating by.

THE SHOWMAN: A sorry sight to see, when all is said. Why don't you set to work?

KING COLE: I have no trade.

THE SHOWMAN: Where is your home?

KING COLE: All gone, a long time past.

THE SHOWMAN: Your children then?

KING COLE: All dead, sir, even the last.
I am a lonely man; no kith nor kin.

THE SHOWMAN: There is no joy in life when deaths begin,
I know it, I. How long is't since you ate?

KING COLE: It was so long ago that I forget.

THE SHOWMAN: The proverb says a man can always find
One sorrier than himself in state and mind.
'Fore George, it's true. Well, come, then, to the van.
Jane, can you find a meal for this poor man?

"Yes," said his wife. "Thank God, we still are able
To help a friend; come in, and sit to table."

"Come," said her man, "I'll help you up aboard,
I'll save your legs as far as Wallingford."

They climbed aboard and sat; the woman spread
Food for King Cole, and watched him as he fed.
Tears trickled down her cheeks and much she sighed.
"My son," she said, "like you, is wandering wide,
I know not where; a beggar in the street,
(For all I know) without a crust to eat.
He never could abide the circus life."

THE SHOWMAN: It was my fault, I always tell my wife,
I put too great constraint upon his will;
Things would be changed if he were with us still.
I ought not to have forced him to the trade.

KING COLE: "A forced thing finds a vent," my father said;
And yet a quickening tells me that your son
Is not far from you now; for I am one
Who feels these things, like comfort in the heart.

The couple watched King Cole and shrank apart,
For brightness covered him with glittering.
"Tell me your present troubles," said the King,
"For you are worn. What sorrow makes you sad?"

THE SHOWMAN: Why, nothing, sir, except that times are bad,
Rain all the season through, and empty tents,
And nothing earned for stock or winter rents.
My wife there, ill, poor soul, from very grief,
And now no hope nor prospect of relief;
The season's done, and we're as we began.

Now one can bear one's troubles, being a man,
But what I cannot bear is loss of friends.

This troupe will scatter when the season ends:
My clown is going, and the Tricksey Three
Who juggle and do turns, have split with me;
And now, to-day, my wife's too ill to dance,
And all my music ask for an advance.
There must be poison in a man's distress
That makes him mad and people like him less.

Well, men are men. But what I cannot bear
Is my poor Bet, my piebald Talking Mare,
Gone curby in her hocks from standing up.
That's the last drop that overfills the cup.
My Bet's been like a Christian friend for years.

KING COLE: Now courage, friend, no good can come from tears.
I know a treatment for a curby hock
Good both for inward sprain or outward knock.
Here's the receipt; it's sure as flowers in spring;
A certain cure, the Ointment of the King.

That cures your mare; your troubles Time will right;
A man's ill-fortune passes like the night.
Times are already mending at their worst;
Think of Spent Simmy when his roof-beam burst.
His ruined roof fell on him in a rain
Of hidden gold that built it up again.
So, courage, and believe God's providence.
Lo, here, the city shining like new pence,
To welcome you; the Prince is lodging there.
Lo, you, the banners flying like a fair.
Your circus will be crowded twenty deep.
This city is a field for you to reap,

For thousands must have come to see the Prince,
And all are here, all wanting fun.
And since
The grass was green, all men have loved a show.
Success is here, so let your trouble go.

THE SHOWMAN: Well, blessings on your heart for speaking so;
It may be that the tide will turn at last.
But royal tours have crossed me in the past
And killed my show, and maybe will again.
One hopes for little after months of rain,
And the little that one hopes one does not get.

THE WIFE: Look, Will, the city gates with sentries set.

THE SHOWMAN: It looks to me as if the road were barred.

KING COLE: They are some soldiers of the bodyguard.
I hope, the heralds of your fortune's change.

"Now take this frowsy circus off the range,"
The soldiers at the city entrance cried;
"Keep clear the town, you cannot pass inside,
The Prince is here, with other things to do
Than stare at gangs of strollers such as you."

THE SHOWMAN: But I am billed to play here; and must play.

THE SOLDIERS: No must at all. You cannot play to-day,
Nor pitch your tents within the city bound.

THE SHOWMAN: Where can I, then?

THE SOLDIERS: Go, find some other ground.

A POLICEMAN: Pass through the city. You can pitch and play
One mile beyond it, after five to-day.

THE SHOWMAN: One mile beyond, what use is that to me?

A POLICEMAN: Those are the rules, here printed, you can see.

THE SHOWMAN: But let me see the Mayor, to make sure.

THE SOLDIERS: These are his printed orders, all secure.
Pass through or back, you must not linger here,
Blocking the road with all this circus gear.

Which will you do, then: back or pass along?

THE SHOWMAN: Pass.

THE SOLDIERS: Then away, and save your breath for song,
We cannot bother with your right and wrong.
George, guide these waggons through the western gate.
Now, march, d'ye hear? and do not stop to bait
This side a mile; for that's the order. March!

The Showman toppled like a broken arch.
The line-squall roared upon them with loud lips.

A green-lit strangeness followed, like eclipse

They passed within, but, when within, King Cole
Slipped from the van to head the leading team.
He breathed into his flute his very soul,
A noise like waters in a pebbly stream,
And straight the spirits that inhabit dream
Came round him, and the rain-squall roared its last,
And bright the wind-vane shifted as it passed.

And in the rush of sun and glittering cloud
That followed on the storm, he led the way,
Fluting the sodden circus through the crowd
That trod the city streets in holiday.
And lo, a marvellous thing, the gouted clay,
Splashed on the waggons and the horses, glowed,
They shone like embers as they trod the road.
And round the tired horses came the Powers
That stir men's spirits, waking or asleep,
To thoughts like planets and to acts like flowers,
Out of the inner wisdom's beauty deep:
These led the horses, and, as marshalled sheep
Fronting a dog, in line, the people stared
At those bright waggons led by the bright-haired.

And, as they marched, the spirits sang, and all
The horses crested to the tune and stept
Like centaurs to a passionate festival
With shining throats that mantling criniers swept.
And all the hearts of all the watchers leapt
To see those horses passing and to hear
That song that came like blessing to the ear.

And, to the crowd, the circus artists seemed
Splendid, because the while that singing quired
Each artist was the part that he had dreamed
And glittered with the Power he desired,
Women and men, no longer wet or tired
From long despair, now shone like queens and kings,
There they were crowned with their imaginings.

And with them, walking by the vans, there came
The wild things from the woodland and the mead,
The red stag, with his tender-stepping dame,
Branched, and high-tongued and ever taking heed.
Nose-wrinkling rabbits nibbling at the weed,
The hares that box by moonlight on the hill,
The bright trout's death, the otter from the mill.

There, with his mask made virtuous, came the fox,
Talking of landscape while he thought of meat;
Blood-loving weasels, honey-harrying brocks,
Stoats, and the mice that build among the wheat,
Dormice, and moles with little hands for feet,
The water-rat that gnaws the yellow flag,
Toads from the stone and merrows from the quag.

And over them flew birds of every kind,
Whose way, or song, or speed, or beauty brings
Delight and understanding to the mind;

The bright-eyed, feathery, thready-leggéd things.
There they, too, sang amid a rush of wings,
With sweet, clear cries and gleams from wing and crest,
Blue, scarlet, white, gold plume and speckled breast.

And all the vans seemed grown with living leaves
And living flowers, the best September knows,
Moist poppies scarlet from the Hilcote sheaves,
Green-fingered bine that runs the barley-rows,
Pale candylips, and those intense blue blows
That trail the porches in the autumn dusk,
Tempting the noiseless moth to tongue their musk.

So, tired thus, so tended, and so sung,
They crossed the city through the marvelling crowd.
Maids with wide eyes from upper windows hung,
The children waved their toys and sang aloud.
But in his van the beaten showman bowed
His head upon his hands, and wept, not knowing
Aught of what passed except that wind was blowing.

All through the town the fluting led them on,
But near the western gate King Cole retired;
And, as he ceased, the vans no longer shone,
The bright procession dimmed like lamps expired;
Again with muddy vans and horses tired,
And artists cross and women out of luck,
The sodden circus plodded through the muck.

The crowd of following children loitered home;
Maids shut the windows lest more rain should come;
The circus left the streets of flowers and flags,
King Cole walked with it, huddling in his rags.
They reached the western gate and sought to pass.

"Take back this frowsy show to where it was,"
The sergeant of the gateway-sentry cried;
"You know quite well you cannot pass outside."

THE SHOWMAN: But we were told to pass here, by the guard.
THE SERGEANT: Here are the printed orders on the card.
No traffic, you can read. Clear out.
THE SHOWMAN: But where?
THE SERGEANT: Where you're not kicked from, or there's room to spare.
Go back and out of town the way you came.
THE SHOWMAN: I've just been sent from there. Is this a game?
THE SERGEANT: You'll find it none, my son, if that's your tone.
THE SHOWMAN: You redcoats; ev'n your boots are not your own.
THE SERGEANT: No, they're the Queen's; I represent the Queen.
THE SHOWMAN: Pipeclay your week's accounts, you red marine.
THE SERGEANT: Thank you, I will. Now vanish. Right-about.
THE SHOWMAN: Right, kick the circus in or kick it out,
But kick us, kick us hard, we've got no friends,
We've no Queen's boots or busbies on our ends;
We're poor, we like it, no one cares; besides
These dirty artists ought to have thick hides.
The dust, like us, is fit for boots to stamp,
None but Queen's redcoats are allowed to camp
In this free country.
A POLICEMAN: What's the trouble here?
THE SHOWMAN: A redcoat dog, in need of a thick ear.
THE POLICEMAN: The show turned back? No, sergeant, let them through.
They can't turn back, because the Prince is due.
Best let them pass.
THE SERGEANT: Then pass· and read the rules
Another time.

THE SHOWMAN: You fat, red-coated fools.
THE POLICEMAN: Pass right along.

They passed. Beyond the town
A farmer gave them leave to settle down
In a green field beside the Oxford road.
There the spent horses ceased to drag the load;
The tent was pitched beneath a dropping sky,
The green-striped tent with all its gear awry.
The men drew close to grumble: in the van
The showman parted from the wandering man.

THE SHOWMAN: You see; denied a chance; denied bare bread.
KING COLE: I know the stony road that artists tread.
THE SHOWMAN: You take it very mildly, if you do
How would you act if this were done to you?
KING COLE: Go to the Mayor.
THE SHOWMAN: I am not that kind,
I'll kneel to no Court prop with painted rind.
You and your snivelling to them may go hang.
I say: "God curse the Prince and all his gang."
THE WIFE: Ah, no, my dear, for Life hurts everyone,
Without our cursing. Let the poor Prince be;
We artist folk are happier folk than he,
Hard as it is.
THE SHOWMAN: I say: God let him see
And taste and know this misery that he makes.
He strains a poor man's spirit till it breaks,
And then he hangs him, while a poor man's gift
He leaves unhelped, to wither or to drift.
Sergeants at city gates are all his care.
We are but outcast artists in despair.
They dress in scarlet and he gives them gold.
KING COLE: Trust still to Life, the day is not yet old.
THE SHOWMAN: By God! our lives are all we have to trust.

KING COLE: Life changes every day and ever must.
THE SHOWMAN: It has not changed with us, this season, yet.
KING COLE: Life is as just as Death; Life pays its debt.
THE SHOWMAN: What justice is there in our suffering so?
KING COLE: This: that not knowing, we should try to know.
THE SHOWMAN: Try. A sweet doctrine for a broken heart.
KING COLE: The best (men say) in every manly part.
THE SHOWMAN: Is it, by Heaven? I have tried it, I.
I tell you, friend, your justice is a lie;
Your comfort is a lie, your peace a fraud;
Your trust a folly and your cheer a gaud.
I know what men are, having gone these roads.
Poor bankrupt devils, sweating under loads
While others suck their blood and smile and smile.
You be an artist on the roads a while,
You'll know what justice comes with suffering then.
KING COLE: Friend, I am one grown old with sorrowing men.
THE SHOWMAN: The old are tamed, they have not blood to feel.
KING COLE: They've blood to hurt, if not enough to heal.
I have seen sorrow close and suffering close.
I know their ways with men, if any knows.
I know the harshness of the way they have
To loose the base and prison up the brave.
I know that some have found the depth they trod
In deepest sorrow is the heart of God.
Up on the bitter iron there is peace.

In the dark night of prison comes release,
In the black midnight still the cock will crow.
There is a help that the abandoned know
Deep in the heart, that conquerors cannot feel.

Abide in hope the turning of the wheel,
The luck will alter and the star will rise.

His presence seemed to change before their eyes.
The old, bent, ragged, glittering, wandering fellow,
With thready blood-streaks in the rided yellow
Of cheek and eye, seemed changed to one who held
Earth and the spirit like a king of eld.
He spoke again: "You have been kind," said he.
"In your own trouble you have thought of me.
God will repay. To him who gives is given,
Corn, water, wine, the world, the starry heaven."

Then, like a poor old man, he took his way
Back to the city, while the showman gazed
After his figure like a man amazed.

THE WIFE: I think that traveller was an angel sent.
THE SHOWMAN: A most strange man. I wonder what he meant.
THE WIFE: Comfort was what he meant, in our distress.
THE SHOWMAN: No words of his can make our trouble less.
THE WIFE: O, Will, he made me feel the luck would change.
Look at him, husband; there is something strange
About him there; a robin redbreast comes
Hopping about his feet as though for crumbs,
And little long-tailed tits and wrens that sing
Perching upon him.
THE SHOWMAN: What a wondrous thing!
I've read of such, but never seen it.
THE WIFE: Look,
These were the dishes and the food he took.
THE SHOWMAN: Yes: those were they. What of it?
THE WIFE: Did he eat?

THE SHOWMAN: Yes; bread and cheese; he would not touch the meat.
THE WIFE: But see, the cheese is whole, the loaf unbroken,
And both are fresh. And see, another token:—
Those hard green apples that the farmer gave
Have grown to these gold globes, like Blenheims brave;
And look, how came these plums of Pershore here?
THE SHOWMAN: We have been sitting with a saint, my dear.
THE WIFE. Look at the butterflies!
Like floating flowers
Came butterflies, the souls of summer hours,
Fluttering about the van; Red Admirals rich,
Scarlet and pale on breathing speeds of pitch,
Brimstones, like yellow poppy petals blown,
Brown ox-eyed Peacocks in their purpled roan,
Blue, silvered things that haunt the grassy chalk,
Green Hairstreaks bright as green shoots on a stalk,
And that dark prince, the oakwood haunting thing
Dyed with blue burnish like the mallard's wing.
"He was a saint of God," the showman cried.

Meanwhile, within the town, from man to man
The talk about the wondrous circus ran.
All were agreed, that nothing ever known
Had thrilled so tense the marrow in their bone.
All were agreed, that sights so beautiful
Made the Queen's court with all its soldiers dull,
Made all the red-wrapped masts and papered strings
Seem fruit of death, not lovely living things.
And some said loudly that though time were short,
Men still might hire the circus for the Court.
And some, agreeing, sought the Mayor's hall,
To press petition for the show's recall.

But as they neared the hall, behold, there came
A stranger to them dressed as though in flame;
An old, thin, grinning glitterer, decked with green,
With thready blood-streaks in his visage lean,
And at his wrinkled eyes a look of mirth
Not common among men who walk the earth;
Yet from his pocket poked a flute of wood,
And little birds were following him for food.

"Sirs," said King Cole (for it was he), "I know
You seek the Mayor, but you need not so;
I have this moment spoken with his grace.
He grants the circus warrant to take place
Within the city, should the Prince see fit
To watch such pastime; here is his permit.
I go this instant to the Prince to learn
His wish herein: wait here till I return."

They waited while the old man passed the sentry
Beside the door, and vanished through the entry.
They thought, "This old man shining like New Spain,
Must be the Prince's lordly chamberlain.
His cloth of gold so shone, it seemed to burn;
Wait till he comes." They stayed for his return.

Meanwhile, above, the Prince stood still to bide
The nightly mercy of the eventide,
Brought nearer by each hour that chimed and ceased.
His head was weary with the city feast
But newly risen from. He stood alone
As heavy as the day's foundation stone.

The room he stood in was an ancient hall.
Portraits of long-dead men were on the wall.
From the dull crimson of their robes there stared

Passionless eyes, long dead, that judged and glared.
Above them were the oaken corbels set,
Of angels reaching hands that never met,
Where in the spring the swallows came to build.

It was the meeting chamber of the Guild.

From where he stood, the Prince could see a yard
Paved with old slabs and cobbles cracked and scarred
Where weeds had pushed, and tiles and broken glass
Had fallen and been trodden in the grass.
A gutter dripped upon it from the rain.

"It puts a crown of lead upon my brain
To live this life of princes," thought the Prince.
"To be a king is to be like a quince,
Bitter himself, yet flavour to the rest.
To be a cat among the hay were best;
There in the upper darkness of the loft,
With green eyes bright, soft-lying, purring soft,
Hearing the rain without; not forced, as I,
To lay foundation stones until I die,
Or sign State-papers till my hand is sick.
The man who plaits straw crowns upon a rick
Is happier in his crown than I, the King.
And yet, this day, a very marvellous thing
Came by me as I walked the chamber here.
Once in my childhood, in my seventh year,
I saw them come, and now they have returned,
Those strangers, riding upon cars that burned,
Or seemed to burn, with gold, while music thrilled,
Then beauty following till my heart was filled,
And life seemed peopled from eternity.

They brought down Beauty and Wisdom from the sky
Into the streets, those strangers; I could see

Beauty and Wisdom looking up at me
As then, in childhood, as they passed below.

Men would not let me know them long ago,
Those strangers bringing joy. They will not now.
I am a prince with gold about my brow;
Duty, not joy, is all a prince's share.

And yet, those strangers from I know not where,
From glittering lands, from unknown cities far
Beyond the sea-plunge of the evening star,
Would give me life, which princedom cannot give.
They would be revelation: I should live.
I may not deal with wisdom, being a king."

There came a noise of someone entering;
He turned his weary head to see who came.

It was King Cole, arrayed as though in flame,
Like a white opal, glowing from within,
He entered there in snowy cramoisin.
The Prince mistook him for a city lord,
He turned to him and waited for his word.

"Sir," said King Cole, "I come to bring you news.
Sir, in the weary life that princes use
There is scant time for any prince or king
To taste delights that artists have and bring.
But here, to-night, no other duty calls,
And circus artists are without the walls.
Will you not see them, sir?"

THE PRINCE: Who are these artists; do they paint or write?
KING COLE: No, but they serve the arts and love delight.
THE PRINCE: What can they do?

KING COLE: They know full many a rite
That holds the watcher spell-bound, and they know
Gay plays of ghosts and jokes of long ago;
And beauty of bright speed their horses bring,
Ridden barebacked at gallop round the ring
By girls who stand upon the racing team.
Jugglers they have, of whom the children dream,
Who pluck live rabbits from between their lips
And balance marbles on their finger-tips.
Will you not see them, sir? And then, they dance.

"Ay," said the Prince, "and thankful for the chance.
So thankful, that these bags of gold shall buy
Leave for all comers to be glad as I.

And yet, I know not if the Court permits.
King's pleasures must be sifted through the wits,
Or want of wit of many a courtly brain.
I get the less and chokings of the drain,
Not the bright rippling that I perish for."

KING COLE: Sir, I will open the forbidden door,
Which, opened, they will enter all in haste.
The life of man is stronger than good taste.
THE PRINCE: Custom is stronger than the life of man.
KING COLE: Custom is but a way that life began.
THE PRINCE: A withering way that makes the leafage fall,
Custom, like Winter, is the King of all.
KING COLE: Winter makes water solid, yet the Spring,
That is but flowers, is a stronger thing.
Custom, the ass man rides, will plod for years,
But laughter kills him and he dies at tears.

One word of love, one spark from beauty's fire,
And custom is a memory; listen, sire.

Then at a window looking on the street
He played his flute like leaves or snowflakes falling,
Till men and women, passing, thought: "How sweet;
These notes are in our hearts like flowers falling."
And then, they thought, "An unknown voice is calling
Like April calling to the seed in earth;
Madness is quickening deadness into birth."

And then, as in the spring when first men hear,
Beyond the black-twigged hedge, the lambling's cry
Coming across the snow, a note of cheer
Before the storm-cock tells that spring is nigh,
Before the first green bramble pushes shy,
And all the blood leaps at the lambling's notes,
The piping brought men's hearts into their throats.

Till all were stirred, however old and grand;
Generals bestarred, old statesmen, courtiers prim
(Whose lips kissed nothing but the Monarch's hand),
Stirred in their courtly minds recesses dim,
The sap of life stirred in the dreary limb.
The old eyes brightened o'er the pouncet-box,
Remembering loves, and brawls, and mains of cocks.

And through the town the liquid piping's gladness
Thrilled on its way, rejoicing all who heard,
To thrust aside their dullness or their sadness
And follow blithely as the fluting stirred
They hurried to the guild like horses spurred.
There in the road they mustered to await,
They knew not what, a dream, a joy, a fate.

And man to man in exaltation cried:
"Something has come to make us young again.
Wisdom has come, and Beauty, Wisdom's bride,
And youth like flowering April after rain."
But still the fluting piped and men were fain
To sing and ring the bells, they knew not why
Save that their hearts were in an ecstasy.

Then to the balcony above them came
King Cole, the shining, in his robe of flame;
Behind him came the Prince, who smiled and bowed.
King Cole made silence: then addressed the crowd.

"Friends, fellow mortals, bearers of the ghost
That burns, and breaks its lamp, but is not lost.
This day, for one brief hour, a key is given
To all, however poor, to enter heaven.
The Bringers-down of Beauty from the stars,
Have reached this city in their golden cars.
They ask, to bring you beauty, if you will.
You do not answer: rightly, you are still.
But you will come, to watch the image move
Of all you dreamed or had the strength to love.

Come to the Ring, the image of the path
That this our planet through the Heaven hath;
Behold man's skill, man's wisdom, man's delight,
And woman's beauty, imaged to the height.

Come, for our rulers come; and Death, whose feet
Tread at the door, permits a minute's sweet;
To each man's soul vouchsafes a glimpse, a gleam,
A touch, a breath of his intensest dream.
Now, to that glimpse, that moment, come with me;
Our rulers come.

O brother let there be
Such welcome to our Prince as never was.
Let there be flowers under foot, not grass,
Flowers and scented rushes and the sprays
Of purple bramble reddening into blaze.
Let there be bells rung backward till the tune
Be as the joy of all the bees in June.
Let float your flags, and let your lanterns rise
Like fruit upon the trees in Paradise,
In many-coloured lights as rich as Rome
O'er road and tent; and let the children come,
It is their world, these Beauty Dwellers bring."

Then, like the song of all the birds of spring
He played his flute, and all who heard it cried,
"Strew flowers before our rulers to the Ring."
The courtiers hurried for their coats of pride.
The upturned faces in that market wide
Glowed in the sunset to a beauty grave
Such as the faces of immortals have.

And work was laid aside on desk and bench,
The red-lined ledger summed no penny more,
From lamp-blacked fingers the mechanic's wrench
Dropped to the kinking wheel chains on the floor,
The farmer shut the hen roost: at the store
The boys put up the shutters and ran hooting
Wild with delight in freedom to the fluting.

And now the fluting led that gathered tide
Of men and women forward through the town,
And flowers seemed to fall from every side,
White starry blossoms such as brooks bow down,
White petals clinging in the hair and gown;

And those who marched there thought that starry flowers
Grew at their sides, as though the streets were bowers.

And all, in marching, thought, "We go to see
Life, not the daily coil, but as it is
Lived in its beauty in eternity,
Above base aim, beyond our miseries;
Life that is speed and colour and bright bliss,
And beauty seen and strained for, and possest
Even as a star forever in the breast."

The fluting led them through the western gate,
From many a tossing torch their faces glowed,
Bright-eyed and ruddy-featured and elate;
They sang and scattered flowers upon the road,
Still in their hair the starry blossoms snowed;
They saw ahead the green-striped tent, their mark,
Lit now and busy in the gathering dark.

There at the vans and in the green-striped tent
The circus artists growled their discontent.
Close to the gate a lighted van there was;
The showman's wife thrust back its window glass.
And leaned her head without to see who came
To buy a ticket for the evening's game.

A roll of tickets and a plate of pence
(For change) lay by her as she leaned from thence.
She heard the crowd afar, but in her thought
She said: "That's in the city; it is nought.
They glorify the Queen."

Though sick at heart
She wore her spangles for her evening's part,
To dance upon the barebacked horse and sing.

Green velvet was her dress, with tinselling.
Her sad, worn face had all the nobleness
That lovely spirits gather from distress.

"No one to-night," she thought, "no one to-night."

Within the tent, a flare gave blowing light.
There, in their scarlet cart, the bandsmen tuned
Bugles that whinnied, flageolets that crooned
And strings that whined and grunted.

Near the band
Piebald and magpie horses stood at hand
Nosing at grass beneath the green-striped dome
While men caressed them with the curry-comb.

The clowns, with whited, raddled faces, heaped
Old horse cloths round them to the chins; they peeped
Above the rugs; their cigarette ends' light
Showing black eyes, and scarlet smears and white.

They watched the empty benches, and the wry
Green curtain door which no one entered by.

Two little children entered and sat still
With bright wide-opened eyes that stared their fill,
And red lips round in wonder smeared with tints
From hands and handkerchiefs and peppermints.

A farm lad entered. That was all the house.

"Strike up the band to give the folk a rouse,"
The showman said, "They must be all outside."
He said it boldly, though he knew he lied.

Sad as a funeral march for pleasure gone
The band lamented out, "He's got them on."
Then paused, as usual, for the crowd to come.
Nobody came, though from without a hum
Of instruments and singing slowly rose.
"Free feast, with fireworks and public shows."
The bandsmen growled, "An empty house again.
Two children and a ploughboy and the rain.
And then a night march through the mud," they said.

Now to the gate, King Cole his piping played.
The showman's wife from out her window peering
Saw, in the road, a crowd with lanterns nearing,
And, just below her perch, a man who shone
As though white flame were his caparison;
One upon whom the great-eyed hawk-moths tense
Settled with feathery feet and quivering sense,
Till the white, gleaming robe seemed stuck with eyes.

It was the grinning glitterer, white and wise,
King Cole, who said, "Madam, the Court is here,
The Court, the Prince, the Queen, all drawing near,
We here, the vanguard, set them on their way.
They come intent to see your circus play.
They ask that all who wish may enter free,
And in their princely hope that this may be
They send you these plump bags of minted gold."
He gave a sack that she could scarcely hold.
She dropped it trembling, muttering thanks, and then
She cried: "O master, I must tell the men."

She rushed out of her van: she reached the Ring;
Called to her husband, "Will, the Queen and King,
Here at the very gate to see the show!"

"Light some more flares," said Will, "to make a glow.
'God save the Queen,' there, bandsmen; lively, boys.
Come on, 'God save our gracious'; make a noise.
Here, John, bring on the piebalds to the centre,
We'll have the horses kneeling as they enter."
All sang, and rushed. Without, the trumpets blared.

Now children, carrying paper lanterns, made
A glowing alley to the circus door;
Then others scattered flowers to pave a floor,
Along the highway leading from the town.

Rust-spotted bracken green they scattered down,
Blue cornflowers and withering poppies red,
Gold charlock, thrift, the purple hardihead,
Harebells, the milfoil white, September clover,
And boughs that berry red when summer's over,
All autumn flowers, with yellow ears of wheat.

Then with bruised, burning gums that made all sweet,
Came censer-bearing pages, and then came
Bearers in white with cressets full of flame,
Whose red tongues made the shadows dance like devils.
Then the blithe flutes that pipe men to the revels
Thrilled to the marrow softly as men marched.
Then, tossing leopard-skins from crests that arched,
The horses of the kettle-drummers stept.
Then with a glitter of bright steel there swept
The guard of knights, each pennon-bearer bold
Girt in a crimson cloak with spangs of gold.
Then came the Sword and Mace, and then the four
Long silver trumpets thrilling to the core
Of people's hearts their sound. Then two by two,
Proud in caparisons of kingly blue,
Bitted with bars of gold, in silver shod,

Treading like kings, cream-coloured stallions trod,
Dragging the carriage with the Prince and Queen.
The Corporation, walking, closed the scene.
Then came the crowd in-surging like the wave
That closes up the gash the clipper clave.

Swift in the path Their Majesties would tread
The showman flung green baize and turkey red.
Within the tent, with bunting, ropes and bags
They made a Royal Box festooned with flags,
Even as the Queen arrived, the work was done.
The seven piebald horses kneeled like one,
The bandsmen blew their best, while, red as beet,
The showman bowed his rulers to their seat.

Then, through the door, came courtiers wigged and starred;
The crimson glitterers of the bodyguard;
The ladies of the Court, broad-browed and noble,
Lovely as evening stars o'er seas in trouble;
The aldermen, in furs, with golden chains,
Old cottagers in smocks from country lanes,
Shepherds half dumb from silence on the down,
And merchants with their households from the town,
And, in the front, two rows of eager-hearted
Children with shining eyes and red lips parted.

Even as the creeping waves that brim the pool
One following other filled the circus full.

The showman stood beside his trembling wife.
"Never," he said, "in all our travelling life
Has this old tent looked thus, the front seats full
With happy little children beautiful.
Then all this glorious Court, tier after tier!
O would our son, the wanderer, were here,
Then we'd die happy!"

Orders were called, steel clinked, and jewels shone,
The watchers climbed the banks and took their stands.

The circus artists shook each others' hands,
Their quarrels were forgotten and forgiven,
Old friendships were restored and sinners shriven.
"We find we cannot part from Will," they said.

And while they talked the juggler took the maid
Molly, the singer, to the hawthorn glade
Behind the green-striped tent, and told his love,
A wild delight, beyond her hope, enough
Beyond her dream to brim her eyes with tears.

Now came a ringing cry to march; and cheers
Rose from the crowd; the bright procession fared
Back to the city while the trumpets blared.

So the night ended, and the Court retired.
Back to the town the swaying torches reeked,
Within the green-striped tent the lights expired,
The dew dript from the canvas where it leaked.
Dark, in the showman's van, a cricket creaked,
But, near the waggons, fire was glowing red
On happy faces where the feast was spread.

Gladly they supped, those artists of the show;
Then by the perfect moon, together timed,
They struck the green-striped tent and laid it low,
Even as the quarter before midnight chimed.
Then putting-to the piebald nags, they climbed
Into their vans and slowly stole away
Along Blown Hilcote on the Icknield Way.

And as the rumbling of the waggons died
By Aston Tirrold and the Moretons twain,

With axle-clatter in the countryside,
Lit by the moon and fragrant from the rain,
King Cole moved softly in the Ring again,
Where now the owls and he were left alone:
The night was loud with water upon stone.

He watched the night; then taking up his flute,
He breathed a piping of this life of ours,
The half-seen prize, the difficult pursuit,
The passionate lusts that shut us in their towers,
The love that helps us on, the fear that lowers,
The pride that makes us and the pride that mars,
The beauty and the truth that are our stars.
And man, the marvellous thing, that in the dark
Works with his little strength to make a light,
His wit that strikes, his hope that tends, a spark,
His sorrow of soul in toil, that brings delight,
His friends, who make salt sweet and blackness bright,
His birth and growth and change; and death the wise,
His peace, that puts a hand upon his eyes.

All these his pipings breathed of, until twelve
Struck on the belfry tower with tremblings numb
(Such as will shudder in the axe's helve
When the head strikes) to tell his hour was come.
Out of the living world of Christendom
He dimmed like mist till one could scarcely note
The robins nestling to his old grey coat.

Dimmer he grew, yet still a glimmering stayed
Like light on cobwebs, but it dimmed and died.
Then there was naught but moonlight in the glade,
Moonlight and water and an owl that cried.
Far overhead a rush of birds' wings sighed,

From migrants going south until the spring.
The night seemed fanned by an immortal wing.

But where the juggler trudged beside his love
Each felt a touching from beyond our ken,
From that bright kingdom where the souls who strove,
Live now forever, helping living men.
And as they kissed each other; even then
Their brows seemed blessed, as though a hand unseen
Had crowned their loves with never-withering green.

THE DREAM OF DANIEL

Weary with many thoughts I went to bed,
And lay for hours staring at the night,
Thinking of all the millions of the dead
Who used man's flesh, as I, and loved the light,
Yet died, for all their power and delight,
For all their love, and never came again,
Never, for all our crying, all our pain.

There, through the open windows at my side,
I saw the stars, and all the tossing wood,
And, in the moonlight, mothy owls that cried,
Floating along the covert for their food.
The night was as a spirit that did brood
Upon the dead, those multitudes of death
That had such colour once and now are breath.

"And all this beauty of the world," I thought,
"This glory given by God, this life that teems,
What can we know of them? for life is nought,
A few short hours of blindness, shot by gleams,
A few short days of mastery of dreams
After long years of effort, then an end,
Then dust on good and bad, on foe and friend."

So, weary with the little time allowed
To use the power that takes so long to learn,
I sorrowed as I lay; now low, now loud
Came music from an hautboy and zithern.
The house was dark, and yet a light did burn
There where they played, and in the wainscotting
The mice that love the dark were junketting.

So, what with sorrow and the noise that seemed
Like voices speaking from the night's dark heart
To tell her secret in a tongue undreamed,
I fell into a dream and walked apart
Into the night (I thought) into the swart,
Thin, lightless air in which the planet rides;
I trod on dark air upward with swift strides.

Though in my dream I gloried as I trod
Because I knew that I was striding there
Far from this trouble to the peace of God
Where all things glow and beauty is made bare.
A dawning seemed beginning everywhere,
And then I came into a grassy place,
Where beauty of bright heart has quiet face.

Lovely it was, and there a castle stood
Mighty and fair, with golden turrets bright,
Crowned with gold vanes that swung at the wind's mood
Full many a hundred feet up in the light.
The walls were all i'-carven with delight
Like stone become alive. I entered in.
Smoke drifted by: I heard a violin.

And as I heard, it seemed, that long before
That music had crept ghostly to my hearing
Even as a ghost along the corridor
Beside dark panelled walls with portraits peering;
It crept into my brain, blessing and spearing
Out of the past, yet all I could recall
Was some dark room with firelight on the wall.

So, entering in, I crossed the mighty hall;
The volleying smoke from firewood blew about.
The wind-gusts stirred the hangings on the wall

So that the woven chivalry stood out
Wave-like and charging, putting all to rout
The evil things they fought with, men like beasts,
Wolf soldiers, tiger kings, hyena priests.

And, steadfast as though frozen, swords on hips,
Old armour stood at sentry with old spears
Clutched in steel gloves that glittered at the grips,
Yet housed the little mouse with pointed ears:
Old banners drooped above, frayed into tears
With age and moth that fret the soldier's glory.
I saw a swallow in the clerestory.

And always from their frames the eyes looked down
Of most intense souls painted in their joy,
Their great brows jewelled bright as by a crown
Of their own thoughts, that nothing can destroy,
Because pure thought is life without alloy,
Life's very essence from the flesh set free
A wonder and delight eternally.

And climbing up the stairs with arras hung,
I looked upon a court of old stones grey,
Where o'er a globe of gold a galleon swung
Creaking with age and showing the wind's way.
There, flattered to a smile, the barn cat lay
Tasting the sun with purrings drowsily
Sun-soaked, content, with drowsed green-slitted eye.

I did not know what power led me on
Save the all-living joy of what came next.
Down the dim passage, doors of glory shone,
Old panels glowed with many a carven text,
Old music came in strays, my mind was vext

With many a leaping thought; beyond each door
I thought to meet some friend, dead long before.

So on I went, and by my side, it seemed,
Paced a great bull, kept from me by a brook
Which lipped the grass about it as it streamed
Over the flagroots that the grayling shook;
Red-felled the bull was, and at times he took
Assayment of the red earth with his horn
And wreaked his rage upon the sod uptorn.

Yet when I looked was nothing but the arras
There at my side, with woven knights that glowed
In coloured silks the running stag to harass,
There was no stream, yet in my mind abode
The sense of both beside me as I strode,
And lovely faces leaned, and pictures came
Of water in a great sheet like a flame;

Water in terror like a great snow falling,
Like wool, like smoke, into a vast abysm,
With thunder of gods fighting and death calling,
And gleaming sunbeams splitted by the prism,
And cliffs that rose and eagles that took chrism
Even in the very seethe, and then a cave
Where at a fire I mocked me at the wave.

Mightily rose the cliffs; and mighty trees
Grew on them; and the caverns, channelled deep,
Cut through them like dark veins; and like the seas,
Roaring, the desperate water took its leap;
Yet dim within the cave, like sound in sleep,
Came the fall's voice; my flitting fire made
More truth to me than all the water said.

Yet when I looked, there was the arras only,
The passage stretching on, the pictured faces,
The violin below complaining lonely,
Creeping with sweetness in the minds' sad places,
And all my mind was trembling with the traces
Of long dead things, of beautiful sweet friends
Long since made one with that which never ends.

And as I went the wall seemed built of flowers,
Long, golden cups of tulips, with firm stems,
Warm-smelling, for the black bees' drunken hours;
Striped roses for princesses' diadems;
And butterflies there were like living gems,
Scarlet and black, blue damaskt, mottled, white,
Colour alive and happy, living light.

Then through a door I passed into a room
Where Daniel stood, as I had seen him erst,
In wisest age, in all its happiest bloom,
Deep in the red and black of books immerst.
I would have spoken to him had I durst,
But might not, I, in that bright chamber strange,
Where, even as I lookt, the walls did change.

For now the walls were as a toppling sea,
Green, with white crest, on which a ship emerging,
Strained, with her topsails whining wrinklingly,
Dark with the glittering sea fires of her surging,
And, now with thundering horses and men urging,
The walls were fields on which men rode in pride,
On horses that tossed firedust in their stride.

And now, the walls were harvest fields whose corn
Trembled beneath the wrinkling wind in waves
All golden ripe and ready to be shorn

By sickling sunburnt reapers singing staves,
And now, the walls were dark with wandering caves
That sometimes glowed with fire and sometimes burned
Where men on anvils fiery secrets learned.

And all these forms of thought, and myriads more,
Passed into books and into Daniel's hand,
So that he smiled at having such great store
All red and black as many as the sand,
Studded with crystals, clasped with many a band
Of hammered steel. I saw him standing there.
After I woke his pleasure filled the air.

THE WOMAN SPEAKS

This poem appeared to me in a dream one winter morning some years ago. In the dream, I was aware of a tall lady dressed for out-of-doors, with furs and a picture hat. I was aware, at the same time, of the whole of her past life, and of the fact that she was looking, for the first time, southwestwards upon Lincoln's Inn Fields, early on a calm, sunny Sunday morning. I saw the Fields as she did, in utter calm, sunny distinctness, as from the north-eastern pavement; the pigeons were picking food, the sun was shining, each brick and stone was distinct. I was aware of the fact that she had suddenly realised that life might be quiet like this, and that were it so, it would be wonderful. At the same time, I was intensely aware of the whole of this poem, which explained her past, what she saw and what she felt. As she passed out of the dream, the whole of the poem appeared engraven in high relief on an oblong metal plate, from which I wrote it down.

Bitter it is, indeed, in human Fate
When Life's supreme temptation comes too late.
I had a ten years' schooling, where I won
Prizes for Headache and Caparison.
I married well; I kept a husband warm
With twenty general years of gentle charm.
We wandered much, where'er our kind resort,
But not till Sunday to the Inns of Court.
So then imagine what a joy to see
The town's grey vast and unappeaséd sea
Suddenly still, and what a hell to learn
Life might be quiet, could I but return.

THE RIDER AT THE GATE

A windy night was blowing on Rome,
The cressets guttered on Cæsar's home,
The fish-boats, moored at the bridge, were breaking
The rush of the river to yellow foam.

The hinges whined to the shutters shaking,
When clip-clop-clep came a horse-hoofs raking
The stones of the road at Cæsar's gate;
The spear-butts jarred at the guard's awaking.

"Who goes there?" said the guard at the gate.
"What is the news, that you ride so late?"
"News most pressing, that must be spoken
To Cæsar alone, and that cannot wait."

"The Cæsar sleeps; you must show a token
That the news suffice that he be awoken.
What is the news, and whence do you come?
For no light cause may his sleep be broken."

"Out of the dark of the sands I come,
From the dark of death, with news from Rome,
A word so fell that it must be uttered
Though it strike the soul of the Cæsar dumb."

Cæsar turned in his bed and muttered,
With a struggle for breath the lamp-flame guttered;
Calpurnia heard her husband moan:
"The house is falling,
The beaten men come into their own."

"Speak your word," said the guard at the gate;
"Yes, but bear it to Cæsar straight,
Say 'Your murderer's knives are honing,
Your killer's gang is lying in wait.'

"Out of the wind that is blowing and moaning,
Through the city palace and the country loaning,
I cry, 'For the world's sake, Cæsar, beware,
And take this warning as my atoning.

" 'Beware of the Court, of the palace stair,
Of the downcast friend who speaks so fair,
Keep from the Senate, for Death is going
On many men's feet to meet you there.'

"I, who am dead, have ways of knowing
Of the crop of death that the quick are sowing.
I, who was Pompey, cry it aloud
From the dark of death, from the wind blowing.

"I, who was Pompey, once was proud,
Now I lie in the sand without a shroud;
I cry to Cæsar out of my pain,
'Cæsar, beware, your death is vowed.'"

The light grew grey on the window-pane,
The windcocks swung in a burst of rain,
The window of Cæsar flung unshuttered,
The horse-hoofs died into wind again.

Cæsar turned in his bed and muttered,
With a struggle for breath the lamp-flame guttered;
Calpurnia heard her husband moan:
"The house is falling,
The beaten men come into their own."

THE BUILDERS

Before the unseen cock had called the time,
  Those workers left their beds and stumbled out
Into the street, where dust lay white as lime
  Under the last star that keeps bats about.
Then blinking still from bed, they trod the street,
  The doors closed up and down; the traveller heard
Doors opened, closed, then silence, then men's feet
  Moving to toil, the men too drowsed for word.
The bean-field was a greyness as they passed,
  The darkness of the hedge was starred with flowers,
The moth, with wings like dead leaves, sucked his last,
  The triumphing cock cried out with all his powers;
His fire of crying made the twilight quick,
Then clink, clink, clink, men's trowels tapped the brick.

I saw the delicate man who built the tower
  Look from the turret at the ground below,
The granite column wavered like a flower,
  But stood in air whatever winds might blow.
Its roots were in the rock, its head stood proud,
  No earthly forest reared a head so high;
Sometimes the eagle came there, sometimes cloud,
  It was man's ultimate footstep to the sky.
And in that peak the builder kept his treasure,
  Books with the symbols of his art, the signs
Of knowledge in excitement, skill in pleasure,
  The edge that cut, the rule that kept the lines.
He who had seen his tower beneath the grass,
Rock in the earth, now smiled, because it was.

How many thousand men had done his will,
  Men who had hands, or arms, or strength to spend,
Or cunning with machines, or art, or skill!
  All had obeyed him, working to this end.
Hundreds in distant lands had given their share
  Of power, to deck it; on its every stone
Their oddity of pleasure was laid bare,
  Yet was the tower his offspring, his alone.
His inner eye had seen, his will had made it,
  All the opposing army of men's minds
Had bowed, had turned, had striven as he bade it,
  Each to his purpose in their myriad kinds.
Now it was done, and in the peak he stood
Seeing his work, and smiled to find it good.

It had been stone, earth's body, hidden deep,
  Lightless and shapeless, where it cooled and hardened,
Now it was as the banner on man's keep
  Or as the Apple in Eden where God gardened.
Lilies of stone ran round it, and like fires
  The tongues of crockets shot from it and paused,
Horsemen who raced were carven on't, the spires
  Were bright with gold; all this the builder caused.
And standing there, it seemed that all the hive
  Of human skill which now it had become,
Was stone no more, nor building, but alive,
  Trying to speak, this tower that was dumb,
Trying to speak, nay, speaking, soul to soul
With powers who are, to raven or control.

THE SETTING OF THE WINDCOCK

The dust lay white upon the chisel-marks,
  The beams still shewed the dimplings of the grain,
Above the chancel's gloom the crimson sparks
  Of Christ's blood glowed upon the window-pane.
No brass or marble of a death was there,
  The painted angels on the wall whirled down
Trumpeting to man's spirit everywhere,
  The spire topped the bell-tower like a crown.
Now, on the tower-top, where the crockets ceased
  Like lace against the sky, they set at pause
The golden wind-vane, that from west to east
  Would turn his beak to tempests or to flaws.
It poised, it swang, it breasted the wind's stream,
The work was done, the hands had wrought the dream.

THE RACER

I saw the racer coming to the jump,
  Staring with fiery eyeballs as he rusht,
I heard the blood within his body thump,
  I saw him launch, I heard the toppings crusht.
And as he landed I beheld his soul
  Kindle, because, in front, he saw the Straight
With all its thousands roaring at the goal,
  He laughed, he took the moment for his mate.
Would that the passionate moods on which we ride
  Might kindle thus to oneness with the will;
Would we might see the end to which we stride,
  And feel, not strain in struggle, only thrill,
And laugh like him and know in all our nerves
Beauty, the spirit, scattering dust and turves.

FROM THE SONG OF ROLAND

Roland gripped his horn with might and main,
Put it to his mouth and blew a great strain;
The hills were high and the sound was very plain,
Thirty leagues thence they heard the strain,
Charles heard it, and all his train.
"Our men are fighting," said Charlemain,
And the Count Guenes answered him again,
"If another said that, we should think him insane."
Ahoy.

Roland was broken by pain and outworn,
In great anguish he blew his horn;
Out of his mouth the bright blood did fall,
The temples of his brain were now all torn:
He blew a great noise as he held the horn.
Charles heard it in the pass forlorn,
Naimes heard it, the Franks listened all.
Then the King said, "I hear Roland's horn,
He would never blow it if he were not overborne."
Guenes answered, "You are old and outworn,
Such words are worthy of a child newborn,
There is no battle at all, neither won nor lorn;
Ahoy.

"Moreover, you know of Roland's great pride,
It is a marvel that God lets him bide.
Without your command and knowing you would chide,
He took Noples and killed the men inside,
With his sword Durendal he smote them hip and side,
Then with water washed the fields where the blood had dried,
So that his killings might never be spied.

All day long he will horn a hare and ride,
Gabbing before his peers, showing his pride,
No man would dare attack him in all the world wide.
Press on your horse now. Why do you abide?
France is still far from us over the divide."

Ahoy.

Count Roland's mouth bled from a vein,
Broken were the temples that held his brain,
He blew his horn with grief and in pain,
The Franks heard it and Charlemain.
The King said, "That horn blows a long strain."
Duke Naimes answered, "Roland is in pain.
There is a battle, by my hope of gain,
He here has betrayed him who did so feign;
Put on your war gear, cry your war-cry again,
Go and succour your noble train,
You hear clearly how Roland does complain."

Ahoy.

The Emperor made his trumpets blow clear,
The Franks mounted and put on their gear,
Hauberks and helmets and swords with gold gear,
Men had shields and many a strong spear,
And banners scarlet, white and blue in the air to rear.
On his war-horse mounted each peer,
And spurred right through the pass among the rocks sheer:
Each man said to his comrade dear,
"If we reach Roland ere he be dead on bier,
We will strike good blows with him and make the pagans fear."
But they had stayed too long, and they were nowhere near:

Ahoy.

THE HAUNTED

Here, in this darkened room of this old house,
  I sit beside the fire. I hear again,
Within, the scutter where the mice carouse,
  Without, the gutter dropping with the rain.
Opposite, are black shelves of wormy books,
  To left, glazed cases, dusty with the same,
Behind, a wall, with rusty guns on hooks,
  To right, the fire, that chokes one panting flame.
Over the mantel, black as funeral cloth,
  A portrait hangs, a man, whose flesh the worm
Has mawed this hundred years, whose clothes the moth
  A century since, has channelled to a term.
I cannot see his face: I only know
He stares at me, that man of long ago.

I light the candles in the long brass sticks,
  I see him now, a pale-eyed, simpering man,
Framed in carved wood, wherein the death-watch ticks,
  A most dead face: yet when the work began
That face, the pale puce coat, the simpering smile,
  The hands that hold a book, the eyes that gaze,
Moved to the touch of mind a little while.
  The painter sat in judgment on his ways:
The painter turned him to and from the light,
  Talked about art, or bade him lift his head,
Judged the lips' paleness and the temples' white,
  And now his work abides; the man is dead.
But is he dead? This dusty study drear
Creaks in its panels that the man is here.

Here, beyond doubt, he lived, in that old day.
"He was a Doctor here," the student thought.
Here, when the puce was new, that now is grey,
That simpering man his daily practice wrought.
Here he let blood, prescribed the pill and drop,
The leech, the diet; here his verdict given
Brought agonies of hoping to a stop,
Here his condemned confessioners were shriven.
What is that book he holds, the key, too dim
To read, to know; some little book he wrote,
Forgotten now, but still the key to him.
He sacrificed his vision for his coat.
I see the man; a simpering mask that hid
A seeing mind that simpering men forbid.

Those are his books no doubt, untoucht, undusted,
Unread, since last he left them on the shelves,
Octavo sermons that the fox has rusted,
Sides splitting off from brown decaying twelves.
This was his room, this darkness of old death,
This coffin-room with lights like embrasures,
The place is poisonous with him; like a breath
On glass, he stains the spirit; he endures.
Here is his name within the sermon book,
And verse, "When hungry Worms my Body eat";
He leans across my shoulder as I look,
He who is God or pasture to the wheat.
He who is Dead is still upon the soul
A check, an inhibition, a control.

I draw the bolts. I am alone within.
  The moonlight through the coloured glass comes faint,
Mottling the passage wall like human skin,
  Pale with the breathings left of withered paint.
But others walk the empty house with me,
  There is no loneliness within these walls
No more than there is stillness in the sea
  Or silence in the eternal waterfalls.
There in the room, to right, they sit at feast;
  The dropping grey-beard with the cold blue eye,
The lad, his son, that should have been a priest,
  And he, the rake, who made his mother die.
And he, the gambling man, who staked the throw,
They look me through, they follow when I go.

They follow with still footing down the hall,
  I know their souls, those fellow-tenants mine,
Their shadows dim those colours on the wall,
  They point my every gesture with a sign.
That grey-beard cast his aged servant forth
  After his forty years of service done,
The gambler supped up riches as the north
  Sups with his death the glories of the sun.
The lad betrayed his trust; the rake was he
  Who broke two women's hearts to ease his own:
They nudge each other as they look at me,
  Shadows, all four, and yet as hard as stone.
And there, he comes, that simpering man, who sold
His mind for coat of puce and penny gold.

O ruinous house, within whose corridors
None but the wicked and the mad go free.
(On the dark stairs they wait, behind the doors
They crouch, they watch, or creep to follow me.)
Deep in old blood your ominous bricks are red,
Firm in old bones your walls' foundations stand,
With dead men's passions built upon the dead,
With broken hearts for lime and oaths for sand.
Terrible house, whose horror I have built,
Sin after sin, unseen, as sand that slips
Telling the time, till now the heapèd guilt
Cries, and the planets circle to eclipse.
You only are the Daunter, you alone
Clutch, till I feel your ivy on the bone.

CAMPEACHY PICTURE

The sloop's sails glow in the sun; the far sky burns,
Over the palm tree-tops wanders the dusk,
About the bows a chuckling ripple churns;
The land wind from the marshes smells of musk.
A star comes out; the moon is a pale husk;
Now, from the galley door, as supper nears,
Comes a sharp scent of meat and Spanish rusk
Fried in a pan. Far aft, where the lamp blears,
A seaman in a red shirt eyes the sails and steers.

Soon he will sight that isle in the dim bay
Where his mates saunter by the camp-fire's glow;
Soon will the birds scream, scared, and the bucks bray,
At the rattle and splash as the anchor is let go;
A block will pipe, and the oars grunt as they row,
He will meet his friends beneath the shadowy trees,
The moon's orb like a large lamp hanging low
Will see him stretched by the red blaze at ease,
Telling of the Indian girls, of ships, and of the seas.

THE SHIP AND HER MAKERS

The Ore

Before Man's labouring wisdom gave me birth
I had not even seen the light of day;
Down in the central darkness of the earth,
Crushed by the weight of continents I lay,
Ground by the weight to heat, not knowing then
The air, the light, the noise, the world of men.

The Trees

We grew on mountains where the glaciers cry,
Infinite sombre armies of us stood
Below the snow-peaks which defy the sky;
A song like the gods moaning filled our wood;
We knew no men—our life was to stand staunch,
Singing our song, against the avalanche.

The Hemp and Flax

We were a million grasses on the hill,
A million herbs which bowed as the wind blew,
Trembling in every fibre, never still;
Out of the summer earth sweet life we drew.
Little blue-flowered grasses up the glen,
Glad of the sun, what did we know of men?

The Workers

We tore the iron from the mountain's hold,
By blasting fires we smithied it to steel;
Out of the shapeless stone we learned to mould
The sweeping bow, the rectilinear keel;

We hewed the pine to plank, we split the fir,
We pulled the myriad flax to fashion her.

Out of a million lives our knowledge came,
A million subtle craftsmen forged the means;
Steam was our handmaid and our servant flame,
Water our strength, all bowed to our machines.
Out of the rock, the tree, the springing herb
We built this wandering beauty so superb.

The Sailors

We, who were born on earth and live by air,
Make this thing pass across the fatal floor,
The speechless sea; alone we commune there
Jesting with death, that ever open door.
Sun, moon and stars are signs by which we drive
This wind-blown iron like a thing alive.

The Ship

I march across great waters like a queen,
I whom so many wisdoms helped to make;
Over the uncruddled billows of seas green
I blanch the bubbled highway of my wake.
By me my wandering tenants clasp the hands,
And know the thoughts of men in other lands.

BEAUTY

When soul's companion fails,
When flesh (that neighed once) ails,
When body shortens sails,

O soul, break through the netting
Of failing and forgetting,
See clearer for sun-setting;

See clearer, and be cheerly,
See thou the image clearly,
Love thou the image dearly.

For out of love and seeing
Beauty herself has being,
  Beauty our queen;
Who with calm spirit guards us
  And with dear love rewards us
In courts forever green.

NIREUS

Once long ago young Nireus was the King
  In Syme Island, so the stories say,
  And at his birth the gods made holiday,
And blessed the child and gave him each one thing,

Courage, and skill, and beauty, and bright eyes,
  Wisdom, and charm, and many another power,
  So that he grew to manhood like a flower
For beauty, and like God for being wise.

Now Nireus' friend was Paris, out of Troy,
  Paris, the prince, the archer, who had seen
  The goddesses within the forest green;
King Priam's son, a peacock of a boy.

At Sparta's court, not far from Syme Isle,
  Bright Helen lived, King Menelaus' Queen,
  The loveliest woman that has ever been,
Who made all mortals love her by her smile.

Nireus and Paris went together there
  To Helen's palace: and when Nireus saw
  Helen the Queen, the lovely without flaw,
He loved her like her shadow everywhere.

And Paris, when he saw her with her mate,
  Helen, the rose, beside that withered weed,
  Loved her no less, but with a young man's greed
That wants the moon from heaven and cannot wait.

Straightway he wooed Queen Helen to be his,
  And won her love, and cried to Nireus then,
  "O Nireus, help to save us from this den,
Lend us your ship to bring us out of this."

So Nireus, though his heart was torn with pain,
  Well knowing what would come, yet took the pair
  To many-towered Troy and left them there,
To live in love and be the city's bane.

When Menelaus knew of Helen's flight,
  He led all Greece in arms to punish Troy,
  Nireus went with him in the fleet, and joy
Ceased in the world, for all men went to fight.

Nine years they fought there in the tamarisk field,
  And in the tenth, in some blind midnight stour,
  Nireus killed Paris underneath the tower.
Men bore him back to Helen on his shield.

Then Troy was sacked and Menelaus took
  Beautiful Helen as his prisoner home,
  And locked her in his castle as a gnome
Might lock a gem on which no man might look.

Thus Nireus lost his love, and killed his friend,
  And knew despair; so going to his ship,
  He sailed to where the constellations dip,
In the great west, to look for the world's end.

When Troy was sacked and all her towers
  Blazed up and shook into the sky
Smoke like great trees and flame like flowers,
  And Priam's bodyguard did die,

Then the Queen's women snatched up spears,
And fought their way out of the gate;
Seized horses from the charioteers
And fled like mountain-streams in spate.

They would not stay for slavery
To some Greek lord until they died,
They rode the forest to be free,
Up on the peaks of snowy Ide.

And in the forest on a peak
They hewed a dwelling with the bronze,
And lived, unconquered by the Greek,
Fierce, sun-burned women, neither tame nor weak,
The panther-women called the Amazons.

They lived there on the heights and knew no men
Having beheld the lusts of men destroy
The town of windy Troy,
They killed all men they met; their only joy
Was hunting for the wild beasts in the glen.

The wild boar and the many-branching stag,
Horse-killing panthers hidden by the brook,
The spotted death among the yellow flag,
All these with their bright spears these women took.
All these, and men, for even to be seen
By men, these hunter-women thought unclean.

So no man saw them save a glimpse afar.
Of panther-skins flung back, and swift feet flying,
And the red stag brought low to the fierce Ha!
Of women's spear-thrusts driven in the dying.
They ruled the crags like wolves, they kept their pride
Savage and sovereign like the snow on Ide.

Nireus sailed; and a strange wind blew him to islands unseen before,
Where the gods sat throned on the crags with peace on their marvellous faces,
Clouds and the smoke of fire, that glittered and changed, they wore!
And unto them came the crying of all man's sorrowful races.

They cried to him as he passed, "You are seeking and you shall find,
Not in the way you hope, not in the way foreseen;
Out of horror of soul, ache, and anguish of mind,
Out of the desert of all, shall come the leaf that is green."

Then the wind blew on to an island where millet is ever in ear,
And the horses that live in the sea come thronging in thousands to eat,
And the horses that live on the island will never let them come near,
But they fight on the beaches forever with flashing and thunder of feet.

Then he sailed by invisible islands, he smelt the fruit on the trees,
And heard the noise in the shipyards and the crowing of cocks unseen,
Then sheered from the roar of breakers and on over unknown seas,
And ever he grieved for Paris, and thought of the beautiful Queen.

Then he came to a sea of terror, where monsters rose from the sea,
Things with the beaks of birds and arms like the suckers of vines:
Things like ghosts in the water coming motionlessly
To tatter the flesh of men with teeth like the cactus-spines.

Over unending water ever he held his course,
 Birds that were curses followed, crying around and above:
"Nireus, broken by beauty, broken again by remorse,
 Goes to the breaking of death for killing his friend and love."

And ever he cursed himself for bringing them both to wreck,
 Helen and Paris, the lovely; and ever the waves seemed filled
With skull-bones hollow in death, that rose and peered on the deck:
 And he thought, "They are those from Troy whom I in my madness killed.

"Had I refused, when they asked for my help to escape,
 Paris would still be alive, Troy, the city, would stand,
And all the killed of the war would be tilling the corn and the grape,
 Not ghosts with a curse in the air and torn bones strewing the land."

So he sailed; but at night in the dark when the lantern bubbled aloft,
 And men lay sleeping, when all save him were asleep,
And the ship slid on with a gurgle of water soft,
 He knew that the dead of Troy came with him over the deep.

Out of the long-backed roller that slid from its crest of foam,
 Gibbered the bloodless dead, white faces with haggard eyes,
Pointing the bones of their hands at him who had forced them from home,
 Their curses came to his ears like little twittering cries.

Whenever he moored at an island for water or food or rest,
 Soon those wraiths of the dead would rise and bid him begone,
To harry the resting gannet out of the roller's crest,
 And carry the curse of his soul to the unknown, on and on.

In the grey of morning
When the stars were paling,
Nireus sailing,
Saw land ahead.
An island shining
With city towers,
Where bells were ringing
And men singing.

As Nireus stepped ashore there
He stood staring,
For all men there
Were the dead of the war:
The Greeks and Trojans,
Beautiful and swift,
Killed in the trampled tamarisks
Beneath Troy town.

Stars were in their hair,
Their brows were crowned with violets,
They stepped like stags,
Comrade with comrade.
They had forgotten
The mud and death,
The heat and flies
Of the plain of Troy.

There among them
Came a prince in scarlet,
With his hands stretched
In welcoming.
It was Paris, his friend,
Paris whom he killed
In the midnight raid
Beneath Troy wall.

Paris cried,
"Nireus, my comrade,
Nireus, my belovèd,
My friend of old!
Here we have forgiven
What my young man's folly bred,
We feast as friends
In the violet fields."

Then he led Nireus
To the hall of feasting.
There they feasted
In the violet fields.
Three summer days and nights,
It seemed, they feasted,
Each summer day and night
Was ten years long.

Paris and the heroes
Cried to Nireus,
"We loved Helen,
When we were men.
Now we love her still
And we see her lonely,
Old, and haunted
By her lovers dead.

"Take to Helen
Gifts from her lovers,
In her old age find her
And give her these:
Beauty and peace
And our forgiveness,
And all our thanks
For what she was."

As they ceased speaking
They faded from him,
The island faded,
Nireus was at sea.
He and his men
Were all grown old,
Thirty years
Had fallen on them.

As old men failing
They came to Sparta;
All unavailing
Their coming was.
Helen was gone
And none knew whither,
To search for peace
Or to find release.

Over the seas
In lands and islands
Nireus sought her,
But could not find.
For the gods retire
When men desire,
Though it burn like fire
And make men blind.

Full of years and wealth and evil, Menelaus died in Sparta,
And Queen Helen at his bedside stood and looked upon him dead,
He who once had bought her beauty, to be bride to him, by barter,
He whom she had loathed and fled from, now lay silenced on the bed.

Bitter thoughts were in her as she looked upon his meanness,
  Thoughts of Paris in his beauty when their love was at its height.
Paris in his morning, and the King in his uncleanness,
  And this dead mean thing, her master, and the winner of the fight.

All was silent in the palace of the King,
Save the soft-foot watchers whispering;
  All was dark, save in the porch
  The wind-blown fire of a torch,
And the sentries still as in a stound,
With their spear-heads drooped upon the ground.

Then she thought: "These two men had me, and a myriad men have sickened
  To a fever of a love for me who saw me passing by:
When they saw me, all their eyes grew bright, and all their pulses quickened,
  And to win me or to keep me they went up to Troy to die.

"Now the earthly moon, my beauty, and the rose, my youth. have dwindled.
  I am old, my hair is grey, and none remembers
What a fire in men's hearts Queen Helen kindled
Ere the fire in Queen Helen turned to embers."

All was silent in the palace of the King,
Save the wind-blown torch-flame guttering,
  And a moth that came
  Beating with his wings about the flame,
And the sentries drawing breath,
With their spear-heads drooped saluting death.

Then she said: "The gods conspired to give gifts of beauty to me,
And the beauty gave the gift of death to all who came to woo me;
Now of all the men who loved me, none remain,
And of both the men who had me neither knew me.
Surely all my past was evil, for its fruit is bitter pain.

"I will go to some lone island where I am not made a story,
Where my beauty made no widow, nor no orphan wanting bread;
Where no human sorrow suffers the disaster of my glory,
And my eyes may lose the vision of the hauntings of the dead."

"Day and night the dead men haunt me, whom the madness of my caring
Brought from home and wives and children to be bones upon the plain;
All the panther-like for beauty, all the lion-like for daring,
And they lie among the bindweed now, uncovered by the rain."

All was silent in the palace of the King,
Save the soft-foot watchers whispering;
All was dark, save in the porch
The wind-blown fire of a torch,
And the sentries still as in a stound
With their spear-heads drooped upon the ground.

Then she rose, and cloaked her face, and hurried swiftly from the city,
And to sea, away from Hellas, but she dared not show her face,

For the women and the orphans would have killed her without pity:
She had sown her crop of death too far, she found no resting-place.

But in inns where people gathered in the evenings after labour,
Where the shepherd's pipe or viol stirred the blind man to his verse,
Till the hearers swayed and trembled and the rough man touched his neighbour,
They would talk of Troy with sadness, but of Helen with a curse.

After long years, when Helen was riding by night
In storm, in the Ida forest, alone, not knowing the road,
She saw a light in the blackness; she turned to the light,
She came to the fort on the crag, the panther-women's abode.

Hearing her horse's stamp, they brought her into the yard,
Those women fierce from the killing of lion or boar or man;
They came with their torches round her, they stared at her hard,
They knew her for Helen the Queen from whom their sorrows began.

For years they had longed for her coming, to have her to kill,
Her beauty a throat for their knives, her body a prey—
Helen, who ruined their lovers, the root of their ill—
She said: "I am Helen. Avenge yourselves on me. You may."

Still they stared at her there in the torchlight; then one of them said:
"God used you to bring things to be; evil things to our city,
Evil things to yourself, for your face declares you have paid;
You have come to the truth like ourselves; we take not vengeance, but pity."

Then they welcomed her into their hold, and when morning
broke clear,
They rode with her down to the ruins of what had been Troy;
There they left her alone in the wreck of the thing overdear
That the gods cannot grant to mankind, but unite to destroy.

Queen Helen left those women of the wood,
She clambered from her horse and stood again
Even on the very hill where Troy had stood,
Where tamarisk shrubs and broom-sprigs and wild grain
Sprouted from bronze and rib-bones of men slain.

There was the palace where her love had been;
Stones blackened by the fire and misplac'd
By roots of vines that fed upon the paste
Of all the pride where she had lived a queen.

Troy was no more than weeds and fireflaked stone,
But still the straits ran roaring to the south,
And still the never-quiet winds were blown
With scent of meadow-sweet from Simois' mouth.

Yet no Greeks were moving on the beaches,
No galleys of the Greeks came oaring in,
Nor did lancer scouts or parties ride the whin,
Bringing in or checking convoys from the river's upper reaches
Where the forest pines begin.

And the forges were all gone, and all the fires
Of the camps and burnings of the dead.
And the grinding of the bronze-shod chariot-tyres
Rang no more.
Both in city and on shore
There were no more shouted orders, clash of arms, or marchers'
tread.

All was manless now, uncared for; both the streams had left their courses.
There was marsh where corn had grown of old, and there, where Paris lay,
Was an apple-tree with fruit which fed the now wild Trojan horses,
That with bright teeth bit each other;
Earth made Greek and Trojan brother,
All the passion that had raged there now was dead and gone away.

Then she cried, "I caused the quarrel that brought death along these beaches,
I alone made Troy this ruin, I alone, from haste of youth,
From a woman's bent, that listens to a lie, if it beseeches;
Now I stand here old and friendless, having nothing but the truth."

There she stopped, for there before her, in the ruins, stood a stranger;
"This is changed indeed," he told her, "since I stood here once before:
Then it flamed all red to heaven and it rang with death and danger,
And I stood here with noble Agamemnon,
In the thunder of the ending of the war."

Something in the old man's bearing made her start and catch her breath.
"You are Nireus, friend," she answered. "You are he who brought me here
When my life and love were dear:
Then I came to life and loving, now I come to grief and death.

"There is no small grass, in plain or water,
But grows from the body of one killed
By the deadly love of me, who am Helen, Leda's daughter:
All the young and swift and lovely, all the quick of heart are stilled;
I was cause of their going to the slaughter.

"Daylong and nightlong their shadows pursue me with evil,
Haunting my thought in the day, killing my rest in the night;
Now they have drawn me here; their multitudinous devil
Bids me die where I sinned.
I hear their cry in the wind,
I see their eyes in the light."

Nireus answered, "Ah, not thus, not so, Queen Helen, surely,
Are those who died for love of you, to win you or to keep!
If they gave their lives, they gave them as a man gives frankly, purely,
Without question, comment or complaint,
The strong heart equal with the faint,
All content to see your beauty and to tread hard ways to sleep.

"Now they know that your beauty made them splendid,
Splendid to the death; for I have seen,
Seen and talked, beloved Helen, with the souls of those who ended
In the ruins of this city that has been,
And they praise your name, they count you still their Queen.

"Now come with me, for the ship waits to receive you,
The wind is fair for Syme; let us start.
Here, where long ago I lost you, I retrieve you;
Let us leave this town of broken heart
For the peace of Syme Harbour and the mirth of Syme mart,
And the calm of knowing sorrow at an end,
And the quiet of the memory of a friend."

Then they sailed for Syme Island, and the gods were with their going,
For their beauty came upon them both, with youth and strength and peace;
Now they rule and live forever in a spring forever blowing,
High in Syme where the sun is bright and skylarks never cease.

THE BEGETTING OF ARTHUR*

Uther, the Prince, succeeding to the post
Of Red Pendragon, or Anointed Chief
Of all the Kings in Britain, saw with grief
How jealousy and spite
King against King, let in the heathen host,
Who, coming in their hundreds, found a land
Of warring Kingdoms owning no command,
And therefore sackt, uncheckt, from Tyne to Wight.

So when he took the purple he began,
Among his friends, to build a league of Kings:
Iddoc of Kent, among the Easterlings;
The Orkney pirate, Lot;
Then, from the North, the golden hero, Ban;
And having these, he greatly longed to win
Old Merchyon, King of Cornwall, rich in tin,
Whose strength would bind the leaguers like a knot.

None loved King Merchyon: Prince Uther knew
That he was aged, savage, mean and grim;
That baron Breuse, the Heartless, lived with him,
Of all bad men the worst;
That in Tintagel, nest-rock of the mew,
His daughters lived with him, the dark Ygraine,
That moon of women; then the bright Elaine,
And little Morgause, whom a witch had curst.

So, knowing that the urger of a cause
Must urge the cause in person, Uther rode
With Kol and Guy, to Merchyon's abode,
And in Tintagel tower

* See also page 412.

Pled eloquently to him without pause,
With all a young man's beauty, flusht and true;
And as he pled, Ygerna watcht, and knew
That of all knights Prince Uther was the flower.

Then Merchyon answered, "I have heard your plea.
I will not mingle in remote affairs,
I can mind mine, let others manage theirs:
What can the East, or Wales,
Or all of northern Britain, mean to me?
No Cornish men shall bleed in the employ
Of you, or others like you, Roman boy.
Your schemes are childish and your fears are tales.

"Or if not so, perhaps the Romans plan
To recommence their empire, for in truth
Taxes and tribute and conscripted youth
Are playthings dear to Rome.
But you, my Roman, come to the wrong man."
So raging, wrapping close his scarlet cloak,
He left the hall: Breuse, as he followed, spoke.
"That was your answer, Uther; make for home."

Breuse and his sworders followed Merchyon out,
Uther had neither welcome nor farewell,
Comfort, nor rest, nor water from the well,
Nor food for man or horse.
He stood a moment, betwixt rage and doubt.
"Sir," said Ygerna, coming from her place,
"Father is old: forgive his want of grace.
To-morrow he'll be broken with remorse."

Then Uther for the first time saw Ygern;
And at her voice and at her wistful glance,
Love stabbed his spirit with her beauty's lance;
While she, made faint with love,

Felt the hot blush upon her temples burn.
Love to both startled mortals made it known
That each was other's to the inward bone
Through some old passion in the stars above.

As in October when the Channel mist
With silent swathes of greyness hides the sea
Until none knows where land or waters be,
And suddenly a blast
Scatters and shreds the vapours into twist
And all is glorious sunlight, wind and foam,
Through which a towering ship comes striding home,
Spray to the rail, with colours at her mast;

Or as, in mild Novembers, when the pack
Whimpers in covert and the hunters wait,
Under slow-dropping oak-leaves falling late,
Making no sound at all,
And suddenly the fox with hollow back
Breaks, with a crying leader at his brush,
And all those riders gathered for the rush
Surge for the fence, not heeding any call;

So, to those two, the greyness and delay
Of all their lives' endeavour and employ,
The hollowness which they had counted joy,
The hopes which had been dear
Until that instant, all were swept away;
They were alone upon an ocean shore
Where nothing meant nor mattered any more
Save their two souls and being without fear.

"O Princess," he began, "O dark-haired Queen,
O moon of women, we have met again,
We who are one yet have been cut atwain
To seek ourselves till now.

Whatever griefs are coming or have been,
Love in his glory grants us to make whole
Our bleeding portions of divided soul
That our last dying sundered with the plough."

And she replied, "Even as a winter bird,
Robin or chaffinch, in the iron day
Mopes, with pufft feathers, on the snowy spray,
Too pincht with cold to fly,
Too starved with bitter need to sing a word,
Till, from the farm, maid Gillian scatters crumbs,
And the bird, gladdened, knows that April comes
And carols his thanksgiving, so am I."

Then, being in the certainty of love,
That cannot doubt, however it be blind,
Those two young lovers plighted mind to mind,
And straightway told the King;
Who cried, "A pretty plot, by Heaven above.
Since I, as King, refused to be allied,
You think to win my power through a bride
Whose loving father grants her everything.

"Not so, my Roman, for I see your plot.
Keep to your own princesses; she shall wed
My Breuse, who has no Latin in his head,
And you shall go out shamed. . . .
You sworders, make this loving swain less hot . . .
Set him ahorseback with his head for home.
And keep from Cornwall henceforth, man of Rome,
Or Cornish hands will swiftly have you tamed."

Then instantly, before Ygraine could plead,
Or Uther answer, he was hustled forth
(He and his Knights) and headed for the north,
With orders not to turn.

Since three alone were helpless, they agreed
To the tide's setting, but they rode in rage,
Vowing to set King Merchyon in a cage
Next Sarum Fair, to suffer and to learn.

Yet, after noon, as Uther stayed to look
West, from the moorland, at Ygerna's home,
There, on the moor, he saw a horseman come
Black against burning sky,
Galloping tow'rds him, by the way he took.
And being near, behold, it was Elaine,
Flusht, tousled, riding on a tautened rein,
Calling, "O Uther, help, or she will die . . .

"Help us to-night, because my Father swears
That Breuse shall wed Ygerna before Prime . . .
Friend, can you help her in so little time? . . .
Not let her go to Breuse . . ."
"Men have plucked women out of dragons' lairs,"
King Uther said, "And I will pluck Ygraine.
O Rose in briars difficult to gain,
Lighten my mind with stratagems to use."

Then, having thought, he said, "This seems a chance.
Your porter's old: suppose I climb the rock,
Dresst like the King your father, and then knock
At midnight on the door.
He, being old and drowsy, may but glance,
Think me your father, bow, and open gates.
Then, when I bring Ygern from where she waits,
He may unfasten for me as before.

"It is worth trying, for, if it succeed,
Ygern and I will be beyond the wall;
And I can see no other chance at all
Of saving her to-night . . .

And if I save her, sister, as God speed,
I swear to take her to the hermit's cell
And marry her before we cross the fell,
Making her Queen from Isis to the Wight.

"You, Kol and Guy, arrange for horse-relays,
From here to where King Merchyon's country ends;
Swift horses, mind. About it: gallop, friends:
And if the luck be fair,
We'll meet again in Sarum in three days.
Sister, be ready when the moon goes west.
The hermit knows me, he is Bran the Blest,
He will assist us: have the horses there."

Who longs for time to pass? The child at school,
Sick for his home where understandings dwell;
He who counts tiles within a prison-cell;
The broken, with her wrongs;
Eagles in cages stared at by the fool;
To all these dreary longers, at the last,
Some bell of blessing tells *the hour is past:*
But none longs for it as the lover longs.

Still, at the last, to Uther, the sun dimmed;
Men drew old sails across the half-built ricks;
The quarrymen trudged home with shouldered picks;
Slow-footed cows turned home;
After the chapel-bell ceast, voices hymned;
Evening came quiet: all the world had turned
To rest and supper where the rushlights burned:
Tintagel blackened like a dragon's comb.

By moonlight Uther came to Bran the Blest
Whose shed now held the horses of Elaine,
Bold-eyed, high-mettled, leaners on the rein,
Waiting their King and Queen.

At moonset, helped by Bran, Prince Uther dresst
With crown and scarlet and a sheep's-wool beard
Like Merchyon's self; then down he went, and neared
The rock-cut stairway slimy with sea-green.

He clambered up, while far above his head,
Black on the sky, the battlements were grim;
The sentries paced above, not seeing him,
Nor hearing how he climbed.
Beneath, within the bay, the ripples spread
One after other slowly to the shore,
Where, gleaming but unbroken, they gave o'er
Like breathing from a sleeper, husht and timed.

Upon the topmost stair he stood intent
Outside the gate, to listen, while the feet
Of drowsy sentries passed upon their beat.
He heard, beyond the door,
The porter, breathing deeply where he leant
Sprawled over table near the charcoal pan.
"Come, courage," thought Uther, "play the man."
He knocked King Merchyon's knocking and gave o'er.

As he had hoped, he heard the porter rouse,
Garble some words, unhook the lantern-ring,
Kick back the bench, and mutter, "It's the King!"
Then fumble on the bar,
Pulling it weakly, gulping down his drowse.
The oaken barbolt loitered slowly back,
The latchet clicked, light yellowed at the crack,
An old man louted with the door ajar.

And as he louted low, Prince Uther passt . . .
There was Elaine, to take him to Ygern,
Telling the porter to expect return
Within few moments more.

All ways are long to lovers, but at last
He found Ygerna waiting in the dim,
Her great eyes bright, her white arms stretcht to him;
He drew her back along the corridor.

They trod the dark stone passage between rooms
Where people slept beneath the sentry's tread;
Tintagel seemed a castle of the dead.
A horse-hoof scraped the stone
Where the King's stallion waked among the grooms.
The porter, with his old eyes full of sleep,
Opened the gate to let them from the keep;
Its clang behind them thrilled them to the bone.

They crept like spies adown the cragside stair,
Into the gully's blackness between crags;
They heard the spear-butts clang upon the flags
At changing of the guard.
No challenge came; the world was unaware
How lovers fled: they reached the castle brook
Where ever-changing gleaming ever shook
An image of the zenith many-starred.

No sentry saw them; no one challenged; no,
Not when they moved across the moorland crest
Leaving the castle black against the west,
Grim guardian of the sea.
Their footsteps made a drowsy cock to crow,
A dog barked at their passing by the farm,
But no one stirred nor answered the alarm:
They reached the hermit's chapel: they were free.

There in the little chapel of the well,
By taper-light, the hermit made them one.
"Now cross the moor," he said, "before the sun.
God be your guard and speed."

They turned the chafing horses to the fell,
That King and bride upon their marriage day;
The nightingale still sang upon the spray,
The glow-worm's lamp still burned among the weed.

All day and night they hurried from pursuit;
Next morning found them out of Merchyon's land
Beside a brook with wood on either hand,
Deep in a dell of green:
Cool water wrinkled at the flag-flower root,
The meadowsweet her heavy fragrance shed:
"Here," the pair thought, "shall be our marriage bed,
Here, in this orchard of the fairy queen."

So there they halted in the summer flowers,
The speedwell blue, the stitchwort starry bright,
The dog-rose not yet opened, pink or white,
But sweet as very love.
Blackbirds and thrushes sang the lovers' hours,
And when the young moon brightened golden-pale
In the blue heaven, lo, a nightingale
Singing her heart out on the spray above.

There the two loved. Alas! ere morning came,
There Breuse and Merchyon, finding them asleep,
Stabbed Uther dead, and took Ygern to weep
In grim Tintagel tower.
There she sat weeping at the weaving-frame,
Waiting to bear her son before she died;
And as she wept, poor woman, hollow-eyed,
She wove the story of her happy hour:—

The creeping from the castle in the dark,
The blinking porter drowsed in lantern light,
The hermit and the chapel and the rite,
The horses tried and true;

Dawn on the moorland with the singing lark,
The ride for safety ever glancing round;
Then the sweet loving-place, where they were found
At dawn among the speedwell in the dew.

And sometimes Merchyon, mindful of his girl,
In mercy of her health, would have her ta'en
To rest beside the Alan with Elaine,
Guarded by Breuse's band.
There as she watcht the water-eddies whirl,
Often a dark-eyed deer with fawn at heel,
Would shyly nuzzle her to share her meal,
And robin redbreasts percht upon her hand.

THE BIRTH OF ARTHUR

When the wind from East changes
Through South into West,
And the hard-frozen brooklets
Thaw out from their rest,

And come shining and leaping
Past the snowdrop's drooped head
Through the green-pushing pastures
Where moles burrow red;

Then the rooks call from elm-tops,
And lambs from the fold;
And the larks joy in heaven
For death of the cold;

And the blackbird calls clearest
Of sweet birds that sing,
And the dear becomes dearest
Because it is Spring;

And a joy of rejoicing
Springs green in the corn;
Such a joy was Ygerna's
When Arthur was born.

When the midsummer dog-rose
Was sweet in each hedge,
She took little Arthur
To Pendragon Ledge,

And at moonrise she laid him
On the Dragon's stone chair
Looking out over ocean,
Grey rock in keen air.

For the wise ones had told her
That to children so laid
Come the Powers who fill them,
And the Helpers who aid.

She laid the child sleeping
When all things were still
Save the sea-water creeping
And wind on the hill,

And the full moon came climbing
Till Time made the hour
For the foot of the Helper
And the wing of the Power.

Then at midnight Ygerna
Bent low at a cry,
For a night-laughing curlew
Laughed loud in the sky;

Such a night-laughing curlew
As never was heard:
It laughed in grey heaven,
But was not a bird.

Then again there was silence;
Then, whirling on wings,
Came the long-ago heroes,
The Queens and the Kings,

All the beast-quelling heroes
Who ruled and made tame,
All the women of glory,
All the spirits of flame

Who had wrought in this island
To make her more fair,
And exist now forever
In the beauty they bare.

There they gazed upon Arthur
With their light-giving eyes,
All the lovely true-hearted,
True-sighted and wise.

And a King said: "Our harvest . . .
This corn coming green."
And a Queen said: "This captain
Will be loved by a Queen."

Then they laughed all together,
And the babe laughed in sleep,
And they said: "Little Arthur,
What we made you will keep."

Then, as seabirds at sunrise
Fly seawards from ken
To a rock of fair fishing
Untrodden by men,

Flying after their leader,
White wings on red sky,
So those heroes flew seawards
And a wonder drew nigh.

For from out of the water
A mailed man arose,
Fierce-eyed as the eagle,
But bearing a rose.

And as manes stream from racers
In wind on the down,
So flames streamed behind him
From under his crown.

He said: "Thoughts are many
But wisdom is one.
Your way being wisdom,
Will shine like the sun.

"You will shine on this island
Till green corn be gold,
And the tale of your harvest
Will never be told.

"All the Power within me
Shall stablish your peace;
But at evening comes darkness
When sunlight must cease."

He ceased into darkness
As meteors that die;
A night-laughing curlew
Laughed loud in the sky:

The night-laughing curlew
Cried loud in the air,
A wonder stole forward
And stood by the chair.

He was dim as an evening
Whose moon sets apace,
Green light as of glow-worms
Was pale on his face.

He said: "Little Arthur,
Our passings will meet:
My moon will be sickle
To garner thy wheat.

"Thyself shall create me
To ruin thy joy,
Yet though I shall break thee,
I cannot destroy."

He ceased into darkness
As sea-mist that dies;
The night-laughing curlew
Made mirth in the skies.

Then a wonder most lovely
Swept in from the west,
As a sea-bird white-pinioned
Who glides to her rest;

Her face had the quiet
Of night at an end,
Her gift was the glory
Of beauty for friend;

In the gold of her crownal
White flowers were fair;
She stood like the morning
With stars in her hair.

And as Arthur woke laughing
And stretcht out his hands,
She said: "The deep currents
Stir even the sands;

"As high as the planets
And deep as the sea
Are the currents of living
That bind you to me.

"To each spirit fashioned,
To each creature born,
Is a Helper from Heaven,
A Rose to the Thorn.

"Myself am your Helper;
My beauty will stir
As a dream in your spirit,
As the prick of a spur:

"Though others' the Power
And yours be the seed,
My beauty as Helper
Will bring it to deed.

"You are frail now as snowdrops
That come before Spring;
My beauty as Helper
Shall crown you the King.

"And thrice in your kingship
Your manhood shall quail;
My beauty as Helper
Shall not let you fail.

"And at passing, my Arthur,
I'll bring you to fold
In the violet meadows
Where nothing grows old."

She ceased into twilight;
A lark carolled sweet,
The blue-blossomed speedwell
Were bright at her feet.

As Ygrain took her baby
The seabirds flew low,
Singing: "Whither man wanders
No mortal can know.

"But rise, little Arthur,
Like the green corn in pride,
And a Power shall fill you
And a Helper shall guide."

THE TAKING OF MORGAUSE

Morgause the Merry played beside the burn:
The otter said: "Go home: return, return."

But no; she wandered down to the seaside:
"Go home, O little friend," the gannets cried.

But no; she strayed to Erbin heaping wrack:
"Morgause," he said, "Beware, my dear; turn back."

But no; she laughed, and ran along the beach:
Blind Erbin cried: "Come back, dear, I beseech."

She ran with naked feet in the bright foam:
The shepherd on the cliff-top called: "Go home."

But no, she did not hear, or could not care.
The little vixen stopped her with "Beware . . .

"Beyond this jutting headland, drawn to land,
A pirate's Drake-Ship lies upon the sand.

"There, filling water, is the pirate's crew . . .
Beware, lest, with the water, they take you."

But no, she heard the sweet-voiced pirates sing,
Filling their earthen beakers at the spring.

Above the cuckoos and the bees of June,
She heard the voices at the ancient tune:—

"My spear will feed me with another's bread,
House me, where once another laid his head,
And bride me with the girl another wed.

"Farewell, you women all, that once were dear;
Lovely is love, but warring makes more near
The man beside me with a fellow spear."

Then little Morgause longed to see and know
These dreaded pirates who were singing so.

She thought: 'One little peep among the fern,
To say I've seen them, then I will return.'

But as she went, the black-backed adder cried:
"You tread the road to trouble; turn aside."

The blunt-tailed field-mouse called with shrilly shrieks:
"Beware of iron claws and horny beaks."

Then the red robin, hopping, twittered: "Flee . . .
These men are wicked, they flung stones at me."

Now, as she crouched among the grasses' stalks,
She saw the Drake-Ship on the roller-balks.

She was red-painted with a sweeping run,
Rowlocked for twelve, with shields for everyone.

A gilded Dragon eyed the way she went,
Aft, were Thor's Hammer and a scarlet tent.

Below the cataract that leapt the rock
The gold-ringed pirates filled their water-stock.

They filled red earthen jars: their King stood near
Whetting the deadly edges of a spear.

He was a young man, smiling, with black eyes;
In all a pirate's wisdom he was wise.

He wore a scarlet cloak above a mail
Of shining silver wrought like salmon-scale.

He eyed the grass where little Morgause lay,
But did not seem to see: he looked away.

He ceased the whetting of his weapon: then
He watched the work and chatted with his men.

At flood, he bade them run the Dragon down
To sea, across the beach-wrack tumbled brown.

They ran her seaward, crying "Heave" and "Hale";
'Now,' (little Morgause thought) 'I'll see her sail.'

They hoisted her red sail, singing to the pull
A song which Morgause thought most beautiful.

The red sail filled and jangled; the calm sea
Lifted and lapsed the vessel not yet free.

The wading pirates loaded her with stores,
Unlasht the steering, shipped the rowing oars.

'There,' (Morgause thought) 'they are about to go,
And I, alone, of all the castle, know . . .

'I shall return and tell them: "Look at me . . .
I saw the pirates whom you did not see.

' "They could not see me hidden in the flowers,
But there I snuggled, watching them for hours.

' "I was as near as you are to the King,
I heard him tell his boatswain what to sing.

' "He never saw me, but he came so near,
I could have touched him with a hunting-spear.

' "Now, after this, I'll wander where I choose,
And when I wish to, nor shall you refuse." '

So Morgause thought, but now the Dragon's sheets
Were homed; the after rowers took their seats;

The moorings slackt; the silver-harnesst lord
Spoke to two seamen as he climbed aboard.

The two men trotted inland: a call blew
Shrill, as the captain passed among his crew.

The oars were tosst together and let fall
Into the rowlocks at the "Ready all."

'Now,' (Morgause thought) 'they go away, away,
Oar-blades green-swirling, Dragon spouting spray;

'Would I could go with them, to see and know
Where all the setting suns and planets go;

'To hear the Mermaids singing, and to see
The spicy Phoenix in her burning tree;

'And all the golden Apples that the Snake
Guards, lest the neighing Centaurs come to take;

'And that dim Valley of the silver corn
Browsed in the moonlight by the Unicorn;

'O would I could . . .' And suddenly she felt
Two pirates grip her grimly as she knelt.

King Lot, the silver-scaled, said, "By-and-by,
When you are wiser, you will make a spy . . .

"Meanwhile, my Morgause, you shall come with me
Over the thoughtless, ship-destroying sea,

"North, to my Orkney kingdom's granite tower;
In that grim garden you shall be the flower."

Thither she went: within that stony place
She grew to loveliness of form and face.

And when the seasons made her seventeen,
King Lot of Orkney took her as his Queen.

THE BEGETTING OF MODRED

When berries were scarlet
In the holly's dark green,
To the court at Caerleon
Came Morgause the Queen,

Being charged by her husband
To spy and report
On the troops under Arthur
From Caerleon court.

There she lived as a lady
From autumn to spring,
But she learned little tidings
To send to her King;

Save that soldiers were mustered
From Uskmouth to Wye,
But for all of her serpent
She could not learn why.

Then she tempted Prince Arthur,
The youth in command,
Till she saw his eyes brighten
At the touch of her hand.

There she baited her beauty
With the lures women use,
But for all of her serpent
She gathered no news.

When the daffodils flowered
In the fields of red clay
And the apple trees blossomed
And the birds sang all day,

When the swallows were building
And the cuckoo had come,
All the camps of Caerleon
Were loud with the drum.

All the troops in Caerleon
Were packing their gear;
All the whets in Caerleon
Whipped sword-edge or spear.

Queen Morgause of Orkney
Knew wars did prepare,
But for all of her serpent
She could not tell where.

In her room hung with purple
She baited her hooks
With her sweet-smelling body,
Sweet words and sweet looks.

There she tempted Prince Arthur
With beauty's delight,
So that love was between them
For one summer night.

Then when first the red cock crew
The trumpet blew shrill,
And the Caerleon legion
Came down from the hill.

And Prince Arthur rode with them
And left her in doubt,
For, for all of her serpent,
She had not found out.

But in Orkney in winter,
When waiting was done,
She bare the boy Modred
From the evil begun,
And the father, the uncle,
Had a nephew for son.

BADON HILL

Loki the Dragon-killer mustered men
To harry through the western isles agen.

Five thousand raiders in a hundred ships
Sailed with him to put Britain in eclipse.

For many days they loitered to the south,
Pausing to raid at every river-mouth.

Always they met good fortune and good reive.
Kol, with his pirates, joined them in the Sleeve.

They sacked the Roman seaport: they laid bare
Down to its plinth, the marble-covered phare.

Then, growing bold, they sacked Augusta town.
Temples of many gods came crashing down.

Then Loki said, "My grand-dad, in his prime,
Burned a great city into building lime.

"Upstream it was and many miles from here.
No man has harried there this many a year.

"Then, as his gang dissolved, he went alone
Upstream from there, exploring the unknown,

"And reached a reed-mere, whence a trackway led
Up to an ancient fort called Badon Head.

"And looking thence (he said) beheld what we
Dream of perhaps but very seldom see:—

"Sway-footed cows in thousands deep in grass,
Unraided reiving such as never was,

"And distant downland stretching, green with keep,
White as its chalk with moving flocks of sheep.

"He swore to raid there with a gang, but Fate
That loves but ruins boldness, shut the gate . . .

"Ambrose the Briton maimed him with a spear
So that he lingered helpless many a year

"And never came to keep his oath, nor saw
That land again, that pasture without flaw;

"Nor did his son, my father: no one has;
Unraided lie those pastures of deep grass.

"Now I will raid them: you and I, my spears,
Will make the greatest raid of fifty years.

"We will go up the river, we will take
That land and sack it for my grand-dad's sake."

"Right," Wolf the Red Fang said; "But people tell
Those Westers' leader is a cub of hell.

"Arthur, they call him: people get their fill
Coming for cattle against Arthur's will."

"Arthur to Hel," said Loki; "I shall go."
"Right," Red Fang answered; "I have warned you though."

Upstream they rowed their Dragons: on the banks
The horsemen scouted, keeping clear their flanks.

O'er many a mudbank jammed with rotting drift
The harnessed horses gave the ships a lift.

After some days, King Loki trod the wracked
Shell of the city that his grand-dad sacked;

Then on he passed, now poling, now with oars,
Now dragged by horse-teams straining on the shores,

Now sailing, till he sailed into the green,
Reed-shadowed mere his ancestor had seen.

There was the trackway, there the Badon Hill
Notched on the skyline by its rampart still.

"This is the place," said Loki. "Here we'll drive
Those sway-foot cattle to the ships alive."

He moored his ships and marched his men ashore.
He eyed those pastures of his ancestor.

No herd, no head, was in those miles of grass.
The fields were empty as the downland was.

No smoke from any house, no noise of men,
Empty the cottage as the cattle-pen.

King Loki pitched his awnings in the camp,
And bade his men new-palisade the ramp.

He said to Wolf the Red Fang, "Mount and scout
West, with the horse, to seek the cattle out."

"Right," Wolf the Red Fang said: "But Arthur calls
All cattle in, and shuts it within walls,

"Soon as he hears of wolf-packs near the house.
Mounting and scouting will not bring you cows."

"Mount," Loki said. "I do not ask advice."
"Right," the Wolf answered. "Now I've warned you twice."

Wolf Red Fang took the horse into the west,
Over green pastures better than the best.

Green though the pastures were, that summer land
Was bare of people as a desert sand.

No scout of all his raiding horsemen heard
Voice of aught living save the summer bird.

Nothing was heard by them, and nothing seen
Save summer blue above the summer green,

Nothing but summer greenness stretching on
Marked by the tracks by which the herds had gone.

"Where have they gone?" they murmured. "We have come
Heel-scenting, sure, or we'd have met with some."

And others said, "We must be under curse . . .
Let's back to camp before we meet with worse."

But Wolf replied, "A man who won't believe
Has got to learn: come, ride ahead and reive."

The sun declined, the misty west grew red,
But still no cattle, not a single head.

The dusk grew dim: they trembled as they rode,
For no dog barked at all, and no light showed.

At star-time they unsaddled for the night
Beside a chalk-brook, water-crowfoot-white.

They did not help again in Loki's plan,
Arthur at dawn destroyed them to a man.

Arthur pushed onward: before dawn next day
He eyed the reed-mere where the longships lay;

Those servants of the water-spooning oar
Lay flank to flank, their noses from the shore.

Their pine-plank, painted red, the hot July
Had burned to be like bonework, blister dry.

Up in the pirate's camp no watch was kept,
Drunk Kol was dicing, drunken Loki slept.

Arthur and Lancelot, the son of Ban,
Took burning touchwood in an iron pan;

They slid into the water among reed,
No pirate saw their coming, none gave heed.

They pushed their gear before them on a raft,
The ripples spread in little gleams that laught.

The weather Dragon-ship rose overhead
Like a house-pale, sun-blistered, painted red.

Arthur and Lancelot together smeared
Tar to the leadings whence her hawsers veered,

Then heaping twigs and pine-cones, they gave touch,
And blew, until the little flames took clutch.

No watcher heard or saw them, no one came.
The little flame became a bigger flame.

It spread along the seams and thrust its tongues
Out, till the straikings looked like ladder-rungs.

First, the wind bowed it down, then, at a gust
The flame, that had been greedy, became lust;

And like a wave that lifts against a rock
Up, into shattering shining at the shock,

So it upshattered into spangs of flame
That writhelled red, and settled, and laid claim

And tore the Dragon's planking from her bones
Roaring: the Dragon sighed with little moans.

Now swearing pirates ran to fight the flame
And Arthur's archers shot them as they came.

And Loki, rising from his drunken sweven,
Saw all his longships blazing red to heaven

And Arthur's army coming with a will
Straight from the fire up the Badon Hill.

All Britons know the stories that are told
Of Arthur's battle for that pirates' hold:—

How first he tried the flank, and failed, and then
Tried at the gate and was repulsed agen;

How at the broken stakes where flints were flying,
He burst a way among the dead and dying,

And held the gap, the while his meyny all
Shovelled and picked, to totter down the wall;

How Loki charged and beat him headlong thence
With pirates in a spear-gang matted dense;

How Lancelot and Hector and Gawaine
Routed the spears and bore him back again;

And how they beat a little breach and stood
Crouched under lifted shields to make it good;

While from the upper wall about their ears
Came flying flints and fire, darts and spears.

And how that lower ditch was filled with dead,
Men taking death there like their daily bread.

How Loki, growing anxious, strove to cut
His passage out but had his pathway shut;

How thrice he tried, with three defeats, and each
Time found him fewer, with a bigger breach.

Then how, like wolves entrapped, those pirates raged,
Horseless, without a navy, foodless, caged,

With Loki sorely wounded and Kol killed.

Men also tell how Arthur's fifers thrilled

Along his front, in that late afternoon,
While all his army, in a demi-lune,

Trod to that fifing up the slope and stayed;
And how the trumpets all together brayed

Along the front, and all the army swarmed
Upward together, till the wall was stormed;

Till, on the crest, beyond the tumbled pales,
They saw all-glorious Fortune turn her scales;

And how the horse came thrusting to the wrench,
Trampling the rampart fallen in the trench;

And how the trumpets all together blew,
And Arthur's army charged and overthrew.

Under the grasses where the cattle browse,
King Loki's army keep eternal house

In Badon earth, for none escaped alive.
Thereafter Arthur's realm was free to thrive.

For many years, no pirates had the will
To band against him, after Badon Hill.

THE SAILING OF HELL RACE

When Arthur came from warring, having won
A name in Britain and a peace secure,
He felt the red horizon cast her lure
To set him hunting of the setting sun,
To take a ship and sail
West, through the grassless pastures of the whale,
West, to the wilderness of nothing sure
But tests for manhood in the deeds undone.

So, in his ship, the Britain, with her crew,
He sailed at all adventure for the west:
The Severn glittered at the Britain's breast
As first her set sail wrinkled and then drew;
She dropped down with the tide,
Then, ere the changing, leaned upon her side
And smote the spindrift from the billow-crest
And strode from raddled waters into blue.

Westward she sailed, beyond familiar seas,
Beyond the landmarks and the ships of home,
To seas where never ship had broken foam,
Past all encounter with man's argosies.
The skies shone blue; the sun
Burned hotter at each marking of the run;
Out of the sea the summer islands clomb;
For many happy days they passt by these.

And there, between the surf-break and the snow
Bright on the pinnacles of crags, the land
Grew fruits of blessing ready to man's hand,
In deathless green an ever-golden glow:

And brown-skinned Indians came
Bringing them wreaths of flowers red as flame,
And plaques of gold-leaf beaten from the sand,
And begged them stay and wept to see them go.

But on they stood, until the sea-most peak
Was sunken as Polaris; till the day
No longer burned with summer but was grey
With iron snow-clouds over waters bleak.
A granite coast appeared,
Beaten by breakers; thither Arthur steered
Into the desolation of a bay
Where the scared seahawks made the echoes shriek.

All still it was, save for the seabird's cry
And for the thunder when the glacier broke
Her seaward iceberg in a spray like smoke.
All iron-grey the land was, like the sky;
But on the beach were heapt
The harvest wreckage which the sea had reapt,
Mastings of pine, fir plankings, ribs of oak;
The bones of ships, suckt bloodless, flung up dry.

There lay the helm, the yard, the figurehead;
Nay, even a ship that had been painted green;
Nay, all the wreckings that had ever been
Seemed to have stored that dockyard of the dead.
And there a cairn of stones
Rose as a tomb above the broken bones,
And on the cairn a wooden box was seen
Which held a script in heart's blood. Thus it read:

"Beyond this harbour are the granite rocks
Which are the gates of Hell, where courage dies.
Brother, I call upon you to be wise;
Return, before the Key turns in the locks,

Return, and do not dare
Death beyond death, the cities of despair.
Return, to where the lark sings in the skies
And on the Down the shepherd keeps his flocks."

Then Arthur said: "We have adventured far,
And tread upon the bones of what has failed;
The door of hell is dark until assailed,
But every night of blackness hides a star.
Come: even if we end,
Courage will bring immortals to befriend,
By whom the precipices shall be scaled
And bolted doors forever flung ajar."

Then: "On," they cried, "good captain, let us go."
Onward they sailed, till sunset, when they neared
Two forms (or were they goddesses?) upreared
On crags with wrack above and foam below,
And from their granite lips
A laughter cackled like the death of ships.
Into the race between them Arthur steered,
Dreading lest they should murder him. But no . . .

Under those awful figures and between
He passed into a race of toppling seas
That broke and back-lasht at the granite knees
And scurft with salt the figure of each queen.
Those Furies' shadows fell
Dark on that channel of the way to hell;
But Arthur's ship was built of sacred trees,
She stood, although the billows swept her clean.

On, through the turmoil of Hell Race, she swept;
The darkness, with her rooky wings of fear,
Covered the starless sunset's crimson smear;
Into the midnight of the sky there crept

Ahead, a glare, as though
The world were all afire smouldering slow.
Black towers on the glaring stood up sheer,
Lit windows in them sleepless vigil kept.

"Friends," Arthur cried, "we have adventured well:
Ahead is all the glittering and pride
Of power of the devils satisfied,
The triple city where destructions dwell.
We will adventure on
And face their death together." Then anon
Furling their sail, they made the Britain glide
Safe to a pier below the citadel.

Hell Race, the channel of the ocean, thrust
Tongue-like throughout the city: her two banks
Glittered and glowed with lamplight, ranks on ranks,
Higher than March's madness flings the dust;
Within some topmost towers
Flames out of cressets tosst like scarlet flowers
Where some exultant devil uttered thanks
For will indulged in executed lust.

Where Arthur lay, the city's dreadful joy
Came to him from the streets, for devils dirled
Pan upon iron pan, for glee; or hurled
Crockery crash, to shatter and destroy;
With shrieking horns they sped;
Explosions burst; the fire rusht up red;
Devils of discord, dancing, shriekt and skirled,
Beating at doors their brothers to annoy.

The naked women devils lured their prey
To dens or corners where, alert, in wait,
Murder stood tiptoe by the side of Hate;
Vice stole in flusht, and, glutted, slunk out grey.

And all life went at speed,
Each for himself and let the other heed.
Life was a fury roaring like a spate,
To fall, and to keep falling, or to slay.

And, drunk with vanity, their poets barkt
The glory of great Hell, the joy, the pride,
Of being devil-born in Hell to bide,
As devil-spawn by other devils sharkt.
The shrieks of women sped:
"Bring us your brother's blood if you would wed;
Blood, that our day-old mantles may be dyed,
That Mammon may be snared and we be markt."

Within his vast and dirty temples sat
Mammon, the god and monarch of that hell,
With sharp suspicion blinking through his fell,
Toad-throated, hooft, yet pinioned like a bat.
Athwart the temple's span,
Across the walls, a fire writing ran,
Blazing the prices of the souls to sell
For all to read, the devils yelled thereat.

Multitudes trampled in the temple nave,
Fighting like wolves in quarrel for a bone;
The brazen forehead with the heart of stone,
Rat with hyena, murderer with knave;
Then from a gallery's height
The tiger devils cast into the fight
Spirits of men like dirty papers blown
That raved in dropping down as madmen rave.

And at the dropping down, the mob beneath
Leapt, like starved dogs at feeding time, to snatch
Each one a dropping from the tempter's catch;
With filthy claws they clutcht, or filthy teeth;

They tattered into rags
Those faded floatings that had once been flags;
Roaring they fought for them with kick and scratch:
They trod the quivering anguish underneath.

Yet more than Mammon, Lady Self was lord
Within that city of the lust for gold,
The jewelled thing, bespiced, bepainted, cold,
Whom Mammon purchased for his bed and board.
A varnisht shell was she,
Exquisite emptiness of vanity,
Unbodied and unminded and unsouled,
The mirror Self, whom all who saw adored.

She, and her mighty husband, and the game,
The roar, the glitter, and the zest of sin,
The prices offered by the Mammon Kin,
The gold all chinking when the moment came,
All these temptations drew
Some of the seamen of King Arthur's crew;
They stole ashore to Mammon, there to win
The worm's eternity in lasting flame.

So ere they all should leave him, and because
The Mammon people, hating foreign breeds,
Denounced him as perverter of their creeds,
One fit for burning by their holy laws,
King Arthur cut his ropes
And thrust to seaward, leaving to their hopes
His nine deserters, there to reap their seeds.
He sailed, with bubbling water at his hawse.

Soon in Hell Race a city loomed ahead,
Unlit, unlovely, under a dark star,
Girded by forts, each scaled with many a scar,
And topped by cloud where fire glittered red.

A roaring filled the air
With thunder and destruction and despair,
As engines flung the fireballs afar
And fireballs Hell's dissolution shed.

And here the Searcher-Devils, grim with steel,
Boarded them out at sea and led them in
Within defences jaw-tootht like a gin
That kept without the port the foeman's keel.
"We are at war," they said,
"The justest war that devils ever made,
Waged as a vengeance on our neighbours' sin,
To blast them into carrion till they kneel.

"Why are we fighting? That's forgotten now;
No matter why; we are, let that suffice . . .
Yes, and those cannibals shall pay the price
Before we end, nor shall we scruple how.
And you . . . remember here
We end all question-askers with the spear.
Wisdom is treason not committed twice;
We make it Death with branding on the brow."

Then did those devils prison ship and crew
Under grim guard, where, natheless, they could tell
The progress of that war of nether hell:
No peace nor any joy that city knew.
The trumpet called the hours,
Trampling of troops had trodden out the flowers,
The trees were rampikes blasted by the shell;
Babes starved and women maddened, and men slew.

Bright-eyed with sharp starvation and with hate,
Twitching their bitter mouths from nerves gone mad,
With homes long since destroyed, in rags half clad,
(No craft save war being practist in the state)

They lusted, like the stoat,
To meet their teeth within a foeman's throat,
Or, like the wolf, to see the corpses shrad
With even thirsty Earth blood-satiate.

All day, all night, the shrieking and the crash
Of battle shook the town, as hate grew worse.
The elements were peopled with the fierce;
Insanity was captain of the rash.
Then cries arose: "Kill, kill! . . .
Those foreigners are workers of our ill,
Spies to a man and bringers of the curse;
Brothers, come slay and burn them to an ash."

Then some of Arthur's crew were killed; and all
Would have been killed, had not the stunt and wizen
Starved doers of the slaughtering arisen
Against their Emperor and General,
And forkt to hideous ends
Those profiters by battle and their friends.
They hurried Arthur and his crew from prison,
Then made their town a pyre of funeral.

As Arthur sailed, he saw a lightning run
Along that city's ramparts with the thirst
Of fire licking up those bricks accurst;
Then thunder blasted from it and did stun;
Then its immense strength shot
Skywards in sooty fire withering hot,
Where trembling planks and figures were immerst
In glare that slowly darkened into dun.

Then as that fiery cloud came scattering down,
Blackness oppresst that city from the sight;
The foeman's fireballs came flaming bright
Into the crater that had been a town;

The devils' laughter cackled,
As fever laughs, like fetters being shackled.
King Arthur's ship drove on into the night;
A darkness toppt the battle like a crown.

Throughout the night they sailed, till morning showed
Mudbanks and salted marshes with sparse hair
Or stubble-stalks of herbage blasted bare.
Then, the wind failing, up the creek they rowed:
Grey wisps of vapour curled
Above that marish of the underworld;
A droning and a whining filled the air
As though small devils in the mist abode.

Then, as the sullen sun rose, they beheld
Smoke rising up from pyres of the dead;
A granite statue sat there without head;
Beyond, arose a city grey with eld,
Nay, green with dropping mould;
That which had ruined her had made her old;
Cricketless were her ovens without bread;
A wind-stirred jangle from her ruins knelled.

There the pale fevers issued from the fen
To yellow human cheeks and cloud the mind;
There tetters dwelt, that writhel skin to rind,
Or rash the forehead with a savage pen;
Palsies, that twitch the lips
Or hamstring men with anguish in the hips;
These, too, were there, and sloughings that make blind,
And all the madnesses that unmake men.

They forced those Britons to that city's queen,
A winged and browless fierceness on the throne,
Vert-adamantine in her hall of bone,
Fang'd, sting'd and mail'd in metal gleaming green:

No thought was in her eyes;
In where her victims' blood ran she was wise;
Her death-horns filled the palace with their drone,
Her dart of death out-quivered and was keen.

"Arthur," she said, "you stand in Nether Hell
Upon the sediments of greed and pride,
The rotted dust of nations that have died,
Amidst the foulness where destructions dwell.
Here the strong hand grows faint;
Here poison saps the manhood of the saint;
Here beauty sickens, joy goes hollow-eyed;
What else of glory is, my minions quell.

"I slay the nations, one by one, that stood
Fierce-eyed in rapine and the fire of sacks,
Bright-eyed in ringing breaches in attacks,
Glad-eyed in glory from the beauty good.
I am the final Death,
Unseen and unsuspected as the breath,
Yet fatal as the crashing of the axe.
I am the ender of all hardihood.

"You, too, with your adventurers, are sealed
As mine already: see, your cheeks are pale,
Your scarlet currents in their courses fail;
However lusty, they will swiftly yield,
And you will dwindle down
To beg among the ruins of the town."
Then Arthur felt a weariness assail,
Nor could he struggle, nor oppose a shield.

And there with yellowing skins his seamen drooped,
Their arms too sick to pull upon the oar,
Forgetting how the sail rose to the roar
Of singing, as the gleaming clipper swooped.

"We've done enough," they cried,
"Leave us alone." There seven of them died:
Their burials were the vulture and the boar,
Whose scavengings the shallow graveyards scooped.

There Arthur saw the chickweed green the deck,
The halliard rot, the anchor-cable rust;
Gone was all order, gone were hope and lust,
The sick mind stared contented with the wreck.
Then in a midnight drear,
As Arthur tossed, a brightness hurried near,
A sudden glory on his senses thrust,
A terror prickt the hair upon his neck.

There, in her blue robe, the immortal queen,
His Helper, stood, the calm one, the benign,
Crowned with forget-me-not and columbine,
And speedwells blue and never-withering green;
No darkness nor disgrace
Could bide the beauty of that steadfast face.
"Arthur," she said, "from birth devoted mine,
Now flung as straw for devils' hands to glean,

"Take power from my touch; arise, arise,
Cast loose these prison-tacklings and begone
Forth from these dens where sunlight never shone,
Nor flower throve, nor spirit saw the skies.
My power gives you strength."
Then spirit kindled Arthur, and at length
It stirred his seamen from the malison
Of that third monarchy of the unwise.

So, with that Helper at the helm, they stood
Clear from that city's mudbanks, and away,
To seas where flying fishes skimmed the spray
And every blowing air gave hardihood.

Homeward the Britain cleft,
Of all her company but seven left.
Soon the blue water dimmed into the grey
And bright Polaris rose as they pursued.

Till, as they sailed, they saw the seaweed float
And felt a changing tide. When darkness came
They watched for sight of land or beacon-flame,
Or any friendly sail or fisher's boat.
The steering lantern purred;
Then through the haze before the dawn they heard
Triumphantly a red cock call his dame,
Making a stallion challenge with full throat.

Then as the haze blew seaward, they beheld
The hills of home, the country green with corn,
Blossom upon the blackness of the thorn,
The hedgerows with the pretty primrose stelled;
They heard the blackbird sing,
They heard the chiff-chaff and the birds of spring,
The early cuckoo wandering forlorn
In woods whose millioned green was still unshelled.

Till noon they coasted, reach by lovely reach,
Beyond King Dyved's, past King Ryence' lands,
Past mountains casting shadows on the sands
And river water shining over beach.
Then lo, a brazen-poled
Bright chariot driving, all aflame with gold,
A chariot driven by princess's hands:—
A princess drove to welcome them with speech.

Two stallions dragged that chariot like a spate,
White stallions lovely as the leaping pard,
Pickt stallions of King Ocvran's bodyguard,
Urged by a green-clad woman, who, elate,

With streaming red-gold hair
And eyes like stars illumined and aware,
Croucht watchful, to the grippt reins straining hard,
As one who lifts a winner up the Straight.

There did the giant Ocvran leave the car
And welcome Arthur to the shining shore;
There Arthur furled the sail and tosst the oar
And dragged the ship where billows could not mar.
The red-gold lady dear
Was Ocvran's daughter, princess Gwenivere,
Whom Arthur worshippt then and evermore,
As in the night the traveller the star.

ARTHUR AND HIS RING

Beauty's Delight, the Princess Gwenivere,
The day she promist marriage to the King
Drew from her hand the gem she held most dear,
Kisst it, to Arthur gave,
Saying, "O love, I plight me with this ring,
This sapphire, my most precious marvellous thing."
Her hair was in it, red as corn in ear.
"This," Arthur said, "I'll carry to my grave."

And being filled with joy, he went to thank
The goddess Venus who had blest his love.
Her image stood before a marble tank
In which, in glittering falls,
A fountain sprinkled water-rings that clove
The shadows of the temple myrtle-grove;
There her bright-breasted pigeons preened and drank,
Sidling and ruckling ever with douce calls.

In marble was the goddess, fashioned well,
Yearning a little forward as she stared;
Men thought her holy bosom rose and fell;
Her robe drooped to her hip,
Fallen in folds, while all above was bared . . .
The myrtle shadows and the water fared
Into the pool before her, there to dwell
With the statue's shadow for companionship.

And Arthur, passing, saw his shadow pass
Along that water on the imaged sky
Wherein the evening planet's glitter was.
He reacht the shape of stone,

Love's very Queen who gives the victory;
He saw her sweet, proud face, her steadfast eye,
Her crown that gleamed, like glow-worms among grass,
Her left hand stretcht, her right hand at her zone.

"O lovely Queen," he cried, "to whom all hearts
That ever suffered Love's intensest ache,
Turn with most passionate crying from all parts,
Take now my thanks, most sweet;
All my heart's deepest thankfulnesses take,
Because, to-day, thy Loveliness didst make
Me, thy poor servant, healed from many smarts
By granted love;" he bent and kisst her feet.

And as he kisst, he felt the marble thrill
As though alive; he felt her garment stir;
Her awful beauty made his heart stand still;
His spirit understood
The cryings of the birds attending her;
Light beat upon him, and the smell of myrrh;
Ecstasy rapt him to a greater will;
A peace that burnt like fire, a pain most good.

"O goddess, risen from the sea," he cried,
"Grant that this ring which my beloved gave
May touch your finger and be sanctified;
And make my love endure
Like to the mountain, not the breaking wave;
Make it my star to shine beyond the grave.
O rose, whom men adore in every bride,
Grant me this boon, most beautiful, most pure.

"Behold the ring." At this, he tendered it
To Venus' self, and with his gentlest touch
Upon her outstretcht finger made it fit . . .
But to his utmost awe,

The finger bent to take the ring in clutch;
Then, instantly, his ecstasy was such
That the green leaf was speaking to his wit
And the gold glow-worm telling him his law.

He felt the goddess' hand caress his head;
He heard the music that the planets sing;
Strange flowers fell upon him, scarlet-red,
And glow-worms gleaming green . . .
Yet in the midmost of his joy, the King
Still strove amidst it all to take the ring,
But, lo, it clippt the hand that never bled,
Merged to the finger of the marble Queen.

And as his fingers pluckt, the glory went;
The twilight's wind was in the myrtle grove,
Rattling the leaves and killing all the scent;
The goddess was but stone,
A marble thing to which his jewel clove;
He wrested at it, but it would not move,
It could not move, the finger being bent,
The goddess meant to keep it for her own.

Even with unguents, even when he smeared
Finger and ring with oil, the gem remained
Fast on the stone; until King Arthur feared
That it was lost indeed.
"And yet," he murmured, "if the stone were planed,
By some good craftsman when to-night has waned,
Then, without any doubt it could be cleared."
He went to bed, praying that dawn might speed.

But being abed, the midnight glowed with fire.
There, standing radiant in her crescent moon,
Was Venus' self, the Granter of Desire,
The Hope forever green.

Her quire of lovebirds carolled all in tune,
Her laughing eyes were glowing like the noon,
Joy was her gift and beauty her attire.
"Arthur," she said, "will you not take your Queen?

"For I am yours, you wedded me this night;
Take me, beloved: I was never won
Before by mortal man beneath the light,
But I am won by you."
Then Arthur cried, "O creature of the sun,
Have pity on me, O immortal one,
Give back the jewel that my lover plight,
It is Queen Gwenivere's and I am true."

"Behold it, set upon my hand," she said;
"You placed it there with many words of love;
Though I am deathless, do not be afraid,
I am your wedded wife."
"O lady, no," he cried. "By heaven above,
By you, the Blesser, and by judging Jove,
My love is Gwenivere, the royal maid,
I neither wooed nor wed you, on my life."

Her crescent moon dimmed down, her eyes seemed stone
Her scarlet lovebirds dimmed and ceast to sing;
He heard the bloodhounds in the courtyard moan.
"So, Arthur, you deny
Me, the immortal, you an earthly King.
God has your words recorded, I your ring,"
The goddess said: "But she whom you disown
Will come again." She dimmed into the sky.

All day he urged his craftsmen, one by one,
To break away the ring; but all from fear
Of goddess or of priest, refused, and none
Would lift a tool or hand.

Then as he sorrowed in the midnight drear,
His bloodhounds whimpered like a stricken steer,
Venus again came shining like the sun,
With eyes not glad, but gleaming like a brand.

"Arthur," she said: "Behold your Queen again . . .
I come out of the brightness of the sky
To seek my husband; must it be in vain?"
Then he, in sore distress,
Said: "Queen, return the jewel. I deny
I ever gave, or thought of giving. I . . .
Goddess, take pity on a mortal's pain."
"So," she said, "twice you spurn my happiness.

"Be wise in time, my Arthur, and beware
A third denial." Then, with dimming light,
She faded from the room and left him there
Shaken at loss and threat.
Unhappy dreams tormented him all night,
Hell-hounds, with yellow eyes and fang-teeth white,
Trotted about his bed with the night-mare.
He rose like one well taken in a net.

And looking at the quay below his tower,
He saw a stranger landing from a ship;
A dark, fierce man, with bright eyes full of power
Blazing beneath a hood . . .
One swift and telling as a cutting whip,
Keen, with a King's decision on his lip.
He smiled on Arthur; Arthur toiled an hour,
Then sought the garden where the statue stood.

And lo, a curse had fallen: fungus grew
Over the goddess in a lace of green;
No sparrows chirruped nor did pigeons coo,
And mat-weed chokt the tank.

The smell of dying made the place unclean,
All withered were the myrtles of the Queen.
"This cannot be the garden that I knew,"
King Arthur thought, and yet his spirit sank.

"Alas," he muttered, "I have brought a curse
Through scorning of the goddess in the night."
Yet in Apollo's house the wreck was worse;
Jove's house was in decay,
The altars bloodless without gift or rite:
No sweet blue incense-smoke, no votive light,
The golden serpents broken from the thyrse,
And no one there to sacrifice or pray.

No pine torch streamed to Mars in tongues of flame,
The sanctuary of the Sun was shut,
And in the Moon's house kittens were at game:
To Mercury no oil
Poured, and to Saturn was no offering put,
Vine-prunings, milk, or cornshoots newly-cut;
No woman called aloud on Juno's name,
Nor brought her wool, or balm, or household spoil.

And no man was at work at field or craft,
Nor loitering in the market or the lanes,
No hawkers cried, no children screamed or laught,
No women tended stall:
The world seemed weary of its fight for gains,
Its daily battle with its daily pains,
Its daily acquiescence in the daft;
A strange awakening had come to all.

But turning tow'rds a lifted voice, he heard,
He found them in the circus at the gates,
Intently listening to a teacher's word.
That same fierce foreign man,

Whom he had seen on quayside midst the freights,
Was speaking to them about life and fates.
His spirit quelled them like the eagle-bird,
The hearers trembled as his message ran.

And when he ceast, those tremblers rose as one,
Eyeing each other for a man to lead;
Then, at a word, they all began to run
Towards the city gate,
Crying, "Destroy the idols, the whole breed . . .
Destroy these statues of the devil's seed!"
Then household idols from their niches spun
Crashing: the stranger bade King Arthur wait.

"Arthur," he said, "I see you have a grief
Tormenting to your spirit: lay it bare."
Then, having heard, he said: "I bring relief;
Their strength begins to fail.
They are but erring thoughts and empty air,
Though some of them are strong and others fair.
My Master is the Master of their chief;
Trust to my Master, for his words avail.

"But, hark. To-night, at midnight, you must go
Out of the city to that open space
Where the three highways all together flow
Before the bridge-gate fort.
You know the spot: it is an evil place:
Blood-sodden spirits haunt there without grace.
Natheless, go boldly, for ere cocks shall crow,
Their King will travel thither with his court.

"Go to that Sovereign and demand your ring
Before he pass the gateway with his crew;
Many and deadly evils do they bring . . .
My Master be your guide.

Ask for that stolen sapphire as your due
And do not blench nor quaver: if you do,
Then truly it will be an evil thing;
But to the valiant nothing is denied."

At midnight Arthur crept outside the gate
Over the causeway to the river bank,
There where the bridge-head tower rose up great
Above three meeting roads.
A fire-basket swung there from a crank,
Lighting the river-ripples rank on rank;
Nothing was there but darkness full of fate
And spirits without pardon or abodes.

And Arthur, standing at the meeting ways,
Lit by the fire swinging from the tower,
Heard voices crying in a meteor-blaze
That streamed across the air.
One voice was calling: "They have had their hour!"
Then one: "All changes, even Beauty and Power."
Then one: "Eternity has many days . . .
The things that will be are the things that were."

Then, from the city, horses' clattering feet,
Trotting upon the causeway, swiftly neared . . .
There came an old King, in a winding-sheet,
Whose gemless crown was lead.
Long-boned he was, sunk-eyed, with scanty beard,
Old beyond human telling, bowed and sered,
Tapping the ass he rode with ancient wheat
That, like a sceptre, dreary lustre shed.

And after him, on horseback, came a crew
Of figures, wrapped in cloaks inscribed with signs,
Each tended by the symbol creature due,
The eagle and the pard,

The wolf, the peacock and the stag with tines,
The ox, the goat, the hedgehog with his spines:
The last was one whose looking almost slew,
Who bore no symbol but a broken shard.

Then Arthur, catching at the donkey's rein,
Challenged the Sovereign as the priest had told,
Saying, "O Saturn, give my ring again!"
Then Saturn slowly spake.
"I, ageless, am most aged: I was old
Ere first a lichen sprouted upon mould,
And now I meet a man who prefers pain
On earth to bliss such as immortals take.

Accept your lesser fortune: take your gem."
Then, with a sudden waft of holy scent,
That loveliest flower of the immortal stem,
Venus herself, the Queen,
To Arthur from her golden saddle leant.
"Take back the troth-plight that you never meant,"
She said, and gave it. "Think not I condemn.
In exile I shall keep your memory green.

"We pass to exile, you to reap your sowing,
We to the violet fields, you to your end,
We into peace and you to ebb and flowing;
But when the Fate cuts short,
When Life has no more penny left to spend,
When Will no longer makes your elbow bend,
Then, from my sea, O Love, I will come rowing,
My Queens and I, to bring you into port.

"And now, farewell." And, as she spoke, a cock
Crowed from the gateway tower; the brazen gate
Jarred, rolling open at King Saturn's knock;

And all the glimmering crowd
Rode slowly through those forces of no date:
Last went the Death that held the broken fate.
Then Arthur, stunned, recovering from his shock,
Kissed his belovèd's ring and sang aloud.

MIDSUMMER NIGHT

Midsummer night had fallen at full moon,
So, being weary of my ancient tale,
I turned into the night,
Up the old trackway leading from the vale.
The downland dimmed before me, dune on dune,
Pale dogrose buds about me shed their scent;
The startled peewits glimmered as they went,
The moonlight made the earth and heaven white;
The heaven and earth together uttered June.

So perfect was the beauty, that the air
Was like immortal presence thrilling all
The downland with deep life:
Presences communed in the white owl's call;
The rampart of the hill-top stood up bare,
High on the windy hill a brightness shone—
I wondered whose, since shepherd-men had gone
Homeward a long time since to food and wife;
Yet brightness shone, as from a lantern there.

Then, as the valley belfries chimed the hour,
I thought: "On summer nights King Arthur's door,
By yonder sarsens shut,
Is said to open to a corridor
Hewn far within the hill to Arthur's bower,
Where he and Gwenivere, with all the tale
Of captains toughened by the weight of mail,
Bide in a hall within the limestone cut:
That is the doorway, this is Arthur's hour."

So, pressing near, behold, a door was wide
Flung open on the steepness of the hill,
Showing a lighted shaft.
A footlift fox was paused upon the sill;
Eyes gleaming green, he fled. I stepped inside.
The passage led within all brightly lit,
Deft limestone hewers' hands had fashioned it.
Behind me (as I thought) the white owl laught.
The lighted way before me was my guide.

Till deep within the hill, I reacht a hall
Lit, but so vast that all aloft was dim.
The chivalry below
Sat at their table stirring not a limb.
Even as frost arrests the waterfall,
So had a power frozen that array,
There at the banquet of the holy day,
Into such stillness that I could not know
If they were dead, or carved, or living all.

Then, entering in, accustomed to the light,
I marked them well: King Arthur, black and keen,
Pale, eager, wise, intense;
Lime-blossom Gwenivere, the red-gold queen;
Ban's son, the kingly, Lancelot the bright;
Gawaine, Bors, Hector; all whom trumpets drew
Up Badon at the falling of the dew:
And over them there brooded the immense
Helper or Spirit with immortal sight.

All was most silent in that carven nave,
Save a far water dripping, drop by drop,
In some dark way of time.
Power had brought that Knighthood to a stop,
Not even their ragged banners seemed to wave.

No whisper stirred the muscle of a cheek,
Yet all seemed waiting for the King to speak.
Far, far below I heard the midnight chime,
The valley bells that buried silence clave.

Then at that distant music Arthur stirred;
His scarlet mantle quivered like a wing.
Each, in his golden stall,
Smiling a little, turned towards the King,
Who from his throne of glory spoke this word:—
"Midsummer Night permits us to declare
How Nature's sickle cut us from the air
And made the splendour of our summer fall."
Then one by one they answered as I heard.

KING ARTHUR:
"I was the cause of the disastrous end . . .
I in my early manhood sowed the seed
That made the Kingdom rend.
I begot Modred in my young man's greed.
When the hot blood betrays us, who gives heed?
Morgause and I were lovers for a night,
Not knowing how the fates had made us kin.
So came the sword to smite,
So was the weapon whetted that made bleed:
That young man's loving let the ruin in."

GWENIVERE:
"I, Gwenivere the Queen, destroyed the realm;
I, by my love of Lancelot the Bright;
Destiny being strong and mortals weak,
And women loving as the summer night.
When I was seized by Kolgrim Dragon Helm,
Lancelot saved me from the Dragon-beak,
Love for my saviour came to overwhelm.

"Too well I loved him, for my only son,
Lacheu, was his, not Arthur's as men thought.
I longed to see my lover's son the King;
But Lacheu, riding into Wales, was caught
By pirates near St. David's and undone . . .
They killed my Lacheu there.
The primroses of spring,
Red with his blood, were scattered in his hair:
Thereafter nothing mattered to me aught . . .

"Save Lancelot perhaps at bitter whiles,
When the long pain was more than I could stand;
He, being Arthur's cousin, was his heir
Till base-born Modred reacht us from the isles.
Thereafter was no comfort anywhere,
But Modred's plottings and my sister's wiles,
And love that lit me ruining the land."

LANCELOT:
"I, who am Lancelot, the son of Ban,
King Arthur's cousin, dealt the land the blow
From which the griefs began.
I, who loved Gwenivere, as all men know,
Was primal cause that brought the kingdom low,
For all was peace until that quarrel fell;
Thereafter red destruction followed fast.
The gates of hell
Hedge every daily track by which men go:
My loving flung them open as I passt."

GWENIVACH:
"I, who am Princess Gwenivach the Fair,
Compasst the kingdom's ruin by my hate,
The poisonous hate I bare
For Gwenivere, my sister, Arthur's mate.

My mind was as a murderer in wait
Behind a door, on tiptoe, with a knife,
Ready to stab her at the slightest chance,
Stab to the life.
I stabbed her to the heart in her estate;
Disaster was my blow's inheritance."

MODRED:

"Not you, with your begettings, father mine;
Not you, my red-gold Queen, adultress proud;
Not you, Sir Lancelot, whom none could beat;
Not you, my princess sweet;
Not one of all you waters was worth wine.
Mine was the hand that smote this royal seat,
Mine was the moving darkness that made cloud;
You were but nerves; I, Modred, was the spine.

"You were poor puppets in a master's game;
I, Modred, was the cause of what befell.
I, Modred, Arthur's bastard, schemed and planned;
I, with my single hand,
Gave but a touch, and, lo, the troubles came;
The royalty was ended in the land.
When shut from Heaven, devils create hell:
Those who ignore this shall repent the same.

"You were at peace, King Arthur (cuckold's peace);
Your queen had both her lover and her son;
And I, your bastard by your aunt, was far,
Where Orkney tide-rips jar.
Your kingdom was all golden with increase.
Then your son's killing happened: Modred's star
Rose; I was heir, my bastardy was done;
Or (with more truth) I swore to make it cease.

"But coming to your court with double claim
(As son and nephew) to the British crown,
You and the Queen named Lancelot the heir:
A brave man and a rare;
Your cousin King, the cuckoo to your dame,
Whom nobody opposed till I was there.
But I opposed, until I tumbled down
The realm to ruin and the Queen to shame."

GWENIVACH:

"And I, your younger sister, whom you slighted,
Loved Modred from the first and took his part.
That made the milk of your sweet fortune sour.
I told you in the tower,
The green-hung tower, by the sunset lighted,
Sunset and moonrise falling the same hour;
Then I declared how Modred had my heart,
That we were lovers, that our troths were plighted.

"You could have won our love, had you been wise;
Then, when, as lovers, we confesst and pled
Together with you for a lasting truce.
No blood would have been shed,
April and June had had their natural use,
And autumn come with brimming granaries.
But no; you gave refusal and abuse;
Therefore I smote your lips so harlot-red . . .
The joy of that one buffet never dies.

"I see you at this moment, standing still,
White, by the window in that green-hung tower,
Just as I struck you, while your great eyes gleamed.
Till then, I had but seemed . . .
My striking showed you how I longed to kill.

O through what years of insult had I dreamed
For that one stroke in the avenging hour!
The devil of my hatred had her will:
God pity me, fate fell not as I deemed."

So, with lamenting of the ancient woe
They told their playings in the tragic plot,
Until their eyes were bright:
The red-gold beauty wept for Lancelot.
Then the church belfries in the vale below
Chimed the first hour of the year's decay,
And Arthur spoke: "Our hour glides away;
Gone is the dim perfection of the night,
Nor yet does any trumpet bid us go.

"But when the trumpet summons, we will rise,
We, who are fibres of the country's soul,
We will take horse and come
To purge the blot and make the broken whole;
And make a green abundance seem more wise,
And build the lasting beauty left unbuilt
Because of all the follies of our guilt.
But now the belfry chimes us to be dumb,
Colour is coming in the eastern skies."

Then as those figures lapsed again to stone,
The horses stamped, the cock his challenge flung,
The gold-wrought banners stirred,
The air was trembling from the belfry's tongue.
Above those forms the Helper stood alone,
Shining with hope. But now the dew was falling,
In unseen downland roosts the cocks were calling,
And dog-rose petals shaken by a bird
Dropped from the blossomed briar and were strown.

THE FIGHT ON THE WALL

Modred was in the Water Tower
At Caerleon-on-Usk,
He saw Queen Gwenivere the flower
Go by at dusk.

She was disguised, but Modred knew her,
No cloak could veil such grace:
She was Queen Gwenivere: what drew her
To such a place?

She passt beneath the phare new-lighted,
He spied a red-gold tress
And gems upon a hand that righted
The wind-blown dress.

"Aha," he said, "My golden plover . . .
What go you out to do?
Queen, you are going to your lover;
I will go, too."

He dogged her through the unbuilt quarter,
Past heaps of brick and slate,
Scantlings and smoking lime and mortar,
To the East Gate.

Behind the East Gate turret-curtain
A rushlight flickered dim.
"Lancelot's room," he said; "It's certain
She goes to him."

He crouched behind her as she listened
And watched, to know all clear.
He thought: "You think it safe. It isn't . . .
Go on, my dear."

Then with a little clink, her sandal
Trod on the East Gate stair . . .
At turret-door one held a candle;
Her Knight was there.

"Lancelot," Modred said. "We take him;
His golden Queen and he;
Arthur will burn the slut and break him.
What joy for me."

Back to the palace Modred fareth
And there he finds Gawaine,
With's brothers Gaheris and Gareth
And Agravaine.

When Agravaine had learned the matter,
He said: "Knights, hearken here:
You thought my charges wicked chatter
Of Gwenivere.

"Now she is trulling with her master,
That Lancelot of fame,
This spotless Queen of alabaster . . .
It is a shame . . .

"It is a shame to them who do it
And worse to us who see.
I say, tell Arthur: let them rue it.
Do you agree?"

Then Gawaine said: "Be silent, brother,
And move no more in this:
Leave evil-speaking to another,
Leave it as 'tis."

Gareth and Gaheris replying
Said: "We will take no part
In dirty treacheries and spying
Foul as your heart."

"But I," Sir Modred answered sour,
"I will make one with you.
Arthur shall know within the hour
About these two.

"You dainty Knights of spotless honour
May watch your Queen's disgrace,
But we will bring a judgment on her
And brand her face.

"And Lancelot, that peer of traitors,
Shall be a public show."
Gawaine said: "You accursed haters
About it: go.

"But know, that what you do will issue
In every grief made worse.
The present world of men will hiss you,
The future curse."

Gawaine and's brothers left in anger:
King Arthur entered in.
Modred said: "Take your Queen and hang her,
She lives in sin.

to next page

"She trulls with Lancelot the splendid
Atop the East Gate stair;
Attack them now and they'll be ended,
Caught unaware."

"If it be so," said Arthur, "surely
The pair of them shall die.
Take men and bind the two securely."
Modred said "Ay."

Modred took Kolgrevance and's brothers,
Kurslin and Petipase,
Galleron, Jouré and seven others,
They went their ways . . .

They crosst the city's narrow alleys,
Now dark, the shops being shut;
They heard the night-wind in the salleys,
The fox in rut:

They heard the screech-owl at his calling
That charms the wood-mouse' ears,
And the tinkle of the water falling
At the bridge piers.

Soon they were near the East Gate tower;
A small light showed aloft.
"See," Modred said, "they're in our power
Now creep in soft.

"There's where the deer lies in her cover,
The red stag keeping guard:
Now we shall take her with her lover.
Bind them both hard."

They tiptoed up the winding stairway,
But Modred tiptoed last.
The jackdaw in the archer's airway
Blinkt as they passt.

They crept out on the paven landing
Atop the city wall.
It had a parapet and banding
Lest men should fall.

Between these ridges ran the footing
To where the tower rose;
The East Gate flanking-tower for shooting,
Loopholed for bows.

Thither they crept and stood there, straining
Their ears at the barred door:
The wind-cock up above complaining,
Creaked and gave o'er.

A silence was within the tower,
Naught touched on wood or stone;
Joure whispered: "This may be the bower,
The birds are flown."

They listened: then, within the hiding,
Gwenivere's voice said: "No . . .
It was the wind-cock spindle griding
As the flaws blow . . ."

Lancelot answered: "Not the spindle . . .
No; but another sound."
The listeners felt their spirits kindle,
The game was found.

Then beating on the door in fury,
They cried: "You traitor Knight!
You are taken now. We're judge and jury,
Come out and fight.

"Come out!" and at the panels rashing
They strove to beat a way,
As through the scrum a pack goes crashing
In football play.

The door held to its bolts, being oaken.
"Come out," the dozen cried.
They rashed again: no bolts were broken,
No hinges wried.

Gwenivere whispered to her lover:
"Alas, we both are lost."
Lancelot had no arms nor cover,
A cloak at most.

"Alas, my Queen," Lancelot muttered,
"That I should die thus tamed;
Snuffed, like a candle that has guttered,
Leaving you shamed."

The arm-chest in the chamber angle
Was bare of points and blades,
He had two hands with which to strangle:
No other aids.

"Come out," the dozen cried: "No quarter
If we are forced to storm."
"Go, Joure," said Modred, "to the dorter . . .
Bring up a form . . .

"We're bringing up a form to batter
The door about your ears . . .
We'll have your head upon a platter,
My prince, sans peers.

"And you, my red-haired quean, your trollop,
Let you make no mistake,
Shall go in smock like a cook's collop
To burn at stake."

Lancelot said: "This filthy crying
Is more than I can stand:
Better than hearing this were dying
Death out of hand.

"O Queen," he said, "the times are over
That you and I have known.
Belovèd Queen, I am your lover,
Body and bone,

"Spirit and all of me, past knowing,
Most beautiful, though sin.
Now the old lovely days are going
And bad begin.

"I shall die here, but whatsoever
May come of me, my friends
Will stand to succour you forever
Until life ends.

"Farewell, belovèd beauty peerless,
My star since I began;
You were my light when life was cheerless,
You made me man.

"In many a foray, many a stour,
In many a deathy place,
Your thought has blesst me like a flower
And given me grace.

"Now would that I had arms upon me
Until my powers fail,
What I would do before they won me
Would make a tale."

At this, the running twelve came battering
Their form against the door,
A panel yielded to the shattering,
They staved two more . . .

They cried: "Three more, and we shall take him,
This captain of the King;
Let this one hit the bolt and break him
Together . . . Ding."

Lancelot said: "Give over knocking,
I will unbar: let be . . .
I will undo . . . I am not mocking . . .
Come capture me."

He drew the bolt and opened to them
And stared into the dark,
By the thin taper's light he knew them
All he could mark.

Even as wolf-hounds snarl and cower
About the wolf at bay,
Those shrank till Kolgrevance of Gower
Leapt at his prey.

Kolgrevance shouted: "Now I have him,"
And slashed, but the cut misst.
Then Lancelot a buffet gave him
With the clencht fist:

A brain-pan blow that laid him sprawling
Dead on the turret floor:
Lancelot, while the corpse was falling,
Bolted the door.

Bolted it just before the others
Charged with their blows, too late.
Lancelot said: "You misst me, brothers,
Now you must wait."

Then as they beat the panels, railing
Like dogs the stag has gored,
Lancelot donned the corpse's mailing
And took his sword.

Modred and Agravaine together
Cried: "Out, you traitor, out."
Lancelot answered: "Cease your blether;
You need not shout.

"Go from the door: I promise truly
That if you go from here,
Naming your place and hour, duly
I will appear

"Before the Court in judgment sitting;
Against what charge you bring
I'll answer all, to my acquitting
From him the King."

"Arthur has damned you both already,
To death," Modred replied,
"To death by us, and we are ready,
So come outside."

"If that be so," he answered, "surely
My portion is but hard.
I warn you, keep yourself securely," . . .
Then he unbarred.

Then storming armoured from his prison
He strode out to the wall.
Since the man's death the moon had risen:
He saw them all.

There was no room in that grim alley
For more than two abreast.
The meyny charged him at his sally,
They smote his crest.

But ducking from their swords uplifted,
He grappled those who led—
Agravaine, Lot's son, called The Gifted,
Lovel the Red.

Agravaine cried to those behind him:
"Stand back, friends; give us room."
He felt a sudden lightning blind him,
He felt Death's doom;

Knew not how Lancelot had stricken,
But felt the blow destroy
The gifts that made his hearers quicken
From calm to joy.

Stumbling, he saw bright waters gleaming
With star-gleams spark on spark,
Then he struck stone, then all was seeming,
Then all was dark.

Before he clanged upon the paving,
Lovel the Red was in,
Crying: "Come, friends; he's ours past saving . . .
Die in your sin . . .

"Die," and he struck, struck twice, but tamely,
Being too near his mark.
Lancelot, closing, gripped him gamely
And struck him stark,

And swung him as a shield before him
As guard to Kurslin's axe,
Which struck Sir Lovel fair and tore him
As cards tear flax.

Lovel fell back upon his slayer
But Kurslin thrust him clear:
He cried: "Where is this Queen's betrayer?
I'll kill him here."

But Lovel's body made him stumble,
And Lancelot cried: "Not so . . .
I betray no one, friend, be humble,
Get out, man . . . go."

And Lancelot struck him surely straightway
Over the gangway wall,
Down to the entrance of the gateway
Men heard the fall.

Thus all knights killed by Lance — dead far below castle wall.

→ To p. 379.

And at the crash the party wavered
And fell back to the stair;
Having four champions dead, they quavered;
He watched them there.

Then Mador, of the White Rock Leaguer
That guards the Wye Mouth Ford,
Lured by the smile of death was eager
And tosst his sword,

And cried: "Now, Lancelot, my brother,
Have at you, with good heart,
One of us two will kill the other
Before we part.

"Remember now our ancient quarrel
About that pasture-right.
Now one of us shall earn a laurel:
Have at you . . . fight."

Then rushing as the wild boar rushes
In some oak glade of Dean,
He scored his gashes with his tushes
So bitter keen.

Two slashes right and left made fire
On Lancelot's armour bright:
Lancelot's sword fell like a geier
From heaven's height,

A geier, that aloft in heaven
Stares at the sun unblind . . .
Then plunges headlong like the leven
Upon the hind:

So swept the broadsword from its eyry
Shrieking to seek its own,
Beating its port and clanging fiery
Through steel, through bone,

Through marrow to the life, so sweeping
Lancelot's smiting scored . . .
And Mador's soul had done with keeping
The swift Wye ford.

And Mador drooped and toppled over,
That loud-voiced ward of Wye,
To feed no more on the green clover
The white-faced kye,

To hear no more sand-raddled Severn
Pass out to sea in song,
But fill a grass-plot at St. Keverne
Not six feet long.

And seeing Mador dead, the seven
Cried: "All together . . . now,
Down with the traitor: help us heaven,
Pull stroke, pull bow."

Petipase led their meyny shouting
The cries of the sea host,
He being a sailor tanned from scouting
The Saxon coast.

He had a short axe poised for striking
Lancelot's skull apart,
Lancelot sent his sword-point spiking
Athwart his heart.

And leaping, Petipase remembered
The red sails of his ships,
Then he collapsed like one dismembered
And in eclipse.

But knew among the gleams and crying
Through which his soul was wrencht,
That other men than he were dying
And that they blencht.

For Lancelot, his point withdrawing,
Struck Florens with the edge
Over the brow, that he fell clawing
Against the ledge.

Then as Joure sprang, the great Knight quickly
So smote him with his shield,
That Joure's manhood was made sickly,
He drooped, he reeled,

And straight, before he fell, the ravage
Of the sharp sword-edge came
Swift as the coming of the savage
Who goes in flame.

And Joure fell and clanged in falling,
But heard before he died
The ring of the triumphant calling
Lancelot cried:

For as the shaken four were backing,
Lancelot cried his cry
That led like trumpets in attacking
To victory,

And charging as he cried, he drove them
Back to the winding stair,
Where, two men making stand, he clove them,
Maelgon and Gare.

Then leaping down the steps pursuing,
He cut down Galleron:
But he who set the trouble brewing,
Modred, was gone . . .

Gone screaming in his dread to cover
Across the sleeping town.
Lancelot turned him to his lover
And sat him down.

Then after all that crash of warring
Came silence, without thrill:
Kolgrevance quiet on the flooring,
The lovers still.

Outside, the city slept; the water
Moaned at the bridge's piers,
The moonlight blancht that place of slaughter,
The dew dripped tears.

The white mist, from the river wreathing,
Shrouded the river ground:
But for the dew and the two breathing,
There was no sound.

Gwenivere spoke at last: "O glory
Of all Knights among men,
This of to-night will be a story
Not matched agen."

A silence followed in the tower
Save for the Knight's deep breath.
Horror had followed on the power
Of dealing death.

By the dim flicker of the taper
Sir Lancelot discerned
How in her face as white as paper
The Queen's eyes burned.

Deep in the panels of the walling
He heard the death-tick knock,
The dewdrops from the aspen falling
Ticked like a clock.

Then in the convent tower a tolling
Called nuns into the tower.
Lancelot said: "Past man's controlling
Are place and hour.

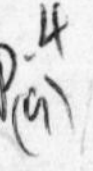

"I had no quarrel with the meyny
Nor did I know them all,
But Life is not at peace with any
And her blows fall.

"Now all our hours of joy together
Are past, our share henceforth
Will be but bitterness, with weather
Out of the north.

"This day, beginning in the quire
Where now the ladies sing,
Will make our glory of desire
Another thing.

"For I foresee the Kingdom breaking
Asunder from all this:
Out of the welter of man's making
What must be is.

"Here is the prelude to the story
That leads us to the grave.
So be it: we have had a glory
Not many have.

"Though what to-morrow may discover
Be harsh to what has been,
No matter, I am still your lover
And you my queen."

to here

How do they spend the rest of night?

Guenevere's confession – p. 360

THE BREAKING OF THE LINKS *

They told King Arthur how the Knights were killed,
He saw the bodies carried by on biers
By torchlight, among faces, under spears;
He knew what misery had been begun;
The doors and shutters banged: the city thrilled.
"The mob will murder Gwenivere," he thought.
The Queen sat haggard like a soul distraught.
"Courage," he whispered; "Much may yet be done."
He led her quaywards as the forum filled.

And while the rabble gathered in the square,
He set her in his galley and bade sail.
He watched the galley whitening a trail
Down eddied Usk for towered Camelot.
"But Lancelot," he thought, "they will not spare,
These widows and these takers of the feud.
He must begone at once before pursued."
Therefore he sent Sir Bors to Lancelot,
Who drew him north, the townsfolk unaware.

Soon, when the colour-giving dawn had come,
The kinsfolk of the dead came, crying all
For vengeance on the killer, to the hall.
"Bring out this royal harlot and her man.
These ruiners of all shall pay for some.
Where are they, Arthur? Bring them out," they cried.
"Where are this strumpet and her homicide?
Burn them, the traitor and his harridan;
Punish their murderings by martyrdom."

* See also page 413.

Then Arthur said, "Keep silence here; the Queen
Is gone from here: so Lancelot has gone.
As to the killings, we shall think thereon
At ripest leisure." Modred answered, "No.
No royalty or loyalty can screen
Treason like theirs; their hot adulteries,
Their plots that sought the Kingdom for a prize,
Their slaughterings, that laid our kinsmen low."
"No," the crowd yelled, "they shall not get off clean."

"No," Modred said. "For, King, you cannot know
The truth of this. Last night at your behest
I went, with friends, with warrant, to arrest
This Lancelot for treasons to the crown.
We summoned him to court: he would not go.
We strove to take him, he resisted: then,
Doing their duty, all those dozen men,
Man after man, were harshly beaten down.
Not by the killer's greater manhood; no . . .

"No, but because within that narrow hold
Only one man could reach him at a time;
Nor was the Queen inactive in the crime . . .
Those dozen sworders held her in regard;
Her presence helped the one a hundredfold;
She helped to arm him; being armed, she stood
So that we dared not tackle nor make good
Our comrades' efforts; our approach was barred,
We must have wounded her had we been bold.

"True, harsher captains might indeed have laid
Hands on the Queen and dragged her headlong thence;
But with what scandal and with what offence?
Mad as we were, we would not shame her thus.

Besides, the only purpose of the raid
Was to take Lancelot; we held no brief
To touch the partner, but arrest the chief . . .
So, holding back, destruction fell on us.
They have escaped, but God will see us paid."

Then Gawaine said: "What need was there to send
Armed men upon the Queen and Lancelot,
The King's wife and King's cousin, as all wot?
The two are daily in the palace here;
At one word spoken, either would attend.
But I perceive that jealousy begins
To conquer wisdom by imputing sins . . .
With Lancelot away and Modred near,
A royal bastard's fortune might amend . . .

"I will not silence, I will speak my word
To you, my cousin Arthur, and to one
At once my mother's and my cousin's son,
Who, with twelve captains, made a night surprise:
Against one lion, thirteen in a herd,
(Or fourteen was it?) By the starry skies
God made His vision of the matter plain.
Yet here this mongrel Modred dares complain . . .
I say he should be branded and unspurred."

Then Arthur said, "But I support him, I,
Against your cavils in the present cause;
He served against a breaker of the laws
At his life's peril, among comrades killed.
And proven treasons, not a jealousy,
Make the foundations upon which we build.
Treasons that amply justified arrest.
As Fate has fallen, I have judged it best
To wait a certain season ere we try . . .

"Therefore the two accused are banisht hence,
Awaiting trial. Meanwhile Modred did,
Or strove to do, exactly as I bid."
"Ay," the crowd shouted, "everybody knows
Gawaine can argue in a trot's defence.
He takes their part." Gawaine said, "I suppose
My cousin-brother now will govern us.
Now I remember what the ship-rat does . . .
When ships begin to leak, he scuttles thence.

"Therefore, my cousin Arthur, chief and King,
I say good-bye: I say you are misled
By plottings from this misbegotten head.
Not lightly will this cloud of evil pass.
I, like the swallow, joined you in your spring,
When first the daisies whitened all the grass;
Now autumn spiders come and leaves are blowing,
The summer being gone, I must be going."
Then Bors and Hector strode into the ring.

Bors said, "I brought Sir Lancelot away
For Gloucester and the north, as I was told.
The time has come for speakers to be bold.
Why was our captain banisht without trial?
Who sent the gang, commanding them to slay?
Since when were Tablers subject to espial?
I say, as Gawaine says, you take advice
From one whose plottings shall not use me twice.
Since Modred governs, I shall not obey."

Sir Hector said, "I do not ask the cause . . .
For men who fling the best and keep the worst
Are men whose fortunes are about to burst,
As yours are, Arthur, acting as you do.

A golden eagle cannot sort with daws,
Nor will this mongrel Modred sort with you;
Nor we with him, by heaven, so farewell.
We choose the Queen and Lancelot and hell,
And leave you folly, Modred and the laws."

Then out the three defiant captains strode.
Their friends and kin, the party of the Queen,
Followed them out: all silent was the scene;
All present knew what breaking of the links
That bound the provinces together bode:
Nothing was heard except the little clinks
Of spurs on flagstones: then the horses sparred,
Sidling from men who mounted in the yard;
Then the slow horse-hoofs died along the road.

And while their going sounded, men were still.
Then Agravaine's gaunt widow, white with hate,
Cried, "Shall our murdered darlings' spirits wait
Thus long for simple justice for their death?"
Then horse-hoofs clattered to the portal-sill,
A rider tottered to them spent for breath;
He cried, "I've galloped from the Kentish prince,
I have not drank these thirty hours since.
Get ready for a second Badon Hill."

Then he sank, panting, till they gave him wine
And splashed his face with water; then he said:
"King Iddoc says this is no common raid,
No, but an over-swarming, such as comes
Only when blazing comets give the sign
And banded nations seek elysiums . . .
Three hundred ships were counted at the first,
More follow fast, we haven't toucht the worst.
They made our army snap like broken twine.

"Who are they? Why, the manhood of a race
Or races, banded by an oath to seize
A Kingdom for themselves beyond the seas:
The summer pirates join with them besides.
Our ships attacked them at the landing-place,
Their ships destroyed them; now their navy rides
Holding the ocean to Augusta tower.
King Iddoc fought them in an evil hour.
They thrashed us out of knowledge and gave chase.

"Briefly, the width of Kent is overrun;
They hold the Channel; beyond any doubt
They will advance before the moon is out
And toss your men-at-arms like meadow-hay;
They are fell fighters, every mother's son.
But will you muster with what men you may
And join King Iddoc? If the truth be told,
Whatever line we take we cannot hold;
They are our masters, Arthur, we are done."

Then Arthur said, "Whatever fair success
These pirates have, I never knew it last.
For when they seem the worst the worst is past;
They conquer first, then suffer for supply.
Therefore be comforted in your distress,
We suffer first and conquer by-and-by.
I start for Camelot at once from here;
By harvest we will have the Kingdom clear
Whatever Iddoc's fears are, I say yes.

"Come, Modred, we must sail for Camelot
Within the hour, or we lose the tide.
Dismiss the court, the other things must bide."
But as he passt, that wraith of Agravaine's
Cried, "You have trickt us, Modred misbegot,
You killed our loves and leave us to our pains.

You shall not go until our cause is heard."
Here the guards seized her, but her witch's gird
Rang through the hall and was forgotten not.

"Modred betrayed us, it is all laid bare.
He used our husbands only to disgrace
The Queen and Lancelot and take their place.
And all our lovely lovers are laid dead,
While he removes to Camelot to share
King Arthur's favour; curses on his head.
But you shall perish by the plots begun,
Son by the sire, sire by the son,
Before one swallow seeks the southern air."

But now King Arthur was aboard his ship,
Rushing from Usk athwart the Severn stream;
War lay ahead, the rest was but a dream:
Modred beside him shared his busy brain.
His galley took a white bone in her grip,
The running bubbles made a noise like rain;
And though he missed two comrades from of old,
His son was by him and his heart was bold
To break the raid by this new comradeship.

GWENIVACH TELLS

I, Gwenivach, King Modred's queen, declare
What happened next: I, Gwenivach, accurst,
Being born very little but most fair.
King Arthur marched his army into Kent
And suffered loss at first:
I said to Modred, "See, the gods prepare
Your fortunes for you; take the chances sent."

Small need had he for prompting; he arose,
He and myself and all our chosen band;
He seized the crown and governed as he chose.
The gutters reddened from our glutted hate.
Had we but laid a hand
On Gwenivere, she should have died, God knows
But she escaped us for a bitterer fate.

Throughout we triumphed: Modred was the King,
I was the Queen, from Gelliwic to Wales.
Sir Kolgrim joined us from his pirating,
Bringing, to swell our army, all the crews
That manned his hundred sails.
Well to our side did Fortune's balance swing:
Then Fortune changed; a rider came with news.

These were the news: that Arthur had destroyed
The heathen fleet and army and had turned
To make our treasoned usurpation void,
Marching like fire on a windy day;
That, when our subjects learned
His coming, they renounced us overjoyed.
So our red morning had an evening grey.

We saw their malice snicker in the street
In Camelot: would God we had had time
To blast their pleasure in my love's defeat;
Some of those sneerers should have had white lips,
And eyeballs seared with lime.
But Modred gave the order to retreat;
We marched to Cornwall to Sir Kolgrim's ships.

And there we waited Fate and Fortune's chance,
Camped above harbour on the windy down.
Spies brought us word of Arthur's swift advance,
Then that he halted like a man in doubt
In that burnt Roman town.
Then lurching at us like a launching lance,
He camped in hail and hung his colours out.

ARTHUR IN THE RUINS

King Arthur watched within the ruined town,
Debating what to do and what avoid;
No sleep was there for his tormented brain.
War lay behind; before, were war and pain,
The column of the Kingdom fallen down,
With all that he had struggled for destroyed.
For if he fought his son,
The heathen would re-win what he had won;
And if he did not . . . there it was again.

So, being heart-sick, saying "I must rest,"
He turned him to his blanket on the stones
Grass-sprouted, of a roofless temple's floor.
The sky above her bright-eyed watchers bore
Now that the youngling moon had wilted west.
Miswandered beetles fumbled out with drones.
And there a woman stood
Star-semée, with a planet in her hood,
Live with such beauty as the morning owns.

"Arthur," she said, "these many weary days
You have desired help where none has been.
To captain souls, in their intensest grief,
No comrade understanding gives relief,
Or brings that balm of the discouraged, praise:
Sweet friendship cannot come to King and Queen;
But we immortals come,
Sometimes, to help them in their martyrdom,
As sunlight comes upon the summer leaf.

"You know that what I counsel will be true,
True as your inmost self at whitest heat
That touches All-Truth, and, as such, endures.
All courses that perplex men with their lures
Perplex you now with anguish, which to do.
So may the summer poppies hide the wheat.
This single thing must be:—
Battle with Modred by the western sea;
Of all man's destined courses, this is yours.

"This will but seem a vision of the night
Rede-ing you falsely: let me prove it true:—
In the grey morning, as you march the Heath,
Left of the road a woman with a wreath,
Broad-browed, like me, in raiment crosst with white,
Yearning towards you there, will welcome you.
'King,' she will say, 'Go on.
Eternal glory waits in Avalon,
In Avalon the sword will find its sheath.'"

At dawn King Arthur bade the trumpets call
"Strike camp and march;" and as King Arthur rode,
Lo, by the crossways in the heathy place,
A broad-browed woman with a noble face,
Wreathed with the little toadflax from the wall,
With white-crosst garments, from the heather strode
Towards him, and declared
Those self-same words: then on King Arthur fared
West, from the downlands to the Cornish chase.

THE FIGHT AT CAMLAN

Soon the two armies were in touch, and soon
Camped, face to face, upon the windy, high,
Thyme-scented barren where the wild bees croon.
Southward and westward was the wrinkled sea
Where Kolgrim's ships lay black.
Now must they treat or battle, since to fly
No longer was a solace that might be.
The season neared midsummer and full moon;
His impulse urged King Arthur to attack.

Then thought, and pity of his son, and hate
Of shedding subjects' blood, made him resolve
To make an offer ere he shut the gate
On every end save battle to the death.
He sent Sir Bedwyr forth
To Modred, to discover what might solve
Their quarrel without quell of living breath.
Modred replied, "Let Arthur abdicate
This southern half the realm, and keep the north.

"If he contemn this, say I shall not treat
Or commune, save as King with equal King.
Here is my army, yonder is my fleet;
Cornwall is mine, I can maintain it mine;
I am prepared to fight.
But if my modest terms can end the thing,
And all this southern realm be paid as fine,
We'll choose ambassadors and let them meet
There on that barrow, in the armies' sight."

So, to be brief, both men empowered peers
To make discussion of the terms of peace.
The barrow, of the King of ancient years,
Topped by a thorn tree, was the meeting-place.
There six from either side
Went, while the heralds bade all warfare cease,
No sword to leave its sheath, no bow its case,
The horsemen to dismount and pile their spears
And all keep camp till all were ratified.

The twelve Knights went unarmed up to the howe
Between the armies, to debate together;
They hung a white flag on the hawthorn bough
And started talking, while the troops in camp
Disarmed, and cleaned their gear,
Or stretcht to sleep upon the matted heather;
Or with their comrades sat upon the ramp,
Sure that the quarrel would be settled now;
Each hailed the other side with mock or cheer.

To eastwards of the campments was a mound
Or rise of earth from some old fallen fence
Of ancient village, camp, or cattle-pound;
Three rebels flung themselves upon its top
With Kolgrim, Modred's friend,
Who mocked and said: "These talkers have no sense."
Then, hours later, "Let this folly stop . . .
There goes King Arthur; let us shoot the hound,
Crown Modred King and bring it to an end."

Prone in the heath the four uncased their bows,
They strung them, on each other's bodies stayed;
Then from their quivers each an arrow chose.
Arthur was sitting with Sir Kai in talk,
Making an easy mark.

Back to the ears the arrow-feathers laid,
Then, as the hornet leaves his hollow balk
Humming with evil, so the arrows rose,
Shot from the string to strike the victim stark.

Sweeping the space those shafted barbings sped,
Like golden birds athwart the light they thrilled:
One pierced Kai's bitter heart and struck him dead,
Another cut King Arthur's purple cloak;
Another, by his hand
Stuck quivering in the table till it stilled;
The last struck sideways on a shield and broke
Below the barbs, its venomed fang unfed.
"Quick, mates, again," said Kolgrim to his band.

But as they drew, King Arthur's herald cried:
"Treason! The men are shooting! Quick. Beware."
Then, leaping up, he thrust the King aside
And shouted "Treason! Fall in, Arthur's men."
And as he snatcht a shield
The second flighting shafted through the air
That struck him through and put him out of ken
Of wife and home by pleasant Severnside.
Then trumpets blew and tumult filled the field.

The counsellors upon the barrow fled,
Each to his camp, not knowing what betid;
King Arthur's men into their cohorts sped,
Swearing, "We'll pay these breakers of the truce,
Oath-breaking, treacherous swine."
The black-backt adder to her cavern glid;
Now Modred's archers let their arrows loose,
And many a grey goose-feather was made red,
Ere either army formed a battle-line.

Now the two armies stood as walls of spears
Beneath the ever-passing shriek and strike
Of arrows wavering in their careers.
Modred came swooping as a falcon swoops,
On horseback down his ranks,
Crying: "Behold your sparrows: play the shrike."
The trumpets blared among the rebel troops,
King Arthur galloped to his front with cheers;
He cried: "If fronts are stubborn, try the flanks."

Then as in thunderstorms the wind-vanes shift
On towers, against blackness, with a gleam,
So did his riders' spearheads glitter swift
Above the blowing pennons as they drooped
As one, down to the charge.
Then did the stallions bare their gums and scream,
The bright bits tightened as the riders stooped;
Then like a lightning from a thunder rift
The squadrons clashed together, lance on targe.

For hours they fought: then Arthur, beaten back
From camp and downland to the planted fields,
Steadied his line against the spent attack;
The armies stopped the battle to re-form.
Thirst-broken soldiers quencht
Their thirsts, and dropped their lances and their shields.
There fell the central quiet of the storm,
And spearmen strayed, to rob the haversack
Of friend or rebel prone with muscles clencht.

And while the battle stayed, Sir Modred found
No plenishment of spears and arrows spent
Save what the fight had scattered on the ground;
But Arthur formed upon his waggon-train
That brought him up new gear.

Archers and lancers took fresh armament
And faced to front, resolved to fight again.
Then Arthur heard a distant trumpet sound,
And, looking, saw strange horsemen in his rear.

And as he moved some lancers as a guard,
Thinking that Modred threatened his retreat,
He saw the banner of the golden pard;
Sir Lancelot was riding in to aid
With squadrons of picked horse.
Lancelot said, "Though banisht, let us meet
To put an ending to this renegade:
See, his line wavers: let us push him hard;
He'll break as sure as prickles grow on gorse."

It was now drawing to the summer dusk,
The sun, low fallen, reddened on the sea,
Dog-rose and honeysuckle shed their musk;
Lancelot's troops moved up upon the left,
King Arthur took the right.
It was the hour of the homing bee.
Then up the bright blades glittered on the heft,
The dragon of red battle bared her tusk,
King Arthur's tattering trumpets sounded Fight.

At a slow trot they started, keeping touch,
Elbow to elbow, upon rested horses
That strove to get the bits within their clutch;
Troop after troop the hoof-beat thunder grew;
Slowly the trot increast
As Lammas torrents grow in watercourses;
Then, utterly triumphant trumpets blew
And as a mounting wave, already much,
Mounts mighty ere it smashes into yeast,

So mounted there that billow ere it broke;
Then, at its breaking, Modred, branch and root,
Horseman and footman, scattered like blown smoke
From burning leaves on an October blast.
Then mile on moorland mile,
King Arthur's army had them in pursuit;
Arthur with six Knights followed Modred fast,
Till on a beach he turned to strike a stroke.
Ten, against Arthur's seven, seemed worth while.

THE FIGHT ON THE BEACH, OR THE PASSING

These were the nine with Modred:—Kolgrim, Gor,
Bein Bloodsark, Stagfoot, Odwin, Addersfang,
Math, Erbin, Breuse, nine scoundrels in a gang,
Three pirates and three outlaws and three knaves.
They turned upon the shore,
And Kolgrim said, "The battle has been lost,
But some beside the beaten shall have graves:
Some of these conquerors shall pay the cost."
These were the six with Arthur:—Owain Mor

(Gwenivere's brother), from the March of Wales,
Bedwyr, the Cornish Knight, whom Tristan fooled;
Lucan, the Golden, whom King Ban had schooled;
Prince Ryence, Girl-Face, beautiful as Spring;
Ambrose, of whom the tales
Still linger by the hearthstones of the west;
And Maximin, the son of Ban the King,
Of all deer-footed runners he was best:
These six now cast their lives into the scales.

And first the giant Owain, called the Red,
Riding in front, put spurs, and with his axe
Killed Math and Sigurd Stagfoot with two hacks;
The Stagfoot, falling, wrenched the haft away.
Here Owain's horse was sped.
He snatched Breuse' javelin as the stallion fell,
He speared Breuse through beneath the shoulder stay,
Addersfang cracked his helmet like a shell;
He grappled Addersfang as Breuse fell dead.

Bein Bloodsark struck him in the back, but he
Brought Addersfang from saddle; then he reeled,
Clutching that panting body as a shield.
Addersfang's horse upset him, Erbin struck,
He could no longer see:
But with his knife he thrust at Addersfang
Under the buckles, twice, and had good luck,
Leaving the hangman but a corpse to hang;
Dying, he muttered, "Four, or was it three?"

King Kolgrim rode at Ryence with a thrust
That speared him through and flung him to the sand;
The lance-head broke, but with the stump in hand
Kolgrim struck Ambrose overthwart the face;
Ambrose reeled back, but just—
Just as King Kolgrim had his axe to strike,
Maximin knocked him over with a mace;
Kolgrim rose dizzy, grinning like a pike,
Ambrose's javelin struck him to the dust.

Bein Bloodsark strode across him and cleared ground.
Men were dismounted now, their horses loose.
Kolgrim rose dying with, "I broke the truce . . .
One other thing I'll break before I die."
His sinews were unbound,
He lapsed face forward slowly and forgot.
Then each man shouted out his battle-cry,
The two sides clashed together in a clot,
Iron with iron meeting, wolf with hound.

Modred killed Ambrose dead, that Knight of Dean;
Erbin sore-wounded Bedwyr; Lucan dropped,
Stunned by a mace-blow which his helmet stopped,
(Odwin the Smiter dealt it as he rushed);

Odwin struck Maximin,
Breaking his guard; he swung and struck again;
The golden leopard of the crest was crushed,
Swift darkness crashed upon the young man's brain,
Dead fell that youngling of the golden Queen.

Then for an instant Arthur fought with five.
He slipped from Modred's blow and swept at Gor
A slash athwart the neck that made them four;
Bein stabbed him at the sword-belt as he smote.
Arthur saw Odwin drive
Towards him, with his mallet swung aloft;
Short'ning his point, he took him in the throat;
Odwin's mace toppled from his grip, he coughed
And fell upon the sand no more alive.

Erbin struck Arthur on the shoulder: Bein
Stabbed him again, a short-arm body-stab:
Then Modred gripped his ankles like a crab,
Meaning to trip, but Arthur shook him clear,
Then slipped in the bright brine,
For now the tide was coming. As he slipped
His left hand clutcht the butt of Erbin's spear;
He wrencht the shaft from Erbin as he dipped
And stabbed him through the heart spoon with the tine.

Modred and Bein came at him as he rose
Among the ripples of the gleaming sea.
He swerved aside and stumbled on his knee:
Bein fell across him, blocking Modred's way.
With moonlight-glinting blows
They struck each other, and the splashings shone,
Like salmon-leapings, as they tried to slay:
Then, at a lunge from Arthur, Bein was gone,
Heart-stricken with his vague hands clutching oaze.

Modred drew backward, seeing Bloodsark killed.
"Modred," King Arthur said, "surrender here.
Your treacheries have cost this Kingdom dear.
They cannot prosper, Modred: let them end."
The brimming ripples spilled
Their brightness on the bodies of the dead.
"I am your father, Modred, and your friend,"
King Arthur pleaded, "and your shot has sped.
I would have granted much of what you willed

"Had you but told me: it is not too late
To come to some agreement, you and I.
Come up, above the tides, and let us try."
He stood near Modred on the moonlit sand.
Modred was still as hate;
He made no answer, but he breathed deep breath.
Sore-wounded Bedwyr, propping with his hand,
Cried, "Arthur, bind me: I shall bleed to death."
"I'll bind you," Lucan answered, "only wait . . .

"One moment, till this dizziness is past."
The ripples swayed the bodies up the beach.
Then Modred said, "A sweet forgiving speech,
More than a bastard rebel can deserve.
I shook the dice and cast
A great throw to be quit of men's contempt.
'Bastard,' they called me; but the bastard's nerve
Came nearer Kingdom's conquest than they dreamt.
I fail; my one endeavor is my last.

"I spit upon your fatherhood and you.
You be my friend, who made me suffer scorn
From every living soul since I was born?
My friend, you think? You sorry cuckold; no.

But an account is due
And shall be paid, O luster that begat.
Down to the hell of all my hatings, go."
Then, leaping forward like an angry cat,
He struck his father on the headpiece, through.

Three blows he struck, not heeding Arthur's thrust;
Then, shaking clear, his features wrenched aside,
Marshlighted deathward, he collapsed and died:
"Thirty years' anguish," were his latest words,
"Made by your idle lust."
Arthur, with both hands groping outward, swayed;
The tide-brink touched his ankles with its curds:
Sick Bedwyr was beginning to upbraid:—
"O come to stop this bleeding! O you must."

Then Arthur reeled towards him, saying "Where?
Where are you wounded, Bedwyr?" Then he knelt,
Tented the wound and bound it with his belt,
And raised Sir Bedwyr's head; his own bled fast.
Then Lucan, crawling, bare
Drink from the brook for Bedwyr, but it spilled.
Then Arthur said, "This hour is my last.
Modred is dead, I killed him; I am killed.
Call, Lucan, if our friends are anywhere."

So Lucan called, a hurt man's feeble cry.
No answer followed save a stir of wings,
That and the creeping water's whisperings
Ant-like about the bodies of the dead.
Then Arthur said, "Good-bye,
O you two faithful who have followed me
With loving service ever since I led.
I give as bitter payment as the sea,
Hard days when living, hard death when you die."

Then, moving from them for a little space,
His spirit felt the promptings of the blood
That now the brimming tides were at the flood,
And that the ebb would carry him afar.
West from the rocks a race
Streamed seawards, speckt with bubble-broken white.
Lamplike before him was the evening star.
He said, "My comrades perish, touch and sight . . .
The feast is finished: let me utter grace."

He faced the western star with lifted hand,
While muddled thoughts and clear thoughts clanged and passt,
Of splendid things, if life could only last,
And long-dead friends, and kindnesses undone
And good things hoped or planned
That life would none of: then he took his sword,
Red once at Badon, red, now, from his son.
He bound about its hilt the priested cord;
He said, "The tide is setting from the land,

"And I, too, set; but yet, before I go,
This that King Uther, yes, and Ambrose bare
In battles with the pirates everywhere,
Our House's Luck, this Britain's Bright Defense,
My Fortune in the flow,
Must take the ebb, if I have strength to fling."
He tottered to the water and stood tense;
The moon and the moon's image watched the King,
The weltering water ceased her to-and-fro.

He gathered up his dying strength, he swung
The weapon thrice and hurled it to the stream;
It whirled like a white gannet with a gleam,
Turning blade up in moonlight as it fell;

Bright-flying foam-drops stung
The steel, the spray leapt as it disappeared.
"No other man shall have you: all is well,"
King Arthur said; and now his moment neared;
The tide was ebbing and his heart was wrung.

A curlew called: he fell upon his knees,
And lo, his failing eyes beheld a ship
Burning a path athwart the water-rip;
The water gleamed about her like soft flame,
Her gear creaked in the breeze;
Towards him, nosing through the soaken sand,
To rest her at his side, the vessel came.
His Helper held the tiller in her hand;
His Friend was come, to comfort his disease.

Then seven queens upraised the dying King
And laid him quiet in a bed aboard,
And balmed the gashes smitten with the sword;
Immortal life upon their faces glowed.
Then they began to sing:—
"We bear him to the isle of Avalon,
Where everlasting summer has abode."
An unheard summons bade the ship begone,
She headed seawards with a stooping wing.

Lucan and Bedwyr, propping as they might,
Watched as she passed: they heard the singing range
Through secrets of things hidden and things strange,
And things of beauty not yet found in thought.
The ship seemed made of light,
She travelled by the thrilling of the hymn;
The race a moment with her passing fought,
Then she was on into the distance dim,
And on beyond, and on, and out of sight.

GWENIVERE TELLS

So Arthur passed, but country-folk believe
He will return, to triumph and achieve;
Men watch for him on each Midsummer Eve.

They watch in vain, for ere that night was sped,
That ship reached Avalon with Arthur dead;
I, Gwenivere, helped cere him, within lead.

I, Gwenivere, helped bury him in crypt,
Under cold flagstones that the ringbolts shipped;
The hangings waved, the yellow candles dripped.

Anon I made profession, and took vows
As nun encloistered: I became Christ's spouse,
At Amesbury, as Abbess to the house.

I changed my ermines for a goat-hair stole,
I broke my beauty there, with dule and dole,
But love remained a flame within my soul.

What though I watched and fasted and did good
Like any saint among my sisterhood,
God could not be deceived, God understood

How night and day my love was as a cry
Calling my lover out of earth and sky
The while I shut the bars against reply.

Years thence a message came: I stood to deal
The lepers' portions through the bars of steel;
A pilgrim thrust me something shut with seal.

I could not know him in his hoodings hid;
Besides, he fled: his package I undid;
Lancelot's leopard-crest was on the lid.

Within, on scarlet ivory, there lay
A withered branchlet, having leaves of grey.
A writing said: "This is an olive spray

"Picked for your blessing from a deathless tree
That shades the garden of Gethsemane;
May it give peace, as it has given me."

Did it give peace? Alas, a woman knows
The rind without may deaden under blows;
But who has peace when all within's a rose?

THE DEATH OF LANCELOT

Then, after many years, a rider came,
An old lame man upon a horse as lame,
Hailing me 'Queen' and calling me by name.

I knew him; he was Bors of Gannis, he.
He said that in his chapel by the sea
My lover on his death-bed longed for me.

No vows could check me at that dying cry,
I cast my abbess-ship and nunhood by . . .
I prayed, "God, let me see him ere he die."

We passt the walls of Camelot: we passt
Sand-raddled Severn shadowing many a mast,
And bright Caerleon where I saw him last.

Westward we went, till, in an evening, lo,
A bay of bareness with the tide at flow,
And one green headland in the sunset's glow.

There was the chapel, at a brooklet's side.
I galloped downhill to it with my guide.
I was too late, for Lancelot had died.

I had last seen him as a flag in air,
A battle banner bidding men out-dare.
Now he lay dead; old, old, with silver hair.

I had not ever thought of him as old . . .
This hurt me most: his sword-hand could not hold
Even the cross upon the sacking-fold.

They had a garden-close outside the church
With Hector's grave, where robins came to perch.
When I could see again, I went to search

For flowers for him dead, my king of men.
I wandered up the brooklet, up the glen:
A robin watched me and a water-hen.

There I picked honeysuckles, many a bine
Of golden trumpets budding red as wine,
With dark green leaves, each with a yellow spine.

We buried him by Hector, covered close
With these, and elder-flower, and wild rose.
His friends are gone thence now: no other goes.

He once so ringing glad among the spears,
Lies where the rabbit browses with droppt ears
And shy-foot stags come when the moon appears.

Myself shall follow, when it be God's will;
But whatsoe'er my death be, good or ill,
Surely my love will burn within me still.

Death cannot make so great a fire drowse;
What though I broke both nun's and marriage-vows,
April will out, however hard the boughs;

And though my spirit be a lost thing blown,
It, in its waste, and, in the grave, my bone,
Will glimmer still from Love, that will atone.

DUST TO DUST

Henry Plantagenet, the English King,
Came with Fair Rosamond, for monkish picks
Had lifted flaggings set in Roman bricks
And cleared a Latin-carven slab which told
That Arthur and his Queen were buried there . . .

They watched: the diggers raised the covering . . .
There lay those great ones placid under pyx;
Arthur enswathed as by a burning wing
Or wave of Gwenivere's undying hair,
Which lit the vaulty darkness with its gold.

Seeing such peace the living lovers knelt
And sought each other's hands: those dead ones lay
Untouched by any semblance of decay,
Liker to things immortal than things dead,
Manhood's undying glory, beauty's queen.

The crimson rose in Rosamunda's belt
Dropped, on the dead, one petal, soft as may.
Like ice that unseen April makes to melt,
Those bodies ceast, as though they had not been;
The petal lay on powder within lead.

ON THE COMING OF ARTHUR

By ways unknown, unseen,
The summer makes things green,
The pastures and the boughs
Wherein birds house.

Summer will come again,
For sick things become sane,
And dead things fat the root
That brings forth fruit.

Arthur, like summer, waits,
For Wit and Will are gates,
Like those the summers pass
To green earth's grass.

Arthur will come like June,
Full meadow and full moon,
With roses up above
As red as love,

And may-bloom down below,
As white as fallen snow,
And no least linnet dumb,
O Arthur, come.

THE OLD TALE OF THE BEGETTING

The men of old, who made the tale for us,
Declare that Uther begat Arthur thus:—

Queen Ygrain sat in her bower
Looking from Tintagel tower.

Uther saw Ygrain the Bright,
His heart went pit-pat at the sight.

He said to Merlin, "Make her mine,
Or you'll be hog's meat for my swine."

Merlin wrought all day with pray'r,
With water, earth and fire and air.

He made a mask that had the look,
Colour and speech of Ygrain's Duke.

Uther wore it and came late
And knocked upon Tintagel gate.

He cried, with the mask's voice, "Fair Ygrain,
Open, it is your lord again."

The dogs howled and the owls cried,
But Uther came to the Queen's side.

As he climbed to the Queen's bed,
Ygrain's Duke on the moors fell dead.

Uther drinks and boasts at his board,
Ygrain sings for her dead lord:
"Would I were pierced through with a sword!"

THE TAKING OF GWENIVERE

French poets write:—That, Lancelot the brave
Fought and defeated Arthur's Knights, to save
Queen Gwenivere, then sentenced to the fire:—

That he and she then lived in heart's desire
At Joyous Gard, for certain months or years.

This is Queen Isolt's tale, not Gwenivere's,
Tristan's, not Lancelot's: but since men know
This version best, I tell it also so.

The trial of Gwenivere:

Soon as the colour-giving dawn was seen,
Arthur bade call
His Court, to judge the sinning of his Queen
There in the hall.
Himself, in scarlet, sat upon his throne
To hear her plead;
She, with her beauty only, stood alone;
Alone indeed.

For round her stood the widows and the young
Of all the Knights
Whose limbs and lives her lover had unstrung
On the wall's heights;
And with them were the rabble of the Court
And Modred's friends,
Thinking the baiting of the Queen a sport
That made amends.

to p. 415

And in the shrilling of the threats and cries
That nothing stilled,
Sir Modred told of Lancelot's emprise
And how he killed
The meyny sent against him to discover
The wicked thing.
"He killed them," Modred cried, "this woman's lover.
Be just, O King."

Then Arthur spoke: "You bid me to be just . . .
Justice decrees
Death for the petty treason of a lust
And brooks no pleas;
'Death for the wife by burning at the stake;'
The law is clear;
No shadow of exception will I make,
It is death here

"Unless the one accused can bring defence
Of such a kind
That we be certain of her innocence . . .
Now let us find
What answer the accused, Queen Gwenivere,
Makes to the tale
Of petty treason brought against her here.
Let truth prevail."

The red-gold Queen replied: "O tender lord
To grant this grace,
To let me answer as you sit at board
To try the case.
A few short hours ago you ordered men
To take and kili
My friend and me. Since murder throve not then,
Now justice will."

"No," Arthur said, "they were not sent to slay,
But to arrest
And bring to me: they charged you to obey
The King's behest.
Resistance to my order was the cause
Of twelve men's death;
For that there shall be answer to the laws
As the law saith.

"But the main question now is treason, Queen.
This Knight and you
Met to be lovers as you long have been.
Is that not true?
You went disguised, in darkness and alone,
To this man's lair, dwelling place
Because you are his woman to the bone
And loved him there.

"If not to love this captain, tell us then
Why did you go
To meet him, hidden from the eyes of men
In darkness so?
Answer us that . . . remember that you stand
On a pit's brink.
Speak truth as one in judgment on God's hand,
But ere speech . . . think."

to p. 417

The colour came to Gwenivere's pale cheek,
Her great eyes shone:
"Why should I think," she asked, "before I speak?
All thought is gone
From you and all the rabble kennelled here
To hear me cast . . .
You mean to burn me living on a bier
By sentence past.

"I say you lie. Your killers never spoke
Of the King's will,
But beat the turret door until it broke,
Meaning to kill.
Then Lancelot to save me (me, the Queen)
From the King's friends,
Made such a story as will last, I ween,
Till the world ends.

"There were thirteen against a man and me;
These two remain:
Modred and Mullet in their infamy,
The things unslain . . .
They disobeyed your orders without cause,
They mocked your will:
No matter: they may much assist your laws
To kill me still."

"Queen," Arthur answered, "if they disobeyed,
That cannot clear
You, the accused one, of the charges made
Against you here.
The chief of which is, that unlawful love
Sways you from me
And has done long, as many people prove
To certainty.

"What the Court asks from you is a defence.
That you must make,
Or our unchanging law will send you hence
To burn at stake.
Why did you go by night to Lancelot
If not for sin?
Let royal indignation be forgot,
Let truth begin."

Then the proud red-gold lady, beauty's peer,
Answered: "Proceed . . .
Burn me, to soothe this kennel barking here,
Your friends in need,
Your haters and your killers and your two
Flee-ers, who ran.
Know, there is warrantise for all you do:
I loved this man."

Then Arthur said: "No need to question more . . .
Since you are his,
Doubly a traitor to the oaths you swore,
Your sentence is
That you be burned within the public ring
Outside the wall,
Before this noon: thus sentences the King . . .
Bear witness all."

Then Gawaine said: "King Arthur, you are mad,
And act from spite . . .
This is no trial that the Queen has had . . .
You have no right
To sentence on confession, without proof,
As the world knows."
Then Arthur said: "Peace, Gawaine, stand aloof.
To stake she goes."

Then Gawaine said: "You turn all upside down
For one hour's rage . . .
She is the chiefest sapphire in your crown,
Star of her age:
And you, because your bastard Modred wills,
Cast her to die.
It is not justice, no, but he that kills . . .
That infamy."

Then Arthur said: "You, for this insolence
To me, the King,
Shall call the bodyguard and take her hence
Out to the Ring,
And there see sentence done as I command."
Gawaine said: "No.
Let Modred be your foul act's dirty hand,
I will not go.

"No; let your bastard do your hangman's task;
I, a King's son,
Refuse it, whether you command or ask."
Then everyone
Cried: "Down with Gawaine!" But Sir Gawaine turned
Scorning them all;
He shouldered through the mob that milled and churned
And left the hall.

Then Arthur cried to Gareth, Gawaine's brother,
Still but a boy:
"You, Gareth, shall not question, like the other,
Your King's employ.
You, on your knightly service, take the Queen,
This proven trash,
And burn her as a felon on the green
To bitter ash.

"About it: go: fall in the bodyguard."
At this he rose
And left the Queen sans counsel or regard,
Alone with foes.
The widows and the children of those killed,
And all the mean
With nails that clutcht and savagery that thrilled,
Assailed the Queen,

So that the spearmen had ado to check
The rush that came
With sharp claws stretching for the victim's neck
And shrieks of shame.
But Gareth with a spear-butt beat them back
And kept space free,
Then said to her: "O lovely Queen, alack
That this should be . . .

"Now I am shamed whatever thing I do:
Letting you live,
I break my oath; and if I murder you,
None will forgive
And nought atone, forever, till I die . . .
These curs at least
Shall all behave or show a reason why."
Then like a beast,

A bull that sees his foe, or wolves made one,
Seeing their prey,
That crowd of haters brought with malison
The Queen to bay . . .
They beat the spearmen back, they spat, they struck,
They overwhelmed . . .
Gareth was gallant but had little luck,
That lad unhelmed;

So, in an instant, Queen and guard were reeds
Tosst in a flood
Of devils utterly possesst by greeds
For human blood.
They screamed: "You golden harlot, once so proud,
Shall now be tame;
Come to the fire, malkin, in your shroud,
And feed the flame."

Then suddenly, while all the building rang
From those who curst,
The bronze doors were forct open with a clang,
And in there burst
Lancelot and his meyny, with Sir Bors,
Ector and Urre,
Cutting a pathway to her from the doors
To rescue her.

In that fierce mellay of the charge none knew
What foe he hit;
Each in his headlong fury struck and slew,
Steel on steel bit.
Lancelot cleared the crowd, his meyny broke
The King's array;
There Lancelot killed Gareth with a stroke,
And Ector, Kai.

And Bors killed Gauter, and Sir Safer clave
Driant the Bright;
There Bel the Proud was toppled to his grave,
And Tor the Knight.
Lancelot at the Queen's side cleared a ring
And shouted: "Swine . . .
I take this royal lady from the King,
She is now mine.

"Tell Arthur therefore that I take her hence . . .
If he demur,
Let him give battle; I will make defence
For love of her."
Then, with his arm about her, forth he stalkt
Out, through the crowd,
Who shrank away from him like jackals baulkt,
Snarling but cowed.

Then at the gateway taking horse, he passt
Usk bridge at trot,
And on the green beyond it trotted fast
From archer's shot.
Th' alarm bell in the tower boomed like surf,
But fear was gone
From all those comrades trotting on the turf
While the sun shone.

Till noon they trotted, then, near Braddoc reach,
They turned aside
From raddled Severn babbling in soft speech,
To a green ride;
Through ancient oakwoods where the ravens built,
All day they went,
Till sunset found them on the western tilt
Of the bare bent.

There, looking back across the misty woods
Topped by red sky,
They saw white Venus star the solitudes
Above the Wye;
They saw the Severn sandy to the mouth,
Arthur's domain,
The forest and the mountains to the south,
Chain in blue chain.

Then Lancelot and Gwenivere were sure
That they were done
With all their past, however long might dure
Their share of sun.
That they were finisht with that realm of gold
As Knight and Queen;
The glory of their living was grown old,
Their joy had been.

Above the rock, above the well, above
The grove of thorn,
That couple stood, those burners in great love,
On the forlorn
Lean neck of hill surmounted by the caer,
The glow of light
Shone in the Captain's eyes and the Queen's hair
Before the night.

They set their tired horses to the east
Over the crest.
Beyond, the colours had already ceast,
Birds were at rest.
The mist was creeping on the Seven Springs
Where no light glowed,
A darkness was upon the face of things:
To that they rode.

SOUTH AND EAST

When good King Arthur ruled these western hursts,
That farmhouse held a farmer with three sons,
Gai, Kai, and Kradoc, so the story runs.
All of the hollow where the water bursts
They reckoned holy land,
For there, they said, the gods came, hand in hand,
At midnight, in full moon, to quench their thirsts.

So by the hollow's western edge they fenc't
With unhewn stone and hawthorn and wild rose,
A little meadow as a holy close
Not to be trodden in by foot uncleanst . . .
And from the harvest rare
Which filled their granaries, they were aware
That the great gods this service recompenst.

Gai was a hunter through the country-side;
Kai was a braggart little prone to truth;
Kradoc was reckoned but a simple youth,
Though kind and good and all his mother's pride.
He loved his mother well;
He loved his mare and dog; but it befell
That sorrow smote him young, for all three died.

Now it befell in grass-time, late in May,
That Gai, the hunter, going out at dawn,
Found the grass trampled in that sacred lawn,
All trodden as by feet the flowers lay.
He thought, "Some godless men
Have done this evil; lest they come agen
I'll watch to-night beside the holy hay."

Yet in his watch he slept, and when the east
Grew bright with primrose-coloured morning, lo,
The grass agen was laid past power to mow;
By godless men, it seemed, not any beast.
So, when the next night fell,
Kai came to watch, but slept, not waking well;
At dawn the trodden portion had increast.

Then, on the third night, Kradoc said, "Let me
Be guard to-night;" so, when the dusk was dim,
He took his hunting-spear and stationed him
Beside the close beneath a hawthorn-tree.
The thin moon westered out,
The midnight covered all things with her doubt,
The summer made the world one mystery.

Then, when the hunting owls had ceast to cry,
There came a sound like birds upon the wing,
And shapes within the close were glimmering,
Hushing, and putting glittering raiment by . . .
Then the shapes moved: they seemed
Three women, dancing, but their moving gleamed:
Or were they birds? because they seemed to fly.

"They are the goddesses," he thought, "at game . . .
Soon they will blast me;" but he watcht intent . . .
Starlight and dawn a little colour lent;
They were three women, each like moving flame
In some old dance of glee,
All lovely, but the leader of the three
Beauty so great as hers can have no name.

For hours he stared, not moving, while they danced;
Then in the brightening dusk a blackbird cried;
The dancing stopped, the women slipped aside,

There to the grey wall where their plumage glanced,
They donned it and were gone
Up, upon wings; across the sky they shone,
Gleams on the darkness where the dawn advanced.

And being vanisht, all his heart was sore
With love of that fair Queen. "Alas, I kept
Ill watch," he said, "and all the grass is stepped
As though it had been danct on o'er and o'er.
To-night I'll try again,
A second night I will not watch in vain."
All day at work love searcht him to the core.

At night, his father and his brothers both
Came with him to the holy close to guard;
But long before the midnight many-starred,
His comrades slept, forgetting boast and oath.
The hours went by: he heard
The darkness laughing with the marvellous bird
Who husht the woodland with her plighting troth.

Then, suddenly, with linnet cryings sweet,
The shapes were near him, putting off their wings;
Then all the close was swift with glimmering
Of silvery figures upon flying feet
White as the thorn that blows,
Skimming the daisies as the swallow goes
Or as the sunlight ripples upon wheat.

Then, as he stared and prayed, the thought came bold.
"There are their wings upon the wall, put by . . .
If I should take them, then they could not fly . . .
But these are gods, immortal from of old,
And they would blast me dead
If I should touch their plumage silver-spread,
Let alone gather it and try to hold."

But as the moth about the candle tries
To know the beauty of the inmost fire,
And feels no burning but his heart's desire,
And even by scorching cannot be made wise,
He took the wings: a lark
Twittered, and colour stood out from the dark;
Those figures sought their wings with passionate cries.

"They are not goddesses," he thought; and then
Seeing who held their wings, those lovely birds
Were pleading with him with caressing words:
"Friend, we shall die if we are seen by men.
Give us our wings, oh, give;
We may not look upon the sun and live:
Sweet mortal, let us have our plumes agen."

Then, to the first, he gave the plumes, from fear;
Then, to the second, gave them out of grace;
Then she, the Queen, was with him, face to face,
Within the touch of hand, she was so near.
The two spread wings and sailed
Up to the summer heaven primrose-paled.
"O lovely Queen," he cried, "for pity, hear.

These two nights now I have beheld your dance,
And nothing matters now, but only you;
You are so beautiful, it shakes me through,
The thought of you is my inheritance.
I am unfit to speak
To such as you, but, lovely Queen, I seek
Only to love you, leaving life to chance.

I am unfit to touch your wings; but quake
At thought of losing you; for pity, tell
How I may reach the Kingdom where you dwell,
There to be slave or servant for your sake;

O bird of beauty bright,
Teach me the way, or come again to-night
And have some pity or my heart will break."

Then looking on the lovely lad's distress,
She loved his love for her and pitied him;
But now the morning made the stars all dim;
She took the wings from his unhappiness.
She said, "We have been seen,
We cannot dance again upon this green,
And where I dwell is past the wilderness."

"O tell me where," he cried, "for I shall find
The way there." "Ah," she answered, "Way is none.
We dwell South of the Earth, East of the Sun,
Beyond the savage rocks and seas unkind;
You have no wings for flight,
No earthly mortal knows the course aright,
Unless the Three Queens have it still in mind."

"And where are they?" he asked. "Far, far," she said,
"Somewhere beyond the sunset in the West;
In seeking me you choose a weary quest.
Now, friend, farewell." "One minute more," he prayed:
"Beloved, I shall try . . .
For I shall love you only till I die . . .
And seeking you, I shall not be afraid."

Her glowing face was noble with sweet thought.
"O friend," she said, "the love of me will bring
Loneliness, toil and many a bitter thing;
Nor can the friend you strive to help in aught.
But I will wait you there . . .
Come, even with palsied limbs and snowy hair,
All things are truly found if truly sought."

Then, leaning suddenly, she kisst his lips,
And presst one glittering feather in his hand,
And swept away above the wakening land
As the white owl at dusk from cover slips . . .
Up the dark wood her gleam
Shone, as adown a basalt shines a stream;
Then she was gone and joy was in eclipse.

At first, he hoped that she would come again:
He watched the next night through: no dancers shone;
Then the next night, until the stars were gone;
Then the third night, but vigil was in vain.
"She cannot come," he cried,
"I will go seek her Kingdom far and wide;
Better to die in search than live in pain."

So at the downland market he enquired
Of all the tinkers, if they knew the way
South of the Earth? "There's no such land," said they;
"We have gone roving Earth till we are tired
And never heard the name."
The wandering merchants told the lad the same:
They knew all lands, but not the one desired.

And in the inn, a travelling minstrel told
Of lands beyond the sea, both East and West,
Lands where the phoenix has her burning nest,
And trees have emerald leaves and fruits of gold,
But no land East the Sun . . .
"Boy, I have been," he said, "There is not one."
"None," Kradoc thought, "There must be, to the bold."

He bade farewell to father, brothers, home,
Friends, and the grasses that her feet had prest;
He sailed to find the Three Queens in the West,

O'er many a billow with a toppling comb,
Till, 'neath the western star,
He trod the forest where the were-wolves are
And spied a hut, as of some witch or gnome.

There sat an old crone wrinkled nose to chin.
"Lady," he said, "Since I have gone astray,
Seeking the Queens to tell me of my way,
Have you some shed that I can rest me in?
In recompense, I'll cut
Your winter's firing and repair your hut."
"O wonderful," she said, "New times begin.

I have reigned here for twenty oak-tree lives,
Yet never once has stranger spoken thus,
Bowing, uncovered, thoughtful, courteous:
What marvellous young noble here arrives?
One who goes South the Earth?
I govern all four-footed beasts from birth,
To-morrow I will ask them and their wives,

If any know the way to that far land.
Rest here to-night." And when the morrow came
All the four-footed creatures, wild and tame,
Ran thither at the lifting of her hand:
Slink tigers yellow-eyed,
The horse, the stag, the rabbit and his bride,
Fur, antlers, horns, as many as the sand.

They listened while she questioned of the way:
"South of the Earth?" they answered, "Madam, no . . .
It is a country where we never go . . .
There is not such a land, the bisons say.
Ask of the birds who fly;
The eagle may have seen it from the sky,
If not the eagle, then the seagull may."

"So," the Queen said, "My people cannot tell.
You must away to ask my Sister Queen
To ask her subject birds if they have seen
A country South the Earth where people dwell.
A year hence, travelling hard,
You may be with her, if no ills retard.
Good luck attend. Commend me to her well."

After a twelvemonths' tramp he reacht a lake
Wide-shimmering, beyond a waste of reeds;
There by a hovel mouldered green with weeds,
An old hag mumbled, gap-tootht as a rake.
"Lady," he pled, "I pray
You grant me shelter, I have lost my way;
All such requital as I can I'll make.

I will re-thatch your house and cut your corn,
And gather in your apples from the tree."
"O wonderful; new times begin," said she.
"I have lived here since roses had a thorn,
Yet never once till now
Has courteous youth addressed me with a bow.
And you go East the Sun and are forlorn?

I govern all the birds that know the air;
Rest here to-night; to-morrow I will ask
If any of them all can help your task
Or know the ways by which men journey there."
When morning came, she cried,
"Come hither, birds," and from the heavens wide
Came erne and geier, heron, finch and stare,

Jay, robin, blackbird, sparrow, croaking crow,
Hawks from the height, their talons brown with blood,
Gannets that snatch the herring from the flood,
And fiery birds that glitter as they go.

"East of the Sun?" they said . . .
"We have flown windy space since wings were made . . .
There's no such land. Perhaps the fish may know."

"So," the Queen said, "My subjects cannot guide.
You must go ask my Sister Queen, who rules
The dwellers in the rivers and the pools
And the green seas that waver, yet abide.
A year's hard travelling hence
Should bring you there: her Kingdom is immense,
Her folk know every country washt by tide."

After another year he trod the beach
Beside an ocean breaking wave by wave.
There an old hag peered from a dripping cave.
"O ocean Queen," he cried, "grant, I beseech,
That I may rest till day.
To-morrow I will labour to repay
Your kindness to me as your wish shall teach."

"O wonderful; new times begin," she said.
"I have lived here since raindrops became sea;
Yet none till now has spoken thus to me,
Courteous and kind and modest as a maid.
South of the Earth you go?
Rest for to-night; to-morrow you shall know
If those I govern know it and can aid."

When morning came, the Queen gave her command,
And straight the bay was white with many a streak
From the swift fins of those that cannot speak:
Whales, dolphins, salmon, hurrying to the land;
Herrings, the pickerels fierce,
Mackerel with blue flanks writ with magic verse,
And cuttles such as eye has never scanned.

The thought passed to and fro, without a word.
"Ah," the Queen said, "They cannot help you, friend,
Between the world's edge and the ocean's end
No fish, no four-foot beast, no flying bird
Has heard of any place
South of the Earth: you say the human race
Knows no such land. Your seeking is absurd.

Why not abandon what is surely vain?
Why not return to all you left at home,
To shear the shining furrow down the loam
Feeling the plough-team lean against the rein?
To marry; and be skilled
In all good crafts, and have your granaries filled
And live till Death comes gently without pain?

Were these not better than the life you choose,
Seeking the thing that is not?" "No," said he;
"This feather, that still shines, she gave to me;
I will go on, though every footstep bruise."
Out in the bay a stir
Broke the land's quiet image into blur . . .
"Wait yet," the Queen said, "something comes with news.

Yes, news of South the Earth . . . the fish that flies,
The thing that beasts and birds and fish disown;
He has a rumour of it, he alone . . .
Go with him therefore, if you think it wise.
These silver wings and fins
Will help you thither; and Desire wins
Though the Desired, won, may prove no prize."

Then with that silvery skimmer of the seas
He sped across the unquiet fatal field,
Now pastured on by haze, now ridged and steeled,

Now low, now loud, but never at its ease;
Till a last leaping flight
Bore him ashore through billows crashing white
Beneath a cliff of granite topped by trees.

And at the scree-top, lo, the crag was sheer,
Hard granite face, nine hundred feet and more,
Gleaming where drifts of cataracts came o'er
And trackless to the foot of mountaineer.
He traced along beneath,
Among the boulders and the stunted heath,
And ever and anon he seemed to hear

From somewhere up above, the cry and bay
Of dogs and hounds together giving tongue,
So that his spirit was with terror wrung
Lest these should be the hunting dogs who slay
Like wolves, what men they meet;
He was defenceless and without retreat,
But thought, "Since hounds are there, there is a way

Up to the summit; and perhaps the hounds
Have huntsmen with them who would succour me."
So thrice he hailed, all unavailingly.
Then o'er the tumbled rocks with leaps and bounds
A dog came swiftly to him,
Barking and wagging tail as though he knew him.
It was his dog, long dead to smells and sounds,

Long buried in that distant Berkshire place,
Now here alive, and crying, "Master, come,
This is our ever-living happy home . . .
Come with me up the track the rabbits trace;
This way, and have no fear.
Climb with me to the forest, Master dear.
We live there always in delightful chase.

All day we hunt whatever game we choose,
Then, in the dusk, we pull it down and eat;
But by the dawn it runs again on feet,
Alive and scattering scent across the dews . . .
Now, up the rock top; lo,
The forest, green as Berkshire long ago.
There run the hounds at game they cannot lose."

And, as he spoke, the precipice was scaled.
There lay a marvellous land of oak-trees high,
With grass where hounds were running in full cry
After immortal game that never failed.
All dogs of every kind
Rooted or hunted as they had the mind,
And all were glad, for all were waggy-tailed.

"Come with me, Master, through the forest green,"
The little dog said, "as we went of old
Along the Icknield underneath the wold.
Here we forget, in time, what we have been;
But I remember well
The rabbits and the moles and the rich smell
Of those old warrens in that happy scene,

And mind your kindness to me." Then they went
For three long days across the forest land,
Until they reacht a desert, white with sand.
"Stay here," the dog said. "Someone will be sent
To guide you further on."
He licked his hand and bounded and was gone.
The desert stretcht its desolate extent.

Its saltness nourisht naught but poisonous things,
The moon in silence looked upon its waste,
Then, towards dawn, a something came in haste
Trotting the sand or skimming it on wings:

It was his long-dead mare,
Coming with whinnyings to greet him there,
Dreading no adder's bite nor scorpion stings.

"Master," she said, "I come out of my rest
To bear you hence upon my wings of flame,
For I can fly now, nothing makes me lame . . .
Mount me and lay both hands upon my crest.
O I remember well,
Deep in my spirit, all the Berkshire fell
And you and I at gallop, heading west.

Now for a time I rest me from the past,
But those old days recur; the huntsman's horn,
The opening of the bin-lid for the corn,
The sweet red apples tumbling to the blast.
You with the bit, which I
Dodged, till the oat-sieve shook too temptingly . . .
And all your kindness to me to the last.

Now mount and ride, together we will go
A swifter gallop than we ever knew."
Then, when he mounted, instantly she flew
Over the desert white with salt like snow;
Skimming the sudden whip
Of the blunt adder with the swollen lip;
Making the sage flow back as waters flow.

Till after three long days she made a halt
Upon the beaches of a sea whose waves
Moaned like to cattle in the glittering caves
And fed the tremulous jellies with their salt.
"O Master mine, farewell,"
The mare said, "Now I gallop back to dwell
In far green pastures without any fault.

For there we dwell together in the plain
Unbitted and unshod, in knee-deep grass,
Where never any gad nor botfly was,
But scarlet apples fall and golden grain.
And there we whinny and race
With streaming tails in the delight of pace,
And muse about old harness with disdain."

So with a whinny as of old she sped,
Out of his sight across the desert sand,
Leaving him lonely on the ocean-strand
Where the spent tide its gathered seaweed spread:
Then, gliding over sea,
A woman came to him; no wings had she,
She moved by love, being his Mother dead.

"O lovely son," she said, "who have given all
For love, despite the hardness of the way,
I come to give such guidance as I may,
And be beside your going, lest you fall.
O often I have been
Close, as you travelled hither, though unseen,
And speaking, though you could not hear my call.

I live in the sweet world that love creates.
It is more beautiful than I can tell,
For we can go with water into hell,
With peace to pain, with gentleness to hates.
We have this joy, to strive
To help the grief of every thing alive
And show where Heaven shines at open gates.

And some, if truly called by mortal need,
Can come, with light and courage and swift strength,
To vanquish the dull snake whose deadly length
Laps and would coil, round every human deed.

Give me your hand, my son,
The darkness shows that morning has begun,
And we have far to travel: let us speed."

She took his hand, and, lo, they footed sure,
Unsunk upon the unsupporting sea;
They trod the air, unfallen, flying free,
High in the cloudless currents, mountain-pure,
Until a land arose,
Peak upon peak, with pinnacles of snows,
East of the Sun, where happy dreams endure.

His mother kissed his brow and then was gone;
He was alone upon the shore, his sight
Dazzled at first by plenitude of light,
For all things in that happy country shone.
A loitering cataract leapt . . .
A glittering people, crying "Welcome," swept
On wings above him, flying on and on.

"This is the land," he cried. "But where is she?
Where shall I find the wonder whom I love?"
Before him ran a brook out of a grove,
Bringing clear water to the clearer sea.
Within the green grove dim
Someone was singing at a morning hymn:
"O you," he cried, "Belovèd, answer me."

He thrust aside the myrtle and the rose:
There was his lover stitching, plume by plume,
Bright silver wings that glittered in the gloom,
And singing out her ballad to the close . . .
Seeing him there, she stood;
She shone as though the light were in her blood;
Gone was the waiting time with all its woes.

"I never ceased to trust," she said, "And lo,
The wings which I have wrought for you are made,
Save for one silver feather which I laid
Bright in your hand, belovèd, long ago.
You have it still, I see.
We win the lovers' heaven, happy we,
The greatest happiness that heart can know."

Then placing on his shoulders the bright pair
Of wings, she took her lover by the hand
And with him swept above that sunny land,
Thrusting aside, like swans, the rushing air,
To some green place of peace
Where love like theirs forever knows increase,
For nothing sad can ever trouble there.

But sometimes, ere the cuckoos lose their tune,
Ere pink has tinged the snowdrifts of the may
Or seething scythe has gleamed into the hay,
Or nightingales stopped singing to the moon
Whose whiteness climbs and rounds;
Then, in the peace which silences earth's sounds
Save the bird's triumph and the water's croon,

Then, sometimes, in the hush, a glimmering glows
Into a brightness in that Berkshire grass.
Those lovers come where their first meeting was
Beside the spring, within the holy close.
They dance there through the night,
Treading adown in patterns of delight
Moon-daisy, vetch, and fallen hawthorn blows.

FULFILMENT

I

Long since, Sir Constans governed here for Rome,
Then northern pirates beat him from his home;
King Cwichelm was the captain of the horde:
He made Sir Constans fly
Into the western wastes, a broken lord.
Cwichelm succeeded to his monarchy;
His wasps made merry in the honeycomb;
He made this Britain England with the sword.

II

Yet, being valiant, Constans often tried
To oust King Cwichelm from the country-side,
By night-alarms and raids against his power:
All failed, King Cwichelm throve . . .
Driving him back until he had to cower
Within his moated manor in a grove
Of old dark elms, abated of his pride,
And Cwichelm's star rose higher, hour by hour.

III

Save that, although he was a conquering King,
He was forever troubled by this thing,
That still he had no heir who should succeed
To what his hands had won.
In all his glory, this was grief indeed,
To win a Kingdom, yet to have no son,
To rule the Kingdom after him and bring
Constans to death and make the rebels bleed.

IV

Yet still, though sonless, he had won a crown,
He and his pirates, dwellers in no town,
Sea-harriers, who harried half the year,
Had made a Kingdom his . . .
Ploughland whose corn had eighty grains an ear,
Sweet-fruited orchards growing all that is,
Green valley-grasses rich, sheep-pasturing down,
"A son," he thought, "would make me without peer."

V

After long years his barren wife conceived,
And he, in hope that all might be retrieved,
Yet harassed by the doubt that she might die,
Rode out, with horse and hound,
And viewed a stag away and went full cry
West over fell beyond his Kingdom's bound,
Till in the savage forest, sombre-leaved,
He found himself alone, with no friend by.

VI

He was alone and lost in the wild woods,
Past cry of hound or horn, in solitudes
Where Constans' rebels rested from their raids,
His horse too blown to stir.
Mist that was drizzle blotted out the glades,
The darkness moaned like tempest among fir,
Then the south-easter gathered all her broods
Of rainstreaks driven and chill that cut like blades.

VII

Leaving his horse, King Cwichelm trod the mire
Backed to the storm which seemed never to tire
But roared in tumult, stabbing as it went.

The rain flung from the trees
Followed like steps of men with fell intent.
King Cwichelm struggled on in little ease
Till in the dark he spied a light or fire
Gleam in a streak as from a shutter's rent.

VIII

And thrusting thither through the wood, he found
A manor without guard or spear or hound,
A black house among elms that the storm smote.
King Cwichelm knocked until
A man unbarred the door and peered to note
What midnight stranger stood upon the sill.
"Cwichelm," he said, "forwandered and half drowned.
Enter. O King, I shall not cut your throat,

IX

Though I am Constans, whom you dispossest.
Come in to supper and to bed and rest,
Take them yourself, I cannot help you, I,
For even now upstairs
My wife is giving birth and like to die."
Thus saying, Constans turned him to his cares
And Cwichelm entered as his foeman's guest,
And ate and drank and warmed him and was dry;

X

Then, being weary, turned him to his bed,
But slept uneasily, for in his head
Voices of angels clamoured, "Take, take, take . . .
A man must take or give . . .
Kill Constans' baby for your Kingdom's sake,
For he will have your Kingdom if he live."
Then others cried, "O Cwichelm, give him bread,
"Give . . . give your crown." Then Cwichelm was awake.

XI

But starting up, he found it only a dream.
The storm in its hurry made the chimneys scream,
The tossing elm-boughs hissed like sea on shingle;
He lapsed and slept again.
Then trumpets blowing made his spirit tingle,
A clear voice cried, "Unless the child be slain,
Constans will beat you, he will be supreme.
Unless you kill the boy, your bloods will mingle."

XII

Rousing at this, he started, but once more
Found it a dream, though clearer than before,
And once again he turned him to his sleep;
And in his dream a form
Whirled to him with bright fire-wings asweep,
And spoke above the tumult of the storm,
"Give, give, King Cwichelm, give the babe good store,
Give even your heart's blood if you wish to keep."

XIII

And starting up, lo, Constans at his side
Crying, "Alas, alas, my wife has died
During this dawn, in bearing of a son;
And now I have no mate.
But rise, King Cwichelm, for the storm is done,
My men have come with horses to the gate,
Eat and begone, my ranger will be guide,
Go to your happy home, from him with none."

XIV

Then Cwichelm, trembling from his visions still,
Bade Constans bow to what was Heaven's will;
But added, "In return for all you gave

Most nobly in my need,
Grant me this privilege, that I may have
Your new-born son, to rear like my own seed."
"Take him," said Constans, "for I saw him kill
My darling wife, for whom they dig the grave."

XV

Then with a shaking voice he bade the nurse
Give up the child whose coming brought such curse;
And she, poor woman, loath to see him sent
Into the winter cold,
Took Constans' gold-embroidered cloak, and rent
Half of its blue away, and warmly rolled
The babe therein, small penny in much purse;
Poor penny hardly won to be so spent.

XVI

So Cwichelm took the child, Sir Constans' heir;
And Constans, bowed by sorrows to despair,
Buried his wife and rode into the west.
Meanwhile as Cwichelm rode
Bearing the tender infant from its nest,
He met his men with news from his abode;
His Queen had borne a little girl most fair,
During the gale, while he was Constans' guest.

XVII

Among the men was Hrut, his marshal grim;
King Cwichelm went aside and spoke with him
And bade him take the child into the wood,
To some dark thicket deep;
"Kill it and give it to the wolves for food,
This brat that Constans offered me to keep.
Go, hack the little bastard limb from limb."
"Right," said the marshal, "I will kill him. Good."

XVIII

Yet being within the yew-grove with his prcy,
Having his knife bare with intent to slay,
The baby smiled and put him from his deed:
He laid him down in fear.
"Lie there," he said, "God help you in your need.
May the wolf suckle you or the she-deer."
Then mounting horse he galloped fast away
And told the King, "I have ended Constans' breed."

XIX

Thereafter Cwichelm prospered, yet no son
Was born to follow when his rule was done,
But still his daughter grew like beauty's rose.
And sometimes Cwichelm mused:
"That night at Constans' house, what forms were those
That trumpeted and ordered and accused?
Dreams of the night, not real beings, none."
And Time moved by, that harvests men and sows.

XX

Then Constans, being old, asked leave to come
To end his life beside his ancient home,
And Cwichelm, seeing him friendless, gave him place
As steward in his court.
There where he once had governed, he was base,
An old sea-battered ship come home to port;
A shadow by the fire with fingers numb
And the beauty that defeat gives in his face.

XXI

It fell that Cwichelm rode his northern leet
To watch his stallion running in a heat;
And in the finish, at the post, a lad

Riding a chestnut mare
Came like a thunderbolt with all he had
And beat the stallion by a short head, bare;
A boy like Constans, like as grains of wheat.
King Cwichelm eyed him strangely and was sad.

XXII

Then questioning about him, he was told
That this same boy, now twenty winters old,
Was found, when newly-born, beneath a yew
Where Constans' son was laid,
Wrapt in a strip of gold-embroidered blue
Like that with which great nobles were arrayed.
"He is Constans' lamb, crept back into the fold,"
Thought Cwichelm. "Hrut has lied; he never slew

XXIII

"Hrut lied and spared him: natheless I shall kill."
He called the lad and praised his riding skill
And offered him employ, to come and go
With messages of state
From court to country, riding to and fro.
This the lad gladly took. Then fear and hate
Wrought upon Cwichelm, till he bent his will
To strike that gallant lad and lay him low.

XXIV

So, writing straightway to Earl Hrut, he said:
"You have both broken oath and disobeyed.
You did not kill the baby as you swore.
Being grown to man, he bears
This letter to you, bidding you, once more,
At your head's peril, kill him unawares,
Kill him at once." The boy no longer stayed,
But took the script, not knowing what it bore.

XXV

Gladly he galloped through the forest pass,
His horse's hurry kicking up the grass,
Till sunset came and all the trees stood still
Black against scarlet sky.
A planet shone: the wood began to thrill
With footsteps and with terror and with cry;
Then midnight tolled another day that was:
He beat the gate at Cwichelm's threshold sill.

XXVI

It was Sir Constans' self who turned the key.
"Earl Hrut, the marshal, is abed," said he;
"See him to-morrow; come within to rest."
He led him to the fire
And brought him food and wine and watched his guest,
This lad most worthy of a Queen's desire.
"He is like my wife in face," he thought. "Let be . . .
No thought of one so beautiful is best."

XXVII

"What are you, lad?" he asked. "A foundling, I.
Found in the western forest, like to die,
A new-born babe, wrapt in a strip of blue.
No more of me is known,
Save that the cloth, gold-broidered, bore a clue:—
The snakes King Constans bore upon his throne."
Then Constans thought, "The living God on high
Has given me back the child she never knew."

XXVIII

And in his heart the misery smote him sore
That he had given the little son she bore
There in such pain, at such a price, to one

Who left him in the hour
To die i' the forest where the wild wolves run.
He hurried to his coffer in the tower;
There lay the strip of blue the midwife tore.
"Such is the cloth that wrapt me," said his son.

XXIX

Then Constans, deeply moved, withdrew to weep;
The lad curled up upon the bench to sleep
Beside the fire within King Cwichelm's hall;
Hour by hour passt:
Then Constans thought, "What weighty matters fall
That Cwichelm sends this messenger so fast?"
The midnight held the castle buried deep,
The lad slept on his bench like dean in stall.

XXX

And gazing at the lad, he saw the script
Sealed by King Cwichelm, from the wallet slipt
On to the hearth whose embers eased the seal.
So Constans took and read.
"O dog, deserving death without appeal,"
He cried, on reading, "Curses on your head!
But those who trip the helpless shall be trippt;
God gives a moment for myself to deal."

XXXI

Then, giving thanks that he might thwart the plan,
He forged a letter thus: "Most trusted man,
As you expect my favour, I, the King,
Command that, instantly,
You marry the young princeling that shall bring
This, to my daughter, never asking why.
This on your peril:" thus the letter ran.
"Fly, wasp," said he, "for I have drawn the sting."

XXXII

What more? The lad delivered the forged screed;
The earl believed it to be Cwichelm's deed,
He caused the lad to marry the princess;
That hour it was done.
When Cwichelm came, he found his wickedness
Had linkt his daughter to his foeman's son.
"Men plot and try," he said, "but God gives heed,
And what God brings to be must surely bless."

POEMS FROM SARD HARKER

SARD HARKER

A calm like Jove's beneath a fiery air.
His hands most beautiful and full of force,
Able to kill the wolf and tame the horse
Or carve the granite into angels' hair.
His brow most noble over eyes that burn
At thought of truth or knowledge wanting aid.
His mind a very sword to make afraid,
A very fire to beacon at the turn.

His step swift as a panther's, his will fierce
To be about the beauty of some deed,
Since beauty's being is his spirit's food.
His voice caressing where it does not pierce;
His wrath like lightning: he is King: indeed
He is much more, a King with gratitude.

*   *   *   *   *

A lean man, silent, behind triple bars
  Of pride, fastidiousness and secret life.
His thought an austere commune with the stars,
  His speech a probing with a surgeon's knife.
His style a chastity whose acid burns
  All slack false fo ml ssness in man or thing;
His face a record of the truth man learns
  Fighting bare-knuckled Nature in the ring.
His self (unseen until a danger breaks)
  Serves as a man, but when the peril comes
And weak souls turn to water, his awakes
  Like bright salvation among martyrdoms.
Then, with the danger mastered, once again
He goes behind his doors and draws the chain.

THE PATHFINDER

She lies at grace, at anchor, head to tide,
  The wind blows by in vain: she lets it be.
Gurgles of water run along her side,
  She does not heed them: they are not the sea.
She is at peace from all her wandering now,
  Quiet is in the very bones of her:
The glad thrust of the leaning of her bow
  Blows bubbles from the ebb but does not stir.

Rust stains her side, her sails are furled, the smoke
Streams from her galley funnel and is gone;
A gull is settled on her skysail truck.
Some dingy seamen, by her deckhouse, joke;
The river loiters by her with its muck,
And takes her image as a benison.

* * * * *

How shall a man describe this resting ship,
  Her heavenly power of lying down at grace,
This quiet bird by whom the bubbles slip,
  This iron home where prisoned seamen pace?
Three slenderest pinnacles, three sloping spires,
  Climbing the sky, supported but by strings
Which whine in the sea wind from all their wires,
  Yet stand the strain however hard it dings.
Then, underneath, the long lean fiery sweep
  Of a proud hull exulting in her sheer,
That rushes like a diver to the leap,
  And is all beauty without spot or peer.
Built on the Clyde, by men, of strips of steel
That once was ore trod by the ass's heel.

A Clyde-built ship of fifteen hundred tons,
  Black-sided, with a tier of painted ports,

Red lead just showing where the water runs,
   Her bow a leaping grace where beauty sports.
Keen as a hawk above the water line
   Though full below it : an elliptic stern :
Her attitude a racer's, stripped and fine,
   Tense to be rushing under spires that yearn.

She crosses a main skysail : her jib-boom
Is one steel spike : her mainsail has a spread
Of eighty-seven feet, earing to earing.
Her wind is a fresh gale, her joy careering
Some two points free before it, nought ahead
But sea, and the gale roaring, and blown spume.

POEMS FROM ODTAA

THE SONNET OF CAMILLA, MOTHER OF DON MANUEL, ON HEARING OF HER SON'S BETROTHAL TO CARLOTTA

Lord, when Thy servant, doubting of Thy grace,
Went in despair from what she judged Thy frown
To search for comfort in an earthly town,
Despairing of all help in any place!

When she was sure, that not in any case
Could her demerits touch the longed for crown,
But rather sorrow, that would bring her down
Where no light comes, nor joy, nor Bridegroom's face:

* * * * *

Then, in the chaos, lo, a plan revealed.
Lo, in the sand, the lilies of the field.
All thy blind servant's darkness of untrust
Proven more wicked than her tongue can speak.
To her unfaith Thou turn'dst the other cheek,
And, to her greed, gavest gold that cannot rust.

LINES, ON THE SAME OCCASION. THIS POEM IS KNOWN IN SANTA BARBARA AS "THE VISION OF CAMILLA CONCERNING MANUEL"

In the dark night I saw Death drawing near
To make me go from here;
In all my sin, with all my work undone,
Leaving behind my son
With no more stay nor path
Than what the wild horse hath.

I saw the souls of all my earthly friends
Laid bare, their aims and ends;
How some might love him, many help, but none
Be wisdom to my son.
Wisdom that is a road
Where no track showed,
A dawn, when no lamp glowed.

Thus in the night I heard Death come, I heard
The mouse shriek at the bird;
My sins came huddled to my bed, the bell
Dead hours did tell:
There was no light: only the tick of time:
Life, strangling in the slime.

Then in the multitude of souls I saw
A bright soul, without flaw,
Wearing a star upon her brow like heaven
In the green light of even.
However black (I knew) the night might turn
That star would burn.

She reached her hand to me and cried: "Death calls,
Time strikes, the hour falls,
And like a flight of birds the souls prepare
To whirl into the air,
To bring to be what none may understand.
I shall but light the hand . . .

Lo, here, the light upon my brow shall lead
Thy son until he bleed;
Until he fail, and falter, and despair.
Even in his blackest night I shall be there;
My star will be his guidance: he will know
What light is, from its glow."

A SONNET UPON EZEKIEL RUST

Son of Isaiah Rust, of Churn, his wage
Was eighteenpence a day, working for Squire,
With rabbits twice a year, and sticks for fire,
In a stoopt cottage, broken-backt with age.

His life was among horses from his birth,
He uttered cries which horses understood,
He handled squire's stallion in his mood,
Strange blood being in him from the ancient earth.

Often, when moons were full, he ranged the Downs,
Much like the fox, but liker to the hare
Who forms in the thymed grass in the hill air,
And sees from the hill edge, as the stars rise,
The glare in heaven above the market towns
And turns back to the midnight, being wise.

THE MEDITATION OF CARLOTTA IN PRISON

This that I understand,
This that I touch with hand,
This body, that is I,
To-day will die.

O given Spirit, now taken,
Keep this to truth unshaken,
That the good thing, well-willed,
Becomes fulfilled.

THE MEDITATION OF HIGHWORTH RIDDEN

I have seen flowers come in stony places;
And kindness done by men with ugly faces;
And the gold cup won by the worst horse at the races;
So I trust, too.

THE COMFORT OF MANUEL, ON SETTING FORTH DEFEATED IN THE *VENTURER*

Bad lies behind, worse lies before.
What stars there were are in us still;
The Moon, the Inconstant, keeps her will,
The Sun still scatters out his store,
And shall not Man do more?

When the worst comes, the worst is going:
As a gate shuts, another opes:
The power of man is as his hopes:
In darkest night the cocks are crowing.
In the sea roaring and wind blowing
Adventure: man the ropes.

POEMS FROM THE *WANDERER*

POEMS FROM THE *WANDERER*

THE SETTING FORTH

Her builder and owner drank tea with her captain below.
He said "Are you bent upon sailing at morning's full flood?"
And Currie, the captain, said "Surely. Determined to sail."
Her owner replied: "It is stormy, and something within
Warns me that worse is approaching; much worse, I imagine.
Stay until Monday, and give the gale time to blow over."

Then Currie replied, "Sir, to-morrow is my lucky day.
The seventeenth day of October, just five years ago,
I first took the *Wayfarer* out, at her first putting forth.
A fortunate day to a fortunate voyage and ship.
I trust to the luck of to-morrow, and sail, storm or no."

"So," said her owner, "so be it: good fortune go with you.
But still, I am sorry you cannot delay till it clear."

In sunlight next morning they hoisted her colours for sea,
Blue Peter in signal of sailing, red ensign abaft,
High at her main truck her house-flag, the swallow-tailed
  burgee,
Blue in the hoist, white in fly, at a summit so lofty
That only two ships in the world carried colours more high.

Now with a crying of catcalls and stumbling and swearing
The crew came aboard in the care of the boarding-house men:
They wore the thin cottons and serges of men of the sea.
Some carried small kit-bags of canvas, or little roped chests,
But many had nothing but rags and a bottle of gin.
Three only were sober, three Welshmen, who went to their work;

The others, all Scands from North Europe, not knowing a word
Of English, all drunken, some fighting, some screeching, some
stunned
Lurched in up the gangway and swore at George Shearer the
mate,
Then stumbled their way to the fo'c'sle and screamed till they
slept.

The Paddle-tug *Wrestler* arrived at an hour ere flood,
Then slowly the hawser was passt and the mooring ropes slackt,
The ship moved away from her berthing, her voyage begun.

In dock, near her berth, lay the famous American ship
The *R. D. Rice*, lofty and lovely, with three skysail yards.
Her captain, there watching the *Wanderer* passing to sea,
Cried to George Currie, "I'll bet you a rosy-cheekt apple
I'll be in San Fr'isco before you": the Wanderers laught
From pride in their racer now trembling to gallop the sea.

Slowly she moved to the gateway that led to the river;
The gates were wide opened, beyond lay the fullness of flood.
There on the pierhead, the dock-gate officials and riggers,
The stevedores and dockers and penniless seamen were buncht.
Watching her ripples advance as she followed her tug.

Now as that queen of the water went out to her kingdom,
As spear-like for diving the spike of her jib-boom was poised
Over the paddle churn foam slapping weeds at the dock gates,
And slowly her gazing white woman moved forward in thought
Between the stone walls, and her boys, coiling gear, paused to
watch,
A man of that muster of dockers went up to the edge,
And took off his cap with, "Three cheers for the *Wanderer*":
then
All of those sea-beaten fellows swung caps, and their cheering

Sent the gulls mewing aloft: then George Shearer, the chief mate,
Up, on her fo'c'sle, replied with "Three cheers for Pierhead, boys."
The boys and the seamen all swinging caps shouted three cheers.
A man from the pierhead jumpt into the rigging aboard.
She passt in procession of masts through the narrow dock gates.

Now in the river she paused as she swung through her quadrant;
Men hurried to watch her as slowly she headed for sea,
At bidding extending her loitering length of delight.

All of the power of muscle of hundreds of builders
Beating out iron and steel into straightness or curving,
All of the knowledge and cunning of hundreds of thinkers
Who make from the stubborn the swanlike and sweeping and swift,
All of the art of the brain that had seen her in vision,
Had gone to the making her perfect in beauty and strength.
Her black painted ports above black showed the curve of her sheer,
Her yellow masts raked as they rose with their burden of yards.
High, high aloft rose her skysails, and over her skysails
Bright in the sun, blowing out, blue and white, were her colours.

As a stallion paws earth at the edge of a forest land,
Snuffing the air as he looks at the grassland below him,
Where all things await him, mares, battles, and clover by springs,
And whinnies for joy, with his ears cockt, his crest hackled high,
And trots down to challenge, all trembling, with flame in his eye;
Or as the sea-eagle aloft in his desolate place
In rock, or in air, all intent on the infinite smile

Of an ocean too quiet to blot out the steamer tracks,
Yet sees in that dove-coloured quiet the silver gleam go
And launches, exulting, his beautiful body as Death;
Or as in a city beleaguered an Angel of God
Moves in the alleys, and eyes bright with famine behold her,
And courage comes out of her beauty and hope from her word,
And as she advances to battle all follow her flag
So trembling and proudly and queenly she trod towards ocean.

Her pinnacled splendour moved westward among the grey gulls,
Past steamers at anchor, whose stewards stoppt work as she
passst,
Past steamers bound outwards or inwards, whose horns blew
salute,
By barges, tan-sailed, lipping under, and schooners from sea,
Past a white-masted ship, towing in, flaunting colours out,
Past Bidston and beaches of pleasure and buoys showing sands,
Past these the *Wanderer* towed, west from the desolate bar.

Next morning beheld her still towing, her pilot discharged,
Clear weather and moderate wind with the southern sky
dark
And promise of worsening weather and freshening wind;
Day-long the heaven grew greyer with gathering storm
Coming with evil of water and evil of moaning
Of wind in the rigging beginning and seas ridging white.
Noontide was pastime of stubbornly butting the hillocks;
But ever the tempest advanced and the hillocks grew steep.
The spurtles of sea from her scuppers were wetting her decks.
In her descendings, the fire-bright shreddings of spray leapt
Over her fo'c'sle; her sails, not yet loost from the gaskets,
Darkened with rain and were dripping: she shone from the
wet
And southward she laboured, with shoutings when watches
were set.

Ere twilight came shrieking, the *Wrestler* made signal to say
"Holyhead's yonder abreast: shall we put in for shelter?
A dangerous sea is now running and stopping our way."
And Currie made answer, "Keep towing: we will not put in."
So on they kept towing in sight of the mountains of Wales
Dark on the anger of heaven; the darkness came early
With streakings of flame in the west and then darkness indeed,
Moonless and starless, a lightning-blencht blackness of tumult,
With seas roaring out from wind roaring, and wind in the shrouds
Shrieking, and iron blocks batting, and swinging ports streaming,
And smoke streaming from her, the ship-shattered water like
smoke.

Onwards she weltered astern of the labouring *Wrestler*,
On, in the teeth of the storm in a blackness so utter
That no gleam was seen save the romping white races of waves
Rushing up, under the sidelights, to thunder down deckward
And hiss out of white into blackness and slowly pour free.
Both of the fo'c'sles were flooded; the draggled drunk seamen
Curst, as the bursting salt water made sodden their pallets:
The night was all anger all banded to stop her advance.

And like a red stag of the forest, who comes from the glens,
Tossing his many tined antlers, adventuring softly
Downhill to the beaches, from hunger of salt of the rock,
And there is engulfed in a quicksand all sodden with well-
springs
And struggles, but cannot escape, being sunk to the knee,
So struggled the *Wanderer*, held by the rush of the storm.

In darkness of tumult the danger came suddenly down.
Some sudden attack of the sworders that smite from the wind,
Some gallop of spearers that smite upon ships from the sea,
No man beheld it, or heard it, or knew it; but sharply,
Suddenly, somehow, the steel-towing hawser was broken,

Snappt, in some heave or descent, and, as suddenly, danger
Leapt at those vessels; the *Wrestler* was towing no longer
But prone on her broadside as helpless as blossom in weir,
As may-blossom caught in a current and whelmed in a sluice;
Swept from the *Wanderer* far, to the brink of destruction,
While she, the fair *Wanderer*, wallowed, not under command,
In breakings of billows that lifted her ropes from her rail.

Then Currie gave order, to get the ship under her sail.
But most of the seamen were drunken and lying asleep:
The others, all new to the ship, in the blackness of storm,
Divided, the some to loose topsails, the rest to sheet home.
Some loost the three topsails and lingered to overhaul gear
But all the sails thundered and bellied aloft like blown flags,
And streamed out to leeward with roaring of quick cannonade,
The chains of the sheets flying skyward in showers of sparks
Tugging their leads like mad horses and shaking the ship;
For those upon deck standing ready to sheet the sails home,
Had all been flung headlong from footing by sea after sea,
And rolled in green water in scuppers with floating ropes' ends.
The sheets all let go, were unroven and flying aloft.
The setting those three lower topsails was playing with Death.

Then Currie, alarmed lest the ship should be blown upon
  Wales,
Called hands to wear ship, and the helm was put up, and she
  paid
Off, with the hands at the braces and steady eyes watching.
Slowly she answered, in thunder on thunder of water
That flooded the line of drencht men at the weather main brace.
Then much as the stallion that follows the hounds, being held
By one full of caution, goes steadily up to the jump,
Some red-berried blackthorn with thrushes' nests still in its
  twigs,
And there flings his rider away, but himself laughs aloud

And kindles from freedom and gallops with stirrups aloft
Free in his glory of speed, in his triumph of power,
So went the *Wanderer* round, through the staggering moment,
Down in the trough, to emerge and go galloping on
Roaring, high streaming, full-flooded, to head to northwestward.

But as she came hurtling to windward, her topsails, all three,
Split into ribbons and rags like to battle-torn banners,
And crash came their gear from aloft on the roof of the house
Over the heads of the helmsmen who screamed in their terror
Lest they should be stricken, while steering, like rats in a trap.

George Currie himself took them aft to the ship's afterwheel,
And set them to steer under cover, with: "There, my men; now
You'll steer her in safety,"—they stood at the wheel steering hard,
Heaving the wheel up and down, though the wheel for the
  moment
Had not been connected; the pintles were presently shipped.
The thunder and lightning made battle in heaven above.

Now, as she laboured, deep-rolling, unsteadied by canvas,
All of her high foretopgallant mast suddenly snapping
Short, at the cap, with its yard and the royal and skysail,
Crasht from its splendour, collapsed in its rigging and swung
  there,
Raining down gear upon deck, blocking the weather foreshrouds.

Then Currie gave order to light the red lights of distress.
The engineman ran to the lamp-room and lighted the lamps,
And carried them aft, there to hoist them aloft at the peak;
But as he was hoisting, the flames were blown out in all three,
He had to return to the lamp-room to light them again.
He was a faithful good servant to Potters, the owners,
Had wrought for them many long years in the Liverpool Dock,
But this was his first going sailing to sea in a ship.

Three times like a fighter he struggled down aft with the lamps;
Thrice, as he hoisted, the wind licked the flames from the burners:
The fourth time he hoisted, the spanker-gaff crasht overboard,
Taking the lanterns along with it under the water.
"O Jasus," the man said. "Thank Jasus, that job's at an end."

Shearer, with all he could gather of seamen and ship's boys,
Waded out forward to set inner jib and stay foresail:
The jib was cast loose, but the halliards were jammed in the throat,
By some of the tangle of gear flying loose from the smash.
Still it was vital to get the jib hoisted and sheeted:
The ship might be lost if she were not brought under command.
Who would go up to that ruin of swinging ship's wreckage
To clear what had jammed? Then Tinsley, the eldest apprentice,
Went up the weather fore-rigging as high as the cross-trees
And cleared what had jammed, dodging Death as he groped in the dark.
Then, as he came from aloft, heavy gear, swinging blindly,
Battered him senseless to deck: he was taken below.
Then, sunken waist-deep at the cope, all the rest, singing "Ho!"
Hoisted the staysail, which scattered to rags as they hoisted.

For now the full fury of tempest was smiting them sore,
Heaving the gasketed sails into tattering ribbons,
And streaming all ropes out to leeward like pennons of pride.
Over the shriek of the gale and the roar of the billows
Beat the continual death-drum of iron sheets smiting;
Chain sheets and blocks smiting masts as a riveter hammers,
And blocks broken loose from the upper spars hitting the poop.
The ship was not under control: she was labouring hard.

Then, as she laboured, her high maintopgallant mast parted,
Snappt at the cap, like the fore, and collapsed in its rigging,
Down crashing with royal and skysail to ruin the crane
And gear of the main topsail-yards, bending iron like clay.
Crashing, the mighty spars fell to the length of their tether
To swingle aloft in the rigging and smash all they met.
Green water broke darkly aboard, for no canvas was set.

Now panic came over the seamen, who scattered below
To hide under bunks in the fo'c'sles, in nooks, behind chests,
Anywhere sheltered and dark to be out of the danger.
The mates in the full flooded fo'c'sles pursuing the men
Dragged them from hiding on deck, but they fled back to hiding:
For men upon deck saw the terrible pendulums swing,
All the wreckt spars swinging over like devils destroying,
Ripping their canvas to ribbons and suddenly stopping
Smash, at the end of a roll, shaking all the ship's fabric.
Those swinging destructions brought terror to all but the best.

Then, as George Currie stood, letting off blue lights, amidships,
Hoping some steamer might see them and come with assistance,
The swinging main skysail swoopt over and struck on his head.
Men laid him, still breathing, full length on the table below,
Where Tinsley lay senseless with five other suffering men.
Then down came the mizzen topgallant, snappt short like the main.

There lay the *Wanderer* helpless, sea-beaten, sail-tattered,
All three topgallant masts broken and swinging aloft still
Raining down pennants and blocks as they tore off in rolling,
Her spanker-gaff vanisht, her jiggermast bent with the strain,
Her captain unconscious, six seamen disabled from wounds,
Half the rest drunken or mutinous, hiding below deck,
The ship heading hither and yonder hove-to with a cloth,
Beaten rail-under by tempest and deluged by billows,
Her mate lighting blue lights and rockets in sign of distress.

The Codling Bank Light showing danger to leeward and near.
Just as the middle watch ended, her signals were answered;
The small coasting steamer, *Merannio*, offered her help,
And lay by with signals and waited for morning to dawn.

Soon after this hailing, the *Wanderer's* captain, George Currie,
Died on the table below; he was known among seamen
As one at his best in a gale driving on under sail;
As learned moreover; a perfect sea captain; and kind;
Strict, never swearing; a trainer of many fine sailors.
Death, and his comrade the sea, took him into their quiet.

When morning from wind-harried heaven showed wind-shattered
sea
The steamer drew nearer attempting to take her in tow,
She hove up to windward and fired her rockets with lines,
But time after time, ere the hawsers were fast for the tow,
The *Wanderer's* sheerline bowed into the run of the sea,
And lipped up the living green water, and rising, deep filled,
Streamed with bright water and plunged, snapping hawsers like
pack thread.
They laboured all morning while slowly the tempest blew by.

At last, when the hawser was passt, the *Merannio* moved
Westwards, to tow her to Kingstown, and heaven's face altered
And sunlight came squally with showers of violent rain
And blue sky grew brighter and seagulls adventured to sea.
At moonrise the tug *Flying Spear* helped the towing uptide,
By moonlight next morning they moored her and made her
secure.

And morning came quietly in upon sandals of peace,
The maiden-eyed morning who wakens the birds in the dew.
With greyness in heaven, and silver in streaks on the sea
She came to that harbour of rest where the *Wanderer* lay

And shone on her ruin all scurfing with patches of salt
Till shadows of beauty were tranquilly stirred at her side.
And weary-eyed men came on deck in the peace of the dawn;
All softly they laboured, all silent, as men in a dream,
As men in a snow in the winter, that muffles all noise.

As gently as rain in the summer those sea-beaten men
Blest her with service, securing the wreckage aloft
And mutely removing the ruin that tempest had wrought.
So dumbly, with depth of devotion will men serve a queen
Whose crown had been lost in a battle, whose beauty remains,
Who rules still by beauty, wherever her crown may have faln.

So hushtly, not speaking, in fear they should waken the hurt,
They tiptoed from cleansing to coiling till all was achieved,
They then crept below upon tiptoe, not liking to speak.
The smoke from the galley went peacefully up to the sky.

* * * * *

Not all was accomplisht, for Shearer went aft with the boys
And hoisted her colours half-mast to the shattered masthead;
Then all day in silence they kept seaman's watch by the dead,
With tears for the captain laid dead there, with prayer for his
peace.

THE ENDING

Once, long before, at her second outgoing down Channel
Re-rigged and re-captained, the tug *Sarah Jolliffe* had towed,
Now at her last putting forth from the port of her building
The tug *Sarah Jolliffe* again took her forth over bar.

Adown the grey river to seaward in ballast she towed
All high and uncomely, but gay as before with her flags,
And gay, in the April, past all the loud toil of the town,
The riveter's hammers, the hooting of sirens, the clang

Of the bells of the ferries, the threshing of screws in the stream,
The rattle of winches, the trample and clatter of drays,
She followed her tug to the gate she would never repass.

So down the grey highway of England she stood to the south
Past beacons that pointed the pathway or warned of the shoal,
The mountains of Wales on the left, underneath her the wreck
Shed from her masts at her first setting forth under Currie.

The April was bright on the water that bore her away.
By Brachy she towed, by the Mumbles, away to the south
Past Bristol, where once she had loaded, past Lundy's north cliff
And away past Bull Point for Tintagel and Pentire Head.

And as she advanct, towing southward, those watchers of ships
Sang from their places a song of the outgoing spirit,
A cry to all farers on ways upon water or earth.

Adventure on, companion, for this
Is God's most greatest gift, the thing that is.
Take it, although it lead to the abyss.

Ceaselessly, like the sunlight, life is spilled
Into these channels till the purpose willed
Meet with the End that is to be fulfilled.

A little hour is given to apprehend
Divine companions from the mortal friend
From mortal hearts a life that cannot end.

Go forth to seek: the quarry never found
Is still a fever to the questing hound,
The skyline is a promise, not a bound.

Therefore, go forth, companion: when you find
No highway more, no track, all being blind,
The way to go shall glimmer in the mind.

Though you have conquered Earth and charted Sea
And planned the courses of all Stars that be,
Adventure on, more wonders are in Thee.

Adventure on, for from the littlest clue
Has come whatever worth man ever knew;
The next to lighten all men may be you.

Adventure on, and if you suffer, swear
That the next venturer shall have less to bear;
Your way will be retrodden, make it fair.

Think, though you thunder on in might, in pride,
Others may follow fainting, without guide,
Burn out a trackway for them; blaze it wide.

Only one banner, Hope: only one star
To steer by, Hope, a dim one seen afar
Yet naught will vanquish Hope and nothing bar.

Your Hope is what you venture for, your Hope
Is but the shadowed semblance of your scope,
The chink of gleaming towards which you grope.

What though the gleam be but a feeble one,
Go on, the man behind you may have none;
Even the dimmest gleam is from the sun.

All beauty is. No paradise of flowers;
No quiet triumph of perfected powers;
It lives in the attempt to make it ours.

All power is; but with retarding thrift
The watching Strengths administer this gift;
Man's paces as a spirit are not swift.

All that has been imagined from of old
Is, but more glorious a thousandfold;
The pebble lightens, and the clay is gold.

And you, the grey thing dragging on the sea,
Go as a man goes in Eternity
Under a crown of stars to Destiny.

Therefore adventure forth with valiant heart
Knowing that in the utmost stretch of art
Life communes with its heavenly counterpart.

So singing, the Watchers beheld her go on in the dusk;
The evening star brightened the dimness; Pentire dimmed down,
The lights of the Land's End were beacons to show her her way.

Now Eastwards she turned by the Land's End, the eater of ships,
The *Khyber* cried to her from seld-litten greenness of gloom
"I once was a swiftness that trampled the billow-tops white
But now I lie broken in darkness with congers and crabs."
The *Peregrine* cried "I was queen: but my crown has been reft;
In darkness destruction came on me, my beauty has faln.
Men called me the beautiful ship in the seaports of home."

And now to the *Wanderer* towing, the Lizard appeared,
The Lizard, the landfall beloved of the homecoming men,
The first light of home they behold after long months away,
An outpost of England, sea-fronted, uplifting her lamp.

And now from the darkness of water the *Cromdale* outcried
"O beautiful passer, I once was the *Cromdale*, a queen
Most lofty, most lovely, most delicate stag of the sea,
Now nothing but jaggings of iron encrusted with shells,

Deep down among swayings of sea weed and whipping of fish.
Yet sweet is the sound of the water about a ship's bows,
And lovely the shadow of ships going by overhead."

And another voice rose from the water, the voice of the Queen,
Queen Margaret, saying, "O *Wanderer*, star of the sea,
I once was the glory of all of the seas of the world.
In sailing I set forty sails, I exulted, I strode,
I rusht like the sea-streaming dolphin, the frigate-bird white
Skimming over the measureless miles, leaping wave on blue wave
And crushing their blueness to greenness, the greenness to white
In a track a mile broad rolling outward all glittering gay.
And seamen remember my running the seas of the Horn
Pursued by the toppling gray combers uplifted astern
Forth thundering eastward all dim with the smoke of my spray.
Now scoured or heapt by the under-sea currents I lie
All crusht out of glory, unseen, save perhaps from the sky
By high-cruising gannets intent upon shadowlike fish."

Then anon from the crags to the northward another voice spoke
"I, too, hoped for home, I, the *Panama Bay*, whom the storm
Set suddenly onto the rocks whence no ship has escapt.
All rusty and ragged with ruin I cumber the swirls,
The sea grants a truce, not a pardon: ships may not live long.
Ships tread on an uncovered grave and their last port is Death."

In bright April weather, the *Wanderer* towed past the coast,
To leeward lay Falmouth where once she had sheltered from storm,
Beyond lay Bolt Tail and the sea-jutting headland of Start,
All the headlands of lights stretching out, all the signalling heads
Which had guided her seawards, or welcomed her home from the sea.

Off Portland another voice spoke from the depths of the sea:—
"I once was the *Siren*, in Queenstown beside you of old.
Of all the world's beautiful ships we were surely the queens.
O would we were racing down Channel again as of old
With skysail poles bending, the lee scuppers flashing with spray,
The leaning high canvas complaining and straining and dark,
Dark with wings dipping, or spindrift: the lean shaving shearing
Of the cutwaters heaving white water as high as the rail,
And the men at the tackles high-crying to board down the tacks.
But Fate smote my going asunder: I gallop no more
On the fenceless green foam-blossomed fields of the horses of storm,
The speechless fish pasture within me: the lobsters' eyes peer
The darkness within me dim-gleaming with shine of the sea.
I once was the *Siren:* we two were the queens, you and I."

So onwards the *Wanderer* towed till the bright April day
Dimmed, and the sunset was crimson and darkness drew on,
And England lay dimly to leeward, and light after light
Cast out her message, and town after town glittered bright,
And the French lights showed faintly as onwards the *Wanderer* towed,
Around the South Foreland and on for the mouth of the Elbe.

And there, in the Altenbruch Road, on a bright afternoon
She came to an anchor: the tug, *Sarah Jolliffe*, cast loose,
For she who had taken her seawards had brought her to rest,
And nothing remained but to steam away westward for home.
The Wanderers watched her steam slowly away down the stream.

They coiled up the hawsers and cleared up the decks for the night.
The east wind blew briskly, the sun set ere seven, the moon
Then new, set directly; they hoisted the riding-lights up,

Men lingered to look at the lights of the city ashore
Then all went below save the anchor-watch seaman on deck.
The midnight passt slowly with lagging steps marked by the
bells.

It chanct, that a big German steamer was going upstream
Full speed, on the flood, in the middle-watch blackness that
night;
Her helmsman and mate saw the *Wanderer's* lights dead ahead
And thought them far distant, then suddenly saw they were
near,
Right under their bows, then they hove the wheel over and rang
The engine-room signal to back: seven seconds dragged by,

* * * * *

The *Wanderer's* watchman beheld the three lights of a ship
Rise suddenly up in the darkness; he saw the ship come,
A white surge of water below her, her fo'c'sle reared high,
And men on her bridge crying anguish and biting their hands.

* * * * *

The seconds of living suspense slowly dropped out their sands.

* * * * *

Then crash on the fenceless port broadside the *Gertrud's* steel
bows
Struck, cutting deep, reeling back, grinding in again deeper,
And over the *Wanderer* reeled at the force of the blow,
Jangling in all of her gear, while with cryings and cursings
Her crew leapt from sleep into action and rusht upon deck.
They saw all the lights of the *Gertrud* draw slowly away,
The men in her shouting and signalling, rushing about;
They saw her back into the darkness to look to herself,
To anchor in darkness and find her bows bent but unburst.

All knew from the roaring of water below in the hold
That in a few moments the *Wanderer* surely would sink.

They lowered a boat, then they let slip the cable, and strove
To tow the ship northward to beach her in safety on sand.
For fifteen swift valorous minutes her heroes wrought hard
While under their feet beat the death-drum, the boom of the
leak,
The ship was fast listing to port from the in-pouring sea.

Too soon she had listed so far that her captain gave word
To cast off the towrope and take to the boat alongside.
They climbed down the side to the lifeboat and cut her adrift.
The overfull boat pushed away from the upheaving bilge
In the darkness upheaving above them: they hove out the oars
And pulled into safety to watch for the ending to come.
The drops from the oarblade drippt gleaming, the oarsmen
could hear
The moan of the *Wanderer* dying the death of a ship.

For now the most beautiful ship having wandered her ways
Was come to her ending, to thrust through the billows no more,
No more to go thundering on under whining wet sheets
In the long leaps from roller to roller, the sea-smiting leaps,
Heaving her bows out, and swaying, and streaming a wake.
No more to creep ghostlike at dawnings with dew dripping gear,
Her seamen, like ghosts in the dimness, removing the lamps,
Or moving all drowsy to pause at the lit galley door.
No more would her beauty come tranquilly in from the sea.
Past the far sunburnt Heads, or the pine solemn Point, or the
Flats,
Gleaming with rice pools, or up the grey Channel for ngland,
Her sails in their gear, being furled, as the tug took her in:
No more would her capstan clink pawls and the anchorage ring
To the song of her seamen aloft on her beautiful bow
Heaving her anchor for Falmouth, her mate at the railing
Watching the growth of the cable; now never, forever
Would tempest receive her, the tempest all flying with spume,

The rain squall, the line squall, the howl of the never checkt
wind
Snatching the sails from their gaskets; her moment had come.

Most gently she slowly leaned over and lay on her side
Her riding lights burning until they were quencht in the flood.
Then, rapidly down, with a gurgling of air and a rush
Of flood beating on her she flung herself over and sank.

And then, in her moment of passing, her Power went forth
West, in the dark, over sea, as a bird going chartless
Speeds in the impulse of April unerringly homewards.
So, as a swallow or pigeon, the *Wanderer's* Power
Sped to her Captain in England, the Captain who took her
First, sweeping southwards in splendour, who first set her
courses
And hoisted her topsails, topgallants and royals and then
Shouted to Tinsley to loose the main skysail, and held her
Under all sail, running free, in all beauty, all swiftness.

There at his bedside, he sleeping, the *Wanderer's* Power
Spoke without word by that impress of spirit on spirit,
So that he saw in his soul what disaster had fallen
And started from sleep crying out that his ship had gone down.
He roused all his household with cries that his ship had gone
down,
All fallen collapsed in the water the deathbed of ships,
Her beauty of sheer in the quicksand, her glory engulft.

Meanwhile in the darkness her crew came to safety unharmed.
The morning rose brightly: men looked at the beautiful wreck,
Thinking to salve her, but quicksands were under her broadside
Drawing her under, engulfing her deeper, enclasping;
While flood thrust her deeper and ebb heaped the sand in her
wound.

*   *   *   *   *

Since nothing could save her, men blasted the wreck from the stream
And left her dead bones in the quicksand full fathom five down,
She lies there deep sunken, unminded, sea-creatures encrust her,
White shells, such as cover the *Siren*, red frond-waving weeds.

Herself is not there, being Beauty Eternal, alive,
She wanders the waters of thought, past disasters, past hates,
Past the world's disapproval, across the black seas of despair,
And on, beyond anguish to havens of peace whence she brings
Hope, Mercy and Courage, all gentle and beautiful things.

She shines on the waters, in summer's mid-daylight she shines
For the hand-shielded brow of her gazer is crowned with a star
And gently and surely she sweeps through the waters of thought
Up, over the curve of the planet, uplifting a song:—

"*Adventure on, companions, the attempt*
At high adventure brings reward undreamt.

The raging sea is grim with reefs unconn'd:
There is a way, a haven is beyond.

Way for yourself, a harbourage for you,
Where every quarry spirit can pursue
Is, in the glory of the dream come true."

So singing, she wanders the waters with white wing on wing
Star-lighted, star-guided, the sea-gleaming beautiful thing.

A MASQUE OF LIVERPOOL

LIVERPOOL

I am the English sea-queen; I am she
Who made the English wealthy by the sea.

The street of this my city is the tide
Where the world's ships, that bring my glory, ride.

Far as the tide along my highway swings,
The iron of my shipwrights clangs and rings.

Far inland as the gulls go are my stores,
Where the world's wealth is lockt with iron doors.

And these my merchants gather day by day
The wealth I bring, the wealth I send away.

THE NORTHERN MERCHANTS

We have been told that in the northern snows
And green icet sea the living sperm whale blows
And narwhals that have ivory in the nose:

And seals, that scrape along the ice and shine
In their sleek coats, and wolves with yellow eyne
And white-pelt bears, with small heads viperine.

And fish beyond all telling in the far
Cold depths wherein the cod's sea pastures are
Where the one sign of home is the North Star.

THE EASTERN MERCHANTS

We have been told that in the East are things
Flame-guarded by the Phœnix' burning wings,
The Sunstones of the Everlasting Kings;

The Moonstones from the Woman of the Sea,
The Changestones that compel Eternity
To that which *is*, but yet can never be.

And myriad balms; and spices such as nard;
The unicorn and the camelopard
White, velvet-horned, in forests moonlit-starred.

And blood-gum, from the dragon poison-tusht,
Such as the Ctesiphon high-priestess crusht
On the sweet altar before swooners husht.

And grain from glittering fields, the which at dark
Strange three-toed stags will rob yet no man mark,
Unseen they come and go before the lark.

And silks, that the worm spins and man refines,
Silk of the East with sunlight in its lines
That, at each turn, with other colour shines.

Berries, and fragrant leaves, and scented wood
Hard as thick glass and smooth, and red as blood,
And painted clays, and all drugs ill and good.

And muslins, delicate as dew, scarce seen;
Jade, carven and uncarven, serpent-green;
Blue from Madras, and scarlet from Cocheen.

Rubies that flame at midnight, pearls like moons
Pluckt from green depth at lulls in the monsoons,
Turquois of Pasht, blush-coloured settaroons.

Salt lamprons, sun-dried waltrons, durians, dates,
Peaches whereon the Paradise Bird baits,
Almonds thick-candy'd from the Mogul's cates.

And perfumes, such as burn by night and day
In Sarn, the city in the Himalay,
Where gods feast nightly, so the travellers say.

THE SOUTHERN MERCHANTS

We have been told that in the South are men
Whom we can buy for beads to sell agen
Betwixt the Trinity and Darien.

And gold in dust, like sand upon the strond,
And soft blue soapstones from the hills beyond
Within whose dullness gleams the diamond.

And wood so dense it sinks, and wood so tough
Not even a blacksmith's rasps can make it rough,
Plank fit for gun-decks and for coaming-stuff.

And palm-oil and palm-matting and palm wine
And palm-rope, hawser-laid for towing line,
And palm wood corded with pajuka-bine.

And beasts for men to stare at, put in cage,
Monkeys like people of a former age,
And shag-maned lions, bound, for all their rage.

And pelts like armour cut from serpents grim,
And striped pelts from the beasts that haunt the dim,
And man-pelts stufft by dwarf folk shrunken slim

And dwarves themselves, that click, but cannot speak,
Of all mankind the smallest and most weak,
Who poison elephants and hew the teak.

And giants, reared on milk, whose two-edged spears
Have foot-wide blades more fatal than Fate's shears,
Who drink a foeman's blood and wear his ears. . . .

But beside these, the lucky man may find
The gold mines that the Kings of Egypt mined,
Rich still in gold though all the shafts are blind.

And in them in the darkness, crowned and throned,
Sits the dead Pharaoh's mummy, staring-boned
Surrounded by the treasure that he owned.

THE WESTERN MERCHANTS

We have been told that in the West the grain
In harvest time so yellows all the plain
That the blue sky seems dippt in a green stain.

And that beyond the grain, the pasture runs
Well watered on, to distant horizons,
Feeding the cattle in their millions.

And that beyond the pastures is the wood,
Mile beyond mile in leafy multitude
Of red-hearts, each dark shadowing a rood.

And that beyond the wood, the mountains are
Gleaming with ore and shimmering with spar,
Wealth like a beacon burning from afar.

And that beyond the mountains there are lakes
Where fish so stuff the net that the mesh breaks,
And men can tread the track the salmon takes.

And that beyond the lakes are glens wherein
The hunter Indian with the painted skin
Has heard the mammoth trumpet to his kin,

And seen from out the dim green forest-hold
Vast tusks outcurve and hairy trunk unfold;
Beyond the glens are mountains made of gold.

ALL THE MERCHANTS

And for these things we offer English wares,
The harvest that the slag-soiled foundry bears,
The fruit of blackened boughs in poison'd airs.

Coal from the mines, and iron, crude and wrought,
Machines, the slaves begotten of man's thought,
Cottons and woollens, these shall be the fraught.

These, and the sons of men, we offer these
To send as our exchange across the seas,
For all the planet's beauty, wealth and ease.

LIVERPOOL

And you, my sailors, see the ships at rest,
Ready to wander Ocean on this quest;

Beauty and worldly power are at one
In all these ships, the finest under sun.

I have these things to sell, these things to buy.
Will you take ship and barter for me?

SAILORS

Ay,
We will take ship and barter as you bid.

LIVERPOOL

The seas are little known, their dangers hid.

SAILORS

Life is a chance, a danger, a chance more.

LIVERPOOL

The sea will lie behind you, sea before.

SAILORS

By sun and moon and star we find a path.

LIVERPOOL

Against you will be wind and sea in wrath;

SAILORS

Against them will be light heart and cool head.

LIVERPOOL

Bitter your drink will be, and hard your bread.

SAILORS

Sweetness and softness will be found ashore.

LIVERPOOL

The washing seas will soak you to the core.

SAILORS

We shall not be the first nor yet the last.

LIVERPOOL

You will be frozen, working on the mast.

SAILORS

We shall be hot enough in lower hold.

LIVERPOOL

Yes, you will sweat enough, for little gold.

SAILORS

Our mothers did not make us thrifty, Queen.

LIVERPOOL

The sleepless nights and toil will make you lean.

SAILORS

Fat men and fatness both belong on land.

LIVERPOOL

Strange deaths await you, many as the sand.

SAILORS

But only one will kill us, as elsewhere.

LIVERPOOL

Death waits to murder vessels as they fare.

SAILORS

Some, Death will take, but some he will not take.

LIVERPOOL

Those that he cannot murder he will break.

SAILORS

That which is only broken we can mend.

LIVERPOOL

The sea gives but hard days and harder end.

SAILORS

We do not heed the end, we only care
To take the ship and wander anywhere;

To mind her, day and night, while underneath
The mouth of Ocean opens, showing teeth.

To give her beauty, though ourselves have none,
And let the others have the wealth that's won.

But for ourselves, a ship, and open space,
Blue water, and a salt wind in the face.

Come brothers, the sea waits, ay, many seas
Wait for the will of men who love not ease.

Come, let us man the windlass and again
Heave, singing up the anchor and its chain.

Come, man the windlass, and heave in, away.

SOLOIST

In Liverpool where I was bred,

SAILORS

A long, long time ago.

SOLOIST

They taught me how to heave the lead

SAILORS

And across the Western Ocean
We're bound away to-day.
They'll give me a donkey's breakfast,
When I sign away my pay;
And across the Western Ocean
We're bound away to-day.

SOLOIST

They taught me how to hand and steer,

SAILORS

A long, long time ago.

SOLOIST

And all the leads of all the gear.

SAILORS

And across the Western Ocean
(*etc. etc., as before*).

SOLOIST

It's hard to starve and freeze and bleed.

SAILORS

A long, long time ago.

SOLOIST

Hell at the end would be hard indeed.

SAILORS

And across the Western Ocean
(*etc. etc., as before*).

LIVERPOOL

Farewell, adventurous hearts, who, in thin rags
For little pay accept the little ease
Of bearing up aloft my merchants' flags
Into the havens of all foreign seas;
Who give your strength, your watchfulness, your care
To things not yours, at all times, everywhere.

THE MERCHANTS

Farewell, O valorous souls, to whom we trust
Our treasure, our magnificence of ships,
In the wind's anger and the billow's lust,
When steel is crumpled and when timber rips,
We know, when the wind howls, that you are there
Awake, on guard, for our sakes, everywhere.

LIVERPOOL

Farewell, and if it be you never come
After long waiting, late, dismantled, tosst,
Again into this river of your home,
But lie on the sad record of things lost;
Farewell, and blessing, for no holier guide
Is here, than those who, in attempting, died.

And know, that He who walkt upon the waves
Will befriend sailors, and at Death and Wreck
Stand by them ever with the Hand that Saves
Even as the roller thunders on the deck
And guide both ship and sailor to the blue
Bay of more peace than any living knew.

ALL

And there, such spirit-voyage as the souls
May take for man on the Eternal Seas
That beat about Man's headlands and Earth's poles,
Surely such great adventurers will make these,
Bringing to men who suffer and despond
In life on earth, good tidings from beyond.

THE *WANDERER*

You swept across the waters like a Queen,
Finding a path where never trackway showed,
Daylong you coultered the ungarnered clean
Casting your travelling shadow as you strode.

And in the nights, when lamps were lit, you sped
With gleams running beside you, like to hounds,
Swift, swift, a dappled glitter of light shed
On snatching sprays above collapsing mounds.

And after many a calm and many a storm,
Nearing the land, your sailors saw arise
The pinnacles of snow where streamers form,
And the ever-dying surf that never dies.

Then, laden with Earth's spoils, you used to come
Back, from the ocean's beauty to the roar
Of all the hammers of the mills of home,
Your wandering sailors dragged you to the shore,

Singing, to leave you muted and inert,
A moping place for sea-gulls in the rain
While city strangers trod you with their dirt,
And landsmen loaded you for sea again.

LIVERPOOL, 1890

Grey sea dim, smoke-blowing, hammer-racket, sirens
Calling from ships, ear-breaking riveting, the calthrops
Of great grey drays, fire-smiting on the cobbles, dragging
The bales of cotton.

The warehouse roofs, wet-gleaming, the ships bedraggled,
Awry-swung yards, backt on the main, the jib booms
Run in, the winches clanking, the slings of cargo
Running up, jolt.

There lie the ships, paint-rusted, each as a person
In rake or sheer or rig, coulters or counters,
Sea-shearing bows, those swords of beauty that thrust
The heart with rapture.

All fair ships, man-killers some, sea-eagles, sluggards.
Tall, too, many: lofty, a dread to look at, dizzy thus:
Among them always one more sky-aspiring, queen,
Remembered always.

LIVERPOOL, 1930

The dockyards of the ancient days are filled
With roads and buildings: of the ships that were
Not any lift their glory to the air;
The singing of their coming-in is stilled.

All has become much greater than of old,
Man has advanced in mastery afar,
The soul of man is conquering his star,
Mud has been changed for granite, dross for gold.

O Capital, whose highway is the sea,
I think of forty years hence, when your spires
Will flame with beauty's intellectual fires,
And what your sons imagine now, will be.

ON SKYSAILS

I saw you often as the crown of Queens
As snow upon a mountain, as the rose
Red in the middest summer's many greens
You were the beauty's final grace, as those.

Or as the spire that lifts aloft in heaven,
Or as the wind-vane on the spiry peak,
Or as the glory glimmering in the sweven,
Caught by the dreamer as he wakens weak.

Or as the rapture of the heart at breaking,
Or Power's last touch, or manhood's winning-place,
Even so were you that set the shadows shaking,
On ever hurrying sea, to leave no trace.

Far, far away, the men beholding knew
A queen the more was passing, seeing you.

The west wind blows the smoke among the rain,
The rigging drips, the iridescent dock
Dimples beneath each following pellet's knock,
From each ship's scupper crawls a rusty stain.

The winches rattle cargo; from a shoot
Coal thunders down; a tugboat threshes past
Towing a ship with colours at her mast;
An orange-bearer scents the air with fruit.

Four boys, two ancient riggers and a mate
Heave round upon a capstan, the pawls clink,
The gathered heaves of purchase fall and kink,
The dangling yard goes up into the sky,
Up on its end it goes and swings awry
And settles square, and is a crown of state.

They reared the pine-tree to its height and held
Its slender taper steady with a stay.
What Nature could not compass they compelled,
There the spar stood, since Nature must obey.

Then, turning pride to use, they crossed the yard,
Itself a triumph with its manly gear,
Theirs was a Queen whom nothing should retard,
They set a sail upon the pointing spear:

And there it gleamed aloft, below the flag,
Over strange seas, impelled by many airs.
What though the waters raged? What heeds the stag,
Running the hills, of stag-hounds, as he fares?

He pays no heed, but canters, as did she,
Billow by crashing billow, sea by sea.

PAY

The world paid but a penny for its toil,
That which was priceless got the beggar's dole;
Men who fetcht beauty, iron, corn or oil
Scarce could keep beggar's bones about the soul.

I saw those sailing seamen, cotton-clad,
Housed in wet kennels, worm-fed, cheated, driven,
Three pounds a month, and small delight they had,
Save the bright water and the winds of heaven.

Yet from their sweated strength an order rose,
The full-rigged ship in her delightful line,
So beautiful and tranquil in repose
But in supremest action so divine.

For in the trampling seas the beauty stood
Trampling those seas, and made her pathway good.

THE CROWD

They had secured their beauty to the dock,
First having decked her to delight the eye.
After long months of water and the sky
These twenty saw the prison doors unlock;

These twenty men were free to quit the ship,
To tread dry land and slumber when they chose,
To count no bells that counted their repose,
To waken free from python Duty's grip.

What they had suffered and had greatly been
Was stamped upon their faces; they were still
Haggard with the indomitable will
That singleness of purpose had made clean.

These twenty threadbare men with frost-bit ears
And canvas bags and little chests of gears.

UNDER THREE LOWER TOPSAILS

Three lower topsails dark with wet are straining
The lower yards to curves, a great sea runs,
Shrouds shriek aloft, the fabric is complaining,
The roaring of the nor'-nor'-easter stuns.

Men stand together waiting for a call,
Their yellow oilskins glisten as they stir.
Each clambering comber toppling wall on wall
Seethes and roars by before its follower.

The ship goes labouring on, until a pause,
A lurch, while a sea mounts and climbs and crowns;
Then like some rapturous instant's loud applause
The thundering billow breaks aboard and drowns:

Flooding the deck rail under, that she lies
Quenched, and the seaman wonders, *Will she rise?*

EIGHT BELLS

Four double strokes repeated on the bells,
And then away, away the shufflers go
Aft to the darkness where the ruler dwells,
Where by the rail he sucks his pipe aglow;
Beside him his relief looks down on those below.

There in the dark they answer to their names,
Those dozen men, and one relieves the wheel,
One the look-out, the others sit to games
In moonlight, backed against the bulkhead's steel,
In the lit patch the hands flick, card by card, the deal.

Meanwhile the men relieved are forward all,
Some in their bunks asleep, while others sing
Low-voiced some ditty of the halliard-fall,
The ship impels them on with stooping wing,
Rolling and roaring on with triumph in her swing.

POSTED

Dream after dream I see the wrecks that lie
Unknown of man, unmarked upon the charts,
Known of the flat-fish with the withered eye,
And seen by women in their aching hearts.

World-wide the scattering is of those fair ships
That trod the billow tops till out of sight:
The cuttle mumbles them with horny lips,
The shells of the sea-insects crust them white.

In silence and in dimness and in greenness
Among the indistinct and leathery leaves
Of fruitless life they lie among the cleanness.
Fish glide and flit, slow under-movement heaves:

But no sound penetrates, not even the lunge
Of live ships passing, nor the gannet's plunge.

IF

If it could be, that in this southern port
They should return upon the south-west gale
To make again the empty bay their court
Queen beyond queen, at rest or under sail.

And if, from every ship, the songs should rise
From those strong throats, and all be as before,
Should we not all be changed and recognize
Their inner power and exalt them more?

Not so, we should not, we should let them be,
Each age must have its unregarded use,
That is but of its time, on land and sea,
Things have their moment, not a longer truce.

Each darkness has her stars, and when each sets
The dawn, that hardly saw her, soon forgets.

I SAW HER HERE

All tranquil is the mirror of the bay,
Empty the anchorage from shore to shore;
A seagull rides the water where she lay,
The ships are gone, they come not any more.

Smoke rises from the town, not any noise
Save from the gulls that mew about the pier,
The shadows in the water stand at poise,
All different from the day when she was here.

For she was here when the tumultuous west
Roared on this granite coast for days together,
And billows rode the Channel under crest
While all the hurt swans sheltered from the weather,

And maddened water seethed along her sides,
Here, in this quiet, where the seagull rides.

WANDERER AND WONDERER

When first the thought of you took steel
I could not know, I could not feel.

When first you thundered down the slip
What more? I had not seen a ship.

When riggers crowned you with your pride
I trod the sunburned country-side,

In cider time, by apple trees,
In stubble, after partridges,

Two hundred miles perhaps from where
Those now-dead sailors made you fair.

* * * *

I could not know, but by some law,
You were the first great ship I saw

Unwitting, I: had I but known
I would have searcht you to the bone.

I saw you in disaster, then,
I sided with you against men.

For beauty, not success, endures.
I saw that queenly soul of yours.

Angels with silver trumpets blew
The song of glory that was you.

They were the self men did not see
Behind the rags of misery.

So is it, in this world, where power
Waits for the rotting of Death's hour.

Which is but for an hour, though shrewd
Its poison is on hardihood.

Out of all death, out of all dream,
I help your spirit to go gleam.

And you, unutterably fair,
Shine on my mind's sea everywhere.

O opportunity let pass;
Beauty that no more is, that was.

Passer that challenged and went by,
A live thing in dead memory,

We two were subtlier linkt than most
By thrilling atoms of the ghost

And shall perhaps be, still, anon,
In wondering and wandering on,

From whence none knows, to where none knows,
Save from the gas-whirl to the rose,

And from the rose to man, and thence
To spirit that has beaten sense.

To that that can annihilate,
To Heat, all Death, to Light, all Fate,

And all is spirit, spark and spur,
Magnificence and minister,
To Wonderer and Wanderer.

* * * * *

And so, farewell, sea-wandering bird,
Whose flight I watcht, whose call I heard,
The time has come
For the last touch, for the last word.

You, with the transitory grace
That gat steel limbs a little space,
Have wandered on
Away, into another place.

I, that have flesh, shall follow soon
As Life commands Death pipe the tune
To change elsewhere
Or here on earth beneath the moon.

However changed upon the chain
Your shape and mine will meet again.
When ship meets ship,
Sea-wanderer, the colours dip.
The hidden then may be made plain.

POEMS FROM MINNIE MAYLOW'S STORY

POEMS FROM MINNIE MAYLOW'S STORY

PROLOGUE

I am a pilgrim come from many lands,
With stories gathered about many fires,
Some, when the moon rose above Asian sands,
Some, when the sun set over English shires.

How often have I told these tales before
To you, the listening pilgrims, who anon
Set out towards the wells you thirsted for
Across the desert, while the planet shone?

Often, perhaps; and often may re-tell,
In distant lands and times, as daylight fails,
When you, the pilgrims, camp beside the well,
And I, the pilgrim, recollect the tales.

MINNIE MAYLOW'S STORY

ONCE (long ago) there was an English King,
Who loved good stories more than anything.

Many a story did the poets tell
To him, who loved their tales and listened well.

But one defect their tales had, that they ended,
Always, at last, the lady was befriended,

The sinner was confounded, lovers blessed.
The story's sun went down into the west.

Then the King said, "Would poets could contrive
An endless tale, whose heroes do not wive;

A story ever fresh and never done,
Like the august procession of the sun

Royally watching mortals from the sky,
That sinks, but rises, and can never die."

Then he proclaimed, "It is our royal will
That poets (duly qualified in skill)

Come to our court, and tell an endless tale."
But those who tried it were of no avail.

Their stories lagged enfeebled and then died,
So that in disappointment the King cried,

"Henceforth it shall be death, to any man,
Who comes to court declaring that he can

Tell me an endless tale and fails therein,
It shall be death, like treason, or great sin,

Upon the headsman's block on Tower Hill.
But any poet who shall have the skill

To tell an endless tale shall have for prize
My daughter's hand and half my baronies;

And, when I die, shall have my crown as heir.
Heralds, go forth: proclaim this everywhere."

It was proclaimed, but, when the threat was known,
The story-tellers left the court alone,

Even though the Princess' beauty was so great
As to tempt any poet to his fate.

Though she was known as Emily the Fair,
Heartsease, and Morning Star, and Golden Hair:

Each story-teller feared to lose his head.
Then the King grieved, for his delight was dead.

No story-teller came with thrilling rhyme
To charm his soul with 'Once upon a time.'

Only his Juggler and the Fool remained:
One he disliked, the other he disdained.

Then silence fell upon the palace hall,
Save for the sentry passing on the wall;

Or some old general coming to report
On army remounts at his frontier fort.

Men with most dreary tales of old attacks,
With half their brains gouged by the battle-axe;

Or ministers with courtesies in their spines,
Or Labour members talking about mines;

Or scarlet admirals, whose breezy tone
Made the King thankful to be left alone.

None who could charm him, as in days of old
The poets with the stories that they told.

And Emily the Fair, with downcast eyes,
Guided the bright silk of her 'broideries,

Loving her father, yet, without offence,
Wishing the loved one might have had more sense,

And not be self-condemned to sit like lead,
Dumb by the fire betwixt meat and bed,

Or snarling, as he poked the burning logs,
"This land of mine is going to the Dogs."

One night the porter came before the King,
Saying, "Behold, my lord, a marvellous thing,

Here at your gate a young man brings a tale
That will go on for ever without fail.

He knows the penalty of unsuccess,
His head upon the gate, but none the less

Determines to adventure for the prize."
"Young," said the King. "The young are never wise

And all their stories are but washy stuff:
Still, youth demands until it has enough.

This man shall have enough, like all the rest.
Bid him go see the chaplain; it were best

He make his peace before he make his trial."
"He would not take advice, nor yet denial,"

The porter said: "but hungers to begin."
"Checking a fool in folly is not sin,"

The King replied, "so let him come to me:
Put up your night's embroidery, Emily.

A tale-teller has come to show his skill."
Now the dark palace-hall began to fill

With knights and men-at-arms and palace dames,
And pine logs on the fire cast ruddy flames

That made the shadows dance upon the wall.
Then the King rose and said, "Friends, listen all.

A story-teller comes to-night to try
His fortune in a tale that cannot die.

Where is he, porter? Let the lad appear."
A young man at the entrance answered "Here."

And coming forward stood before the King,
Bright as the golden pheasant in the Spring,

Cool as the antlered royal on the crag,
Tense as the racehorse waiting for the flag.

Then the King said, "You doubtless know the rules
That hedge our Throne from the attempts of fools.

Those who begin and fail in the attempt
Stand self-condemned and none shall be exempt,

Steel lops away the peccant proser's head.
Your person seems unready to be dead."

"Sire," the youth said, "I understand the terms.
I dread no headsman's axe, nor coffin worms,

I venture all things gladly for the stake:—
This fair Princess for whom so many ache.

I do not come for glory nor for land
But as a suitor striving for her hand.

If I succeed, and she will have me . . . well.
If not, come headsman with the burial knell:

And shut me from the presence of her worth.
For the most beautiful princess on earth,

I come to tell a story without end."
Then the King answered, "Very well, my friend.

If you can tell a tale that will endure
Daily as sunrise and as season-sure,

This fair Princess and half my land shall be
Yours, now, and all my kingdom after me.

But if you fail, you die: are you content?"
"Yes," the youth said: "the terms are excellent.

If you permit, I will begin my story:—
Our ancient poets, excellent in glory,

Say that of old this England had a King
Who dreaded Famine above everything . . .

Dreaded, lest anywhere, in toft or street,
Subject of his should lack enough to eat,

And he behold his people wanting food.
So, being eager for his country's good,

He swore, on coming to his father's throne,
That, while he ruled, hunger should be unknown

To woman, child or man throughout his realm.
Then being crowned, and settled at the helm,

He called for England's chiefest architect,
Firstly to draw, and after to erect

A granary with cellars, walls and roof
Water proof, tempest proof, and earthquake proof.

When this was done he bade his Treasury
Purchase all corn, and fill the granary.

* * *

The granary was filled, up to the hatch
With peerless wheat and barley without match.

'Now we are saved,' the King cried, 'from our dread
And we can sleep with an untroubled head,

And shall not dream of hunger, nor of towns
With all their people starved to skeletons;

With their lips green from biting on the grass.
Men shall forget that ever Famine was.

This grain will last through ten lean years together;
Let blight, or smut, or rust, or rainy weather,

Or wind, that lays the blade and earths the ear,
Let them all come, I say: We need not fear;

We have destroyed what has destroyed mankind.'
So, with glad heart, contented in his mind,

He bade them seal the granary hatch with lead.
'Let Famine fall,' he thought, 'we shall be fed.'

But mark, O King, upon how small a point
A mortal craft will shipwreck and disjoint.

In that gigantic granary's topmost wall
One tiny scrap of mortar came to fall,

Leaving a chink that no man's eye could see,
Being aloft where men could never be.

Now, King, this vasty mass of gathered wheat
Sent forth a smell, unknown by man, but sweet

To all the locusts of the world, who flew,
Longing to see where so much eating grew,

So that the skies were dark with locusts flying.
Then for three days men saw the locusts trying

To find some entrance to that shuttered store:
And in the end one lively locust tore

Through that small chink from which the mortar fell
And stole away one grain. O King, I tell

Nothing but truth. Another locust came
And struggled through the hole and did the same.
And then another locust did the same.

As secretly as sickness in a bone,
So wrought these locusts utterly unknown.

Who could suspect a cranny? Who suspect
The building Guild, the royal Architect?

Unseen as poison breathed in with the breath,
Each of three locusts dealt a corn a death.

Then came a fourth and took a corn and went;
Then a fifth locust, who was bulky, bent

And almost blocked the chink, but struggled through
And took a grain, and a sixth locust, too.

And then a seventh crept into the hole;
And then an eighth; and eighth and seventh stole

Each one a grain, and carried it away.
And then a ninth one, having seen the way,

Crept in and took a barleycorn and fled.
The tenth was a king-locust, spotted red.

He took three grains, being of royal blood.
The eleventh took a grain and found it good.

Then the twelfth locust, shining in the sun,
Crept in and took a grain. The thirteenth one

Followed and took a corn. The fourteenth came
And took a corn. The fifteenth did the same
And then the sixteenth locust did the same.

And another locust carried off another.
And another locust came, the first one's brother.

He took a corn, and then his brother drew
It through the hole, and took another, too.

And then another locust found the place
And another locust followed him in chase,

And another locust followed close behind
And another locust, hungry as the wind,

Leaped in upon his tracks and took a corn;
And a battered locust, who was all forlorn,

Lame in one leg, and sorry on the wing,
Came in and took another grain, O King.

Sometimes in hot Septembers one may see
On grey cathedral roofs the wasps in glee

Whirling against the blue sky overhead
From papery nests hung underneath the lead;

So men beheld these locusts, but none guessed
That greed of grain had given them such zest.

There came a black Saturnian one, there came
A stalwart Jovian, with crest of flame.

A glittering, dainty Venus-locust flew
Questing for corn, red Martians followed, too.

Each took a grain, and then, a marvellous sight,
A locust bowed with age, whose hair was white,

Thrust to the corn. . . ."
But here the King cried, "Hold.
Boy, by our Father's Corpse down in the mould

Stop this unworthy folly of the flies.
Get to your tale." The young man said, "Be wise . . .

Govern your kingdom, Sire, as seems good
But leave a story-teller to his mood.

I tell the tale of what the locusts did.
Another locust crept within and hid

Under a pile of wheat and took two grains.
And then a locust suffering from pains

Searched for a peppercorn to warm his marrow:
Then a sow-locust with her twenty farrow

Crept one by one into the chink and stole,
And then another locust found the hole

And crept within and pillaged like the last,
And then another locust followed fast.

And then another locust followed soon.
Then one, with wits unsettled by the moon,

Strayed crooning through the hole and did the same.
And then another, and another came.

And then another and another followed
And soon the space between the bricks was hollowed,

So as to hold a locust and a quarter;
And then another locust pressed the mortar.

And then another came and wore it smooth,
And then another came and fleshed his tooth

Right to the bitter kernel of an oat.
Then yet another, with a greedy throat,

Came in, and then his cousin, and his aunt."
"Stop!" said the King. The young man said, "I can't.

I have to tell my story as it was.
I serve poetic truth, a noble cause.

I will not stop for conqueror or king.
Another locust came upon the wing."

"Silence," the King said. "Silence. Tell me, friend,
How soon this locust incident will end?"

"It will not end," the youth said. "It will go
As it has gone for ever. You will know

All that each locust of those millions did.
Give ear, my King." The King said, "Jove forbid!"

"It is my tale," the youth said, "and you shall.
I staked my life upon it in this hall,

To tell a story for your prize, and now
Many might think you meant to break your vow.

Let me proceed. Another locust came."
"Young man," the King said, "you have missed your aim.

Your story fails, although I grant you clever;
Those locusts could not carry corn for ever.

They might have for a year, but in the end
That granary was bare. What then, my friend?"

"Sire," the youth said, "the King, who made the store,
Filled it again, much fuller than before.

And another locust came and took a corn."
"O readiest story-teller ever born,"

The King cried, "you have conquered; we submit
And, as my Daughter seems rejoiced at it,

Son, you shall marry Emily the Fair,
Have half my kingdom now, and be my heir.

My heralds shall design you a device,
On a field wavy, semée wheat and rice,

Three locusts proper, bearing each a grain.
Girl, never let him tell that tale again!"

ADAMAS AND EVA

WHILOM there was, dwellyng in Paradys,
Our fader Adamas with Eve hys wyf.
They nere not sinful folk in any wys
But angelyk they lived, withouten stryf:
They moughte so have lived all her lyf,
Dronk the clene wel withouten Dethe's curse
But out, allas, al fel as I reherse.

O hellish Sathanas, feend dampnable.
O corsed foule wrecche, soth to say,
Thou wast so wlatsom, so abhominable,
And eke so mordrous without any nay,
Thou didst persuade Eva welaway
To take the greene pomme from the tre.
O fatal apple, seed of miserie!

For as hit fel by dominacioun
Of thise derke sterres, as I gesse,
Or rede Mars in Opposicioun
To Fortune's brighte sterres, More or Lesse,
Or declinacioun of lukkinesse,
God wot, I nis no more than a babe.
Redith thise clerkes on the Astrolabe.

But so hit fel that Adam is ygo
Out of thys garden for a day or twey,
Him liste se the wilde horses go,
Thise litel prety Centaures, soth to sey,
So forth he goth, though Eva said him nay;
He careth never a del, forth is he went.
Now Sathanas, let launch thy fel intent.

This corsed wrecche, I mene this Sathanas,
Upon his bely sobtilely doth crawl
Into thys garden on the grene gras

Ther as the thikke hegge has i-fal,
Or els a mous had eten through the wal
And left an hole: he on his bely crepith
To the grene bour thereas Eva slepith.

O Judas of dissimulacioun,
O false Ganelon of evil lukke,
Fly, sparwe, fly, with informacioun,
Beth Adam 'ware the feend is with hys chukke:
O pypen, blisful goos, o quakke dukke,
Warn sely Eva sleeping in the bour
Ther comth this false corsed tregetour.

But as thys Cato saith in Scipioun,
In his old bokë that thise clerkes rede,
"Though all men shryken Morder in the toun
What botes it if the wrecche have done the deed?"
The woful cors, forblodied, skarlet-reed,
Gettith no gost, for al they cry Allas.
Now comth this Sathanas where Eva was.

O sely Eva, moder of us al,
Thou wast to nice and grene, ye, God woot,
The rede apple round as is a bal
Goth doun the sclendre golet of thy throot;
Thou ettist it when thou was tolde noot . . .
Wepe, Adam, wepe, thy wyf has lost hir sense,
Sewith thy napron, farewel innocence.

For ye han herd how Adamas and Eve
For apple-take were chased out of hir bour,
Where the swete birdis sang in the grene leve
They might not stop a minute ne an hour.
Their salte teres wetted many a flour;
Hem listed nat to wenden wel away,
But out they went, ther nis namore to say.

SON OF ADAM

ONCE on a time there was a lusty Lion
Just come of age, within the Libyan desert,
A handsome he, all shiny with manly beauty.

So on his coming-of-age-day out he went
Forth from his father's palace, caring no straw
For how his Mother begged him to be careful:
For "Oh," she cried, out of the palace turret,
"Beware, my lovely boy, of Son of Adam.
Of all the dangerous deadly beasts of Earth,
He is the dangerousest and the deadliest."

This shiny Lion, full of beauty of youth,
Went to the drinking-pools where the gazelles went,
But not to seek gazelles. Into the water
He peered a long, long time at his reflection,
And smiled and said: "Perhaps not beautiful,
But oh, how interesting and how virile.
Let Son of Adam come here: only let him."
Then, rising up, he paced into the desert
Shewing his teeth, lashing his flank with his tail,
And with deep coughing roars calling aloud
"Come, Son of Adam, with your deadly danger."

And lo, out of the air there came a stranger,
A grey bird ghastly, with all tail feathers gone,
Part plucked, part moulted, altogether battered.

"What Animal are you?" the Lion asked it.

"I'm a Goose Animal," the creature answered.
"And I am running away from Son of Adam
Who longs to cook and eat me: he has ravished
My feathers, as you see: it is his custom

To eat us geese with apple sauce and sages;
Our feathers stuff his beds, our grease, out-melted,
He rubs upon his skin to make him shiny.
He is a deadly thing, the Son of Adam."

The Lion answered: "Leave the matter to Me.
Myself will deal with him and see you righted."

He paced a little further upon his way
And lo, another creature, withered and gray,
Came hobbling, stumbling, ribbed and shoulder-sorry
A lop-eared, pondering thing, clever, perverse.

"What Animal are you?" the Lion asked it.

"I am a Donkey Animal," it answered.
"And I am running away from Son of Adam,
Who bangs me with a stick and makes me labour
Dragging the load of barley sacks to market.
Beatings and kicks and curses are my portion,
The chaff the horses leave, the hay the cows leave,
The meal the pigs refuse, and autumn wind-falls:
These, and, sometimes, a happy dream of carrots.
A dream, I say, a vision, that on waking
Fades to an empty crib with the rain dripping.

"Such is my life, but even when pale Death comes
To end my life of sorrows and release me
Still Son of Adam comes, he takes my skin off
And moulds it into what he knows as vellum
On which his devilish deep ones write their deeds.
Dangerous are the deeds of Son of Adam."

"Leave him to me, my friend," the Lion answered,
"Myself will deal with him and see you righted."

Onward he paced, engrossed in his importance,
And as he felt the wiseness of his wisdom,
Lo, coming thither was another creature
A little like the Donkey in his feature
But shorter in the ear and sadder-looking,
The ribs more staring and the knees more broken,
Such as a cats'-meat man would rub his hands at.

"What Animal are *you?*" the Lion asked it.

"I am a Pack-Horse Animal," it answered.
"And I am running away from Son of Adam.
Deadly and dangerous is Son of Adam:
He makes my life a burden beyond bearing,
With ploughing, harrowing and homing harvest,
Taking the sacks to mill, turning the mill-stone,
Then dragging back the flour to the baker.
And always being ridden, having my jaw jabbed
With snatchings on the bit and 'Back there, will you.'
And always getting saddle-galls and spavins
And curby hocks and colic and the staggers.
And for my food, to give me strength to labour
I ask you what, and Echo answers with me.
Chaff that a sailor would reject in biscuit;
Hay that a politician would not purchase
During a war, and corn the forage merchants
Could not dispose of, even to a general.
And in the green time, in the happy summer,
When the pink clover blossoms in the hayfield,
And all beasts banquet, never think that I do,
Not with a Son of Adam for a master.
I snatch a dusty mouthful from the roadside
The while I drag the hayload to the hayrick
And even then am struck, and Son of Adam
Cries, 'You're not here to gormandize but labour.

Pull up, now, to your collar; pull, you cab-horse.'
And even when I perish, Son of Adam
Makes profit of me, selling me to kennels
To boil with barley into broth for foxhounds,
And others boil my horny hoofs for jelly
And sell my flesh for cats'-meat or for sausage;
Unhappy Pack-Horse, deadly Son of Adam."

"Leave him to me, my friend," the Lion answered.
"Myself will deal with him and see you righted."

So, pacing on, he mused, "In after ages
These paltry beasts will raise a temple to me,
The Lion of all Lions of all Lions
Loud roaring vanquisher of Son of Adam
Where is this Son of Adam? Let me see him."

And as he spoke, behold, coming towards him,
There was a Something of a mildewed aspect
So sorrowful, so furless and so feeble
That it was doubtful what it could be reckoned;
Whether an Animal or only Nightmare.

It had no teeth to speak of, and no talons,
No fur upon its head, but moulted baldness,
Two wretched legs it had, and one a lame one,
A coat all ragged, shewing rags beneath it.
Across its back was slung a builder's wallet
And on its shoulders, staggeringly, it bore
A load of planks and also an iron door.

And seeing it, at first, the Lion doubted
Whether to stoop to speak to such a creature.
Then with extreme misliking and disfavour
He asked the thing: "What Animal are you then?"

The creature, putting down his burdens, panted
And touched his brow, and said, "To tell the truth, sir,
I am a Builder-Animal, so please you.
And I am running away from Son of Adam,
Because I can't agree with Son of Adam.
And why? Because this Son of Adam asks me
To build at things I cannot reckon building.
They are not building, no, but jerry-building,
These bungalows in ribbons down a roadside,
These cottages constructed by the Council.
Workers like me can't reckon them as building.
Give me to build at building that *is* building;
One of these towers like a minaret now
Or pyramid all pointed for a Pharaoh . . .

"But tripe, not taste, is Son of Adam's fancy.
No use to talk to him of architecture.
Besides he wants no workers, no, but wage-slaves
That he can grind to do his deeds of darkness.
I tell him plain I'll do no jerry-building . . .
Since Builder-Animals must die like others,
I say 'Die building palaces not pigsties.'
So here I come, to build a palace, *and* die."
Salt tears were glistening in the Builder's eye.
"I come," he said, "prepared to build a palace
For him they call the King of Beasts, the Monarch
Of all live things, the Conqueror and Captain,
The Emperor of Animals, the Leopard."

"Leopard?" the Lion said. "You are mistaken.
The Leopard is not Emperor nor Captain,
Nor Conqueror, nor Monarch; he is nothing . . .
The certain spotty grace that we accord him
He shares with currant dumplings and hyænas . . .
And as for King, he's less a King than you are.

Lions have palaces and Leopards lairs, sir . . .
And that if Lions choose. I am a Lion . . .
Build me a palace: talk no more of Leopards . . .
For by the Lion Sun who ranges Heaven
Tossing his mane of fire from his shoulders,
To talk of Leopards in such terms is treason."

"Forgive me my mistake, sir," said the Builder.
"It comes from all that Son of Adam taught me.
Leopards indeed! Indeed I see my error,
Seeing a royal Lion like yourself, sir
(That is, as far as I can see, from dazzle).
O what great joy and rapture and promotion
For this poor wage slave 'scaped from Son of Adam
To build a palace for a Royal Lion,
A Conqueror and Emperor and Sultan.
To think that with these plankings and this hammer
These hands will build a palace for your Kingship
To see your smiles and echo with your singing
And gleam with the reflection of your beauty.
For, sir, when I beheld your beauty coming
I thought, 'This is some planet or some angel.'
And now, to think I am to build your palace.
O happy Builder-Animal, thrice happy:
O lucky nails, O blessed plank and hammer."

And as he spoke, he built a little palace
Then turned it upside down, and through the bottom
Drove four and five inch nails, so that the points stuck
Up, through the floors, and each one pointing inward.

"Why drive the nails like that?" the Lion asked him.
"In royal palaces we always put them,"
The Builder said. "It is the royal hall mark.
The palace is now ready, if it please you.
Will you walk in?"

"It is not very big," the Lion answered.
"There's lots of room inside, I do assure you,"
The Builder said. "As sweet a little palace,
Ay, and as roomy as a King could look for.
Just step inside and see it for yourself, sir."

So stooping down the Lion crawled within it,
And instantly the Builder clapped the door to,
The iron door, and locked it with a padlock.
Then went away, but soon returned rejoicing,
Riding the Donkey Animal, and plucking
The Goose for dinner, while he drove the Pack-Horse.

He halted there, and hove the Lion palace,
The Lion still inside, onto the Pack-Horse
And drove him to the Sultan, where he sold him.

THE LOVE GIFT

In King Marc's palace at the valley-head
All seemed in happiness: Isolt the Queen
And Marc the King were lovers newly wed;
Brangwen, the maiden, watched them with soft eyes;
Tristan would pluck his harp-strings till they pled
To all hearts there, and April flourished green.
Men said, "Our kingdom becomes Paradise."

But Tristan and the Queen were lovers sworn
Both having drunk the love-drink meant for Marc
Brangwen in bitter anguish went forlorn,
Loving the King: she, too, had drunk the dram,
Had played the Queen that marriage night till morn,
And lived upon her memory of the dark.
These souls, like petals in a mill-race swam.

It fell that Marc, upon Midsummer Eve,
Went to the holy hill above the wood
And saw the moon steal slowly up and cleave
The white, still clouds that glittered as she came.
And lo, he saw the forest-goddess leave
The aged Oak of Watching that there stood;
She sped to him, and called him by his name.

She was a mighty lady crowned with oak
In its young green, with oak-apple; she held
In her left hand a spear clutched to her cloak,
Her marvellous hair was gathered to her head.
Her sandals were bright fire without smoke.
Her robe was of fresh beechen leaves all stelled
With hawthorn blossom that never would be dead.

Antlers she bore, and from her leafy dress
Peered squirrels' eyes intelligencing quick
All things that happened with all suddenness.
The swiftness of the forest life was hers
All, from the ousel running 'neath the cress
To soft-foot stags that never snap the stick;
Her voice was as the forest when it stirs.

"King Marc," she said, "since you have honored me
At all times, having kept this holy copse
From hunting horn and hound forever free,
Nor let the woodmen's axes lop and split
The branches of my oaken dwelling-tree,
Where falcons nest and the red squirrel hops,
Now you shall joy in my reward for it.

"I have three gifts to offer to your choice:
Wisdom and Power and Immortality,
Wisdom that makes the spinning stars rejoice;
Power that makes the singing stars to spin;
And last, that Death shall never still your voice,
Eternal Living, Marc, from Death set free.
Which shall I give you? you shall choose: begin.

"Each of the three gifts you may give away
But must not share: I cannot help you choose:—
Each is a glory wrested from the clay
By spirit striving against mortal odds
To hive a little sunlight from the day.
Each is a splendour for immortal use,
Each, being had, will make you like the gods."

She waited, while Marc pondered which to take
Of those three glowing fruits the goddess had.
Rejecting any would be such mistake.

But this he thought: "Since any may be given,
Which were the loveliest gift for me to make
To my beloved Queen, to make her glad?
Which would my Isolt love, my bird of Heaven?"

And thought: "The gift of Immortality
Would be the loveliest gift, it would ensure
That Death would spare that living ecstasy,
That April, at whose passing the grass springs;
Death should be powerless on such as she;
That White Rose of Midsummer should endure,
Bringing forever the beauty that she brings . . .

"Therefore" (he told the goddess), "I will choose
Immortal Life of what you offer here,
Healing to every cut, balm to each bruise,
Life, flowing in wherever fever is,
Life, the advancing knight who cannot lose,
Life, that is enemy to death and fear,
Life, that brings vision to the mind amiss."

The goddess gave the central glowing fruit,
"This gives immortal life to whoso eats,"
She said. "It grows upon a deathless root;
Men see it glimmer if they give their lives.
Breath cannot falter nor the pulse be mute
Of whoso swallows its exciting sweets.
Eat and be quit of all that Death contrives:

"Or give (you may not share) if give you must . . .
Only a god's gift should not lightly pass
At greedy bidding from a mortal lust.
God chooses the recipients of his gifts,
As earthly kings their messengers of trust,
The golden vessels not the things of brass,
Not clay that crumbles nor the sand that shifts."

Then she was gone as stilly as the moon
Creeps into mist: not any hazel stirred.
Marc looked upon the goddess' glowing boon:—
A quince, like living ember to the sight;
Of intense tint, but ever changing soon,
As gorget jewels on the humming-bird;
Now drawing to itself, now giving, light.

Then hastening back to palace, Marc repaired
Straight to the Queen and cried: "Isolt, my own,
I bring you here Life's very essence bared.
Accept the fruit of immortality;
The spirit powers forbid it to be shared;
Its excellence must be for you alone,
Life at its fullest, for eternity.

"The goddess gave this wonder even now
And said: 'The Eater cannot taste of Death.'
This apple grew on an immortal bough
Whose roots are thrusted in eternal things.
Beloved, with this gift I Thee endow.
Eat, my beloved, that your blood and breath
May be exempt from mortal sorrowings.

"And be, forever, beauty, as they are
Now, to myself, O treasure of the West.
My joy, my Morning and my Evening Star,
I have so longed for such a gift to give . . .
The winds will blow my perished dust afar,
This dust that loves you and that you have blessed.
What matters that, beloved: you will live."

Then Isolt took the Fruit of Life and said,
"Marc, you were ever generous, to the soul;
I take this precious gift that you have made.

But for the eating of this living fruit . . .
That is a question to be deeply weighed.
How beautiful it is . . . like glowing coal . . .
Ask me not what I purpose, but be mute

"About it: it were better if we both
Kept silence about this most marvellous gift.
My husband, ever since we plighted troth
You have been royal to me, gift and thought.
I who have profited have suffered sloth
To check the gratitude that should be swift
And generous as the gift, and as unsought."

She bowed her lips upon the fruit and went.
That following afternoon at milking time
When all the palace hinds were up the bent
(Save the smiths shoeing and the men at mill)
She stole into the gallery and lent
Over the rail, and softly sang a rhyme,
And Tristan came at call to know her will.

"Tristan," she said, "my heart's beloved friend,
This fire-glowing fruit that has been given,
Gives to the Eater Life without an end.
I cannot share it; but I cannot eat
Taking a joy I cannot give nor lend
To you, beloved soul, my earthly Heaven.
Take it from me, and be immortal, sweet.

"For then I shall be happy, knowing this,
'My Tristan is alive, through love of mine.'
Out of our loving and the joy it is
I give this golden apple of the sun;
Beloved, take it, though it once was his . . .
Marc's . . . it is yours, I kiss it for a sign,
Kiss it for my sake, my beloved one."

So Tristan took the fruit, and as he took,
An aged crone beside the fire awoke
In the dark settle in the chimney nook,
And whimpered: "Ai, my little grandchild's late,
And I'm forgotten being palsy-strook;
My breath is shocking and my heart is broke."
Tristan slipped sidelong thence and out at gate.

But being by himself he thought, "Alack,
I cannot take the gift that Marc has given
(Doubtless with passion), I must give it back.
How could I live forever without her?
We are two wild-duck in a single track
Bound to a mere whose reeds are tempest-driven,
But we are utterly one amid the stir."

So, when he next met Isolt in the hall,
He said: "I cannot keep your precious gift.
We are each other's, let us share in all,
Living or dying, O beloved heart.
Love is most royal, without self, or thrift,
Or wisdom, or concern for what may fall,
Beyond the longing for the counterpart.

"But Isolt, sweet, when first we plotted here
We tricked King Marc, that on his marriage night
He drank the philtre that makes people dear,
With Brangwen, not with you: and that offence
Leaves Brangwen sorrowing in love, and drear
With miseries of shame: it would be right
To give this fruit to her in recompense.

"But I refuse a life you cannot share:—
Therefore let Brangwen eat the fruit and live."
Isolt agreed and calling Brangwen there

They gave the fruit to her, and Brangwen took.
Brangwen the sweet-faced woman with brown hair;
Eternal life, but peace they could not give
To her whom Love's devouring fever shook.

All day the gentle Brangwen pondered long
Trying to dare, but checked by shame-facedness,
Then Love, which ever ventures and is strong,
Drove her to presence of King Marc to speak.
"O King," she said, "forgive me if I wrong
Custom or rule in daring to address
Your Majesty uncalled: I do not seek

"Aught for myself, but humbly offer you
This fruit which makes immortal him who eats —
Immortal, as the shining retinue
Of bringers of the Light of God to earth.
All sickness flesh of mortal ever knew
Fades from the eater of these living sweets.
It is for you: man cannot share its worth."

Then Marc, in taking Brangwen's gift, was sure
That Isolt had betrayed him to the full,
Loving another someone beyond cure.
He said, "I thank you, Brangwen, for this gift.
Life is a precious boon, if Love endure.
This way and that the angry passions pull;
Many are eager that the end be swift.

"I shall remember that you gave this thing,
And how you gave it, and be ever proud
That subject has so reckoned of her King."
Then carrying the gift he left the hall
And anguish from the poison of the sting
Wrought in him till he wept with forehead bowed
Nor heeded whither he was bent at all.

But at the last, he sat beside a brook
And lo, beyond, a little seven year lad
Was weeping with such grief his body shook
Choking with sobs and moaning in between
That Marc, remembering childish sorrows, took
Pity, and asked what misery he had?
What bitterness had happed to cut so keen?

Then the child answered "Mother's going to die,
So Doctor says, of weakness; when she's dead
Bran says that she'll be somewhere in the sky
Where she can never talk to us, nor see.
And Father beats when Mother isn't by;
When drunk, he's beaten me until I've bled.
But Mother's kind: she makes him let us be."

"But, courage," said King Marc, "and lead me, straight,
To where your Mother lies"; then, being brought,
He paused beside the broken cottage-gate
And said, "Go swiftly: make your Mother eat
This Fruit of Living ere it be too late."
The lad ran to the cottage swift as thought.
And laughter followed after, that was sweet.

Then the King turned for home, no longer blest,
No longer home, but now the tragic place
Of passionate love's betrayal manifest.
But deeper sorrows than his own were bare,
The inmost ache within the mortal breast,
The pitiful child's crying of the race
For comfort of a soul no longer there.

TRISTAN'S SINGING

PART I

When Isolt quarrelled with her Tristan there
In the green forest, and returned to Marc,
Tristan was in the uttermost despair
And fled into the wilds and lived on bark
And found a cavern, once a hermit's lair,
And dwelled there raving for that lovely thing
Gone from him, back to Cornwall and her King.

And in his madman's rage, he fashioned bows,
And pointed arrows in the flame, and slew
The red stags of the mountain and their does,
The wolves of the mid-forest and their crew;
He killed, and flung their bodies to the crows,
But took their skins, and pricking with a thorn
Wrote on them in his blood his love forlorn.

Then, shrieking like the she-wolf gaunt and dire,
He would run raging like a fiend in hell,
Thro' berry-bramble, gorse and forest-fire,
Hunted by love remembered but too well;
Love gone and living torment of desire:
Then dropping wretched he would rock with pain
Weeping for Isolt gone to Marc again.

Thus in a madman's misery he dwelled
More than a year, then, on a summer night,
He wandered from his cavern and beheld
The moon in heaven beautiful with light,
And saw the glowing dog-rose many-stelled,
And joy returned to him: he wept that things
So beautiful should bless this world of stings.

And as he wept, his spirit was aware
Of joy within him, lightening his mind
To marvels that had lain unnoticed there;
Custom had made him deaf and passion blind.
But now the universe was riven bare,
The very grass was singing from the ground,
The life within him carolled at the sound.

The sallow clover-clusters tinged with red
Were rooted in immortal life and spoke
Of earth and living beauty, wine and bread,
That yet are starry in their mortal yoke;
The hairy and dark-crimson basil shed
Wisdom and peace: a moth with jewelled eyes
Perched on his hand and sang of Paradise.

And all the glittering dusts upon his wings
Expanded and contracted singing too
Their unison and joy as living things,
The unison and joy that Tristan knew.
Life flowed within him from eternal springs.
"O Heaven," he cried, "I am so gulfed in bliss,
Burn me away and let me live in this."

But, in his joy, a flash of sorrow came:
"This, being dream, will vanish with the night."
But lo, the morning touched the East with flame,
The forest tree-tops shivered and grew bright,
Cocks from the little tofts without a name
Cried, and the blackbirds leaped out from the thorn.
Intenser rapture came with day new-born.

For every waking bird and opening flower
And leaf upon the tree and four-foot beast
Cried out his exaltation in the hour,

And brighter and still brighter grew the East.
Then the great Sun strode up into his tower
And looked and laughed upon this world of men,
This world of joy for all was singing then.

Then, from the forest of old, lichened oak
That had so often bowed before the blast,
Leaf-crowned immortals in procession broke;
Tristan beheld the spirits who outlast
Men, ravens, trees; they smiled on him, they spoke,
Those spirits of the waters and the woods,
Whose presence sanctifies the solitudes.

Brown-limbed and starry-eyed the Queens of hills
And Kings of glens came, and the Nymphs who rule
Brooks, lipping pastures glad with daffodils,
Or water from the chalk up-bubbling cool;
And spirits of the Peace whose beauty fills
Shy places, that the comer kneels in prayer
That the eternal felt may bless him there.

And lesser spirits, lovely or austere,
Came from the summer bracken and the heather,
The speedwell, harebell and the mouse's ear
And water-guarding reeds with tossing feather
And fox-gloves, that the humble-bee holds dear
All these he saw, all Summer's queens and kings,
Followed by mortal troops of forest-things.

The red-tongue-lolling wolves out of the rocks;
Badgers that root the wasp-nests and the bees;
The kindreds of the poultry-murdering fox;
Stoats from the barren, squirrels from the trees:
And solitary birds and birds in flocks,
Curlews, and little snipe that in the spring
Make heaven noisy with their whinnying.

And there were otters from the mere, and voles
Out of the brook, still nibbling at the cress,
The herons who stand fishing in the shoals
Watching the shadows in the glassiness;
And kingfishers as bright as blazing coals
Burning blue skimmings where the minnows rise
And glittering winged green-gleaming dragonflies.

All these went pressing up the Ancient Way
And Tristan followed, for a Summer King
Said, "Follow, Tristan; all rejoice to-day,
The lost make merry and the broken sing."
Within the rampart on the hill-top lay
A sheltered field, stone-mossy, scantly grassed;
To this those singers and rejoicers passed.

There they formed circle, but as waiting still
For something greater that should crown the hour;
Joy made the spirit within Tristan thrill.
Rapture was his again and peace and power
And all were singing on the holy hill,
Bird, beast and spirit, grass and mossy stone,
Joy, yet foretelling greater joy unknown.

And then upon the summit of the year
So burning blue, so crooning with the dove,
Nature herself swept thither with her spear,
Nature the naked swiftness, fierce as love,
With mad eyes full of lightning, striking fear,
Hawk-winged she was, wing-footed, antler-helmed,
Compact of joy that drew and overwhelmed.

"Spirits and subject creatures all," she cried,
"In this midsummer hour the ruling sun
Sends rapture into every heart, full tide,

Even now his glory quickens every one.
Sing for midsummer and the full year's pride
And sunlight flooding." At her word they sang,
Bird, beast and spirit, till the forest rang.

Then Tristan, leaping to her, caught her hand,
And cried, "O passionate swiftness, strike and kill . . .
I cannot care, being so sown with sand,
But, lovely fierceness, first declare your will;
Null me to dust, but let me understand . . .
What are you, fiery beast or goddess? Tell."
Then Nature's voice made answer like a bell.

"I am so swift, that mortals think me slow;
I am so patient, mortals think me dead;
I am too little for men's eyes to know,
Too vast for what I blazon to be read;
Too jubilant with energy for woe;
Too truthful in my justice to be fierce.
All men must suffer, or annul, my curse.

"But you, forsaken soul, by passion burned
Into one hunger, being daft and driven,
Bitten by watch-dogs, outcast, outlawed, spurned,
To mortal nothingness, shall now have Heaven."
Then Nature told him all and Tristan learned
The tale of Changing, never young nor old,
Dust into man and angel, clay to gold.

Then, having told, she sped, and Tristan went
Back to his cave, but trembling with such peace
As made his spirit seem omnipotent . . .
He wrote what Nature told, he could not cease
Though the moon rose, and southt, and westward leaned
And morning stars beheld him as he wrought
Burned into beauty by consuming thought.

All summer long, from day dawn until night,
The glory of the poem kept him glad,
So that he heeded neither wet nor bright.
Nor the rank chitch, the only meat he had.
But beauty welled from out him in delight
As from the hollow in the chalk the cool
Water comes bubbling to the sunny pool.

Till, when the summer waned and leaves were dying
To brown and red, and evening mists were chill,
And yellow crabs had fallen and were lying,
And morning frosts were white upon the hill
And heaven sighed with flocks of migrants flying
On Summer's heel, Tristan arose and said
"Isolt must hear these poems I have made."

So forth he went, a ragged, starving thing
Gaunt as a famine, staring as an owl,
His matty hair and beard like tangled string,
His body burned like brick, his tatters foul.
On Severn bank he heard a church-bell ring
For the first time for months, the sound of man.
Then in the dusk an evening hymn began.

Then, lowing as they loitered home, the cows
Came swaying up the lane before a hind
Who whistled ballads of the milking house,
And tears of very joy made Tristan blind.
His living soul was come out of its drowse
Of love and madness, he was Man again,
Who had been mad as any fiend in pain.

Southward he went, until, behold, ahead
The river and the palace of the King,
The courtyard and the stag-hounds being fed,

And horses on the cobbles clattering
And Isolt, too, and Marc, like lovers wed
That morning, there together, entering in
After their gallop on the windy whin.

He knew them, but none present recognized
Himself, the wreck with bracken in his beard,
Him the dogs barked at and the cats despised
And women shrank from and the children feared.
The porters marked him closely and surmised
He came for scraps, they watched he did not steal
A bone from any stag-hound for his meal.

Then Kai, the steward, flaunted to the gate
To bid the porters close it on the throng;
And, seeing Tristan, asked, "Why do you wait?
You, dirty gangrel? Off where you belong."
And Tristan said "I come to supplicate
Leave to approach Queen Isolt, and to sing
One poem to her from this pack I bring."

Kai looked upon the written skins, and frowned
And said "But that His Majesty has bidden
That poets shall find Cornwall friendly ground,
Such skins as these should go upon the midden,
And you, yourself, be hunted by the hound
Over the border . . . I will take your pack
In, to King Marc. Await my coming back."

Soon he returned and said "The King has glanced
At some of all this scribble: your request
To see the Queen cannot be countenanced.
She sees no lazar smelling of the pest.
The prospects of your verse might be enhanced
Were yourself cleaner; but the King, even so
Dislikes it. Take your rubbish. Kindly go."

Marc passed upon the instant and said: "Stay,
You Severn poet. Though I cannot care
For what you write, you must not go away
From this my palace, guerdonless and bare.
Give him a cloak and wine and victuals, Kai.
And for your journey westward, take this purse."
Then Tristan flung it from him with a curse.

"No, Marc," he said, "I am Tristan, come again
To win back Isolt to me if I can.
Let Isolt tell me if I come in vain.
Let Isolt choose between us, man and man."
"Tristan," Marc said, "I vowed you should be slain:
Hunted and torn to pieces by the hounds
If you were seen within my Kingdom's bounds.

"You have wrought harm enough in Isolt's life;
You have disgraced her, you have brought her pain.
She has renounced you and is now my wife.
You shall not look upon her face again.
If you attempt it, boy, the hangman's knife
Shall have you into quarters in the yard.
Now you shall leave this Kingdom under guard."

Then the guards, closing on him, dragged him thence,
Bound him, and flung him in a cart, and drove
Over the frontier to the forest dense
Where slink and savage wild wolves used to rove.
Then, flogging him, they left him without sense
And so returned: the rime-frost striking cold
Revived their victim lying on the mould.

PART II

When morning came, he gathered up the sheaf
Of poems flung beside him: like a deer
That limps into dark covert for relief

Being sore hurt, so Tristan trod the drear
Dark, water-dripping forest, full of grief
Not knowing where, but wandering amiss
Towards the camp where Isolt had been his.

And limping on, at dusk he reached the place
So beautiful when it had held and shrined
Their summer love together, Isolt's grace,
And all the ecstasy of being blind
To all things but the beauty of a face.
Autumn had wrought her change, the bower now
Was sodden grass and leafless hawthorn bough.

There, with a flint and rags, he lighted fire
And burned his poems, all, except the last
That was the song of Nature and Desire,
And of Eternity and Time long past;
Of Doing, Good and Ill, and of its Hire
That never sleeps, but waits, and has its Turn;
This, being Isolt's song, he could not burn.

Daylong he crooned it until even-fall,
Praying for Death to come to give him peace;
And Autumn chilled, until the oak trees tall
Had dropped the last brown shred of summer's fleece.
Then the snug dormouse curled into a ball
Deep under knotty roots in nibbled wool
And silent-footed snow came beautiful.

All winter-long he wandered, living hard,
On roots and dulse and mussels of the rock,
And grain forgotten at the thrashing-yard,
And barley-porridge that the fattening stock
Left (or the upland swineherd did not guard),
And green cow-parsley thrusting from the snow,
And other pasture such as thrushes know.

Then Spring began again and at the stir
Of Earth's green fire thrusting into leaf
Again old passion pricked him with the spur
And April's beauty only added grief.
April was only beautiful through her,
But rocking in his woe the tune took power;
Nature and he were knitted for an hour.

And living beauty ridded his despair
Till joy compelled him to arise and sing
The song that Nature taught him to its air
That pierced like the green fire of the Spring.
Clear as a challenge rang his singing there;
The rabbit-bucks crept cock-eared out of holes
And stags came tip-toe upon velvet soles.

Still louder rang the challenge of the song
The great, white, black-eared cattle rowsed and came —
The bull's chin chiselling as he licked his thong
His brooding eyes alight with sullen flame,
The stallion, whickering answer, snapped his thong
And ran to hear: and from the marsh the geese
Trumpeted out to birds the end of peace.

And ducks out of the pond, and cock and hen
Flapped and took wing at hearing of the call,
Sheep from the moors turned thither, hogs from pen,
Horses at ploughing, hunters in the stall.
And now it arrowed in the hearts of men,
It struck in Isolt's heart the while she wove,
In King Marc's palace, tapestries of love.

And at the sound she said: "That song of power
Is Tristan calling me: I inly know
That here begins the striking of the hour;
The ebbing ends and here begins the flow,

To sweep us on its crest." She left her bower
And caught her horse and galloped to the cry
That seemed to draw the winds out of the sky.

And in the forest beast and hurrying beast
Thronged to the singing; birds from bough to bough
Flitted like blackbirds to the cherry feast;
Rapine and mating both forgotten now.
There she found Tristan singing, facing East
Ringed by the birds and beasts that crooned and swayed
As Nature's song went ringing down the glade.

Then, flinging from her horse, she passed the throng
And cried: "O Tristan, I have come again . . .
Forget that we have wrought each other wrong
We are as one as western wind and rain.
Forget my cruelty and teach your song,
And let us sing together, you and I,
And be away together in the sky."

And then they sang together until space
And Time were over for them: Dinan's son
Rapt by the song to that enchanted place
Heard their two voices merging into one
And saw the lovers drawing face to face,
Shining with beauty such as seldom shines
On faces, here, where roses have such spines.

And then, lo, they were one, and all was over
Their rags and robes were fallen and gleaming things,
Spirits, a lover wing in wing with lover
Were laughing in the air and spreading wings
Shining like stars and flying like the plover
Laughing aloft and singing and away
Into some Summer knowing no decay.

* * *

Men never saw them more, but Dinan's son
Gathered those relics of the fallen gear
And bore them to the Saint within the Dun
Who sent for precious woods and wrought a bier
Inlaid with goldwork gleaming like the sun
And laid the relics on it and with prayer
For those two lovers' souls displayed them there.

They lie there still within the holy shrine
And lovers sick with loving go to pray:—
"O God of Love, be such love hers and mine
As to touch Life that nothing can decay
And be at one forever and so shine
Singing forever, blessing sorrowing men,
Like these immortal ones, Amen, Amen."

SIMKIN, TOMKIN AND JACK

BEFORE old Tencombe of the Barrows died,
He called his sons, and said, "Simkin, and you,
Tomkin and Jack, I am at Jordanside.
When I have passed the river you shall have
Each one, a thousand pounds, and this thereto,
This farm and downland where the Barrows stand;
Share it; all happy virtue is in land."
He died, the three sons carried him to grave.

Then the three sons debated how to spend
Each one, his heritage; first Simkin spoke:
"I'm not for farming, here at the World's End:
The bailiff can do that; myself am fixed
On Science, to attempt some happy stroke
To make synthetic Man's Flesh which will do
Whatever menial jobs we put it to.
Flesh is but hydrogen and carbon mixed."

Then Tomkin spoke: "A beautiful resolve,
And yet less beautiful than what I plan.
I hope to catch the electrons that revolve
Within the excited brains of splendid men
And make an Essence of the Soul of Man.
Injecting this will make the silly sane;
The normal splendid: it will kindle brain.
That done, perhaps I'll think of farming then."

Jack said, "And I, who am a Business Man,
Reject your plans, and farming, which will leave
The practisers more poor than they began.
I shall go Citywards to Stocks and Shares
To venture at a profit and achieve.
Then, having money, haply I'll finance
Your Flesh and Spirit ventures, and advance
This farmstead for week-enders with cheap fares."

They went to work: then, on a holiday,
Spent at the ruined farm, Jack said, "The Press
Mentions our Barrow on the Roman Way,
And quotes the old Wives' Fable that within
There sits a giant in a golden dress.
Let's dig the Barrow open to make sure."
"Right," said the brothers. "Practice is the cure
For theories of all sorts: let's begin."

So, out upon the Antient Way they drove.
There was the Barrow forty feet aloft;
Beeches were green about it in a grove;
Rabbits had burrowed deep into its sides.
The brothers settled on a site and doffed
Their coats and collars; then their swinging picks
Rang on the scattered flints with little clicks.
Blisters made bubbles on their fingers' hides.

Three days they dug into the Barrow's heart —
The shepherd on the downland thought them mad.
Then, upon sunset, roofing fell apart,
The Sun shone in upon a central cave.
There sat a mighty Bone Thing, golden-clad,
A skeleton, gold-helmeted, who grinned
Sitting below the beech-roots and the wind;
Kingly, tho' fifteen centuries in the grave.

Then Simkin said "So the tradition's true . . .
Cro-Magnon skull . . ." And Tomkin: "He is big.
Look, on the bone, the markings of the thew" . . .
And Jack, "This gold will speedily be ours.
A happy end to a successful dig."
Then Simkin said: "Synthetic flesh would go
Well, on these bones: a looker-on would know
The kind of chap he was, and all his powers."

Then Tomkin said "If you would clothe his bones,
I'd squirt Synthetic Spirit in his veins.
Then he would speak, I think, in monotones,
And tell us something precious about dates."
But Jack said "Brothers, after all our pains,
Let's cover him until the morning: then
Have in the Press and Moving-Picture men
And also charge admission at the gates.

"But first, our duty is to take the gold,
It is not safe to leave it as it is."
He took the armour, fold on gleaming fold,
Leaving the rib-bones open to the air.
He said "Collectors will be mad for this;
Authentic armour fetches any price
And no such armour will be offered twice.
To-morrow we'll be famous everywhere."

That night he clamoured to invite the Press.
Simkin and Tomkin checked him as they toiled
Making in test-tubes many a smelling mess,
Or at a wire-end a spitting spark
Or violet glowings from the wires coiled.
They met at breakfast-time with amplest store —
Simkin had outer husking, Tomkin core;
Jack was by much less cheerful than at dark.

"You know," he said, "this making flesh and soul,
Is going far: I'm not a squeamish man . . .
But in the play the Robots took control . . .
Besides, it's witchcraft, which is counted wrong
By every people since the world began.
The Witchcraft Statutes are not yet repealed . . ."
"Rats," Simkin said. "The plough is put to field."
"Bunkum," said Tomkin. "Up, and come along."

So out they went along the dewy grass
Up to the Barrow where the giant sat
Bone upright like the warrior that he was.
Tomkin took off his jacket, rolled his shirt,
Simkin upon the skullbones set his hat.
"Come, Father Noah," Tomkin said. "At last
We'll get authentic datings of the past.
First body, Simkin. Then the Soul with squirt."

So Simkin wrought his wondrous chymic clay.
The figure, like an image made of wax,
Stared listlessly along the antient way.
"You've made him like a warrior," Tomkin said.
"Now for the soul, to stir him in his tracks."
But Jack in terror cried, "No, not the last . . .
This creature is so awful and so vast . . .
If once you give him life he'll smite us dead."

"Rubbish," said Simkin. "If we give him life
It will be elemental in its form;
If fractious you can stick him with a knife.
Go on with Spirit, Tomkin, fill the gland."
"No, no," Jack pleaded, "you will raise a storm."
"Bosh," Tomkin said. "Now for it . . . Look at me."
"Mercy," Jack pleaded. "Let me climb a tree
I would not watch it for all English land."

"Get up your tree," said Tomkin, "and be still."
Jack climbed a little beech tree: Tomkin took
Transmitting wires for the vital thrill
To make the giant lively: Simkin helped.
"When I count Three," said Tomkin, "you can look.
One . . . No, the wire's jammed. Two . . . There's a short.
Now the thing's working . . . Waken up, old sport.
Three . . . there she goes." Jack cowered down and yelped.

And lo, a marvellous thing, the figure stirred,
It trembled, then its mighty jointings cracked,
Bones grided in their sockets, as they heard.
Then the thing stood upon its feet and breathed.
Nothing of living man his glory lacked . . .
He strode into the sunlight, facing east,
At every pulse his majesty increased.
He stood like light in something glowing sheathed.

Then, looking at the Sun, the figure spoke
Meanings, not words: his hearers understood.
Like morning in their minds his meaning broke:
"O Sun that I have worshipped: Sun that brings
The living green upon the wintry wood,
Sun that brings thought into the barren mind,
Sun that puts beauty into hearts unkind,
Lord of all Life and Order, King of Kings,

"I once more look upon you and obey
The call to Likeness with the Force that sends
Poetry in the shining of the ray
And Wisdom in the summer of your touch.
All Energy and Beauty are your friends.
Your fires shout for rapture but confess
A power supreme above their mightiness
Who captains Heaven and many millions such.

"I have been buried long and now awake,
I who was Arthur's comrade long ago.
Man is no longer manhood but mistake.
O spirits of the Morning, come like fire
Come, Arthur, from the dead; let trumpets blow."
Then, lifting to his mouth his mighty hand,
He cried "Come, comrades to this holy land.
O Light, breathe Light upon this land's desire."

Once he called thus, and all the trees stood still;
Twice he called thus, and all the air grew tense;
Thrice he cried thus, and over Barrow Hill
A rush came, like the coming-by of birds,
As spirits never seen by commonsense
Gathered, and gazed, and gleamed upon the view
Waiting, calm-eyed, for orders what to do
From some great trumpet call transcending words.

The brothers saw their many coloured wings
Fold, on their breasts: their beauty was so calm
Each spirit seemed a King of many Kings.
They came to carry light to human souls.
None of those victors carried sword, but palm.
The brothers knew that Arthur's comrade's cry
Had called to England lights that cannot die,
Beauties and powers wearing aureoles.

And then . . . what then? . . . the warrior's figure died.
The body drooped, as all the aged bones
Dropped into dust upon the downland side.
Nothing was there except a chymic mess,
The Barrow's tumbled earth and scattered stones.
Then the three brothers heard a cry begin
"Open your doors and let the new life in."
And skylarks rose and sang in nothingness.

THE ROSE OF THE WORLD

DARK Eleanor and Henry sat at meat
At Woodstock in the royal hunting-seat.

Eleanor said: "The wind blows bitter chill . . .
Will you go out?" King Henry said, "I will."

Eleanor said: "But on so black a night . . .
Will you still go?" He said, "I take delight . . .

"In these wild windy nights with branches swaying
And the wolves howling and the nightmare neighing."

She said, "May I come, too?" "But no," said he;
"No, for at night, if robbers set on me

"I can defend myself . . . I could not you
In the pitch darkness without retinue."

Eleanor said, "Why is it that you go
Thus, and alone?" He said: "You cannot know.

"Leave the King's secrets: let the fact suffice;
Duty demands it and I pay the price."

While Henry reached his sword-belt from the ledge
She pinned a tassel in his mantle's edge,

A clue of white silk that would glimmer pale
About his ankles as he trod the gale.

* * *

Henry went swiftly in the roaring night,
Eleanor saw her token glimmer white.

She followed down the hill, along the brook,
Just seeing by the clue the way he took.

He reached the forest where the hazels swayed . . .
Her soul was too intent to be afraid.

He pushed within the forest and was gone
But still among the scrub her token shone.

In the blind forest many trackways led,
The hazels swayed, the token shewed ahead.

And as she followed she untwined a skein
Of silken floss to lead her out again.

The gale roared in the branches: the beasts shook
Not knowing which direction the step took.

Eleanor knew: she followed thro' the night
King Henry's mantle with its patch of white.

A long, long way she followed: but at last . . .
A clearing in the forest sweetly-grassed

With apple-trees in blossom that the gale
Tore and flung forth; the token glimmered pale.

Beyond the apple-garth a little house
Stood, shuttered close among the tossing boughs.

Light shone from out the bower window-chinks;
Eleanor crept as cat-like as the lynx.

The white patch lingered at the door: she heard
A signal knock: within doors someone stirred.

All stealthily and still as though for sin
The door undid and Henry passed within.

Then the lock turned and Eleanor crept near.
In the gale's roaring she could nothing hear.

Yet near the door a fragrance in the air
Told that a red rose had been crumpled there.

Then in the breaking storm a wild moon shewed
The fashion of that secret wood abode.

The windows high: each crevice tightly shut.
Over the lintel-piece a rose was cut . . .

Eleanor crept about as a cat creeps
In evil midnights when the master sleeps.

No dog was there: no sign of life was there,
Save the faint smell of roses in the air;

And hours passed and hurrying showers passed.
Eleanor watched what fish would come to cast.

Then suddenly, before the East grew gray,
The bolt withdrew to let the King away . . .

Eleanor had but time to crouch and hush
Close in the green of a sweet-briar bush.

She heard no word, but someone whispered close
In the King's ear, a someone like a rose.

And white arms, with their clinking bangles, drew
The King's head downward in a long adieu.

Then the King turned and quietly the door
Closed, and the house was silent as before.

* * *

Eleanor watched, but, lo, the patch of white
Was gone, that should have led her through the night.

Yet following on his steps she saw his frame
Retread in front of her the way he came.

And suddenly she saw him halting dead:
His scabbard's end had caught her guiding thread.

She heard him snap it, but she inly knew
He had not guessed the thread to be a clue.

Afterwards Henry hurried, for the day
Came swiftly, now the storm had blown away.

And lo, the beanfield sweet and blackbirds waking
Leaping from hedge and setting brambles shaking,

And Woodstock dim in trees with nothing stirring
Save the cats homing after nights of erring.

* * *

Eleanor decked herself in all her pride,
All that had graced her as King Henry's bride.

"Were you out late?" she asked. He answered, "No . . .
It was not midnight when we rose to go.

"These midnight councils seldom sit for long."
Eleanor hummed a merry scrap of song.

She went into her turret and undid
Her chest with iron bandings on the lid.

She took a drowsy and a biting draught
And mixed them both and as she mixed she laughed . . .

"This is as heavy sleep upon the life . . .
And this is cutting as an Eastern knife,

"Together they will still the April grace
Of Mistress White-Arms in the rosy place."

She put the potion in a golden flask,
King Henry's gift, and went upon her task.

King Henry asked her, "Whither are you bound?"
"On charity," she said, "my daily round . . .

"The Christian charity I must not spare
To those poor women lying suffering there."

He said, "God bless your charity." And she
Replied "Amen," and went forth quietly.

She visited her sick with bread and wine,
Then searched the forest for her silken sign.

She found the floss still clinging, leading in.
"The hunt is up," she said. "The hounds begin."

The forest was all thicket, but the lane
To tread was blazoned by the silken skein.

Though it was dark in covert, her delight
In what her spirit purposed gave her light.

Then lo, the clearing, and the little house
So fair among the blossomed apple-boughs,

And once again her spirit was aware
Of midmost summer's roses present there.

Within the house she heard a woman sing.
Eleanor knocked the signal of the King.

The chain undid, the bolt was drawn, the key
Turned, and the door was opened, it was she . . .

A girl more beautiful than summer's rose
That in the mid June's beauty burns and glows;

A golden lady graced from foot to tress,
With every simpleness and loveliness,

Who, in the second when she saw the Queen,
Knew that her Death had come, for what had been.

Eleanor like a striking python seized
That golden child and dragged her as she pleased.

"O darling of the King," she said, "behold . . .
I, who am Queen, have brought this flask of gold,

"Also the common hangman and his crew.
I, being royal, give a choice to you.

"Either you drink this poison, and so end . . .
Or I will call the hangmen who attend

"And they shall strip you naked and so hoot
And beat you to the Woodstock gallows-foot

"Where they shall hang you: choose, then, sweetest heart."
The girl beheld Death present with his dart.

The present Death with which man cannot strive.
Death that makes beauty be no more alive,

And is so strange the hot blood can but shrink.
"Threaten me not," she said, "for I will drink.

"I, too, am royal: and no way remains."
She drank the golden flasket to its drains,

And straight the savage poison in her side
Thrust on her heart-strings that she sank and died.

* * *

Eleanor dragged the body to the bed,
"Lie there and welcome Henry, Golden Head."

Then forth the grim Queen went, and licked her lips
To think of June's bright beauty in eclipse

And Henry going to his love to find
The candle quenched that shone behind the blind.

"He will thrust in, and find her lying cold."
So Henry did and found the flask of gold

And knew the Queen's contrivance in the Death.
That night the Queen cried "Open . . . give me breath . . .

"Open the window, for I cannot breathe,
The golden roses' tendrils wreathe and wreathe

"Over my mouth. O who has crushed a rose,
The perfume stifles me: unclose, unclose."

They told her that she dreamed; but she replied—
"The roses choke me: open windows wide.

"Someone had crushed a white rose or a red . . .
Can you not smell the perfume that is shed?

"It comes so close, I cannot breathe the air."
Thenceforward every day and everywhere

The grim Queen cowered from the haunting scent
Of roses crushed, of sweet rose-petals blent

Red, white and golden, coming where she trod.
Henry and Eleanor are now with God,

Whose Face is in all Beauty, as I say.
The pure White Nuns took Rosamund away.

Within their Quire they showed for many years
A little chest or scatolin of hers,

Painted with birds, that Henry once had given.
There the White Sisters prayed her into Heaven

That is the rest for lovers: there they wrought
A white-rose tomb for her from loving thought

So that none thought of her, nor ever will
Save as a lovely thing that suffered ill.

There every May the grass above her bosom
Is strown with hawthorn bloom and apple-blossom.

And on the wild-rose spray the blackbirds sing
"O Rose of all the World, O lovely thing."

YOUNG JOHN OF CHANCE'S STRETCH

PART I

WHEN Father died, my Mother ran
Our Farm at Chance's like a man.

When I was turned eighteen there fell
This venture that I come to tell.

Out cubbing, Mother bruised her knee
(Jumping a gap) against a tree,

So that she could not go to Fair
To buy us a new plough-team there.
She would not trust the bailiff . . . So
"John," said my Mother, "you must go.
Here's fifty pounds in notes. In town
The one safe tavern is the Crown,
Therefore stay there. A Fair-time stranger,
Remember, 's probably a danger . . .
And with a horse to sell, he's worse.
So, John, be careful of your purse.
These Fair-time rogues can so persuade
I marvel any girl's a maid.
Only last Fair time, two men came
To Squire's Hall at Wick-on-Tame,
And said they'd come 'to free the tanks.'
The girl (one of these dolls) said 'Thanks,
Come in,' and led them hand in hand
Upstairs to where the cisterns stand.
There one man said 'Now you be gone
Downstairs and turn the water on,
And watch it as it runs away . . .
And, mind: the instant it turns grey
Or brown, call out to me at once.'

So down the silly creature runs
To sink, and turns on all the taps
And watched, if they'd run wine perhaps.

"And up above, the two men ramped
Through every room and then decamped
While she was watching underneath.
Even the Squire's spare false teeth
Were taken: and of course the men
And things were never seen again.

"That shows how risky 't is to trust:
Never believe unless you must,
And never then about a horse.
But there: you're my wise boy, of course."

I took the money and the trap;
I drove to town without mishap
The day before the Fair began.

Many a gilded swing-boat van,
And horse-go-round, with varnished nags
And bright brass rails and flying flags
And burning furnace shedding glare
Stood by the pavement in the Square;
And showmen fitted up the Fair
Heaving with spanners, lamming mawls.

The gipsy-women with bright shawls
And thick brass earrings and big plumes
Hawked posies made of autumn-blooms
Stolen from gardens on their way.

Towards the closing-in of day
As I was listening to the cries
Of men with pots and dames with pies

My good old Nurse from Tuttocks Rise
Came by: I stopped and greeted her
And edging outwards from the stir
We stood and talked by Grocer's door
Of old times over long before,
Three minutes, I suppose, or four.

And while we talked, a woman stood
Fingering Grocer's poultry food
Close to us, looking at the grain.
She moved away, but came again
And eyed me hard, and entering in
Ordered some hen-food from the bin
And paid and went.
I may be wrong
But thinking of it late and long
Both day and night, in hope of solving,
I think she set the ball revolving,
That all the game began with her.

About some points I cannot err.
She heard Nurse name me: then she heard
My home, and things that had occurred,
And what had brought me to the Fair.
And though she stood before me there
Two minutes, in that crowded place
I never really marked her face.

Then, after sauntering up and down
Seeing the sights, I reached the Crown,
Made sure the nag was snug, and saw
Him happy, fetlock-deep in straw.
The sun was down, the lamps were lighting,
The Fair's noise came like battles fighting:
The Cheap Jack's cries, the songs and shouts,
And brazen patter from the touts

Arose and lifted lad and girl
Into the mad steam-organ's whirl.
It being time, I went to sup.

And at the cheese, the maid came up
And said that someone wanted me.

So, wondering who this could be,
I went into the hall, and there
A girl with two long plaits of hair,
A school-girl, not eleven gone,
Came up and said, "O, Mr. John,
Please, sir, but would you come anon . . .
To see your sister for a minute?"

"Why, girl," I said, "the Devil's in it . . .
I have no sister . . . never had."

She said, "But please, sir, I was bade
To bring you to her, if you'll come."

"But who are you? Whence are you from?"
I asked, and stared upon the child . . .

Her eyes were innocent, she smiled,
She was well dressed, and trim and clean,
"I'm Maggie Hill, from Tuttocks Green,"
She said, "and stopping for the Fair,
With Mrs. Roberts, Market Square."

"Yes, and who sent you here to me?"

"Your sister, Mrs. Peck," said she.

"Where does she live?"
"Up Laurence Lane,
At Rector's Close," she said again . . .
"She's Rector's House-keeper at present."

The girl seemed merry, straight and pleasant.

"All very well, my girl," I said,
"But listen: some mistake's been made.
Who was it you were sent to fetch?"

"Young Mr. John of Chance's Stretch,
Please sir," she said, "lodged at the Crown.
Perhaps if you would just step down
And speak with Mrs. Peck a second
She could explain . . ."
And I, I reckoned
That that was simplest.
"Right," said I.
"Something or someone's gone awry . . .
We'll put it straight, so lead the way."

The West still smouldered with the day
And Maggie prattled as she led
About the wonders overhead,
The flares, the flags, the horses whirling,
And pendulum-like swing-boats swirling.
We turned up Laurence Lane and there
An old house jutted, carven fair . . .
The Rector's house as I knew well.

My leader never rang the bell.
She upped the steps and opened wide
The door for me to pass inside
Then showed me to a little room
Already darkened into gloom
And said "I'll tell them that you're here."
She vanished down a passage near
And down some stairs.
Myself, alone,
Leaned back against the mantel-stone,

Or straining forward strove to see
What Rector's photographs might be . . .
And saw the bare legs and the dates
Of football teams and rowing eights.

The last light of the sunken sun
Gleamed upon silver flagons won
At school or college: in a rack
Some briar pipes gleamed, cindered black;
Then the gleams died: but no one came.
I struck a match and by the flame
Saw Rector's books and college oar.

An owl cried somewhere out of door.
I thought "I'll go, since no one's coming."
Yet downstairs stealthy speech was humming,
A rapid whispered gabble stirred
Designed not to be overheard.
So thinking "If they don't intend
To come, this joke had better end,"
I moved to window.
In the sky
A gnat-pursuing bat went by
And from the Church two shuffling crones
Passed by upon the cobble stones.

Then, just as my resolve grew stronger
To wait there in the dark no longer,
One came with candle down the hall
And shadows moved along the wall,
Gigantic fingers screening light.
A woman came, her face dead-white
And great dark rings of eyes: she laid
The candle down: "O John," she said,
"Forgive me: I was so afraid,
I really could not come before."

She turned again and shut the door,
And plucked the window-curtains to.
She said, "O John, I wish you knew
The joy it is to see you here.
And you are wondering, my dear,

"Both who I am and all about me
And more than half inclined to doubt me;
But if you'll listen, I'll explain.
It starts in a great deal of pain
All over many a year ago,
In ways they never let you know:
And so, may shock you when you hear.

* * *

"Listen . . . Your Father, John, my dear,
Many long years ago was wed
To my poor Mother, long since dead.
He farmed in Dorset then, and she
Died a year later, bearing me.
You never heard of that? Alas . . .
This photo shows you what she was.

* * *

"My Father in his grief, gave over
Me, the poor babe who killed his lover,
To Mother's sisters to be reared . . .

* * *

"Afterwards, Father disappeared.
He never knew nor saw again
Me, the poor cause of so much pain.
He left the district and the past,
Settled at Chance's, and at last
Married your Mother and began
Anew, like every married man.

"My Aunts would never let us meet.
But Life's a very little street,
And people knock against each other.
Destiny brought me near my Brother
To house-keep for the Rector here.

"And like a spy or pioneer
I've been to Chance's, just to see
If Brother John resembled me.
I had not courage to go in.

"I never meant to claim my kin . . .
But seeing you alone to-night
I hungered to, and thought I might.
And then I thought, 'But if I do
He'll disbelieve; he's certain to;
What man would credit such a tale?'

"Since most refrain who fear to fail,
I did not speak, but let you pass.
Then afterwards I thought, 'Alas . . .
The heart within my bosom cries
To that young Brother with dear eyes . .
Why did I let him go?'
And you . . .
Knew nothing of me: never knew . . .
And then I thought: 'It isn't sin
Or fault, to tell him we're akin . . .
But still, he may not care to know.
Or else will disbelieve,' and so
I wandered to the Church and sought
My Husband out, for what he thought.

"My Husband hadn't doubts nor fear.
He said 'Send Maggie round, my dear,

To ask the lad to see you here.'
Maggie's the neighbour's child: and now
I've told you all the manner how.

"And now, my dear, since I have waited
These years for you as things have fated,
Now let me hold you close and kiss.

"Why, what a man my Brother is . . .
So tall: so powerfully made.
And all boy-modest and afraid.

"Now come below: we've supper laid.
My husband's waiting: come to sup."

All full of honey is the cup
And bitter is the morning's taste.

She slipped her arm about my waist
And led me to another room,
Lit by a lamp but still in gloom,
Close-curtained where a table stood
With glasses, dishes, plates and food,
A loaf, a cheese, and watercress.
And in one wall was a recess
From which a man (with a black beard)
Holding a jug of wine appeared.
"This is my husband, John," said she.
He took my hand and welcomed me.

Somehow I didn't like his eyes.

"Have you got over your surprise
At hearing you'd a sister here?"
He asked. "Come, sit, and make good cheer;
But drink, first, to the happy meeting.
Come, drink it to the dregs, no cheating,

It's only claret, mulled. Come, Ann . . .
This John of yours is grown a man . . .
Here's your glass, Ann; here's yours, here's mine."

He leaned across and poured the wine.
And smiled, our glasses clinked, we drank.

Then surging billows rank on rank
Rose somehow out of wall and table
And all the room became unstable
And hummed a tune which droned and rose
And flooded as a river flows.
And I, within it, was as dead
Lapped within rising swathes of red
Thinking "This is great bliss . . . great bliss . . ."

I know not what the next thing is.
I was turned endlong, lifted, hauled
Up-ended, held, supported, mauled,
Why, where or how I had no notion
Save that there somehow was an ocean
Of great red surging waves about.

But somehow someone got me out
To darkness and the open air
And wheeled me in a barrow there,
Then tipped me, but I didn't care
Having such glory in my mind
Watching the surges wave and wind.
Then all was dumb: then all was blind.

* * *

From vasty distance and with pain
I came to consciousness again.
I wondered at the dark and cold
And why I lay upon the mould,

And why the sky was over me.
Then in great sickness wearily
I forced myself to sit upright
And found myself all dressed in white
In woodland, in the middle night.
I marvelled, and was ill, and drowsed.
Then, as the drug passed off, I roused
And knew I had been drugged and stripped.
I was a pigeon plucked and clipped . . .
My money, clothes and shoes all gone.
The long white coat that I had on
Was Rector's cricket-umpire coat,
Tied by the sleeves about my throat
But for that mercy I was bare.

I staggered out into the air
And knew not where I was, but knew
That I had fallen on a crew
Of thieves, in spite of every warning.
And what would happen in the morning
When Mother learned the kind of ass
Her well-belovéd first-born was?

How I had been a fool and taken
The simplest bait a knave had shaken.
Fifty pound bank-notes and my pride
Lost utterly: I sat and cried.

Still dizzy with the drug I trod
Out of the woodland to a road.
There, by the moonlight and a brook
I recognized the way I took
And knelt in the cool mud and drank
Like a parched horse and gave God thank
And drank again, and yet again
Like meadows in the May in rain,

And splashed my face, then tottered down
Bare-footed to the sleeping town;
And as I went each stone beneath
Seemed full of thorn and foxes' teeth,
And I was cold and sick and sad.
O friends, I was a sorry lad.

PART II

I had no count of Time at all
But resting there on turnpike wall
Not sure of getting to the Station
To tell the police my ruination
I saw a dim light move and falter
In the Lady Chapel, near the altar.
And though the old monks' ghostly lights
Are seen there on the Feast Day Nights
I didn't think of those, nor feared.
The very thought of helpers cheered.
I thought: "O joy, the Rector's there;
Some midnight service 't is, or prayer;
Or quire practice, where there'll be
Somebody to look after me."

At that the church-clock sounded One.
And as the echoes ceased to stun
And no strokes followed, Nine or Ten,
I thought "The light is not of men
But spirits: ghosts are walking there."
I felt a pricking in my hair.

This Lady Chapel's builded fair
Out from the Church's end: it stands
Like something thought, not made with hands.
Why, at that hour, was it lit?
I gripped the wall and looked at it.

* * *

The light would now be dim, now glowing
Like candle-light when winds are blowing.
I shook to think of what thin crowds
Might there be flitting in their shrouds.
And then Clink, clink, I heard a pick
Strike stone and falling fragments click.
I said "Whoever works on stone,
It isn't ghosts, but flesh and bone."

So up I rose and crept anear.
Within the Chapel I could hear
Work of some sort, like an assault
With crowbars on a burial vault.
I crept right round it, to the door.

And all old tales, heard long before
Of body-snatchers, thrilled me through.
I trod the graves all wet with dew.
The chapel door was opened wide
And lantern candle-light inside
Wavered and made the shadows shake.

I crept. A muffled voice said "Take . . .
Catch hold your end. There. Got him? Hoist."

The sweat upon my brows was moist.
But still, I peeped within to see
What all this midnight work could be.

I saw a man bent at a hole
Dragging with all his very soul,
Cursing, at something hard to drag.
A pick lay on a broken flag.
A lantern lit the scene: below
A voice said "Heave and make her go."

And at the heave a leaden roll,
Corpse-shaped, came endwise from the hole.
And as the coffin jolted forth
A Newgate face, all fringed with swarth,
Peered from the hole: a man crawled out.

He said: "We won't be long in doubt.
Cut open: where's the chisel, Jack?"

They cut and bent the cover back,
They held the light to the cut gash.

Jim said: "His Lordship's not so brash
As when they put him in: but, look . . .
Gold rings and chain and golden crook.
Empty him out, his noble nibs."

A jawbone and some scraps of ribs
And dust and gold and femur bones
Were emptied out upon the stones
And those two ruffians with delight
Held up the gold against the light
And pawed the dust and scraped the lead.

"That's all," said Jack. "Now let's to bed.
There's more in this night's work than beer."

The moon had risen high and clear
Though waning, when they rose to go.

What prompted me I cannot know,
But as they left the door I raised
One hand, and held them as though crazed.
I cried "Why are you robbing me?
Restore my corpse's property."

I, the half-naked thing in white
Half seen in moon and lantern-light,
Must have seemed walking-corpse or ghost.

The robbers bleated like the lost
Then they both screamed and darted past
Screaming, and as they ran they cast
Their takings from them, right and left.

And one thing, scattered from their theft,
Hit me: I picked it up: a ring
Set with a ruby for a king.

Before St. Laurence' bell struck Two
I told my tale t' Inspector Drew.
He called his men, and by Two-twenty
They found that Rector's house was empty . . .
Rector on holiday, my thieves
Gone, having sacked it, floor to eaves.
Maggie, the neighbour's child, and Ann,
My so-called sister, and her man
All gone, that three who kept a school
For teaching wisdom to a fool.
All vanished somewhere, not by train.
I never had my notes again.

Years afterwards, it chanced I saw
At trial in a court of law,
A man condemned for poisoning.
If I am sure of anything,
I'm sure the prisoner was he
Who wiled and drugged and plundered me.
And one poor woman bent with sobbing
Was Ann who lured me to the robbing.

Victims need never rage and curse,
Life's justices will punish worse.

As for the robbers, Joe and Jack,
Who fled, they never ventured back.
They disappeared into the Fair
The better Christians for the scare.

The gold that they had scattered, proved
To be a crozier, chased and grooved,
A ring and crucifix and chain
Of some old Abbot who had lain
Down in the vault six hundred years,
Some Abbot Hayward, it appears.

My ruby ring, as treasure found,
Was valued at a thousand pound
Of which eight hundred came to me.

I bought the best team that could be,
I gave the village-school a tea.
I bought my Mother all a store
Of things I'd heard her hanker for,
Beside a watch and silken gown.
I had the orphans out of town
For cake and sports: the rest I banked,
And so I ended, God be thanked.

EVAN ROBERTS, A.B., OF H.M.S. *ANDROMACHE*

This gallant act is told by the late Montagu Burrows, on page 67 of his *Autobiography* (Macmillan & Co., 1908, 8s. 6d.). I thank his son, Sir Montagu Burrows, K.C.I.E., for permission to make this use of it. The act was done in the night of the 29th-30th October, 1836, on and near the main topsail yard of H.M.S. *Andromache*, twenty-eight guns, then at sea in a cyclone not far from Madras.

The hero, Evan Roberts, was a merchant seaman of Liverpool, born at Temple Lane, and living, when ashore, at Rice Street, in that city. He was a single man, aged twenty-four at the time, had been nine years at sea, and had joined the *Andromache*, as a volunteer, at Capsingmoon, on 4th October, 1834. He remained in the *Andromache* as a main topman, till she paid off (probably at Spithead) on September 28th, 1837.

I cannot learn what became of him. He was "a quiet steady fellow" who "had through temperance become a religious man." He was of a ruddy complexion, with brown hair and gray eyes; he stood five feet four inches in height; he was tattooed with a cross on his left arm, a man and a woman on his right arm, and an anchor and A R on his right hand. If anyone who reads this can tell me more of him, I shall be grateful if he or she will write to me, in the care of the publishers of this volume.

About the ship *Andromache* the cyclone blew,
After heavy running they had to heave her to,
Seas broke green aboard her, men couldn't keep their feet,
The weather main topsail parted at the sheet.

The topsail lifted and split to seven rags
That streamed like banners and bellowed like stags;
Buntlines and cluelines snapped like lady's lace,
And snap at both the yardarms went the topsail brace.

They steadied on the lifts, but the lifts broke, too;
The topsail yard lifted and shook the frigate through;
The topsail yard lifted and the parrel gave . . .
And the yard went flying till the heart-strings clave.

Out it streamed to leeward like a wind-blown vane,
Flogged its tattered topsail and thundered in again;
Outboard at the rising, inboard at the 'scend,
At each in crashing as though it were the end.

As the topmen struggled to bring it to a check
It struck on Robert Eadie and knocked him to the deck.
Fifty feet of timber with will and strength to strike
None of all the topmen had ever seen the like.

It was blind black midnight, blowing like the Pit,
The yard was flying with Death to whom it hit;
Roberts took a brace-end, bit upon it hard,
When the yard crashed inboard he leaped upon the yard.

Now he was above it, now he was beneath,
He bit upon the brace-end and kept it in his teeth;
Tattered topsail flogged him, the blind yard banged,
The top said "Glory . . . he is born to be hanged."

Roberts reached the yardarm and grovelled to the block,
The yard boxed compass like hands upon a clock.
Tongues of flying topsail licked away his skin;
He rove his weather brace-end from outboard in.

Roberts bit the brace-end, and gathered as she swang,
Ready for the life-spring a second ere the bang;
As the yard crashed inboard he leaped into the top,
The topmen snatched the brace-end and the yard came stop.

The topsail yard jolted, but the curb came taut,
They dragged it into harness like a mad bull caught.
Underneath a staysail she pointed to the blow.
Roberts and the topmen were piped below.

In case some find it difficult to follow what happened, it may be said that the topsail yard, a spar of wood fifty feet long, dangerous with tattered gear, was flying about in the night in the gale, held only by the halliards. In the confusion and fury of darkness and storm those aloft could not explain to those on deck, nor these see. Not one man in ten million could have imagined that a yard so flying could be bridled by leaping onto it in the dark, dragging a rope, groping out to the yardarm as it flew, passing the rope through a block, bringing the rope's end in, and then leaping with it from the yard into the comparative stability of the top, all this in a furious gale at midnight with the ship so labouring that the masts threatened to go overboard at every roll. Not one man in a million could have been strong, quick and ready enough to do the deed; nor could the valour of the man have availed without the skill and courage of his shipmates.

RICHARD WHITTINGTON

PERSONS

FORTUNE	RICHARD WHITTINGTON
MISTRESS MERCER	ALICE
MESSENGER	MAPONGO

FORTUNE:

I am Fortune: I give as is fitting to each of my souls,
Therein, as their strength is, they follow or fashion their fate.
Though his embers be almost extinct, if I breathe on the coals,
The man reddens into a glory and gleams and is great.
When I breathe not, the glow of his state
Dies down into ash on the bars.
I pass over men with my stars.

Now here, from the red clay compounded, a lad from the west,
The son of a lord of a manor, a fortunate child . . .
My dark stars were passing, his Fortune was darkened with pest;
Since then, in the years he has suffered, I have not once smiled.
The poisonous words that make wild,
And tears, are his portion of late.
My darkness will pass, if men wait.

[*She goes.*]

RICHARD WHITTINGTON:

When I was but a babe, my Father died
In the Great Death, with half his folk beside.

My Mother married with another man;
A bitter time for me then soon began.

Not being wanted in my Mother's home,
And hating him she loved, I used to roam

About the forest in that hilly land
Which the Great Death had utterly unmanned.

For I could wander all day long and find
No house with any dweller save the wind;

Chapels with red deer muzzling at the paint,
Still blue and gold, of some forgotten saint,

And dog-rose thrusting past the carven piers
And altars where wild dogs killed the wild steers.

And skeletons of women dead of pest . . .
With their long hair the chaffinch wove her nest.

There was a little town where all were dead,
The winds jangled the church bell overhead;

And cats came snarling: you may judge the joy
That Dead Man's Land was to a little boy.

When I was nine years old, my mother's mate
Said "He must go, this Richard, with his hate,

"Off to my sister's husband there, in Cheap,
To learn a Mercer's trade and earn his keep.

"No longer lurk here skulking, eyeing me
With that glum hate which I am sick to see."

So here I came to learn a Mercer's trade.
This is the fourteenth year that I have stayed:

The business droops, the Mercer is now dead,
His half-mad widow governs here instead.

Her hatred hinders me from chance or wage;
My Mother's Husband holds my heritage:

By hate from both, my Fortune is opposed.
Last June, before the Summer Term had closed,

A Shipman came here, making up his trade.
"Adventure everything," my instinct said.

But luckless I, with nothing but a Cat
To stake in trade could only venture that:

Now I regret I did not venture this
Body and mind, and that which in them is.

Adventured that and on a reckless die
For Death or Fortune risked this grumbling I.

I would have, too, but for the love I bear
To Mistress Alice, beautiful and fair;

Daughter of Arlingham, King Richard's Knight.
She only is my pleasure and delight.

Penniless I, unhappy, love her so
That though I hate my life, I cannot go

Away from here, lest I should never see
Her blessed sunlight shining upon me.

She comes here sometimes as a sunbeam falls
Once in a year, perhaps, on prison-walls,

Then, passing, leaves the knowledge that light is.
Would I had greatly ventured, ending this,

Staking myself for all that I have dreamt.
Love is not love that risks not in attempt.

I should have ventured seaward and have found
Way to my heart's desire, or have drowned . . .

Not rotted here . . . The tyrant enters. Peace.

[*He goes.*]

[*Enter* MISTRESS MERCER.]

MISTRESS MERCER:

He shall not rob this old ewe of her fleece,
Whittington shall not, though he be the son
Of that old Knight who perished in the pest.
My Brother wed the old Knight's widow, true;
And took her manors, but he found no peace
Dogged daily by this Richard Whittington.
Would he had cut the infant's neckbone through
And flung him to the hounds: it had been best.
Would he might cease.
Hate of him leaves me utterly undone.

It was my Husband's being partly mad
And love for Brother made me take the lad.
Here throughout boyhood he has learned the trade.
Now the ungrateful scoundrel would be paid . . .
Paid, after all the charity he has had.

I know he longs to murder me and seize
My Husband's place and work-rooms: oh, I know
The greed of gold possessing him like lust . . .
Why, when the Captain came, some months ago,
This Richard sent his cat abroad in trade;
Ventured his cat for profit over-seas . . .
O dog, so greedy for the golden dust,
Small profit, God be thanked, your venture made;
Ship, cat and captain must have drowned ere this;
None has had tidings of them since they weighed.

Would that my thought were poison in his cup,
I hate him so; for I am growing old,
My star is sinking, his is rising up.
This Richard rises and my heart forebodes,

For I am in a dangerous enterprise: —
My Brother, who usurps this Richard's lands,
Plots for the post of Warden of the West
Which the King gives to Arlingham the Knight.
My Brother and myself have sworn to lies
Against this Arlingham: and now, to-night,
Our joint denouncing comes to the King's hands.
God, put belief within the royal breast,
Let him believe our charges and smite down
This Arlingham, and make my Brother Warden.

But lo, the white rose comes from the rose-garden,
Arlingham's daughter, Alice, London's crown,
Comes hither with her simper: come, sweet Miss,
Heaven shall change that simper into tears,
And hoist your Father's head aloft on spears,
Before to-morrow's dawn, if Heaven hear me.
This poisonous Richard loves you from afar.
My hate shall drag you under, moth and star,
I am old and quaking upon Death's abyss,
Before I fall, your dying groans shall cheer me.

[ALICE *enters*. *She calls.*]

ALICE:

Is Mistress Mercer here? Is Richard here?
I will call Hob, the foreman, for I fear
That both are out, and I must leave a word.

[*Enter* RICHARD.]

RICHARD:

Greetings, sweet lady.

ALICE:

Richard, you have heard
How latterly the King, in his great grace,
Has honoured us in Court with pride of place.

He has made my Father Warden of the West
To hold the Marches that the Welsh infest,
And we must start at once, and shall be gone
Three years, my Father thinks, or thereupon.
I come to tell you this, and say farewell.
I know this bitter place has been a hell
To you, these latter years, and is so still.
Believe that Life will better and it will;
I, as your Friend, most fixedly believe
That you will conquer Fortune, and achieve,
And soon, an end to all your misery.
I shall think often of you: now good-bye.
If I can help in friendship in the West
In righting you where you were dispossessed
Count upon me, upon my Father, too.
But of your own strength you will struggle through
These bitter times and be the man I think.

RICHARD:

'Couraged by you a man will never sink.
I am happy at the honour that has come.
May you be happy in your Western home;
I shall think much of you and wish you well.
What you have been to me, no tongue can tell.
Through these last months, your sometimes coming here
Has been like sun in April of the year.
May all good angels be about your ways;
And if, as God forbid, unhappy days
Should ever come, that you should need a friend,
I am devoted yours till the world's end
And should be proud to aid you till I die.

ALICE:

I know it, Richard, thank you: now good-bye.
Good fortune to you in the days to be.

[*She goes.*]

RICHARD:

Love flows like Severn, but it ebbs like sea.
She mounts, she rides away, and she is gone . . .
Three years, her Father thinks, or thereupon . . .
How can a life continue without sun,
Without the hope of light or coming Spring?
Would men were as the swallows that can wing
After their heart's desire anywhere.
Would I had ventured with the sailors there
With my poor cat, to better Fate or end.

MISTRESS MERCER:

Believe in Life, good Richard: it will mend,
And you will conquer Fortune very soon
And be as glad as April in the moon
And follow Alice on the swallow's wing.
Why, you bone-idle, gormandizing thing,
Why, you shall have your wouldings to the top:
I here dismiss you, both from works and shop,
Go venture with the sailors like your cat,
Or after Alice as the swallows do.
The world's your mistress now: I've done with you.
Forth with you to the beggary and rope
Henceforth to be your portion as I hope.

[*She goes.*]

RICHARD:

Since I am cast, I will go westaway,
After my heart's beloved, and assay
Adventure for her, though I nothing have
Beyond the wits and thews that Nature gave.

Her Father may engage me in his troop
Riding the Marches beyond Severn Loop,
And I will serve him well, serving for her,
And it is good to plunge into the stir

For her who is the banner of my mind.
Therefore I go, to seek what I shall find.

[*He goes out.*]

FORTUNE:

I am that Lady Fortune whom men paint
With globe or turning wheel, forever swift,
Whom many men implore, as to a saint,
Out of the drowning waters as they drift.
My weathercock, that shows how the winds shift,
I bear aloft, for wandering men to see,
It swings in the bright sun on the blue lift,
And men beholding are aware of me.

About a central calm the currents turn,
Gently or turbulently, never still;
As round a rock the tidal eddies churn,
So these, as the Mood passes at my will.
And as men lift their eyes towards a hill
For marching-mark when wayless in a plain,
So, in the darkness of the roaring ill,
Men question this, "Does Fortune turn again?"

O shifting winds of passion, changing tides
Of living nations that the women bare,
Seek out the central quiet that abides,
Within yourselves are Peace and Everywhere;
But since the running star with the bright hair
Lures, and men follow, to disaster strange,
Think this, that I am just, and am aware,
And that, however fixed, the wind will change.

[*She goes.*]

RICHARD:

Alas! for changing Fortune; for a blow
Has laid my Alice and her Father low.

I left this city for the West, I passed
Into the springless Cotswolds, scanty-grassed,

And saw the raddled Severn running red,
With Worcester green, and Malvern blue, ahead.

Then learned that on some traitor's false report
Alice's Father was disgraced at Court

And had returned to London to await
Sentence (men told me) and a traitor's fate,

With ruin to himself and to his girl.
Thus, with my wits and passions in a whirl,

Helpless in Alice's need as in my own,
I sat me down upon a boundary stone

Not knowing where to turn, nor what to do.
And as well-water, ever-clean and new,

Comes from the unknown hollow underground
Into the light, and dances, and makes sound,

So, from within me and without me, wells
Of message sounded with the voice of bells,

Saying again and yet again, these words.
"Turn again, Whittington,
Lord Mayor of London Town;
Turn again, Whittington,
Lord Mayor of London Town;
Of London Town
Three times Lord Mayor."
The April wind and all the April birds

Repeated this, so that I could not doubt
My Life within was touched by Life without.

Therefore I have returned as the words bade.
I hear sad news of my beloved maid.

Her Father's goods escheated to the Crown,
Herself in some mean lodging in the town,

Deserted in her need, and helpless I,
Her friend forever, sunk in poverty,

But I am in the cockcrow of my day
After the dark, the morning becomes gray.

Beauty will triumph, Love will find a way.
[*He goes out.*]

[ALICE *enters.*]

ALICE:

Since we are ruined, since my Father's fine
Is far too heavy ever to be paid
I have forgotten that the sun can shine
And thought the story of my fortunes said.
Father, unjustly 'prisoned in the Tower,
Lives with small hope of ever issuing thence:
He tells the dreary stones and counts the hour
And prays that God may show his innocence.

While I, deserted by the world, am now
Come to this Mercer's, seeking work to do
I have never worked; good angels, show me how.

MISTRESS MERCER:

Who's there without? O Mistress Alice, you?

ALICE:

I, Mistress Mercer. May I speak a word?
I am in sorrow, as you may have heard.
And come to ask, if you can give me work?

MISTRESS MERCER:

Lace-work, or broiderer's work, or needlework?

ALICE:

I will learn any honest work you give.

MISTRESS MERCER:

For your amusement?

ALICE:

No, as means to live.

MISTRESS MERCER:

To live, God spare us, you are rich and proud.

ALICE:

The sun once shone: now heaven is in cloud.

MISTRESS MERCER:

Where is your Father?

ALICE:

In the Tower.

MISTRESS MERCER:

In jail?

Ah yes, for Treason; true, I heard the tale.

ALICE:

No, never Treason: men have falsely sworn.

MISTRESS MERCER:

Where are your friends, then: you are nobly born.

ALICE:

Some are beyond the sea; some disbelieve.

MISTRESS MERCER:

They may have grounds for doubting, by your leave.

ALICE:

No grounds, but jealousy and envious hate.

MISTRESS MERCER:

So you want work?

ALICE:

I do, I supplicate.

MISTRESS MERCER:

What sort of wages would you reckon fair?

ALICE:

Those paid in open market everywhere.

MISTRESS MERCER:

And bed and board besides, and holidays?

ALICE:

Whatever usual wage the Mercer pays.

MISTRESS MERCER:

I've got no work for idlers such as you.
Work is for workers, not a useless crew
Who never did a turn and never can.
You are less use than a blind, crippled man.
You that have had your riches should have kept.
You have lived daintily and ate and slept
And now will taste the difference. And besides
Treason is as the gracious King decides . . .
I'll have no traitors here, nor traitors' kin.
Find other means to feed your pretty skin,
You'll get none here and so I tell you plain.

[*She goes.*]

ALICE:

Can any offer everything in vain?
Now I perceive in what a tottering cage
Man thinks he stands above the whirlpool's rage.

RICHARD:

Courage, sweet lady, for the darkest hour
Prepares the dawn, the darkest bud the flower.

Though all malignance all its malice spend
Spirits that hate malignance come to friend.

And I can friend, for everything I have
Is consecrated yours unto the grave,

Sweet lady, while I live, you shall not starve.
This city's granite block this soul shall carve

Into a setting for you, worthy you.

[*Enter* MISTRESS MERCER.]

MISTRESS MERCER:

Away from here, you outcast beggars' crew.
You cast apprentice with his callat, hence.
Away, Miss Dolly and Sir Insolence.
Off, from my doorstep, to your tavern den,
To rags of women and the wrecks of men,
To gutter-pick by moonlight for your bread.
This is no lazar house nor loitering shed
For beggars such as you to stretch and shake you.
Hence, or I'll call the watchmen who will make you.
And do you dare to brave me to my face?

[*Enter* MESSENGER.]

THE MESSENGER:

Is Mistress Mercer keeper of this place?

MISTRESS MERCER:

Yes, I am she, a widow, but still able
To keep a roof, and bread upon the table
For all a pack that plot to beggar me.

MESSENGER:

One Whittington was with you. Where is he?

MISTRESS MERCER:

He *was* with me: not now.

RICHARD:

But I am here.

MESSENGER:

In the King's name, I greet you, with good cheer.

RICHARD:

I bow to the King's grace.

MESSENGER:

God save the King,
I bear a knot for your unravelling.
So you are Richard Whittington?

RICHARD:

I am.

MESSENGER:

You recollect the queenly ship that swam
Within the Pool last year, the *London Ark?*

RICHARD:

Yes, and her Captain. Have they prospered?

MESSENGER:

Mark!

My tale is about them: they are no more;
Their bones are in the ocean far from shore;
Green water washes them and fishes eat.

MISTRESS MERCER:

Yes, and your cat's become the herring's meat,
Your cat that you adventured in your greed.

MESSENGER:

Madam, you interrupt me: pray give heed.
Although the Captain and the ship are gone
It was in battle with the Moors: anon
The mate and sailors flung themselves aboard
The Moorish ship and took her by the sword
And, ere their own ship sank, installed them there,
Saving your cat, that pride with glossy hair.

RICHARD:

I am glad I did not send the cat to death.

MESSENGER:

You sent her to more life, for she gave breath
Soon after this to seven little ones.
She kittened, to be plain, between the guns,
And reared her kittens to a stalwart seven
Such as the cats (if there be mice) in Heaven.

The ship went loitering onward, moon by moon,
And reached the capital of Settaroon,
Mapongo City on Mapong' Lagoon.

But, ah, Mapongo City, once so glad
With roaring life, was desolate and sad;
Curse had undone the glory it had had.

Of all the roaring life that used to run
To cheer incoming bark or galleon
With songs and splashing spray, we saw not one.

Voiceless, with empty streets, the city lay,
The palm-thatch blown to tatters, withered grey,
Doors blowing to and fro, walls in decay.

And when the sailors landed, they espied
No man at all, but yet on every side
Myriads of Mice, quick-flitting, glitter-eyed.

And in the palace on his throne of state
The King of Settaroon, Mapongo, sate
Grey with his fear, but constant under Fate.

But King Mapongo comes himself to tell
How Settaroon was smitten with such hell
And how his people fled and what befell.

[MAPONGO *enters.*]

MAPONGO:

I am Mapongo. Ere my Father died,
Two years ago, he called me to his side.

He said, "I tell you what my Father told
Myself, when I was young and he was old . . .

"*All Evil that afflicts this land of ours*
Comes from a wizard who has Devil's powers.

"*He dwells within a man-bone scattered tract*
A moon's march hence, beneath the Cataract.

"*He who shall kill this Devil will deliver*
This Kingdom from all Evil whatsoever.

"*As Battle, Revolution, Murrain, Blight,*
The Pest by day, man-killing Beasts by night.

"Therefore I bid you (as my Father me)
Seek out this Devil (as did I and he),

"And spear him if you can, ourselves have failed."

My Father having died, myself was hailed

King, in his place, and therefore took a spear
And sought that Devil in his cave of fear.

He dwells within a gash of mile-high walls
Into which wrench of earth a river falls

So that a smoke of water rises grey
All rainbow-lit and soaking earth with spray
The water-eagles cruise there, seeking prey.

I found a trackway narrow as a girth
Leading below into that gash in earth

Beneath; the water roared in the abyss.
I heard the eagles mew, the serpents hiss.

I reached the beach below, the slippery stones
Were heaped with driftwood and with dead men's bones.

I reached the falls, that ever-dropping cloak
Of water torn as wool and flung as smoke.

I reached the cave, that grimness ever grey
With ever-changing spectres of the spray.

I entered in those galleries of stone:—
I heard no sound, but I was not alone.

The black glass alleys gleamed : I could not see
Aught else, but something else was there with me.

Its breath was just behind me as I crept,
Its footstep was like echo when I stepped.

At every corner, it was there in front,
My spirit was the quarry of its hunt.

And when I reached the central cave I knew
The thing was present, evil as doom due.

And nothing shewed : a small red fire burned :
Yet the whole cavern threatened me and girned.

I cried : "I am Mapongo : meet me here
O Cavern Devil, spear to flying spear."

No answer came, yet something seemed to mock
With silent laughter in the cavern rock.

Then suddenly I felt the cavern fill
With many unseen shapes of evil will.

And suddenly a myriad little eyes
Peered at me from the cavern's galleries.

No word was said, but at a secret sign
A myriad teeth went 'chatter' : so did mine.

Then at a sign that none could hear or see
Those myriad little Devils rushed at me.

And I ? I fled, and from that hellish place
I ran to Settaroon, with them in chase . . .

And though we slaughtered myriads, myriads more
Came in upon us all and overbore.

We had to fly for life, and having flown
They picked our city to the inner bone,
Nothing was left that was not shut in stone.

Hiding in forest boughs we saw beneath
The million tails, bead-eyes, and gnawing teeth,

The Mice had dispossessed us of our all.
Woe for Mapongo's melancholy fall.

THE MESSENGER:

But vengeance followed on those conquering Mice . . .
This Richard's cat and kittens, brought ashore,
Smote them, as blowing fire shatters ice . . .
And as November beech-leaves fly before
A gale from the Atlantic, so did these
Fly, from the terror taloning them dead,
Some, to swift ending in the breaking seas,
The rest, to darkness in the forest, fled.

The cat and kittens finished every mouse;
Down from the trees came warriors and their wives,
Children again met parent, mate met spouse.
And thanks were sent to him who saved their lives.

MAPONGO:

Our friend will read the list of what we send
To Richard Whittington, Mapongo's Friend.

THE MESSENGER:

To Richard Whittington, to have and hold.
One ton of gold-dust, one ton *solid* gold.

Ten emeralds of Sarras, each as green
As hawthorn leaves in April, when first seen.
Ten rubies of Ratanga, each as red

As dog-rose berries when the rose is dead.
Ten sapphires of Solyma, each as blue
As heaven is to girls when love is new.
Ten alabaster caskets of cut stones,
Amethysts, beryls, jacynths, chalcedones.
Ten sherris sapphires coloured like cut corn;
Ten moon spikes of the icy unicorn;
Ten pearls like moonlight on a quiet pond;
Ten black pearls, and a frosty diamond.
Eleven hundred ostrich plumes which foam
Over at edge in flounce as billows comb.
Eleven hundred tusks, some white and some
Yellow, some scarlet from blood-coloured gum.
Eleven hundred baskets of a bark
So sweet men cannot handle it till dark.
Eleven hundred boxes of such balm
As mollifies all anger into calm.
Eleven hundred buckets of such spice
As burns the Phœnix in her sacrifice.

But topping all together comes beside
The Crimson Settaroon, Mapongo's Pride,
The jewel that gives light from inner fire,
Round as the orb, outflowing as desire,
Out of the passion of whose globe there burns
Ray after ray that lightens and returns.
Itself alone such wealth as never yet
Came Europe-wards for crown or coronet.

In all, such treasure as has never come
In any ship to any port of home.

MAPONGO:

Here is the deed of gift, the treasure waits
At Tower Wharf beside the Tower gates.

For Richard Whittington, Mapongo's Friend.
May your delight in living never end.

[MAPONGO *goes.*]

THE MESSENGER [*to* ALICE]:

Another thing, King Richard bids me say
He learns your Father never did betray,
Never, as Mistress Mercer's brother swore.
Your Father is as free as heretofore,
And has the King's great favour as of old.
But Mistress Mercer's brother is in hold
For falsely swearing, and as does appear
Usurping the estates of Richard here.
And, Mistress Mercer, I am charged to bring
Yourself to trial now before the King,
Lest you were with your brother in the plot.
Endure such fate as Fortune shall allot.

[*To* RICHARD.]

The King will greet you here when we are gone.
Long life and luck to Richard Whittington.

[*He goes with* MISTRESS M.]

RICHARD:

I am glad that your Father is saved from the hatred of men.

ALICE:

I am thankful to you for your gladness and glad of your luck.

RICHARD:

I am stunned by my fortune, your gladness alone makes it real.

ALICE:

It is stablished four square at the Pier like the Tower itself.

RICHARD:

It is fortune past telling; I long for yet greater in dream.

ALICE:

All the world is a ball at the feet of the fortunate man.

RICHARD:

Sweet lady, my fortune and world are yourself standing there,
Without you, my fortune is nothing, my world is despair,
I love you so dearly, I cannot find words for my love.

ALICE:

I love you so dearly, I need not the words, but the love.

RICHARD:

O lovely beloved, you are beauty and hope and all peace;

ALICE:

You are gladness and comfort without whom all comfort would
cease.

RICHARD:

You are joy beyond telling and glory that thrills like the sun,

ALICE:

You are desolate days put away and a new life begun.

RICHARD:

You are all my endeavour and longing made real, made mine.

ALICE:

Having all, each in each, let us offer up gifts as a sign.

RICHARD:

Let us build for the wretched in prison a shelter and home.

ALICE:

Let us build a fair study of books where poor scholars can come.

RICHARD:

Let us dower an almshouse where bedesmen may pass happy age.

ALICE:

Let us dower a spital with doctor to heal and assuage.

RICHARD:

Let us build, to Saints Spirit and Mary, a church white and fair.

ALICE:

Let us give it a College of Priests to sing services there.

RICHARD:

Let them sing night and day, that the Angels of Beauty may hear.

ALICE:

And the Angels of Beauty spread feathers of gold and draw near.

RICHARD:

And shine in this City and take each a soul to his fold.

ALICE:

And the souls of this City shine bright with their Helpers of gold.

RICHARD:

May spirits so brightened imagine the Earth that may be.

ALICE:

May hands so encouraged create what the vision can see.

BOTH TOGETHER:

May Earth be so happy with Heaven that all souls shall sing
As the stars and the planets above
The Order, the Beauty, the Love
Of the Might that directs them as King.

THE HOUR STRIKES

PERSONS

THE SEEKER
DESTINY

KATHARINE

WOLSEY

ANNE

HENRY

THE SEEKER:

The shepherds warned me not to climb this hill
To-night, Midsummer Night, "Because," they said,
"The Past goes by, with power to do ill.
And all the Kings, with Arthur at their head,
Return to life and are no longer dumb
But commune of Times past and things to come."

Yet I have climbed the hill in hope to see,
Before the mist is white with the moon's power,
Those workers of our country's destiny,
And hear them talk for their allotted hour:—
And lo, great figures sitting with a Queen,
Spirits of that which will be or has been:—

O, if a mortal's question may find grace,
What are you, Lady of the starry face?

DESTINY:

Nothing, perhaps, save urging to the race.

SEEKER:

Who are the veiled attendants at your side?

DESTINY:

Forces that spirits struck, that have not died.

SEEKER:

May I ask on, or do your laws forbid?

DESTINY:

To those who ask aright nothing is hid.

SEEKER:

Then I would ask if these are Queens and Kings
Come from this windy downland's burial rings,
Or from old tombs, on this most sacred night
To see again the land of their delight?
If so, I'll kneel.

DESTINY:

Nay, ask themselves to speak,
They were once strengths for sifting out the weak,
And resolute for ends, as you are now.
To Life's uncoultered pasture they were plough;
To Life's unscattered fallow they were seed.
They lived and suffered torture and had need.

And I, I dealt with them; for I am one
That trumpet up the sleepers with the sun,
And urge them on all day and blow the call
For the red sunset at the evenfall,
And new souls for the morrow. I am she
Who urges from the depths the things to be:
And millions come at call, and from their pain
Are sweated out the radiants that remain
Before I fling them by: what they achieve
I cannot count: I cannot joy nor grieve,
Only sweep on: and yet I inly know

That what they do will be my overthrow.
They will be conquerors, and I, destroyed,
Flung forth with past abortions to the void.

But question: for at summer's topmost peak
All powers in my domination speak:
And these will speak, if questioned: but for me
I question nothing: only bring to be.

THE SEEKER:

Spirits, unveil to me.

[THEY *unveil.*]

You have the mien,
Figure and bearing of an English Queen.
O speak to me out of the night of Death.
Who were you, when your beauty drew sweet breath
Here on this Downland? May a mortal know?
Ha; she awakes: her life comes pulsing slow:—
She is about to answer me: she speaks.

K. OF ARAGON:

I am that Katharine brought out of Spain to be wed
To Arthur, the Prince; I was wedded, then widowed, then wooed
By Henry the brother of Arthur, my prince who was dead:
I came to be Queen beside Henry, and sorrows ensued
Not singly but brood upon brood,
Till my heart was made sick, and my faith
Like a rag under feet of the rude,
And I died of the shame and the scathe.

It is scant happiness, sisters, to be as a pawn
In the chess of the Kings of the nations, a pawn to be played,
Exchanged for advantage, or lost, or advanced or withdrawn,
But the game is the game of God's will, and His will be obeyed.

Like Him are the Kings He has made
To rule as He rules, and to bring
Into Earth the Idea of the King:
Knowing this I endured unafraid.

I was a child when I was wedded to Arthur,
A child when Arthur died: yet, being a child
I saw the old King plotting to save my dowry
By marrying me to his surviving son,
Henry the Prince: he had his will and the dowry,
And I was married to that most hopeful prince.

The old King died, my Henry was crowned as the King.
I was the Queen of England, with bright hopes shining.
No prince in Europe had royaller hopes than mine.

How shall I speak of him that was
Of all Kings' sons the chrysopras?
He was built stalwart as the bull,
His countenance was beautiful,
His body perfect, his feet swift,
His mind filled full with every gift,
With every talent, for he knew
The things that men of genius do
And did them as a master might.
Music was ever his delight,
He sang, he played, he wrote sweet airs
Which the Court minstrels wished were theirs:
He was an architect whose schemes
Surpassed the living master's dreams:
He knew the known tongues and could speak
Latin, French, German, Spanish, Greek;
And in his speech such sweetness hung
He witched all comers with his tongue:
He knew all law, he could debate

All questions touching his estate:
In all disputes he could take part
With the best doctors in each art:
And in himself he had such force,
Such mastery and grace of horse,
Such swiftness and such skill in play,
Wrestling or tennis, that men say
None ever equalled him, or near.

In courtesy, none was his peer.
In gifts, none matched him, nor in grace
Of body, spirit, parts or face.
None was more loved, none was more served
With constancy that never swerved;
And none began a reign so stored
With things that men and angels hoard.

His treasuries were filled; his land
Was well content beneath his hand;
His counsellors were good; his friends
Secure; he sought no wicked ends.
The sun seemed rising in his might
To fill the English realm with light;
And hourly the thinkers wrought
More beauty out of subtle thought.
And life, to all alive, was even
With the bright boundaries of Heaven,
And angels walked the earth with men.
England was surely Heaven then.

And had my sons survived, my Fate
Would have been ever fortunate . . .
My sons all died, I brought no heir
For all the little babes I bare.

And other bitternesses grew,
France and her influences drew
The English out of touch with Spain;
And Wolsey smarting with the pain
Of being thwarted in his hope,
Of coming to be made the Pope,
Was hostile both to Spain and me.
And Henry glowered lustfully
On courtesans: and everywhere
Spoke of his longing for an heir
Who should ensure the Kingdom's peace.

And trouble-makers did not cease
To tell him that my barrenness
Came from his godless wickedness
In marrying his brother's wife.

Henry was coming into life,
Not reverencing aught that stood
Between him and a fancied good.
His want was master of his will.
When he determined on an ill,
All bent to that . . .

So he resolved
To have his link with me dissolved,
By Papal means, if that might be.
Long, long he wrought for that decree
By threat and bribe and argument . . .
All pretexts cloaking his intent
To leave me and to live with Anne.
I pleaded when the suit began,
Not afterward, I stood aside.
I pitied those who in their pride
Helped Henry, then, for I had learned
What devil in his spirit burned,

What worship of himself, what will
In all things to be master still;
To be the axle or the pin
On which another world might spin.
I knew how deadly he would be
To all who helped in ousting me;
And as I knew it would, it fell:
Their moment's glory led to hell.

I was what I had ever been,
A queen, the daughter of a queen,
Anointed and appointed great;
Death only could annul my state;
But Death came slowly: I could see
My ousters ruined before me.

That was no joy; I also saw
My Henry falling from all law
Into all headlong lust of will.
I saw him lie and rob and kill,
Smite at the holy, wreck the brave,
Do all things as his devil drave,
With no good counsellor or friend.
It made my very heart-strings rend
To see his soul in devil's hands.

God, who allowed it, understands.
And, for myself, I took the bad
That followed on the good I had had.
I learned how pitifully kind
Friends may be to a tortured mind.
I learned that peace may be attained
By sinners racked and many-pained;
Peace that is south wind after east,
Quiet to greatest and to least,
Quiet in which Earth's feverish things,

The wills and fiercenesses of Kings,
Sink to proportion, and the soul
Perceives the universe unroll
Star beyond singing star, immense
Beyond all dream, beyond all sense,
All order, all magnificence.

God in His Mercy let me see
Through darknesses that covered me
Bright planets that his angels be.

[*She sinks back to her chair.*]

THE SEEKER:

Ah, noble lady, and through you we still
Behold that light in darkness . . .

[WOLSEY *rises.*]

but he speaks
To whom peers spoke bareheaded: it is Wolsey.

THOMAS WOLSEY:

I am that Wolsey the Cardinal, prelate and proud,
I who was King of my King, who was sceptre and sway.
To me, not to Henry, the princes and potentates bowed.
I strode like the sun in his glory on Midsummer Day.
My splendour all crashed in decay,
The web that my spirit had spun
Was swept into dust and undone;
I died as the gambler who fails.

I was a butcher's son, but royally dowered
With wit and Fortune, which dower smoothed my pathway.
Men gave me place: men made me a priest: and helped me.

One man there was who checked me, I then being priest,
One Paulet, a country gentle, set me in stocks.
It is dangerous to check beginning Fortune:—

Lads grow; priests become bishops, princes take Kingdoms;
And I, that priest in the stocks, was soon most trusted,
Chaplain to Calais' treasurer, employed, besought,
My advice asked and taken, and my young wisdom
Praised to the King himself, who took me to service.
I think that Paulet repented before he died.

Henry the Seventh gave me my chance, as follows:
He sent me upon a mission to Maximilian,
The Emperor, then in Flanders: I staked my all
On doing that mission like an angel of God.

Therefore, on leaving the King, I sped down river,
Helped by the wind and the ebbing tide to Gravesend,
Where taking horse I galloped: and all night galloped
From post to post across Kent, rousing the ostlers,
Flinging myself from reeking horse to the fresh one
And galloping through the night with owls and foxes,
Till lo, cocks crowed and Heaven grew gray at Dover . . .
There, tottering down the beach, I found fair fortune,
A ship with her sails cast loose at point of sailing
For Calais. I climbed aboard her; in three hours more
I was in France upon horseback galloping on.

That night I was with the Emperor, in treaty.
None ever beat or out-braved me in any treaty
When I was facing my man, nor did the Emperor.
Next day my treaties were settled: all that next night
I galloped for Calais, got there at morning gun
Again, found ship; and, getting aboard, wind favoured,
In three hours more I was galloping from Dover,
And late that night I came to the Court at Richmond.
King Henry being abed, I too could take rest
After eighty hours spurring from post to post,
But I was afoot ere dawn, awaiting Henry
As he passed from bed to chapel to early Mass.

He, seeing me, chid my not having started forth.
I said "I have been: I have now returned, O King."
He seemed both startled and not well pleased, for he said:
"That is the worse, for, after you hurried away
I thought of a needful point that I had not urged
In your commission: nay, a point that was vital,
And sent one after you straight to stop and warn you.
Did he overtake you?"
I answered, "No, Your Grace.
As I returned I met him and learned his errand.
But as for the needful point, may it please Your Grace,
I thought of it myself on my journey Eastwards,
How vital it was; and greatly presuming dared
(Though without warrant from you) to urge the matter.
The Emperor's self was pleased to agree and seal.
Pardon your servant's assumption in so doing."

Then the King said "I not only pardon, but thank
A servant so thoughtful, eager and fortunate."

Friends, from that mission's happy speed
Came Fortune glorious indeed.
The old King honoured me: his son
Heaped honours on my head: I won
Glory and gratitude from men:
I was made thrice a Bishop, then
Lord Chancellor, Archbishop . . . more,
Legate and Cardinal; priests bore
Great silver crosses as a show

Before me: riches fell like snow
About me: and the gay young King
Left me to govern everything.
My will was Law in Church and State,
Through Christendom my will was great.
I said and Europe did: one hope,

One only, failed me, to be Pope.
The Emperor Charles betrayed me there.

I was like sunlight making fair
All that I shone upon: my house
Was beyond telling glorious .
With quaintly twisted chimneys red
Above the dormers and the lead,
And halls and galleries made good
With joinery in precious wood
And flutings running down the grain.
I had stories leaded pane by pane
Into the windows, that they shewed
Shagged Centaurs in the mountain-road
Coming towards the haunts of men
To ravish women: and agen
The Rapes and Loves that Ovid told.
And hanging upon rods of gold
I had tapestries of silk whereon
The Loves of Mars and Venus shone.
I had golden cups and plates enough
To fit the King with household stuff;
Of silver plate I took no heed.

My gardens sprang from foreign seed.
All that is excellent in fruit,
Or beautiful in flower, took root
There, with such fragrance, and so bright,
Spirits were trancéd with delight . . .
And I had many a joy beside:
Green woodlands for my stags of pride;
Cock-shutes and coney-warrens, stews
For many a swift pike and slow luce . . .
Half a shire grew meat and bread
That my great household might be fed.

They who beheld my state, I wis,
They only, know what glory is.
My state was greater than the King's.
My Herald went with trumpetings
Before, with the two crosses, then
My mace-man and my pillar-men,
Then ushers crying "Way, make way!"
Then three and three my picked array
In velvet, bearing golden chains.
Then sumpter mules and baggage trains.
Then spearmen in a bodyguard
In scarlet tunics golden starred,
And bowmen wearing tawny coats.
Then to the cheering of all throats
Came the Great Seal majestical,
And the Red Hat of the Cardinal,
Both borne by noblemen; and then
I, the great crimson King of men,
Rode stately on a mule of state;
Four men with pollaxes of plate
Were at my sides, and after me
Were seventy horsemen, three and three,
Riding great horses, scarlet hung.
And men and children sweet of tongue
Sang to me as I rode or stayed.
I was a god to whom men prayed,
A wise god, taking thought for all.
In scarlet, under golden pall,
I sat like godhead and gave doom.

There were five hundred men to whom
My daily state gave daily bread.

But Henry's lust to be unwed
From Katharine and wed to Anne

Was ruin to me: there began
Problems I could not shelve nor solve.
I strove to change the King's resolve . . .
That failed . . . then I was forced to strive
To win him licence to re-wive . . .

Yet the Pope saw what wars would be
If he should grant the King's decree.
Straight Katharine's nephew would invade
Rome, to avenge her: so he stayed.
I saw that if the Pope refused
The King's divorce, there would be loosed
On Rome in England, on the Church,
Utter destruction that would search
Rome's hold on England and outroot.

Such was the seed, such was the fruit.
Even as I saw, it came to pass . . .
That heart of flint and brow of brass
Broke Rome in England for his lust.
Myself was stricken to the dust;
That black-eyed mistress and her lord
Put some few martyrs to the sword,
And smote me to the broken form
Wrapped up in linen for the worm,
A dead man without power to stir.
I, Cardinal and Minister,
I, Chancellor and Legate, lay
Under the quire in the clay,
Dropping to dust, and all my schemes
Dust too, forgotten as men's dreams
Forgotten as the star that lights
A trail thro' Heaven on winter-nights
And falling fades and leaves no trace.

I, the Pope's Legate, the King's Grace,
Am vanished: there remain behind
Some gleams, however, from my mind
From which men know that there was one
Once, who was splendid as the sun;
Who bent great brows upon affairs
And made Kings' wills his ploughing-shares,
And was the central pin whereon
Revolved that Europe that is gone.

While I was Sun, the planets shone.

[WOLSEY *sinks back.* ANNE *rises.*]

THE SEEKER:

As you supplanted Katharine, another
Supplanted you: this beautiful blithe figure.

ANNE:

I am the beautiful Queen who was ruined and lost.
I am Anne Bullen, whom men still remember with pity.
Few have bought terrible days at more pitiful cost.
Falling from Queen to the hatred of country and city,
Like a rudderless ship I was tossed.
Powers made use of my being,
Changes too vast for man's seeing,
The Will of the Time passing by.

I was a black-eyed witty girl of old
When, with my sixteen summers hardly told,
I came from France into the English Court.

Promptly King Henry wooed me for his sport,
As he had wooed my sister (so men said);
But I escaped the amorous traps he laid.
I was the Queen's maid, dedicate and vowed
To the Queen's service, and besides was proud.

And yet it thrilled me, knowing that the King
Loved me past doubt, beyond imagining . . .

That that grim palace-bull with bloody horn
Came like a ring-dove to my hand for corn.

Then, for the Queen, men muttered everywhere:
"A barren Queen, and England needs an heir . . .

"God has pronounced against her: it is plain.
Henry should be divorced and wed again,

"The State demands it . . . If his second choice
Were English, surely England would rejoice."

Dignities fell into my father's hand,
Jewels and moneys, titles, manor-land . . .

And people whispered: "Lady, if you choose,
You can be Queen of England: why refuse?"

And others said: "If you were England's Queen
The Reformed Faith would prosper and be green

"Where now its martyrs perish at the stake.
Anne, become Queen for sweet religion's sake."

Others (and my ambitions) said their say:
"How grand to hear the heralds clear the way . . .

"'Way for Queen Anne!'; how exquisite to lead
All England's peeresses as Queen indeed;

"Call lilied France my brother, ay and bear
A future King of England, Henry's heir . . ."

When Henry sought divorce and Rome refused,
Bitterer tongues spoke, angrier pleas were used:—

"Make the King paramount within his realm,
Strike off this Roman guidance from the helm,

"Abase this Spanish Queen who uses Rome.
The English King must be supreme at home."

Those whom I knew spoke thus.
And hour by hour
My spirit saw the images of power,

The crown, the scarlet and the pride of place,
The thousand eyes on one unseeing face,

My Father, Mother, Brother, Sister, all
Splendid with gold-work, bearing up my pall.

King Henry's hand on mine, King Henry's son
Mine, to be King when Henry's reign was done,

Were not these glories to a girl, beside
Having the great King wooing her for bride?

'Tis but a step to Hell; but getting back
Takes many a march up jagged rocks, alack!

I, who had only youth and Henry's greed,
Staked those for Henry and was queen indeed.

Rome was defied, dishonoured, dispossessed,
A flooding spring, with me upon its crest,

Swept over England, bearing me to power;
Men rang the bells for me in that my hour . . .

All England's bells . . . and London's thousands massed,
Scattering roses on me as I passed
To have the crown upon my brows at last.

Then great guns thundered, trumpets silver-keen
Shrilled, and the Prelate cried "God save the Queen!"

I was the Queen, and all the battle won
If but my little child might be a son.

My child was a Princess, thereafter came
Griefs and disasters putting me to shame . . .

Daily the foothold underneath me failed,
King Henry wearied of me; foes assailed.

Men shouted insults at me in the street,
The Court spies sought my blood on catlike feet.

When foreign Kings' ambassadors appeared
They did not hail me Queen, they smiled and sneered

And called me the King's woman: but, alas,
I was not that . . . another woman was.

Jane Seymour, once my waiting-woman, stepped
Into the heart that I no longer kept.

Henry and she were lovers to the full;
I was not merciful nor dutiful;

The broken heart is often mad in head.
Then was my princely little son born dead,

And I was lost.

The King deserted me;
Round me were enemy on enemy;

Some I had humbled or had thwarted, some
The friends and followers of the Queen to come.

Then I was paid that I had once reviled
And used with spite my predecessor's child;

Then I was paid that once I moved the King
In wanton hatred to a darker thing.

I was well paid in those few weeks of hate,
Lost beyond hope, but having still to wait.

None but the lovely stand by misery.
My brother and some others stood by me.

One loyal and a lover to one lost,
Such surely is the soul God treasures most.

Bitter and utter was the death that fell
On those who comforted my weeks of hell.

In those few weeks, though nothing outward changed,
My death and Henry's wedding were arranged,

My headsman ordered, and most savage ends
Prepared by all my foes for all my friends.

Then at the tourney as the trumpets blew,
Henry arose like one with death to do.

One merciless fat sidelong look he gave,
From which I knew that he had dug my grave;

Then he was gone at gallop, and the fawn
Myself was netted and the toils were drawn.

I who was England's Queen, had now to die.
That is forgotten where my ashes lie,

And where my spirit is, it is forgiven.
O living men, for pity and sweet Heaven,

Forgive what misery my thoughtlessness
Wrought ere my life was smitten with distress.

I, the White Falcon with the starry rod
Of roses, am a lesser bird with God.

I am in peace where flowers shine like stars.
The hates and angers beat against the bars

Of Love, that shuts this sunny garden close.
When the bells chime the loving overflows

Out of the garden and the angers cease;
Men's souls behold a morning star of peace

And cry: "O silvery one,
Companion of the Sun,
Mark not the thing ill-done
In the blind Night,
But mark the Life begun,
The Race still to be run,
The Hope that may be won,
Now we have light."

[HENRY VIII *rises.*]

HENRY:

And I am your King and your leader who stood by his strength,
You thought you could sway him or hold him, or rule in his name;
All three of you prospered, but found out your error at length,
All you who attempted to rule me, I made you all tame;
You three were but pawns in a game,
I used you and let you be lost.
Be glad you were worth what you cost,
But think not to vex me with blame.

I might have been priest, but my brother's death made me a King;
I planned to be worthy the office, a master indeed;
I fashioned myself as a goldsmith who fashions a ring,
That none in the Kingdom but I should have power to lead.
I was not a puppet nor reed,
But a master in body and soul,
And the weeds that I could not control
I cut, as is best for a weed.

What if I found myself in earliest youth
Bound to a Spanish policy through you?
This country also has a part to play,
Not at another's bidding, but her own.
Your Spanish friends betrayed me and France failed me,
But England did not fail me, nor I her.

* * *

And you, my Prelate, who made use of England
In your Italian game, you also felt
A better player than yourself at hand,
Who wrecked the Roman scheme.

* * *

And you, sweet minion,
You charmed me many hours, but did not bring
The heir the Kingdom wanted: — tales were told
Of plottings that should bring the wanted heir:
You say, false tales.
Perhaps, but they seemed likely to be true
To one who knew your nature: you were cast out
And with you all your fellows, utterly.

I found this Kingdom swayed by foreign powers
And left her free of them: I builded up
A fleet to keep her: I uprooted all

Those states within a state which ruin states;
I made myself the head: and any head
Which had not wit to bow, I lopped away . . .
Good heads among them, too; better than yours.

Would I had had a stalwart son or two
From those six flimsy women whom I tried.

But that which must be is: —
One thing I hated: —
Disorder; — and another, want of splendour: —
Both coming from the want of resolute will
In a King's spirit. Men must think of me
As splendid in a splendid time; I did
My will as King: and ruled to greater purpose
Then any English King since Arthur's time.

K. OF ARAGON:

You had great greed
Of mastery: no other quality.

WOLSEY:

And men rejoiced that the dogs licked your blood.

ANNE:

For all our love, that made your subjects glad.

HENRY:

A horse rolls when his saddle is taken off,
So will a land: but not while this King rode.

DESTINY:

The star is southing. The year is near to the height,
When you must hush till another year be perfect.
Back to your quiet, spirits; the midnight comes.
[*The* FIGURES *sink back.*]

SEEKER:

O spirits, linger: tell me one thing more.

DESTINY:

What is it that the mortal hungers for?

SEEKER:

What follows Death?

DESTINY:

Come to me, I will tell.

[SEEKER *goes up the stage. The hour strikes.*]

KATHARINE:

O April flowers,

WOLSEY:

And summer hours,

ANNE:

And autumn showers,

HENRY:

And winter cold!

KATHARINE:

O days and hours,

WOLSEY:

And pride and powers,

ANNE:

We call them ours,

HENRY:

But cannot hold.

DESTINY:

The hour passes, the tale is told.

PENELOPE

PENELOPE

ODYSSEUS

EURYCLEIA

ATHENE

SCENE: — *A room in* PENELOPE'S *palace.* PENELOPE *seated centre on throne.* ODYSSEUS *on bench right.*

PENELOPE:

O guest, I would first ask you this: who are you, whence you come
And what is your city, and who are your parents?

ODYSSEUS:

O lady,
Not any man living upon the wide earth would refuse you;
Your glory has reached unto heaven, like that of your lord.
Would that that godlike one ruled over many brave men
Upholding the right, while his black soil grew barley and corn
And his trees bent with fruit and his sheep bore strong lambs, and the sea
Brought fish, thro' his ruling, and all of his commonwealth prospered.
But now, as I sit in your house, I would ask that you ask
Other things, not my kin, not my land, lest you o'erbrim my heart
With sorrow in calling to mind: I am one many-sorrowed
Nor is it right I should sit in another man's house
Moaning and mourning, for unceasing mourning is evil,
And one of your maids, or yourself, being angry, might say
That my eyes swam with tears because all of my wits swam with wine.

PENELOPE:

O stranger, the Deathless Ones ruined my beauty and body,
When the Argives went up against Troy with my husband Odysseus.
If he could return and be minister tending my life
My glory and beauty would surely be better than now.
Now I mourn; for the powers of evil so press me with evil.
For the chieftains who rule in the islands, in wooded Zakynthos.
Dulichium, Same, or neighbours in clearly seen Ithaca,
Woo my unwilling person and scatter the wealth of my home.
Therefore I cannot heed guests, no, nor suppliant men,
Nor heralds, though sent from the Elders, but pine for Odysseus,
Longing at heart, while they press on their suits, and I plot.
First, God breathed this to my wits, that I set up a loom
In my room, and weave cloth there, a broadcloth of delicate kind.
I said to the suitors, "O nobles, my wooers, hear this.
Since godlike Odysseus is dead, cease the urging my marriage
Till the cloth has been finished, lest all of my wool-work be waste.
A shroud for the hero Laertes to wrap him when Fate
Destroy him in length-stretching Death, lest the women should blame me
That he should lie shroudless that once had so many possessions."
So I said, and their kingly hearts trusted: then daily I wove
There at the great loom, but nightly unpicked it by torchlight.
So for three years I triumphed: and all the Achaeans believed.
But ah, when the fourth year came round, and the seasons were changing
In the dying of months and fulfilment of many long days
Then through my house-maids, the heedless sluts, lo, I was caught
Unpicking, and blamed, so I finished, unwilling, needs must.
Now I can neither fly marriage nor think of a wile.
My parents much urge me to marry: my son is much shocked
(Now that he knows it) at having our living devoured.

For he is a man now, most able to manage a house,
May God give him glory . . . But even so, tell me your kin,
Whence you come, for you are not the son of a rock, nor the son
Of some oak of old stories . . .

ODYSSEUS:

O Lady, the much honoured wife
Of Odysseus, the son of Laertes, why will you not cease
From asking my kindred? I'll tell you: although it will give me
More sorrows than mine are already: for so it must be
To a man who has been from his country as long as I have now,
Much drifting through cities and peoples and suffering sorrows.
But now I will tell what you ask me.
There is a land called Crete in the midst of the wine-bright sea
Lovely and wealthy, sea-girdled, with many men in it,
Countless, and ninety cities, their tongues all mixed with each other,
Achaeans live there, and great-heart Eteocretans.
Kydonians, plume-tossing Dorians, godlike Pelasgi.
Among them Knossos, the mighty city where Minos
Was nine years King and the companion of God.
It was there that I saw King Odysseus and gave him my guest gifts,
When tumult of tempest had blown him on Crete in his going
Troyward, astray from Malea.
I, taking him up to my palace, well welcomed him there,
With heartiest friendship, there being much plenty at home.
And, to those other companions, who followed him there,
I gave barley-bread from the storehouse and brought gleaming wine
And sacrifice-oxen, that they might be happy at heart.
And there for twelve days the godlike Achaeans stayed with us.
On the thirteenth day as the wind fell, then he put forth.

PENELOPE:

Now truly, O stranger, I think I will prove if indeed
You guested my lord with his godlike companions abroad
There in your palace. Tell me, what clothes did he wear?
What was he like? Who were the comrades who followed him?

ODYSSEUS:

O lady, it's hard, after such length of time, to declare;
It is now twenty years since he went, setting sail from my
country.
But yet I will tell you of how he appears in my heart.
The godlike Odysseus was wearing a cloak of fine purple
Double, and clasped with a gold brooch doubly grooved.
The front of the brooch was wrought with a cunning work:—
A dog in his forefeet grappled a dappled fawn
That gasped as he gripped: and all folk marvelled to see
How, altho' only gold-work, he throttled the deer,
While the deer strove with his feet, being minded to fly.
I noticed the glittering shirt on Odysseus' body.
Because it was like to the withered dry skin of an onion . . .
It had just that soft smoothness, and glossy it was in the sun;
A great many women stared at it.
A herald, too, followed him; one little older than he.
Him, too, I'll describe, what he was: he was round in the
shoulder,
Swarthy-skinned, curly-haired and had for his name Eurybates.
Odysseus honoured him most out of all of his crew
Because at heart they were one.

PENELOPE:

Now, verily, stranger,
You, who were pitied before, shall now be both honoured
And dear, in my palace: for I, myself, gave him those clothes
You tell of, all folded, from out of my room; and I added
The glittering brooch to be precious to him; but alas,

Not again shall I welcome him home to his dear fatherland.
By a fatal decree of the gods he went into his ship
To go forth to behold Evil Troy, that is not to be named.

ODYSSEUS:

O honoured wife of Odysseus, son of Laertes,
Destroy not your beautiful body nor perish your heart
With mourning your husband. I will not in any way blame it;
For indeed any woman would mourn for a husband destroyed,
For the man unto whom, in her love, she bare children, although
He were worse than Odysseus, who (men say) is peer to the gods.
But cease now from mourning and lay me up this in your heart.
I will tell you the utterest truth, nor deceive you at all.
I have heard of Odysseus returning to home; he is near.
Alive, in the fertile land of the men of Thesprotia.
And brings many treasures and rich as he strays thro' the land.
But his hollow ship and his trusty companions are lost
In the wine-bright sea.

Not long will the King be far from his friends and country: —
Nevertheless I will give you now my oath . . .
Now first may Zeus, the highest and best of gods,
Bear witness here at the hearth of noble Odysseus
To which I have come, that this shall be all fulfilled.

Odysseus will come back here within this sun's cycle,
At the old moon's death and the coming-in of the new.

PENELOPE:

O guest, I would that this word might be fulfilled.
Swiftly then should you know my friendship and gifts
So that any meeting with you should call you blessed.
But this does my heart forebode and thus it shall be:
Odysseus will not come home, nor will you find escort
Since there are not now such rulers within the palace

As Odysseus was among men — if he really was —
To welcome the honoured guests and to speed them forth.

[*She goes over to the left.*]

But, handmaidens, wash this guest's feet and prepare him a bed
Pallet and mantles and glittering rugs, that he come
Warmly and snugly to golden-throned Morning to-morrow.
And then very early at dawn you must bathe and anoint him
So that he dine with Telemachus there in the hall,
And it shall be the worse for the one of the wooers
Who injures this man, *his* business shall not thrive
However he rage.

For how would you learn, O guest,
That I am wiser and shrewder than other women
If I let you dine in the hall, ill-clad, sun-beaten?

ODYSSEUS:

O honoured wife of Odysseus, Laertes' son,
Mantles and glittering rugs have been hateful to me,
Since first I drew away from the snowy mountains
Of Crete, out-bound in the long-oared ship.

I'll lie
As formerly in the sleepless nights I stretched,
Ay, many a night, in a bed not like a bed
Stretched, to await the well-throned glittering morning.
And washing of feet is no longer the joy of my heart.
Nor shall one of the women now servants here in your house
Touch my foot, save some old dame here of old
Trusty of heart, who has borne such grief as I.
I would not grudge such an one to touch my feet.

PENELOPE:

Dear guest, not yet has any such wise man come
To my house, of all dear guests out of distant lands,
To speak such eloquent right in all that he says.
I have an old servant here who is wise at heart

Who nursed and fostered yonder ill-fated man
And carried him in her arms when his mother bare him.
She shall wash your feet, although she is feeble now.

[PENELOPE *claps her hands.*]

But come now, rise now, wise-hearted Eurycleia,
And wash one like to your lord . . .
for the feet and hands
Of Odysseus now will be even as these of his.
For men among evils swiftly grow old.

EURYCLEIA:

Alas!
Woe's me, child, unable to help you, surely our God
Loathed you above all mortals although you were righteous
For never has mortal yet burned so many thighs
Or offerings picked, to God Delighting in Thunder,
As you once gave with prayer that yourself might come
To a smooth old age and rear your glorious son.
Now God has taken from you all day of returning.

[EURYCLEIA *now turns to* ODYSSEUS' *self, the Stranger.* PENELOPE *goes off left.*]

And perhaps the women are mocking Odysseus now
In a far-off stranger land in a famous house
As the shameless sluts all mock at your presence here.
It is to avoid their outrage and many insults
That you will not let them bathe your feet.
Icarius' daughter, the prudent Penclope
Has ordered me, who am not unwilling, to bathe them
For Penelope's sake and also because of yours.
Since my heart is moved within me with pity for you.
But come now, 'tend to the word that I shall speak.
Many much-suffering strangers have drifted hither,
But I say, I have not yet seen one so much like
As you, to Odysseus, body and voice and feet.

ODYSSEUS:

So all men say, who have seen us both with eyes,
That we're very much like each other, as now you notice.

[EURYCLEIA *kneels to the washing, the curtain is drawn.* ATHENE *goes rapidly to the centre stage as the curtain closes behind her.*]

ATHENE:

Now Odysseus sat turned from the hearth.
Then swiftly he turned to the darkness, he feared in his heart
Lest handling his scar she might know it, and facts become clear.
She went to her master to bathe him and straightway she knew
The wound which the boar had once dealt him with white tusk of old.
When the early-born rose-fingered Dawn shone,
He went out to hunt with the hounds and Autolycus' sons.
Up the steep, forest-garmented mountain Parnassus, he went
And swiftly came up to the windy ravines as the Sun
From the soft-flowing deep-flowing Ocean struck bright on the fields.
Then the hunters went into a glen, and in front of them went
The hounds, on a scent, and behind them Autolycus' sons,
And with them the godlike Odysseus went close to the hounds
Poising a long-shadowed spear. There a mighty boar lay
In a harbour so tangled that neither the might of wet winds
Might blow through its cover, nor bright Sun beat through it with rays,
Nor thunderstorm pierce it, but masses of many dead leaves lay.
Then the noise of the feet of the men and the dogs reached the boar
As they came, setting on, and he leaped out in front of his lair
Well bristling his hackles and gleaming with flame in his eyes,
And stood up against them, and first of them all King Odysseus,
Charged, lifting long spear in grapple intending to smite.

And rushing, the wild boar forestalled him and struck above knee,
Ripping it sideways and tearing much flesh with his tusk,
Not reaching the bone of the man. And Odysseus smote him
Home, in right shoulder, the point of the bright spear went through.
And he fell in the dust with a scream and his life fluttered out.
Then the dear sons of Autolycus brittled the boar
And bandaged the gash of the noble, godlike Odysseus
Staunching the black blood with song: then they straightway returned
Back to Autolycus' palace, and there they well healed him,
Giving him glorious gifts, and speedily sent him
To Ithaca home in love, glad hosts, glad guest.

[*Here* ATHENE *comes to lower stage, extreme left.*]

Now Eurycleia, seeing the scar, at once
Knew that she touched Odysseus' self and straight
Her joy and grief took hold of her wits, her eyes
Filled with tears, and her clear voice checked, as she said:

[*Here* ATHENE *goes off the stage, the curtain is drawn and displays* EURYCLEIA *kneeling at* ODYSSEUS' *feet, touching his chin as a suppliant.*]

EURYCLEIA:

You are Odysseus' self, dear child, and I did not know
Before, until I had handled my Lord all over.

[ODYSSEUS *grips her throat with his right hand and draws her to him with his left.*]

ODYSSEUS:

Nurse, why do you wish to destroy me? — You, too, who once nursed me
On your own breast — now, when after enduring much woe,
I come, in the twentieth year, to my fatherland?

But since you have known me, since God has put this in your mind,
Silence, lest any one else in the hall spy me out.
Or I tell you this, and it will be brought to fulfilment,
If God subdues these excellent wooers to me
I will not spare you, not though you be my nurse
When I kill the other women who serve in my halls.

EURYCLEIA:

My child, what word has crossed the hedge of your teeth?
You know how my mind is firm and not to be won.
I'll stand as stark as a stone or steel; and I tell you
(You keep it well in your heart) that if God should grant
That you subdue these excellent wooers, I'll tell you
Which of the women dishonour you, which are guiltless.

ODYSSEUS:

Nurse, why do you speak of these, when there is not need?
I'll notice them well myself and mark each one.
You hold to a silent mind and trust to the gods.

[EURYCLEIA *goes off, left front:* ODYSSEUS *covers his scar:* PENELOPE *enters, left back.*]

PENELOPE:

Stranger, I yet must ask you one little thing.
Swiftly the hour for untroubled resting is coming
To him whom the sweet sleep takes, however much harassed.
But to me God gives measureless sorrow, for daylong I mourn,
Weeping, appointing the tasks of the maids in the house,
Yet when the night comes, and all sleep, I am there in my bed
And sharp sorrows thronging about me are thick at my heart,
Rousing my sorrowing like as the daughter of Pandarus
The olive-green singer, sweet singing in new-comen spring,
Perched in the thick leaves of trees, often altering mode
Pours many-toned song in lamenting her child, her dear Itylus

(Son of Zethus, the prince), whom she slew with the bronze
through mistake.
So hither and thither my mind is tormented asunder,
Whether to stay with my son and guard all things unchanged,
My treasures, my house-folk, my high-roofed great palace,
respecting
My vows to my husband, and also the voice of the people,
Or go with the best of the Greeks wooing here in the hall?
While my son was a child and a light-heart, I could not well
marry
Nor go from the house of my husband, but now he is grown
And come to the measure of manhood, and now he implores me
To go from this house, being vexed for his wealth, which the
wooers
Devour together.
But come, now, and hark to my dream and interpret it to me.

I keep twenty geese at the farm, eating grain from the pool,
I am happy to see them. Now out of the mountain there came
A great crook-beaked eagle that struck on their necks and killed
all.
They lay heaped in hall while he lifted aloft through bright air.
And I cried and made clamour although it was only a dream.
And the women of Greece with the beautiful hair gathered round
me
To my pitiful cry that the eagle had slaughtered my geese.
But the eagle came back and was perched on an outjutting
cornice.
And ending my weeping he spoke with the voice of a man.

"Courage, O daughter of far-famed Icarius, listen . . .
This is no dream but the truth: you shall see it fulfilled.
The geese are the wooers, and I was the eagle but now.
But *now* am your husband returned who will bring shameful
death

On all of the wooers." So said he. Then sweet sleep released
me
And I saw all the geese in the hall eating corn from the bin
Where they formerly were.

ODYSSEUS:

O lady, man cannot interpret
Your dream, wresting meanings awry, since Odysseus himself
Shows how he means to fulfil it: Death comes to the wooers
To all of them, all; not a man shall escape death and doom.

PENELOPE:

Stranger, a dream and the judging a dream are both baffling.
Nor are all dreams fulfilled among men.
There are two gates of powerless dreams, one of horn, one of
ivory,
Those which come through the ivory gate, cheat the hope, bear-
ing nothings;
Those which come through the doors of wrought horn, they are
truly fulfilled
To the mortal who sees them; but my dream, I think, came not
thence.
Good to me, to myself, and my son were it so. I say thus:
mind it well.
Even now is the evil dawn breaking that sweeps me away
From the house of Odysseus, for now I must set up a contest
With the axes Odysseus was used to set up in his halls
Like the oak blocks of keels, twelve in all; he would stand far
apart
And hurtle an arrow through all; this I'll set for the wooers.
He who most easily strings my lord's bow with his hands
And shoots through the rings of twelve axes, I'll follow that man,
I'll abandon this house of my marriage, this beautiful house
All full of good living . . .
I think I shall think of it always, ay, even in dreams.

ODYSSEUS:

O Lady, the wife of Odysseus, the son of Laertes,
Delay not this contest, because many-crafted Odysseus
Will be here before these who fondle the well-polished bow
Shall string it with sinew and hurtle a shaft through the iron.

PENELOPE:

O guest, if you would but sit thus in my halls giving comfort
Beside me, sleep would not be laid on my eyelids at all.
But men may not always be sleepless; the Deathless have made
A Fate for each thing among men on the corn-giving world,
I shall go to my high upper room and there lay me to bed,
All made with my sorrows and soiled with my weeping since he,
Odysseus went forth to see Evil Troy not to be named.
There I shall rest; but yourself will lie here in the house,
Either stretched on the ground, or let some set a bed for you here.

[PENELOPE *goes off, left, down stage.* ODYSSEUS *spreads mats on the ground as though for his bed. He goes up right, and listens.*]

ODYSSEUS:

Those women go out from the house: they are bound for the Wooers . . .
Shall I rush out and kill them, each one? Shall I leave them to love
Those proud ones this last latest time? For I rage at their evil . . .
But bear it, my heart, you have borne a more dog-like thing once,
In the day when the unchecked mad Cyclops devoured my mates,
You bore it, till cunning had led you safe out of the cave
Where you reckoned to die . . .

[ATHENE *appears above.*]

ATHENE:

Why are you watching, most luckless of all men alive?

This is your palace, your wife is within the house,
And your son, such a captain as any would wish for a son.

ODYSSEUS:

Yes, all of these things are the truth, Goddess; rightly you speak,
But my heart in my bosom debates, how to put out my hands
On these shameless ones, being but one, and themselves always many.
But still more I think in my heart. If by God's help and yours
I kill them, how 'scape the Avengers? Advise and command.

ATHENE:

O doubter, men trust in a sorrier comrade than I,
In a mortal, who knows no such counsel; but I am a God
Who will faithfully guard you in all of your troubles whatever.
I tell you this plainly, should fifty picked squadrons of men
Surround us, all minded to kill us, yet still you should win
And drive off their cattle and flocks. But let sleep take you now.
It is pain to guard all night awake. You shall soon rise from troubles.

[*She pours slumber upon* ODYSSEUS: *he sleeps.*]

A TALE OF TROY

A TALE OF TROY

THE TAKING OF HELEN

Menelaus, the Spartan King,
Was a fighting man in his early spring,
With a war-cry loud as a steer's bellow,
And long yellow hair, so the poets sing.

But he wearied of war, and longed to bide
In quiet at home by his fireside;
He wooed and wedded the beautiful Helen
And carried her home to be his bride.

And little delight was hers, poor thing,
To be tied till death to the Spartan King,
She moved in the cage of the Spartan court
Like a bright sea-bird with a broken wing.

Paris came from a Trojan glen,
The prince of the world's young famous men,
With a panther's eye and a peacock air,
Even the goddesses wooed him then.

He came from Troy to the Spartan port,
He moored his galley: he rode to court
In a scarlet mantle spanged with gold
On a delicate stallion stepping short.

Helen and he knew each from each
That a red ripe apple was there in reach,
The loveliest girl and the loveliest lad
Ready to learn and ready to teach.

He said "O Helen, why linger here
With the King your husband year by year?
What life is this to a star like you,
The brightest star in the atmosphere?

"O beautiful girl, I love but you,
And a life of love is your rightful due:
Come with me over the sea to Troy,
Where Queens shall ride in your retinue."

She said to him, "O Paris, my own,
Since I married him I have lived so lone
That life is bleak as a withered bone.
O take me hence into light and life,
My spirit within me turns to stone."

Then Paris said, "But we will not fly
Like thieves that have heard a step draw nigh.
You are the Queen and I am I;
I'll carry you off to my golden ship
At noonday under your husband's eye."

So it was planned, so it was done,
Paris and she were there at one,
The sentry bribed and the door undone,
With a waiting ship and a rising wind
Helen was off with Priam's son.

THE GOING TO TROY

He took her to Troy, the windy town,
Where the exploit gave him great renown.
Helen was bright as a golden crown.
But Menelaus in Sparta swore:—
"This shall topple their towers down."

Agamemnon, his brother, vowed :—
"Troy shall be sacked that is so proud.
The sites of her temples shall be ploughed.
We have waited long, but the cup is brimmed,
The glory of Asia shall be bowed."

By lying and threats and fraud and force
He gathered his ships and spears and horse.
As many as thorns on April gorse
He sent them aboard in Argos Bay,
And away to Troy they took their course.

But difficult fortunes wait on ships,
For the winds may blow their sails to strips
And the waves may knock their planks to chips,
Or the wind may stop their going at all,
And Death come salt on the seamen's lips.

It was not triumph and prize they found,
But a wind that kept them harbour-bound
Week after week in Kalkis Sound,
Dying of fever, under a curse,
Till a tenth were under the burial mound.

What did they do, that might avail
To appease the gods that the ships might sail?
A horror that makes the cheek turn pale,
A horror that Agamemnon did :
But the Queen herself shall tell the tale.

KLYTAIMNESTRA

(*Enters*)

I am that Klytaimnestra whom Agamemnon wedded,
Queen of a beautiful land in a city rich in gold.
Would that my happy fortune might strike me suddenly dead.

The cause of the Trojan war was not Queen Helen,
That lovely fool of a girl, with her painted boy,
But lust for the spoil of the peaceful Trojan towns,
And the vanity of Agamemnon, the King,
Who raged, after all those years, because King Priam
Was chosen to walk before him at Zeus's rites.
Those children, drunken with youth, were but the pretext.

Such was the "righteous war" that my Husband preached of.
And all the youth of all the cities and kingdoms
Went at the bidding of Agamemnon to Troy.

We women and little children and aged men
Were left behind to the work that the fighters left,
To raise the food and wine that the fighters wasted
And forge the weapons to kill some woman's dear one.

Months passed by, with never a message, but orders
To press more youths, to hurry them on to the war.
And the youths marched singing away and none returned.

Never a message of love came, none, but rumours
From each blind beggar that passed, of ruin and death.
And the daily bread of our lives was pain of mind.

Then, after months, a herald came from my Husband,
Giving his ring as sign, speaking these very words:—
"The spearmen and all the ships are drawn in a port ashore,
Waiting to fall on Troy when the Trojans least expect us.
But, while we wait for the day,
Fortune provides a means of linking our House of Atreus
With the House of Peleus' self, that the Halves of Greece be linked.
We plan that our Daughter Iphigenia be married
To Achilles, Prince of Phthia, thus linking the kingdoms.
Therefore, Queen, we will, that you send our Daughter to Aulis
Under the guard we send, that so she may marry the prince."

I sent my darling Daughter away to Aulis.

It was all a lie of the King's, from end to end;
There was no marriage prepared; the fleet was wind-bound,
Unable to sail for Troy, and the food was scarce,
The camp was sickly, mutinous; quarrels were hot.
My Husband knew, when he sent that message of lies,
That within two weeks his League would dissolve in rage.
So he schemed to kill my girl as a sacrifice,
That the gods might change the wind and the fleet set sail.
My Daughter went with the guards, thinking she went to be bride.
They say that her Father smiled, that his plot had thriven so well.
She was decked as they deck cows, she was bound as they bind
beasts,
And he and his filthy beasts prayed loud to the gods to hear;
And a thousand men stood near; not one of them lifted hand;
In the light, on the sea-sand, he killed his child with a prayer.
And after he burned her there, and took an oath at her dust
That all should be faith and trust, since brotherly love was best.
And the wind swung round to the west; they shouted there
in their joy.
They left a poor little tomb behind on the trampled beach.
With singing and merry speech those heroes sailed towards Troy.

If there be any Curse, Fury or Evil
Able to leap from the Hurt Heart, to follow
The causer of the Hurt, and grapple, biting
Until the Fangs have riven his very life,
Let such curse follow Agamemnon always
And all his men.
Open, you kennels of Hell,
Come all you hounds of hell, red-eared, red-eyed,
Come Quarrel, Insult, Outrage, Misery, Shame,
Come lolling-tongued, tireless, hellish-hearted,
Hunt them down shrieking to untimely Death.

This hatred is but misery, daylong, nightlong.
Vengeance will not bring back my little daughter.
Would that a happy fortune would strike me dead!

THE SPEARMAN

You have heard the lady, making her complaints.
It was at Aulis: the gods were angry with us:
They had to be appeased by the King's child.
When that was done, at once the whole curse lifted,
The gods were with us, we sailed, we were successful.

We sacked the little cities in league with Troy.
Then we landed in force three miles from Troy,
Drew up our ships and fenced them with ditch and wall.
We learned, later, that Hektor, Priam's son,
Urged that all Troy should fall on us with fire
Then, while we dug; but old fools in the council
Caused Priam to refuse: lucky for us.
One good attack, pushed then, would have destroyed us.

And afterwards our state was none too safe.
The pestilence that had begun at Aulis
Began again, and raged, and the Kings quarrelled.
Chances were missed and foolish chances taken
That ended ill: there was much bitterness.

It was a working life there, sieging Troy.
Sometimes we went on foray with the horse,
And gathered cattle, corn and wine and oil.
That was delightful to a lad at first.
But later, when the plunder had grown scarce,
And every raider had to fight for it,
Going, and gathering, and getting home,
It was rough service: needing many men.

Yet necessary service, for we starved else.
And when, after a night march and a raid,
And running fighting, driving back the cattle,
We entered camp, perhaps a gang from Troy
Would shoot into the camp and fire a ship.
Then out the parties had to go again,
To drive the bowmen back and quench the fire.
And when the darkness came we stood to arms
And slept upon our arms under our wall,
Those who were lucky: many watched, as sentries.

Then there was work: an everlasting work,
Mending the palisades, digging the ditches.
Digging the clearance channels after rain,
Unloading ships that brought us stores or horses,
Taking the horses to the tanks for water;
Going up river to cut forage for them,
And bearing back the forage under spear-shot.
Building and mending huts, bringing in wood,
Wood for the forges, wood for ship repair,
Barricades, palisades and burial pyres.
And daily fights and frequent night alarms;
And many night patrols and constant danger,
On scanty food and bad, in stench and flies;
Many men dying, very many sick,
None really well, and always in the need
Of showing we were longing for a battle.

Often they marched us to the city walls
"To show that we defied them," as they said.
It only made us envy them the more
Snug in their homes within the walls of Troy,
Singing (we heard them singing) and contemptuous.

Had they attacked us then, with all their strength . . .

And yet we hoped and longed to capture Troy,
To break them in a battle and so enter.
But with our quarrelling Kings what chance had we?

The prince Achilles quarrelled with Agamemnon
And would not fight, which meant, one third of us
Sulked in the tents, yes, even while the Trojans
Stormed over-thwart the wall to burn the ships.

For while Achilles sulked, the Trojan King
Put Hektor in command of all his host;
And then we suffered: night and day they raided,
Penning us into camp: and blazing arrows
Fell everywhere to set the ships afire.
And then all Troy burst on us and burst in;
They filled the ditch, they broke the wall, they entered
Right into camp; they killed men in the ships.
Had they but had another hundred men
And one half hour of summer daylight more,
They would have finished every man of us.
It was as near as that. The darkness saved us.

Yet still Achilles sulked, with all his tribe.

He would have carried all his sulkers home,
Meant to, prepared to, but his friend was killed,
A fine young fellow, I forget his name.
I met him once. He ventured out too far,
The Trojans got about him and so killed him
And took his armour.
Had they let him go,
I verily believe they would have won.
Achilles would have gone with all his men
And we without him should have had to go.
But no, they killed him: and Achilles' rage

Was like the fury of a god: he went
Straight against Troy, and slew and slew and slew,
Raging for vengeance, till he met with Hektor
And killed him underneath the walls of Troy.

And Hektor's death was blessed joy to us
And grief to them, but fortune changes face
Quickly in war: only a few days later
The Trojans killed Achilles in an ambush.
Our luck was gone that day and theirs was in.
We thought "Now Agamemnon will make peace."

And on that very night the Trojan Paris,
Who caused the war by bearing off Queen Helen,
Was killed patrolling at the Skaian Gate.
We said "Now this will certainly bring peace.
Helen will be returned to Menelaus."

The King sent into Troy suggesting peace
On that one point, that Helen be returned.
But young Deiphobus, Prince Paris' brother,
Said "No. I swore to Paris to save Helen
From Menelaus always, come what may.
And so I will: she is my wife henceforth.
And Troy and I will keep her against all men."
He took command in Troy and stopped all thought
Of peace or treaty: so our Herald told us.

And Agamemnon knew that he was beaten.
For what with pestilence and mutiny,
His want of wit, and winter coming on,
There was no taking Troy.
For, friends, remember,
Troy was a miracle of strength, with walls
Built by the gods themselves, as they maintained.

It was not so: they tricked Egyptian builders
To come to build them, and then cheated them.
But still, the walls were wonders of the world.

They were great, sloping walls of masonry
Twenty feet high, and on the top there stood
Twelve feet of upright rampart in addition.
Thirty-two feet of wall stood everywhere
All round the city, with square flanking towers
Jutting at intervals on every length.
Impossible to storm: we tried it once
And not one stormer of us reached the top.
Impossible to batter to a breach,
We had not men enough to do the work.
We and the ramparts being what they were,
We could not capture Troy, and knew we could not.

And so we growled, on this side mutiny,
While the Kings quarrelled, and the summer burned.

We did not know the truth till afterwards.
This is what happened. Agamemnon called
A council of the Kings most secretly
Where they debated: "How to leave with honour,
Without disgrace, without a mutiny,
Troy being takeless and the winter coming."

Some were for crazy deed or crazy flight,
And Nestor wished that he were young again,
His usual wish, at more than usual length;
And nothing was decided in the end.
But when the Kings had gone, Odysseus said:
"Take this suggestion, mighty Agamemnon:
Send word to Troy that the Troy god Apollo
Has come to you in dream and ordered you

To end the war with Priam and begone:
That, before sailing, you and yours must make
An image of Apollo's sacred Horse
Precious with bronze and gold, in expiation
Of Greek pollution on Troy's holy soil.
That this great image should be left to Trojans
To drag into the city to the shrine
Of great Apollo.
That within few days,
Soon as this image has been wrought and decked,
You and your allies will break camp and sail.
That, in the meantime, all your Trojan prisoners
Will be released at once without a ransom.

"For thus," he said, "you gain a holy warrant
For doing what you have to do, go home.
Epeios and myself will make the Horse.
Send you to Troy the message I have bidden,
Send it by all your prisoners released,
And tell the allies here that bright Apollo
Commands us to withdraw. So trust Apollo."

Odysseus had his will: the King agreed.

So Agamemnon called his Trojan prisoners,
Told them what bright Apollo had commanded,
Promised the Horse, and sent them back to Troy
With gifts for each: and we were bidden launch
The ships into the sea, ready to sail.
And we were thankful to be going thence.

Then only, when Apollo's will was known
To Greeks and Trojans, was Odysseus' will
Made known to Agamemnon.
"King," he said,
"Inside the Horse we'll hide our champions.

The Horse will go into Apollo's temple:
The men will wait within him until cockcrow:
Then creep out of the Horse down to the gate,
Murder the keepers of it and unbar.
Our host, come secretly ashore again,
Shall be outside, ready to enter in.
The Trojans will be taken by surprise;
Utterly startled without will or way
They will surrender: we shall sack the city."

Men without plan succumb to any plan:
The King agreed to all Odysseus' plan.

Others will tell you of the Horse: myself
Only just saw him as I went aboard.
He was a stalwart stallion, plated over
With bronze and gold, upon a frame with wheels.

We left him in the ruins of our camp
And so set sail away from windy Troy.
What happened later, I will tell you later:
The story of the Horse waits to be told.

THE HORSE

My Father, King Epeios of the Islands,
Fashioned the Horse, after Odysseus' plan.
His shipwrights helped: this was the fashion of it:

The body of the horse was a hooped hollow
Of staves of wood, shaped to the horse's shape.
Within it, on each side, and at the chest
Were seats, covered with fleeces against noise,
To take five men, close-sitting two a side
Bent forward somewhat, and the fifth at end

Who sat more upright since his head had space
Within the horse's neck.
The entry hatch
Was in the beast's back, bolted from within
And covered with a saddle-piece of gold.

All this was made most secretly, unknown
By any, save Odysseus and my Father,
Who worked in a locked hut, under a guard,
"The work," they said, "being consecrate to god."

The pinewood workers made neck, head and legs.
Then all the parts were tenoned to each other
And treenailed fast, and shod to the wheeled stand.
Then the rough wood was polished with sea-sand
As smooth as ivory; then bronze workers
Plated the wood with bronze from battle gear
And ran fine goldwork over all the seams,
And horse-hair helmet-plumes made mane and tail.

When done, he seemed to march like a proud stallion
Bitted and decked, with an erect crest arched.

Then, when the Horse was finished, the five men
Were picked to go within: Odysseus, captain:
It was his plan; and he had been in Troy
A dozen times, dressed as a beggar, spying.
Next, Menelaus, as Queen Helen's husband,
The man with bitterest grievance against Troy.
Next, Neoptolemus, Achilles' son,
Longing to avenge his father, newly killed.
Next, Sthenelus, our best, after Achilles.
Lastly, my Father, who had made the Horse,
And claimed to share its fortunes.
All these five
From gazing at the City, and from study

Of a model of the city walls and ways
Wrought by Odysseus out of river clay,
Learned all the alleys to the southern gate
That they would open . . . if their fortune held.

My Father said: "I felt like to a swimmer
Who has betted all his having on the point
That he will swim a rapid, without harm,
And then, in the cold morning, sees the torrent
That he is pledged to swim, all jagged rocks
And gliddery boulders, antlers of dead trees,
Whirlpools and waterfalls and water-snakes,
Spikes, and a rushing shriek of bloated water,
Mangling and horrid death in every yard,
And dreadful hags of water with grey arms
Tossing to pluck him to their yellow teeth;
And wishes himself far, or the deed over. . . .
But still," he said, "Odysseus never doubted."
Odysseus said: "I answer for success
If once the Trojans bring us through the gates."

His captaincy turned doubt into a Hope,
And what the Hope became, another tells.

STHENELUS' DAUGHTER

The Entry into Troy

King Sthenelus, my Father, has often told me
The adventure of the Horse: I tell as he told.

"When the time came to put it to the proof,
Only we five and Agamemnon knew
What had been planned: then Diomed was told.

"When the Greeks struck the camp and launched the ships,
We five went openly aboard a ship;
We said that we were bound to holy Chrysa,
To sacrifice to great Apollo there.
Men cheered us as we went and thought us gone.

"But when we were beyond the Point, we landed,
And slept until a little before dawn,
When we returned unseen to Agamemnon,
And stole into the stable of the Horse.

"There we anointed, prayed, and saw all ready
And took a meal together cheerfully,
Since it might be our last. Odysseus ordered
King Menelaus to the Horse's neck,
Himself to the King's right, me to the left,
Epeios on my left, facing the boy.
We waited for King Agamemnon's signal.

"At the appointed time the trumpeters
Blew the long blast to bid the Greeks aboard.
There came a long long cheer and grating of pebbles,
And cheering and still more cheering.
We five shook hands
And said good-bye to light and clambered in.
When we were in our seats Odysseus drew
The cunning lid across and bolted it.
We were in darkness then, like five men buried.
Should we ever see the light of day again?

"Then we heard Agamemnon at the hut,
Bidding men strike it: this was swiftly done.
Some glimmer of the daylight came to us.
Then workers felt about the Horse's body,
Fixing his golden trappings with small pins.
Then Agamemnon said: 'This Argive Horse

Is offered to Apollo's Trojan shrine.
We pray that Troy receive it and admit it
Within the shrine: and that it bring to Troy
The blessings that we pray for her: so be it.'
We heard him spill the wine in the libation;
Then the men muttered prayers: then the King
Ordered 'About turn. March. Aboard your ships.'
We heard the singing as they hoisted sail,
The cries of men heaving: the plash of oars:
The griding, rib on rib, the oaths and cheering:
And the crackle of the flames from the great bonfire
Of burning hut-wood well to leeward from us.
The noise of our friends' cheering slowly died,
We knew ourselves alone within the camp.

"And then a crow perched on the Horse's head
And cawed and flapped, and cried an eager cry
Seeing a morsel, and with creaked wings went.
Then the seagulls perched upon the Horse together:
They talked their sea speech as they preened themselves;
Then, after shifting leg for leg, they slept
There in the sun above us, while the heat
Grew greater in the oven where we were.

"We five were packed into a narrow space
With fresh air only from the Horse's nostrils:
Outside the sun was beating on the wood
In full midsummer. We had taken oath
Never to speak, but suffer silently
Whatever came: we panted: the sweat trickled.
Being so shut away, we could not tell
How long we had endured or had to suffer:
It seemed another life since the ships sailed.
Then suddenly Odysseus put his hand
Upon my knee: he had heard horses coming.

"They were the Trojan chariots drawing near.

"Our hearts thumped: the adventure had begun.

"Then, as the horses and the chariots halted,
One of their stallions whinnied at our Horse.
We heard the men leap down to hold the teams
And the harness jingling, as the horses tossed.
Then Priam and the princes came about us.

"And first they praised the beauty of the work.
'It was a well-made Horse, handsomely decked.'
But then one or two voices, which Odysseus,
Who knew Troy well, could recognise, not I,
Asked, 'Why should Agamemnon leave a Horse
Instead of gold or beasts for sacrifice?'
But Priam said: 'The god appeared to him;
Apollo's self ordered a Horse's image.'
One said: 'He bears at least ten pounds of gold.'
We heard the princes comment on our fleet
Now sailing past the Point to Tenedos.
And citizens of Troy came round the Horse
And stared and wondered at him; many praised.
They dared not touch, thinking him consecrated.
We heard them poking in the sites of huts
For relics of our stay, to carry home,
Spear-heads and arrow-heads and armour buckles.
Then Priam and the princes came again.
Then Priam put his hands upon the Horse
And shook, to test if it were strongly fixed.
He said: 'It is well made and heavy. Feel it.
The body must be made of solid wood.'
He tapped the body, but the plate and trappings
Made the blow dull. He could not prove it hollow.

"We heard them bring up teams and waggon-traces,
Four teams were harnessed to the float, and men
Stood to side-traces and to guiding-traces.
Then, as the sweat came pouring down our faces,
We felt our prison moving towards Troy.

"We were able to forget the heat a little
In the thought of what might meet us on the way.
My thought was, 'If the Horse break from its stand . . .
Or stick within the river at the ford . . .
Or fall and break asunder in the ford . . .'
But we had set ourselves upon the chance
And had to take what came.

"It often happens
That a thing dreaded ere it come, is nothing
In the doing when it comes. We crossed the ford,
Scarce knowing we were there.

"Long hours seemed to pass, then, suddenly,
There came a blast of trumpets and a cry,
A long wild cry of cheering and exaltation:
We were near Troy gate, and the citizens
Had crowded to the ramparts. We were there.

"Here we were halted while they took the horses
And changed the traces for long ropes of leather,
Then all Troy's strongest, singing all together,
Hauled, and the girls flung flowers, pipers blew
Apollo's hymn, and so the Trojans drew
The Horse within the Waggon Gate of Troy.

"Then our wheels rumbled on the paven ways
Up a steep slope: and ever hymns of praise
With lyres and with cymbals greeted us.
We went with music and with singing thus

Round all the city (to our seeming) thrice.
At the third round we thought: 'The sacrifice
Will follow this; shall we be burnt, or thrown
Over the walls to break upon the stone?'

"We halted: then the singers ceased their song.
We felt that all about us was a throng
Of men and women pressing, touching, peering . . .
The heralds of the Trojans called a hearing.
When there was silence old King Priam spoke.
He was so near, we felt his left hand stroke
The Horse's neck and pat it when he paused."

My sister here shall tell you what he said.

THE TROJANS ABOUT THE HORSE

What Priam Said

"Apollo's self commanded Agamemnon
To make this image for the Trojan shrine,
In expiation of the long pollution
Of all Apollo's land by acts of war.
Here is the image, and the Greeks are gone
South of the headland, bound for Tenedos.
Now you, the elders, priestesses and priests,
Debate here in the council, and decide
What shall be done with this. There are three courses:
Bring it within Apollo's temple here,
Burn it with holy fire where it stands,
Or fling it from the ramparts to the rocks.
I urge that it be placed within the temple,
As bright Apollo bade the Argive King."

After a moment's pause another spoke:
"This city wants no offering from the Greeks.

This that the Greeks have made has been received.
I move that it be offered now to god
With holy fire, even where it stands.
When it is ashes, let us take the ashes
And fling them from the city to the wind,
And so be done with Greeks and offerings."

Another said : "We cannot understand
Why anyone should bring an Argive image
Into this city. We have suffered much
Since the first Argive image entered Troy.
We have her still, and suffer from the having.
I say let Princess Helen mount the Horse
And ride on him over the walls to hell.
Then, when we have tilled the fields again,
Replanted all our vineyards, stocked our byres,
And put aside the memory of our sons
Dead in this war for Helen and her boy,
We may forget a little what we owe
To Agamemnon and his company.
At present we owe death to him and his,
And I say smash this image into fragments,
Here or upon the rocks below the walls."
And instantly the mob assailed the Horse
With tooth and hand, and would have torn it piecemeal
But for the press and the beast's size and strength.
But heavy blows fell on the beast, and hands
Snatched at the trappings, and a woman screamed
"Tear it to pieces, put it in the fire !"

We felt that we were ended, without hope.

Then, just as the Horse tottered under press,
There came something that made our blood run cold,
And checked the raging of those wolves of Troy
With horror.

There came a cry like mad laughter or weeping,
A sobbing like one laughing over a corpse.
And the mob froze, and people shrank aside,
Horror had put her hand on everyone.
It was the worst thing that we suffered there.

KASSANDRA

I was the thing they heard, I am Kassandra.
I am as one blind from too much light.
The pure air, the pure light and the pure fire
And the ecstasy that comes, considering these,
Are all my having. All else is touched with Death.

I saw that golden Horse, Apollo's Horse,
With all those Deaths about Him in Troy Town.
Men with their carrion arms and bloodstained hands,
And the skeleton fingers of the women stretched
And the skulls of all, all gibbering, showing teeth,
All rotting, all Death, about Apollo's Horse,
The stallion of Pure Fire on which He rides.
O terrible pollution, those living dead.

So I crept among them . . . and I am like the Light,
Death shrinks away from me, those shrank away. . .
I touched Apollo's Horse and instantly
Light came to me: I spoke the Light, the Truth.

This is Apollo's Horse. Take off your hands
From this immortal work and holy gold.
This Wood is from the Holy Grove of Ida,
Where nothing mortal comes on foot or wing
Nor crawls, for it is lifeless, save for trees,
Pine trees immense, together ever-living,
A forest of the pine trees, nothing else,

Only the dark green trees, murmuring wisdom,
Daylong murmuring wisdom like the sea.
But at night, lo, they are mountain goddesses
Singing by moonlight terrible songs of god . . .
This Wood is of their Flesh, Goddesses' Flesh.

This Bronze, that was the armour of dead men,
Has since been through the fire, Apollo's fire;
The purity of fire has made it deathless.
This Gold is from the inmost mountain glen
Beyond all Life whatever, beyond all noise,
Save sometimes the rocks crack and the stones fall.

All day the rocks stand up among the glare,
All night they face the frost, the moon, the stars;
Not even the shadow of a cloud dare cross there.

And in its secrecy a water trickles
Out of the rock, the purest, brightest water,
Into a pool whose sand is dust of gold.
And there Apollo plunges from the rock.
This Gold is from Apollo's wing-feathers.

And Apollo will come into Troy at sunrise
To claim his Horse and ride: I see him riding
Bright, bright, bright, through the city . . .
O so bright . . .
Bright as pure gold: I see him riding here,
Brighter than gold, like something in a flame . . .
Yes, he will ride like fire, bright fire in Troy,
And, yes, the fire will redden as red as blood,
These ways, these walls, these towers, will glow like sunset,
A ruby of red, an ember, all heart's blood spilt.
And roaring fire will raven and lightnings sear.
His sword will bring bright death upon all of Troy;
O joy, joy, joy, when Apollo rides the ways.

Bring precious gums, bring gold,
The cobwebbed winejar old,
The pure work of the bees,
And Indian spice.
Bring milk, barley, and oil,
Bring salt, ashes and soil;
Gather all these.
We have a god to please,
Apollo to appease,
With sacrifice.

And strew down Indian silks, green silks, all woven
With sunbirds in gold thread, at the bright feet
That soon shall trample fire from the street
And dart his lightnings till the Wall be cloven.
Apollo shall come riding into Troy,
O joy, O joy.

Friends, beautiful Apollo tells me this:
That I shall ride on his immortal Horse
Far, far from Troy, in triumph, like a Queen,
Past lions, up a stair all strewn with purple
Straight into fire . . .
Straight to my lover Apollo waiting for me.

STHENELUS' DAUGHTER

In the Horse, till Sunset

That was the voice those hidden in the Horse heard.

She strayed back, lightly singing, to the temple.
My Father said, "Even within the Horse,
We felt the horror of those shrinking from her,
That priestess whom the god loved and had maddened.

After her song had ceased, King Priam said
'Draw this into the temple, as god bids.'

The men tautened the ropes to drag us in,
Starting a hymn, when a fierce voice behind us
Cried: 'I'll not welcome any Greekish gift;
Never. Let Agamemnon's Horse take that!'

And crash, a spear struck in the Horse's side,
Cracking the bronze and sticking in the wood.
Men wrenched it out and beat the flinger with it.

'Put him in bonds,' King Priam said: 'Sing on.
Bring bright Apollo's Horse into his home.'
We knew that we were dragged out of the light
Into a dimness sweet with burning gums.
We stopped: our dragging team unhooked the traces
And quietly went from us upon tiptoe:
We were within the temple: we were there.

Sweating and stifling as we were, we felt
Thanksgiving at our greatest danger over.
Fear having died, the hope of victory
Began to grow: our chance seemed to be coming.

The priests gathered about us with their incense.

Outside the temple there was still a crowd
Of men and women jabbering together.
Street-singers sang, and then the crowd would listen:
Street jokers, mountebanks and public mimics
Mimicked and mocked, and then the crowd would laugh
And then a man whose comrade had been killed,
And a half-mad woman, cried aloud again
For lovely dead lads lying in the rain,

And rage leaped up against the Greekish gift,
And grew, till the priests closed the brazen doors
And drew the bars: and then the rabble beat,
Beat on the doors, crying, 'Have out that image.'
There was a passage from King Priam's palace
Into the temple. Priam's spearmen came
Into the temple by it as a guard.

And presently they cleared the crowd away
And kept the precincts free: we heard them pacing,
Shifting their spears, grounding their spear-butts, calling
'Stand back there, you. Keep back there. Stand away.'
Little boys shouted mockings and then fled,
And spearmen leaned their spears against the Horse:
They diced and joked and told each other stories.
One mounted on the Horse and switched and cried:—
'Get up now. Watch us gallop for the Cup.'
And we, half stifled in the Horse, were glad
Of anything that passed the time or showed
That time was passing. But the thought occurred
'What if these spearmen watch us all night long?
What if they sleep here, all about the Horse,
And take us as we open?'
But for that
We had small fear: the heat and the discomfort
And knowledge of the hours still to pass
Ere we could hope to stir, were pain enough,
We would face the other trouble when it came.
Then singing priests bore offerings in procession,
Men, women and children came with gifts.
Kassandra took them. She offered them to god.

There was some little riot near the doors
During all this, but the guards silenced it.

Kassandra and the offerers withdrew;
The hours began again, of waiting, waiting.

The hours passed, leaving not even misery.
After long hours, it was sunset time:
We heard the water-sellers in the streets
Blowing their gurgling bird-calls and then crying
'Water; fresh Xanthus water; crystal water.
Fresh water from the Idan springs; so cold.
A penny the double-pitcher, but worth gold.'

It would have seemed worth minted gold to us.

One brought it to our sentries in the temple.

Then from the towers came the cry of 'Sunset.'
And trumpets blew the Closing of the Gates.
And every bell in Troy jangled or chimed
And children cheered: and women called to supper:
And men came thronging home: and shops were shut:
And the hammers that had beaten on the anvil
Since we reached Troy, were silent, we thanked god.
And almost instantly a coolness came,
And in the silence that fell suddenly
We heard again the never-ceasing wind
Running in every cranny, shaking shutters,
Flinging the dust against the masonry,
The wind of Troy, that blows all summer long."

In the Horse, Sunset till Cockcrow

Then, to our joy, quick steps came up the courtyard,
A voice cried, 'Come, fall in, the First and Third.
Back to the Palace with you, into quarters.
The Second Watch will guard here until midnight.'

Then two out of the three watches of guards
Formed, and marched off: the third undid their cloaks
And slept upon the floor: all save two men,
A sentry, marching: and a sergeant pacing.
Sometimes the couple talked together there
(Leaning upon the Horse) of wine and women.

At the second changing of the sentinel
The priests entered with lights and sang their song
How beautiful Apollo sailed the sea
In a red ship, into the midnight lands,
But soon would turn, and drive his flaming horses
Up from the world's rim, bringing light again.
Then, as they ceased their hymn, Kassandra came.
She stood beside the Horse next to Odysseus.
She said: 'The Trojan people are gone mad,
Quite mad, to bring this Horse into the City.
They should have burned it in the Argive camp.
Or burned it here, or flung it from the walls.
Apollo tells me truly; it brings Death,
A fivefold Death into the City's heart.
Death of the Man, Death of the Woman and Child,
Death of the Home they made, Death of the City.
Apollo says, *the image should be burnt*
Even if it scream, like burnt men, in the burning;
As it will scream, he says.
Will you not burn it?'

'No,' the men said, 'the orders are precise . . .
To bring it here and guard it, until midnight.'

'But Apollo bids me say *it must be burned*.'

'Go, tell King Priam so, priestess,' they said.

'King Priam has forbidden me the palace
Because I am a priestess consecrate.
Go, tell him, you.'

'We have strict orders, priestess,
Not to disturb King Priam before dawn.
When the King wakes he shall be told at once.'

She seemed to ponder this in agony.
Then she cried: 'Telling him at dawn will be
Too late for Troy: Apollo tells me truth.
I see nothing but burning: nothing but Death.'

Then, suddenly, Kassandra struck the Horse
And cried: 'I name the fivefold Death within.
Odysseus, King of craft, hater of Troy;
Menelaus, who let Helen loose upon us;
Epeios, the contriver of the Image;
Neoptolemus, avenger of Achilles;
And Sthenelus, the Red-with-Trojan-blood.
These are the Deaths: Apollo cries *Destroy them.*'

She then went slowly back into the darkness,
Wailing *Destroy them. Burn the image now.*

When she had gone, the priests muttered their pity.
The spearmen murmured: then the captain said:—
'You priests ought to be guided by a warning,
Given by god; you ought to waken Priam
And tell him that the image must be burned.'

A priest replied: 'Kassandra has gone mad.
We cannot waken Priam for such madness.
He has forbidden us to listen to her,
Apollo speaks through the bright brain of man
Not through the clouded.'

Then the priests withdrew.

When they had gone, the captain said: 'And yet
I am for taking warnings sent by god.
I say we ought to send to tell the King.'

The guard agreed that Priam should be waked:
But who should wake that turbulent old King
Against his urgent orders: no man dared.
'But still,' the captain said, 'he should be told' . . .

While they debated, sentries on the towers
Blew a soft trumpet call and voices cried,
'It is now a rainless midnight and All's well.'

'Cease watch,' the captain said. 'To quarters. March.'
Those spearmen of the temple stood to arms,
Clashed their bronze spear-butts on the temple floor,
Shifted and turned and marched away from us:
And silence fell.
We listened. All was still.
Then wise Odysseus swiftly drew the bolt
And thrust the hatchway up. 'Come on,' he said.
Those men will waken Priam and return
And burn the Horse: we have a moment's truce.'

He clambered out, we others after him,
So cramped, so stifled, we could hardly do it.
Odysseus snatched the weapons and the fleeces,
Reclosed the hatch, recovered it with trappings,
And whispered, 'Follow me: utter no sound.'

He led us deep into the temple's darkness.
There, at the north-east angle was a ladder;
He led us up it to a gallery,
Doubtless the passage to the treasure room.
'Drink, everyone,' he said, 'then lie and stretch.'

We drank the lukewarm water from our bottles
And stretched and felt new life come into us.

We had not lain five minutes at our ease
Before the guards returned, dragged out the Horse,
Smashed it with axes, in the temple close,
And brought out blazing straw and burned it there.
Odysseus' wisdom saved us, barely saved us.

The fire from the Horse lighted the temple.
We saw the glare and people dodging by
Screening their eyes: within an hour it died,
Though smoke from smouldering embers blew about.
I was so weary that I slept: all slept
Except Odysseus: he kept watch for us.
And in my sleep I knew that Troy was quiet,
That danger was all past, or not yet come,
That of a hundred chances, ninety blessed us,
And that the long, long trouble of the war,
The toil, the watching, hunger, danger, death,
Loss of dear comrades, all these things, might end,
Soon end, in Victory, the lovely thing,
The spirit with the crown coming from Heaven,
Life after all that Death, Life, Life itself,
The Sun climbing aloft out of the Night.

And lo, in the dark rafters over us,
Within an unseen roost, Apollo's Herald,
A cock half-rousing, flapped his wings and crowed,
Crowed for the Sun still far under the rim
Of the dark land beyond Mount Ida there.
We waked at that clear summons of the cock.
'Come on,' Odysseus said. He led the way
Down, through the temple, through the open doors
Into the close, where still the embers smouldered,
And cats glided, and little Troy lay sleeping.

THE SURPRISE

You have heard the story of the Horse of Troy.

We left him on the sea-beach when we sailed.
We sailed all day, but when the darkness fell
The captains ordered all the fleet ashore.
We beached the black ships out of sight of Troy.

Then quietly the captains of the hundreds
Were told that a surprise would be attempted.
Orders were given: then most stringent watch
Was made, lest any traitor should give warning.

We supped and slept, till somewhere after midnight,
Then roused, and tied bleached linen on our arms,
And took short spears and swords: no other weapons:
And forth we went by fifties towards Troy.
Absolute silence upon pain of death
The order was: we crept along like ghosts.

Soon we were in the Plain among the graves
Of men half-buried, whom we used to know,
And how they died, a dozen known to me.
And Trojan bodies, too; familiar landmarks.
It was all cold and windy, with bright stars,
No moon, dry summer going, and the wind
Beating the withered grass and shrivelled leaves.
Then we were at the ford and passing through
I remember water gurgling at a flag-root.

Beyond the ford we were in Trojan land.
There was the black mass of the walls of Troy
With towers (and a light in one of them).
No other sign of life, except a glow,

Before Apollo's temple as we judged,
Some sacrificial fire not yet quenched.
The city was dead still, but for the wind.

They halted us below the waggon track
Between the Spartans and the Ithacans,
And there we huddled in the bitter cold,
Wondering what had happened in the city
And why the city should be still as death:
Whether the Horse were burning in the fire
With all our men inside it sacrifice:
Whether the trap door in the Horse had jammed
So that they could not leave it: or perhaps
(We thought) the Horse is guarded in the temple,
Surrounded by men praying all night long.
Or had they ventured out, and all been killed?
And if the men were killed, the stratagem
Was surely known, and we half-armed and freezing,
Would be attacked at dawn and ridden down.

A temple bell jangled within the city,
A lesser bell tinkled; then all was silent.

And all this time the little owls from Ida
Came hooting over us: and presently
A mighty, savage owl perched upon Troy
And snapped his iron lips, and flapped, and screamed,
Almost one saw the yellow of his eyes.
Then he launched forth, stealing into the air.
It seemed like many ages in the cold
Before the whisper reached the Ithacans
To creep a little nearer to the wall.
When they had passed, unchallenged, others went.
Word passed that there were sentries on the wall.

And though the orders were against all speech,
Yet whispers let us know that Diomed
Was at the South Gate underneath the tower,
With the picked fighters.
Hours seemed to pass
While we froze slowly in our companies.
My eyes were so accustomed to the dark
That I could see the great wall with its ramparts,
A tower, and a gate, close-fastened, brazen,
With men of ours heaped near it like to stones.

Then there was whispering in the ranks behind me:
A captain whispered, "Who knows Diomed?
Do you?" I whispered, "Yes."
"Why, then," he whispered
"Creep forward there, and find him by the gate
Under the tower with the forward party.
Tell him *King Agamemnon is convinced*
That this has failed, and that we must withdraw.
Be ready to fall back as we retire."

I crept the seventy yards up to the front,
One whispered, "Diomed is on the right,
Nearest the wall." I found him lying there
And whispered him the message of the King.
"What?" he said, "What? Withdraw from where we are?
Who says so? What authority have you?"
I told him, "Verbal orders from a captain."
"Lie still," he said, "and not another word.
I'll learn of your authority when day dawns."

Then suddenly there came a little noise.
Someone within the gate was lifting down
The heavy bars that barred it, one by one.
Each of us nudged his fellow and drew breath.
Diomed stood: we others raised ourselves.

One half the narrow brazen door moved back,
Showing a dark gash that grew wider and lighter;
A lamp wavered and flickered in a lane,
The damp glistened on wallwork; a man peered
Round the half-opened door; and "Sst, Sst, Sst,"
He hissed. It was Odysseus, from the Horse.

Diomed signalled to us: he himself
Was first within the gate: I helped him there
To lay the gate wide open to our men.
Then we pressed in, up the steep narrow lane
Past the still flickering lamp, over a Trojan
Sentry or watchman, newly murdered there,
Killed by Odysseus: no one challenged us.
We were in Troy: the city was surprised.

The dogs had all been killed some weeks before,
There were no watch-dogs. When we reached the Ways,
The Wide Ways running round within the walls,
Some horses, tethered there, whinnied and stamped,
And drowsy horse-boys mumbled in their sleep,
But no one challenged; Troy was in a drowse
In the deep morning sleep before the dawn
Now faint upon the distant tops of Ida.

And we were seen by watchmen on the tower
On that side Troy, but none of them suspected
That we were Greeks: they thought that we were Lycians,
Old allies of the Trojans, mustering
Up to the temples for a sacrifice
Before we marched from Troia to our homes.

We were within the second ring of road,
Outside King Priam's palace and the temples,
Before a sentry challenged us, and then

It was too late for the alarm to help.
The man paused at the turning of his beat,
Looked round and saw us, gave a cry, then challenged,
Then died, stabbed through the throat by Diomed.

My party rushed into Apollo's temple
And burst into the palace to the guards
Sleeping in quarters, some of them half drunk,
All without arms: we herded them like sheep.

And by the time the guards were bound, the city
Was lit with blazing thatches, and awake,
Dawn coming, fire burning, women screaming,
And war-cries, and loud trumpets and clashed armour.
There was hard fighting in a dozen spots.

We came out of the guard-room by a gate
Into a blaze all red with fire flying:
A palace court it was, the inner court,
Where Menelaus and his Spartan spearmen
Were killing Priam's sons.
Just as we reached the court a dozen spearmen
Were all attacking young Deiphobus.

I knew the lad by sight, for he had come
On embassy to Agamemnon once,
And Menelaus meant to have him killed
And flung to the camp-dogs, because of Helen.

There he was, fighting for his life with twelve.

A fine young man, like Hektor in the face,
A bright, clean-cut face, tanned with sun and wind,
Smiling and cool and swift with parry on parry.

He had been surprised: he had no body-armour,
Nothing but spear and shield, and there he stood,
Checking each thrust, swift, marvellously.
One minute
He stood, matchless in skill in the red glare,
Then someone crept above and stabbed him down.

The city was all ours in the hour.
Many were killed in fighting: many more
Escaped, during the burning and confusion,
Out, to the mountains, by the Eastern gate.
The rest we took: some of the prisoners,
The little children and old men and women,
We drove out of the gates into the wild.
The rest we kept: young women skilled in crafts
And men who might make slaves.
We made them quench
The fires that were burning here and there
And then we sacked the city utterly.

When we had sacked her utterly, we forced
Our Trojan slaves to lever down the ramparts
Over the walls, until the city seemed
A mound of fallen stones and roofless houses.
We lit the wreck.

Then as we sailed for home with slaves and plunder,
We saw the ruins burning, and the smoke
Streaming across the sunburnt Trojan plain.
With all that world of murder on our backs
We bore our load of misery from Asia.

EPILOGUE

Spoken by Kassandra

Though many died and many fled
To live as beasts do, without bread,
Or home, or bed,

Yet many, like myself, am slave,
Weeping the life the spirit gave
Into the grave.

However long our lives may be,
There is no hope of getting free
To such as we.

Swallows will come again, and flowers,
Not Troy, who guarded with her towers
That life of ours.

What help in giving way to tears?
To those most hurt by Fortune's spears
A spirit nears.

The spirit whom the prisoner knows,
And broken wretches faint from blows;
It comes most close.

And though I tread the unknown stair
Up, into Death, I shall not care,
It will be there.

RECENT POEMS

RECENT POEMS

MUSIC 1939–40

Speak to us, Music, for the discord jars;
The world's unwisdom brings or threatens Death.
Speak, and redeem this misery of breath
With that which keeps the stars
Each to her point in the eternal wheel
That all clear skies reveal.

Speak to us; lift the nightmare from us; sing.
The screams of chaos make the daylight mad.
Where are the dew-drenched mornings that we had
When the lithe lark took wing?
Where the still summers, when more golden time
Spoke to us, from the lime?

Though these be gone, yet, still, Thy various voice
May help assuage the pangs of our distress,
May hush the yelling where the fiends rejoice,
Quiet the sleepless, making sorrow less.
Speak, therefore, Music; speak.
Calm our despair; bring courage to the weak.

Ah, lovely Friend, bring wisdom to the strong,
Before a senseless strength has all destroyed.
Be sunlight on the night of brooding wrong,
Be form upon the chaos of the void.
Be Music; be Thyself; a prompting given
Of Peace, of Beauty waiting, and sin shriven.

IN PRAISE OF NURSES

Dedicated to
MARY CLIFFORD
LAURA FRANKLIN
HELEN MC KENNA
PHYLLIS SIMMONDS
JOAN WILLS

Man, in his gallant power, goes in pride,
Confident, self-sufficient, gleaming-eyed,
Till, with its poison on an unseen point
A sickness strikes and all his strengths disjoint.
Then, helpless, useless, hideous, stinking, mad,
He lies bereft of what he was and had,
Incapable of effort, limb and brain,
A living fog of fantasies of pain.

And yet, today, as ever, since man was,
Even mad Man a healing impulse has.
Doctors there are, whose wisdoms know and check
The deadly things that bring the body's wreck,
Who minish agony, relieve and heal
Evils once mortal in Man's commonweal.
All honour Doctors; let me honour those
Who tend the patient when the doctor goes.

Daily and nightly, little praised or paid,
Those ordered, lovely spirits bring their aid,
Cheering the tired when the pain is grim
Restoring power to the helpless limb.

Watching through darkness, driving away fear
When madness brings her many spectres near;
Cleansing the foul, and smiling through the pique
Of nerves unstrung or overstrained or weak,
Bringing to all a knowledge, hardly won,
Of body's peace and spirit's unison;

And blessing pillows with a touch that brings
Some little ease to all man's broken strings.

All that they do is utter sacrifice
Of all themselves and precious beyond price;
And what a joy, through them, to re-survey
That narrow, sweet, now half-forgotten way
Of selfless service as a way to live
Based not on what you win but what you give.

Daily these gentle souls give pain relief:
Deferring dying they diminish grief;
The one they succour need not be a friend,
Only a wreck with anguish to amend.
Anguishes such as lately made me see
Such day-and-night-devotion given to me.

To you, most beautiful, devoted friends
My gratitude will go until life ends.
Never, while living, may I fail to bless
The thought of you about my wretchedness.

I thank and bless you: that I write at all
Is, by itself, your work's memorial.

THE KINGS AT MIDNIGHT

That starry night when Christ was born,
The shepherds watched by Dead Man's Thorn.
They shared their supper with the dogs,
And watched the sparks flick from the logs
Where coppings from the holly burned.

Then the dogs growled, and faced turned,
To horsemen coming from the hill.

A Captain called to them, "Keep still . . .
We're riding, seeking for a sign
That human beings are divine.
Is there such marvel, hereabout?"

The shepherds said, "Us don't know nowt,
We're Mr. Jones's shepherd chaps.
Old Mr. Jones might know, perhaps. . . .
But if you've come this country road,
You've passed his house and never knowed.
There's someone in the town might know;
A mile on, keeping as you go."

Long after all had disappeared,
More horsemen, from the woodland, neared;
And one, a King, with a dark skin,
Cried: "Friends, are gods and men akin?
A wonder tells of this, they say.
Is it near here? Is this the way?"

"Why; No;" the shepherds said. "Perhaps.
We're Mr. Jones's shepherd chaps.
Old Mr. Jones would know, I wis.
But he'll be gone to bed by this."

After the troop had passed away,
A third came, from the River way,
And cried, "Good friends, we seek to find
Some guidance for the questing mind.
Eternity, in all this Death;
Some life outliving flesh and breath.
Can we find this, the way we ride?"

"You'd better picket down and bide,"
The shepherds said, "and rest your bones.
We're shepherds here, to Mr. Jones.
When morning comes, you ask of he,
For he'd know more of that than we.
We're only shepherds here; so bide."

"We cannot wait," the horseman cried.
"Life cannot wait; Death cannot stay;
This midnight is our only day.
Push on, friends; shepherds all, farewell.
This living without Life is hell."

The clatter of the horse-hoofs failed,
Along the wood a barn-owl wailed;
The small mice rustled in the wood;
The stars burned in their multitude.

Meanwhile, within the little town,
The camping horsemen settled down;
The horses drank at stream and fed
On chaff, from nose bags, picketed.
The men rolled blankets out and stretched;
Black Nim their hard-cheese supper fetched;
Then, after spirit from the gourd,
Each turned to sleep without a word,
But shortly roused again to curse

A some-one calling for the nurse
To help a woman in her woe.

All this was very long ago.

ON THE HILL

No I know not;
Yet the framework has a beauty and an order
Over which illusion passes in the never-counted leaves,
That are whirled away in Autumn, if they go not
From Nature any further than the border
That re-gives as it receives.

Bare the hill stood.
Rabbit-scuffled chalk was on its trenching;
And the leafless beeches listened to the silence of the sky.
Purple as a cloud of thunder brooded Kills Wood;
In the Vale, a running white of smoke was blenching
As the West Express went by.

No; I knew not;
But the setting had a vastness and a power,
And the long illusion passing never passed, though seemed to
pass.
It was green a little season, and then grew not:
Fruited sometimes; often never came to flower,
Then was wind above dead grass.

No; I see not
More than this, a living greatness of procession,
Part of infinite procession hurled in fire through the sky,
Bearing things that seem to be, then seem to be not,
Human things, in living faulty with obsession,
Leaving anguish when they die.

THE HILL

This remains here.
This was here, I well remember, over fifty years ago.
Subject to untiring Nature as to many dying creatures,
Altered always, crop and colour, but preserving living features
That we love and seem to know.

Here the Norther
Brings its death upon the bastion till the laurustinus dies.
Here the Easter comes with coughings and the tower death-bell tolling,
Here the Souther drives the rain-streaks out of darkness over-rolling,
And the Wester clears the skies.

Thought is nothing
To this scene on which the plant of man puts out its million leaves
It has neither brain nor feeling; neither planning nor progression;
Only infinite diversion of an on and on procession
Heedless of what man believes.

I am of it.
Know that I am wholly kin, if partly set astray.
Know that in it is the healing of the sorrow of a nation,
And the glory of deliverance from crime and usurpation
With Eternity today

Man is nothing
To this quiet, full of power, to this effort, full of peace,
Nothing, even as a rebel, blind with anger and forgettal;
Nothing, even as a turmoil that his madness cannot settle
That his death makes swiftly cease.

But the power
And its quiet and its effort reassert a silent sway.
Man by man a spirit listens, soul by soul, a mortal answers,
Then a cry for better order moves the frenzy of the dancers
And the madnesses obey.

I am gazing
Into what is man's foundation, the enduring scene that stands,
Comforted by sun and water, glad of either in their season,
Something that outlasts our minute, and has majesty for reason,
While its granites wear to sands.

Much I wonder.
Much I long for this to speak, for an Incarnate Scene to come
With a word for me to utter: so I ponder; so I hearken,
Watching closely that I see it ere my fading eye-balls darken,
And repeat, ere I be dumb.

All my knowledge,
All my being is summed up in this, the scene, that is a friend
That is comfort through the evil and the agony of living,
That, if heeding, and if judging, seems forgetting and forgiving
And will seem so to the end.

Here I leave it.
Here it leaves me in the twilight, the imperfect wax it prest;
Knowing this, that it has shaped me, or mis-shaped me, for the telling
Of the purpose of the spirit that possesses this, indwelling,
Knowing change, but never rest.

Is it heedless?
Is it heartless, or unjudging, or forgetful, or immune?
Do we apprehend its nature, can we comprehend its power,

We, as mortal as the sparrow, and as fading as the flower,
And as changing as the Moon?

Let them answer
Who reply to every question, as befits an iron time.
I can only see a valley with a million grass-blades blowing
And a hill with clouds above it whither many larks are going
Singing paeans as they climb.